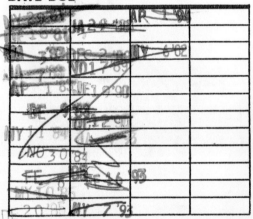

MONEY AND BANKING

MONEY AND BANKING

SECOND EDITION

Dudley G. Luckett

IOWA STATE UNIVERSITY

McGraw-Hill Book Company

New York   St. Louis   San Francisco   Auckland
Bogotá   Düsseldorf   Johannesburg   London   Madrid
Mexico   Montreal   New Delhi   Panama   Paris
São Paulo   Singapore   Sydney   Tokyo   Toronto

This book was set in Times Roman by Cobb/Dunlop
Publisher Services Incorporated.
The editor was Bonnie E. Lieberman;
the cover was designed by Robin Hessel;
the production supervisor was Gayle Angelson.
Fairfield Graphics was printer and binder.

MONEY AND BANKING

1 2 3 4 5 6 7 8 9 0   FGRFGR   7 8 3 2 1 0 9

Library of Congress Cataloging in Publication Data

Luckett, Dudley G
    Money and banking.

    Includes bibliographical references and indexes.
    1. Money. 2. Monetary policy. 3. Banks
and banking. I. Title.
HG221.L882 1980   332   79-14224
ISBN 0-07-038956-X

FOR
Elaine
Jim
Tom
Brian

WITH LOVE

CONTENTS

PREFACE TO THE SECOND EDITION

I have been most gratified by the response to the first edition of this text. Both instructors and students have apparently found the use of simple regression analysis to be helpful in understanding the subject matter of monetary economics. One instructor wrote that the book "combined analytical rigor in key areas with empirical evidence on the crucial parameters." Another wrote that he liked the book because his students could now understand why they were required to take a course in elementary statistics. And, best of all, a student wrote that, after having taken both micro- and macro-economic theory, my text had finally made economics "believable" to her. If these reactions are at all representative of users of the book generally, then my purpose in writing it has, in some measure, been achieved.

Naturally, along with the praise there has come some blame. A number of errors—typographical, factual, and interpretative—have been pointed out to me, as well as certain areas where the user would have preferred a different emphasis or approach. In the present edition, I have tried to be as responsive as possible to these comments and suggestions, while at the same time acknowledging that I cannot follow conflicting suggestions, and that I must ultimately exercise my own pedagogical judgment. In any case, virtually all of the comments I have received have been constructive, and many have been incorporated into the new edition. I would like to extend a blanket word of gratitude to those instructors and students who have cared enough about their subject to write me, and a blanket invitation to users of this edition to do the same.

There is one point of blame, however, which, if valid, I am happy to acknowledge. In the first edition I was brash enough to suggest to those instructors who found I had placed too much emphasis on the statistical method, that they "should probably adopt another text." Apparently, I was wrong. Two instructors have independently commented to me that they make little or no use of the regression technique contained in the text, either in the classroom or on examinations, but that this raises no barriers to student acceptance. I happily acknowledge my error.

There is hardly a chapter of the old edition that has not in some way been revised significantly. Perhaps the most obvious difference between the two editions is that the present edition contains two new chapters. The first of these, Chapter 5, uses portfolio theory to introduce the student to financial intermediation. This has three advantages. First, it gives the student a much better answer to the question of why financial intermediaries exist. Second, it gives the student—especially the business-school student—at least a nodding acquaintance with a subject that he or she is likely to encounter in more advanced courses. And finally, from the instructor's viewpoint, it introduces some analytical material into a part of the book that is otherwise almost unrelievedly institutional.

The second new chapter, Chapter 19, deals with the modern quantity theory of money. A part of this chapter was contained in the first edition's single-chapter discussion of the quantity theory. Breaking the quantity theory down into two chapters has a number of advantages: For one thing, it gives the quantity theory parallel treatment, and a more nearly equal quantitative emphasis, with the Keynesian theory. But the main advantage is that it gives latitude for a discussion of some of the more recent developments of the monetarist school, such as rational expectations.

The most heavily revised chapters are those dealing with banking, and with international finance. American commercial banking is changing so rapidly that I have little doubt that this edition, like the last, will to some extent be out of date as soon as it is published. In the case of the present edition, however, I have tried to write the banking chapters with an eye to the future, giving emphasis to such matters as the holding company movement, electronic banking, and the growing similarity between thrift institutions and commercial banks. I believe that I should add, nevertheless, that I have deliberately tried to eschew too much speculation about the "future of banking." Such speculation is, I believe, out of place in a textbook.

The chapters on international finance have been completely rewritten, for two reasons. First, the world has moved from fixed to floating exchange rates, and this has required extensive rearrangement and revision. Beyond this, some users of the first edition complained that it went well beyond what was necessary for an under-graduate money and banking text, especially with respect to covered-interest arbi-trage and a debit-and-credit approach to balance of payments accounting. Upon reflection, I agreed. I have accordingly dropped these discussions and substituted an extended discussion of international banking. Particularly because American com-mercial banking has become so active in the international sphere in recent years, I feel that the present content of these chapters is much more satisfactory.

I would like to extend more than merely token thanks to the people who have assisted me in revising this book. Among these, Tom Boggess has been particularly helpful. Tom spent a summer as my research assistant, and his aid in updating tables, figures, and other data was invaluable. Among those who were kind enough to comment on various parts of the book, I would like to thank, without implicating, Walter Enders of Iowa State University; Adrian W. Throop of the Federal Reserve Bank of Dallas and Southern Methodist University; James Barth of George Wash-ington University; Richard B. Baltz of Millsaps College; James R. Gale of Michigan Technological University; Stuart Greenfield of the University of Texas at Austin; Timothy Kersten of California Polytechnic State University; Stephen A. Meyer of the University of Pennsylvania; Duane B. Oyen of University of Wisconsin at Eau Claire.

Dudley G. Luckett

PREFACE TO THE FIRST EDITION

I may as well say candidly and at the outset that my primary motive in writing this book was to make money. While my pedagogical instincts are, I think, as highly developed as those of most professors, they are not so overweening that I couldn't think what else to do with my nights and weekends. I must add that I do not consider the money-making motive either base or crass. If an economist cannot unblushingly confess to commercial motivation, who can?

Having (I hope) established my credibility by exposing the warts of my "primary" motive, now let me tell you the second reason why I wrote this book. It has long seemed to me that there is a marked discrepancy between the way economics is practiced and the way it is taught. Pick up almost any professional journal and you will find that eight articles out of ten consist of three parts: institutional description (frequently implicit), model building, and hypothesis testing. But pick up any undergraduate text and you will find only the first two of these—description and theory. For some reason, the undergraduate teaching of economics has traditionally eschewed hypothesis testing. This has had, I believe, a number of unfortunate consequences. For one thing, we have been cheating the students by giving them a lopsided view of what economics is all about. For another, it has forced us into making what must sound to students like *ex cathedra* pronouncements. We use such glib phrases as "economists believe . . . ," "studies show . . . ," and "the evidence indicates . . ." without any explanation of the type of evidence on which we base our conclusions. To mention only one other shortcoming, confining ourselves to theory and description has had the effect of compartmentalizing the subject. It is common-place to hear teachers of economics complain that the theoretical and institutional material is "not integrated." In my view, such integration is impossible absent hypothesis testing. It is this method which permits economists to organize factual material into a cause-and-effect framework.

In short, I believe hypothesis testing to be as important as description and theory in applied economics. I have accordingly tried to write what is essentially an orthodox text, but one which makes use of the least-squares regression technique. For those students with zero training in statistics, a self-contained appendix is provided at the end of Chapter 1. No mathematics is required, and no attempt is made to instruct the student on how to calculate a regression. The exclusive aim of the appendix is to give the student the basis for an intuitive interpretation of a regression equation. The appendix is intended to be a reading assignment for those students who need it but not to be lectured on in class.

Throughout the remainder of the text, I have attempted to use only very simple regressions, and these sparingly. With the exception of the chapter that compares the modern quantity and Keynesian theories, my purpose has been to introduce a regression equation in about every other chapter. Beyond this, I have tried to illustrate the extraordinary flexibility of this tool of the economist's trade.

Some professors will doubtless feel that I have placed too much emphasis on the statistical method. If so, they should probably adopt another text. Others may feel that too little emphasis has been placed on it. In this case, I would urge them to bring additional examples to class, either from the extant literature or from their own research activities. In using this method in my own classes, I have found that one of its major advantages is the feeling it gives students of participating in current research issues.

It is customary to indicate in a preface how the book can be adapted to a one-quarter or one-semester course. I consider this presumptuous. Instructors know much better than I how they wish to teach their courses. I will only say that most parts of the book, and many chapters within parts, are self-contained and can be either turned into reading assignments or omitted entirely.

A number of professional economists helped me greatly by reviewing the text in manuscript form. Among these, Ronald Teigen of the University of Michigan saw the book through in its entirety. Others who commented critically on particular parts of the manuscript were: Jack Francis, Bernard Baruch College of the City University of New York; Timothy Kersten, California Polytechnic Institute; Will Mason, Pennsylvania State University; Marvin Rozen, Pennsylvania State University; Dennis Starleaf, Iowa State University; Steve Steib, University of Tulsa; and Dwayne Wrightsman, University of New Hampshire. I must add that I have not always taken the advice of these gentlemen; they are in no way to blame for any of what follows.

Dudley G. Luckett

PART 1

INTRODUCTION

The purpose of Chapter 1 is to introduce the remainder of the book. To be candid, introductions are usually a bore; they tell you what they are going to tell you, rather than telling you what they're telling you. Students may understandably become impatient at being treated like this, especially since the book was bought with their money. Nevertheless, *some* introduction is necessary if for no other reason than that the reader needs to have an initial orientation to the material. Without such an orientation, it is possible to become lost among the trees of finance and consequently never see the forest of monetary policy.

Beyond this, Chapter 1 will also serve to introduce the reader to the method of contemporary economics. Like other applied areas in economics, the field of money and banking rests to a considerable extent on factual evidence. The following chapter attempts to explain the sorts of evidence economists find persuasive. For those students with no background at all in statistics, an appendix is provided at the end of Chapter 1 that explains a few basic statistical concepts in very elementary terms. The Appendix is meant to be read by those students who need it but not discussed by the instructor. It is sufficient for an understanding of the remainder of the book.

1

Introduction and Plan of Book

As the title implies, this book is about two things: It is about the role played by *money* in the economy, and it is about *banking.* It is necessary to emphasize the dual purpose of the book at the outset in order to avoid confusion. For while the subjects of money and banking are closely related to one another, they are not inseparable. One could study money—or, more generally, monetary policy—with only a sketchy understanding of commercial banking. And, by the same token, one could study banking while having only a limited knowledge of monetary policy. This book, however, deals with both topics. And therein lies a danger.

The danger is that readers may become so enmeshed in the details of one topic that they lose sight of the other. This danger is particularly acute in the study of banks. The inner workings of the financial machinery of the United States is a subject of considerable interest for many people. And it is all too easy to become so involved with the details of finance that one loses sight of monetary policy. Accordingly, the purpose of this chapter is to orient the reader with respect to the way that money and banking fit together.

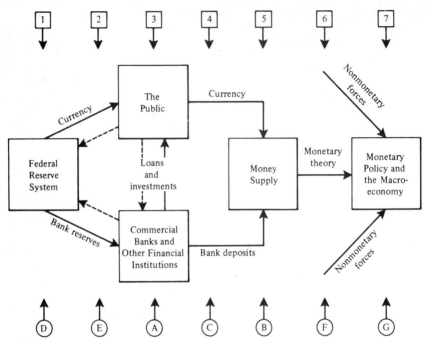

Figure 1-1 Schematic of monetary policy.

1-1 AN OUTLINE OF MONETARY POLICY

How monetary policy works can be understood in very general terms with the aid of Figure 1-1. The reader should become familiar with this figure since it will be referred to again in the introduction to each of the remaining eight parts of the book. Its purpose is to keep the reader oriented with respect to the way the material of each part fits into the overall structure of monetary policy.

Look first at the extreme right-hand side of Figure 1-1, at the box numbered "7" on top. (For the moment, ignore the letters along the bottom of the figure.) This box represents the *macroeconomy,* that is, aggregate economic activity. Our concern with the macroeconomy ultimately lies in the behavior of various performance indicators such as the price level, percentage of the labor force that is unemployed, and rate of economic growth. Naturally, we would like to have these performance indicators behave as well as they can; that is, we would like to have a stable price level (no inflation), full employment (no involuntary unemployment), and so forth. But bear in mind that the United States has a free-enterprise economy, which means that these goals cannot be attained through *direct* governmental intervention. In our economy, the government cannot tell businesses what prices they must charge or how many people they must hire. Some other, *indirect* method must therefore be found to achieve these goals. This is where monetary policy comes in.

In the United States, the governmental agency charged with the formulation and execution of monetary policy is the Federal Reserve System. The Federal Reserve System is to be found in Figure 1-1 in the box on the extreme left, marked

"1" on top. The purpose of the figure is to relate boxes 1 and 7 to show, in a very general way, the process by which a monetary policy decision taken by the Federal Reserve affects the macroeconomy. To see how this process works, note the arrows marked "2." The upper arrow shows that the Federal Reserve is the ultimate source of currency to the public; that is, if the public (Figure 1-1, box 3) wants more dollar bills and coins, it is ultimately the Federal Reserve that supplies them.

The lower of the arrows marked "2," the one labeled "Bank reserves," constitutes a somewhat more complex arrangement. To understand this it is first necessary to understand that the United States has what is called a *fractional reserve banking system.* By this is meant that commercial banks are required by law to maintain cash reserves equal to some percentage (fraction) of their deposits. For example, if the law stipulates that the reserve requirement of banks is 15 percent, then a bank with $10 million of deposits would have to hold $1.5 million (15 percent of $10 million) in cash reserves. What the lower arrow 2 indicates, therefore, is that the Federal Reserve is the ultimate source of these cash reserves to the commercial banks (Figure 1-1, box 3) just as it is the source of currency to the public.

The implementation of monetary policy by the Federal Reserve means, basically, changing the cash reserves of the commercial banking system. And the banks, in turn, will then change the amount of loans and investments they make to the public (Figure 1-1, arrow 3). When they do this, a complicated series of interactions is set in motion among the banks, the public, and the Federal Reserve. These interactions are shown in Figure 1-1 by the dashed arrows 2 and 3. While the process itself is too complex to be described in a few words, the *result* of the process is comparatively simple: Both the amount of currency and the amount of bank deposits in the economy are changed (Figure 1-1, arrows 4).

The full significance of this last statement can be appreciated only when it is realized that *bank deposits are money* (Figure 1-1, box 5). Most people are accustomed to thinking of money only as bills and coins, something one puts in a wallet or purse. But from an economic viewpoint, money is whatever is currently being used to make payments, and most payments in the United States today are made by check—that is, by transferring bank deposits from one person to another. Thus, when you buy electricity, you don't go to the power company and give them dollar bills; rather, you send them a check in the mail.

There is thus a connecting link between the Federal Reserve and the total quantity of money in the economy. While it would be inaccurate to say that the Federal Reserve controls the money supply in a day-to-day sense, in the longer run it is the dominating influence on our money supply. The importance of this statement can hardly be exaggerated. One need not have a Ph.D. in economics to realize that a large expansion or contraction of the money supply can lead to inflations and depressions—which can, more than incidentally, lead to wars and race riots.

It has been said "money will not manage itself," and the truth of this statement has been demonstrated on countless occasions. If money is mismanaged or not managed at all, the social, political, and economic consequences can be catastrophic. It is literally true that presidential elections and international alliances may turn on decisions made by officials of the Federal Reserve System. It is therefore of the utmost importance that the Federal Reserve use its influence over the nation's money supply wisely.

But it is not enough simply to shake a finger at the monetary authorities and admonish them to be wise. For what is wise? How, that is, *should* the Federal Reserve behave in any given situation? The answer to this question is by no means obvious. To answer it requires a detailed understanding of the role played by money in the functioning of the macroeconomy. This is the task of *monetary theory* (Figure 1-1, arrow 6). Basically, monetary theory asks the question, If we change the quantity of money in the economy by a given amount, how will this affect income, employment, and prices? The question is simple; the answer is not. Just for openers, note that we must have a pretty firm idea of how income, employment, and prices are determined in a free-enterprise economy (macroeconomic theory) before we can make any fruitful hypotheses about the specific role played by money. We must also know something about how money is used—why people and businesses hold it or spend it—and how these economic units react when the price of money (interest rates) changes.

Keep in mind that we cannot answer these questions by direct observation; we cannot put a tag on each dollar of currency and demand deposits, and ask every individual in the country why he or she did or didn't spend that piece of money. Thus, a *theory* of money is necessary in understanding the monetary process. It tells us which relationships are important and which are not. We can then use statistical analysis to find out the nature of the important relationships. From this point of view, the purpose of theory is simply to suggest meaningful and testable hypotheses. (We shall discuss this viewpoint more fully in section 1-3.)

To summarize the process of monetary policy outlined in this section: The Federal Reserve System makes a decision that it is going to try to improve the overall performance of the economy—for example, that it is going to try to change total employment. It will then implement this decision by causing the cash reserves of the commercial banking system to change. The banks then will interact with the public and the Federal Reserve in such a way that the total amount of money in the economy is changed. And this change in the quantity of money will (hopefully) have the desired effect on the level of employment. The entire process is indirect; no one anywhere has been told what to do. It is really quite remarkable.

1-2 AN OUTLINE OF THIS BOOK

At this point readers may feel that they see exactly how a textbook on money and banking should be organized: Start with the Federal Reserve System and proceed through its relations with the public and banks to the determination of the money supply. Then develop the theory necessary to link the money supply and the macro-economy. Right?

Wrong. Although this may be the "natural" organization of the material, it is pedagogically awkward. That is, the order in which these events occur in practice is not necessarily the best order in which to learn them. Perhaps the main reason for this has already been mentioned: the dual purpose of the book. For in addition to explaining monetary policy, our goal is also to describe the financial machinery of the United States economy. And this being the case, it is necessary to go into commercial banks and related financial institutions in much greater depth than can be justified by a study of monetary policy alone. To interrupt the flow of the material on monetary policy with a lengthy discussion of commercial banking would rupture the thread of the argument. Beyond this, it is easier to understand monetary policy after one has mastered the background of finance than to try to understand the Federal Reserve in an institutional vacuum.

For both these reasons, it is best to begin the study of monetary policy with the commercial banking system. But it is very important that students understand that to do so involves a paradox: The *logically correct* arrangement of the material would make the subject matter more difficult to learn and would almost certainly prove tedious. The *pedagogically correct* arrangement of the material is more interesting and lively but puts the various pieces of monetary policy together in a jumbled fashion, so that students may have a difficult time understanding how they fit together.

Referring again to Figure 1-1, note the letters A to G along the bottom. These letters indicate the sequence of the material as taken up in this book, as opposed to the numbers along the top of the figure, which indicate the logical development of the subject. Thus, we shall begin with a detailed description of the commercial banking system and related financial institutions (A) and move from there to the money supply (B). Currency and deposit creation (C) are then discussed. We shall consider next the Federal Reserve System (D) and how it is able to control the flow of reserves into the commercial banks (E). At this point students should know (if they have rearranged the jumbled pieces) how the Federal Reserve is able to influence the amount of money in the economy. The remaining task, therefore, is to determine how changes in the money supply affect the economy (F) and how effective this method of economic control is in practice (G). It need hardly be mentioned that there is a wealth of descriptive and analytic detail, as well as many important questions of public policy, involved in each of these steps.

Before turning to the substantive material of the monetary economy, it is desirable to say a few words on the method of economics—how do economists know what they know?

1-3 THE EMPIRICAL METHOD IN APPLIED ECONOMICS

Looking again at Figure 1-1, note that it is made up of two kinds of elements: boxes and arrows. We can think of the boxes as representing economic *institutions,* and the arrows as representing the economic *relationships* among these institutions. Thus, the Federal Reserve System and the commercial banking system are institutions in the sense that they each have a formal legal structure, defined rights and duties, specified officers, and so forth. A substantial knowledge of these institutions is a necessary first condition to understanding any area of economics; we could not hope to understand monetary policy without a working knowledge of the formal nature of the Federal Reserve or the financial machinery of the economy. But finding out the facts about such institutions presents no real difficulties; it is only necessary to look up what the law says about how many people are on the Board of Governors of the Federal Reserve System, counting the number of commercial banks in the United States, and so on. This is the *descriptive* part of economics.

While learning the descriptive details of economic institutions is frequently an interesting and rewarding activity, it is not enough to satisfy the inquisitive nature of the human animal. Nor can we hope to arrive at an understanding of the process of monetary policy by confining ourselves to description. It alone cannot tell us how the money supply is determined or what difference it makes. In order to study the relationships among economic institutions, it has been necessary to develop the *analytic* (as opposed to the descriptive) part of economics.

Economic analysis is not a simple procedure. We can't just look it up in the law books or even observe it directly in practice. Many people, of course, *believe* they know how various economic relationships work, basing their beliefs on the fact that they work in business, read the *Wall Street Journal* every day, or once made money in the stock market (they seldom tell you about the money they lost). Economists call this kind of thing *casual empiricism,* meaning, basically, that it is an opinion based on some kind of informal experience.

Of course, many people do learn from experience, and opinions and insights based on this learning process should not be dismissed lightly. Nevertheless, casual empiricism is not a very reliable method of investigation because, in this case, the word "casual" means "unsystematic." No two human beings ever have exactly the same experience or see the world in exactly the same way. Thus, radicals will interpret their experiences with the American business system in one way, and conservatives in another. Even two people in business in the same industry and with essentially the same social, economic, and political philosophies will interpret technical events—for example, a fall in stock prices—in widely different ways. And who is to say one is right and the other wrong? All casual empiricism is equal.

If we are to deal scientifically with cause-and-effect relationships among economic institutions, therefore, we need some systematic method of investigation—a method with commonly agreed upon rules, and where the same "experience" (evidence) is simultaneously available to all investigators. Economists have such a method. It has evolved slowly over literally hundreds of years, and it is a very difficult subject indeed. Yet it can be summarized in two words: *hypothesis testing.* Behind these two small words, however, lie two very big questions: Where do the hypotheses come from? and, How do we test them?

Sources of Hypotheses

In economics, as opposed to the physical sciences, many empirical relationships between two events tend to be spurious. By *spurious* is meant that the relationship is accidental—more apparent than real. For example, we might uncover a persistent statistical relationship between the price of eggs in Goose Bay, Labrador, and the per capita whiskey consumption in Blue Eye, Missouri (there really are such places). But even if we did so, we would nevertheless be inclined to dismiss such results as silly. We would feel this way because there is simply no reason to believe that the two sets of data are causally related to one another. In other words, we would reject out of hand the hypothesis that per capita whiskey consumption in Blue Eye determines egg prices in Goose Bay; we would immediately recognize such a hypothesis as absurd, whatever empirical support we might be able to garner for it.

To recognize a poor or trivial hypothesis is one thing; to explain what makes a hypothesis good is quite another. A good hypothesis is rather like Lord Acton's elephant: "A beast difficult to define but easy to recognize." Perhaps the best that can be done here is to suggest that a good hypothesis should appeal directly to at least one (and hopefully all) of the following: economic theory, intuition, and experience.

Economic Theory   Economic theory is primarily a way of looking at the social world around us; it is a mental framework which aids us in sorting and classifying social phenomena. But it is more than just a scheme of classification, for it also includes statements involving cause-and-effect relationships among economic events. Such statements, based on hypotheses about human behavior, lie at the heart of economic theory.

There are several criteria that might be listed for judging the "goodness" of a theory. For example, a good theory should be internally consistent in the sense that a conclusion derived from one part of it should not contradict a conclusion derived from another part. Or again, a good theory should be an abstraction from reality; it should *not* be developed at such a minute level of detail that it becomes mere description (beginning students frequently have a difficult time understanding this point). But from the viewpoint of applied economics, there are two basic aspects of economic theory which especially need to be noted: first, that it be able to guide the empirical investigator in distinguishing the important from the trivial; and, second, that it be stated in such a fashion that it generates testable hypotheses about how the world works.

It is essential that we be able to distinguish important and unimportant relationships in the economy, and it is impossible to make such distinctions without a theory. For example, try asking yourself the following question: If we want to stop inflation, is it more important to control the quantity of money or the quantity of peanut butter? The point of the question (which may surprise you) is that it really doesn't matter whether you answer money or peanut butter. *Either* answer implies a theory of the cause of inflation. In the absence of any theory at all, no answer is possible. Thus we must have a theory if we are to make any statement at all about how the economy functions. Many people who should know better refuse to accept this self-evident truth.

But a theory needs to go beyond merely pointing to important relationships. It needs also to be stated in terms that are operationally meaningful—that is, in terms which can be shown to be consistent or inconsistent with factual evidence. An example of a nonoperational theory might be the following statement: Inflation occurs because the spirit of Daniel Boone is unhappy. (Don't think that to hold to such a theory would be totally absurd; there are some very peculiar theories in this world.) The trouble with such a statement is that there is no test we can make to disprove it. We have no way of knowing the emotional state of Daniel Boone's spirit and hence no way of judging the accuracy of the hypothesis.

The purpose of economic theory might thus be thought of, for our purposes at least, as a source of testable hypotheses about important economic relationships. We might, indeed, define a good theory simply as a consistent set of such hypotheses. But it is necessary to go still one step further and ask ourselves what happens when we investigate a hypothesis and find it inconsistent with the evidence—that is, when we *disprove* it? Note, first, that disproving a hypothesis is a slow and laborious process, involving many subtle questions of interpretation and many technical questions of statistical method. But suppose we do disprove it. What then? Clearly it is then necessary to go back and rethink the theory so that this new information is taken into account. In this fashion economic theory and the testing of hypotheses interact upon one another. The process is one of mutual interdependence, with concepts and methods constantly evolving and changing over time.

Intuition and Experience   While theory is easily the best source of economic hypotheses, intuition is more common. Unfortunately, it is also more difficult to say anything very sensible about. For example, we do not need economic theory to support the hypothesis that big cities will have more banks than small towns. Such a statement appeals to us intuitively and we would, indeed, think it queer if no such relationship existed. Nevertheless, one should be cautious in accepting uncritically hypotheses based on intuitive appeal. Upon closer inspection, or after examining the empirical evidence, these hypotheses sometimes prove erroneous.

A third source of economic hypotheses is experience based on a thorough and detailed knowledge of economic institutions. Such experience may be gained either directly, e.g., by working in a particular business, or indirectly, e.g., by constantly studying developments and trends in a particular industry. Experience of this sort can provide a very rich vein of hypotheses for the empirical investigator to tap, frequently at a level of detail that economic theory cannot reach. Again, however, a couple of qualifications should be borne in mind: First, there is the all-too-human tendency to make generalized statements on the basis of particular examples. A business person who "knows" how some economic relationship "really" works may be basing this belief on only one or two very narrow and specific occurrences. Second, there is the trap into which we all fall from time to time—believing something is so because we want it to be that way. Scholars and business people, radicals and conservatives, men and women—we all have pet prejudices that we don't want the world to destroy. And our hypotheses are therefore likely to contain subtle biases that cause the evidence to show what we want it to show.

It is frequently possible to take hypotheses derived from intuition and experience and state them in terms of economic theory. When this can be done, it should be done. Not only does it provide an appropriate check on intuition and experience, but it often helps us also to gain insights into the nature of economic theory—its strengths and weaknesses, its generality and limitations. Indeed, one of the most fascinating things an economic investigator can do is to take a situation in which economic theory runs counter to what "everyone knows" and then devise a testable hypothesis to find out which is right.

Hypothesis Testing in Economics

The method economists use to test hypotheses about how the economy functions is called *statistical inference;* that is, we *infer* economic relationships through the application of statistical techniques to economic data.[1] The use of such techniques is as fundamental to the practice of contemporary economics as either economic theory or economic description. Indeed, properly understood, it is the statistical method that provides the necessary link between description and theory. In its absence, economics would be locked up into two watertight compartments, with description unable to tell us *how* things work and theory unable to tell us *if* they work. The statistical method permits us to arrange factual, or descriptive, material into the cause-and-effect framework of economic theory.

In this book we shall make limited use of only one of the statistical methods employed by economists: the technique of *regression analysis.* The purpose of using regression analysis is, very simply, to give the student some insight into how economists know what they know. Rather than making *ex cathedra* statements from the Olympian heights of the professional economist, we shall try to present and explain the kinds of evidence economists find persuasive, especially about controversial matters of public policy. Having examined the evidence students may then, of course, either accept or reject it; at the least they will understand the nature of the evidence upon which a particular conclusion rests.

Hypothesis testing in the discipline of economics typically proceeds by first developing an economic "model" of the real world—that is, a carefully constructed theory of the interrelationship between two or more observable facts. In the nature of the case, these models are usually of such complexity that to attempt to explain them would require more space than the results warrant. In addition, the testing of such models frequently requires the use of sophisticated statistical analysis, and much of this analysis requires training in statistical methods that cannot be expected of undergraduates. As a consequence only the most straightforward results will actually be given, although passing references will be made to other pertinent research. The student who has done any work at all in statistics will easily be able to interpret the regressions given in this book. For the student with no statistical training, an appendix is provided at the end of this chapter which gives an intuitive explanation of the few techniques used. No special knowledge (e.g., mathematics) is needed to understand the Appendix.

The Limits of Statistical Inference   A few precautionary words about the use of regression analysis are in order. In the first place, a hypothesis cannot be *proved* by statistical methods; the most that can be done in this respect is to show that the data are *consistent with* a hypothesis. The reason for this is that a regression equation cannot, by itself, demonstrate anything conclusive about cause and effect. For example, we might use regression analysis to show that changes in the money supply and

---

[1]The student with no background in statistics should probably read the Appendix to this chapter before reading this section.

national income are associated with one another. But does this prove that the quantity of money in the economy determines national income? Clearly not. We might argue as well that national income determines the quantity of money, or that they are both being determined together by some (unspecified) third force. In other words, a regression analysis will always be consistent with more than one hypothesis, and we must ultimately rely on economic theory to decide which hypothesis is correct.

But while a hypothesis cannot be proved correct by statistical methods, it can be proved wrong, that is, shown to be inconsistent with the factual evidence. Even here, however, it is necessary to exercise a good deal of caution. Setting up the precisely appropriate regression equation and then correctly interpreting the results is a very tricky business. In economics it is commonplace for different studies of the same phenomenon to give different results. The reason for these "mixed" results does not usually lie in the statistical method itself, but rather in the specification of the underlying model, different data sources, and so forth. Particularly when an economic relationship is well established in theory, one should not be too ready to disavow it on the basis of a single regression equation. Indeed, the same statement may be made for the *acceptance* of a hypothesis because it is consistent with a regression equation; here, too, more than a single test is required. Economists often speak of a *robust* relationship, by which they mean a relationship that continues to hold up in study after study.[2]

The Uses of Regression Analysis   Finally, it should be noted that there are many different ways in which regression analysis is used in economics. For example, we may be primarily interested in whether a relationship is "significant" (in the statistical sense) and much less interested in the precise nature of the relationship. Or we may be interested in *how much* of the behavior of one variable can be "explained" (r^2) by another. Or our interest may lie predominantly in the algebraic sign (i.e., plus or minus) of a particular coefficient and not so much in its actual value. Or, to give one last example, we may want to compare the predictive power of two competing theories with each other rather than comparing each one separately with the "real world." Regression analysis is a highly flexible tool and can be made to serve many different purposes.

Many issues of contemporary economics—theoretical as well as policy issues —turn ultimately on the answers to empirical questions. Some progress has been made in the past thirty years in providing answers to these questions, though much still remains to be done. In the remainder of the book, the attempt has been made to integrate both empirical questions and answers with the more traditional approach of description and theory.

[2]The meaning given here to *robust* is related to, but not the same as, the technical definition given it by statisticians.

1-4 REVIEW QUESTIONS

1 Why is this book organized differently from the way monetary policy works itself out in practice?
2 Distinguish among: (1) economic theory, (2) institutional description, and (3) hypothesis testing in economics.
3 Where do economic hypotheses come from?
4 What is meant by "casual empiricism"? How does this differ from "statistical inference"?

APPENDIX TO
CHAPTER ONE:
REGRESSION
ANALYSIS

One of the most curious aspects of contemporary economics is that the evidence upon which economists base even their most elementary conclusions is not generally "available" to the public. This is not true in the physical and biological sciences. Even grade-school children conduct experiments, and even preschool children have direct and immediate experiences with practical applications of scientific principles —doorknobs and television sets, for example. Yet the statistical method used in economics (and in the social sciences generally) is certainly no more difficult to understand than the experimental method used in physics.

The purpose of this appendix is accordingly to make the evidence of economics "available" to readers—"available" in the sense that they will be able to interpret a very few key statistical measures. It should be noted immediately that this is not a textbook in statistics; no attempt will be made to give instruction on *how* to conduct statistical experiments, or on any of the underlying mathematics. Rather, all that this section is intended to convey is a common-sense, intuitive "feel" for the essential meaning of a small number of statistical concepts. *Warning:* Without the knowledge of these concepts, the reader will find that certain parts of the rest of the book will be unintelligible. *Promise:* With the knowledge of these concepts, the reader will end up with a much better grasp, not just of money and banking, but of the entire discipline of economics.

We shall consider the following four statistical measures in turn:

1. The variance and standard deviation
2. The least-squares regression equation
3. The coefficient of determination (r^2)
4. Significance

A-1 THE VARIANCE AND STANDARD DEVIATION

The *variance* is a statistical measure that deals with a single collection of similar data —for example, a collection of data on the number of banks in a particular area. Because the variance deals only with a single collection of data, it cannot by itself tell us anything about cause-and-effect relationships. Its purpose is not analytical, but descriptive.

The variance, as the name implies, is a measure of the variability, or dispersion, of a collection of data. For example, suppose that we are interested in describing the locational convenience (to the public) of banks in a particular geographic area. We might want to know, for instance, if another bank should be permitted to open in this area. Since we could hardly expect the banks to conduct their business in the rural parts of the area, an examination of the numbers of banks in the various towns in the area is a reasonable way to delimit the study.

The first two columns of Table A-1 describe the banking situation in (hypothetical) geographic area 1. The area contains five towns, each with a different number of banks; town 1A has three banks, town 1B has four banks, and so forth. As shown, the data given in columns 1 and 2 of Table A-1 are perhaps sufficiently brief and direct that these figures alone would suffice for the problem. But if the table were to be made much longer and more complicated by adding on additional towns and

Table A-1

1 Towns in area no. 1	2 No. of banks in town	3 Average no. of banks in all five towns	4 No. of banks minus average no. of banks (col. 2 minus col. 3)	5 Squared no. of banks minus average no. of banks (col. 4 squared)
Town 1A	3	5	−2	4
Town 1B	4	5	−1	1
Town 1C	5	5	0	0
Town 1D	6	5	1	1
Town 1E	7	5	2	4

Total: 10

Variance = $^{10}/_5$ = 2

Standard deviation

= $\sqrt{\text{variance}}$ = $\sqrt{2}$

= 1.4

Table A–2

1	2	3	4	5
Town	No. of banks in town	Average no. of banks in all five towns	No. of banks minus average no. of banks (col. 2 minus col. 3)	Squared no. of banks minus average no. of banks (col. 4 squared)
Town 2A	0	5	−5	25
Town 2B	1	5	−4	16
Town 2C	5	5	0	0
Town 2D	9	5	4	16
Town 2E	10	5	5	25

Total: 82

Variance = $82/5$ = 18.4

Standard deviation

$$= \sqrt{\text{variance}} = \sqrt{18.4}$$
$$= 4.3$$

a wider variety of bank numbers, it would obviously be convenient to be able to summarize these data with a single number, or *statistic.* The most "natural" statistic to use for this summary is the *average,* or *mean,* number of banks per town in area 1. We, obtain the average, of course, by adding the number of banks in each town and then dividing by the number of towns. Thus in the case of area 1, there are five banks per town, on the average.

The trouble with using the average as a summary statistic to describe a particular set of data is that it frequently hides almost as much as it reveals. Specifically, it tells us nothing about the diversity of the different cases to be found in the data. Town 1A has only three banks, and town 1E has seven; the average tells us nothing about this. To illustrate this point, consider Table A-2, which describes a second (hypothetical) geographic area and gives in its first two columns the same type of data for area 2 as Table A-1 does for area 1. Now compare the two areas. The point of the exercise is that they both have exactly the same average number of banks per town, even though it is obvious from the data that the banks are spread out much more evenly in area 1 than they are in area 2. Town 2A, for example, has zero banks (a situation that does not occur in area 1), while towns 2D and 2E both have more banks than *any* town in area 1. It may thus be that because of the lumpiness of banking facilities in area 2, an additional bank should be permitted to open there, whereas there is no need for another bank in area 1. The average number of banks per town gives us no clue to this; it is identical in both cases. What we need, therefore, is another descriptive statistic (in addition to the average) that will give us some idea of the diversity of the data we are dealing with. The *variance* is the statistic most commonly used for this purpose.[1] It has almost the same intuitive appeal as the average.

Consider Table A-1 again. The first three columns give us six pieces of information: the number of banks in each of the five towns plus the average number of banks in all towns. We want to try to answer the question, How well does the average

[1]Actually, the *standard deviation* is the most frequently used statistic, but since the standard deviation is just the square root of the variance, the two are related in a simple and straightforward way and the distinction needn't bother us now. The standard deviation is discussed on p. 17.

describe these data? It seems clear that we can answer this question best by using *all* the information we have. We can also answer it best by focusing our attention on the average; it is, after all, the accuracy of the average that is the heart of the issue. The most logical way to begin, therefore, would seem to be to find out by how much the number of banks in each town differs from the average, or *norm*. This can be done by subtracting the average for all towns from what is true of each town. For example, town 1A has only three banks, whereas the average for all towns is five. Town 1A thus has two fewer banks than the average, and so we record this information as –2 in the first entry in column 4 (Table A-1). We do the same for each of the other towns, and in this fashion fill out all entries in column 4. Now what is needed is a single statistic that will describe all these deviations from the average. Note that we cannot simply take the average of column 4, since column 4 sums to 0 because the number of towns with below-average banking facilities is offset by the number of towns with above-average facilities. It turns out that the best way to get around this problem is to eliminate the minus signs by squaring each term in column 4, which gives column 5 (Table A-1). To obtain the variance, we simply take the average of these squared deviations; that is, we add the figures in column 5 and then divide by the number of entries. The variance of banks in the towns of area 1 is thus $10/5 = 2$.

Note that if we perform the same set of arithmetic calculations on the number of banks in the towns of geographic area 2 (Table A-2), we obtain a variance of $82/5 = 18.4$. Contrasting the variances of the two areas, we thus see that the variance for area 2 is larger than the variance for area 1. This is, of course, what we want: a single statistic which will tell us that the figures for area 1 are more tightly clustered about their average than are those of area 2. After inspecting the variances of the two areas, it thus seems reasonable to make the following interpretation: The average of five banks per town is a better description of area 1 than of area 2.

Still and all, the reader may feel some uneasiness with the variance as a descriptive statistic comparable to the average. This is probably because the variance is still in its squared form and has no direct intuitive interpretation. In other words, although a variance of 2 for area 1 may have some meaning, a variance of 18.4 for area 2 seems to have no meaning at all; it is substantially larger than any entry in column 2. The reason for this, of course, is that the figures in column 4 were squared, which results in very large numbers. But to understand the cause is to recognize the cure. The variance may be put back into an order of magnitude comparable to the original data simply by taking its square root. This square root of the variance is called the *standard deviation*. Thus the standard deviation of area 1 is approximately equal to 1.4, and the standard deviation of area 2 is about 4.3. While the standard deviation is a more "natural" descriptive statistic than the variance, our limited purposes here require an understanding only of the variance.

A-2 THE LEAST-SQUARES REGRESSION EQUATION

Our interest in the statistical method lies in our ability to use it to investigate cause-and-effect economic relationships. Since our ultimate aim is to be able to influence the economy in order to make it work better, it is necessary to understand how one thing will change if we change something else—for example, how interest rates will change if we change the quantity of money. The most common way to express such relationships in our daily lives is, of course, by using words. Thus, one frequently hears the statement that labor unions cause higher prices. The difficulty with such a statement is that (even if it's true) it doesn't tell us very much—it is not at all precise. The exact nature of the relationship remains unspecified. If there were more people in labor unions, would prices be still higher? How much higher? And so forth. What we need is a more careful method of saying the same thing, one that will permit us to quantify the relationship in addition to making the statement. But, of course, when we begin talking about a quantifiable cause-and-effect statement, we are really talking about a mathematical relationship.

In economics, many important relationships are most conveniently expressed in mathematical terms. Unfortunately, many people are frightened by mathematical relationships even though they in fact use them all the time. Consider, for example, the following simple statement: One British pound is worth two dollars. Another way of saying the same thing is to say, One British pound is *equal* to two dollars. The latter is a mathematical statement which can also be expressed as

One British pound = two dollars   (1)

If we now let $ be a symbol which stands for a dollar, and, similarly, let £ stand for a British pound, we can further simplify the statement by writing

$$£1 = \$2 \qquad\qquad\qquad\qquad (2)$$

Equation (2) says exactly the same thing as eq. (1) except that it says it much more briefly. But eq. (2) also tells us something a great deal more useful than the original statement (One British pound is worth two dollars). It tells us that this statement is not limited to the relationship between *one* pound and $2; it tells us, in fact, that we may convert any number of pounds into 2 times as many dollars *no matter how many pounds we have.* Thus, if we have 17 pounds, we can simply multiply both sides of eq. (2) by 17 to find the equivalent amount of dollars. Hence we can write

$$£(17) = \$2(17) \qquad\qquad\qquad\qquad (3)$$

or, performing the arithmetic,

$$£17 = \$34 \qquad\qquad\qquad\qquad (4)$$

Since we can make this same set of calculations for *any* number of British pounds, it is possible to show this same relationship between British pounds and dollars on a graph. It is frequently more convenient to show information in this form, for then we can read pound and dollar equivalents directly off the graph. A graph of eq. (2) is given in Figure A-1.

Figure A-1 is, in fact, a graph of a very simple *functional relationship.* By a functional relationship is meant only that the quantity of one thing determines the quantity of another. In this case, the number of British pounds determines the

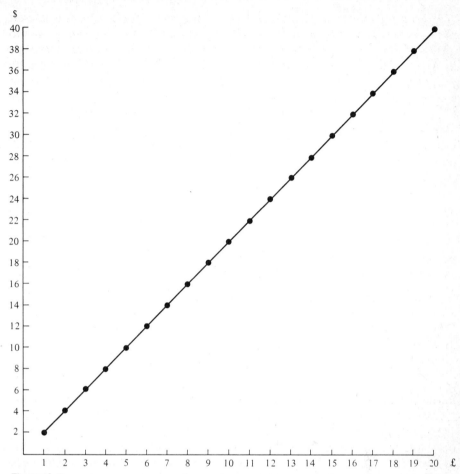

Figure A-1

number of dollars; or, expressing the same thing in more formal mathematical terms, the quantity of dollars *is a function of* the quantity of pounds.

This particular functional relationship has the advantage of being very precise. Look at Figure A-1 again and you will see that *all* pound-dollar equivalents lie exactly on the straight line of a graph (in fact, of course, the line is simply made up of a lot of these points). Unfortunately, most economic relationships are not so precise. Other factors, which the investigator doesn't know anything about, will enter into the relationship between the two variables being studied.

Consider, again, the question of the number of banks in each of the five towns in geographic area 1 (see section A-2). Since we are interested in whether to open another bank in this area, an obvious question to ask is: Why do some towns have more banks than others? Or, putting the question more generally, What *causes* the number of banks in a town? One reasonable possibility, or *hypothesis,* is that the number of banks in a town depends on (is a function of) the size of the town.

Table A-3

Town	No. of banks in town	Population of town
Town 1A	3	5,000
Town 1B	4	8,000
Town 1C	5	7,000
Town 1D	6	12,000
Town 1E	7	13,000

Moreover, we would expect the relationship to be positive—i.e., the larger the town, the more banks it will have.

The first two columns of Table A-3 repeat the information contained in the first two columns of Table A-1. Additionally, Table A-3 contains a third column giving the data on the population of each of the five towns in area 1. It is clear, simply from looking at Table A-3, that there is *some* positive relationship between population and banks per town. But it is also clear that the relationship is not at all exact. Town 1B has more people and fewer banks than town 1C, for example, and town 1D is much larger than town 1C but has only one more bank. What we need, then, is a method of expressing the *inexact relationship* between population and banks per town that is similar to the method we used to express the exact relationship between British pounds and dollars.

As a first step in analyzing the relationship among the data given in Table A-3, we might show them in graphic form, as we did with the pound-dollar relationship. Figure A-2 does this. The vertical axis measures the number of banks per town, while the horizontal axis measures the population. Each town has a unique combination

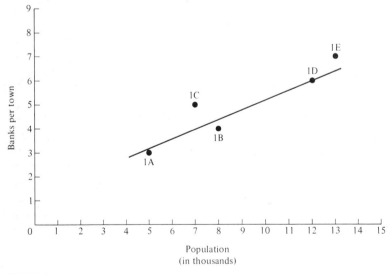

Figure A-2

of banks and people that can be described by only one point in this figure. For example, town 1B has 4 banks and 8,000 people, and hence a dot labeled "1B" is placed at the intersection of a horizontal line extended from 4 banks and a vertical line extended from 8,000 people; the other four points in Figure A-2 are located in a similar manner.

It is apparent from an inspection of Figure A-2 that we have some sort of a systematic relationship at work here, and it is desirable to be able to describe this relationship in the same way we did the pound-dollar relationship—by drawing a single straight line. The trouble is, which straight line? Any number of straight lines can be drawn in and around the five points of Figure A-2. What is thus needed is, first, a uniform method that will give all investigators the same straight line; and, second, a line that in some sense "best" describes the relationship between banks per town and population. The method most commonly used by economists is the *least-squares regression equation.*

While no attempt will be made here to go through the arithmetic of deriving the least-squares regression equation for the example given in Table A-3 (as we did for the variance), the general idea can be explained in fairly simple terms. The least-squares regression equation is that line which minimizes the sum of the squares of the "distances" between each observation and the line itself. Since such a statement as this is apt to be confusing on a first reading, let's take it a step at a time.

Suppose we were to draw just any old line through the dots, or *observations,* shown in Figure A-2. Having drawn such a line, we could then measure the vertical distance between this line and any one of the dots shown. Consider, for example, the dot labeled "1C" in Figure A-2. This dot lies a distance of +1.1 banks per town *above* the line shown in Figure A-2 (hence the plus sign). The dot labeled "1B," on the other hand, lies a distance of – 0.3 banks per town *below* the line shown in Figure A-2 (hence the minus sign). Now suppose we do this for each dot and then take each of these distances and square it. For example, the square of the distance for dot 1C would be +1.22 (1.1 squared), and the square of the distance for dot 1B would be +0.09 (– 0.3 squared).

If, finally, we add together all these squared distances, we get a sum of the squares. The size of this sum will obviously be larger or smaller depending on what line we draw; one line will give us one sum, another line another sum. The problem is, Which of these lines is "best" in the sense that it best describes the relationship between banks per town and population? Viewed in this way, it seems intuitively obvious that the best line is the one that gives us the smallest sum of these squared distances. This is what the least-squares regression equation does (the meaning of *least squares* should now be clear). The regression equation is unique—there is no other line that will give a smaller sum of squared distances—and can be calculated from a standard mathematical formula. (This formula may be found in any elementary text on statistics.)

The regression equation for the data given in Table A-3 is

$$\text{Banks per town in area 1} = 1.09 + .0004 \text{ population} \tag{5}$$

or, if we let the symbol B stand for "banks per town in area 1," and the symbol P stand for "population,"

$$B = 1.09 + .0004P \tag{6}$$

This is the equation of the regression line shown in Figure A-2.

To interpret eq. (6), look first at the numbers in it: 1.09 and .0004. These numbers are called the *coefficients* of the equation. Consider first the coefficient 1.09. What this *might* tell us (under other circumstances) is the value that B would take on if P were equal to zero; that is, if $P = 0$, then

$$\begin{aligned} B &= 1.09 + .0004(0) \\ &= 1.09 \end{aligned}$$

In words, this means that a town with no one in it (zero population) would, according to the regression equation, nevertheless have 1.09 banks. Such a result is clearly nonsensical and, in fact, is caused by overinterpreting the regression equation. The fact is that we have no observations in our data for towns with a population of less than 5,000, and therefore we cannot make any legitimate inferences about such towns. In much the same way, if we were to use this regression equation to estimate the number of banks in a town of 1 million people, we would have

$$\begin{aligned} B &= 1.09 + .0004(1,000,000) \\ &= 1.09 + 400 \\ &= 401.09 \end{aligned} \tag{7}$$

Although this result may seem reasonable, it is actually just as nonsensical as our previous calculation. We simply don't know *anything* about towns this size insofar as our data are concerned. The student should be very cautious in extrapolating a regression equation beyond the bounds of the data.

Consider next the second coefficient .0004. The first thing to note is that the number is meaningless taken by itself. Unless we know the units of the variable with which it is multiplied (in this case P), the number tells us nothing. However, once it is realized that this coefficient is multiplied by population (or number of people), it tells us a great deal. In fact, it is this coefficient which really gives us the basic nature of the estimated relationship between banks per town and population. Specifically, it tells us that a town in this area will add 1 bank for every 2,500 people (this is not at all realistic; keep in mind that the numbers have been picked for convenience, not realism). This is evident from the fact that .0004(2,500) = 1. Consider, for example, how many banks there would be in a town of 5,000 people:

$$\begin{aligned} B &= 1.09 + .0004(5,000) \\ &= 1.09 + 2 \\ &= 3.09 \end{aligned} \tag{8}$$

Now perform the same arithmetic for a town with a population of 7,500 people. Then

$$B = 1.09 + .0004(7,500)$$
$$= 1.09 + 3$$
$$= 4.09 \tag{9}$$

By comparing eqs. (8) and (9), it will be seen that the population has gone up by 2,500 and the number of banks has gone up by 1. This will be true in general of this estimated relationship no matter what population figure we begin with: If the population increases by 2,500, the number of banks will increase by 1.

Now return to the problem with which we began: Should we permit an additional bank to be opened in this area? The regression equation can give us a good deal of help in answering this question. It probably depends on which town we want to open a new bank in. Look again at Figure A-2. Obviously, town 1C would be a poor choice for starting up a new bank since this town lies well above the regression line. In other words, town 1C already has more banks than it should have, at least according to the estimated relationship between banks and population. On the other hand, town 1B lies below the regression line and might very well be able to support an additional bank. It would at least be worthy of further investigation.

One final point should be made concerning the regression equation, a point that is extremely important for the student to understand: By a straightforward extension of the method of least squares, more than one variable can be included in the regression equation. Since most economic relationships are not of the simple "one thing causes one other thing" variety, it is necessary to emphasize this point. For example, in the problem we have just considered, the number of banks per town in area 1 may be a function not only of town population, but also of, say, per capita income in each of the towns. If so, the least-squares method of regression can still handle it. We would then get an equation of the form

Number of banks per town in area 1
$$= a + b \text{ (population)} + c \text{ (per capita income)} \tag{10}$$

where a, b, and c are the coefficients. Equation (10) is to be interpreted just like eq. (5).

A-3   THE COEFFICIENT OF DETERMINATION (r^2)

In our discussion of the regression equation, the point was made that least-squares regression is basically a systematic method for dealing with *imprecise* relationships. Thus in the example we have been using, the number of banks in a town is obviously related somehow to the population of the town, but the relationship is by no means exact. Yet we run into a paradox here. For while we admit that the relationship is not exact, we nevertheless describe it with an equation which is mathematically precise. Something more is clearly needed.

Table A–4

Town	No. of banks in town	Population of town
Town 2A	0	2,000
Town 2B	1	25,000
Town 2C	5	50,000
Town 2D	9	31,000
Town 2E	10	34,000

As an example, suppose that we were to collect population data for the towns in area 2 just as we did for area 1. These hypothetical data are given in Table A-4 and shown in Figure A-3. The regression equation for the data in area 2 is

$$B = .69 + .0002P \tag{11}$$

This equation is plotted as the straight line in Figure A-3. Now compare eq. (6), the regression equation describing the relationship in area 1, with eq. (11), the regression equation dealing with area 2. While the coefficients in the two equations are different, there is nothing in the *form* of either equation to distinguish between them. But now take a look at Figures A-2 and A-3. Even a casual glance will show you that the regression line in Figure A-2 "fits" the data for area 1 much better than the regression line of Figure A-3 fits the data for area 2. In Figure A-2, the dots are fairly tightly clustered around the regression line; in Figure A-3, the dots are scattered all over the place. Obviously, the regression line of Figure A-2 describes the relationship much better than does the regression line of Figure A-3. But eqs. (6) and (11) give no clue to this. What is needed, therefore, is some additional statistic describing how well a regression equation "fits" the data. This statistic is the *coefficient of determination.*

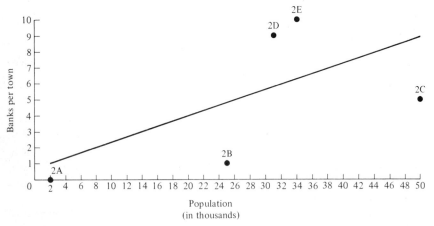

Figure A-3

To understand the rationale behind the coefficient of determination, let us put the matter in a slightly different way. Go back to the basic problem. We are trying to find out what causes, or *determines,* the number of banks per town in each of the two areas. On a priori grounds, we decided that the size of the town probably has a lot to do with the number of banks in it. Now we are trying to see if this is so. In short, first we formulated a hypothesis, and now we are trying to test it. What we really want to know, then, is the answer to the question, How good is our hypothesis? That is, how well does population "explain" the number of banks per town?

The key to understanding the coefficient of determination is to understand what is meant by the word "explain" in this context. Of course, statistical analysis cannot explain something in any very profound sense of the word. Only the reasonableness of the hypothesis can do that; a regression equation is never any better than the hypothesis underlying it, and is certainly no substitute for common sense. So when we use the word "explain" here, we use it only in a very narrow and superficial way. What is meant, and *all* that is meant, is this: How much of the variance in the number of banks per town is associated with the population per town? Note that giving the word "explain" this meaning involves a trick. We have deliberately avoided a big question that we can't answer (why?) and substituted instead a small question that we can answer (how much?). For we can measure the variance of the banks per town, and we can measure the population in the different towns, and all else that is needed is some rule for relating these two things in a meaningful way.

Looked at in this fashion, it seems a logical first step to break down the variance of the number of banks per town into two parts: that part which is "explained by" or associated with, the populations of the towns, and that part which is not explained by these populations. That is, we can say that

Total variance of B
= variance of B explained by P + unexplained variance of B (12)

Rearranging terms, we have

Variance of B explained by P
= total variance of B–unexplained variance of B (13)

Now clearly it would be convenient to have the statistic we are looking for have a uniform range over which to move, so that we can interpret it easily as we move from problem to problem. Equation (13), for example, is awkward to work with because the variance of B is expressed in units of number of banks per town; other problems might be expressed in dollars, rates of interest, and so on. The simplest and most natural way to eliminate this problem is to put everything in proportional terms. This can be done by dividing both sides of eq. (13) by the total variance of B. Thus

$$\frac{\begin{array}{c}\text{Variance of } B\\ \text{explained by } P\end{array}}{\text{Total variance of } B} = \frac{\text{total variance of } B}{\text{total variance of } B} - \frac{\text{unexplained variance of } B}{\text{total variance of } B} \qquad (14)$$

The left-hand side of eq. (14) is the coefficient of determination; it is that proportion of the total variance which is explained by the regression equation. The symbol generally used for the coefficient of determination is r^2. Using this symbol and simplifying the right-hand side of eq. (14) gives

$$r^2 = 1 - \frac{\text{unexplained variance of } B}{\text{total variance of } B} \qquad (15)$$

Thus, all we really need to know is what is meant by the *unexplained variance of B*. But this is easy. It is simply that part of the changes in B which is not explained by the regression equation. For example, according to the regression equation for area 1, a town with a population of 7,000 should have 3.89 banks. But town 1C, in fact, has five banks. Thus 1.11 (5.00 – 3.89) banks in town 1C are not explained by the regression equation. If we make the same calculation for each observation and then take the variance of the resulting numbers, we have that part of B's variance which is not explained by our hypothesis that the populations of the towns in area 1 determine the number of banks in the town.

Now look at eq. (15) more closely. Suppose that the regression equation fitted the data exactly, i.e., that all observed points fell exactly on the regression line, as with the pound-dollar example. Then *all* the total variance would be explained by the regression equation, and so, of course, the proportion left unexplained would be zero. But if the unexplained part equals zero, then $r^2 = 1$. Contrariwise, suppose that the regression equation indicated no functional relationship between the two variables. (This would be the case if the regression line were perfectly flat, with no slope at all.) In this case, the unexplained variance would exactly equal the total variance, and hence, according to eq. (15), $r^2 = 0$. Since we can't explain less than none or more than all of something, the coefficient of determination must therefore lie somewhere between 0 and 1; that is, $0 \leq r^2 \leq 1$. In general, the closer r^2 is to 1, the more we have explained and the better the "fit" of the regression equation; the closer r^2 is to 0, the less we have explained and the worse the fit of the regression equation.

Finally, let us return to our point of departure: how well the regression lines of Figures A-2 and A-3 fit the data. Simply by looking at the figures, it was apparent that the line of Figure A-2 gave a better fit than that of Figure A-3. (If we had had several dozen observations in each case, however, the goodness of fit would not be so obvious.) We are now in a position to say something more definite on this subject. Specifically, for the data in area 1 (Table A-3 and Figure A-2), $r^2 = .89$; for the data in area 2 (Table A-4 and Figure A-3), $r^2 = .39$. Thus, the calculation of the coefficient of determination bears out in a more precise way what we decided on the basis of casual inspection. In area 1, the population "explains" 89 percent of the variation of banks per town; in area 2, it explains only 39 percent.

A-4 SIGNIFICANCE

The meaning of *significance* in regression analysis rests on the field of mathematics known as *probability theory*. Because of this dependence on the underlying mathematics, an intuitive understanding of the concept is much more difficult to convey; tests for significance lack the common-sense appeal of the statistical concepts already discussed. For this reason, the explanation of statistical significance given here will be comparatively brief.

When we speak of the *significance* of a particular statistic, we are really making a probability statement. To get some idea of what is meant by this, consider the following example. Suppose that we were to take a very large pot and dump into it 500 white golf balls and 500 red golf balls, mixing them thoroughly. We then blindfold a passing stranger and ask our subject to choose six balls at random. Obviously, under such circumstances, we would expect the stranger to choose *something like* three red and three white balls, but we would not be particularly surprised if four white and two red balls were selected. We would be absolutely astonished, however, if all six balls chosen turned out to be red. If we were asked the reason for our astonishment, we would very likely say that the probability of the blindfolded stranger choosing six red balls at random was very low—that there was only about 1 chance out of 100 of this happening. What exactly would we mean by this? We would mean that if we were to repeat this same experiment 100 times, we would expect 6 red balls to be chosen only once in all those 100 experiments.

Now let's turn the problem around. Suppose that we are the blindfolded stranger, that no one tells us what the mixture of red and white balls is, but that we do know how many red and white balls we picked in our random selection. Since the pot hasn't changed, and since the balls haven't changed, we can consequently make a logical inference about the mixture of red and white balls in the pot. For example, if we were to choose six red balls, we would still be entitled to say that there was only 1 chance in 100 of this happening if the red and white balls were present in equal amounts. On saying this, we would mean exactly what we did before: If we repeated this experiment 100 times, we would expect to choose six red balls only once if there were an equal number of red and white balls.

Now suppose the economic investigator is the blindfolded stranger and the "experiment" is the regression equation. What the economist tries to do is to apply these same laws of probability to gain a better understanding of economic relationships. But the question asked by the economist is slightly different than the one just posed. To understand this, consider again the regression lines of either Figure A-2 or Figure A-3. Since these lines slope upward and to the right, we are inclined to argue that they are consistent with the hypothesis that banks per town and population per town are positively related. But how confident are we of this hypothesis? If the regression lines had been flat, with no slope, we would have said that there was no functional relation between number of banks and population, and we would have rejected the hypothesis. The amount of confidence we can place in our regression results, then, really boils down to this: What is the probability that, even if the "true" regression line were flat, we would still obtain the results shown? If the probability were 50 percent—that is, if the odds were even—then we would be pretty skeptical of attaching any meaning, or *significance,* to our results. But if there were only 1 chance in 100 that we would obtain the relationship shown if, in fact, there were no relationship, we would be much more confident—much more inclined to base subsequent actions on these results.

Note that when we ask whether the regression *line* is flat, we are really asking about only a single element in the regression *equation.* For it is the coefficient on the explanatory variable—e.g., the .0004 in eq. (6)—that determines the slope of the regression line. If this coefficient is zero, then the regression line is absolutely flat. Look again at eq. (6), for example. If the coefficient on P is equal to zero, then $B = 1.09$ no matter what the population is. Thus when we ask the question, What is the probability that the regression line is flat? we are really asking, What is the probability that the coefficient on the explanatory variable could be equal to zero? Or, more accurately, we are asking the question, What is the probability that I could have obtained the coefficient I did obtain even if the true coefficient were zero? This is what the economist means by *significance.*

By custom, more than anything else, economists tend to use a cutoff point of 5 or 1 percent in judging whether a coefficient is significant. By *5 percent* or *1 percent* is simply meant that there is only 1 chance in 20 or 1 chance in a 100 that the economist would have obtained the coefficient that was obtained in the regression equation even if, in fact, the true coefficient were zero. Thus, when an economist says that a particular statistical relationship is significant, the word "significant" is being used as an abbreviation; it means that the coefficient is significantly different from zero at the 1 (or 5) percent level.

A-5 SUMMARY

The four statistical concepts just discussed will be used throughout the remainder of this book. If they are not already familiar to the student, it may be convenient to have a summary statement of them to be referred to later.

1 *Variance and Standard Deviation* The variance is a measure of the variability, or dispersion, of a collection of data about its average, or mean, value. The *standard deviation* is the square root of the variance.

2 *The Least-squares Regression Equation* The least-squares regression equation is a method of describing the cause-and-effect relationship between two variables by fitting a straight line, or linear equation, to the data.

3 *The Coefficient of Determination* (r^2) The coefficient of determination (r^2) tells us what proportion of the changes in one variable is explained by the changes in another variable. Alternatively, it is a measure of how well the regression equation describes the relationship between the variables.

4 *Significance* Statistical significance tells us the probability that a particular relationship between two variables could have been obtained by chance if, in fact, no such relationship actually exists. It is most commonly applied to

the coefficient on the explanatory variable and tells us the probability that this coefficient is actually equal to zero.

A-6 REVIEW QUESTIONS

1   Suppose two groups of people, group A and group B. Both groups have an average income of $15,000 per year, but group A incomes have a variance of $3,000 and group B incomes have a variance of $11,000. What does this tell you about how income is distributed in the two groups?

2   Give a common-sense interpretation of the meaning of the words "least squares" in the phrase "least-squares regression equation."

3   What does an r^2 of .89 mean?

4   What does it mean to say that a coefficient is significant at the 5 percent level?

PART 2

THE COMMERCIAL BANKING INDUSTRY

The purpose of the following three chapters is to acquaint the student with the commercial banking industry of the United States. That is, the primary objective of this part of the book is to begin to fill in that portion of Figure 1-1 labeled "3" above and "A" below. This is shown as Figure II-1.

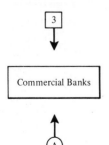

Figure II-1 Detail of Figure 1-1.

The material to be covered in Part Two is predominantly descriptive. It is a part of that field of economics commonly called industrial organization, that is, the study of how various industries are organized for the purpose of producing goods and services for sale in the market. Thus in the next three chapters we shall examine questions involving various legal forms of banking, whether the banking industry is competitive or monopolistic, the extent and form of governmental regulation and supervision, and so on. But while the basic purpose of Part Two is descriptive, we shall also enter into a number of controversial areas of public policy, areas where theoretical and empirical analyses are required.

2

The Banking
Structure
of the United States

Visitors from abroad are frequently perplexed by the many different forms of American commercial banking. What may confuse the foreigner as apparently unnecessary complexity, however, may in fact appeal to Americans as a wholly desirable diversity of institutional arrangements. In a nation spanning an entire continent, it would seem necessary to have institutions capable of being adapted to local circumstances. Most Americans would probably regard a single banking law and a single legal type of bank organization as too rigid and constraining. Nevertheless, it must be admitted that this diversity may at times result in confusion and inefficiency, not only for students of banking, but for bankers and the regulatory authorities as well. In this chapter we shall describe the major kinds of banking in the United States.

Before beginning the description of the organizational aspects of banking, however, a warning is in order: American commercial banking is changing very fundamentally and very rapidly. Things that were true just a few years ago are no longer true today, and things that are true today may not be true a few years hence. A description of the current banking structure of the United States is, therefore, rather like a still photograph of a horse race: The picture is accurate enough, but the real story is in the action.

While no one, of course, can predict the future, certain trends in banking today appear so dominant that they will almost certainly shape the future nature of banking. In this and the following two chapters we shall try to highlight these trends, while at the same time giving an accurate portrait of banking as it currently exists. As you read on, here are the things to look for: the holding company movement in banking; electronic banking; and the growing similarities between nonbank deposit institutions and commercial banks.

2-1 COMMERCIAL BANKING

The phrase *commercial banking* has been used several times but has not yet been defined. Actually, the term is something of a misnomer—or more accurately, it is an expression that may have been descriptively valid 150 years ago but which does not clearly distinguish banks from other financial institutions today. The word "commercial" is a throwback to the so-called *commercial loan* theory of banking[1] that held sway during the nineteenth century. This theory argued that bank assets (except for cash) should consist exclusively of commercial loans—that is, short-term loans to businesses for financing the production and transportation of goods and the holding of inventories. Putting it the other way around, the theory held that banks should *not* invest in long-term loans, such as those used for financing real estate and the purchase of capital equipment (buildings, machinery, and so on).

The term *commercial banking* is no longer a particularly good one for two reasons: First, banks are no longer the exclusive suppliers of credit for financing short-term business needs, and thus the term does not adequately distinguish banks from certain other financial institutions. Second, commercial banks have long since ceased to adhere to the commercial loan theory of banking in the types of assets they acquire. Today banks hold many long-term assets, including long-term loans to businesses and governments, and the expression *commercial banking* can therefore be misleading if taken literally. Nevertheless, the weight of tradition is such that the term *commercial banking* is still widely used to differentiate banks from other financial institutions, and consequently we shall continue to use it here.

In fact, it is very difficult to devise a functional (as opposed to legal) definition of banks that would set them off from all other financial institutions. As recently as ten years ago it would have been accurate to define commercial banks as the only institutions that handled *demand deposits,* or what the public usually calls *checking accounts.* In the past few years, however, savings and loans associations in some parts of the country have been authorized to issue *negotiable orders of withdrawal* (commonly called NOW accounts), and credit unions authorized to issue *share drafts.* Both of these instruments function like checks—that is, bills can be paid with them by ordering the institution involved to pay part of a deposit to a third party.[2] But while demand deposits are no longer unique to commercial banks, it is neverthe-

---

[1]See Chapter 8 for a more complete explanation of the commercial loan theory of banking.
[2]NOW accounts and share drafts are discussed more fully in Chapters 3 and 4.

less true that the overwhelming bulk of *third-party transfers* (as all forms of checks are called) are handled by commercial banks. Thus most people and corporations in the United States pay their bills by writing checks against their demand deposits in commercial banks. In consequence, commercial banks are by far the major institutions responsible for our country's *payments mechanism,* that is, the mechanism whereby people and corporations make payments to one another. As such, the importance of commercial banks for the smooth functioning of our economy can hardly be exaggerated. It is precisely this aspect of banking that accounts for the economist's peculiar interest in it.

But to identify commercial banks solely with their function as a repository of demand deposits would be misleading. Banks are much more than that. From the viewpoint of both the banker and the public, the essence of the commercial bank can best be captured if it is thought of as a department store of financial services. Other institutions ("specialty shops") may offer a few of these services, but only the bank offers them all within the context of a single organization. Because these other aspects of banking (e.g., factoring, trusts, safety deposit boxes, foreign exchange) have comparatively little to do with monetary policy, they will not be discussed much in this book. But keep in mind that from the workaday viewpoint of the individual banker, these aspects of banking are equally as compelling as demand deposits.

2-2 DUAL BANKING

Because of its importance in the functioning of the economy, commercial banking in the United States is a highly regulated business. In order to start a new bank, it is first necessary to obtain the permission of the government. This permission, when granted, is obtained in the form of what is called a *charter.* A charter to engage in the business of commercial banking may be obtained from either the federal government or from one of the various state governments. If the charter is granted by the federal government, the bank is known as a *national bank* and is part of what is called the *national banking system* (all federally chartered banks considered collectively). All national banks, and *only* national banks, must have the word "national" in their titles.[3] Banks that are not national banks receive their charters from the state governments. Thus the First National Bank of Anytown is a national bank that is chartered and regulated by the federal government; and the Peoples Bank of Anytown is chartered and regulated by the banking authorities of the state in which it does business. In every state, therefore, two sets of banks exist side by side: national banks and state banks. This legal arrangement is known as *dual banking.*[4]

Table 2-1 shows the number of state and national banks in the United States since 1960. As of the end of 1977, there were 14,718 commercial banks in the United States. Of these, 4,701, or about one-third, were national banks and the remaining 10,017 were chartered by various state governments. As can be seen from Table 2-1,

---

[3]National banks may also identify themselves by the addition of the letters "NBA" to their titles.
[4]The reasons why the United States has a dual banking system are largely historical. United States banking history is discussed in Chapter 13.

Table 2-1   Commercial Banks According to Type of Charter

Year	National banks	State banks	Total banks
1960	4,530	8,944	13,474
1961	4,513	8,920	13,433
1962	4,503	8,924	13,427
1963	4,615	8,954	13,569
1964	4,773	8,988	13,761
1965	4,815	8,989	13,804
1966	4,799	8,971	13,770
1967	4,758	8,963	13,721
1968	4,716	8,963	13,679
1969	4,669	8,993	13,662
1970	4,621	9,067	13,688
1971	4,600	9,184	13,784
1972	4,613	9,315	13,928
1973	4,659	9,512	14,171
1974	4,706	9,759	14,465
1975	4,741	9,892	14,633
1976	4,735	9,937	14,672
1977	4,701	10,017	14,718

Source: 1977 (to June 30th), Federal Reserve Bulletin, March, 1978, p. A17. Previous years: various issues of the Federal Reserve Bulletin.

these proportions have remained comparatively steady for the past two decades; there is no strong trend in favor of one type of bank or the other.

The existence of dual banking accounts for much of the complexity of the American banking industry. The laws governing national banks are different from the laws governing state banks, and the banking laws of each state are different from those of every other state. Banking practices that are legally permitted and, indeed, even encouraged in one state may be absolutely prohibited in another state; and practices permitted national banks in a state may be denied state-chartered banks in the same state. The resulting complexity of the banking structure is hardly surprising.

This profusion of regulations, statutes, and supervisory authorities caused by dual banking is frequently defended on the grounds already noted at the beginning of this chapter—that it permits a closer adaption of banking structure to local circumstances. Beyond this, it is sometimes also argued that the various possible chartering sources for banks perform a sort of experimental service to the banking community. This argument runs as follows. If we had only a single banking law governing all banks, then any changes in the law would have to be done on an all-or-nothing basis; that is, every bank in the country would be affected to the same extent and at the same time. Since such all-or-nothing changes might have fairly drastic consequences, it is held that a single, uniform banking code for all banks would prove too rigid, incapable of adapting to changing times. In contrast, the present arrangement makes it possible for changes in the law to be carried out in a single state and for the other states to wait and see how this "experiment" works before deciding whether they try it. As a corollary to this argument, many bankers seem to feel that their ability to choose between a national or a state charter gives them a sort of competitive leverage with the regulatory agencies. If one agency or the other becomes too hidebound, the bankers feel, they can change the source of their charter, and even the *threat* of substantial amounts of charter switching is enough to keep the agencies on their toes. To the possible counterargument, that competition among regulators may lead to increasing laxity, it is answered that the existence of the Federal Deposit Insurance Corporation, which examines virtually all banks in the United States, is sufficient to prevent widespread abuses in banking.

As a general proposition, large banks tend to be national banks while small banks tend to have charters from state governments. For example, although the national banks constitute slightly less than one-third of the *number* of commercial banks in the United States, they hold almost 60 percent of the assets of all commercial banks.

The advantage to a bank of having a state charter lies primarily in the amount and kinds of reserve assets it is required by law to maintain.[5] All commercial banks in the United States are required to maintain part of their assets in the form of reserves. For national banks, these reserves are comparatively large and must be held either as cash on hand or as funds deposited in the district Federal Reserve Bank. The important point to note is that such reserves are *nonearning assets;* that is, they do not earn the bank interest or buy services, as do its other assets. By contrast, the state laws dealing with bank reserves tend to be more liberal. They may require smaller reserves, or they may permit the bank to use selected earning assets (such as government securities) to satisfy its reserve requirements. Since in the final analysis banks are in business to make a profit, they naturally want their nonearning assets to be as small as possible. Most banks consequently choose state charters.

The advantages to a bank of having a national charter lie in the kinds of business it may engage in. In general, the laws and regulations governing the behavior of national banks tend to be more flexible than those governing state banks.[6] This flexibility is meaningful, however, only if the bank is large enough to take advantage of it. A small bank in a small town in the Midwest would have no interest in the flexibility of the laws governing its foreign exchange department, for example, since it doesn't have one. Thus small banks tend to prefer the reserve-requirement advantages of state laws, and large banks tend to prefer the flexibility of the national laws. In the past few years, however, a few large banks have switched from a national to a state charter to avoid the comparatively large amount of nonearning assets associated with being a national bank. Whether such charter switching constitutes a trend remains to be seen. It has concerned the federal authorities enough that the Federal Reserve System has requested Congress to permit it to pay interest on bank reserves. So far, Congress has not seen fit to grant such permission.

[5]This is not the only advantage of a state charter. For example, the capital requirements of state-chartered banks, especially as they apply to the establishment of branches, tend to be lower than for national banks.

[6]See William J. Brown, *The Dual Banking System in the United States,* The American Bankers Association, New York, not dated; reprinted in *Compendium of Issues Relating to Branching by Financial Institutions,* Committee on Banking, Housing and Urban Affairs, Subcommittee on Financial Institutions, United States Senate, October 1976, pp. 239–311. See also E. S. Redford, "Dual Banking," *Law and Contemporary Problems,* Autumn 1966, pp. 749–774.

2-3 UNIT BANKING

The United States is unique among the industrial nations of the world in having as many banks as it does. Most nations have only a few banks. For example, Canada has ten banks and England has thirteen. The United States, in contrast, has almost fifteen *thousand* banks. The difference between the United States banking system and that of other countries is that the United States has a great many *unit banks*. A formal definition of a unit bank is that it is a single commercial banking organization operating a single banking office, is not controlled by another corporation, and is not controlled by a person who also controls another bank. In other words, a unit bank is one that is *not:* (1) a branch bank (more than one office); a holding-company affiliate (bank holding company); or a member of a chain of banks (noncorporate common ownership of two or more banks).

Until very recently, the United States could be accurately described as a unit banking country in the sense that more than half the banks in the country were unit banks. However, in the past decade there has been such a rapid growth in bank holding companies that this is probably no longer the case. Nevertheless, the concept of the locally owned and locally managed unit bank continues to dominate a great deal of public policy concerning banking, much as the concept of the family farm continues to dominate much of the public policy concerned with agriculture.

2-4 BRANCH BANKING

A *branch bank* is just what the name sounds like: a single banking corporation that offers a full line of banking services in two or more offices. The largest branch in the system (measured in terms of deposits) is generally known as the *head office,* although it may occasionally happen that one of the branches will grow larger than the head office. Branching may occur in either of two ways: *de novo branching,* where a branch is developed from scratch, or *branching by merger,* where one bank takes over another bank and then operates the acquired bank as a branch.

The extent of branch banking in the United States is controlled by the banking laws of the various state governments. National banks are permitted to branch to the extent, but only to the extent, that the banks chartered by the government of the state in which they do business are permitted to branch. There is no constitutional issue involved in this arrangement. Congress has voluntarily subordinated the branch banking question to the state governments—a sort of local option—and could change the arrangement at any time. Indeed, legislation is periodically introduced in Congress to permit national banks to branch on a regional basis regardless of state laws. But Congress has never seen fit to pass such legislation, apparently feeling that to do so would be to strike a fundamental blow to the dual banking system. There is very little likelihood of such legislation being passed in the foreseeable future.

One consequence of the subordination of national to state branch banking policy is that there is almost no branch banking that crosses state lines. Within the states, however, there is a wide variety of branching arrangements, running from

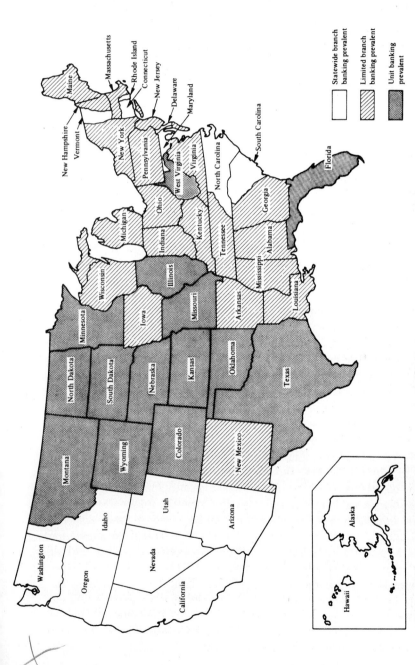

* This classification is made for the purpose of discussing changes in the banking structure and is based on the type of banking seemingly prevalent in each state and not necessarily on the current status of legal provisions. The classification of some states in this list depends on the interpretation of the key words *prevalent, limited, severely limited,* and *prohibited,* and this classification may differ in respect to a few states from similar classifications made for other purposes. Missouri is classified as of December 1971.

Figure 2-1 Classification of states according to types of branching prevalent, December 31, 1976.
Source: Annual Statistical Digest *of the Board of Governors of the Federal Reserve System, 1972–1976, p. 310.*

those states that permit unlimited statewide branching to those that absolutely prohibit branch banking of any kind. In between these two extremes there is so-called limited branch banking. For example: Some states permit branching only on a city-wide or countywide basis; some states limit the type of banking business a branch may engage in; Virginia permits statewide branching by merger but only limited *de novo* branching; and so forth. Figure 2-1 shows the branching arrangements in each of the states. Note that the states which permit some form of branching tend to be on the East and West Coasts, while those states prohibiting branching tend to cluster in Midwest and South.

There has been an enormous growth in branch banking in the United States since about 1950 in terms of both the number of banks that operate branches and the actual number of branches themselves. In 1950, out of 14,146 banks in the United States, 12,905 were unit banks and 1,241 were branch banks that were operating 4,721 branches. In 1975, the number of banks in the United States was 14,632; of these, 9,111 were unit banks and 5,521 were branch banks with a total of 29,795 branches. Thus, during these 25 years, the number of banks increased by 486 and the number of banking offices increased by 25,560. Putting the matter somewhat differently, in 1950, branches (including the head office) of commercial banks accounted for 31.6 percent of all banking offices in the United States; by 1975 this figure had risen to 79.5 percent.

Despite this phenomenal growth in branch banking, it would be wrong to conclude that the United States is on the verge of becoming a branch banking country comparable to Canada. The primary reason for the increase in branch offices in the United States in recent years is the suburbanization of America: As the affluent middle-class has moved to the outskirts of town, the downtown banks have felt it a business necessity to move with them. Accordingly, the laws of a number of states have been modified to accommodate this movement. Consequently, where in 1950 less than 10 percent of the banks in the United States maintained one or more branches, today this figure is almost 40 percent. Thus, despite the growth in branch banking, much of the essence of unit banking—the underlying concept of local ownership and management—has been preserved.

Branch Banking versus Unit Banking

Perhaps the most controversial political issue involved in banking structure is the question of whether branch banking should be permitted or prohibited. Generally speaking, it is the big city banks located in unit banking states that push the hardest for some form of branch banking. Contrariwise, it is typically the small town unit banks that resist branch banking with all the political power at their disposal. Particularly in states having both a large urban and also a large rural population (such as Illinois, Missouri, and Texas), therefore, attempts to change unit banking laws frequently result in bitter political disputes.

Such disputes usually generate more heat than light. The appeal is to the emotions rather than the intellect, and such appeal is seldom based on careful empirical and theoretical analysis. In the past several years, however, a number of scholars have addressed themselves to the branch banking question using the methods of economic analysis. While we are still far from having settled all the issues involved, enough results are in for us to be able to reach some conclusions on specific questions.

The issues involved in the branch banking controversy can generally be classified under three headings: *concentration in banking, operating efficiency,* and *allocational efficiency.*

Concentration in Banking   Opponents of branch banking place their emphasis on the argument that branch banking will lead to greater concentration in the banking industry—that is, to fewer and larger banks—which, in turn, will lead to monopoly. Indeed, probably the most fundamental reason that American banking developed along unit banking lines was our traditional fear of the concentration of economic power in general, and of the concentration of financial power in particular. The extreme statement of this viewpoint, which most students have probably heard at one time or another, is that the United States is actually run by a small group of "Wall Street bankers."

The argument that branch banking leads to monopoly would appear to rest on two assumptions: first, that branch banking is associated with greater concentration in the banking industry; and, second, that greater concentration in the banking industry leads to monopolistic practices. While the first assumption may be correct in very general terms, it greatly oversimplifies the actual situation. It is necessary to observe that the sheer existence of a large number of banks in the country does not guarantee competition. The small business person in a town of 10,000 people may have no choice but to buy banking services from the only bank in town; the fact that there are about 14,500 other banks in the country is simply not relevant. Thus, it is necessary to think of concentration in terms of a *market area.* While it is not a wholly satisfactory definition, the small towns of the United States are generally used as bank market areas for the nonmetropolitan regions of the country.

Table 2-2 shows the average number of banking choices available to residents of a sample of ninety small towns. In the sample, thirty small towns were randomly selected from two unit banking states (Arkansas and Missouri), thirty from two limited branch banking states (Kentucky and Tennessee), and thirty from two

Table 2–2 Average Number of Banking Choices of Ninety Rural Towns, Year-End 1970, Classified by Type of Branching Law

Type of branching law	Average number of banking choices within the town	Average number of banking choices within a 5-mile radius of the town	Average number of banking choices within a 10-mile radius of the town
Unit banking state	1.7	2.0	2.8
Limited branch banking state	2.3	2.5	3.7
Statewide branch banking state	1.9	2.8	3.8

Source: Adapted from Paul F. Jessup and Richard W. Stolz, "Customer Alternatives among Rural Banks," *Journal of Bank Research*, Summer 1975, Figure 2, p. 138.

Table 2-3   Average Number of Banks per Standard Metropolitan Area by Type of Branching Law, June 1974

Population of metropolitan area	Statewide branching	Limited branching	Unit banking	United States
50,000–99,999	6.7	6.7	7.4	7.0
100,000–499,999	10.3	12.7	19.6	13.9
500,000–999,999	19.8	24.0	56.0	28.7
1,000,000 and over	36.6	56.7	171.5	77.2
All metropolitan areas	15.7	19.7	39.6	23.9

Source: Jack M. Gottentag, "Branch Banking: A Summary of the Issues and the Evidence," in *Compendium of Issues Relating to Branching by Financial Institutions*, Committee on Banking, Housing and Urban Affairs, Subcommittee on Financial Institutions, United States Senate, October 1976, p. 112.

statewide branching states (North and South Carolina). The main thing to note about the table is that unit banking does not provide more choices than statewide branching for the residents of these towns; indeed, when the market area is defined to include 5-mile and 10-mile radii around the towns, statewide branching actually increases the number of banks available to customers. Based on studies such as this, it seems clear that for nonmetropolitan areas, branch banking may actually *decrease* banking concentration.

In the cities we get a different story. Table 2-3 shows that banking concentration tends to be greater in metropolitan areas in branch banking states than in metropolitan areas in unit banking states. For example, in cities with over a million population, the average number of banks is about 37 in statewide branching states, and about 172 in unit banking states. Thus, branch banking seems clearly to result in fewer and larger banks in the cities.

But does this *prove* that branch banking leads to monopoly in the cities? The answer is no. Why not? Because the relevant *market area* is almost certainly larger in cities that permit unlimited branching than in those that don't. Look at it this way. Imagine a unit-banking city that is divided into two neighborhoods, and suppose that the inhabitants of this city never leave their own neighborhood. Then a bank in one neighborhood is not in competition with a bank in the other neighborhood, even though both are in the same city. But now suppose that the law is changed to permit branch banking, and that each bank establishes a branch in the other neighborhood. Then each bank *is* in competition with the other, even though the number of banks is the same and people still don't leave their own neighborhood. The point of the illustration is that branch banking typically services a much larger market area than do unit banks. And because of this, twenty city-wide branching systems may provide a greater competitive atmosphere than forty unit banks that service only their own neighborhoods. Thus, even given that branch banking tends to lead to greater concentration in the banking industry, it is by no means obvious that branch banking is inherently monopolistic. Nor can the issue be settled by casual empiricism. Careful analysis of the facts is required.

Studies using the regression technique indicate the following tentative conclusions about the effect of branch banking on the pricing of bank services. (1) Interest rates on loans in *metropolitan* areas appear to be raised slightly by banking concentration. However, the movement of branch banking into *nonmetropolitan* areas appears to decrease the interest rates on small business loans. (These findings have caused some researchers to suggest that branching be permitted only *outside* the head-office county rather than only *within* the head-office county, as is now generally true in states with limited branching.[7]) (2) It seems fairly clear that branch banking has a tendency to raise the interest rates paid by banks on savings deposits. Within metropolitan areas, this result appears to be caused by the typically larger sizes of branch banks. In other words, a unit city bank *of the same size* as a branch bank will pay the same or higher interest rate; but because branch banks tend to be larger than unit banks on the average, a branch bank will pay a higher interest rate. Moreover, the evidence seems fairly clear that competition from branch banks will cause unit banks to pay higher interest rates on savings deposits. (In a multiple-regression study of 106 unit banks in nonmetropolitan communities, it was found that the interest rates on savings deposits paid by unit banks located in branch banking states were significantly higher than those paid by unit banks located in unit banking states.[8]) (3) Finally, the evidence seems overwhelming that the spread of branch banking results in higher service charges on checking accounts.[9] It is not wholly clear why this is so, but it seems to be related to the systemwide pricing practices of branch banks and the fact that service charges on checking accounts are higher in the cities.

In summary, it seems fair to conclude that there is little factual basis for the charge that branch banking leads to monopolistic practices in the banking industry. In fact, in the small towns throughout the country, branch banking may actually lead to a more competitive banking structure.

Operating Efficiency   Those people who favor branch banking have traditionally rested their case largely on the argument that economies of scale exist in banking. By *economies of scale* is meant simply that as a business grows larger, it is able to produce its products at a lower average cost. For example, the cost per automobile would be very high for a company that produced only 1,000 cars a year, but if the company could mass-produce 500,000 cars a year, the average, or per unit, cost would fall drastically. Banking, it is argued, is just such an industry; the larger the bank, the lower the average operating cost. Since in many cases the only practical way to achieve bigness in banking is through branching, it is argued that branch banking is therefore a more *efficient* (lower average cost) form of bank organization than unit banking.

Are there economies of scale in banking? A number of studies have been done

---

[7] A good summary of the research on this question is found in Jack M. Guttentag and Edward S. Herman, "Banking Structure and Performance," *The Bulletin (of New York University),* February 1967, pp. 89–98.

[8] Paul M. Horvitz and Bernard Shull, "The Impact of Branch Banking on Bank Performance," *The National Banking Review,* December 1964, pp. 171–178.

[9] Guttentag and Herman, op. cit., pp. 98–103. This conclusion is based on studies made before the movement to "free" checking accounts.

in an attempt to answer this question, and although the precise results of the studies vary somewhat, the answer appears to be yes.[10] Average costs of doing business appear to fall fairly rapidly *for unit banks* up to a deposit size of about $10 million, with much more moderate economies of scale being experienced after that point. Does this prove that branch banking, with its typically greater size, is more efficient than unit banking? Not really. For the studies also indicate that branching is a very expensive way for a bank to acquire size. In other words, if one compares the operating expenses of a branch and unit bank *of the same size,* the branch bank will have higher average costs. A moment's thought will indicate why this is so. At a minimum, the branch bank is providing one major service that the unit bank is not, namely, the convenience of having more than one office where the public can conduct its banking business. Like any other service, this service costs money to provide.

The comparison between branch and unit banks of the same size is not, however, the most relevant comparison for questions of public policy. The choice faced by the public is whether to liberalize branching restrictions, which would mean having fewer and larger (branch) banks. Thus, the important public policy question is whether average operating costs would go down if, say, ten independent unit banks were to be merged into a single branch bank with ten offices. The studies done on this question are mixed. Early studies suggested that costs associated with branching would just about offset economies of scale, so that little, if any, operating efficiency would be gained.[11] However, more recent studies conclude that a branch bank with many large offices has lower operating costs than a unit bank with a size comparable to one of the branch bank's offices.[12] Thus, perhaps the best that can be said at this point is that branch banking is no less efficient than unit banking, and is perhaps more efficient.

Allocational Efficiency   By *allocational efficiency* is meant how well resources are channeled into appropriate uses for the benefit of the overall community. From the standpoint of the unit versus branch banking controversy, the issue boils down to two questions: First, how good a job do branch and unit banks do in providing credit to the local community? And, second, which type of bank organization is able to furnish a broader range of services to the community?

Opponents of branch banking have long held that branches of big city banks

[10]Two studies in particular should be noted: George J. Benston, "Economies of Scale and Marginal Costs in Banking Operations," *The National Banking Review,* June 1965, pp. 507–549; Frederick W. Bell and Neil B. Murphy, "Costs in Commercial Banking: A Quantitative Analysis of Bank Behavior and Its Relation to Bank Regulation," *Research Report* 41, Federal Reserve Bank of Boston, 1968. For an interesting comparison of these and other studies, see Federal Reserve Bank of Chicago, *Midwest Banking in the Sixties,* March 1970, pp. 186–193. See also George J. Benston, "Economies of Scale in Financial Institutions," *Journal of Money, Credit and Banking,* May 1972, pp. 312–341; and William A. Longbrake and John A. Haslem, "Productive Efficiency in Commercial Banking," *Journal of Money, Credit and Banking,* August 1975, pp. 317–330.

[11]See especially Bell and Murphy, op. cit., pp. 65–68.

[12]See the discussion by Jack Guttentag, "Branch Banking: A Summary of the Issues and the Evidence," in *Compendium of Issues Relating to Branching by Financial Institutions,* op. cit., pp. 100–101.

are insensitive to the needs of small communities and tend to exploit them. Thus it is argued that the survival of the unit bank is intimately connected with the survival of the community: The unit bank prospers if the community prospers and dies if the community dies. The unit bank's self-interest therefore lies in doing all it can to promote the well-being of the community. In contrast, it is held that a branch bank's allegiances, if it has any, are to the head-office city; it is not dependent on any single branch and therefore not dependent on the survival of any single community. Consequently, it is argued, the branch bank will tend to divert money away from smaller communities and toward the head-office city. It will do this by taking in deposits in the small communities, transferring the money to the head office, and then lending it out.

In the first place, it should be noted with respect to this argument that even if it's true, the transfer of money from small communities to big cities isn't necessarily bad. The economic system of capitalism depends on businesses making as much profit as they can. If higher profits can be made in the cities than in the small towns, it is because people want the things the cities can provide and investment funds *should* move to the cities. From this standpoint, the greater mobility of funds that branch banking can provide is a positive virtue and should be regarded as such. For example, there are several specific cases where branch offices in growing communities actually have a loan/deposit ratio greater than 1; that is, they actually lend out more money than they have taken in. Practically speaking, this would be impossible for a unit bank. But even so, is the argument true? Do branch banks "exploit" small communities? The evidence overwhelmingly indicates that they do not. For example, research has shown that the amount of loans made locally by branch banks is considerably greater than for unit banks.[13] Moreover, "before-and-after" studies of branches acquired by merger have shown that loans usually rise when a unit bank in a small community is taken over and operated as a branch by a city bank.

Whether branch banks offer a wider variety of services to their customers than unit banks is also a testable hypothesis. Since branch banks tend to be larger than unit banks, it is sufficient to demonstrate a relationship between bank size and the number of services offered. The following regression equation between services offered and bank size was derived from data for the Seventh (Chicago) Federal Reserve District:[14]

$$S = 16.4 + .05D$$

$$r^2 = 0.91$$

Coefficients significant at the 1% level .

In this regression equation, S is the percent of banks offering nineteen different services and D is the size of the bank measured in millions of dollars of deposits.

[13]Robert A. Eisenbeis, "The Allocative Effects of Branch Banking Restrictions on Business Loan Markets," *Journal of Bank Research,* Spring 1975, pp. 43–47.

[14]The regression is based on data given in Federal Reserve Bank of Chicago, op. cit.

To understand the meaning of the regression, let us solve the equation for banks of two different sizes: a bank with $10 million of deposits, and a bank with $500 million of deposits. Taking the smaller bank first gives

$$S = 16.4 + .05(10)$$
$$= 16.4 + .5$$
$$= 16.9$$

For the bank with $500 million deposits, we have

$$S = 16.4 + .05(500)$$
$$= 16.4 + 25.0$$
$$= 41.4$$

Thus, according to the regression equation, only 16.9 percent of the banks with $10 million of deposits would offer all nineteen services, as opposed to 41.4 percent of those banks with $500 million of deposits. The relationship is what we would expect, of course; the larger the bank, the greater its ability to offer its customers specialized services. Other studies have achieved similar statistical results.[15]

Conclusion   Economic analysis cannot tell you, of course, whether to favor branch banking or unit banking. What it can do, and what we have tried to do in this section, is to tell you which of the common arguments surrounding this controversy are factually well founded and which are not. Having done that, the economist rests. Make up your own mind.

2-5 BANK HOLDING COMPANIES

Easily the most dramatic development in American commercial banking during the decade of the 1970s was the bank holding company movement. As currently constituted, a *bank holding company* (BHC) is a holding company that owns the controlling interest in one or more banks. A holding company, in turn, is a corporation that owns stock in other corporations. Thus a typical BHC might control five banks and several other, nonbank business firms. Table 2-4 shows the extent of all holding-company activity in banking at year-end, 1976. As will be seen from that table, half of the banking offices in the United States were part of a holding-company-affiliated bank; additionally, holding-company banks held about two-thirds of all bank deposits in the United States. Note that there are no restrictions on the types of bank that may belong to a holding company—they may be either unit banks or branch banks. Note further that holding-company activity may extend across state lines.

As with branch banking, state regulation of BHCs is varied. Bank holding company activity is not restricted in thirty-eight states (including the District of Columbia), while thirteen states prohibit or restrict it in some way. Holding-com-

[15]For a good summary of these studies, see Guttentag, op. cit.

Table 2-4   Banking Offices and Deposits in Holding Company Groups, December 31, 1976

Number of holding companies	Number of banking offices			Holding company offices as a percentage of all commercial banking offices	Deposits as a percentage of all commercial bank deposits
	Banks	Branches	Total		
1,912	3,791	19,199	22,990	50.0	66.0

Source: Annual Statistical Digest of the Board of Governors of the Federal Reserve System, 1972–1976, pp. 309 and 311.

pany activity is most prevalent in unit banking states that permit bank holding companies, although it is common in other states too.

The main federal legislation dealing with BHCs is the Bank Holding Company Act of 1956. This act, which was significantly amended in 1970, provides that all bank holding companies must register with the Federal Reserve System, and gives the Federal Reserve considerable authority to regulate the kinds of nonbank business a BHC may acquire, as well as the acquisition of new banks by a BHC. The criteria the Federal Reserve is required to consider in approving or disapproving BHC applications to acquire bank and nonbank businesses are: (1) the effect on competition; (2) the convenience and needs of the public; (3) the operating efficiency of the acquired organization; (4) the effect on bank soundness; and (5) the effect on the concentration of resources.

BHCs versus Independent Banking

There has been a good deal of alarm expressed in certain quarters over the rapid growth of bank holding companies. In general, the fear is of a monopolistic web of financial interconnections, with the holding company at the center of the web. At the same time, a number of people have staunchly defended the BHC as a highly flexible, efficient, and dynamic form of corporate organization. In the past few years, a good deal of economic research has been undertaken to try to determine who is right and who is wrong in these arguments.[16] We shall briefly describe the results of this research.

Effect of BHCs on Bank Competition   To understand the effects of the holding-company movement on the competitive structure of banking, it is necessary to distinguish among three ways that a BHC may acquire additional banks: (1) A BHC may grow by a *de novo* acquisition. In this case, a brand new bank is constructed and chartered. (2) A second means of growth for a BHC is through *foothold entry*.

[16]Two very good summaries of this research are: Robert J. Lawrence and Samuel H. Talley, "An Assessment of Bank Holding Companies," *Federal Reserve Bulletin,* January 1976, pp. 15–21; and Dale S. Drum, "MBHCs: Evidence after Two Decades of Regulation," Federal Reserve Bank of Chicago *Business Conditions,* December 1976, pp. 3–15. For a more extensive discussion, together with some original research, see Michael A. Jessee and Steven A. Seelig, *Bank Holding Companies and the Public Interest,* Lexington Books, Lexington, Mass., 1977.

When this occurs, a BHC acquires (purchases the controlling stock in) an established *small* bank in a banking market that the BHC was not previously represented in. (3) Finally, a BHC may expand through *leading bank entry*. Here the BHC acquires one of the large banks in a market. It is generally believed that BHC expansion *increases* competition when it occurs through *de novo* or foothold entry into a market, and decreases competition when it occurs through leading bank entry. Research studies seem to bear out this hypothesis. When foothold entry occurs, for example, the market share of the acquired bank generally rises. And because the Federal Reserve will typically not grant permission for leading bank entry into a market, very little of this type of expansion occurs. Most research has consequently concluded that the BHC movement has had procompetitive effects on banking.

Effect of BHCs on Nonbank Competition   As previously noted, the 1970 amendments to the Bank Holding Company Act allowed BHCs to expand into nonbank areas. According to the amendments, however, these nonbank affiliates had to be "bank-related," and permission of the Federal Reserve System had to be obtained before they could be acquired. Since 1970, BHCs have acquired control of a number of bank-related, nonbank businesses, such as mortgage banking companies, finance companies, financial consulting firms, data processing companies, and the like. The acquisition of such firms has naturally raised the specter of increased concentration in each of these industries specifically, and in the financial sector of the economy generally. However, while there is comparatively little evidence one way or the other on this issue, many observers feel that BHCs have actually increased the amount of competition in these industries. This impression rests largely on the observation that a great deal of the expansion of BHCs into nonbank activities has been on a *de novo* basis, which, of course, results in more firms in the industry.

Convenience and Needs of the Public   BHCs are frequently defended on the basis that an *affiliated bank* (i.e., a bank controlled by a BHC) is, because of its linkage to a holding-company network, able to offer more and better services to the public than an *independent bank* (a bank not connected to a BHC). While the benefits to the public are probably not so great as most BHCs claim, research studies do seem to support the contention that affiliated banks outperform independent banks in this respect. For example, it seems fairly clear that BHC banks make more credit available to the local community than do comparable independent banks. Moreover, in "before-and-after" studies of acquired banks, there does seem to be a tendency for the number and quality of the services offered the public to increase.

Operating Efficiency and Profits   As with branch banking, one of the major claims made for holding-company banking is that it is more efficient than independent banking because of economies of scale. This claim, however, does not seem to be borne out by the evidence. Indeed, most studies seem to indicate that affiliated banks have *higher* operating costs than their independent counterparts. In particular, the "miscellaneous" costs of affiliated banks are quite high relative to nonaffiliated banks. Since there is no breakdown of these miscellaneous expenses, the reasons they are higher is unknown, but there is a strong suspicion that it is because the parent holding company assesses "management fees" to their affiliates, thereby raising costs. For much the same reason, apparently, profits of affiliated banks are no greater than for independent banks. In other words, the accounting practices of the parent holding company can cause profits of affiliates to show up elsewhere in the system.

Bank Soundness   Bank *soundness* refers to the risk exposure of the bank. In general terms, the more sound a bank, the greater is its ability to withstand adverse economic conditions, such as a local or national recession. The relationship between bank soundness and holding-company affiliation is quite complex. On the one hand, it is claimed that because an affiliated bank is only a single unit of a much broader organization, it is therefore sounder because it is able to "spread the risk." On the other hand, fear is frequently expressed that an affiliated bank could be forced by the parent holding company to make risky loans to a nonbank affiliate in financial difficulties. Evidence on these and related matters is, in the nature of the case, indirect. What does seem to be true is that affiliated banks hold, on the average, riskier assets than independent banks; and that affiliated banks have lower capital/asset ratios. Neither of these facts, however, is conclusive evidence of the relative soundness of affiliated banks.

Conclusion   The very rapid growth of BHCs in the 1970s has fundamentally changed the nature of American commercial banking. Where in 1965 it was accurate to describe the United States as a "unit banking country," in 1980 it must be described as a branch-banking and holding-company banking country. Like most such pell-mell historical changes, BHCs are a mixed bag, carrying with them both opportunity and danger.

2-6   CHAIN BANKING

Chain banking is very similar to holding-company banking, except that the holding-company device is not used. Instead, a banking chain is held together through ownership of two or more banks by the same individual, by members of the same family, by common membership on the boards of directors of the banks (interlocking directorates), and the like. There is virtually no state or federal legislation specifically dealing with chain banking, although the antitrust acts can be used in cases where actual or potential monopolistic abuses can be demonstrated.

We know very little about chain banking in the United States. In the nature of the case, individual ownership of bank stock is a private matter, and systematic data are difficult to get. Moreover, there are severe problems of definition. An individual who owns less than 1 percent of the stock of two banks can hardly be thought of as "controlling" the banks in any meaningful sense of the word. But it is equally clear that control over a business may be exercised with considerably less than 50 percent of its stock. Indeed, the exact breaking point probably varies from case to case, so that precise definition is not even possible. Using an arbitrary cutoff of 5 percent plus some additional conditions, one researcher[17] estimated that in 1962 there were about 2,300 banks in the United States that were members of a chain. However, these data, based on a computerized matching of names and addresses of stockholders, represented only a rough order of magnitude at that time, and are obviously well out of date today. There is some speculation that chain banking has grown in the United States in the past few years, particularly in those states (such as Oklahoma) where bank holding companies are prohibited, but where considerable lobbying activity is going on to change the law. In such cases, groups of wealthy individuals might put together chains in anticipation of converting them to BHCs when BHCs become legal.

Most chain banking systems are apparently rather small, involving only two or three banks, although a few are substantially larger. Evidently, many member banks in a chain feel that membership gives them substantial advantages over their independent competitors, including a better exchange of credit information, joint participation in large loans, sharing of specialized equipment, and the like. It should also be noted that chain banking, like holding-company banking, appears to be largely a substitute for branch banking. Over 85 percent of the chain banks in the United States are located in states that prohibit branch banking.

2-7   CORRESPONDENT BANKING

The existence of branch, holding-company, and chain banking in the United States should not cause the reader to overlook what is perhaps the most obvious feature of our banking system: that it is comprised of almost 15,000 separately incorporated banks. These separate banks are not, however, unconnected with one another. As has been stressed, the banking system plays a central role in the *payments mechanism* of the United States, and to be effective in a country such as ours a payments mechanism must be nationwide. A check written on a bank in Miami, Florida, must be capable of being cashed in Seattle, Washington.

The mechanism knitting the banking system together is known as *correspondent banking.* Correspondent banking is simple in principle, if not in fact. It consists, basically, in some banks holding demand deposits in other banks just as individuals and other businesses do. In general, the pattern is that small banks in small communities place deposits in nearby city banks; these banks, in turn, hold deposits in the giant banks of the great regional capitols—San Francisco, Chicago, New York, and so on; and these banks, in turn, hold reciprocal deposits with one another. In this way a web of banking interrelationships is built up that ultimately connects every bank in the United States with every other bank. Actually, the correspondent banking system is more complicated than this since small banks will typically maintain five or six correspondent relationships and large banks may have as many as thirty or forty.

---

[17]Jerome C. Darnell, "Chain Banking," *The National Banking Review,* March 1966, p. 317.

We shall call the small bank that owns the deposit in the city bank the *respondent* bank, and the city bank that holds the deposit for the small bank, the *correspondent* bank. To understand the correspondent banking system, it is necessary to realize that the system is mutually advantageous (profitable) for both the country respondents and their city correspondents. From the viewpoint of the city correspondent, the deposits it accepts from respondent banks benefit it in precisely the same way as do other deposits. Because the bank knows from experience that all these deposits will not be withdrawn in full at the same time, it can accept the deposits, set aside a small amount for cash reserves, and invest the rest of the money in interest-bearing assets such as government securities and business and consumer loans. Thus the acceptance of interbank deposits is a very profitable line of business for city correspondents—so profitable, in fact, that the large city banks compete vigorously with one another for these deposits. Since it is against the law for commercial banks to pay interest on demand deposits, this competition takes the form of offering to provide specialized services to the country respondent banks. It is these services, of course, that provide the benefits derived by the respondent banks from the correspondent banking system. Recent studies[18] of correspondent banking indicate that two of these services are especially important: *nonlocal check clearing* and *loan participation.*

Check clearing is the method whereby a check is sent for collection to the bank it is written on. Local items (checks written on a bank in the same town they are cashed in) are fairly easy to collect, and clearing them is usually done through an arrangement among the local banks called a *clearinghouse.* For nonlocal items (checks written on a bank in another town), the Federal Reserve System provides free check clearing for all member banks. Notwithstanding this service, small banks prefer to clear virtually all their nonlocal checks through their city correspondents. Moreover, even large city banks apparently clear some 40 percent of their nonlocal items through the correspondent system.

The reason for this preference for correspondent clearing is rather technical. The Federal Reserve requires a prior sorting of checks before they will accept them for clearing; city correspondents do not. Apparently this check sorting is sufficiently difficult that most small banks prefer to avoid it. It should be noted also that check clearing through the correspondent system does not necessarily reduce check clearing through the Federal Reserve by the same number of checks; checks sent *initially* to a correspondent may ultimately be re-sent to the district Reserve Bank.

The second major service performed by correspondent banks for respondent banks is that of *loan participation.* Part of the government regulations surrounding commercial banking in the United States involves limits on the size of the loan that a bank may make. Since these loan limits vary with the size of the bank, for small

[18]See especially the following articles by Robert E. Knight in the *Monthly Review* of the Federal Reserve Bank of Kansas City: "Correspondent Banking, Part I: Balances and Services," November 1970, pp. 3–14; "Correspondent Banking, Part II: Loan Participation and Fund Flows," December 1970, pp. 12–24; "Correspondent Banking, Part III: Account Analysis," December 1971, pp. 3–17; and "Account Analysis in Correspondent Banking," March 1976, pp. 11–20.

banks in particular this restriction may mean that they cannot fully satisfy the financial needs of some of their big customers. A respondent bank faced with such a situation can ask its city correspondent to *participate* in the loan—that is, to lend the difference between the customer's needs and the respondent bank's loan limit. If the city bank is willing, the small bank can keep its big customers happy in this fashion.

Although check clearing and loan participation are the major services performed by correspondents for the respondent banks, they are by no means the only services offered. A full discussion of the other services would be tedious, but they include: interbank borrowing, safekeeping of securities, investment and management advice, international banking services, insurance and retirement plans for bank employees, and a number of personal services for the country banker (in a recent survey, one city bank reported that it had bought a live alligator for a respondent bank customer).

One final point concerning the correspondent banking system should be noted. In the previous discussion of branch banking and BHCs, it was pointed out that one of the main advantages claimed for them is that they can offer more services to customers than unit and independent banks. To some extent, this advantage is offset by correspondent banking. Even though they cannot offer certain services themselves, small banks can frequently arrange for customers to get these services through their city correspondent banks. Are these correspondent-offered services fully satisfactory substitutes for the services offered by branch and affiliated banks? Apparently not. Either because of a lack of communication or because of conflicts of interest, the small unit banker is unable to match completely the quality and variety of services that branch and affiliated banks can provide within the context of a single organization.[19]

2-8 ELECTRONIC BANKING

Just as bank holding companies fundamentally altered the structure of American commercial banking during the 1970s, so *electronic banking* seems likely to result in sweeping changes in the nature of banking during the decade of the 1980s. Electronic banking, more commonly called the *electronic funds transfer system,* or EFTS, is simply the application of computer technology to banking, especially the payments (deposit transfer) aspects of banking. Most students have probably used one or more of the machines that banks have available for routine customer transactions, and those students who haven't used them have probably seen them advertised on television. Even though EFTS is now in use, it is still in its infancy. The technology now available can be, and almost certainly will be, used much more extensively in the future.

[19] *Correspondent Relations: A Survey of Banker Opinion,* Committee on Banking and Currency, 88th Cong., 2d Sess., 1964.

Technology of EFTS

Although the phrase "electronic funds transfer system" makes electronic banking sound like a single thing, in fact it isn't. There are three fairly distinct pieces of hardware that comprise it: the automated teller machine (ATM), the point-of-sale (POS) system, and the automated clearing house (ACH).

Automated Teller Machines   The type of system that the student is most likely to be aware of is the *automated teller machine.* As the name implies, an AMT can perform most of the routine banking functions that are now done by bank tellers—deposits can be made, funds withdrawn, funds transferred between savings and checking accounts, and so forth. The customer operates the ATM by using a plastic card plus a personal identification number (PIN) known only to him or herself. While it is currently true that most ATMs are found on bank premises, there is no technological necessity for this. Indeed, not only is it possible for a bank to have an ATM located elsewhere, but there is also no reason that banks cannot share ATMs through a computer linkage. Thus, it is technically feasible for the system to be set up so that a person who lives in Gainesville, Florida, and is vacationing in Denver, Colorado, may go to the supermarket and withdraw currency *directly* from her own account.

Point-of-Sale System   Imagine that you are in a department store and decide to buy something. If you don't have enough currency with you, you can write a check. But the check typically involves a good deal of hassle—writing it out, showing identification, and so on. Moreover, many merchants regularly lose a lot of money in bad checks, and these losses are passed on to customers through higher prices. Such costs can be eliminated through a *point-of-sale* system. Such a system involves a computer terminal in retail stores that will transfer funds instantly from the bank deposit of the customer to the bank deposit of the store. In the process, the computer will verify that the customer has sufficient funds to cover the purchase, and will inform the customer of the new bank balance. The customer can also arrange for overdrafts at the bank, so that "instant loans" (up to a preset limit) can be made.

Automated Clearing Houses   Another type of EFTS, quite different from the two just described, is the *automated clearing house.* The ACH is largely designed to transfer funds among banks electronically, although customers may also become involved. For example, a company might, with the authorization of its employees, record its monthly payroll on electronic tape. The company then takes this tape to its bank, and that bank then uses the tape to deposit (in other banks) salaries directly to the credit of the employees. The ACH can also be used for preauthorized payments of a recurring nature. For example, many people now have various utility and mortgage bills deducted directly from their bank accounts, rather than writing checks at the end of the month.

Institutional Barriers to the Adoption of EFTS

The primary advantage to electronic banking lies in its ability to reduce costs. It has been estimated that there are some 30 billion checks written in the United States each year. Each of these checks must, at some point, be processed at least once by hand, and most checks are handled many more times than this. The cost is enormous. EFTS can reduce these costs drastically. But if this is so, one may reasonably ask, then why hasn't EFTS moved much more rapidly than it has? There are two answers to this. In the first place, the legal status of EFTS is not at all clear. Consider an AMT in a grocery store, for example. Is it merely a "data processing machine," as many banks claim? Or is it a branch bank? If it is the latter (and the courts have overwhelmingly held that it is) then is it legal in unit banking states? And even in branch banking states many questions arise about such matters as competition. For example, it is clearly uneconomic for each of two banks to put its own ATM in a grocery store when one machine can as readily handle the transactions of both banks. But if the banks share a single machine, are they colluding? These and similar legal problems need to be worked out before EFTS can become widespread.

The second major barrier to the adoption of EFTS is, unexpectedly, the prohibition against banks paying interest on demand deposits. (The explanation is a little tricky so—you there!—pay attention.) Since banks cannot legally pay interest on demand deposits, they compete for these by offering customers free checking accounts (frequently with some minimum deposit). Now, surveys have shown that bank customers *like* the present check-writing system. That is, given a choice between free checks and a free EFTS, most customers would choose checks. They prefer checks for a variety of reasons: It gives them unequivocal evidence (a signed check) that they, and no one else, has spent the money; they don't like and don't trust computers; they are familiar with checks; and so forth. But—and here comes the rub—the EFTS is a very high fixed-cost operation. In other words, most of the costs of EFTS are incurred at the beginning. What this means is that the EFTS needs a very high volume to be economical—i.e., it needs to spread those fixed costs over a lot of transactions. But it can't get the volume so long as people can write checks free of charge. And banks will continue to provide free checking accounts so long as they cannot pay interest on demand deposits.

One can therefore imagine the following scenario. Congress passes a law that permits banks to pay interest on demand deposits. This raises the costs of checking accounts to banks, and banks pass these costs on to customers in the form of service charges against checks. Bank customers, who are now receiving interest on their demand deposits, are then faced with the choice of paying 15 to 20 cents per check, or paying 1 cent or less for an EFTS transaction. Thus, EFTS becomes the common means of payment.

Whether this scenario will come about is, of course, by no means certain. But do not underestimate the possibility; the economic motive is very powerful.

2-9 REVIEW QUESTIONS

1 How can we have both *dual banking* and *unit banking* in the United States? Isn't this a contradiction in terms?

2 Do you think that nationwide branch banking would result in more monopoly in the banking industry? What are the arguments for this viewpoint? What are the arguments against it?

3 Why do you think that bank holding companies have grown so rapidly in the past fifteen years? Do you think that bank holding companies should be regulated? Why or why not?

4 What are the main impediments to the widespread adoption of electronic banking (EFTS)? Do you think we will have a checkless society by the year 2000?

3

Bank Regulation and Supervision

Banking is a highly regulated industry. It is, moreover, regulated in an unusual way. Most industrial regulation in the United States is carried out in terms of pricing policies. For example, power companies, telephone companies, and railroads are generally supervised by governmental commissions, which establish lists of the maximum prices these industries may charge for the various goods and services they sell to the public. This is not true of the banking industry. There is, for example, no regulation of the rate of interest banks may charge on loans (except for state usury laws) and no determination of the service charges banks may impose on checking accounts. In fact, the major pricing restrictions on commercial banks are the ceilings imposed on the prices they may *pay* (not charge) the customer—a maximum rate of interest on savings accounts and a zero rate of interest on checking accounts. Rather than having their pricing policies determined by the government, in the United States the regulation of commercial banking has taken the form of laying down certain operating rules that banks must follow. These rules encompass virtually every aspect of banking, such as whether a new bank may be opened in a particular locale, the sorts of investments a bank can make with depositors' money, and the types of business a bank may engage in.

The reason for the particular regulatory approach taken by this country toward commercial banking is to be found in the nature of banking and in our banking history. We shall consider United States financial history in some detail in Chapter 13. It is sufficient to point out here that the basic weakness of our banking system has historically been its *instability*. Even in the relatively prosperous decade of the 1920s, literally hundreds of banks failed each year; and in the dark depression days of the early 1930s the annual figure for bank suspensions rose into the thousands. Of course, many other businesses failed too. But banking is not just an ordinary business. When a shoe store failed, it was too bad for the employees and owners, but the community in general didn't suffer much. When a bank failed, everyone who deposited money in it lost, other banks were put in jeopardy, and the integrity of the payments mechanism for the entire economic system was thrown into doubt. An annual rate of several hundred such failures was an intolerable burden for a developing industrial economy to sustain.

The basic purpose of bank regulation has thus been to stabilize the banking industry, that is, to eliminate bank failures. It seems a fair generalization to say that the form this regulation has taken is to protect bankers from themselves. This is done in two ways: First, the *internal* affairs of banks are supervised in the sense that bankers are given a set of constraints (regulations) within which they must operate. This supervision is policed primarily through bank examination procedures. Second, the banking authorities attempt a careful control of the *external* structure of the banking industry as a whole. This is accomplished largely through policies dealing with the chartering of new banks, bank mergers, *de novo* branching, and holding-company affiliation.

In the remainder of this chapter, we shall first briefly describe the various regulatory agencies, then consider their methods of regulation, and finally discuss a controversial regulatory change that has been proposed for the banking industry.

3-1 REGULATORY AGENCIES

There are three federal agencies that have regulatory authority over commercial banking in the United States, plus each of the state banking authorities—fifty-three in all. We shall discuss the three federal agencies separately and the state banking authorities as a group.

The Comptroller of the Currency (Established in 1863)

The Office of the Comptroller (pronounced "controller") of the Currency is part of the U.S. Treasury Department and is the agency responsible for supervising all national banks. The Office is headed by a single individual (the Comptroller) who is nominated by the Secretary of the Treasury and appointed by the President (subject to Senate approval) for a five-year term. Although the law specifies that the Office of the Comptroller "shall be under the general direction of the Secretary of the Treasury," in fact it is virtually autonomous; it can be (and has been) run as though it had no official ties with the Treasury. Moreover, although the Office of the Comptroller must submit an annual report to Congress and, of course, must obey the laws Congress passes concerning it, it is not dependent on the Congress for annual appropriations. All its funds come from assessments on national banks, which gives it a further degree of autonomy.

Because it is run by a single individual and not by a commission or board, the Office of the Comptroller tends to vary its organizational structure according to the character and interests of the incumbent Comptroller.[1] Currently, the country is broken down into fourteen different regions for administrative purposes, with each region having its own set of bank examiners, its own legal staff, and so on. The Washington headquarters supervises the regional offices, checks field reports of bank examinations, approves or disapproves new bank charters, bank mergers, and *de novo* branching, handles other banking litigation, and collects statistics and conducts economic research on topics of particular interest to the national banking system.

The Federal Reserve System (Established in 1913)

The Federal Reserve System is called the *central bank* of the United States. This means that it is the agency responsible for the conduct of United States monetary policy, and it is this aspect of the "Fed" that will ultimately be of primary interest to us. Consequently, we shall postpone giving a detailed description of it until Chapter 14; we present only a thumbnail sketch here.

The Federal Reserve is an *independent* agency, which means that it is not attached to any other bureau, department, or agency in the federal government. (The student should not confuse the Treasury and the Federal Reserve; they are quite distinct.) Although its ruling seven-person Board of Governors is appointed by the President, these people are appointed for very long terms (fourteen years) that cannot be revoked. Like the Office of the Comptroller, the Federal Reserve is not dependent on congressional appropriations for its operating expenses.

All national banks are required to join the Federal Reserve System. State-chartered banks may join if they wish to and if they are willing to meet certain conditions imposed by Federal Reserve membership. In practice, only a comparatively small number of state banks have joined; thus, of the 10,017 state-chartered banks in the United States in 1977, only 1,019 (10 percent) have chosen to join the Federal Reserve System.

In addition to having responsibilities for the conduct of monetary policy, the Federal Reserve has rather wide supervisory powers over its member banks. Although it does not grant charters, it does conduct bank examinations, grant permission for mergers, branching, and holding-company acquisitions, regulate the maximum interest rates that member banks may pay on savings accounts, set legal reserve requirements on bank deposits, and so on.

[1]Ross M. Robertson, *The Comptroller and Bank Supervision,* Office of the Comptroller of the Currency, Washington, D.C., 1968.

The Federal Deposit Insurance Corporation (Established in 1934)

In 1933 the United States experienced the worst banking crisis in its history (before or since that time). In that year an unbelievable 4,000 commercial banks suspended operations. Hundreds of thousands of people lost their life's savings overnight as bank after bank failed. One immediate outgrowth of this crisis was the establishment of the Federal Deposit Insurance Corporation (FDIC). Several state plans of deposit protection had been tried previously but without success. The establishment of the FDIC marked the recognition of bank failures as a national problem, one which could be successfully solved only at the federal level.

As currently constituted, the FDIC insures the deposits of its member commercial banks to a maximum of $40,000. All member banks of the Federal Reserve System are required to join, and other banks may belong if they are willing to accept the conditions of membership. In fact, it is virtually a competitive necessity for commercial banks to join the FDIC, and all but a handful (344 in 1977) have done so. Thus, the FDIC comes closest to being that agency with supervisory authority over all banks in the United States.

Like the Office of the Comptroller, the FDIC does not receive congressional appropriations but instead is financed by annual insurance premiums paid by its member banks. By statute, the premium for each bank is set at 1/12 of 1 percent of its total (not just insured) deposits. Out of this premium income the FDIC pays its operating expenses, makes an assignment of funds to its reserves, and returns the remainder to its member banks on a pro rata basis. The large banks complain that the system of assigning premiums by total deposits forces an outright subsidy of small banks by big banks in two ways: First, small banks historically[2] have had a higher failure rate than large banks, so that to treat them equally for insurance purposes is to penalize the large banks for something they haven't done. Second, and more important, the large banks typically will have a much higher proportion of deposits that are not covered by insurance (i.e., are greater than $40,000) than small banks. The large banks thus feel that they are paying for something they are not getting and argue that insurance premiums should be based only on the insured part of a bank's deposits. Such a proposal, if it were to be carried out, would alter drastically the existing pattern of payments for deposit insurance. Thus, while about 98 percent of the *number* of commercial bank deposits are insured, only about 67 percent of the *dollar amount* of deposits are covered.

Although the most dramatic way that the FDIC protects deposits is by the prompt payment of insured accounts at defaulted banks, in fact it has at its disposal a number of less conspicuous but equally effective means of accomplishing this goal. Foremost among these, of course, is bank examination and supervision, which protects depositors by preventing bank failures from occurring. The FDIC has been quite successful in imposing uniform standards of sound bank management throughout the banking system, in particular on the small state-chartered banks that do not belong to the Federal Reserve System. Beyond this, the FDIC is also empowered

[2]This has not been true in the past few years, however.

to facilitate mergers between an insured bank in financial distress and a sound insured bank in the same vicinity. It does this by lending funds to or buying some of the assets of the distressed bank, so that the merger becomes attractive to the second bank. Finally, the FDIC is authorized to make loans, buy assets, or make deposits in an insured bank if it is in danger of failing and if its failure would leave the community without banking facilities. It is to be noted particularly that in these ways the FDIC is protecting (but not insuring) *all* deposits of its member banks, not just the insured portion. To this extent, a good deal of force is taken out of the argument of the big banks that they are paying more than their fair share for deposit insurance.

The State Banking Authorities

Each state in the union has some sort of supervisory authority over the commercial banks chartered by that state. These authorities have various names (superintendent of banking, banking commission, and so on), but, in general, their duties with respect to state-chartered banks are analogous to those of the Comptroller for national banks. They approve charters, conduct examinations, promulgate regulations, rule on mergers and acquisitions, and so forth. In addition, they are frequently given similar supervisory authority over other state-chartered financial institutions, such as savings and loan associations, credit unions, personal loan companies, and the like.

Perhaps the only valid generalization that can be made concerning these state banking authorities is that the quality of their supervision varies enormously from one state to another. Some states have highly qualified examiners and research personnel, fully comparable to the best in the federal agencies. Other state banking agencies are notoriously weak, riddled by the political patronage system, and are controlled by the very banks they are supposed to be regulating. This variability in the quality of the state banking offices frequently makes it difficult to coordinate the

Table 3-1　Bank Supervision in the United States*

	Banks supervised by			
Comptroller of the currency	Federal Reserve System	FDIC	State banking authorities	Banks also supervised by
4,701 (55.3%)	4,701 (55.3%)	4,701 (55.3%)	None	Comptroller of the currency
4,701 (55.3%)	5,720 (73%)	5,720 (73%)	1,019 (17.7%)	Federal Reserve System
4,701 (55.3%)	5,720 (73%)	14,425 (98.3%)	9,724 (43%)	Federal Deposit Insurance Corporation
None	1,019 (17.7%)	9,724 (43%)	10,017 (47.7%)	State banking authorities

*Percentage of total commercial bank deposits are shown in parentheses. Figures are as of June 30, 1977.

Source: *Federal Reserve Bulletin*, March 1978, A17.

overlapping authorities of the various agencies charged with supervising the banking industry.

Summary of Regulatory Agencies

Table 3-1 shows the numbers of banks of the United States subject to supervision by the various agencies just discussed. Also shown (in parentheses) is the percentage of total bank deposits held by each agency.

3-2 BANK SUPERVISION AND REGULATION

Chartering

When economists speak of *entry barriers,* they mean the ease or difficulty of starting a new firm in an industry. As a broad generalization (with some notable exceptions), public policy in the United States has followed the path of permitting industries with low entry barriers to go unregulated, in the belief that competition will force these industries to operate in the public interest, and regulating only those industries with very high entry barriers, for example, public utilities.

The banking industry is peculiar in that the "natural" entry barriers are relatively low but very high "artificial" entry barriers have been erected by governmental decree. Thus the amounts of capital, technical knowledge, equipment, and so on, required to open a small bank are probably no greater than those required to begin a modern farm of average size. In the absence of natural barriers, the government has seen fit to severely restrict entry into banking by erecting legal barriers, which are primarily in the form of requirements necessary to obtain a *bank charter.* No one is permitted to open a new bank without receiving a charter from either the federal or state government, and in recent decades both governments have been very selective in granting such charters.

The reasons for this selectivity in granting charters can best be understood within an historical context. Figure 3-1 shows new bank charters granted, bank failures, and the total number of banks in the United States from 1921 to 1976. Note in particular the large number of bank charters granted, the large number of banks, and the large number of bank failures prior to 1935. In trying to analyze the causes of the high bank-failure rate, especially in the early 1930s, public officials reached the conclusion that the country had been *overbanked.* Like so many pseudotechnical terms in popular usage, the term *overbanked* was never clearly defined, but it seemed to mean that there were more banks in the country than could be supported by public demand for banking services. As a result, it was argued, banks were forced into "unhealthy" competition with one another, individual banks engaged in "unsound" management practices in competitive desperation, and many banks failed.

If this analysis is correct, part of the answer to the problem of excessive bank failures seemed to lie in restricting entry into the banking industry. As shown in Figure 3-1, new bank charters were granted quite liberally during the 1920s. One reason for this was that the federal government had no control over bank charters granted by the states. As a consequence, an application for a charter that was denied

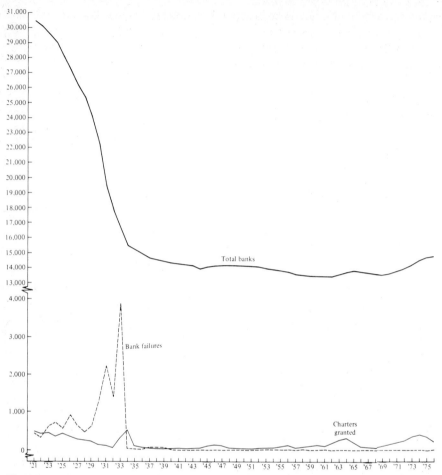

Figure 3-1   Changes in the number of commercial banks, 1921–1976. *(Source: Gerald C. Fisher,*
American Banking Structure, *Columbia University Press, New York, 1968, p. 204. Based on and*
updated by information in the Federal Reserve Bulletin. *For years 1973–1976: Annual Report of*
the Board of Governors of the Federal Reserve System, various years. See index under Banking
Offices; Numbers, changes in.)

by the Comptroller of the Currency nevertheless stood a good chance of being
accepted by a state banking authority, and vice versa. Bureaucrats being what they
are, neither agency was prepared to drive all new banks into the other's camp, and
therefore a permissive attitude toward bank charters resulted.

In 1935 the Federal Deposit Insurance Corporation was set up on a permanent
basis. Although the law required that the FDIC had to insure all national banks and
all state banks belonging to the Federal Reserve System, it could deny insurance to
other state-chartered banks at its own discretion. Since deposit insurance was a
virtual necessity for any new bank, for the first time in our history an agency of the
federal government was, in effect, given a veto power over state bank charters. The

consequences of this change can be inferred from the data. The number of new bank charters granted since 1935 has been comparatively small. In fact, largely owing to the disappearance of banks through mergers, the number of commercial banks in the United States in 1977 was actually less than in 1935.

Worthiness and Need Criteria The factors that authorities now investigate before approving a new bank charter may generally be classed under two headings: *worthiness* and *need.* By *worthiness* is meant that the proposed bank is soundly constituted in terms of its capital structure and the background and expertise of its management. The charter applicants must demonstrate that they have (or are able to get) sufficient money to buy the bank building and fixtures, assign funds to capital and paid-in surplus, and, in general, be able to operate the bank without undue risk. They must also show that the proposed management has successful banking and business experience and is of good reputation and character. These matters are examined in considerable detail before a charter is approved. The purpose of such a thorough investigation, of course, is to keep wheeler-dealers and shady operators out of banking and hence minimize bank failures.

While few economists would quarrel with the general principle underlying the worthiness criterion, the *need* criterion is considerably more controversial. Under the Banking Act of 1935, new national bank charters are to be approved only if a proposed bank has adequate "future earnings prospects" and promises to meet the "convenience and needs of the community to be served by the bank." Since the FDIC was instructed to make a judgment on these same criteria for insurance purposes, the "needs test" has been effectively imposed on the granting of all new bank charters, both federal and state.

There are two basic difficulties with the needs test: First, it substitutes the judgment of the supervisory authorities for that of the investors. Does the proposed bank have adequate future earnings prospects? The presumption is that the stock-holders would not be willing to risk their money unless they thought so. But the authorities are specifically required to arrive at an independent judgment about this, and if their judgment differs from that of the stockholders, they must deny the application. Since market forecasts are more of an art than a science, it can never be demonstrated definitely who is right and who is wrong.

The second difficulty with the needs test is that it can be (and undoubtedly has been) used to shelter a market area from the rigors of competition. It is very difficult to prove that a community *needs* a new bank if there are other banks in the area. Not only is there a presumption that the needs of the community are already being met, but the already-existing banks are prepared to go to considerable lengths to prove this point. Like most self-interested business people, bank personnel are in favor of competition primarily for others. Moreover, if a new bank can be successful only by taking business away from other banks, there is always a danger of causing bank failures by following a too-liberal chartering policy. As a consequence, a distinctly noncompetitive atmosphere has been engendered in the banking industry through the strict application of the needs test and the resulting high entry barriers into the banking industry. One researcher, for example, using regression analysis, has estimated that federal regulation has curbed the rate of new entry into banking since the 1930s to less than half of what it would otherwise have been.[3]

Finally, it should be noted that the same entry restrictions that apply to new bank charters also apply to *de novo* branching. Thus, permission of either the Comptroller, the Federal Reserve, or the FDIC is required before a new branch office may be opened, and such permission may be granted only in those cases where the needs test can be met. However, the authorities are apparently a good deal more lenient in granting permission for new branch offices than for new banks, especially if the branch comes into competition only with the branch of another bank. The general presumption is that a branch bank has the necessary expertise to judge whether a new branch will be profitable; and even if it isn't profitable, the consequence is not failure of the bank but just the orderly shutting down of that particular office.

Bank Supervision and Examination

Banking is a highly regulated business. There are detailed state and federal laws governing the types of assets a bank may acquire, the types of services it may offer its customers, the kinds of other businesses it may affiliate with, the prices it may pay for its raw materials (deposits), its overall capital structure, and so forth. There are laws covering virtually every aspect of banking. Moreover, at one time or another many of these laws have been the subject of legal action, so that the bank must be aware of and comply with, not just what it thinks the law says, but what the courts have held the law to mean. Finally, each and every law is itself the subject of an even more detailed set of regulations and instructions issued to the bank by banking authorities. And look again at Table 3-1. Virtually all banks are subject to the regulatory decisions of at least two separate agencies, and many are subject to three. It is small wonder bankers frequently feel harassed and put upon; the wonder would be if they didn't.

It is one thing to pass laws and promulgate regulations. It is quite another thing to encorce them. Given the detailed nature of banking regulations, the overlapping jurisdiction of the authorities, with the inevitable interagency rivalries, and the fact that actual cases seldom fit regulations precisely, the ordinary banker would be hard-pressed to comply with regulations on a wholly voluntary basis. In consequence, an elaborate system of bank examination procedures has been developed. The purpose of bank examinations is to make sure the individual bank is being soundly managed within the existing framework of rules and regulations.

Coordination of Bank Examinations   The first problem, of course, is that of coordination. If each supervisory agency exercised its full authority over all the banks under its jurisdiction, the average banker would scarcely have time for anything else. In general, the system of bank examinations has been reasonably well coordinated, at least among the federal agencies. The Comptroller of the Currency

---

[3]Adrian W. Throop, "Capital Investment and Entry in Commercial Banking," *Journal of Money, Credit and Banking,* May 1975, pp. 193–214.

examines the 4,701 national banks; the Federal Reserve System examines the 1,019 state-chartered member banks but not the national banks; and the FDIC examines those insured banks that do not belong to the Federal Reserve System (8,705). Of course, each of these agencies makes its "report of examination" available to the other two, and the FDIC in particular reserves the right to conduct special examinations. Paradoxically, the banks that are subject to the fewest authorities have the most severe problem of dual examination. These are the 8,705 state-chartered insured banks that do not belong to the Federal Reserve. Both the FDIC and the state banking authorities insist on exercising their right of examining these banks. Even here, however, the attempt is made to conduct simultaneous examinations by both agencies, so that the time loss to the banker is minimized. Although simultaneous examinations clearly do help, there remain difficulties in scheduling, in examiners wanting slightly different information, and so on. The whole thing is rather a mess.

The problem of overlapping jurisdiction among the various regulatory agencies has led some people to advocate a single centralized banking authority having primary responsibility for the examination and supervision of all commercial banks.[4] Various schemes have been proposed either for transferring all authority to an existing agency or for setting up an entirely new agency. In the absence of a major banking crisis, however, such schemes have very little chance of being enacted into law.

Bank Examination Procedures   Banks are examined basically in two ways: First, there are the *call reports,* which are detailed statements of the condition of the bank that the bank is required to send to the appropriate authority four times a year. A summary statement of condition, based on the call reports, is usually published in the local newspaper in early January and early June, and these can make interesting reading if the reader knows what to look for. Second, there are the on-the-premises examinations, in which examiners show up unannounced and begin inspecting the books of the bank. Generally the law provides that at least one such examination will be conducted annually.

It is important to note that a bank examination is not a bank audit. Examiners are not looking for embezzlers, defalcators, or other crooks. They do not verify all the assets and liabilities of banks and do not ask if the information given is true. Rather, examiners assume such information is correct and instead ask if the banks are being soundly managed—for example, if the bank loans have been made to credit-worthy borrowers, or if the capital of a bank is sufficient given its size and the kinds of assets it owns. Examiners do occasionally catch embezzlers, but it is usually by accident. A clever bank fraud may go on over a period of several years, and no blame should be attached to the examiners.

Bank Mergers

One of the major trends in contemporary commercial banking is the *merger movement*—the "urge to merge," as someone has called it. Beginning in the early 1950s,

---

[4]For a discussion of this issue and a substantially different proposal, see Jack M. Guttentag, "Reflections on Bank Regulatory Structure and Large Bank Failures," in Federal Reserve Bank of Chicago, *Bank Structure and Competition,* May 1975, pp. 136–149.

the annual number of bank mergers rose substantially and has been running at a high rate ever since. Figure 3-2 gives the data.

What lies behind the bank merger movement? In part, it is related to the broader question of the economic development of the United States. As the suburbs have grown, the banking system has changed to accommodate this growth. And, as we have seen, the altered life-style of the country has affected the banking structure largely in the expansion of multiple-office banking. One way this expansion of offices has occurred has been through branching and holding-company affiliation by merger; in recent years, between 85 and 90 percent of the banks taken over have been converted into branches or affiliates of the acquiring bank.

Needless to say, the bank merger movement has been viewed with alarm. In an industry already sheltered from intensive competition by restrictive chartering and supervisory policies, the consolidation of banks into larger units has led many people to believe bank mergers should be strictly controlled. As a consequence, in 1960 the Bank Merger Act was passed by Congress.

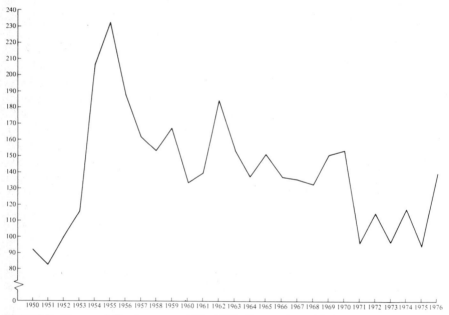

Figure 3-2 Commercial bank mergers, 1950–1977. *(Source: Annual Report of the Board of Governors of the Federal Reserve System, various years. See index under Banking Offices; Number, changes in.)*

The Bank Merger Act   As it now stands, the Bank Merger Act requires the prior approval of one of the three federal banking agencies before a merger may take place: the Comptroller of the Currency for national banks, the Federal Reserve for state-chartered member banks, and the FDIC for insured, nonmember banks. Before making a decision, the relevant agency must seek an advisory opinion on the competitive aspects of a bank merger from the other two agencies and from the antitrust division of the Attorney General's office. These opinions are only advisory, however, and are in no way binding on the agency having primary jurisdiction. In the event of an emergency, where a merger is necessary to avoid a bank failure, the provision for advisory opinions is waived.

Of particular interest are the factors that the supervisory agencies are instructed to consider before approving or denying a bank merger. These are divided into two general categories: the so-called *banking factors* and the *competitive factors*. The banking factors are standard. They require the agency to investigate the financial history and condition of each of the banks involved, the adequacy of its capital structure, the general character of its management, and the convenience and needs of the community to be served. In fact, these banking factors are taken almost verbatim from the FDIC act and, in effect, simply apply the same criteria to mergers that had previously been applied to chartering.

More important are the *competitive factors* to be considered in a bank merger case, and the relationship between these and banking factors. The amended Bank Merger Act requires that the supervisory agency should not approve any merger where the effect would be to substantially reduce competition, except in those cases where the anticompetitive consequences of the merger would clearly be outweighed by the public interest in terms of the *convenience* and *needs* of the community. Thus, it would appear that the law says, in effect, that we are willing to accept some greater element of concentration in banking provided that we obtain better banking services. It is the responsibility of the supervisory agency to make a judgment about this trade-off between greater concentration and better services.

The intent of the Bank Merger Act was twofold: to slow down the number of mergers in banking, and to establish uniform criteria among the regulatory agencies in approving or disapproving bank mergers. The act has been notably unsuccessful in both of these intentions. As can be seen from Figure 3-2, the number of mergers since 1960 has not been markedly reduced. And so far as the uniformity of criteria is concerned, recent studies[5] have shown that the three federal regulatory agencies and the Attorney General have emphasized different aspects of merger proposals.

Bank Failures

Prior to the establishment of the FDIC, many bank failures occurred because of poor bank management—making risky loans that went sour and couldn't be repaid, for example. Additionally, many bank failures in those times had their roots in forces over which the individual bank had no control: crop failures in agricultural communities, the closing down of the local textile mill, or (most disastrous of all) a nationwide economic depression. Because there was no deposit insurance, banks would be "run" by panicked depositors at the slightest hint of trouble, and a run (general deposit withdrawal) could break even a well-managed bank.

[5]See Roberta Grower Carey, "Evaluation under the Bank Merger Act of 1960 of the Competitive Factors Involved in Bank Mergers," *Journal of Monetary Economics,* July 1975, pp. 275–308; and Robert A. Eisenbies, "Differences in Federal Regulatory Agencies: Bank Merger Policies," *Journal of Money, Credit and Banking,* February 1975, pp. 93–104.

Circumstances have changed, and so have the causes of bank failures. Deposit insurance has virtually eliminated runs on banks, and the accompanying nationwide system of bank examination has forced at least minimal standards of sound management on virtually every bank in the country. Most important of all, perhaps, is that the national economy has on the whole performed with remarkable stability during the last forty years. Where bank failures used to be common, they are now rare; where in the 1920s literally hundreds of banks failed each year, in recent years the average annual failure rate of insured banks is about eight. These bank failures are almost always due, moreover, to the use of bank funds for the personal gain of some one individual—sometimes outright fraud, sometimes just skirting the edge of legality.

Primarily because of the *nature*, rather than the number, of recent bank failures, in 1966 Congress passed the Financial Institutions Supervisory Act. This act considerably broadened the powers of the federal banking agencies to enforce their control over the banking system. Before the passage of this act, about the only remedy at the disposal of the agencies was the withdrawal of insured status from a commercial bank. This remedy was deemed too harsh for minor infractions of the rules, and in cases of this sort the supervisory agencies had to rely largely on the voluntary cooperation of the commercial banks. The Financial Institutions Supervisory Act gave the agencies an intermediate set of powers. They may now issue cease-and-desist orders for specific activities of banks, and, under certain circumstances, they may cause the removal of a particular individual as an officer or director of a bank.

3-3 THE CASE FOR BANK FAILURES

As has been emphasized throughout this chapter, the purpose of regulating the banking system is to eliminate bank failures. Charters, examinations, supervision— all are intended to stabilize banking and prevent the sort of debacle that occurred in the 1930s from happening again. Yet, when one thinks about it, what is at issue is not the prevention of bank failures per se, but rather the protection of the depositing public from the *consequences* of bank failures. In other words, it is not the bank itself we are worried about, but the loss of deposits to the public. Yet, in order to protect the public, we have apparently found it necessary to protect the management and stockholders of banks as well. We seem to have adopted a particularly roundabout method of achieving our goal.

Many economists feel that a strong case can be made for allowing some banks to fail as long as bank depositors do not suffer the consequences of these failures. The case, in fact, is precisely as strong as the economic theory of capitalism itself. While no one wants business failures for their own sake, it cannot be denied that they perform a valuable function for the economy. To the extent that business failures are caused by factors beyond the control of the business—shifts in population and changes in consumer tastes, for example—they give the economy a certain flexibility, a capacity for adaptation to changing circumstances. To the extent that business failures are caused by bad management, they weed out the incompetent managers and inefficient firms. Precisely the same argument can be applied to commercial banks. Population changes can result in excess banks in an area, and banks can be woefully mismanaged and grossly inefficient. Yet, because of our concern for depositors, we have created a system of bank regulations that makes it almost impossible for a bank to fail.

Is it really necessary to protect bank depositors by eliminating bank failures? Many economists feel that the two problems can be separated. These economists propose that the FDIC be expanded so that all deposits (not just the first $40,000) are fully insured. At the same time, they would remove much of the enormous amount of regulation currently surrounding the banking industry and let banks compete like other business firms. If, in the rough and tumble of a competitive business environment, some banks should fail, it would be unfortunate for the owners and managers. But that, after all, is the risk any business person takes. The public's deposits would be fully protected, and the integrity of the payments mechanism would be guaranteed.

3-4 REVIEW QUESTIONS

1 How does the approach to governmental regulation of banking differ from the approach to governmental regulation of telephone companies? Why?

2 Name the three federal agencies that supervise banks, and identify which group of banks each agency supervises.

3 What is the difference between the *worthiness* and the *need* criteria for chartering new banks?

4 If the FDIC were to insure all bank deposits fully, could we do away with bank regulation completely?

4

Competition and Monopoly in Commercial Banking

So far we have discussed competition in the commercial banking industry only incidentally in connection with branch banking and bank holding companies (Chapter 2) and bank regulation (Chapter 3). Our purpose now is to bring these issues into focus at a single point: To what extent do monopolistic practices exist in the banking industry? This is not a simple question, and since the question isn't simple, neither is the answer. Attempts to answer it necessarily involve economic theory, statistical analysis, and court decisions about antitrust laws. If you're the sort of person who likes nice, unqualified, easy to understand answers, you may find yourself a bit discouraged by what follows. But if you enjoy a good argument, with something to be said for both sides, read on!

4-1 BANKING MARKETS

The concept of economic concentration in an industry necessarily involves the idea of *market power*. Indeed, properly understood, monopoly *is* market power: the extent to which a single firm or a small group of firms can impose its will on its customers, especially with respect to prices. Before one can hope to say anything sensible about monopoly and competition in the banking industry, therefore, it is necessary to specify what the banking *market* is. Is it a market for consumer loans, or is it a market for business loans? Is it a market for savings deposits, or is it a market for demand deposits? Is it a national market, or is it a local market?

Product Markets

In fact, the banking market is all these things. Or, putting the matter somewhat differently, banks do business in many different markets. A bank is, in the first place, what economists call a *multiproduct firm,* that is, a firm that produces many different products. The products are, of course, services—all different kinds of deposits and loans. Each of these products constitutes a separate market in which the bank operates. In these *product markets,* the individual bank faces competition in varying degrees both from other banks and from nonbank financial institutions. Banks may compete with one another for demand deposits, with savings and loan associations for savings deposits, and with credit unions for consumer loans. It would seem, therefore, that we cannot sensibly discuss competition in banking without first specifying which product market we're talking about.

Geographic Markets

Delineating the appropriate product markets of banks is further complicated by the concept of the *geographic market.* The problem may be illustrated by the following example: Imagine two banks, each of which is the only bank in town, and where the towns are located in the same county. Do these banks compete with each other? That is, if we are trying to assess the degree of banking concentration in this area, do we emphasize the fact that each bank is the only bank in town or the fact that there are two banks in the county? Which is the appropriate geographic market, the town or the county?

How we answer this question will probably depend on which product market we're talking about. If what we have in mind is the demand deposit of the typical individual, then the town (or, in a city, the neighborhood) is probably the appropriate market area; holding one's checking account in a bank in another town is simply too awkward to be tolerated by most people. On the other hand, if the bank product we're talking about is a loan to a large business, then the county may well define the appropriate market area; the business is big enough to "shop around" for its loan and indifferent as to which bank it uses.

That banks operate in different geographic markets has been demonstrated many times. For example, one study[1] of 2,000 metropolitan banks showed that less than half of the large businesses ($5 to $25 million in assets) in these areas obtained all their loans from banks in the same area. By contrast, about 90 percent of the smaller businesses borrowed exclusively from banks in that area. In other words, the

[1]Franklin R. Edwards, "Concentration in Banking and Its Effect on Business Loan Rates," *The Review of Economics and Statistics,* August 1964, p. 295. See also Robert A. Eisenbeis, "The Allocative Effects of Branch Banking Restrictions on Business Loan Markets," *Journal of Bank Research,* Spring 1975, pp. 43–47.

bank market for big business loans is national in scope; for small business loans, it is local.

In the discussion that follows, it is particularly important that the reader keep in mind the concepts of product and geographic markets; much of the data can be meaningfully interpreted only within this framework. Needless to say, the type of market relevant to the discussion will be made explicit throughout.

4-2 CONCENTRATION RATIOS AND TRENDS

A *concentration ratio* is a bit like one's parents: simple-minded but endearing. It is simple-minded in the sense that it is a very unsophisticated measure of monopolistic power in an industry, subject to serious misinterpretation unless supplemented with other factual material. It is endearing because no other measure seems to have the same dramatic appeal—simple to calculate and easy to understand.

To reckon a concentration ratio, we first decide on an appropriate number of firms—say three. Then we simply calculate the percentage of business of an entire industry done by the largest three firms in that industry. For example, we might find that in the steel industry the largest three firms produce 75 percent of all steel produced in the United States. That's all there is to it. The game is not just to observe current concentration ratios, but to track them over time to see if the industry in question is becoming more or less concentrated.

There are a number of possible pitfalls in an uncritical use of concentration ratios. When dealing with the banking industry in particular, the major danger is the one discussed in the preceding section: the appropriate market, both product and geographic. The small business looking for an inventory loan is not interested in the competition its bank faces nationally; it simply isn't relevant. In this case, therefore, the proper concentration ratio would be confined to the local market—for example, the percent of local small business loans made by the largest bank in town. Other bank products might require other market definitions.

To get around the problem (to some extent) of the appropriate product market, concentration ratios in banking are usually measured in terms of total (demand and savings) deposits. The use of total bank deposits to delineate the product market of banking, however, leaves a great deal to be desired. Not only do banks face stiff competition from other financial institutions for savings deposits, but these same institutions are to an increasing extent offering demand deposit services to the public. We shall discuss these matters later on in this chapter; for the moment we will accept the traditional approach to banking concentration as measured by total bank deposits.

To eliminate the problem of where to draw the boundaries for geographic markets, concentration ratios are usually struck for three separate areas: national, state, and local.

National Concentration Ratios

At the end of 1976, approximately 0.8 percent of the commercial banks in the United States held about 42 percent of all bank deposits; at the other end of the scale, about 83 percent of the commercial banks held only 21 percent of bank deposits. Most

Table 4-1   Percentage of Total Deposits Held by the Largest 100 Commercial Banking Organizations in the United States, 1961-1975

Year	1961	1966	1968	1975
Percentage of total deposits	49.44	49.27	48.99	48.10

Source: Bernard Shull, "Multiple Office Banking and Competition: A Review of the Literature" in *Compendium of Issues Relating to Branching by Financial Institutions*, United States Senate Committee on Banking, Housing and Urban Affairs, Subcommittee on Financial Institutions, October 1976, p. 123.

people find such statistics startling and, indeed, alarming. They seem to indicate an industrial structure dominated by a few very large banks, with a lot of little banks of no particular consequence. This, in turn, seems to suggest that there are vast monopoly powers in banking. Are there?

Table 4-1 shows the percentage of deposits held by the 100 largest banking organizations in the United States for selected past dates. (Note that these data refer to banking *organizations*—i.e., a bank holding company is treated as a single organization, even though it may encompass several separately incorporated banks.) As may be seen from these data, there is certainly no evidence that banking is becoming increasingly concentrated at the national level—indeed, if anything there is a very slight downward trend in these concentration ratios. It therefore seems a safe generalization to say that the largest 100 banking organizations in the United States hold about one-half the total bank deposits in the country, and that this situation has not changed markedly in the last twenty years. The question is, Does this represent a high degree of concentration?

The answer is no. The first thing to note is that we are here dealing with a national market. The customer relevant to this market is the nationwide corporation. The borrowing of such a corporation is by no means confined to commercial banks. It has the alternative of borrowing on the open market—selling bonds and stock, for example. Additionally, the large corporation may retain its own earnings and borrow from nonbank institutional investors such as insurance companies. In short, the large corporation has so many borrowing alternatives open to it that the market power of the banking system is quite limited.

The second point to note is that these national concentration ratios are really quite low, at least as compared with many other American industries. Think of automobiles, steel, aluminum, and cigarettes, for example. In these industries, the number of firms doing the bulk of the business can be counted on the toes of one foot. In the banking industry, in contrast, it requires 100 firms to approximate 50 percent of the business. One can be reasonably sure that 100 firms in a market are sufficient to establish effective competition. Indeed, large deposits in large banks are notoriously migratory—they will move from bank to bank according to shifting circumstances. Our conclusion, that banking concentration in the national market is relatively low, necessarily follows.

State Concentration Ratios

Although they seem to interest a number of people, most economists regard statewide bank concentration ratios as being of questionable value. In the first place, state

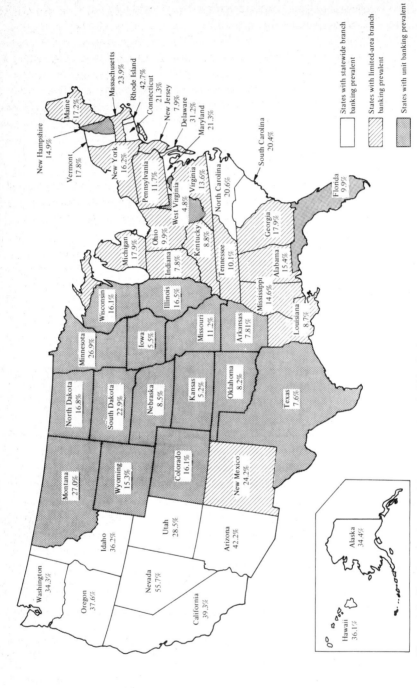

Figure 4-1 Percentage of commercial bank deposits held by the largest commercial bank or bank group in each state, classified by status of branch banking. *(Source:* FDIC's Summary of Accounts and Deposits in All Commercial and Mutual Savings Banks *1975 (biennial), Table K, p. 17.)*

New Hampshire 14.9%
Maine 17.2%
Massachusetts 23.9%
Rhode Island 42.7%
Connecticut 21.3%
New Jersey 7.9%
Delaware 31.2%
Maryland 21.3%
South Carolina 20.4%
Vermont 17.8%
New York 16.2%
Pennsylvania 11.7%
West Virginia 4.8%
Virginia 13.6%
North Carolina 20.6%
Florida 9.9%
Georgia 17.9%
Michigan 17.9%
Ohio 9.9%
Kentucky 8.8%
Tennessee 10.1%
Alabama 15.4%
Indiana 7.8%
Illinois 16.5%
Mississippi 14.6%
Louisiana 8.7%
Wisconsin 16.1%
Iowa 5.5%
Missouri 11.2%
Arkansas 7.81%
Minnesota 26.9%
North Dakota 16.8%
South Dakota 22.9%
Nebraska 8.5%
Kansas 5.2%
Oklahoma 8.2%
Texas 7.6%
Montana 27.0%
Wyoming 15.3%
Colorado 16.1%
New Mexico 24.2%
Idaho 36.2%
Utah 28.5%
Arizona 42.2%
Washington 34.3%
Oregon 37.6%
Nevada 55.7%
California 39.3%
Alaska 34.4%
Hawaii 36.1%

States with statewide branch banking prevalent

States with limited-area branch banking prevalent

States with unit banking prevalent

Table 4-2 Number of States in which Specified Percentages of Deposits are Held by the Largest Banking Organization and the Five Largest Banking Organizations, June 30, 1975

Percentage of deposits	Largest bank	Five largest banks
90–100	—	4
80–89.9	—	4
70–79.9	—	4
60–69.9	—	8
50–59.9	1	6
40–49.9	2	7
30–39.9	7	9
20–29.9	10	4
10–19.9	16	4
Under 10	14	—
Total	50	50

Source: FDIC's Summary of Accounts and Deposits in All Commercial and Mutual Savings Banks 1975 (biennial), Table K, p. 17.

concentration ratios seem to suggest that there is an intermediate banking market somewhere between the national and local markets. While such a market may in fact exist, there is no evidence to support this contention. The second and more serious objection to state concentration ratios is that, even if intermediate markets exist, there is no sensible reason why they should end at state borders. The state is a political concept, not an economic one. It is by no means obvious why New York and New Jersey should be identified as separate geographic markets.

Perhaps the only valid reasons for calculating bank concentration ratios by states are the hope that state political boundaries may roughly approximate (correlate with) meaningful economic regions; and the fact that, in any case, this is the form in which the data are available. Whatever their shortcomings, people find state concentration ratios interesting, especially for their own state.

Figure 4-1 gives concentration ratios for the largest banking organization in each state, with the states grouped by branch, limited branch, or unit banking laws. Examination of similar data for earlier years shows, predictably, different trends for different states. In general, however, the data indicate that states permitting statewide branching are more heavily concentrated than states with unit banking, although the increase in the number of banking offices has been substantially greater in states with branch banking than in states with unit banking.

Table 4-2 summarizes the data shown in Figure 4-1 and also includes similar data on five-bank concentration ratios. As can be seen, bank concentration at the state level is not particularly great. In only one state does the largest bank control more than 50 percent of deposits, and in forty states the largest bank controls less than 30 percent of total deposits. As one would expect, using the largest five banks (rather than the largest one bank) shifts this distribution upward, but even so twenty-four states have five-bank concentration ratios of less than 50 percent.

Bank Concentration in Local Markets

Local market concentration ratios have some of the same drawbacks as state concentration ratios, though not to such a severe degree. In large financial centers, such as Chicago or New York City, the metropolitan area may encompass several local submarkets; in nonmetropolitan areas, the local market may include more than one town. Our knowledge of these matters is very limited. Nevertheless, it seems a fair assumption that metropolitan areas and towns constitute a reasonable approximation of local banking markets.

Nonmetropolitan Areas About 90 percent of all unit banks in the United States are located in population centers of 25,000 or less. About one-half of these are the only bank in town, and most of the remaining banks face competition from only one other bank in town. In addition, it has been estimated that there are about 5,800 other towns with populations below 25,000 with no banking facilities at all. For the United States as a whole, including states with unit, statewide branch, and limited branch banking, the average number of banks in towns with populations from 15,000 to 25,000 was about 2.4. It seems clear that, especially with respect to demand deposits and short-term business loans, where banks have no effective "outside" competitors, nonmetropolitan banking markets are very highly concentrated.

Metropolitan Areas Local banking markets also appear to be very heavily concentrated in metropolitan areas. Table 4-3 shows average one-bank and three-bank concentration ratios for metropolitan areas of different sizes. The data are broken down by the types of branching laws applicable to the state in which the metropolitan area is located. Note that the concentration ratios are generally high, particularly the three-bank ratios, and become higher the smaller the size of the metropolitan area. Thus the largest three banks in metropolitan areas with a population of 50,000 to 99,999 with unit banking hold 85.4 percent of deposits, while the comparable figure for metropolitan areas with a population of over 1 million is only 45.3 percent. Note also that areas located in states with branch banking have uniformly higher ratios than those located in states with unit banking. (This point has already been discussed in Chapter 2.) Finally, note that ratios for areas having limited branch banking fall in between the other two.

Trends in Local Banking Markets Studies of local banking markets in both metropolitan and nonmetropolitan areas strongly suggest that these markets have become more competitive in recent years. Table 4-4, for example, shows that during the nine-year period from 1966 to 1975, the three-bank organization concentration ratio declined in most areas of the country. Further analysis of these data indicates that the concentration ratios fell most in those markets that were the most heavily concentrated in 1966. The reason for this general decline in concentration ratios is probably the bank holding company movement. As discussed in Chapter 2, most studies indicate that when a BHC acquires a small bank in an area (foothold entry),

Table 4–3 Average Percentage of Demand Deposits Accounted for by the Largest Banking Organization and Largest Three Banking Organizations in Metropolitan Areas, by Size of Metropolitan Area and Branching Law, December 1975

	Population 50,000–99,000			Population 100,000–499,999			Population 500,000–999,999			Population 1 million and over		
	Unit banking	Limited branch banking	Statewide branch banking	Unit banking	Limited branch banking	Statewide branch banking	Unit banking	Limited branch banking	Statewide branch banking	Unit banking	Limited branch banking	Statewide branch banking
Percent of deposits in the largest bank or bank group	41.3	39.6	40.8	26.7	35.7	37.0	25.7	28.7	35.5	20.9	30.8	36.2
Percent of deposits in the three largest banks or bank groups	85.4	81.3	81.2	59.6	73.3	75.0	54.9	64.9	68.7	45.3	64.4	72.7
Number of SMSA's	13	7	5	55	74	46	7	16	13	9	14	11

Source: Federal Deposit Insurance Corporation, *Summary of Accounts and Deposits in All Commercial and Mutual Savings Banks*, Table L; combined with SMSA population information from Appendix II, *Statistical Abstract of the United States, 1977.*

77

Table 4-4   Change in Bank-Market Structure for 213 Metropolitan Areas and 213 Non-metropolitan Counties, 1966–1975

Bank markets	213 Metropolitan areas	213 Nonmetropolitan counties
Number experiencing an increase in the three-firm concentration ratio	29	54
Number experiencing a decrease in the three-firm concentration ratio	184	163
Number experiencing no change in the three-firm concentration ratio	0	16

Source: Based on Samuel H. Talley, "Recent Trends in Local Banking Market Structure," Board of Governors of the Federal Reserve System, *Staff Economic Study Number 89*, 1977, Tables 1 and 2.

that bank's share of the market usually rises. Naturally, this rise in the market share of the small bank tends to decrease the market shares of the larger banks in the area, and thus decrease the concentration ratio in that market.

4-3   ENTRY BARRIERS

Entry barriers in banking—the ease or difficulty of establishing a new bank—were discussed in Chapter 3. It was pointed out there that the regulatory authorities have adopted a policy of severely restricting the granting of new bank charters, with the result that entry barriers in banking are quite high. The discussion will not be repeated here, but it is worth making the point explicitly that, notwithstanding the recent trend toward more competition, concentration ratios in local banking markets (especially in nonmetropolitan areas) are likely to remain high as long as these entry barriers persist.

4-4   COLLUSIVE BEHAVIOR IN BANKING

While an examination of such things as concentration ratios and entry barriers can give us valuable factual information that reflects the nature of banking markets, they cannot, by themselves, tell us anything conclusive about the extent of competition in banking. Economists generally *assume* that, human nature being what it is, the smaller the number of firms in a market the larger is the probability of collusive agreements to fix prices, standardize services, and the like. But this is *only* an assumption. A high concentration ratio doesn't *prove* a lack of competition. For this reason it is necessary to go beyond the mere facts of banking market structure and look for evidence of anticompetitive behavior. One such bit of evidence is the existence (or nonexistence) of *collusive behavior*—banks getting together and agreeing not to compete with one another.

Although several cases of collusive behavior in banking have been documented, most of these are quite dated. For example, in 1961 the Department of Justice brought a civil suit against banks in a small New Jersey town for agreeing on service charges on checking accounts. And in 1963 certain banks in Minnesota were charged with fixing prices on service charges, correspondent-bank services, and some types of loans. But one swallow doesn't make a summer, and isolated cases don't establish general rules, especially where the cases occurred almost twenty years ago. There is, however, one general practice in banking that most economists believe exhibits some of the characteristics of oligopolistic price setting: the *prime rate convention*.

The Prime Rate Convention

The *prime rate* is that rate of interest which banks charge their very best customers; the interest rates charged to less creditworthy customers are scaled up from this basic rate. For most banks,[2] the determination of the prime rate appears to fit very closely the theoretical model economists call *price leadership,* which means that a price in an industry is not determined continuously by supply and demand pressures in a competitive market, but instead is set periodically by a leading firm, with other firms quickly following suit. It is held that the prime rate, or the "price" of borrowing money, is determined in a price leadership fashion rather than competitively. Typically, one of the large banks in the country will set a new prime rate, this fact will be given widespread publicity, and other banks will quickly fall into line. In the past few years, moreover, a few large banks have apparently been setting what has come to be called a *superprime* for a few very large multinational corporations.[3] Since it is generally believed that such corporations are very sensitive to interest rates (i.e., have an elastic demand), while smaller corporations are not so sensitive (have an inelastic demand), the bank will maximize its profits by charging two different prime rates of interest. In doing so, these banks are again conforming closely to a theoretical model of pricing behavior called that of a *discriminating monopolist.*

4-5   BANK CONCENTRATION AND PRICING

With the exception of the prime rate convention, we have very little *direct* evidence on the relationship between bank concentration and bank pricing policies. It is, however, possible to use the indirect method of regression analysis to shed additional light on this issue.

A great deal of statistical research has been done on the consequences of bank concentration. Although the results of this research have been mixed, the weight of the evidence seems to indicate a small but positive relationship between concentration and bank loan rates. However, the pitfalls in this type of study are numerous, and this conclusion should not be taken as firm.

Trying to pin down the relationship between bank concentration and bank pricing policies is not a simple matter of regressing loan rates on concentration ratios. The difficulty is that average rates of interest charged by banks are determined by many different factors besides the degrees of concentration. The "mix" of different kinds of loans made by the bank, demand conditions in the local loan market,

[2]A few large banks have what is called a "formula prime" or a "floating prime." The formula prime is "tied" to some well-known, open-market rate of interest. For example, one of these banks might set its prime rate each week at ½ percent above the interest rate on prime commercial paper.

[3]Randall C. Merris, "Prime Rate Update," Federal Reserve Bank of Chicago, *Economic Perspectives,* May/June 1978, pp. 14–16.

the size of the bank—all these factors and more may affect the rate charged by a particular bank to a particular customer at a particular time. The first problem is therefore to isolate the effects of bank concentration from all these other things. Basically, we want to ask the question, If we were to hold everything else constant in banking markets and change only the degree of concentration, what would be the effect on loan rates? This can be done with a *multiple-regression equation,* a straight-forward extension of a simple regression equation, except that more than one explanatory variable is used (see the Appendix to Chapter 1).

The second problem is that we rarely have exactly the information, or data, we need in order to quantify such concepts as "demand in the local loan market." This problem is handled (in an admittedly imperfect manner) by using *proxy* variables. A *proxy variable* is information you *can* obtain that is related to information you *can't* obtain. Thus, a proxy variable for demand conditions in a particular market area might be the change in employment in that area; the underlying assumption would be that employment and loan demand vary together and in approximately the same proportions.

Both these techniques—multiple regression and proxy variables—are needed to investigate our problem. Specifically, we wish to test the hypothesis that higher interest rates will be charged by banks in those areas where banking is more heavily concentrated. One study[4] of this question, which may be considered typical, found the following relationship for banks in thirty-six metropolitan areas of the United States:

$$I = 4.68 + .012C - .0004B + .003P + .033L$$
$$r^2 = .42$$

Coefficient on C significant at 5% level
Coefficient on L significant at 1% level
Coefficients on B and P not significant

where I (interest) = average interest rate charged on bank loans
      C (concentration) = percentage of bank deposits in the area held by the largest two banks
      B (bank) = bank size
      P (population) = percentage change in population in the area (a proxy for the demand for bank loans)
      L (loans) = ratio of consumer to total loans in the two banks (a proxy for the "mix" of loans)

Of particular interest in this equation is the coefficient of C, the measure of bank concentration. Suppose that mentally we hold all other variables (B, P, and L) in the equation constant but change C by 10 percent. What happens to I, the interest

[4]Franklin R. Edwards, "Concentration in Banking and Its Effects on Business Loan Rates," *The Review of Economics and Statistics,* August 1964, pp. 294–300.

rate on bank loans? It will go up by about 0.12 percent; that is, .012 (the coefficient of C) times 10 percent $= 0.12$ percent. Thus if banks are charging, say, a 7 percent rate of interest in a market with a 50 percent concentration ratio, *other things equal,* they will charge 7.12 percent on these loans if the concentration ratio rises to 60 percent. From this it is possible to conclude that a highly concentrated banking market will exploit its monopolistic power by charging higher interest rates on loans.

But note that this conclusion is not wholly satisfactory. In the equation just given, the coefficient of determination r^2 is low at .42. The proxy variables P and L do not measure exactly what we want them to measure, and the coefficients B and P are not statistically significant. Also, although the coefficient on the concentration variable C is significant at the 5 percent level, it is nevertheless very small.

Another approach to this problem that has been taken in recent studies is to focus on the relationship between bank-market concentration and some very specific, and very narrow, aspect of banking—e.g., the interest rate on new car loans, or the service charges on demand deposits. One recent research study,[5] for example, investigated the relation between consumer installment loans and bank concentration. Consumer installment loans were chosen on the assumption that they are a homogeneous product, so that problems of defining the "product market" are minimized; and that these loans are sufficiently small that the geographic market is quite limited. This study, like similar studies, generally concludes that the relation between market concentration and bank loan rates is positive but quite small.

4-6 NONPRICE COMPETITION

When economists talk about *competition,* they usually mean *price competition.* They have in mind a *model,* or theory, of a market consisting of many buyers and sellers, with prices as their only means of competing with one another. In fact, however, most American industries do not conform to this model; in industry after industry, each firm has *some* advantage over its rival: The products are somewhat different, locations of outlets vary, repairs are better, and so forth. Industries composed of such firms are said to be engaged in *nonprice competition.*

There are a number of ways in which banks compete with one another on a nonprice basis. Probably the most obvious of these is through advertising: television and radio commercials and newspaper ads. Beyond this, banks may offer new or better financial services to their customers—for example, longer banking hours, drive-in windows, and free travelers' checks. Since we can find, statistically, only a weak relation between banking concentration and bank *price* competition, the question naturally arises as to whether we can discern a relation between bank-market concentration and *nonprice* competition. Note that in this latter case, we would expect an inverse relationship. That is, our hypothesis is that the more heavily a market is concentrated, the weaker is nonprice competition and hence the fewer the services that will be offered.

[5]H. Prescott Beighley and Alan S. McCall, "Market Power and Commercial Bank Installment Credit," *Journal of Money, Credit and Banking,* November 1975, pp. 449–467.

This hypothesis has only recently been investigated, but the studies so far done suggest a strong inverse relationship between bank services offered in a market and the degree of banking concentration in that market. One such research study,[6] for example, was based on a telephone survey of 332 banks in sixty-nine metropolitan areas. The banks were asked a number of questions about such matters as trust department services, banking hours, overdraft arrangements on checking accounts, automated teller machines, and the like. These responses were then related, with the use of regression analysis, to a measure of bank concentration in the respondent's market. The results very strongly supported the hypothesis that the more highly concentrated a bank market is, the fewer services the bank is likely to offer its customers. Since offering fewer services lowers the bank's costs, the authors conclude that studies that focus on a *single* performance indicator in banking, such as loan rates, strongly understate the influence of bank concentration.[7]

4-7 BANKS AND THE ANTITRUST LAWS

The Sherman Antitrust Act was passed in 1890. The Clayton Antitrust Act, which greatly strengthened the Sherman Act, was passed in 1914. Until about 1960, it was generally believed by bankers, lawyers, and economists that the commercial banking industry was exempt from prosecution under these laws. This belief rested on two bases: First, the antitrust statutes had been enacted under the power of Congress to regulate interstate "commerce," and earlier court cases had seemed to indicate that banking was not a commercial activity—that banks traded in money, not in goods. Second, it was held that banking, like public utilities, was a regulated industry and therefore not subject to the antitrust laws. In the early 1960s, however, this situation was completely altered by a landmark Supreme Court case involving a bank merger.

The Philadelphia National Bank Case (1963)

The case involved an application for a merger between two banks in Philadelphia, Pennsylvania: the Philadelphia National Bank (PNB) and the Girard Trust Corn Exchange Bank (Girard). The facts are briefly as follows: In 1960, the PNB, a national bank, applied to the Comptroller of the Currency for approval of a proposed merger with the Girard. At that time, the PNB was the second largest bank in the Philadelphia metropolitan area, and the Girard was the third largest bank. The merger, if approved, would have made the consolidated bank the largest bank in that area (about 36 percent of total bank deposits) and the sixteenth largest bank ($1.8 billion of assets) in the United States.

Under the provisions of the Bank Merger Act, the Comptroller was required to ask for an advisory opinion about the proposed merger from the Federal Reserve

[6]Arnold J. Heggestad and John J. Mingo, "Prices, Nonprices, and Concentration in Commercial Banking," *Journal of Money, Credit and Banking,* February 1976, pp. 107–117.

[7]For similar studies that reach a similar conclusion, see Laurence J. White, "Price Regulation and Quality Rivalry in a Profit-Maximizing Model," *Journal of Money, Credit and Banking,* February 1976, pp. 97–106; and Lewis Mandell, "Diffusion of EFTS among National Banks," *Journal of Money, Credit and Banking,* May 1977, pp. 341–348.

System, the FDIC, and the Antitrust Division of the Attorney General's office. Although all three agencies apparently recommended that the request for a merger be denied, the Comptroller nevertheless approved it. In February 1961, the Attorney General filed suit in the district court to prevent the merger. The suit alleged, in part, that the merger would violate the Clayton Act by causing a significant increase in the concentration of firms in the market, thereby lessening competition. The district court ruled in favor of the merger, and the government appealed the case to the Supreme Court. In June 1963, the Supreme Court ruled in favor of the government and enjoined the proposed merger. In doing so, it established once and for all the principle that banking was subject to antitrust prosecution under the Clayton Act.[8]

Legal issues were not the only ones involved, however. In making its decision, the Court was also obliged to rule on three economic questions: What is the appropriate product market? What is the appropriate geographic market? and What degree of concentration constitutes a threat to competition? With respect to the first of these issues, the Supreme Court held that banking was a *line of commerce,* that is, that the appropriate product market is the single market of banking, not the several markets of savings and demand deposits, consumer and business loans, and so on. In making this decision, the Court appears to have greatly oversimplified a complicated economic question.

Given that the product market is simply *banking*—that banking is a separate and distinguishable line of commerce—the Supreme Court then decided that the proper geographic market was the four Pennsylvania counties comprising the Philadelphia metropolitan area. The lawyers for the PNB had argued (and the district court had agreed) that a more appropriate geographic market was an eight-county area, including three counties in New Jersey. The Supreme Court evidently ruled as it did because the limited branch banking laws of Pennsylvania would have confined the merged bank to establishing branches within these four counties. (It is not clear what the Court would have done if the state of Pennsylvania had permitted statewide branching.) Whatever the merits of the two geographic markets, again the Court seems to have made its decision on the basis of a rather simplistic criterion, at least from the economist's viewpoint.

Finally, given that banking is the appropriate product and that the four Pennsylvania counties are the approprate area, the question still remained as to how much concentration was too much concentration. It will be recalled that if the PNB and Girard had been allowed to merge, the resulting bank would have controlled 36 percent of bank deposits in the area. In considering this concentration ratio, the Supreme Court said: "Without attempting to specify the smallest market share which would still be considered to threaten undue concentration, we are clear that 30 percent presents that threat." Again, it is not clear on exactly what basis the Court chose this figure of 30 percent. As we have seen, the theoretical and statistical basis for such a figure is quite questionable.

[8]The Philadelphia case involved a violation of the Clayton Antitrust Act. In 1964, in a case involving the proposed merger of two banks in Lexington, Kentucky, the Supreme Court enjoined the merger on the basis of the Sherman Antitrust Act. The Court thus made it absolutely clear that banks were subject to the antitrust laws, just like other businesses.

4-8   THE GROWING SIMILARITY BETWEEN BANKS AND OTHER FINANCIAL INSTITUTIONS

As has just been discussed, in 1963 the Supreme Court decided that banking constituted a product market all by itself. While most economists felt that the issue was more complex than the Supreme Court made it out to be, nevertheless in 1963 the decision was not wholly unreasonable. However, in 1974, in the *Connecticut National Bank Case,* the Supreme Court reaffirmed its position that commercial banking is a specific line of commerce, and that commercial banks and other depository financial institutions are not in competition with one another. But by 1974 a trend was evident in the financial sector of the economy that made the Supreme Court's position on this issue highly questionable. This trend, which has grown markedly stronger since 1974, involves the growing similarity between banks and certain other nonbank financial institutions.[9] As these institutions become more and more like commercial banks, and as banks become more like them, the whole issue of competition in banking markets will be profoundly affected.

The financial institutions that are becoming more like banks are generally called "thrift institutions" (or, more simply, "thrifts"). These thrift institutions, which are described more fully in Chapter 6, are of three kinds: *Savings and loan associations* (S&Ls), which accept savings deposits from the public and invest these funds primarily in home mortgages; *credit unions* (CUs), which also accept savings deposits and make consumer loans; and *mutual savings banks* (MSBs), which are very much like S&Ls, and are found in only eighteen states (mostly in the northeastern part of the United States). The ways in which these institutions are becoming like commercial banks involve both their *liabilities* (the kinds of deposit services people can get from them), and their *assets* (the kinds of investments they make).

Deposit Liabilities

To understand how thrifts and commercial banks are converging in terms of their deposit liabilities, it is necessary to understand that as recently as 1972 it was generally considered illegal for thrift institutions to offer demand deposit services to the public. Thrifts, that is, were limited to offering interest-bearing savings deposits. Commercial banks, on the other hand, were prohibited by law from paying *any* interest on demand deposits, and had to pay ¼% less interest on savings accounts than S&Ls and MSBs. It was under this set of legal constraints that thrifts and banks were generally held not to compete with one another.

In 1972, however, certain mutual savings banks in Massachusetts found a

---

[9]For discussions of this trend, see: Jack S. Light, "Increasing Competition between Financial Institutions," Federal Reserve Bank of Chicago, *Economic Perspectives,* May/June 1977, pp. 23–31; Jean M. Lovati, "The Growing Similarity among Financial Institutions," Federal Reserve Bank of St. Louis *Review,* October 1977, pp. 2–11; and Jean M. Lovati, "The Changing Competition between Commercial Banks and Thrift Institutions for Deposits," Federal Reserve Bank of St. Louis *Review,* July 1975, pp. 2–8.

loophole in the law and began to offer their customers a checklike instrument called a *negotiable order of withdrawal,* or *NOW,* account. These NOW accounts worked just like checking accounts, but with one major difference: they paid a rate of interest. Naturally, they proved to be popular with customers, and spread rapidly —first to New Hampshire, then to Maine. The commercial banks in these states, and all depository institutions in nearby states, were not too happy about this, of course, considering it unfair competition. In 1976, therefore, Congress authorized all depository institutions (including commercial banks) in the six New England states to issue NOW accounts. In essence, this meant that in these states the traditional distinctions between bank demand deposits and thrift savings deposits had been obliterated.

Meanwhile, the thrift institutions in the rest of the country were not idle. Some states began permitting thrifts to offer *noninterest-bearing negotiable orders of withdrawal* (NINOW) accounts; other states and the Federal government (for federally chartered S&Ls) began permitting such innovations as preauthorized withdrawals from thrifts (e. g., you could have your mortgage payment automatically deducted from your savings account) and off-the-premises automated teller machines for withdrawing currency from an S&L or MSB savings account. Credit unions got into the act in 1974 by offering so-called *share drafts,* which, like NOW accounts, were essentially an interest-bearing checking account. Banks, to stay competitive, began offering preauthorized withdrawals and telephone transfers from savings accounts to checking accounts. In 1978, the Federal Reserve System authorized for its member banks an *automatic* transfer of funds from a savings account to a checking account. This meant that if you wrote a check against your checking account when you didn't have enough funds in it, the bank was authorized to automatically shift enough funds from your savings account to your checking account. In the meantime, you earn interest on the money.

The profusion of new types of accounts in both thrifts and commercial banks in recent years is both overwhelming and confusing. But the essence of the matter is this: Thrift institutions can now offer either checking accounts, or very close substitutes for checking accounts, that have the added attraction of paying the customer a rate of interest. And commercial banks, while they are still technically prohibited from paying interest on demand deposits, have found a number of ways to get around this. If, as seems very likely, this trend continues, there will soon be virtually no difference to the individual customer between thrift deposits and demand deposits. Obviously, this will mean that banks will find themselves in a much more competitive market than they faced a few years ago.*

*Author's note added in proof: In April 1979 the U.S. Court of Appeals in the District of Columbia made a very fundamental decision concerning these matters. In a decision encompassing three separate cases, the court held that federal regulatory agencies had exceeded their authority in permitting the automatic transfer of funds from savings to checking accounts by commercial banks, the use of remote service units by savings and loan associations, and the issuance of share drafts by credit unions. The court held that these devices were in violation of the laws prohibiting interest payments on checking accounts, and the issuance of checking accounts by nonbank financial institutions. The court therefore ordered that these practices be stopped, but at the same time stayed its own order until January 1, 1980, to give Congress time to review the situation. The court's decision may be appealed to the Supreme Court.

Assets

When a depository institution, such as a commercial bank or an S&L, takes in your money as a deposit, it generally will set aside a certain amount in cash and then use the rest to buy interest-bearing *assets*. It is from these assets, of course, that the institution makes its profits. Both traditionally and by law, the various institutions have specialized in different kinds of assets—commercial banks in business loans, S&Ls and MSBs in home mortgages, and credit unions in personal loans (financing new car purchases, and the like).

Increasingly, however, all four of these depository institutions are acquiring assets that were previously the special province of only one of them. Commercial banks, for example, have for many years been heavy investors in mortgages and personal loans. More recently, S&Ls and MSBs have been acquiring such assets as government bonds, municipal securities, and consumer loans at a very high rate. Credit unions were authorized in 1977 to make mortgage loans of up to thirty years in maturity. In short, the composition of the assets of these institutions are overlapping more and more.

Conclusion

The market structure of American commercial banking is currently in a state of flux. Thrift institutions more and more resemble commercial banks, and commercial banks more and more resemble thrift institutions. This trend is so pronounced that it is doubtful that it can be deflected. Thus, the day may well come when there is no real difference among the various depository institutions. If and when such a day does arrive, the amount of competition in "banking" will be greatly increased.

4-9 REVIEW QUESTIONS

1   Explain why it is necessary to specify both the product market and the geographic market before discussing monopoly in banking.
2   Is banking becoming more concentrated at the local level? Why or why not?
3   What is the *prime rate?* What has this to do with *price leadership* in an industry?
4   How are loan rates and concentration ratios related in metropolitan banking markets? Is this relationship a strong one?
5   Does bank concentration in metropolitan markets affect the quality of bank services?
6   If commercial banks and nonbank thrift institutions become identical, what effect will this have on: (1) bank holding companies; (2) branch banking; (3) competition in banking?

PART 3

FINANCIAL INTERMEDIARIES AND FINANCIAL MARKETS

In our description of the financial machinery of the United States' economy, we have to this point concentrated exclusively on the commercial banking industry. But, of course, there is a great deal more to it than that. While banks are easily the single most important type of financial institution in the United States, they are certainly not the only type. There are many others, ranging from savings and loan associations to small-loan companies.

Moreover, all these institutions (and banks, too) have dealings in the great financial markets of the United States—for example, the stock market and the government securities market—where standardized financial instruments are bought and sold impersonally. Clearly, our background description of the functioning of the money side of the economic system will be seriously incomplete until the reader has gained at least a rudimentary working knowledge of these matters. Accordingly, the immediate purpose of the following three chapters is to round out the student's knowledge of financial institutions and markets. Thus, in terms of Figure 1-1, we now need to fill in the rest of the material in the box marked "3" above and "A" below. This additional material is indicated in boldface type in Figure III-1.

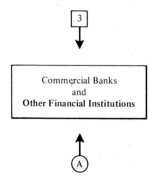

Figure III-1   Detail of Figure 1-1.

5

The Theory
of Portfolio Selection

Nonbank financial institutions are frequently called *financial intermediaries*. By this is meant that they serve as intermediates between two groups of people. They do this by selling a particular type of financial service to one group of people and then taking this money and selling another type of financial service to another group of people. The question naturally arises (as it always does with an intermediary), as to why each group cannot perform these services for themselves? Who, that is, needs a middleman? Isn't the intermediary function just an extra expense, which we could all do without?

There are two answers to this question—one which is fairly obvious and intuitive, and one which is rather subtle and complicated. The intuitive answer is that the financial services sold by intermediaries are ones that individuals would find it difficult, if not impossible, to provide for themselves. Consider an insurance company, for example. The service it sells to the public is protection—protection against the financial disasters of fire, theft, sickness, death, and so on. The funds thus collected are then lent (a financial service) by the insurance companies, largely to corporations. Clearly, ordinary persons would find it impossible to insure themselves against financial disaster, and large corporations would find it very difficult to borrow huge sums in small amounts from a great many small investors. The insurance company has thus *intermediated* between the public on the one hand, and the corporations on the other.

But while this answer may seem intuitive when we think about insurance companies, it is not so obvious if we consider other types of financial intermediaries. For example, a savings and loan association is an institution that, basically, sells interest-bearing savings certificates to the public and then lends these funds out in the form of home mortgages. The S&L, of course, is able to do this because the interest rate it receives on the mortgages is greater than the interest rate it pays on savings accounts. But in this case, it is not so obvious that ordinary persons couldn't perform this intermediary function for themselves. Surely, one feels, it would be possible for many people to lend money directly to home buyers, using the house as collateral.[1] And if they can, why don't they? This brings us to the second answer to the question posed at the outset of this chapter, the one that is rather subtle and complicated. For as it turns out, there is an inherent advantage to all financial intermediation, an advantage that very few people would have the resources to capture fully. This advantage is frequently expressed in popular parlance as "spreading the risk" or "not putting all your eggs in one basket." In financial circles, it is called *portfolio theory.* Portfolio theory goes well beyond the intuitive, however, and has general applicability in such diverse areas as the stock market, personal finance, and monetary theory. While our immediate interest in portfolio theory will be confined to its applicability to financial intermediaries, we will return to it when we consider monetary theory.

5-1 PORTFOLIO THEORY

As a point of departure, imagine the following situation: Suppose someone gives you $10,000 in cash and at the same time hands you a list of various *financial assets—* i.e., financial instruments that you can buy. He then instructs you to spend (invest) the $10,000 on some combination of these assets; that is, you are to choose an asset *portfolio.* You may put the entire $10,000 into a single asset, such as a government bond; you may spread the $10,000 among several assets, such as cash, bonds, and common stocks; or you may do anything else you wish as long as you buy only the assets listed. The question is, How will you make your choice among all the possibilities open to you?

To answer this question, consider first the *goals* of an investor when choosing a portfolio. One goal is immediately apparent: The investor wants to earn a rate of return on his portfolio. If this were his only goal, then the selection of his portfolio would be a simple matter; he would just choose that single asset which he expected would give him the greatest return in the future. Unfortunately, there *is* more to the matter than this. For the investor is concerned not only with the return he obtains, but also with the safety of his investment. That is, he wants not only a high rate of

---

[1]Indeed, some people do this. It is called selling (or buying) "on contract."

return, but also a low level of *risk.* But, as we all know, risk and return are positively associated with one another. Thus, if the investor wants a high return, he must be willing to accept a high level of risk; or, alternatively, if he wants a low level of risk, he must be willing to accept a low rate of return.

Risk-Return Indifference Curves

We can lend precision to these ideas in the following way: Consider Figure 5-1, which measures expected return on the vertical axis and risk on the horizontal axis. Thus, any point on the graph gives some unique combination of risk and return. The point marked *A,* for example, is a point of high risk and high return; the point marked *B* is a low-risk, low-return combination. Suppose that an investor is at point *B,* which implies that she is willing to accept R_1 of risk and r_1 of return, i.e., the risk-return combination of (R_1, r_1). Next, imagine that we arbitrarily choose some slightly higher level of risk—say, R_2—and then ask the investor how much more return she would have to receive in order to accept the risk level R_2? If we phrased the question properly, she would give us the *minimum* amount of return that would just compensate her for the higher risk. Suppose, when we do this, that the investor indicates that she would be willing to move from risk level R_1 to risk level R_2 if her expected return were to rise from r_1 to r_2. This would give the point marked *C* in Figure 5-1, and we would say that this investor was *indifferent* between points *B* and *C,* that is, between the risk-return combinations (R_1, r_1) and (R_2, r_2). If we kept repeating this experiment with very small changes in risk, eventually we would generate the entire curve marked *BCA* in Figure 5-1. We shall call this curve the investor's *risk-return indifference curve* (or sometimes just the *indifference curve* for short).

There are two things to note in particular about the risk-return indifference curve of Figure 5-1: The first is that the curve *BCA* slopes upward. This property of the curve marks the underlying assumption that people do not like risk, that is, that they are what economists call *risk averters.*[2] That this state of mind does,

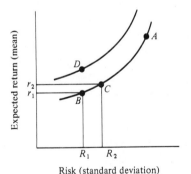

Figure 5-1 Risk-return indifference curves.

[2]This assumption is by no means necessary. We could as easily analyze the behavior of people who enjoy taking risks *(risk lovers)* or people who don't care about risk one way or the other *(risk neutral).* Since it is widely believed that risk aversion is the most typical attitude of investors, we shall not inquire into these other cases.

indeed, underlie the indifference curve can be seen simply by noting that as we move farther out on the risk axis, a higher expected return will be needed to compensate for the greater risk. The second point to note is that the investor will *prefer* any point *above* the curve *BCA* to any point on it. The point *D,* for example, which lies directly above point *B,* will be preferred to point *B,* for at point *D* the investor obtains a *higher* expected return with exactly the *same* risk. But note also that we could begin at point *D* and, by repeating the process just described, generate another indifference curve such as the one of which point *D* is a part. Thus we can, in this fashion, develop an entire set, or *family,* of risk-return indifference curves. Any point on a higher indifference curve is preferred to any point on a lower indifference curve.

The Mean-Variance Portfolio

We now have an analytic tool that provides us with a basis for developing a theory of investor behavior. But we need something more. We also need to be able to describe financial assets in terms of the same two characteristics, risk and return, that were used to describe the choice process of the investor. Moreover, we would like to be able to put this matter into terms that can be measured. We can do this by recalling two statistical concepts that were described in the Appendix to Chapter 1: the *average (mean)* and the *standard deviation.* The average, of course, is familiar to everyone. The standard deviation, remember, is the square root of the variance and is a measure of the dispersion of a series of numbers about their average. (At this point the reader may wish to review the discussion of the variance and standard deviation in the Appendix to Chapter 1.) We can use these statistical concepts for the problem at hand.

Let's suppose that, based on the past behavior of an asset, an investor has some notion of what it is going to do in the future. However, he is not certain of this expectation. For example, he may feel that *on the average* a particular stock will probably pay him an 8 percent return over the following year, but the return *could* (i.e., with some probability) go as high as 10 percent or be as low as 6 percent. Thus the investor is seen as forecasting a set of probable outcomes with respect to the returns on an asset. The average of these outcomes, weighted by their probability, is taken as his *expected* return; the standard deviation of the outcomes is his *risk.*

To see that this is a sensible interpretation of the ideas of risk and return, consider the following example. Suppose that we have two common stocks and, based on their past performance, we expect that on the average both will pay us an 8 percent return over the following year. We also know, however, that the past price movements of stock 1 have been over a very limited range—it has never paid more than 10 percent or less than 6 percent. Stock 2, on the other hand, has behaved quite erratically in the past, sometimes paying as much as 16 percent and other times paying nothing at all. Even though both stocks have the same expected return, therefore, we would regard stock 2 as being riskier than stock 1. *If* we were forced to choose either one stock or the other and *if* we dislike risk (as most people do), *then* we would choose stock 1 to invest our money in.

Now let us move one step further. Suppose we add a third common stock, stock 3, to the possibilities before us. That is, suppose now that we may invest our money in either stock 1, 2, or 3 (but we continue to assume that we must invest all our money in only one stock). Stock 3 has the following characteristics: Its expected (average) rate of return is 10 percent, and its risk (standard deviation) is the same as stock 2. Which stock do we now choose? We can organize our thoughts about how to answer this question by comparing the stocks two at a time. Thus, comparing stocks 1 and 2, it continues to be true that we would prefer stock 1 because it gives us the same return (8 percent) at less risk. Comparing stocks 2 and 3, we would prefer stock 3 because stock 3 has the *same* standard deviation as stock 2 but a higher average rate of return.

But what about the choice between stocks 1 and 3? How do we choose between these stocks? The problem is that stock 1 has less risk but stock 3 has greater return. In choosing one of these stocks, therefore, we must decide what our trade-off is between risk and return. But this is precisely what the risk-return indifference curves of Figure 5-1 show. Suppose, for example, that Figure 5-2 is our indifference map. Let the point marked "$S1$" be the risk-return combination of stock 1. Then if the point $S3*$ is the risk-return combination for stock 3, we would prefer buying stock 3 because it lies on a higher indifference curve. Alternatively, if $S3'$ is the appropriate point, we would buy stock 1 since in this case stock 1 is on the higher indifference curve. If both stocks 1 and 3 lie on the same indifference curve, we would be indifferent between them. (This last situation is not shown in Figure 5-2.)

We now have a theoretical construct that begins to explain, in reasonable terms, how investors choose among financial assets. But the theory remains incomplete because we are still operating under a very restrictive assumption—that investors must put all their money into only one asset. Such an assumption is unrealistic, of course; an investor may instead want to have a composite portfolio, a blend of several different stocks. We now want to incorporate this possibility into the theory. In order to do so, it will be necessary to state some somewhat advanced statistical concepts without rigorous proof, although an intuitive explanation can be given.

Let us continue to work with stocks 1 and 3 and with the proposition that an investor has a fixed sum of money ($10,000) to invest. We shall now assume, however, that the investor may divide this money in any way she sees fit between stocks 1 and 3; that is, she may invest $0 in stock 1 and $10,000 in stock 3, $3,861 in stock 1 and $6,139 in stock 3, or any other combination. The question we want to analyze is this: How much will she invest in each asset?

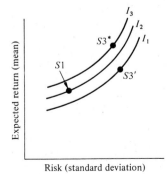

Expected return (mean)

Risk (standard deviation)   **Figure 5-2**   Asset choice in an unmixed portfolio.

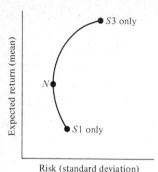

Figure 5-3   Risk and return in a mixed asset portfolio.

To help us answer this question we shall use Figure 5-3, which, as usual, measures expected return on the vertical axis and risk on the horizontal axis. However, these two concepts must now be understood in a broader context. For what we now want to measure is the risk and return, not just of a single asset, but of the *total* portfolio—that is, of *all* the various *combinations* of the two stocks that are available to the investor. Within this context, we can immediately locate two points in Figure 5-3: the points labeled "*S*1 only" and "*S*3 only." These are the extreme cases. At the point *S*1 only, the investor will have invested $10,000 in stock 1 and $0 in stock 3; at the point *S*3 only, the investor will have invested $0 in stock 1 and $10,000 in stock 3. But what about the in-between cases, the mixed portfolios?

Consider, first, the expected return. By combining stocks 1 and 3 in different proportions, the investor can achieve any desired expected return she wants as long as it lies between the extreme points. Suppose, for example, the expected rate of return on stock 3 is 10 percent and on stock 1 it is 8 percent. Then if the investor puts her entire $10,000 into stock 3, her expected return will be $1,000 (10 percent of $10,000). Now suppose that the investor takes $100 out of stock 3 and invests it in stock 1. Then her expected return on the $9,900 in stock 3 will be $990 (10 percent of $9,900), and on the $100 in stock 1 it will be $8 (8 percent of $100). Adding these together gives an expected return of $998 ($990 + $8) on the mixed portfolio. Proceeding in this fashion, the investor could achieve any expected return desired down to $800, where she would have the entire $10,000 invested in stock 1. Naturally, as the expected return changes, so does the risk, and it is with the behavior of risk that we generate some surprising, and most interesting, theoretical results.

To understand the behavior of risk in a portfolio of mixed assets, it is necessary to emphasize that by *risk* we now mean the standard deviation of the *entire* portfolio —that is, of the two stocks mixed together in some proportion. Before we can analyze the behavior of the mixed portfolio, it is necessary to make some assumption about the relationship between the standard deviations of each stock considered separately. The assumption we shall make is that of *independence*.[3] Formally, we

[3]This assumption is not necessary. We could also deal with the case where the risks of the two assets are positively correlated and with the case where they are negatively correlated. These cases will not

shall assume that the standard deviation of stock 1 has zero correlation with the standard deviation of stock 3. Less formally, we assume that the risk of one stock is completely unrelated to the risk of the other. Given this assumption, a very interesting thing happens to the risk of the mixed portfolio as we move between the extremes of $S1$ only and $S3$ only in Figure 5-3: Over some range of combinations, the risk of the mixed portfolio actually *becomes less than the risk of either stock.* Thus, in Figure 5-3, the curve connecting the extreme points $S1$ only and $S3$ only passes through the point N. And point N lies to the left of either $S1$ only or $S3$ only, indicating less risk. In other words, a mixed, or diversified, portfolio may actually have less risk than the least risky stock in it.

The theoretical result described in the previous paragraph is certainly not an obvious one, and the question naturally arises, Why does it work this way? Although a rigorous proof would carry us too far into statistical theory, it is fortunately possible to answer this question in common-sense terms. Recall that the standard deviation is a measure of the dispersion about the mean and is calculated by taking deviations from the mean. When we calculate the standard deviation of a series of numbers, therefore, some of the numbers will be above the mean and hence be a positive deviation, while others will lie below the mean and hence be a negative deviation. Now, if we combine two series of numbers, some of the positive deviations of one series will be offset by the negative deviations of the other series, and vice versa (assuming independence). The combined series will consequently have a smaller standard deviation than either of the other two series considered separately. The risks tend to cancel one another.

Let us now return to our original question: If the investor can buy a mixed portfolio of stocks 1 and 3, in what proportion will she buy them? This question can be answered by combining the risk-return indifference curves of Figure 5-1 with the risk-return portfolio combinations of Figure 5-3. This is done in Figure 5-4. To understand Figure 5-4, remember that the investor wants to reach the highest

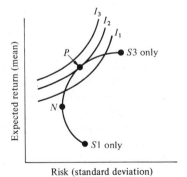

Figure 5-4 Asset choice in a mixed portfolio.

---

change the general nature of our conclusions. However, the case of independence (zero correlation) between the standard deviations is the easiest to understand, and consequently we shall not inquire further into the other two cases.

indifference curve possible. Her optimum portfolio, therefore, is described by the point marked P, where the portfolio possibility curve $S1$ only-N-$S3$ only is just tangent to the indifference curve I_2. At point P the investor is getting the best deal possible, given the $10,000 she has to invest.

One final point about portfolio theory needs to be made, an important point that should be kept firmly in mind: The theory can be extended to include any number of assets. We have confined the discussion here to only two assets because to deal with three requires some rather complicated geometry and to deal with more than three requires mathematics. But just as we can calculate the standard deviation of a portfolio composed of two assets, so also can we calculate the standard deviation of a portfolio composed of three or more assets; the principles involved and the conclusions reached are the same. This is important because of our point of departure—the inherent advantage of financial intermediaries.

5-2 PORTFOLIO THEORY AND FINANCIAL INTERMEDIARIES

What our discussion of portfolio theory has shown is that a *diversified*, or mixed, portfolio of assets may reduce risk for a given rate of return. The difficulty is, however, that many persons do not have enough financial resources at their disposal to take advantage of this aspect of investment behavior. Consider, for example, the hypothetical portfolio we constructed in section 5-1. We assumed that the investor had $10,000 at her disposal. Most readers (faculty included) would consider this a fairly large sum of money. Yet if you bought 100 shares of a common stock (which is the cheapest way to buy common stock) priced at $50 per share, it would cost you $5,000. In other words, with $10,000 to invest, you could only make two such purchases of common stock. Obviously, two different assets isn't much diversification of a portfolio of assets. Thus, for most people the primary difficulty in achieving the risk reduction potential of portfolio diversification is that they can't afford it.

This is where financial intermediaries come in. For what small investors *can* do is to "pool" their money by using a financial intermediary. Consider a *mutual fund*, for example. What a mutual fund does is to sell stock to the public and then use this money to buy a lot of *different kinds* of other stocks.[4] In other words, what a mutual fund does is to sell the public shares in a diversified portfolio—something that most investors are unable to do for themselves because they lack the financial resources. And while the mutual fund is probably the most straightforward example of how financial intermediaries use portfolio theory in practice, it is certainly not the only one. Savings and loan associations, for example, by pooling the riskiness of a large number of mortgages, are able to offer depositors a much safer asset than if individual depositors tried to lend their money directly in the mortgage market. Similarly, life insurance companies are able to pool the risk of death. Indeed, all financial intermediaries (including commercial banks) are able to offer the services they do because pooled risks are less than individual risks.

[4]Mutual funds are described more fully in Chapter 6.

In the following chapter, we shall examine the various services offered to the public by the various financial intermediaries, and the types of asset portfolios these intermediaries acquire.

5-3 REVIEW QUESTIONS

1 What is a financial intermediary? Who do they intermediate between? Are commercial banks financial intermediaries?
2 Try to plot a risk-return indifference curve of your own. Start with a stock with an expected return of 10 percent and a standard deviation of 5. How much more return would you want if the standard deviation rose to 7? to 10?
3 Explain in your own words why a combination of two stocks, A and B, might be less risky than either stock A or stock B.
4 Explain why portfolio theory helps us understand the economic function of financial intermediaries.

6

Nonbank Financial Institutions

Although commercial banks are easily the dominant type of financial intermediary in the United States, they are certainly not the only type. Indeed, as was discussed in Chapter 4, the traditional dominance of commercial banking is increasingly being challenged by other financial institutions. Between 1969 and 1975, for example, the volume of deposits held in credit unions (CUs) grew by 145 percent, and deposits of savings and loans associations (S&Ls) grew by 111 percent. Commercial banks, in contrast, increased their deposits by only 80 percent—certainly not a slow rate of growth, but not so high as CUs and S&Ls. Nor are depository institutions the only types of financial intermediaries. There are many others, ranging from pension funds to sales finance companies. Our purpose in this chapter is to describe these nonbank financial intermediaries. In doing so, we shall deal with many of the same issues dealt with in connection with commercial banking in Chapters 2 to 4, but the discussion will be much less detailed.

6-1 KINDS OF NONBANK FINANCIAL INSTITUTIONS

Savings and Loan Associations

Except for commercial banks, probably the best-known financial institution in the
United States is the *savings and loan association* (S&L) (sometimes also called
building and loan association). As with other financial intermediaries, S&Ls sell a
financial service to the public and invest the funds thus acquired. The services sold
in this case are passbook *savings* accounts, *certificates of deposit,* and, in the New
England states, *negotiable orders of withdrawal* (NOW) accounts. A passbook savings account is simply a deposit in the S&L that can, in practice, be withdrawn at
any time (although, legally, owners of savings accounts may be required to wait
thirty days before they can withdraw their funds). Because money put into a savings
account is immediately available to the deposit holder, these deposits carry a relatively low rate of interest—currently, 5 ¼ percent. If the S&L customer chooses to
put funds into a certificate of deposit instead, then there is a specified waiting period
before the money can be recovered without penalty. The waiting period typically
varies from three months to four years or more, with the longer periods carrying
a higher rate of interest. NOW accounts are very similar to the checking accounts
of commercial banks, except that they pay a rate of interest. While at the moment
their use in the United States is limited, it seems likely that they will be used much
more extensively in the future.[1] These various deposits, especially the passbook
savings account, often carry with them certain other services to the customer—for
example, off-premises automatic teller machines, bill payment with push-button
telephones, telephone transfer of funds to the customer's checking account in a
commercial bank, and the like. These types of services have proven very popular
with customers, since they are close substitutes to checking accounts and permit
funds to earn interest until they are used. As a result, the growth rate of the savings
and loan industry has been very rapid in the past few years—considerably more
rapid, for example, than that of commercial banks.

Because such a large part of their liabilities are in savings and time deposits,
S&Ls invest a large proportion of their funds in long-term loans such as home
mortgages. In general, S&Ls are not subject to sudden and severe withdrawals of
deposits and are therefore able to keep quite a high percentage of their assets tied
up in long-term investments. In practice, about 84 percent of the assets of S&Ls are
invested in the mortgage market, with the remainder being invested mostly in cash
and government securities. Table 6-1 shows the principal assets and liabilities of all
S&Ls in the United States.

S&Ls receive their charters to do business from either the federal government
or one of the state governments. Of the approximately 4,751 S&Ls in the United
States, about 41 percent hold federal charters; this 41 percent, however, hold about
58 percent of total S&L deposits. Federally chartered S&Ls are required to be
mutual-type savings institutions; that is, they are technically owned by their savings-
account holders. State-chartered institutions may be either of the *mutual type* or

---

[1]See Chapter 4 for a fuller discussion of this point.

Table 6-1   Principal Assets and Liabilities of United States Savings and Loan Associations, January 1978 (Millions of Dollars)

Assets	
Mortgages	384,192
Investment securities	40,305
Cash	
Other	39,688
Liabilities	
Savings capital	389,625
Reserves and undivided profits	25,441
Borrowed money	27,797
Loans in process	9,847
Other	11,475

Source: Federal Reserve *Bulletin*, March, 1978, p. A29.

so-called *stock* companies, which are owned by shareholders, not by depositors. In fact the number of stock-type S&Ls is comparatively small, constituting about 31 percent of the state-chartered associations and about 15 percent of the total number of S&Ls.

Branching restrictions on S&Ls are considerably more liberal than on commercial banks. Unlike commercial banks, state laws do not take precedence in determining the structure of the industry. Thus, in only two states (Montana and West Virginia) are state-chartered S&Ls prohibited from branching, and in no states are federally chartered S&Ls so prohibited. Many states do, however, restrict the branching activities of S&Ls. There are currently about 2,500 branch associations operating about 10,000 offices (including the head office). Holding-company activity in the S&L industry is very limited. In 1959, Congress prohibited the formation of new S&L holding companies and barred existing holding companies from acquiring additional insured associations. As a consequence, the existing number of holding companies in the S&L industry is virtually frozen at twenty-five.

Savings and loan associations are subject to federal regulation through the Federal Home Loan Bank (FHLB) system. Membership in the FHLB system is mandatory for federally chartered S&Ls and optional for those with state charters. About 2,500 of the latter have chosen to join the system, which means that about 82 percent of all S&Ls belong; these associations hold about 98 percent of the total resources of the industry. The FHLB is empowered to examine member associations and set the maximum interest rates they may pay on savings deposits. Also, through its twelve regional offices, it may make *advances,* or loans, to individual associations. These advances may be of two types: (1) short-term loans, which enable the association to meet deposit withdrawals, and (2) long-term loans, which give the association additional mortgage-buying ability if local sources of funds are not adequate. The FHLB, in turn, obtains the funds it lends to member associations by selling debt obligations in the capital market.

Deposits in S&Ls may be insured by the Federal Savings and Loan Insurance Corporation (FSLIC). The FSLIC is to S&Ls as the FDIC (see Chapter 3) is to commercial banks. All federally chartered S&Ls are required to join the FSLIC, but membership is optional for state-chartered associations. Since some states (Massachusetts, Ohio, and Maryland) have their own S&L insurance, the coverage of the FSLIC is less extensive than that of the FDIC; only about three-fourths of S&Ls belong to the Corporation. Otherwise, the FSLIC and the FDIC are very similar in structure, operation, and coverage.

Mutual Savings Banks

Like S&Ls, *mutual savings banks* (MSBs) sell interest-bearing savings deposits to the public and acquire assets largely in the form of urban residential mortgages. Indeed, the distinction between (mutual) S&Ls and mutual savings banks is largely technical; from the viewpoint of the depositing public the two types of savings institutions are essentially interchangeable. There are three basic distinctions: (1) the MSBs are chartered only by state governments; in fact, there are only eighteen states that charter MSBs, and almost all of these are in the northeastern section of the United States. (2) Although they are mutually owned, MSBs are managed by a self-perpetuating board of trustees. As members of the board retire or die, successors are elected by the remaining members of the board. (3) State laws usually set a *maximum* (not a minimum) on the size of the individual deposit, for example, $15,000. The purpose of this provision dates back to the original purpose of the MSB movement, which was to provide a safe outlet for small investors. A lot of small deposits will typically be more stable (have a smaller variance) than a few large deposits.

MSBs are regulated by the banking authorities of the states in which they do business. They are insured by the Federal Deposit Insurance Corporation (not the FSLIC), although, because of state insurance plans, only about 65 percent have joined. They may also join the Federal Home Loan Bank System, but only a handful (about fifty) have chosen to do so. Currently there are about 475 mutual savings banks in the United States.

Credit Unions

Credit unions are small, nonprofit thrift and lending institutions organized around some common bond of membership, typically a common employer, but sometimes a church or club. They may be chartered either by state governments or by the federal government under the Federal Credit Union Act of 1934. Currently there are about 22,800 credit unions in the United States, with over 17 million members. They have outstanding loans of about $44 billion.

Credit unions are typically small, as compared with S&Ls or mutual savings banks. They accept deposits (on which they pay interest or dividends) only from their membership and make small loans only to their members (usually for the purpose of buying consumer-durable goods, such as automobiles). Interest charged on these loans is typically limited to 1 percent per month on the unpaid balance (a true 12 percent per annum), which is quite low for small loans. These interest charges are kept low by voluntary help and by employer subsidies in the form of office space, heat, light, and released employee time.

Although credit unions hold only about 3 percent of total deposits in the United States, in the past few years they have experienced an annual growth rate that is more rapid than any other depository institution. This very high growth rate is apparently the result of three factors: (1) the introduction, in 1970, of deposit insurance by the National Credit Union Share Insurance Fund, which is comparable to the FDIC and FSLIC; (2) a loosening of the "common bond" requirement, so that many more people have become eligible to join credit unions; (3) the development of *share draft accounts,* which are similar to checking accounts, except that they pay interest, and which have permitted credit unions to become more competitive with commercial banks, S&Ls, and MSBs.

Life Insurance Companies

The service offered to the public by life insurance companies is, of course, some measure of financial protection against life's various misfortunes. As a necessary consequence of these insurance activities, the insurance companies have built up huge amounts of funds, which they invest in order to minimize the cost of this protection to the public. Thus, life insurance companies have become one of the major investors in the United States, and the policyholding public shares indirectly in these investments. Table 6-2 shows the principal assets of life insurance companies for selected dates from 1955 to 1977.

The activities of life insurance companies are regulated by the governments of the states in which they do business. Since the liabilities of life insurance companies are long-term and are actuarially predictable to a fairly fine point, they are generally given a good deal more latitude in the types of assets they may buy than, say, commercial banks where deposits are subject to withdrawal at any time. In practice, life insurance companies generally hold a substantial part of their assets in such long-term instruments as mortgages, corporate bonds, and the common stock issues of large corporations. Additionally, they extend credit on mortgage notes against business property, and in this way they are perhaps the chief source of long-term credit for many unincorporated small business firms.

Private Pension Funds

One aftermath of the Great Depression of the 1930s was that it left most Americans with an itch for economic security. The strengthened bargaining position of labor

Table 6-2 Assets of Life Insurance Companies, 1955–1977 (Billions of Dollars)

Assets	1955	1960	1965	1970	1975	1977
U.S. government securities	8.6	6.4	4.8	4.6	4.7	5.7
State and local obligations	2.0	3.6	3.1	3.3	4.5	6.0
Foreign securities	1.2	1.7	2.9	3.2	4.5	7.8
Corporate bonds	35.9	46.9	61.1	73.1	107.3	142.1
Corporate stocks	3.6	5.0	7.5	15.4	28.1	33.1
Mortgages	29.4	41.8	64.7	74.4	89.2	96.8
Real estate	2.6	3.8	4.9	6.3	9.3	11.2
Policy loans	3.3	5.2	9.1	16.1	24.5	27.5
Other financial assets	3.7	5.3	8.8	10.9	17.0	20.3
Total	90.4	119.6	167.0	207.3	289.3	350.5

Source: for 1955, Federal Reserve *Bulletin*, January 1957, p. 55; for 1960, 1965, Federal Reserve *Bulletin*, July 1968, p. A36; for 1970, Federal Reserve *Bulletin*, May 1972, p. A39; for 1975, 1977, Federal Reserve *Bulletin*, March 1978, p. A29. Numbers may not sum due to rounding.

unions, together with the comparative prosperity of the country in the last thirty-five years, has enabled us to scratch this itch. In particular, there has been an enormous growth in private, i.e., nongovernmental, *pension funds.* Today, most corporations of any size offer their employees a retirement plan as a benefit of employment. The financial service offered the public is, of course, the accumulation and investment of employer and employee contributions to these funds. Because these contributions far exceed the payments from the funds to retired persons, the private pension funds annually have very large sums to invest in capital markets.

In general, there are two types of pension funds: insured and noninsured. Insured pension funds are managed by insurance companies, and the investment of these funds is frequently subject to the same governmental restrictions that are placed on funds collected for insurance purposes. The managers of noninsured funds have a considerably wider latitude in the types of assets they may acquire, particularly with respect to common stocks. Table 6-3 shows the principal assets of noninsured pension funds for several recent years.

Investment Companies

Investment companies sell diversification. By *diversification* is meant the ability to buy and own a wide variety of different financial assets[2] —for example, United States government bonds, corporate bonds, and common stock shares of corporations in different industries. While this may seem a much less concrete financial service than insurance or a retirement plan, it is nevertheless a very popular one, especially with small investors. In principle, a diversified group of assets will be subject to much narrower swings in value than a single asset because a fall in the price of some securities will be offset by a rise in the price of others. Small investors (persons with only a few hundred dollars to invest) lack adequate financial resources to diversify their assets. The investment company, by combining the funds of a great many small investors and investing them in a variety of securities, can thus provide its shareholders with a financial service they are unable to obtain individually.

There are two main types of investment companies: open end, or mutual fund, and closed end. Open-end companies have no fixed number of their own stock shares

Table 6-3 Assets of Private Noninsured Pension Funds, 1955–1977 (Market Value; Billions of Dollars)

Assets	1955	1960	1965	1970	1975	1977
U.S. government securities	2.9	2.0	3.0	3.0	11.1	20.0
Corporate bonds	7.9	13.2	21.5	25.0	34.5	42.7
Mortgages	0.3	0.9	3.3	3.5	2.1	2.4
Other financial assets	0.4	1.5	3.8	6.2	9.3	14.5
Total	17.6	32.2	71.4	104.7	145.6	181.5

Source: 1970, 1975, 1977, *Statistical Bulletin* of the Securities and Exchange Commission, May 1977, p. 7; 1965, *Statistical Bulletin* of the Securities and Exchange Commission, August 1967, Table 1, p. 271; 1960, *Statistical Bulletin* of the Securities and Exchange Commission, June 1963, Table 1, p. 30. Data may not sum exactly due to rounding.

[2]See Chapter 5.

Table 6-4　Open-End Investment Companies, 1955–1977 (Billions of Dollars)

Assets	1955	1960	1965	1970	1975	1976
Corporate and foreign bonds	0.5	1.2	2.6	4.3	4.8	7.0
Corporate stocks	6.9	14.8	30.9	39.7	33.7	37.3
Other assets	0.4	1.0	1.7	3.6		
Total	7.8	17.0	35.2	47.6	42.2	47.0

Source: Years 1965, 1970, 1975 and 1976 from *Annual Statistical Digest* of the Board of Governors of the Federal Reserve System, 1972–1976, p. 223.

outstanding, but instead continuously offer to sell shares to and redeem shares from the investing public. Since new investments in mutual funds typically are greater than redemptions, the managers of these funds have a steady stream of new money to invest in capital markets. Table 6-4 shows the volume of assets held by open-end investment companies in recent years. Closed-end companies acquire funds through an initial sale of a fixed number of shares, which are then traded in the secondary markets.

Finance Companies (Small-Loan Companies)

The financial institutions discussed up to this point characteristically intermediate by taking in money in small amounts and then lending it out in large chunks. Personal *finance companies* reverse this process: They borrow large sums in the money and capital markets and then lend it in small amounts to individuals and small businesses. The rationale for this kind of intermediation stems in large measure from state usury laws. Most states have laws that prohibit lenders from charging a borrower a rate of interest above some maximum (usury). Although the intent of these laws—preventing the poor, the ignorant, and the weak from being exploited by high interest charges—is exemplary, in most cases they appear to have been drawn up with no appreciation of economic principles.

Lending money is subject to sharply decreasing average costs. In terms of the amount of employee time involved, credit investigation, collection of payments, and so on, the total cost of lending $1,000 is little more than the total cost of lending $100. Per dollar lent, therefore, the smaller the loan, the higher the cost. The effect of state usury laws on small borrowers, consequently, has been to make small loans uneconomic and therefore unobtainable legally. But since people still need small loans, illegal lending operations (loan sharks) have been set up, which cannot, of course, be regulated.

A more realistic approach has been to permit the establishment of finance companies, or small-loan companies. These companies are exempt from the usury laws, but their activities are subject to government supervision. Finance companies are geared to making loans up to some maximum amount; in turn, they obtain their funds either by selling debt on the open market or by borrowing from commercial banks.

It should also be noted that there are a variety of other cash-lending institutions available to consumers, such as pawnbrokers, industrial (Morris Plan) banks, and remedial loan associations. And, of course, illegal lending continues to flourish despite attempts to stop it.

Sales-Finance Companies

Much consumer credit is extended by retail stores directly to the customer when goods are purchased, either by installment buying (easy purchase plans) or by end-of-month billing (charge accounts). There is a wide variety of other devices of a similar nature that are also very popular—for example, credit cards, revolving credit, and lines of credit.

Much of the credit extended by retail stores is, in fact, financed by *sales-finance companies.* These companies are specialists in financing the installment sales contracts of automobile dealers, large retail stores, mail-order houses, and other merchants. Typically they do not lend directly to the consumer but instead buy a consumer's sales contract from the retailer. Some of them are so-called captive companies, which are controlled by a large retail firm and confine their activities to the financing of the parent company's credit business. Like small-loan companies, sales-finance companies obtain their funds largely by borrowing in the money market. Because of their very high credit ratings, these companies are usually able to sell their paper at low rates of interest.

Government Regulation of Consumer Credit

Most of the governmental regulation surrounding the extension of consumer credit has already been noted: usury laws and supervision of small-loan companies and credit unions. One additional law of more recent vintage should also be mentioned. In 1969, Congress passed the Truth in Lending Act, requiring retailers and lenders to state explicitly to customers the interest charges they are paying for credit. Although no attempt is made to regulate these charges, the presumption is that if the consumers are better informed about them, they will be more cautious about overextending themselves.

6-2 FINANCIAL AGENCIES OF THE GOVERNMENT

In the past several decades, a number of federal agencies with distinct financial purposes have been established in the United States. These agencies typically do not make loans directly to the ultimate borrower but instead either guarantee loans made by private institutions or make funds available to such institutions, which then relend them to the final borrower. The purposes of these governmental programs are varied, of course, but in general the idea has been to bolster some sector of the private market in order to promote a goal deemed socially desirable—for example, to strengthen the mortgage market in order to encourage home ownership. Other economic sectors in which governmental financial agencies have been established are agriculture and small business.

Table 6–5   Investors in Mortgage Debt Outstanding (Billions of Dollars)

Investors	1955	1960	1965	1970	1975	1977
S&Ls	31.5	60.1	110.3	150.3	278.6	381.2
	(24%)*	(29%)	(34%)	(33%)	(35%)	(37%)
Life insurance companies	29.4	41.8	60.0	74.4	89.2	95.7
	(23%)	(20%)	(18%)	(16%)	(11%)	(9%)
Commercial banks	21.0	28.8	49.7	73.2	136.2	176.7
	(16%)	(14%)	(15%)	(16%)	(17%)	(17%)
Mutual savings banks	17.5	26.9	44.6	57.9	77.2	88.0
	(13%)	(13%)	(14%)	(13%)	(10%)*	(9%)
All others†	30.3	49.2	61.2	95.9	220.3	278.1
	(23%)	(24%)	(19%)	(21%)	(27%)	(27%)
Total	129.7	206.8	325.8	451.7	801.5	1,019.7

† Includes individuals and Federal investors.
*Numbers in parentheses represent the percentage of total mortgage debt outstanding.
   Sources: 1955, Federal Reserve *Bulletin*, January 1957, pp. 65–66; 1960, Federal Reserve *Bulletin*, December 1966, pp. 1820–21; 1965, Federal Reserve *Bulletin*, December 1968, pp. A48–49; 1970, Federal Reserve *Bulletin*, January 1974, pp. A49–51; 1975, 1977, Federal Reserve *Bulletin*, April 1978, p. A41.

Mortgage Credit

One of the most notable developments in the American economy during the past forty years has been the rise in home ownership. This development has in turn given rise to a national mortgage market of very substantial proportions. By the end of 1977, there were about $1,019 billion of mortgage debt outstanding. Of this, about 60 percent dealt with one-family to four-family houses, with the remainder applicable to apartment houses, commercial property, and farm mortgages. Most of this debt is held by four of the institutional investors already described: S&Ls, MSBs, commercial banks, and insurance companies. Table 6-5 shows the amounts and percentages held by each of these investors.

The United States government has consistently taken the position that home ownership is a socially desirable goal of high priority. To implement this view, a variety of governmental programs have been established to encourage people to own their own homes. Some of these programs will be discussed here.

Federal Housing Administration   The Federal Housing Administration (FHA) was established on a permanent basis in 1934 as part of the New Deal legislation. The FHA does not make mortgage loans. However, it does insure mortgages against loss to the lender, and, by requiring standardized terms, it has been instrumental in creating a truly national market in home mortgages.

Veterans Administration   The Veterans Administration (VA) was authorized in 1944 to aid exservicemen in obtaining mortgages to finance the purchase of residential and business property (so-called GI loans). It does this in the same general way as the FHA: by guaranteeing mortgage loans to the lender. There are two basic differences between the FHA and the VA: (1) VA-guaranteed mortgage loan terms are more liberal to the borrower in terms of the minimum downpayment and maximum years to maturity of the mortgage. (2) The VA is authorized to make direct loans to the borrower if local mortgage credit is not sufficient to meet the demand. (In fact, the VA has made only minimal use of this authorization: Slightly over 3 percent of its loans have been made directly to borrowers.)

Federal National Mortgage Association   The Federal National Mortgage Association (Fannie Mae) operates in the secondary market for mortgages. It is authorized to "intermediate" by selling its own short-term notes and buying government-guaranteed mortgages. By doing so, it redirects funds toward home mortgages. In 1968, Fannie Mae became a private association; it continues to operate in a quasi-governmental fashion, however.

Public Housing Administration   The purpose of the Public Housing Administration (PHA) is to give financial assistance to state and metropolitan housing authorities in order to clear slums and construct rental housing for low-income families. To achieve this objective, the PHA essentially puts the guarantee of the credit standing of the federal government behind the debt issues of various local public housing authorities. Under certain conditions, however, it may also provide funds to local authorities.

Agricultural Credit

Perhaps the oldest of the financial aids to a particular sector of the economy has been in the area of agricultural credit. Probably more than any other occupation, farming is considered a way of life, a situation in which family, social gatherings, and earning a living are integrated into a single whole. Although this view of farming is becoming increasingly less valid, it remains true that Americans have a traditional nostalgia for the family farm. Together with the exaggerated political power of farmers, this attitude toward farming has led to an extensive and comprehensive government program of credit agencies servicing the agricultural sector. Virtually every part of the financial needs of farming and ranching has its counterpart in a government-sponsored program. In general, these programs involve local ownership and control, with the government agency making indirect loans to the final borrower.

Farm Credit Administration   The Farm Credit Administration was established in 1933 to consolidate various existing farm programs. It is now a part of the Department of Agriculture and encompasses three distinct programs in long-term lending, short-term and intermediate-term lending, and lending to farmers' cooperatives.

The Federal Land Bank System   One of the most persistent needs of people in American agriculture has been for long-term credit. In the first place, modern farming requires a substantial capital investment in machinery, such as tractors and combines, and in outbuildings. Perhaps more important, our adherence to the concept of the family farm means that every generation farms are divided among the children of the family, and it is typical for one child to buy out the others (rather than physically subdividing the farm). As a consequence, substantial amounts of mortgage credit must be channeled annually into agriculture. Although this long-term credit comes from a variety of sources, one of the main sources is credit made available through *Federal Land Banks* (FLB).

There are twelve FLBs in the United States, each servicing its own district. These FLBs do not lend directly to farmers, but instead make funds available through local farm-loan associations that are controlled cooperatively by the farmers themselves. The FLBs acquire their funds through the Farm Credit System (to be discussed), which, in turn, obtains its funds by issuing various debt instruments in the money and capital markets.

Federal Intermediate Credit Banks In addition to long-term credit, farmers also have a substantial need for short-term and intermediate-term credit in order to meet expenses for such things as crop production (feed, seed, and fertilizer), "feeder" livestock, various kinds of machinery and equipment, and land improvements. The Farm Credit Administration also makes these types of loans available through *Federal Intermediate Credit Banks.* Like the FLBs, the twelve credit banks do not lend directly to farmers but instead make funds available through locally owned and controlled production credit associations.

Cooperative Farm Credit System Farmers' cooperatives have been estab-lished extensively in the rural areas of the United States. These cooperatives are voluntary associations of farmers and ranchers organized primarily for the purposes of marketing farm products and purchasing farm supplies. Such activities require financing, and as a consequence the Cooperative Farm Credit System has been organized within the Farm Credit Administration. The Farm Credit System makes funds available to cooperatives through twelve regional banks for cooperatives. Additionally, it contains a central bank for cooperatives, which has a primary function of servicing national (as opposed to local) cooperatives.

Farmers Home Administration The Farmers Home Administration is *not* a part of the Farm Credit System, although it, too, is a part of the Department of Agriculture. Its primary purpose is to strengthen the family farm and rural commu-nities by making direct and guaranteed loans. Many of these loans are made in response to emergency situations, such as drought and flood, although "ordinary" loans for such things as watershed development and rural housing are also made.

Small Business Administration

In 1958 the federal government established the Small Business Administration (SBA) as a federal agency. Its responsibility is to provide help and guidance for small business firms. The SBA has developed a variety of programs, ranging from manage-ment aids and research on the problems of small businesses to several types of credit programs. In general, these credit programs involve either direct loans or partial guarantees of long-term loans made by banks to small businesses. By making these guarantees, the SBA probably enables some firms to acquire capital funds that they could not otherwise obtain.

6-3 THE SIGNIFICANCE OF INTERMEDIATION

Just as most economists feel that the importance of commercial banks extends far beyond their role as mere lending and depositing institutions, so many economists feel that nonbank financial institutions perform an essential task for the economy which transcends their obvious and immediate functions as suppliers of financial services. In order to understand this viewpoint, it is necessary to consider financial intermediation at a higher level of abstraction than we have been doing so far; that is, it is necessary to broaden our perspective and consider these institutions within the more general context of the economy as a whole. When this is done, it becomes clear that intermediaries occupy at least one, and perhaps two, strategic positions in our economic system: They are pivotal in the savings-investment process, and they are creators of *near money.*

Financial Intermediaries and the Savings-Investment Process

A modern, complex, industrial economy cannot function without massive injections of new capital equipment each year. By *capital equipment* is meant the buildings and machinery used in the process of producing the goods and services we all depend on for survival and for the pleasantries of life. Capital equipment must be produced to replace worn-out machinery and expand output. But this equipment doesn't just appear spontaneously; in order to be able to produce it, someone in the economy must save, that is, must forego the immediate gratification of buying consumer goods. Having saved, an act of investment must then occur. In other words, for capital to be produced, the savings of individuals and corporations must somehow be translated into the investments in the plants and equipment necessary to keep the production process operating.

It is this translation of savings into investments that is the primary economic function of savings intermediaries. In general, they may be thought of as collecting the savings of a lot of small savers and then providing loans and investments in large chunks to corporations needing capital equipment and families needing housing. This intermediation is vital to the functioning of the economy. Clearly, most small savers are in no position to invest directly in machinery, plants, housing, inventory, and so on; and most corporations are in no position to borrow a few hundred dollars each from hundreds of thousands of savers.

Financial Intermediaries as Creators of "Near Money"

In Chapter 1, the point was made that commercial banks are the main creators of money in the form of checking accounts. Although it is true, this statement is also an oversimplification. It is correct, for example, that an insurance company cannot create checking accounts; but it is also correct that an insurance policy has a cash-surrender value—that it is a liquid asset, or what economists call *near money.*

Checking-account money may be spent directly; you can use it to buy hamburgers and airline tickets and pay the rent. You can't do this with an S&L savings account or with the loan value of an insurance policy. But you can do something almost as good: You can convert these liquid assets into cash and *then* spend them. Arguing in this fashion, many economists have hypothesized that the amount of near money affects spending decisions and that these spending decisions affect the behavior of the economy. If this hypothesis is correct, then financial intermediaries are extremely important institutions, with (collectively) the same potential for creating economic stability or instability as commercial banks. (We shall return to this discussion in Chapter 22.)

6-4 REVIEW QUESTIONS

1 What is the difference between a commercial bank and an S&L? an MSB?
2 What is the most rapidly growing type of depository institution?
3 What do insurance companies do with the insurance premiums they collect?
4 What does the phrase "near money" mean? What has this to do with financial intermediaries?

7

The Capital Market, the Money Market, and the Behavior of Interest Rates

The description of the financial machinery of the United States has to this point dealt with a variety of financial institutions treated in isolation from one another. But of course this is an inaccurate picture of the situation. In practice, all these financial institutions, including particularly commercial banks, are interconnected within a tightly woven mesh of financial markets. A "market," in this context, is to be understood as any exchange of a variety of financial instruments. Thus the various financial institutions described in previous chapters buy and sell securities from and to each other and to third parties.

Financial markets may be broadly classified as *negotiated-loan markets* and *open markets.* The negotiated-loan market is a market in which lender and borrower personally negotiate the terms of the loan agreement. A business person borrowing from a bank and an individual borrowing from a small loan company are examples of negotiated loans. In contrast, the open market is an impersonal market in which standardized securities are traded in large volumes. Buyers and sellers may never meet, and there is comparatively little latitude for tailoring an instrument to the precise needs of a given issuer. The stock market is an example of an open market. Through it, equity securities[1] of giant American corporations are bought and sold by a myriad of investors, large and small, from all over the country. Thus, the open market provides the binding that ties the country's financial institutions together into an integrated whole. It is with the open market that we shall be concerned in this chapter.

7-1 THE CAPITAL MARKET

Suppose you were the treasurer of a corporation that needed money to build another plant. Where would you get it? One possibility would be to have your corporation sell stocks and bonds. If it did so, it would sell them in the *capital market*. The capital market is just what the name implies: a market for capital funds. The word "capital," used in this context, infers a long-term commitment on the part of the lender(s) and a long-term need for the funds on the part of the borrower. Thus, strictly speaking, the capital market encompasses any transaction involving long-term debt or equity obligations.

The capital market can be usefully subdivided into the *primary market* and the *secondary market*. The primary market deals with the selling of new securities when they are first issued by the issuing corporation. Since many of the initial buyers of these securities will eventually want to resell them, there is also a secondary market for "second-hand," or previously issued, securities. The stock market, for example, is a secondary market in corporate securities.

The Primary Market

The institution that dominates the primary market is the *investment banking house*. When a corporation decides that it wants to acquire new funds from the outside, it will frequently do so through the intermediation of an investment banker. Investment bankers are specialists in the marketing of new securities. They advise corporations in the design of the security—what type of security it should be (common stock, preferred stock, or bond), if a bond, what rate of interest it should bear, what its maturity provisions should be, and so on—so that it will best serve the needs of the corporation and the buying public. Although there are a number of possible arrangements, the investment banking house will typically *underwrite* a new issue of securities. By *underwrite* is meant, in this case, that the investment banker buys the securities from the issuing corporation and then sells them to the public, making its profit like any other merchant on the spread between its buying and selling price. Because the investment house assumes a substantial measure of risk in an underwriting operation, large issues of new securities usually will be syndicated among several investment banking firms.

[1] A *stock* indicates ownership, or *equity*, in a corporation; a *bond* is evidence of a debt obligation by the corporation. Stocks pay dividends, i.e., a share of the corporation's profits; bonds pay interest, a fixed contractual obligation that must be met before corporate profits are calculated. The word "securities" is used generically to encompass all kinds of financial instruments, including both stocks and bonds.

Prior to 1933, commercial banks were an important part of the investment banking field. The banking crisis of the early 1930s, however, convinced many observers that bank participation in this area had weakened the banking system by inducing banks to acquire questionable assets as part of their underwriting activities. In consequence, the Banking Act of 1933 required commercial banks to divorce themselves from investment banking, and now they do not participate directly in the market.[2]

In addition to placing new issues through the intermediation of investment bankers, many corporations engage in the *private placement* of securities. Private placement means that the issuer of the securities sells them directly to investors, without the underwriting services of an investment banker. This method of marketing new issues has a number of advantages; foremost among these are that it is cheaper since underwriting costs are avoided,[3] that it involves less red tape with the Securities and Exchange Commission, and that the terms of the securities can be closely tailored to the needs of the buyer. Table 7-1 shows the comparative volumes of public offerings and private placements of new securities during the past several years.

Table 7-1   Total New Issues, Gross Proceeds, and Corporate Issues* (Millions of Dollars)

		Bonds		Stocks	
Period	Total	Publicly offered	Privately placed	Preferred	Common
1960	8,081	4,806	3,275	409	1,664
1961	8,420	4,700	4,720	450	3,294
1962	8,969	4,440	4,529	422	1,314
1963	10,856	4,713	6,143	343	1,011
1964	10,866	3,623	7,243	412	2,679
1965	13,720	5,570	8,150	725	1,547
1966	15,560	8,018	7,542	574	1,939
1967	21,954	14,990	6,964	885	1,959
1968	17,383	10,732	6,651	637	3,946
1969	18,347	12,734	5,613	682	7,714
1970	30,315	25,384	4,931	1,390	7,240
1971	31,999	24,790	7,209	3,679	9,236
1972	28,896	19,434	9,462	3,367	9,694
1973	22,269	13,649	8,620	3,372	7,750
1974	32,063	25,903	6,160	2,253	3,994
1975	42,755	32,583	10,172	3,458	7,405
1976	42,261	26,453	15,808	2,789	8,305
1977	39,673	24,185	15,488	3,344	7,846

*Gross proceeds are derived by multiplying principal amounts or number of units by offering price.
   Source: Federal Reserve *Bulletin*: 1974, March 1978, p. A36; 1975–77, April 1978, p. A36; Previous years from various issues.

[2]Banks may participate in underwriting *municipal securities,* however. Municipal securities are issued by state and local governments.
[3]Privately placed securities usually carry a higher rate of interest, however.

The Secondary Market

The secondary market in corporate securities can be subdivided into two parts: the registered *stock exchanges* and the *over-the-counter market.*

Stock Exchanges   There are currently fourteen stock exchanges registered with the Securities and Exchange Commission, of which the largest and by far the most important is the New York Stock Exchange. These exchanges are voluntary associations of members who come together for the purpose of buying and selling for the general public the securities of the great American corporations. Only certain securities are traded on the exchanges—the so-called listed stocks—and these are bought and sold by auction. Since the members of these exchanges have branches throughout the country, the stock exchanges are truly a national market in which virtually anyone may participate.

Over-the-Counter Market   The over-the-counter market is the market for those securities not listed on the stock exchanges. Used in its broadest sense, it includes all transactions in securities other than those taking place on the national stock exchanges. In practice, however, the term is usually limited to the activities of dealers and brokers[4] specializing in unlisted securities. The over-the-counter market has very low entry barriers, and traders may range in size from very large houses doing an international business to one-person firms that trade only in local markets.

Economic Function of the Stock Markets   It seems to be a common misconception that the stock markets are a sort of national casino, whose sole economic function is to provide Americans with a comparatively harmless outlet for their gambling instincts. This is not true, of course. While there is undeniably a considerable element of risk and uncertainty in stock trading, the stock markets also play an indispensible role in the functioning of the American economy.[5] The role of the secondary market is to make the primary market possible. Suppose, for example, that a corporation needs to buy a machine with a life expectancy of twenty years. It may want to issue a twenty-year bond to do this. But who would buy such a bond if they had to hold it the full twenty years? Yet this would be necessary in the absence of a secondary market. *With* a secondary market, the initial purchaser of the bond knows that it can be resold to someone else in a year or two. In this fashion, the secondary market in securities is said to give *liquidity* to primary issues, and this liquidity is an essential ingredient in the capital formation process of the American economy.

---

[4]Properly speaking, a *dealer* is a principal in a transaction, and a *broker* is an agent in a transaction. Thus, when you buy something from a dealer, he is selling you something that he himself owns; when you buy something from a broker, she is selling you something that someone else owns—she is acting only as an intermediary.

[5]This is not to say that a different kind of economic system would have to have a stock market. But that is a much broader question.

Government Regulation   Because the capital markets are so huge and involve so many people, opportunities abound for the unscrupulous to engage in unfair and fraudulent activities. To prevent this, there is extensive federal and state regulation of the securities business. In particular, the Securities and Exchange Commission was established in 1934 to protect the public against malpractices in the securities markets. To do so, it requires registration and licensing of dealers and brokers, registration of specific issues, public disclosure of pertinent facts about new stock issues, and it engages in civil and criminal prosecutions for fraudulent acts.

The Long-Term Government Securities Market

The size of the public debt is a topic that seems an endless source of fascination to most Americans. Newspapers feature it on their front pages, entertainers feature it in their comedy routines, and middle-class Americans feature it in their dinner-table conversations. What seems frequently to go unappreciated, however, is that the public debt is composed of large amounts and varieties of debt obligations, and has given rise to one of the most active financial markets in the world.

State and Local Securities   Although the phrase *public debt* is generally interpreted to mean the debt of the United States Government, in fact there is a very substantial amount of state and local government debt outstanding. (*Local* governments, in this case, are to be taken to include such things as school districts and highway authorities, not necessarily conterminous with political subdivisions.) This debt is called *municipal securities,* and it comes in all kinds and varieties.

The popularity of municipal securities among investors stems primarily from their tax-exempt feature: Income derived from municipals is not subject to the federal income tax and in some cases is also exempt from state income taxes. For wealthy individuals and for corporations subject to a 48 percent marginal corporate income-tax rate, this feature is obviously very attractive. Interest rates on municipal securities are correspondingly lower than those on comparable but taxable securities.

The idea behind making municipal securities tax exempt is to provide an indirect subsidy (in the form of lower interest rates) to the issuing body. Unfortunately, this same feature, when viewed from the standpoint of the ordinary taxpayer, can best be described as a loophole. Most of the people one reads about who have annual incomes in excess of $1 million but who pay no income taxes have invested their money in municipal securities. Legislation to change this situation has been introduced in Congress periodically, but so far with no success.

Federal Government Securities   People who work for the Treasury Department spend a good deal of time managing the outstanding debt of the United States government. The process is comparable to the trick of juggling several balls of different sizes at varying rates of speed. The trick is to smile while you're doing it.

Nonmarketable Federal Debt   A substantial part of the federal debt is in what are called *nonmarketable securities,* that is, securities that cannot be resold in a secondary market. The best known of these are *savings bonds,* ownership of which may not be transferred but which may be redeemed with the government before maturity at a stipulated price. In general, savings bonds have proved to be quite popular with small savers, although from time to time their administratively determined (as opposed to market-determined) interest rates have led to substantial redemptions when other savings instruments earned more. There are currently about $77 billion worth of savings bonds outstanding.

In addition to savings bonds, the federal government also has a variety of other nonmarketable securities outstanding, such as depository bonds, retirement-plan bonds, and foreign-currency bonds. There are also about $155 billion of special issues outstanding, which are held only by United States government agencies and hence do not enter into the active markets.

Marketable Federal Debt   About 35 percent of the marketable public debt outstanding is in the form of short-term securities (Treasury bills); the rest is in long-term securities—notes (55 percent) and bonds (10 percent). We shall consider short-term federal debt later in our discussion of the money market and here confine our attention to notes and bonds. Notes generally carry a maturity of two to seven years when issued; bonds carry a maturity of over ten years. Both notes and bonds have explicit (coupon) rates of interest, which pay the owner a stipulated number of dollars per year. For our purposes, it will be sufficient to treat notes and bonds similarly under the generic term *bonds*.

United States government bonds are issued irregularly and in large chunks by the U.S. Treasury, with months of preparation going into designing the terms of the issue. Generally, bonds are designed to appeal to particular investor groups, such as insurance companies and pension funds. Because these groups buy them to hold and not for resale, trading activity in bonds is considerably less than in Treasury bills even though the outstanding volume is greater.

A new issue of government bonds is made either by a cash offering or by a refunding. If a cash offering is made, the bonds are offered to the public in exchange for cash; if a refunding is made, a new bond is offered in exchange for a maturing bond. The Treasury also engages in so-called advance refundings, that is, a refunding in which the Treasury offers to exchange a new bond for an old one several years before the old bond is scheduled to mature. The purpose of advance refunding is to keep the bond in the hands of the original buyer and thus prevent market "churning" as the bond approaches maturity. For example, an insurance company may have bought a twenty-year bond fifteen years ago, so that it still has five years to run. Since the insurance company has a distinct preference for long-term investments, they may soon decide to sell the bond and buy a longer-term issue. By making a direct offer of a swap now, the Treasury will be able to keep this sale and purchase out of the market.

Ownership of the Public Debt   Who owns the public debt? As Table 7-2 indicates, among private investors commercial banks are by far the single most important holders, with state and local governments running a poor second, and the remainder (except for savings bond holders) being spread more or less evenly among other investor groups.

Table 7-2 Ownership of Public Debt (Par Value, Billions of Dollars)

| | | Held by | | | | | | | | | Individuals | | |
Year	Total gross public debt	U.S. government agencies and trust funds	Federal Reserve banks	Total held by private investors	Commercial banks	Mutual savings banks	Insurance companies	Other corporations	State and local governments	Savings bonds	Other securities	Miscellaneous
1955	280.8	51.7	24.8	204.3	62.0	8.5	14.6	23.5	15.1	50.2	14.8	15.6
1960	290.4	55.0	27.4	207.9	62.1	6.3	11.9	19.7	18.7	45.7	19.3	24.2
1965	321.0	59.7	40.8	220.5	60.7	5.3	10.3	15.8	22.9	49.7	22.4	33.4
1970	389.2	97.1	62.1	230.0	62.7	3.1	7.4	7.3	27.8	52.1	29.1	40.5
1975	576.6	139.3	87.9	349.4	85.1	4.5	9.5	20.2	34.2	67.3	24.0	104.5
1977	718.9	154.8	102.5	461.3	102.4	6.0	15.6	22.2	55.1	76.7	28.6	154.6

Source: Federal Reserve Bulletin, 1975, 1977 data from March 1977, p. A32. Other data from previous years.

7-2 THE MONEY MARKET

The *money market* is a market for *short-term* (less than one-year) loans; in fact, its very name suggests that it is *money* that is being bought and sold. It is used by business firms for the purchase and shipment of inventories, by sales-finance companies to finance consumer credit, by banks to finance temporary reserve shortages, and by governments to bridge the gap between tax receipts and expenditures. The money market is not a place (like the stock market) but an activity: Transactions are carried out by telephone among people who may never meet one another. Although almost all large cities have local money markets, the national (and international, for that matter) money market of the United States is centered in the financial district of New York City. Here, literally billions of dollars are traded daily by buyers and sellers located throughout the world.

A supplier of funds to the money market can be virtually anyone with a temporary excess of funds. For example, a corporation may be accumulating funds for a quarterly income-tax payment, and rather than holding the funds in (non-interest-bearing) demand deposits, the corporation may decide to lend them out at short term. Or a state treasurer may have a temporary excess of tax receipts over disbursements and decide to invest them. Or a commercial bank may know from experience that it will have large seasonal deposit withdrawals shortly, but in the meantime it may invest the money in earning assets. The motives of the lenders are, in fact, as varied as the American economy itself. But there is one principle common to all of them: the desire to earn interest on money that they don't need right away. Such funds may be lent for as long a time as a year or for as short a time as a day.

Probably the best way to obtain a clear impression of the money market is to understand the mechanics of the various debt instruments traded on it. The discussion that follows explains the operation of these debt instruments.

Treasury Bills

By far the largest volume of business done in the money market is carried out in *United States Treasury bills.* These are obligations of the United States government and, as such, are of the very highest quality. They are issued weekly and carry maturities ranging from three months to a year. Like most money market instruments, Treasury bills do not carry an explicit rate of interest but are sold on a discount basis, with the difference between the buying price and the maturity value functioning as an implicit yield to the lender. For example, if you pay $9,500 today for a Treasury bill that will be worth $10,000 one year from now, then at the end of the year you will have earned $500 or 5.263 percent on your investment.

The primary market for Treasury bills is a regular weekly auction at which the Treasury offers to sell approximately $3 billion of 91-day and 182-day bills. Since the bills are sold on a discount basis and do not carry an explicit coupon rate of interest, the submitted bid prices determine the rate of interest the investor will earn.

Because of the very specialized knowledge that is required to know what is an appropriate price to bid, and because of the very large amounts involved, this auction market tends to be an "insider" market, with few bidders relative to the size of the market.[6] Most medium-sized banks and nonfinancial corporations prefer to buy their Treasury bills through the twenty government security dealers operating in the secondary market. This is one of the largest markets in the world. The *daily* volume of trading carried out in the secondary market for Treasury bills approaches $2 *billion.*

In addition to the weekly Treasury offering of three-month and six-month bills, there is also a regular monthly auction of nine-month and one-year bills. Finally, the Treasury also offers, on an irregular basis, so-called tax anticipation bills (TABs) with a maturity of less than one year. TABs have the interesting feature of being scheduled to mature one week after quarterly corporate tax payments are due but are acceptable on the tax date at par in lieu of cash. Thus corporations may accumulate funds for tax payments in these earning assets and also earn an extra week's interest.

Mutual Funds in Treasury Bills   Before 1970, Treasury bills were sold in minimum denominations of $1,000. The issuance of Treasury bills in such small denominations, however, created problems for thrift institutions. When open market rates of interest rose very high (as they did, e.g., in 1969), people would withdraw their savings from thrift institutions and reinvest them in higher-yielding Treasury bills. This process, known as *disintermediation,* resulted in savings outflows from thrift institutions and threatened, according to some observers, the stability of the entire savings industry. As a consequence, in 1970 the Treasury raised the minimum denomination on Treasury bills from $1,000 to $10,000. This change was, at least temporarily, quite effective in keeping small savers out of the Treasury bill market.[7] However, there soon developed *mutual funds in Treasury bills.* These mutual funds sell shares for small accounts (usually $1,000) and then invest the money in Treasury bills. Thus small savers can now accomplish indirectly what they used to be able to accomplish directly. Because the Treasury's policy is consequently no longer effective, many economists feel that the Treasury should return to $1,000 minimum denominations for Treasury bills.

Bankers' Acceptances

Bankers' acceptances are a very old form of commercial credit. They provide, in essence, a method whereby a bank may add its good name and reputation to the promissory note of a borrower, thereby making the note much more marketable than it would otherwise be. Specifically, the mechanics of the operation work like this. A corporation in need of short-term funds will issue a draft on a bank ordering the

[6] *Noncompetitive* bids up to $200,000 are accepted, however. In this case, the sale price of the bill is fixed by the Treasury at the average price (to three decimal places) bid that week.

[7] See Peter Fortune, "The Effectiveness of Recent Policies to Maintain Thrift-Deposit Flows," *Journal of Money, Credit and Banking,* August 1975, pp. 297–315.

bank to pay a certain sum of money to the holder of the draft at some future date. The corporation then takes the draft to the bank, and the bank stamps "accepted" across the face of it. By accepting the note, the bank has obligated itself to pay the draft when it becomes due. The draft is now a negotiable, marketable debt instrument and may change hands several times in a secondary market. When the due date arrives, the draft is presented to the bank for payment. Simultaneously, the original issuing corporation is expected to pay into its demand account at the bank funds sufficient to cover the draft. The bank then simply takes the money out of the corporation's account and pays it over to the holder of the draft. The bank charges the corporation a fee for this service.

If everything goes smoothly (i.e., if the corporation pays the bank on the due date), no bank funds are involved in this transaction; the bank has merely added its guarantee to the draft. A bank could therefore, in principle, do an unlimited amount of acceptance business. There are no "natural" limits on it as there are with loans, where the bank cannot lend more money than it has. Nevertheless, the more acceptance business a bank does, the greater is its risk exposure. Therefore there are legal limits imposed on the volume of a bank's acceptances outstanding—typically 50 percent of the bank's capital and surplus, although exceptions to this may be permitted.

The acceptance market is rather small compared to those of other money market instruments. Nevertheless, the market has grown steadily in the past few years, with the volume outstanding now about $27 billion. About half of this volume is based on international trade, with the other half based on domestic commerce.

Commercial Paper

Commercial paper consists, very simply, of the promissory notes of large corporations. The corporations are sufficiently well known so that their credit worthiness is not in doubt. Their promises to pay can consequently be bought and sold in an organized market. Commercial paper generally carries a maturity of from four to six months and is used by the issuers as a supplement to borrowing from commercial banks.

Commercial paper may either be *dealer placed* or *directly placed.* If it is dealer placed, the issuing corporation sells its promissory notes to one of the ten regular commercial paper dealers, which, in turn, sells it to others. If commercial paper is directly placed, the issuing corporation sells its notes directly in the market, without the intermediation of the middleman dealer. This is the method used primarily by sales-finance companies because they participate in the market on a virtually continuous basis. Sales-finance companies are companies that supply the credit for the installment purchase of major consumer items, for example, automobiles, refrigerators, and television sets. These companies find the commercial paper market particularly well suited to their needs since it enables them to adjust to swings in demand for installment purchases.

Commercial banks are still a major buyer of commercial paper, though today they are not as important in this market as they used to be. Over half the commercial paper outstanding is held by nonbank financial institutions wanting a short-term outlet for their funds. There has been a marked growth in the volume of commercial paper in recent years. By the end of 1977, about $65 billion were reported outstanding, of which about one-fifth was directly placed and about four-fifths dealer placed.

Broker and Dealer Loans

Securities brokers and dealers represent a substantial source of demand for short-term funds. Dealers need funds for financing their inventories of securities, and brokers need funds to relend to their customers who wish to borrow money to finance stock purchases (buy on margin). Loans to dealers and brokers may be either *call* or *time* loans. Call loans are payable on demand (may be *called*) at any time the lender wants the money back. Time loans are made for a definite period of time. Loans to brokers and dealers at one time dominated the money market. However, with the growth of other money market instruments, particularly Treasury bills and federal funds, they have come to play a comparatively minor role in the market. Total volume outstanding is currently about $10 billion.

Negotiable Certificates of Deposit

One of the major developments in the money market in the 1960s was the dramatic growth in *negotiable certificates of deposit* (CDs). A negotiable CD is a receipt given by a commercial bank for a deposit of funds, which stipulates that the holder of the receipt at maturity will be paid interest plus principal. The CD may not be redeemed by the bank before it matures, but because it is negotiable, it may be sold by the initial buyer on a secondary market. The volume of such CDs outstanding grew from a very small amount in 1960 to nearly $82 billion in 1978.

Banks issue CDs in order to acquire new funds and to be able to hold onto the funds they already have. Thus the rise in interest rates in the early 1960s induced a number of large corporations to shift funds out of demand deposits and into short-term money market instruments. Faced with the possibility of a serious drop in their deposits, some of the large New York City banks began issuing CDs—a money market instrument of their own—to these corporations in order to stem their drop in deposits. The instrument proved popular and spread throughout the banking system. Banks then began using negotiable CDs as a source of new funds to be used when they needed more money to satisfy customer loan demands.

By using CD money to make customer loans, note that banks are acting just like any other financial intermediary: They are selling a financial service (short-term, marketable debt) to one group of people and using the funds thus acquired to invest with another group of people (bank-loan customers). Note also that by using CDs, banks are no longer simply passive acceptors of deposit liabilities with no control over the amount of deposits they accept. With the rise of CDs, a bank can within limits actually determine its own size. In recent years, this fact has given rise to a completely new concept of bank management called *liability management.* (We shall return to this point in Chapter 8.)

Federal Funds

The federal funds' market is one of the most interesting in the money market. It is interesting because it is a market composed mostly of banks, both as buyers and sellers, because purchases and sales are made in very large amounts (the typical minimum being $1 million), and because the minimum maturity of the instrument is one day.

Federal funds are balances held in the Federal Reserve System. As mentioned previously, member banks of the Federal Reserve System are required by law to hold a certain percentage of their deposits as cash-reserve assets. These reserves, except for vault cash, are held in the form of deposit balances at the district Federal Reserve Bank. If a member bank holds less than the required amount of reserves, it is penalized; and if it holds more, it has tied up money in nonearning assets and thus has lost profits. As one would expect, on any given week some banks have reserve deficiencies while other banks have excess reserves. Of such stuff are markets made. The federal funds' market is largely a market wherein banks with too many reserves lend them to banks with too few reserves. Additionally, the federal funds market is used by brokers and dealers, especially government securities dealers.

Not all banks trade directly in federal funds. In fact, most do not. But many small banks will put federal funds temporarily into the market through their city correspondents. Notwithstanding the limited number of banks actively and directly engaged in the market, the volume of trading is huge. Gross transactions in 1978 totaled more than $1.5 trillion.

Eurodollars

Eurodollars are dollar-denominated deposits in foreign commercial banks and in foreign branches of United States banks. By *dollar denominated* is meant that the amounts on deposit are stated in terms of dollars rather than in the monetary unit of the country in which they are held, such as pounds in England or marks in Germany. Eurodollars are lent and borrowed freely at market-determined rates of interest. The maturity of Eurodollar loans varies, but it is usually for less than a year and typically for shorter periods of time than that.

While London is the center of Eurodollar activity, Eurodollars are actively traded in all the major financial cities of the world, including some non-European cities such as Singapore. The Eurodollar market constitutes, in truth, an international money market that is used by all the major commercial banks of the world. But since extensive use is made of it by some American banks, Eurodollars may also be regarded as a domestic money market instrument fully comparable to those already discussed (e.g., federal funds). American banks in need of funds to lend to their customers may acquire these funds by borrowing Eurodollars, and American corporations may lend in this market when interest rates paid there are high enough to induce them to do so. In fact, only a few United States banks are active in this market primarily because of the required expertise and because the minimum trade is for $10 million. Interest rates paid on Eurodollar borrowings typically are above domestic United States rates for comparable maturities.[8]

---

[8]The Eurodollar market is discussed more fully in Chapter 24.

The Interest Rate Futures Market

One very interesting development in the money and capital markets that has occurred recently is the emergence of a *futures market*. A futures market, as the name implies, is a contract to deliver something in the future for a price that is stipulated now. Such contracts have existed for a long time in agricultural commodities, but were initiated only in 1975 in financial instruments.

The advantage of a futures market is that it allows people with known future needs to *hedge*—that is, to avoid risk. Suppose, for example, that on March 1 the manager of a pension fund expects to have $1 million available for investment on June 1 (i.e., three months from now). The fund manager may consider interest rates high now, and want to be sure that he can get this yield when the $1 million becomes available. To do so, he can buy a future contract for the delivery to him, on June 1, of $1 million in United States government bonds. Since the price at which the bonds are to be delivered is stipulated in the future contract, the fund manager has, in this manner, avoided adverse interest rate movements.

Futures markets generally come into being only for commodities whose price is volatile, such as agricultural commodities. Historically, interest rates have been fairly stable, and have been less than 6 percent. In the past fifteen years, however, interest rates have risen well above 6 percent, and have become subject to sudden and sharp fluctuations. It is this increased volatility of interest rates that has prompted the futures market in debt instruments. Futures contracts can now be arranged, through the Chicago Board of Trade, on GNMA mortgages, long-term United States bonds, and commercial paper.

7-3 INTEREST RATES IN THE MONEY AND CAPITAL MARKETS

A market implies a price, of course. Generally there is no difficulty in grasping this concept. For example, the hog market implies a certain number of dollars at which pork is bought and sold per some standardized measure of weight and quality. In principle, prices in the money and capital markets are just as simple as they are in the hog market. But there are difficulties of terminology and definition in financial markets that frequently prove a source of confusion to the beginning student, and it will be best to clear away these obstacles at the outset of our discussion of interest rates. The most convenient vehicle for explaining the meaning of the various terms to be used will be specific examples.

Some Definitions

Let us begin with some definitions. A *bond* is a contractual obligation on the part of the seller of the bond (that is, the borrower of the money) to pay a fixed number of dollars per year for a set number of years to the buyer of the bond (that is, the lender of the money). At the end of the set number of years, the borrower also repays the original sum borrowed. The number of dollars paid the lender per year is called the *coupon;* the number of years over which the bond runs is called its *maturity;* and the number of dollars paid the owner of the bond when it matures is called its *par value,* or *principal.* The coupon, expressed as a percentage of the par value, is known as the *coupon rate* of the bond.

An example may help to fix these terms in the reader's mind. Suppose you and I enter into a written contract, the terms of which are as follows: You agree to lend me $1,000 for ten years. In return for lending me this money, I agree to pay you $50 per year for each of the ten years, plus, of course, paying you back the $1,000 at the end of the tenth year. In this case, the written contract is the *bond,* the bond's *maturity* is ten years, the bond's *coupon* is $50, and the *par value* of the bond is $1,000. Since $50/$1,000 = .05, or 5 percent, we may also say that the bond bears a 5 percent *coupon rate.* It is important to keep in mind that since both the coupon and par value are invariant over the life of the bond, so also is the coupon rate.

An obvious question that arises is, How do we decide on the terms of the bond, that is, on its maturity, coupon, and par value? As long as just you and I are involved, all sorts of things might enter into the agreement, such as friendship, social status, and relative bargaining power. But our concern here really lies in asking how the terms of a bond issue are determined in the open market when, say, a large corporation sells bonds to hundreds of investors. There are various answers to this question. In the first place, the par value of the bond is determined simply by convention. By tradition, most bonds are issued in $1,000 denominations, and the issuing corporation will, of course, simply issue as many of these as it needs to obtain the total amount of money it wants. Generally speaking, the maturity of the bond will be linked to the purpose for which the money is borrowed. A corporation needing money to build a new plant might thus issue twenty-five-year bonds, whereas a corporation wanting only to modernize some of its equipment might issue five-year bonds. While the setting of the par value and maturity are not quite as simple as this in practice, these explanations will serve well enough for our purposes here.

Establishing the coupon rate (or, equivalently, the coupon) is a bit more complicated, and it is essential that the reader understand the procedure. Basically, the establishment of the coupon rate on a new bond issue is a matter of competitive pricing. That is, the coupon rate is set so that the bond will be able to compete with comparable bonds already outstanding in the market (by *comparable* is meant bonds of similar maturity and credit risk—matters to which we shall return in a moment). This competition is carried on in terms of the *market rate of interest,* or *yield,* currently available on that type of bond. Do not confuse the coupon rate and the market rate. The two are quite different. As has been emphasized, the coupon rate is constant throughout the life of the bond. The market rate, on the contrary, changes all the time as money becomes more difficult ("tight" money) or less difficult ("easy" money) to borrow. The reason that the yield on a bond may vary even though its coupon rate remains the same is that the price for which the bond is sold on the secondary market can change *between* when it is issued and when it matures at par. Indeed, it is the combination of the fixed coupon and the variable price that determines a bond's yield.

Again, an example may help clarify these terms. Suppose you buy a ten-year bond that was issued nine years ago and therefore has only one more year until it matures at par. Suppose, additionally, that the bond carries a coupon of $50. Then if you buy the bond today for $990, at the end of the year you will receive the $50 coupon plus the $1,000 par value. You will thus have made $60 (the $50 plus the $10 price appreciation) on a $990 investment, or approximately 6 percent ($60/$990 $\approx$ .06). This 6 percent is the *yield* on that bond; when referring to all bonds of a particular maturity and risk, the 6 percent would be called the *market rate of interest* on that class of bond.

It is the existence of the variable market price and market rate of interest that makes bond pricing appear more complicated than hog pricing. But this complexity is only apparent. The difficulty is that many people are not precise in their language. The *price of borrowing money* is the market rate of interest; the *price of a bond* is its market price, that is, what it is currently selling for in the secondary bond market. In fact, in a competitive market situation these two prices are tied together in a strict mathematical relationship so that given either one the other can be derived. Two aspects of this relationship are of particular interest: the inverse relationship between bond prices and bond yields, and the relationship between bond prices and maturity. We shall first explain these relationships intuitively, and then explain the underlying mathematics.

The Inverse Relationship between Bond Prices and Yield

We wish to show that bond prices and market rates of interest vary inversely with each other—that when one decreases the other must increase, and vice versa. As before, this relationship can be understood most readily by using an arithmetic example. Suppose that on January 1, 1980, we issued bond A for $1,000. When issued, bond A had a two-year maturity (it matures on January 1, 1982) and carried a coupon rate of 5 percent, which at the time of issue was equal to the market rate of interest. As we have seen, this means that the seller of bond A would pay its owner $50 on January 1, 1981, and another $50 on January 1, 1982; additionally, the seller would repay the principal, or par value, of $1,000 on January 1, 1982. Now imagine that it is January 2, 1981. The owner of bond A has just received the first coupon payment of $50 and is thinking of selling the bond. Since the previous year, money has gotten tighter and the market rate of interest on one-year bonds is now 6 percent. Query: What price will bond A sell for on January 2, 1981?

The answer to this question is intuitively clear. On January 2, 1981, bond A will sell for a price such that the one remaining coupon plus the price appreciation between January 2, 1981, and January 2, 1982, when the bond matures, will give the investor a 6 percent yield on the investment. For clearly, no one would buy the bond if its yield were less than this since they have the alternative of buying some other bond that *will* yield 6 percent, and the holder of the bond need not sell it for a greater yield since there is competitive bidding. Arithmetically, therefore, we may answer the question by solving the following equation, where P is the price of the bond:

$$.06P = \$50 + (\$1{,}000 - P)$$

The first term on the right ($50) is the remaining coupon; the second term ($1,000 − P) is the dollar appreciation on the bond as its price goes to par at maturity.

The sum of these two amounts must be such that they equal 6 percent of the buyer's investment (the term on the left). Solving the equation, we get

$$.06P = \$50 + (\$1,000 - P)$$
$$.06P = \$1,050 - P$$
$$P + .06P = \$1,050$$
$$P(1.06) = \$1,050$$
$$P = \frac{\$1,050}{1.06}$$
$$= \$990.57$$

The point of the exercise is that because the market rate of interest *increased* (from 5 to 6 percent), the price of the bond *decreased* (from $1,000 to $990.57). This will be true in general: As market rates rise, bond prices will fall.

What about the reverse case? If the market rate of interest decreases, will bond prices increase? The answer, of course, is yes. To illustrate, take the same example, except assume that on January 2, 1981, the market rate of interest has decreased to 4 percent. Then our equation becomes

$$.04P = \$50 + (\$1,000 - P)$$
$$P(1.04) = \$1,050$$
$$P = \$1,009.62$$

That is, as the market rate decreased (from 5 to 4 percent), the price of the bond increased (from $1,000 to $1,009.62).

It is extremely important that the student keep this inverse relationship between prices and yields in mind. It is a point to which we shall return again and again.

The Relationship between Bond Prices and Maturity

Before discussing the mathematics of interest rates, we must explain one further aspect of the relationship between bond prices and yield: *For a given change in yield, the price of the bond will change more, the longer is its term to maturity.* In other words, if the market rate of interest on *both* long-term and short-term bonds increases by 1 percent, the price of the short-term bond will decrease only a little while the price of the long-term bond will decrease a lot.

To see that this is so, let us compare the price behavior of bond A of the previous example with a very long-term bond, bond B. In fact, the simplest case (paradoxically) is to suppose that bond B is a bond that never matures; that is, it runs in perpetuity. (Such bonds are not issued in the United States, but they are issued in other countries; probably the best known are the British "consols.") In other words, the original seller of the bond promises to pay the holder a stipulated number of dollars per year *forever*. What we want to do, of course, is to make bond B just like bond A in every respect except maturity. Let us therefore suppose that bond B was originally issued for $1,000 on January 1, 1980, with a 5 percent coupon rate, and that at that time this coupon rate was equal to the market rate of interest. Now move forward a year, January 2, 1981. Again, suppose that the market rate of interest has risen to 6 percent by this time. What will be the current market price of bond B? Clearly, bond B must now be priced such that its buyer will receive a 6 percent return on the investment. That is, the coupon on bond B ($50) must be 6 percent of its selling price *(P)*. Thus:

$$.06P = \$50$$

$$P = \frac{\$50}{.06}$$

$$= \$822.22$$

Now compare the prices of bonds A and B as of January 2, 1981. A 1 percent rise in the market rate of interest caused the price of bond A (a one-year bond) to decrease from $1,000 to $990.57, a loss of only $9.43 for its owner. But, under exactly the same circumstances, the price of bond B decreased from $1,000 to $822.22, a whopping loss of $177.78. Thus a given rise in the market rate of interest has had a considerably greater effect on the price of the long-term bond than on the price of the short-term bond. The reader may be persuaded that this is true in general by examining the reproduction of a page from a bond table shown in Figure 7-1.

The Algebra of Bond Prices, Yields, and Maturity

The discussion of the relationships among bond price, yield, and maturity has so far been carried on at the intuitive level, using arithmetic examples. We now want to move a step further, and explain these relationships in more generalized terms. To do so, it is desirable to use mathematics.

Suppose that you were to invest $943.40 for one year at an annual yield of 6 percent. How much would you get back at the end of the year? Clearly, you would get back your original investment of $943.40 *plus* 6 percent of $943.40, or $56.60. Stated in equation form, you would get back

$$\$943.40 + (.06)\$943.40 = \$943.40 + \$56.60$$

or

$$943.40(1.06) = \$1,000 \tag{1}$$

One way of expressing this relationship is to say that $943.40 *today* is worth $1,000 *one year from today* (assuming an interest rate of 6 percent). However, the more common way to write eq. (1) is to divide both sides by 1 plus the interest rate:

$$\$943.40 = \frac{\$1,000}{1.06} \tag{2}$$

The amount on the left-hand side of eq. (2) ($943.40) is called the *present value,* meaning that the value *today* (at present) of $1,000 due one year from today is $943.40 (assuming an interest rate of 6 percent).

Now let us drop the numbers and use symbols instead. Let P be the present

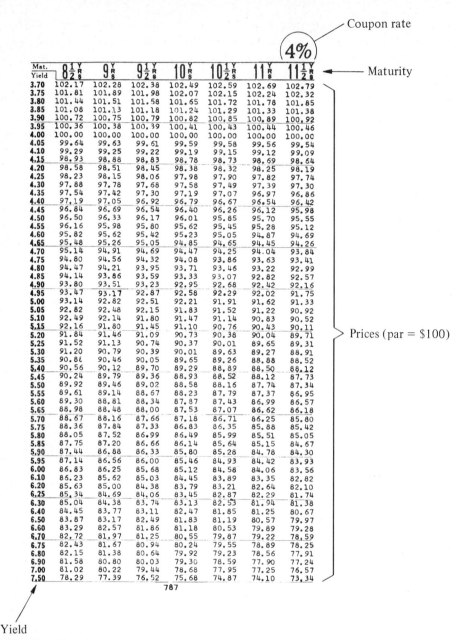

Figure 7-1 Page from a standard bond table. Note that, except where yield and coupon rate are equal, bond price changes as maturity lengthens. This can be seen by reading along any such row and noting the change in prices. Note also that, holding coupon rate and maturity constant, bond price falls as yield rises. This can be seen by reading down any column and noting the decline in price. (*Source: Reproduced with permission from* Comprehensive Bond Value Tables, *4th pocket ed., publ. no. 161, p. 787, copyright 1958, Financial Publishing Company, Boston, Mass.*)

value ($943.40 in the example), M be the maturity value ($1,000 in the example), and i be the interest rate (6 percent in the example). Then the *present value formula* of eq. (2) can be written more generally as

$$P = \frac{M}{(1 + i)} \tag{3}$$

We are now in a position to explain the inverse relationship between bond prices and interest rates. For clearly, for a given M, the larger is i the smaller is P, and vice versa. For example, if $i = .08$ ($> .06$), then $P = \$925.93$; that is,

$$\$925.93 = \frac{\$1,000}{1.08}$$

Conversely, if $i = .04$ ($< .06$) then $P = \$961.54$; that is,

$$\$961.54 = \frac{\$1,000}{1.04}$$

To understand the second relationship, that between present value and maturity, it is necessary to take one more step and consider *compound interest.* [9] To explain, suppose that you were to take some amount of money—say $60—and invest it for *two* years at 6 percent. Then at the end of *one* year, you would have

$$\$60(1.06) = \$63.60$$

If you left all this money in your investment (still at 6 percent), then at the end of two years, you would have

$$[\$60(1.06)](1.06) = \$63.60(1.06)$$

or

$$\$60(1.06)^2 = \$67.42$$

Dividing both sides by $(1.06)^2$ gives

$$\$60 = \frac{\$67.42}{(1.06)^2}$$

In other words, the present value of $67.42 due *two* years from now is $60 (assuming a 6 percent rate of interest). Using the same symbols as were used in the previous example, the present value formula for a sum of money due two years from now is

[9] We here deal only with the case of *annually* compounded interest.

$$P = \frac{M}{(1 + i)^2}$$

Clearly, if the money were due in three years, then the formula would be $P = [M /(1 + i)^3]$, and so forth. In general, the present value formula for a sum of money due in n years is

$$P = \frac{M}{(1 + i)^n}$$

Now consider a bond of, say, a three-year maturity that has an annual coupon payment of $\$A$. Then the present value of the payment made at the end of the first year is $A/(1 + i)$; the present value of the payment made at the end of the second year is $A/(1 + i)^2$; the present value of the payment made at the end of the third year is $A/(1 + i)^3$; and the present value of the maturity value of the bond (M) is $M/(1 + i)^3$. Putting all this together gives a present value (P) of the bond as:

$$P = \frac{A}{(1 + i)} + \frac{A}{(1 + i)^2} + \frac{A}{(1 + i)^3} + \frac{M}{(1 + i)^3}$$

In general, for a bond of n years to maturity, the present value formula is

$$P = \frac{A}{(1 + i)} + \frac{A}{(1 + i)^2} + \ldots + \frac{A}{(1 + i)^n} + \frac{M}{(1 + i)^n}$$

On the basis of this formula, we can now explain why, for a given change in the rate of interest, the present value of the bond will change more the longer is its maturity: The reason is that the larger is n, the number of years to maturity, the more terms there are on the right-hand side of the equation to affect the price, P. Additionally, the larger is n the larger is the denominator in these extra terms. Putting the matter somewhat more technically, P is a function of n as well as of i.

The Significance of the Relationship Among Price, Yield, and Maturity

The importance of the relationship among price, maturity, and yield has to do with the concept of *liquidity*, the ability to convert a financial asset into cash for a sum of money that is approximately known in advance. The greater price stability of short-term assets thus means that they are more liquid. In other words, the owner of a three-month Treasury bill knows to a fairly fine point what price it will bring if it is necessary to sell the bill before it matures, but the owner of a twenty-year bond will be much less certain about what price it will fetch in the market. Thus, other things equal, the shorter the term to maturity, the more liquid is a financial asset.

The importance of the concept of liquidity can hardly be exaggerated. It occupies a strategic position in the day-to-day management, not only of all financial institutions, but also of the financial management of all business firms and households as well. In rural communities, for example, it is commonplace to refer to someone as being "land poor," meaning that the person has put all available assets into real estate that cannot be readily converted to cash. This person may thus be quite rich in terms of total asset value but quite poor in terms of ability to spend money. Such a person has ignored the concept of liquidity.

The Term Structure of Interest Rates

In our discussion of interest rates, we have until now referred to *the* market rate of interest, as though there were only a single such animal. But in practice, of course, the market presents us with a profusion of interest rates in bewildering variety. Many of these differences in rates can be traced back to special features of the bonds, to market imperfections of various sorts, and to the financial soundness of the issuing corporation. Some bonds contain a feature that permits them to be converted to common stocks, for example; others are purchased predominantly by highly special-ized investors; the risk of default (nonpayment of interest or principal) varies from one issuer to the next; some bonds, such as municipals, carry special tax provisions; and so forth. Trying to determine why the yield on any given bond is precisely what it is is the special province of investment analysis, which is an entire field of study in itself. There is, however, one aspect of the relationships among market rates of interest that traditionally has interested economists because of its relevance for questions of public policy and monetary theory. This is the relationship between short-term and long-term interest rates—what has come to be called the *term* (to maturity) *structure of interest rates.*

To understand more clearly what is meant by the term structure of interest rates, let us pose the following questions: Suppose that we could eliminate all differences in debt securities except maturity. Would the market rates on these securities then form a recognizable pattern that changed systematically as maturity changed? And, if so, can we then explain why the pattern behaves as it does? The first question is the easiest to answer. For we do have a series of market yields where the only fundamental differences among the securities is term to maturity. This series consists of the rates of interest on marketable United States government securities. Note that these securities are issued in a variety of maturities, are totally free of default risk, and are regularly traded in a very active market. That they do indeed conform to a regular pattern can be seen from Figure 7-2 (reproduced from the *Treasury Bulletin*), which shows market yields on the vertical axis and years to maturity on the horizontal axis. The reader should note in particular that the data plotted in Figure 7-2 are as of a single point in time—February 28, 1978. That is, the figure does not depict a time series but instead shows the government securities market on a single day; it is not a movie but a snapshot.

It is also to be noted that although the rate pattern shown in Figure 7-2 is undeniably regular, it is not precisely so. If we were to draw a line connecting all the *x*'s in the figure, the line would seem a bit jagged, or saw-toothed. This jagged-ness is believed to be caused by such things as the tax laws on capital gains and mathematical subtleties in the yield-price relationship. As a consequence, it is cus-tomary to draw a smooth freehand curve through the yield data, such as that shown in the figure. This line is known as the *yield curve* and is well known to market

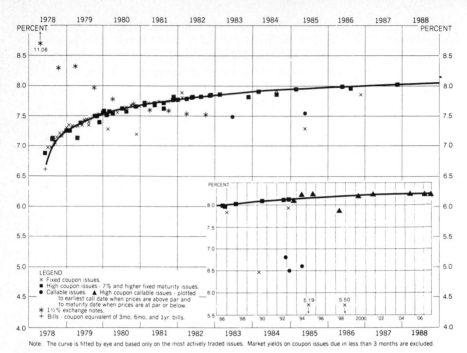

Figure 7-2 Yields of treasury securities, February 28, 1978, based on closing bid quotations. *(Source:* Treasury Bulletin, *March 1978, p. 81.)*

participants and economists. The shape of the yield curve changes over time. The four basic types are shown in Figure 7-3*a* to *d*. The question that intrigues economists, and that has proved central to a number of issues in monetary economics, is simply this: Under what circumstances, and for what reasons, will one type of yield curve emerge in the market rather than another?

The Hedging Theory of the Term Structure   Perhaps the simplest explanation of the term structure is the *hedging theory.* In its purest form,[10] this view holds that the government securities' market is, in fact, composed of several submarkets that are sealed off from one another. This compartmentalization occurs because investors are interested in aspects of securities other than just yield. For example, commercial banks have large amounts of demand liabilities (checking and savings accounts) that are payable whenever their owners want their money. Banks are therefore obliged to match, or *hedge,* these liabilities with highly liquid assets that can be converted into cash at an almost-known price at any time. Banks are thus interested in buying short-term securities and will hesitate to move into the long-term market no matter how high long-term yields may go; they are *locked in* in the short-term market.

[10]There probably are no advocates of a "pure" hedging theory, so that what follows is something of a caricature. The standard reference for this view is J. M. Culbertson, "The Structure of Interest Rates," *Quarterly Journal of Economics,* November 1957, pp. 485–517.

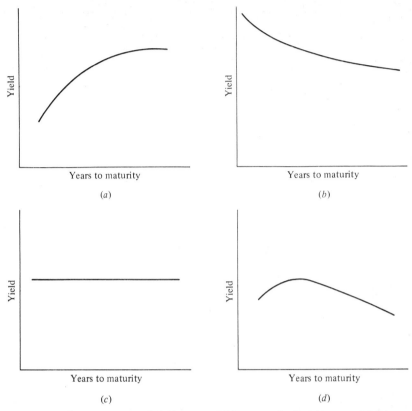

Figure 7-3   Common types of yield curves: (a) "upsweeping" yield curve; (b) "downsweeping" yield curve; (c) "flat" yield curve; (d) "humped" yield curve.

Insurance companies, in contrast, have highly predictable long-term obligations and consequently want to hedge these obligations with a predictable cash inflow. They are therefore primarily interested in long-term bonds, where the fixed-dollar coupons are contractually set and therefore predictable; they are locked-in in the long-term market. The hedging theory holds that both buyers and (for nongovernment bonds) sellers of open-market debt are generally like banks and insurance companies and that therefore the market is sealed off into distinct submarkets. Thus, each yield is determined by supply and demand pressures within its own compartment, and the term structure of interest rates emerges as a sort of by-product of these pressures.

The hedging theory is widely held among market participants but is generally regarded as inadequate by economists. Two criticisms are generally made of it: First, if the hedging theory is correct, then how can we account for the apparent regularity of the yield curve? One would think that if the yield in each submarket is set in isolation from the yields in all other submarkets, then these yields would bear no necessary relation to one another. Second, how can this theory account for the apparent fact that particular yield curves are associated with particular states of the economy—that an *upsweeping* curve is characteristic of an easy money period and a *downsweeping* curve typical of a tight money period. These criticisms do not, of course, necessarily deny the influence of *some* hedging as an important element in the market, but they do argue forcibly that some additional explanation is needed.

The Expectational Theory of the Term Structure   Perhaps the most widely held theory of the term structure among academic economists is that the shape of the yield curve results primarily from investor *expectations* about the future course of interest rates.[11] While this theory can become very messy algebraically, most of the mess can be avoided, and the essence of the theory nevertheless retained, by using *simple interest*—that is, interest that is not compounded from one year to the next.

To see how the expectational theory works, consider the following example: Suppose an investor has $1,000 to invest over the next two years. There are two possible choices: The individual may buy a bond that matures in two years. Alternatively, she may buy a bond that matures in one year and at the end of that year reinvest the money in another one-year bond. In other words, the investor has a choice between 1 two-year bond or 2 one-year bonds, sequentially held. The question is, On what basis should the investor make this choice?

In general terms, the answer to this question is that the individual should choose that investment path which promises to maximize the rate of return over the two-year period. But the specific question remains, How is this done? To lend concreteness to the problem, suppose that the following bond yields currently prevail in the market:

On a one-year bond, the yield is 5%.
On a two-year bond, the yield is 6%.

Thus if the individual invests $1,000 in a two-year bond, at the end of the two years the return will be $1,120—$1,000 in principal and $60 for each of the two years (remember that we are considering only simple interest). If, on the other hand, the individual decides to invest in 2 one-year bonds, the return will be $1,050 at the end of the first year plus whatever the yield is on a one-year bond during the *second* year. But since the individual doesn't know for certain what the one-year rate will be during the second year, the choice must be made on the basis of her *expectations* about that yield. Suppose that she expects the one-year bond yield to be 8 percent in the second year; then the total return for the two-year period will be $1,130 ($1,000 principal plus $50 in the first year and $80 in the second year). Clearly, $1,130 is greater than the $1,120 return on investing in the two-year bond at the outset, and therefore the investor will prefer this investment path. Alternatively, if she expects the one-year bond yield to be only 5 percent in the second year, then the total return will be only $1,100 and the individual will prefer the two-year bond

---

[11]The expectational theory of the term structure of interest rates can be found in a number of places. Probably the most frequently cited reference is Friedrich A. Lutz, "The Structure of Interest Rates," *Quarterly Journal of Economics,* February 1940, pp. 36–63; reprinted in American Economic Association, *Readings in the Theory of Income Distribution,* W. Fellner and B. Haley (eds.), Philadelphia, 1946.

to the sequential purchase of 2 one-year bonds. If she expects the second-year yield to be exactly 7 percent, then the total receipts will be the same whichever path is chosen, and the investor will consequently be indifferent between the two.

It is next necessary to broaden the focus of this analysis from the individual to the market as a whole. According to the expectational theory, this is easily done. If all investors in the market act on the basis of their expectations in the manner just described, then they will sort themselves out according to their expectations about the second-year market rate of interest. In the example of the previous paragraph, all those who believe that the second-year rate will be *above* 7 percent will buy one-year bonds and all those who believe it will be *below* 7 percent will buy two-year bonds.

So far, so good. But at this point things get a bit tricky, and the reader should follow the next step closely. For as it turns out, it is the expectation about what the one-year rate will be in the second year that determines the current two-year bond rate, and not the other way around. To see how this works, again assume that the current one-year rate is 5 percent and the current two-year rate is 6 percent. In contrast to our previous example, however, let us suppose that *all* market investors, without exception, expect that the one-year rate in the second year will be above 7 percent. In this case, no one will be willing to buy two-year bonds; they will all prefer to buy one-year bonds and then invest again in one-year bonds during the second year. But if no one is willing to buy two-year bonds, the price of these bonds must fall, just as the price of pork must fall if there is no demand for it. But, as we have seen, when the price of a bond decreases, its yield increases. Thus the yield on two-year bonds must rise above 6 percent under the assumed circumstances. How far will this rise go? It must continue until the market sorts itself out again, that is, until all investors are in either the one-year or two-year-bond market *according to their expectations about the second-year rate.* For example, suppose that the rise in the two-year-bond rate stabilizes at 7 percent, so that the new current yield curve is:

On a one-year bond, the yield is 5%.
On a two-year bond, the yield is 7%.

This yield curve implies that all those investors who believe that the one-year rate will rise above 9 percent in the second year have bought one-year bonds, while all those who expect that the second-year rate will not rise as far as 9 percent have bought two-year bonds. The market is thus in a state of equilibrium; there is no tendency for rates to change because everyone is where he or she wants to be.

This same analysis is applicable in the opposite case. That is, suppose that we once again have current one-year and two-year bond rates of 5 and 6 percent, respectively. If, now, we assume that no one expects that the one-year rate in the second year will go as high as 7 percent, then *everyone* will want to buy two-year bonds and no one will want to buy one-year bonds. But if everyone wants to buy two-year bonds, then their price will be bid up and consequently their yield will fall. Once more, equilibrium will be restored to the market only when everyone is holding that type of bond which, *according to expectations,* will maximize his or her rate of return over the two-year period.

The central point to note about the analysis is that the yield on two-year bonds is actually being determined by expectations about the one-year rate that will prevail in the second year. In fact, the expectational theory of the term structure of interest rates holds that long-term bond rates are simply an average of current and expected one-year rates. For example, if the current one-year rate is 5 percent and the one-year rate expected for next year is 7 percent, then the current rate on two-year bonds will be 6 percent, or the average of the 2 one-year rates (5% + 7%/2 = 6%). The numbers used in this example are the same numbers that were used in the example on page 135, but there is a subtle difference between this example and the previous one. For whereas before we were determining expectations from the current rate structure, now we are determining the current rate structure from expectations. It is precisely this latter case that constitutes the expectational theory of the term structure of interest rates. Thus, the central hypothesis of the expectational theory is that *long-term interest rates are an average of current and expected short-term interest rates.*

Before we test this hypothesis, let us note that, at the very least, it gives us a reasonable explanation of the basic types of yield curves shown in Figure 7-3a to d. Consider the upsweeping yield curve of Figure 7-3a, for example. If long-term rates are above the short-term rates, and if long-term rates are an *average* of expected short-term rates, then these expected short-term rates must be rising. This is so simply because of the nature of averages: To keep an average rising smoothly as you add more numbers to it, each number you add must be larger than the previous number. Thus if we accept the expectational theory of the term structure of interest rates, an upsweeping yield curve is interpreted to mean that on the average the market expects short-term interest rates to rise in the future. Is this reasonable? Yes, it is. For, as we have noted, an upsweeping yield curve is characteristic of an easy money period when rates are low. And what could seem more sensible than that if rates are low in the present, they will rise in the future?

The other types of yield curves are subject to similar interpretations. A down-sweeping yield curve is interpreted to mean that on the average the market expects short-term interest rates to fall in the future. (Note that a downsweeping yield curve is characteristic of tight money, i.e., high current interest rates.) A flat yield curve means that the market expects short-term rates to remain unchanged, and a humped curve means that expectations are that short-term rates will first rise and then fall.

The expectational theory of the term structure thus seems to be a sensible hypothesis. But keep in mind that it is *only* an hypothesis. We have not as yet established any statistical link between the expected short-term rates *implied* by a yield curve and *actual* expectations. To establish such a link is, of course, difficult, if for no other reason than that actual expectations are not directly observable. That is, we don't know what expected short-term rates *actually* are, nor have we any way of finding out. Consequently there is no direct way to relate actual expectations to implied expectations. Nevertheless, a most ingenious test of this hypothesis was devised several years ago by a researcher named David Meiselman.[12]

Meiselman's test of the expectational hypothesis is based on what is called an *error-learning model.* All this means, really, is that people learn from their past mistakes (errors) and that this learning process will modify their current behavior. To see how this idea may be used for a statistical test of the expectations theory, consider the following hypothetical set of expectations about future one-year rates of interest:

In 1980, the one-year rate expected to prevail in 1981 is 5%.

In 1980, the one-year rate expected to prevail in 1982 is 6%.

Now assume that it is 1981. Last year (1980) we forecasted that the one-year interest rate in 1981 would be 5 percent; but now (1981) we *know* what the one-year rate is because it is an actual rate. Suppose that the rate is 5½ percent, that is, ½ percent above what we had expected it to be. We now realize, therefore, that a year ago (1980) we made an error in our expectations. According to Meiselman's error-learning model, this realization of the past forecasting error will cause us to revise our expectations about what the one-year rate will be next year (1982). In other words, the knowledge that we made a mistake in the past will modify our behavior in the present. How will our expectations about the one-year rate in 1982 be changed? The assumption is that since the actual rate in 1981 turned out to be *higher* than expected, we shall revise our expectations about the 1982 rate *upward.* That is, the revision in expectations will be positively related to (vary in the same direction as) the forecasting error.

Note that we now have an hypothesis that is susceptible to statistical investigation. Using past yield curves, we may derive the implied expectations about future one-year interest rates; by then moving forward a year, we can find out what the forecasting error was and what the next year's expectations were; and by using regression analysis, we can then see if there is a systematic relationship between forecasting errors and the revision of expectations. This is precisely what Meiselman did. An example of his results is as follows:

$$\Delta r_1 = 0.00 + .70E$$

$$r^2 = .91$$

Significance of the coefficient on E is not given

In this equation, Δr_1 is the revised (changed) expectation about what the one-year rate will be one year from now (i.e., the date of a given yield curve) and E is the forecasting error made last year. As can be seen, E and Δr_1 are positively

[12]David Meiselman, *The Term Structure of Interest Rates,* Prentice-Hall, Inc., Englewood Cliffs, N.J., 1962.

related, as hypothesized, and the coefficient of determination (r^2) is quite high at .91. Moreover, as the expectations deal with short-term rates further and further into the future, r^2 and the coefficient on E decline. Thus, e.g., Meiselman's researches also show that

$$\Delta r_4 = -.03 + .33E$$

$$r^2 = .47$$

Significance of the coefficient on E is not given

where Δr_4 is the revised expectation about what the one-year rate will be four years from now and E is as previously defined. Meiselman interpreted this decline in r^2 and the E coefficient to mean that expectations about the distant future are more vague and more tentatively held by market investors than expectations about the near future.

Meiselman's results obviously lend support to the expectational theory of the term structure of interest rates, but they certainly do not *prove* the validity of the theory. In fact, his work sparked a whole host of other studies dealing with this issue. These studies have raised many theoretical and empirical questions which remain unanswered, with the result that the theory of the term structure of interest rates continues to be a controversial matter among economists. Nevertheless, it seems fair to say that the bulk of the evidence supports the view that expectations of future interest rates play a major role in determining yield curves.

7-4 REVIEW QUESTIONS

1 Would a corporation wanting to finance the construction of a new plant be more likely to use the capital market or the money market? Why? Suppose the corporation wanted to finance an inventory for a seasonal sales peak?

2 Array the following securities from the most to the least liquid: a newly issued twenty-year government bond; a banker's acceptance; a twenty-year municipal bond that now has five years to maturity; a newly issued one-year Treasury bill. Why did you put them in the order you did?

3 In your own words, explain why a security that has only one day to go before it matures will not change its price much no matter what happens to the market rate of interest. Compare this to a bond that still has twenty-five years to go before it matures.

4 Suppose that the term structure of interest rates is:

On a one-year security, the yield is 7%.
On a two-year security, the yield is 8%.

What does this imply about investor expectations about the one-year rate one year from now?

PART 4

COMMERCIAL
BANK
MANAGEMENT

We have to this point considered the financial apparatus of the American economy from an overall viewpoint. Our purpose so far has been to understand the financial sector as an integrated system, where each type of institution plays a particular role but where all institutions taken together form an interlocking pattern. Thus, in terms of Figure 1-1, the reader should now have a good working knowledge of the contents of the box labeled "Commercial Banks and Other Financial Institutions" (shown as Figure IV-1).

The purpose of the next three chapters is to zoom in on this scene and examine the microeconomic principles of financial management. In doing so, we must necessarily consider the relationship between financial institutions and the general public. That is, we now take another step in assembling the various pieces of Figure 1-1. To the material contained in the box of Figure IV-1, we now add the additional box of the public shown in Figure IV-2 plus the arrows (loans and investments) connecting the two boxes.

While the center of interest in the next three chapters will be the commercial

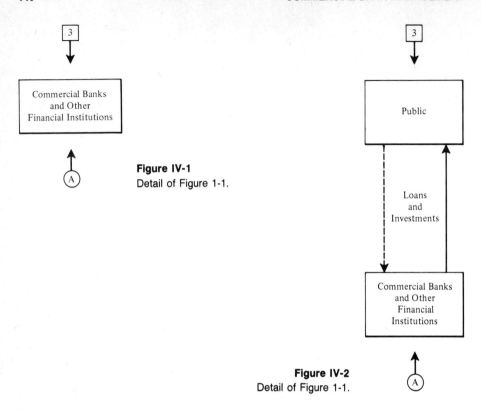

Figure IV-1
Detail of Figure 1-1.

Figure IV-2
Detail of Figure 1-1.

bank, it should be understood that the basic principles of financial management are applicable to all financial institutions; it is only necessary to modify the principles to fit the particular circumstances of other institutions. We begin Chapter 8 with an historical survey of banking theory, since financial management has traditionally meant bank management. Then, having derived the underlying principles, in Chapters 9 and 10 we shall see how these principles are currently applied in practice.

8

Theories of Banking

The phrase *theory of banking* may sound strange to most readers. Surely, one feels, banking is something people do, not something they build armchair theories about. But in fact, theories of banking—abstract arguments dealing with the pros and cons of how banks should and do behave—have been with us for hundreds of years. The reason for this is that for centuries commercial banks have been recognized as institutions occupying a strategic position in the overall functioning of the economy. So important is this position, indeed, that it has long been recognized that we cannot hope to solve many of the major social problems that beset us, such as inflation and unemployment, without some general knowledge of the internal workings of a commercial bank. A bank is not just another business like a furniture store or a lumberyard. The decisions made by bankers quite literally permeate the entire economy, affecting the decisions made by other business people, housewives, and government officials. In fact, reduced to its simplest terms, the whole idea behind central banking and monetary policy is that if we can somehow influence the decisions made by bankers, then these decisions in turn will influence the decisions made by everyone else. In this indirect fashion we can control the overall functioning of the economy. In order to implement such a method of control, it is necessary to understand why bankers do what they do—what their motives are and the particular problems they face.

It should not be inferred, however, that banking theory is simply a sort of abstract description of what bankers do. The relationship between banking theory and banking practice is more complex than this. For the decisions of bankers are as much influenced by the prevailing theory of banking as the theory is by current banking practices. Thus, for example, the *commercial loan theory* held banking practices in its grip throughout the nineteenth century and had profound influences on the historical development of banking in the United States. Moreover, legislators, bank examiners, and regulatory officials, as well as bankers, are influenced by banking theory. In banking, as in so many areas, theory and practice interact with one another; causality does not run in a single direction.

Before discussing banking theory, it is necessary to say a few words about balance sheets. (Those readers who have studied any accounting at all may skip this discussion.)

8-1 THE CONCEPT OF THE BALANCE SHEET

Suppose you owned a small business—a shoe store, say—and you decided to sell the store and retire to Florida. How would you go about it? The first thing you would do is to collect all your debts and sell everything you owned—inventory, building, equipment, and so on. What the business owns and what is owed to it are called the *assets* of the business. After converting all your assets into cash, the next thing you would need to do is to pay off all your debts. What the business owes is called its *liabilities.* When you have sold your assets and paid off your liabilities, what you have left is what you can use to retire to Florida. This difference between assets and liabilities is called *capital.* [1]

We can express these relationships in the form of a very simple equation:

Assets − liabilities = capital

Or, putting the equation in its more typical form,

Assets = capital + liabilities

This is the basic *balance-sheet equation* (really an identity). Note that the equation must hold true under all circumstances because capital is *defined* as the difference between assets and liabilities. When the liabilities of a business are greater than its assets, the business is said to be bankrupt, or insolvent, and its capital will take on a negative algebraic sign; but the equation nevertheless continues to hold.

[1]More generally, it is called *net worth,* but in banking it is called *capital,* or (more accurately) the bank's *capital accounts.*

A *balance sheet* is simply the enumeration of the various assets of a business on one side of a ledger and the enumeration of its various liabilities and capital accounts on the other side. The two sides *must* be equal, or *balance,* because of the underlying equation. Only one further point should be noted: A balance sheet refers to a single point in time, for example, the close of business on December 31. Taken by itself, a balance sheet does not show changes over time. It is what economists call a *stock* concept, not a *flow* concept. That is, the balance sheet shows the stock of goods a firm has on hand at any particular instant and does not show the flow of goods through the firm over time. For this reason, a balance sheet does not show business profits, which are a flow.

8-2 THE NATURE OF BANKING

Two fundamental aspects of the business of commercial banking color all its activities. The first of these is that the capital of a bank is typically very small. On April 26, 1978, for example, the average commercial bank in the United States had capital accounts equal to only 7 percent of its assets. Consider what this means: Only 7 percent of the assets that banks have bought have been purchased with money provided by the owners of the banks. In other words, 93 percent of bank-owned assets have been bought with other people's money. This fact is of paramount importance in banking. If you should spend an hour or two someday chatting with a commercial banker about the banking business, it wouldn't be long before you would be told that bankers lend other people's money. When the banker says this, listen. It is not merely a cliché; it is almost the literal truth.

Why is the low capital/asset ratio in banking important? Think about it a moment. If bankers were to invest all their funds in government bonds that then fell in price by only 7 percent, they would be bankrupt. If they were to put all their money into loans and if only 93 percent of them were repaid, they would be bankrupt. Bankers are known for their conservatism, and well they should be. There are very few businesses where faulty business judgment can be so disastrous.

Nor is this all. The second aspect of banking that makes it different from other businesses is that most of its liabilities are payable on demand. In other words, on any business day any number of a bank's depositors may walk in and withdraw all their money. Thus, not only is the bank lending other people's money, but these "other people" may and do ask for their money back at any time. Small wonder that bankers are conservative!

These two aspects of banking lead to what is generally regarded as the central problem of bank management: reconciling the conflicting bank goals of solvency, liquidity, and profits. By *solvency* is meant not going bankrupt, and it is a particularly acute problem in banking because of the low capital/asset ratios. By *liquidity* is meant the bank's ability to pay its depositors on demand. And, of course, since the bank is a business, it must earn a *profit* for its stockholders. That these goals of bank management conflict with one another can be easily seen by reflecting on the fact that a bank could be perfectly liquid only if it held all its assets in cash, but then it would earn no profits. Or again, if the bank makes risky loans, it may increase its profits but it will also increase it potential for going bankrupt *(insolvency).*

One way or another, the various banking theories we shall now consider have as their common focal point a theory of how banks should behave in order to reconcile these conflicting goals.

8-3 BANKING THEORY: HISTORICAL

The oldest theory of banking is the *commercial loan theory,* also called the *real bills doctrine* (the terms are used interchangeably). This theory dates back at least two centuries, and a discussion of it can be found in Adam Smith's *Wealth of Nations,* first published in 1776.

The Commercial Loan Theory

Stated in its most succinct form, the commercial loan theory[2] holds that banks should lend only on "short-term, self-liquidating, commercial paper." Naturally, each of these terms needs defining. In banking, a *short-term loan* is a loan maturing in less than one year from when it is first made. Such loans carry the connotation of seasonality; that is, the inference is that they are made to accommodate the seasonal aspects of a business, not for the purpose of furnishing a firm with permanent capital. *Self-liquidating* means that the loan contains within itself its own means of repayment; that is, the very nature of the loan generates the funds necessary to pay it off. A good example would be a retail toy store that did its peak volume of business in the three months preceding Christmas. Such a store might borrow from a bank to finance the purchase of inventory in September; during October, November, and December, the toys are sold and the bank loan is then repaid out of the proceeds of these sales. The loan is thus self-liquidating in the sense that it has liquidated, or repaid, itself. *Commercial paper* refers to debts that arise in the course of commerce—the processing, moving, and marketing of goods. The intent here is to emphasize that the loan is solidly based on "real" goods as opposed to loans for speculative or purely financial purposes. The alternative phrase for the commercial loan theory, the *real bills doctrine,* highlights this aspect of the theory.

To repeat, the commercial loan theory states that banks should lend *only* on short-term, self-liquidating, commercial paper. Why? This can best be understood by enumerating some of the types of loans that the theory maintains a bank should *not* make. First of all, all long-term loans are excluded. For example, a bank should not make real estate loans or loans for the purpose of financing the purchase of plant and equipment. Such loans are considered too illiquid. The controlling factor is that a bank has liabilities payable on demand, and it cannot meet these obligations if its assets are tied up for long periods of time. Rather, a bank needs a continual and substantial flow of cash moving through it in order to maintain its own liquidity, and this cash flow can be attained only if the bank limits its lending activities to short-term maturities. Moreover, the theory argues, even short-term loans are not an appropriate object of bank lending unless they are backed up by real, physical,

---

[2]The definitive study of the commercial loan theory is Lloyd W. Mints, *A History of Banking Theory in Great Britain and the United States,* University of Chicago Press, Chicago, Ill., 1945.

tangible goods. For example, a bank should not make funds available to customers so that they can use them for speculating in the stock market. A bank should avoid making such loans because they increase the bank's risk exposure, and the bank is lending other people's money. There is no end to the trouble speculative loans can cause. As a committee of the Kentucky legislature put it in 1837: "The bill business is limited by the actual operations of commerce, while the accommodation business is as limitless as the want of money, the rage of speculation, or the spirit of gambling."

The commercial loan theory had as its primary objective the stabilization of the banking system. Remember that this theory reached its heyday during the nineteenth century, before the establishment of the Federal Reserve System and the FDIC. A bank had to remain liquid, solvent, and profitable on its own; there was no government agency charged with the responsibility of bailing it out if it got into trouble. Given the times, the real bills doctrine may well have been the best rule of thumb available for bankers to follow. Nevertheless, the commercial loan theory is flawed by serious misconceptions, both analytical and historical.

On a theoretical level, the most basic weakness of the real bills doctrine is that it misconceived the nature of what is and is not "real." It is true, of course, that an inventory of toys is real in the sense that toys are actual things that one can see and touch. But in fact the bank isn't making loans on the goods themselves. Rather, it is lending on the *value* of the goods, which is quite a different matter altogether. For the value of an inventory of toys may decrease even though the toys themselves remain unchanged. And if the price of the merchandise goes down far enough, the bank's loan becomes uncollectable, notwithstanding the fact that it is a "real bill." In short, there is a speculative element to any loan, whether or not it has as its immediate source real goods. Even had all banks adhered rigidly to the tenets of the commercial loan theory, therefore, they would nevertheless have been vulnerable to bankruptcy during the periodic depressions of the nineteenth century.

Not only was the real bills doctrine theoretically unsound, it also grew to be fundamentally out of touch with historical reality, particularly in the latter half of the nineteenth century.[3] By 1850 the industrial revolution in the United States was well underway. Heavy industry and manufacturing were growing rapidly, and the railroads were in the process of opening up the West for farming and ranching. This economic development of the country created heavy and insistent demands for long-term capital, demands that could be met only in part through the capital markets. As a consequence, banks were put under a great deal of pressure to make long-term loan commitments, particularly in the agrarian Midwest and South. The nation's commercial interests, however, which had long been associated with short-term credit and the real bills doctrine, recognized the threat to the stability of the banking system posed by long-term bank loans and urged the banks to resist this pressure. The banks got caught in the middle. The trouble was that both the industrial and commercial interests were right in their own way, but neither group was willing to admit the legitimacy of the other's position. The legitimate demand

---

[3]See Bray Hammond, "Long and Short-term Credit in Early American Banking," *Quarterly Journal of Economics,* November 1934.

for financing capital formation with long-term credit was regularly translated into attacks on the stability of the banking system; and the equally legitimate defense of the banking system was regularly translated into an attempt to strangle agriculture and small busienss. Much of the political history of the latter part of the nineteenth century—the inflationist *greenback* and *free-silver* movements, in particular—can be interpreted in these terms.

Faced with conflicting demands, many banks unwisely tried to compromise. They preserved the letter of the commercial loan theory but not its spirit. For example, it became common practice among some banks to write what were essentially long-term loans under the guise of a series of short-term loans that were automatically renewed at maturity. Needless to say, this sort of lip-service adherence to the dictates of the commercial loan theory just made matters worse. Bankers deceived not only their customers and examiners, but themselves as well. As a result, even greater instability was insinuated into the banking industry, an instability that was ultimately resolved only by the establishment of the FDIC in 1933.

The commercial loan theory, or real bills doctrine, has been a persistent theory of banking. Vestiges of it still remain in the structure of bank regulatory agencies, bank examination procedures, and the thinking of many bankers. One cannot understand contemporary banking without an understanding of our banking history, and one cannot understand banking history without an understanding of the commercial loan theory.

The Shiftability Theory

Beginning roughly at the turn of the century, a new theory of banking emerged in the American banking scene: the so-called *shiftability theory* of banking. It is necessary to take careful note of the fact that the shiftability theory did not replace the commercial loan theory in the sense that the latter was completely scrapped and held to be invalid. Instead, the shiftability theory took a more general view of the banking business by broadening the list of assets deemed legitimate for bank ownership. The shiftability theory does not say that commercial loans are inappropriate bank assets; it does say that commercial loans are not the *only* appropriate asset.

The central thesis of the shiftability theory may be stated very simply. This theory holds that the liquidity of a bank depends on its ability to shift its assets to someone else at a predictable price. Thus, for example, it would be quite acceptable for a bank to hold short-term open market investments in its portfolio of assets. If, under these circumstances, a large number of depositors should decide to withdraw their money, the bank need only sell these investments, take the money thus acquired, and pay off its depositors. In the words of one of the originators of the theory, "Liquidity is tantamount to shiftability."[4]

That the shiftability theory had a profound effect on banking practices can hardly be denied. What it did, basically, was to redirect the attention of bankers and the banking authorities from loans to investments as a source of bank liquidity.

[4]Harold G. Moulton, "Commercial Banking and Capital Formation," *Journal of Political Economy,* July 1918, p. 723.

Indeed, proponents of the theory argued that the liquidity of short-term, commercial loans was largely fictional in any case. If a meat processer, they said, was financed by a bank during the time it took to process the meat, then *that* loan was terminated at maturity. But then the wholesale distributor of the meat required short-term financing from some other bank, so that, in effect, the first bank's loan had just been shifted to the second bank. Thus, the author cited previously also observed: "In ordinary times the problem of liquidity is not a problem of maturing loans so much as it is a problem of shifting assets to other banks in exchange for cash."[5] A bank holding short-term money market instruments such as Treasurey bills or call loans is actually in a better position to shift its assets than a bank holding customer notes, since the open market debt can be sold before maturity if necessary. The liquidity position of a bank consequently came to be closely associated with the amount of money market instruments it was holding—so-called *secondary reserves.*

In the early 1900s only a handful of banks made use of the shiftability theory in their management practices. The reason the number of banks was small was primarily the lack of an adequate volume of money market instruments capable of serving as secondary reserves. But World War I in 1917 resulted in a substantial growth in the public debt and the subsequent issuing of Treasury bills by the federal government, an instrument that was almost perfectly suited to the shiftability theory. Additionally, call loans, secured by stock exchange collateral and repayable on demand, came much into vogue in the 1920s. These two instruments made it possible for virtually all banks to switch to the management practice of shiftability, and by the 1940s the commercial loan theory had been broadly supplemented by the shiftability theory.

As with the commercial loan theory, however, the shiftability theory contained a serious flaw. (Actually, this flaw did not lie so much in the theory itself—it was well understood by the various writers on the subject—as it did in the bank management practices to which the theory led.) The defect of the theory was simply this: Although *one* bank could obtain needed liquidity by shifting its assets, the same thing was not true of *all* banks taken together. This is what logicians call the *fallacy of composition,* that is, the supposition that what is true when one member of a set behaves in a certain way will continue to be true when all members of a set behave that way. For, clearly, *all* banks cannot gain additional cash reserves by shifting their earning assets to each other, just as we cannot all earn a living by taking in one another's wash. The problem became acute, of course, only in times of crisis. But the crisis—the worst one of them all—finally came in 1929–1933. It is elementary that for every seller there must be a buyer. But in 1929–1933, all the banks wanted to be sellers and none of them wanted to buy. What was needed was some agency outside the banking system with the ability to pour massive doses of liquid reserves into *all* banks by buying what they all wanted to sell. This was, indeed, the role for which the Federal Reserve System had been designed and which it should have played. But the Federal Reserve, to put it charitably, behaved with excessive timidity in the early 1930s; to put it uncharitably, they acted perversely. However

[5] *Ibid.*

put, the result was that the necessary liquidity was not forthcoming, and literally thousands of banks failed throughout the country.

Nevertheless, after the banking crisis was over, the banking system once again reverted to management practices based on the concept of asset shiftability. Nor was it unreasonable of them to do so. The problem of the liquidity of the whole banking system is simply not solvable by commercial banks alone. A central bank, such as the Federal Reserve, that is prepared to act quickly and decisively, is an absolute necessity.

The Anticipated Income Theory

In the late 1940s a new theory of banking became prominent in the United States: the *anticipated income theory*. [6] Properly understood, this theory was a rival only to the commercial loan theory, not to the shiftability theory. It did not question the shiftability view that a bank's most fundamental source of liquidity is its secondary reserves. Rather, it again focused attention on the types of loans appropriate for a bank to make but came to quite a different conclusion than that reached by the advocates of the commercial loan theory. For the anticipated income theory, in contrast with the commercial loan theory, concluded that it was quite all right for a bank to make long-term and nonbusiness loans. In reaching this conclusion, the theory delivered the *coup de grace* to the real bills doctrine.

Recall that the commercial loan theory holds that a bank should make only *self-liquidating* loans. According to the anticipated income theory, there is no such thing as a self-liquidating loan. Goods will not sell themselves, nor is there any guarantee that the goods will be as valuable tomorrow as they are today. Instead, even a "real bill" is repaid out of the future earnings of the borrower, that is, out of anticipated income. But if anticipated or future income is the true source of bank-loan repayment, then there is no reason to confine bank lending to the traditional commercial loan. What is critically at issue is the borrower's ability to repay the loan out of future earnings, nothing more. Thus, under the anticipated income thoery, it became acceptable for banks to engage in a much broader range of lending. Specifically, banks began to make long-term loans to businesses, consumer installment loans, and amortized real estate mortgage loans. Today, these three categories constitute well over half of all commercial bank loans.

8-4 BANKING THEORY: CONTEMPORARY

The three theories of banking discussed in the previous section all have one thing in common: They deal exclusively with the asset side of a bank's balance sheet. This preoccupation with assets is typical of the traditional view of a bank as being a passive accepter of liabilities. In other words, historically a bank has been thought of as having no control over the size or mix of its liabilities; it simply waits patiently

[6]See Herbert V. Prochnow, *Term Loans and Theories of Banking,* Prentice-Hall, Inc., New York, 1949.

for customers to bring money to it and then gives them whatever kind of deposit they want—demand deposit, savings deposit, and so on. Several significant developments in banking practices during the 1960s radically changed this traditional view of banking. Out of these new practices emerged a new theory, the *liability management theory* of banking.

The Liability Management Theory

Liability management is something of a misnomer. It does not mean that the bank manages *only* its liabilities and is passive with respect to its assets. Rather, the theory continues to recognize that the asset structure of the bank has a prominent role to play in providing the bank with liquidity. But the theory goes beyond this one-dimensional approach to liquidity and argues that the bank can also use its liabilities for liquidity purposes.

How can a bank manage its liabilities so that they actually become a source of liquidity? The short answer is that when the bank needs money, it "just goes out and buys it." But this answer is *too* short; it does not adequately convey the fundamental nature of the change in banking practices caused by the concept of liability management.

Consider, first, why a bank wants liquidity. We have already mentioned one reason: deposit withdrawals. A bank is, of course, legally required to pay its demand deposits whenever its customers want them, which alone is sufficient to dictate the bank's concern for liquidity. But there is also a second reason why a bank needs liquidity, a reason which, while not a legal necessity, is almost equally as compelling: The bank needs to be able to meet the reasonable loan requests of its customers. Not only are bank loans very profitable, but a bank that won't or can't make loans to its depositors when they need funds is not likely to keep those depositors for very long.

Now suppose that for either or both these reasons—a sudden drop in deposits and/or a sudden demand for loans—a bank finds itself in need of ready cash. What does it do? As we have seen, traditional approaches to banking would suggest that the bank sell secondary reserve assets—for example, Treasury bills and bankers acceptances. In contrast, the liability management approach would suggest that the bank *borrow* the funds it needs. How? By means of the various bank-related money market instruments: federal funds, negotiable certificates of deposit, and Eurodollars. For example, the bank might borrow federal funds and then use this money to take care of unexpected deposit withdrawals; or it might issue new CDs and then lend the money thus acquired to accommodate the loan demands of good customers. It is in this sense that the bank "just goes out and buys" the liquidity it needs. It almost literally borrows from Peter to pay, or lend to, Paul. And as long as Paul is willing to pay a higher rate of interest than Peter is charging, why not? This kind of intermediation is good business from the bank's viewpoint.

As with the theories discussed previously, banking theory and practice interacted with one another in the development of the liability management concept of banking. Liability management began with the rapid growth of the federal funds market in the late 1950s. Although trading in federal funds dates back to the 1920s, the market was dormant during the 1930s and 1940s. In the 1950s and 1960s, however, banks were put under heavy pressure to meet the credit demands of customers and, as a consequence, once again began borrowing reserves from each other. As the market became strong and active, banks increasingly began to view it as a ready source of cash, an alternative to selling secondary reserves. Negotiable CDs were the next liability instrument developed by the banking system. From virtually nothing in early 1961, the volume of CDs rose to $18 billion in 1966. Where the federal funds market gave banks an easy channel for borrowing from one another, the development of the CD market gave banks ready access to nonbank funds; that is, CDs could be sold to corporations, state and local governments, and private individuals. Eurodollar borrowing, which became prominent in the mid 1960s, added the ability to borrow internationally.

The practice of liability management may eventually have profound consequences for the structure of American commercial banking. It is a concept that is well suited to large banks but poorly suited to small banks. A small bank simply does not have the necessary access to the money market needed to engage in liability management as a routine matter (although it can to some extent do so indirectly through its city correspondent). And note that, within limits, the practice of liability management permits a bank to determine its own size. Liability management may thus ultimately lead to increasing both the qualitative and quantitative differences between large and small banks.

Modeling Bank Behavior

So what else is new in banking theory? Increasingly, banks are making use of financial *models* to help guide them in their decision-making process. The word "model," used in this context, means simply that the relationships between and among the bank's assets and liabilities are specified in mathematical terms, with the end goal of making the bank more profitable. Once the basic model is developed, statistical analysis is used to take it out of the realm of the abstract and put it into the concrete world of reality so that the bank can use it. The bank may use the model, for example, by programming it onto a high-speed computer and then seeing what the consequences of various alternative choices might be.

In the nature of the case, bank models are complicated. Their whole purpose is to give bankers a means of handling numerous, subtle, and simultaneous interactions among their balance-sheet items, interactions much too complex to be worked out mentally or on the back of an old envelope. Both the mathematical and statistical methods used in these models are consequently too advanced to be discussed here. But perhaps the general idea of bank *model building* can be conveyed to the reader through the use of an example. (Keep in mind that the example is for illustrative purposes only and is not meant to be realistic.)

Suppose that you are a banker and that you know that tomorrow an outstanding loan in the amount of $X will be repaid. You have two choices as to what to do with the money. You can lend it out in the municipal securities market at a net (after-tax) yield of i_m percent. Alternatively, you can lend it to customers at an after-tax yield of i_c percent. To keep the problem from degenerating into the trivial matter of choosing the highest net rate of interest, let us also add the following condition: If you *don't* make the customer loans, some of your customers will get mad and withdraw their deposits. We may express this deposit loss as a fraction a of the potential customer loans; thus the deposit paydown resulting from *not* making the customer loans will be aX.

We can now state the two choices open to you in abstract algebraic terms:

1 If you put the money into customer loans, you will earn i_cX, that is, the net customer loan rate times the number of dollars invested.
2 If you put the money into the municipal securities market, you will earn $i_m(\$X - \$aX)$, that is, the net return on the amount put into municipal securities, where this amount is less than $\$X$ by the number of dollars used to take care of the deposit withdrawal ($\$aX$).

The question is, Is $\$i_cX$ greater than, equal to, or less than $i_m(\$X - \$aX)$?

In order to answer this question, it is necessary to *quantify* the problem by moving from the abstract realm of algebra to the concrete world of actual numbers. We do this by using accounting and market information and statistical methods. By checking our books and the current market, for example, we might find that $\$X = \$1$ million, $i_m = 6$ percent, and $i_c = 5$ percent. By using regression analysis, we might estimate that $a = \frac{1}{4}$. Plugging these numbers into the algebraic expression then gives

$$\$i_cX = .05(\$1 \text{ million})$$
$$= \$50,000$$
$$i_m(\$X - \$aX) = .06[\$1 \text{ million} - \frac{1}{4}(\$1 \text{ million})]$$
$$= \$45,000$$

If this were all there were to it, clearly we would be better off putting the money into the customer loan market.

Although this example is simplistic, it does highlight some of the major features of bank models: the estimation of cash flows through the bank, the need for accurate cost and market information, the interdependence between the asset and liability sides of the bank's balance sheet, and the bank's goal of profit maximization. If to these considerations we add liquidity and solvency constraints, a multitude of other possible choices, regulations imposed by the banking authorities, and so on, and then try to conceive of the whole thing within a probabilistic framework, the reader may begin to catch some of the flavor of bank models.

But the reader may nevertheless have a puzzlement. In what sense do models of banks constitute a *theory* of banking, comparable to the real bills doctrine? The answer is that all banking theories try to establish rules of behavior for banks under various possible circumstances. The commercial loan theory tells bankers what kind of loans to make; the shiftability theory indicates appropriate investments; liability management rationalizes the buying of liquidity; and so forth. The only difference between these theories and banking models is that the latter try to consider the bank as a whole, that is, as a multidimensional unit with a wide variety of choices open to it. The traditional concerns of bankers for liquidity, solvency, and profits are not ignored. Rather, they are built into the models, and the models are then used to help the banker choose the best path for attaining and reconciling these goals.

A final word of caution: Bank model building is still in its formative stages. No definitive model has as yet been developed—no model that everyone would agree is an accurate representation of a bank. A great deal of research continues to be needed in this field. But if and when such a model is developed, it will continue to be an aid to, not a substitute for, thinking. Creative bank management will remain an art.[7]

8-5 LIQUIDITY OF THE BANKING SYSTEM

One point already made in this chapter needs to be repeated for emphasis: The problem of the liquidity of the individual bank is quite different from the problem of the liquidity of the banking *system.* A particular bank can acquire needed liquidity from any one of the variety of sources discussed in our survey of banking theory. But ultimately all these sources trace back to some other bank, which must give up the liquidity that the first bank gets. The banking *system,* that is, cannot increase its *total* liquidity by purchasing federal funds, selling Treasury bills, or anything else. The system can acquire liquidity only through some outside agency, an agency that can "create" bank liquidity when, as, and if needed. This agency is the central bank; in the United States, it is the Federal Reserve System. How and why the Federal Reserve creates bank liquidity is clearly a matter of great importance and will constitute the main theme of the last half of this book (Parts Six through Nine).

8-6 REVIEW QUESTIONS

1 Draw up your own personal balance sheet, listing all your assets (money owed you, value of your car, clothes, and so forth) and all your liabilities (debts). What is your net worth?
2 When it was originally established in 1914, the Federal Reserve *rediscounted* bills for commercial banks, that is, bought such things as bankers acceptances from commercial banks at a discount. What theory of banking does this sound like? Why?
3 Why may liability management have different effects on large and small banks?
4 Has the development of the negotiable CD market eliminated the problem of liquidity for the banking *system?* Why or why not?

---

[7]For a good discussion by a commercial banker of both the benefits and limitations of bank models, see George W. McKinney, Jr., "A Perspective on the Use of Models in the Management of Bank Funds," *Journal of Bank Research,* Summer 1977, pp. 122–126.

9

Bank Management: Liabilities and Capital

We move now from the rarefied atmosphere of banking theory to the workaday world of the individual commercial banker. What sorts of problems beset the banker in the course of an ordinary day? What kinds of decisions must be made routinely? And what tools may be used to implement these decisions?

9-1 SOURCES AND USES OF BANK FUNDS

Because the activities of commercial bankers have such fundamental and widespread implications for the behavior of the economy, at times one might be tempted to forget that they are business men and women and think of them as a kind of public servant. Unlike most temptations, this one should be resisted. Bankers are interested in earning a living by making a profit for their stockholders. And like other people in business, the activities of bankers can be usefully classified into two categories:

the getting and spending of money. In high-class financial circles, it is customary to dress up this somewhat grubby phrase by calling it the *sources and uses of funds.*

A full explanation of what is meant by the sources and uses of funds in a formal accounting sense would take us too far afield for our limited purposes here. But the general idea can be readily understood by performing the following imaginary experiment: Think of a bank as a business with a certain amount of cash in its vaults. Now mentally list all of the bank's *other* balance-sheet items,[1] and in each case ask yourself if an *increase* in the item would increase or decrease the bank's vault cash. If an increase in the item would increase the bank's cash, then the item is a *source* of funds to the bank; if an increase in the item would decrease the bank's cash, then it is a *use* of bank funds. For example, an increase in the bank's deposits is a source since a deposit of funds increases the bank's cash, and an increase in the bank's loans is a use since lending draws down the bank's cash.

If you now take a sheet of paper and list all the sources of bank funds in one column and all the uses of funds in another, you will notice an interesting thing: Under "Sources of Funds" you will have listed all the bank's liability and capital items, and under "Uses of Funds" you will have listed all its asset items. In short, you will have duplicated the balance sheet you began with, except that changes in *assets* are now called *uses* and changes in *liabilities and capital* are now called *sources.* The purpose of the experiment, of course, is to make precisely this point. But the game is not a trivial one, designed only to test the reader's patience. For in performing the experiment you will have gained two insights: First, you now have

Table 9–1   Principal Assets, Liabilities, and Capital Accounts of United States Commercial Banks, March 20, 1978 (Billions of Dollars)

Assets	
Cash assets	131.4
Investments	
United States Treasury securities	97.9
Other securities	159.2
Loans	677.2
Other	68.9
Total assets	1,134.6
Liabilities and capital accounts	
Demand deposits	
Interbank	37.6
United States government	4.8
Other	279.4
Time deposits	
Interbank	9.1
Other	561.5
Borrowings	107.3
Capital accounts	83.2
Other	51.7
Total liabilities and capital accounts	1,134.6

Source: *Federal Reserve Bulletin*, April 1978, p. A16. Figures partly estimated.

[1]Vault cash is a use of funds, of course.

an alternative and meaningful interpretation of the nature of a balance sheet; and second, you should now have a more intuitive understanding of the nature of banking. In the long run a bank *gets* money (source) from its capital and liabilities accounts and *spends* this money (use) on its asset accounts. It is the interest earned on these assets that constitutes the main source of a bank's earnings, or profits. The major categories of the balance-sheet items of the United States commercial banking system are shown in Table 9-1.

Because the balance sheet is both a meaningful and familiar system of classification, the discussion of banking in the remainder of this chapter will be organized along similar lines. Before beginning this discussion, however, a few warnings to the reader seem in order. First, the reader should be clear about exactly what it means to say that a change in a liability is a source of funds and a change in an asset a use of funds. It means that if a liability item goes *up,* the bank's resources also go *up.* But the reverse is also true: If a liability item goes *down,* the bank's resources go *down.* In other words, liabilities and resources vary in the same direction, and assets and bank resources vary in opposite directions. In the long run, over a period of years, the liabilities of the banking system will grow as the economy grows, and hence *on the average* liabilities will be a source of funds, and assets a use of funds. But in the short run, on a day-to-day basis, liabilities and assets may move in either direction, and hence each may be both a source and a use of funds. Thus a fall in the demand deposits of the bank (deposit withdrawals) will use bank resources, and a decrease in bank loans (loan repayments) will be a source of funds to the bank. In short, a negative use is a source, and a negative source is a use.

On a day-to-day operating level, it is the banker's job to constantly juggle all these daily asset and liability changes so that the bank's goals of liquidity, solvency, and profitability are achieved. This brings us to the second warning to the reader:

Table 9-2   Controllable and Uncontrollable Factors in Short-Run Bank Adjustments

---

Controllable balance sheet items

Excess cash reserves (asset)
Open market investments (assets)*
Negotiable certificates of deposit (liability)
Borrowing from the Federal Reserve (liability)
Federal funds (liability)

Partially controllable balance sheet items

Loans (assets)
Correspondent balances (asset)

Uncontrollable balance sheet items

Cash items in the process of collection (asset)
Demand deposits (liability)
Time and savings deposits, except negotiable CDs (liabilities)
Capital accounts (capital)

---

*Some of the bank's open market investments are pledged against the repayment of specific deposits. These investments are not available for sale by the bank in the short run. See page 161 for a discussion of these *secured deposits.*

In the short run, all balance-sheet items are not equally under the banker's control. Changes in demand deposits, for example, are something that, from the workaday viewpoint of the individual banker, "just happen." Although the bank may be able to *predict* deposit fluctuations, it cannot *control* them. Changes in the bank's holdings of Treasury bills, on the contrary, are wholly under the control of the bank; within the limits set by its size, it can buy and sell exactly as many of these as it wants. In addition to the "sources and uses" classification of balance-sheet items, therefore, it is equally revealing to classify these items according to the degree of short-run bank control over them. This is done in Table 9-2. Note that the classification of Table 9-2 is not unambiguous. That is, there are some items over which the bank has some control, but not complete control. The most conspicuous of these is bank loans. It may seem strange to suggest that the bank lacks complete control over the size of its loan portfolio, but it is nevertheless true—although not in a legal sense, of course. Legally, the bank may refuse a loan to anyone at any time. But as a practical matter, the bank is obliged to take care of the loan needs of many of its customers.

Viewed together, Tables 9-1 and 9-2 explain a great deal about both the long-run and short-run behavior of the typical commercial bank. In the long run (Table 9-1), the bank earns a profit for its owners by expanding its liabilities (sources) and using the funds thus acquired to buy assets (uses). In the short run (Table 9-2), the bank manages those items over which it has control to adjust to fluctuations in those items over which it does not have control. It is this latter activity in particular that requires most of the skill needed to manage a commercial bank.

9-2 THE BANK'S CAPITAL ACCOUNTS

As explained previously in Chapter 8, the equity, or ownership, of a bank's stockholders is represented by the bank's *capital accounts.* The capital accounts are subdivided into four categories: capital stock, surplus, undivided profits, and other. The *capital stock* of a bank is a dollar amount calculated by multiplying the number of shares of the bank's common stock outstanding by the par value of each share.[2] Thus if a bank has issued 2,000 shares of stock at a par value of $100 per share, its capital stock account will be $200,000. The *par value* of the bank's stock is simply the value of a share of stock stated on the face of the share. It should not be confused with the market value of the stock, which is the price the stock will actually fetch in the market.

A bank's *surplus* account is a legal category, not to be confused with the paid-in or earned surplus account of other business firms. It represents an assignment of bank profits to a special account and is meant to give extra protection to depositors (see page 157). The *undivided profits* of a bank are what other businesses call earned surplus. These are the past profits of a bank that have been *retained* or plowed back into the business. The *other* category of bank capital accounts represents a variety

---

[2]Banks also have subordinated capital notes and debentures outstanding. These have a claim on bank earnings prior to equity interests but do not have voting privileges in managing the bank. The amount of such notes and debentures is relatively small, representing only about 7 percent of total capital accounts and about ½ percent of total assets. They are used primarily by large banks.

of special accounts, such as reserves for bad debts and dividends declared but not yet paid to shareholders.

Purpose of Bank Capital

Bank regulatory authorities traditionally have been concerned with the size of a bank's capital relative to the size of the bank. The reason for this concern is that the capital accounts have traditionally been viewed as representing a buffer between the mismanagement of the bank and losses suffered by depositors. Consider, for example, a bank with $9 million of deposits, $10 million of assets, and $1 million of capital accounts. Such a bank can undergo a shrinkage (through making bad loans, and so forth) of $1 million in the value of its assets and still be able to pay its depositors in full. In other words, the authorities' concern about bank capital is basically a concern about the solvency of banks—their potential for paying off their debts (deposits) during hard times. Obviously, the larger a bank's capital accounts are relative to its assets, the safer the bank is for depositors.

This way of viewing the capital accounts has led to a number of regulatory devices having bank capital as their focal point. One such device, for example, is the minimum capital requirements of federal and state laws relating to the chartering of new banks. These laws typically require progressively higher capital for a bank, the larger the size of the town in which it does business. Another such provision is that national banks are prohibited from paying dividends to their stockholders until they have built up a surplus account at least equal to the size of their capital stock.

Trends in Bank Capital

Since the regulatory authorities are motivated largely by a desire to protect the interest of the depositing public, they have traditionally favored high capital/asset ratios for commercial banks. The difficulty with this attitude is that it tends to run directly counter to the interest of the banks. Bank shareholders, like other business people, are concerned with managing their affairs so as to maximize their *profit rate.* Generally speaking, the profit rate is simply the ratio of bank earnings to invested capital. The usual way of increasing this ratio is to increase earnings. But it is also possible—and this is particularly true in banking—to increase the ratio by decreasing its denominator, that is, by decreasing the amount of capital invested in the business. As a consequence, there has been a strong long-run tendency in banking for the capital/asset ratio of banks to decline. For example, in 1900 the average capital/asset ratio of all commercial banks in the United States was about 20 percent; by 1978 the ratio had fallen to about 7 percent. The question is, Who is right—the banking authorities or the banks? How much capital is enough capital?

Adequacy of Bank Capital

When you think about it for a moment, it becomes apparent that the question of enough capital cannot be answered with a single number like 10 percent of assets. The answer has to be more complicated if for no other reason than that banks differ from one another in many respects besides size. Thus if the purpose of bank capital is to offer some measure of protection to depositors, one would immediately think that the safer a bank is in other respects, the lower its capital/asset ratio might be permitted to be. This line of reasoning has led to a variety of measures that attempt a more sophisticated analysis of the adequacy of bank capital than the somewhat simplistic capital/asset ratio. We shall describe briefly three such measures.

The Capital/Risk-Asset Ratio   The first attempt at a more sophisticated answer to the question of "enough" capital came about largely as a response to the very substantial rise in bank-held government securities during World War II. In general, bankers argued that the increased percentage of their assets held in the form of government securities made them much safer repositories of depositors' funds. Consequently, the bankers said, they should be permitted lower capital/asset ratios. Out of this line of reasoning grew a new measure of capital adequacy, the *capital/ risk-asset ratio*. By *risk assets* is meant all assets that are neither United States government securities nor cash. Using this measure, those banks with fewer loans and more cash and government securities than other banks would be permitted smaller capital accounts relative to their size. Many banking authorities—in particular, the Comptroller of the Currency and some state authorities—accepted this argument as valid and subsequently used it in their examination procedures.

The Secondary Risk-Asset Ratio   Although the capital/risk-asset ratio is an improvement over the capital/asset ratio, it is nevertheless an arbitrary measure. What is arbitrary about it is the definition of risk assets as all assets except cash and United States government securities. For why should United States government securities be considered "riskless" and loans guaranteed by the United States government (for example, VA mortgages) *not* be considered riskless? There is obviously a problem of consistency of definition here. Many assets held by banks may be considered virtually as riskless as government securities. Federal funds, loans collateralized by government securities, passbook savings loans, and so on, involve virtually no risk of default insofar as the bank is concerned. Therefore why not also exclude them from risk assets? Following this line of reasoning (and under pressure from the banks), many supervisory authorities began calculating a *secondary risk-asset ratio,* which also defined these types of assets as riskless.

The secondary risk-asset ratio is generally used as a supplement to, rather than a substitute for, the more conventional risk-asset ratio. That is, in examining a bank, the examiner first calculates the capital/risk-asset ratio. If this ratio is "in line" with the average ratio of other banks, then no further calculations are made. But if it is below the average, this ratio is not taken as absolute proof that the bank has inadequate capital accounts. Instead, the secondary risk-asset ratio is calculated, and if this ratio is high enough, it can be used to compensate for the low capital/risk-asset ratio. In other words, government-guaranteed loans can be used as a partial offset to a lack of government securities.

The Uniform Interagency Bank Rating System   In 1978, the three federal bank-regulatory agencies began using a new system for evaluating banks—the Uniform Interagency Rating System (UIRS). Since one of the federal regulatory agencies using the UIRS was the FDIC, it is applicable to virtually every bank in the country.

The UIRS does not focus exclusively on the adequacy of bank capital. Instead, it is concerned with the overall soundness of the bank, of which capital adequacy is only a part. The other aspects of the bank that are considered in rating soundness are: the quality of the bank's assets, the ability of the bank's management, bank earnings, and the liquidity of the bank. These five areas of the bank are given a numerical score, and then a "composite rating" from 1 through 5 is computed, with 1 being the best and 5 being the weakest.

With respect to capital adequacy specifically, examiners are required to assess the bank's current position with respect to such things as the volume of risk assets, the loan-loss experience of the bank, and recent growth experience and prospects for the future. Additionally, the access of the bank to capital markets may be taken into account. While it is too early to make a judgment about how well the UIRS will work out, it does seem a sensible approach to rate the bank on many different bases, rather than just one.

One final point should be made about the measures of capital adequacy just discussed: In general, what is deemed "adequate" depends on the average of all banks, not on some absolute standard. The fundamental rule of thumb for a bank is that it "stay in line" with other banks. In banking, as elsewhere, it seems, there is safety in numbers.

9-3 COMMERCIAL BANK PROFITS

A story that is currently popular among accounting majors is that when you are asked in a job interview, "How much is two and two?" the correct answer is not "Four" but, "What number would you like?" The story isn't true, of course, but it does illustrate a point that needs to be made in any discussion of bank profits: The concept of *profits,* although seemingly simple, is in practice rather vague. Profits can be measured in a number of different ways, and each way has some logical support. Probably the most commonly used measure is the *rate of return on capital,* which is the ratio of net income (after taxes) to capital. Thus:

$$\text{Profits} = \text{rate of return on capital} = \frac{\text{net income}}{\text{capital}}$$

Note that, since both *net income* and *capital* are dollar amounts, their ratio is a rate, or percent. The behavior of this percentage figure over the period 1963–1976 is shown in Figure 9-1.

Figure 9-1 indicates that bank profits have tended to rise since the 1960s, and have fluctuated quite a bit in the 1970s. What has caused this movement in bank profits? We can gain some insight into this question by reworking the previous equation.

$$\begin{aligned} \text{Profits} &= \left(\frac{\text{net income}}{\text{capital}}\right)\left(\frac{\text{assets}}{\text{assets}}\right) \\ &= \left(\frac{\text{net income}}{\text{assets}}\right)\left(\frac{\text{assets}}{\text{capital}}\right) \\ &= \frac{\text{net income/assets}}{\text{capital/assets}} \end{aligned}$$

This new form of the equation gives us profits expressed as the consequence of two other ratios. The ratio in the denominator is our old friend the capital/asset ratio, discussed in the previous section. The ratio in the numerator indicates the average rate of return that banks make on their total assets. Clearly, anything which increases the numerator or decreases the donominator will increase the profit rate. Figure 9-2 shows the behavior of these two ratios for the same period as shown in Figure 9-1.

The behavior of the two ratios shown in Figure 9-2 illustrates very nicely the dependency of bank profits on the capital/asset ratio. Note, in the first place, the long-run tendency of this ratio to decline. Thus, during the late 1960s and early 1970s, two factors were at work increasing bank profits: a declining capital/asset ratio and a rising ratio of net bank income to bank assets. This latter ratio was rising because of generally higher interest rates, and because of a shift in the *composition* of bank assets from low-yielding United States government securities to high-yielding loans. In the latter part of the 1970s, however, the return on bank assets generally stabilized, while the capital/asset ratio rose slightly. The consequence was the decline in bank profits shown in Figure 9-1.

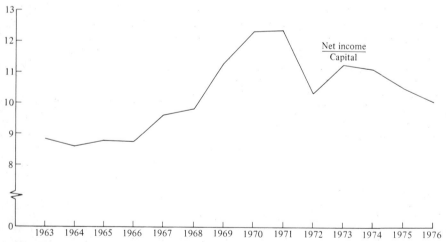

Figure 9-1   Ratio of net income to capital accounts, insured commercial banks, 1963–1976 (percent). *(Source: 1973–1976 net income data from* Federal Reserve Bulletin, *July 1977, p. 634; 1973, 1974 capital data from* Federal Reserve Bulletin, *January 1976, p. A14; 1975, 1976 capital data from* Federal Reserve Bulletin, *July 1977, p. A16; other data from previous issues.)*

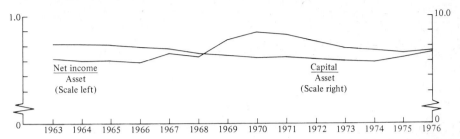

Figure 9-2 Net income/asset and capital/asset ratios, insured commercial banks, 1963–1976 (percent). *(Sources: Data for net income and capital from* Federal Reserve Bulletin, *July 1977, p. 634; 1973, 1974 asset data from* Federal Reserve Bulletin, *January 1976, p. A14; 1975, 1976 asset data from* Federal Reserve Bulletin, *July 1977, p. A16.*

9-4 COMMERCIAL BANK LIABILITIES

It may sound a bit odd, but it is nevertheless the case that the profitability of banking depends on the ability of banks to go into debt—the bigger their debts, the more their profits. The reason for this, of course, is that banks earn interest on their assets, and, in general, the amount of their assets is limited by the amount of their liabilities. All of this is simply another way of saying that in the long run the liabilities of banks are their major sources of funds. These liabilities can be classified into two categories: bank deposits and bank borrowings.

Bank Deposits

As the "department stores of finance," banks offer a wide product line of deposits for sale to consumers, businesses, and governments. These deposits may be classified in a number of meaningful ways. Probably the most familiar of these is to distinguish among deposits by term to maturity—basically, to distinguish among demand deposits and the various time deposits.

    Demand Deposits The demand deposits of commercial banks in the United States can be classified into five categories: *interbank deposits; United States government deposits; state and local governments' deposits; deposits of individuals, partnerships, and corporations;* and *other.* Table 9-3 gives the breakdown of total demand deposits into these categories as of September 30, 1977.

    Interbank deposits are the deposits held by one bank in another bank, that is, the *correspondent* balances discussed at the end of Chapter 2. As indicated previously, these balances are held because they are mutually advantageous for both the depositing *(respondent)* bank and the recipient *(correspondent)* bank. The *United States government deposits* in commercial banks are referred to by banks as their *tax and loan* (T&L) accounts because they arise from the governmental processes of taxation and borrowing. The United States government does not actually write checks against the T&L accounts, but instead it first transfers the funds from

Table 9-3   Demand Deposits of Insured Commercial Banks, September 30, 1977
(Millions of Dollars)

Type of deposit	Amount	Percent of total
Interbank deposits		
Domestic	$ 34,016	10
Foreign	6,713	2
United States government deposits	5,279	2
State and local governments' deposits	16,719	5
Deposits of individuals, partnerships, and		
corporations (IPC deposits)	255,804	76
Other	16,349	5
Total demand deposits	$334,880	100

Source: Federal Reserve Bulletin, April 1978, p. A19.

commercial banks to the Federal Reserve System and then writes checks against the Federal Reserve account. The reason for this rather peculiar bookkeeping arrangement is to prevent the periodic collection of taxes and loan flotations from seriously depleting the cash reserves of the banking system. If the U.S. Treasury were to take all the money it collects at income-tax time and deposit it directly into its Federal Reserve account, there would be a sudden and sharp transfer of deposits from commercial banks to the Federal Reserve. So, instead of doing this, the Treasury keeps the money in T&L accounts until it is ready to spend it. The *state and local governments' deposits* are obviously the deposits of various political subdivisions (including school districts, and so on) other than the United States government. The *other* category of Table 9-3 consists largely of certain special accounts, such as certified and cashiers' checks.

As can be seen from Table 9-3, by far the largest category of demand deposits is held by individuals, partnerships, and corporations—so-called *IPC deposits*. Table 9-4 gives a further breakdown of the ownership of the IPC deposits. Nonfinancial corporate business firms own about one-half of these deposits, with "consumers" owning about another third. As one would expect, studies indicate that on the average consumer deposits are much smaller than business accounts. Nonfinancial corporate deposits account for only 11 percent of the *number* of deposits while consumers account for about 80 percent.

Secured Deposits   All United States government deposits and many state and local deposits in commercial banks are *secured,* which means that certain assets of the bank are pledged against the payment of these deposits. If the bank were to go bankrupt, these assets would be sold and the money would be used to pay off these deposit liabilities. In this way, the government is a preferred creditor of the bank —it gets paid in full, and other depositors have to share what's left. The most usual asset pledged against secured deposits is United States government securities. Municipal securities are also sometimes used.

Table 9–4   Ownership of IPC Demand Deposits, December 1977
(Billions of Dollars)

Owner	Amount	Percent of total
Financial business	$ 25.0	9
Nonfinancial business	142.9	52
Consumer	91.0	33
Foreign	2.5	1
All other	12.9	5
Total demand deposits	$274.4	100

Source: Federal Reserve Bulletin, April 1978, p. A25; numbers may not sum due to rounding.

Time and Savings Deposits   Unlike demand deposits, which are generally homogeneous in type, time and savings deposits are offered in a variety of different forms. Their common characteristics are that they pay a rate of interest and that the bank may require a waiting period before the deposits can be withdrawn. There are three basic forms of the time and savings deposits: *passbook savings deposits; time certificates of deposit;* and *time deposits, open account.*

Passbook savings deposits (or just *savings deposits*) are probably the most familiar of the various interest-bearing accounts held by commercial banks. They are held predominantly by individuals and generally contain no more than a few thousand dollars. There is no specific maturity on savings deposits, and, in practice, funds deposited in these accounts may be added to and withdrawn at the convenience of the depositor. Savings deposits typically pay a lower rate of interest than any of the time accounts.

Certificates of deposit are evidences (certificates) that a person or corporation has deposited a specified sum of money in a bank. The most basic characteristics of these accounts are that the owners of the deposited funds cannot withdraw their money for at least thirty days (usually longer), and that the certificates are sold by the bank in fixed denominations, such as $1,000, $5,000, and $100,000. One type of certificate of deposit was described in Chapter 7: the *negotiable certificate of deposit,* a bank-issued money market instrument. There are also *nonnegotiable certificates of deposit.* The basic difference between the two is that a negotiable CD may be sold before maturity by the original depositor while a nonnegotiable CD may not; that is, the original purchaser of a nonnegotiable CD is the only one who can cash it in. Nonnegotiable CDs are frequently tailored to the needs of a particular bank customer and sometimes permit premature redemption providing the holder is willing to accept some kind of penalty, such as a partial loss of interest.

The main difference between a certificate of deposit and a *time deposit, open account,* is that with the latter account the amount of money on deposit is not set by the bank. In other words, the word "open" in *open account* means that depositors may add to their deposits at their option. The rules concerning no withdrawals until maturity are enforced, however. Table 9-5 gives the data on the various types of time

Table 9-5 Types of Time and Savings Deposits Held by Insured Commercial Banks on January 25, 1978 (Millions of Dollars)

Type of deposit	Amount	Percent of total
Savings deposits	$218,539	39.9
IRA and Keogh Plan time deposits with original maturities of 3 years or more	2,084	0.4
Other interest-bearing time deposits in denominations of less than $100,000	166,717	30.4
Interest-bearing time deposits in denominations of $100,000 or more	156,122	28.5
Non-interest-bearing time deposits* in denominations of:		
Less than $100,000	692	0.1
$100,000 or more	3,327	0.6
Club accounts (Christmas savings, vacation, or similar club accounts)	813	0.1
Total time and savings deposits	$548,294	100.0

* Non-interest-bearing time deposits are principally escrow accounts and compensating balances held against loans.
Source: Federal Reserve Bulletin, May 1978, p. 368.

and savings accounts owned by individuals, partnerships, and corporations. Note that savings accounts, despite their lower interest rates, nevertheless make up almost 40 percent of the total.

Interest Rates on Time and Savings Deposits As discussed in Chapter 4, commercial banks are currently prohibited by law from paying interest on demand deposits. However, they do pay interest on time and savings deposits. These rates of interest are regulated with respect to the maximum amounts that banks are permitted to pay. The maximum rates are set by the Federal Reserve for member banks and by the FDIC for insured nonmember banks. The maximum rate structures set by the two agencies are identical[3] and are shown in Table 9-6.

It is interesting to note that there is no legal maximum rate payable by banks on large negotiable CDs; that is, banks may offer any rate they choose on these instruments. It is also interesting to compare Table 9-7 with Table 9-6. Table 9-7 shows the average rate actually being paid on time and savings deposits as of January 25, 1978, the same time when the maximum rates shown in Table 9-6 were in effect. Note that, in general, the actual rates being paid were very close to their legal maximum. In other words, it seems safe to say that the legal ceilings are, in fact, binding constraints for most banks.

Comparative Growth Rates of Demand and Time Deposits Historically, demand deposits and time (including savings) deposits have grown at roughly similar rates. More recently, however, there has been a marked tendency for time deposits to grow much more rapidly than demand deposits. These aspects of growth rates

[3]In practice, the Federal Reserve sets these maximum rates and the FDIC goes along with them.

Table 9-6 Maximum Interest Rates Payable on Time and Savings Deposits, in Effect April 30, 1978 (Percent)

Type of deposit	Maximum rate
Savings deposits	5
Other time deposits (multiple and single maturity)*:	
Less than $100,000	
30–89 days	5
90 days to 1 year	$5\frac{1}{2}$
1 to $2\frac{1}{2}$ years	6
$2\frac{1}{2}$ to 4 years	$6\frac{1}{2}$
4 to 6 years in minimum denomination of $1,000	$7\frac{1}{4}$
6 years or more in minimum denomination of $1,000	$7\frac{1}{2}$
$100,000 or more	None

    *Multiple maturity means that the deposit is automatically renewable at maturity without action by the depositor and is payable only after written notice of withdrawal is given the bank. Single maturity means that the deposit matures on a specified date.
    Source: Federal Reserve Bulletin, May 1978, p. A10.

of time and demand deposits can be nicely illustrated by computing the *trend lines* for each kind of deposit for the periods 1950–1960 and 1961–1978. A *trend line* is simply a regression against time. Since all that is needed to compute a regression equation is two columns of figures, there is no reason why one of these columns can't be a series of years; and, if it is, the resulting equation describes the *trend* of the other data over time. For the 1950–1960 period, the *trend equation* for demand and time deposits is

$$D = 91,818 + 2,230T$$
$$r^2 = .93$$
Coefficient significant at 1% level

Table 9-7 Average of Most Common Interest Rates Paid on Various Categories of Time and Savings Deposits at Insured Commercial Banks on January 25, 1978

Types of deposit	Bank size (total deposits in millions of dollars)						
	All size groups	Less than 20	20 up to 50	50 up to 100	100 up to 500	500 up to 1,000	1,000 and over
Savings and small-denomination time deposits	5.58	5.77	5.73	5.62	5.54	5.50	5.44
Savings, total	4.92	4.95	4.91	4.92	4.93	4.90	4.92
LRA and Keogh plan time deposits with maturity of 3 years or more	7.55	7.48	7.48	7.49	7.57	7.54	7.63
Other time deposits in denominations of less than $100,000, total	6.43	6.39	6.54	6.44	6.41	6.41	6.36
Domestic governmental units, total	5.84	5.94	5.99	5.60	5.56	6.20	5.71
Other than domestic governmental units, total	6.44	6.41	6.56	6.46	6.43	6.42	6.37

    Source: Federal Reserve Bulletin, May 1978, p. 371.

$$S = 28{,}111 + 3{,}487\,T$$
$$r^2 = .97$$
Coefficient significant at 1% level

where

    D = demand deposits, millions of dollars

    S = time and savings deposits, millions of dollars

    T = time, in years (beginning with 1950)

In contrast, for the 1961–1978 period, the trend equation is

$$D = 131{,}351 + 12{,}599\,T$$
$$r^2 = .97$$
Coefficient significant at 1% level

$$S = 5{,}085 + 28{,}407\,T$$
$$r^2 = .94$$
Coefficient significant at 1% level

    In comparing these equations, note first that in the 1950–1960 period demand and savings deposits grew by about the same amount. This is readily seen by comparing the coefficient on T (time) in the two equations. For the demand deposits equation, this coefficient is 2,230; for the savings deposits equation, it is 3,487—not too much different. Now look at the 1961–1978 period. The coefficient on the time variable for demand deposits has increased to 12,599, but the coefficient on the time variable for savings deposits has increased much more, from 3,487 to 28,407. Thus time deposits grew much more rapidly in the latter period. In fact, so fast was their growth rate that time and savings deposits became larger than demand deposits for the first time in history in 1971.

    The reason for this phenomenal growth in time and savings deposits is complicated. In the early 1960s the open market interest rate began to move upward substantially. Business firms found it to their advantage to skimp on their demand deposit balances and invest any idle funds in money market instruments such as Treasury bills. The banks began to feel threatened by the possibility of large withdrawals, and consequently the Federal Reserve raised the ceiling rates on time deposits to permit banks to attract and hold these deposits. Not only did the banks do this, but they also developed the negotiable CD instrument to compete with other money market instruments in order to hold onto large corporate deposits. Ceiling rates have been raised several times since the early 1960s, and the time deposits of commercial banks have continued to spurt upward.

Bank Borrowings

Although the vast bulk of their liabilities lie in deposits, banks also have other liabilities, most of which have already been described, notably the borrowing of federal funds and Eurodollars (Chapter 7). However, one bank liability has not been mentioned as yet because it is not a money market instrument and because it is small compared with such things as time and demand deposits: This is the ability of member banks to borrow from the Federal Reserve System, known as *member bank discounting.* This liability is quite important.

Member Bank Discounting The Federal Reserve System is sometimes called a *banker's bank* because it lends money to member banks in much the same way that banks lend money to individuals and corporations. This process of Federal Reserve lending is called *discounting,* and the rate of interest charged by the Federal Reserve is known as the *discount rate.* The importance of this process does not lie so much in the dollar volume of Federal Reserve loans to member banks (which amounted to about $0.5 billion in mid-1978), as it does in the fact that discounting and the setting of the discount rate are one of the three main channels through which monetary policy is conducted. At this point it would be premature to attempt to explain how this process works, but keep at least the following two points in mind: (1) Member banks of the Federal Reserve System have an emergency source of funds available to them—borrowing from the Federal Reserve; (2) when the Federal Reserve changes its discount rate, this fact is likely to be publicized on the front pages of newspapers throughout the country and influence bankers in setting their loan rates.

9-5 REVIEW QUESTIONS

1 What is the significance of dividing balance sheet items into those over which banks have short-run control, and those over which it does not have such control?
2 Why is the capital/asset ratio important to bank regulatory agencies? to bankers? Which group would like to see it higher? lower? Why?
3 Why are bank profits higher today than they were in the early 1960s?
4 Which is growing faster, bank time deposits or bank demand deposits? How do you account for this?

10

Managing
the Bank's Assets

It is worth repeating at this point that a commercial bank, considered as a business firm, has two highly unusual aspects associated with the capital and liabilities side of its balance sheet: First, it has a very thin margin of owner equity; only about 7 percent of its total resources represents funds invested by its owners, with the other 93 percent being borrowed money (mostly deposits). Second, the money the bank has borrowed is, for the most part, payable on demand; that is, payment can be required (deposits withdrawn) by the lender on any business day. What keeps banks viable organizations is the sure knowledge, based on experience, that *all* depositors will not demand *all* their money at the same time. As a matter of daily routine, bankers know that deposit withdrawals will be at least partially offset by additions to deposits. As a matter of experience, they know that movements in aggregate deposits and loan demands will follow familiar seasonal patterns, which can be planned for in advance.

But the future is uncertain for bankers no less than the rest of us. Seasonal patterns shift, periods of prosperity alternate with periods of recession, the unexpected occurs. Banks must accommodate themselves to change and uncertainty. The traditional way they do this is by structuring their assets in such a manner as to be able to meet a priority ordering of their goals. Although *liability management banking* has modified the importance of asset management, it nevertheless remains true that banks in the United States must rely to some extent on the proper structuring of their assets for the attainment of their goals.

What are these goals? Like firms in other industries, the goals of the bank are to stay in business and to make as much profit as it can while doing so. But because of its unusual qualities, "staying in business" has a special meaning for a bank. Because of its thin equity position, the bank is obliged to take great care in avoiding risk; because of its demand liabilities, it must be constantly concerned about its liquidity; and because it is a business, it must make a profit. All three factors influence the bank in its choice of assets. The difficulty is that there is no such thing as a high-liquidity, low-risk, high-profit asset. In general, the more the liquidity and the less the risk, the lower the yield of an asset. Thus, in choosing to buy any given asset, the bank must sacrifice profit for liquidity and risklessness, or vice versa. But the bank is not confined to a *single* asset. What it strives to do, therefore, is to develop the appropriate structure, or mixture, of assets to reconcile these conflicts.[1] It does this by assigning *priorities* to its asset acquisitions.

1 *Primary Reserves* The highest priority item for any bank is to meet its primary reserve needs. These reserves are required partly for legal reasons and partly for the everyday working balances of the bank. Their distinguishing characteristic is that they are *cash* assets; that is, they do not directly earn the bank any income.
2 *Secondary Reserves* After the bank has satisfied its needs for primary reserves, its next goal is to develop adequate liquidity. This is done by acquiring so-called secondary reserve assets. Although the main purpose of these assets is to impart liquidity to the bank, they are also earning assets.
3 *Loans* Once the bank has sufficient liquidity, it next concentrates on lending. Generally speaking, loans are less liquid and more risky than other bank assets, but they are also very profitable.
4 *Investments for Income* Finally, after the bank has satisfied its loan demand, residual funds are put into open market investments. These investments are longer term than secondary reserve assets, their main function being to provide income rather than liquidity to the bank.

The following discussion of bank assets will be organized according to these priorities.

10-1 PRIMARY RESERVES

As indicated, a bank's nonearning assets constitute its *primary reserves*. These primary reserve assets can be further subdivided into *required reserves* and *working reserves*.

[1]See Chapter 5 for the advantages of portfolio diversification.

Required Reserves

As the name implies, *required reserves* are the cash assets that the bank is required by law to hold. The law typically stipulates that required reserves be some definite percentage of the bank's demand and time deposits. These reserves have two functions: First, they give the bank short-run liquidity. The bank is not expected to hold the exact amount of its required reserves every minute of every day, but instead is only required to hold *average* reserves as a percent of *average* deposits, where these items are averaged over a week or more (and sometimes with a lag). Thus, on any given day a bank may pay off depositors completely out of its required reserves as long as it makes up such a deficiency within the next few days; it can "buy time" with its required reserves until it can make more fundamental adjustments either in its assets or by borrowing. The second function of required reserves has to do with the conduct of monetary policy. However, since monetary policy will be discussed at considerable length later in the book, we shall not dwell on this function now.

Required Reserves of Member Banks   The percentage reserve requirements for member banks of the Federal Reserve System are shown in Table 10-1. These reserves are calculated separately against the member bank's time deposits and *net demand deposits,* or gross demand deposits minus cash items in the process of collection (checks that are clearing) and any correspondent balances it is holding in other banks. Deposits are averaged over a one-week period, and similarly reserves are a weekly average of daily figures. The period over which reserves are averaged is two weeks later than the deposit-averaging period to give banks time to adjust to deposit changes. A bank with deficient reserves must pay a penalty rate of interest on such reserves, the penalty rate being equal to the current discount rate plus 2 percent.[2] Only vault cash and balances held in the Federal Reserve banks may be used to satisfy the required reserves of member banks.

Table 10-1   Reserve Requirements on Deposits of Member Banks of the Federal Reserve System as of April 30, 1978* (Percent)

Net demand deposits[†]						Time deposits	
							Other
On the first $2 million	$2–10 million	$10–100 million	$100–400 million	Over $400 million	Savings deposits	On the[‡] first $5 million	Over $5[‡] million
7	$9\frac{1}{2}$	$11\frac{3}{4}$	$12\frac{3}{4}$	$16\frac{1}{4}$	3	3	6

* Legally permissible range of reserve requirements:
   Net demand deposits
     $400 million and over (10 to 22%)
     Below $400 million (7 to 14%)
   Time deposits (3 to 10%)
[†] Net demand deposits = gross demand deposits minus cash items in the process of collection and demand balances due from domestic banks.
[‡] Maturing in 30–179 days.
Source: Federal Reserve Bulletin, May 1978, p. A9.

[2] Except that a bank may be as much as 2 percent deficient in any averaging period provided it makes up such a deficiency by an equivalent surplus in the following period.

As can be seen from Table 10-1, the reserve requirement on demand deposits becomes progressively higher the more deposits a bank holds, reaching a maximum of 16¼ percent on deposits over $400 million. The reasons for this are largely historical, dating back to the nineteenth century, when the banking system *pyramided* reserves. Pyramiding occurred because national banks could at that time count correspondent balances as part of their reserves. Thus a small-town bank could deposit money in its city correspondent to meet its reserve requirement, and the city correspondent could then use the same money as part of *its* reserves. Because of this, it was deemed wise to have big city (or *reserve city*) banks hold larger reserves than small-town *(country)* banks. Although member banks of the Federal Reserve System may not use correspondent balances to satisfy reserve requirements, authorities continue to believe that the more deposits a bank has, the more likely it is to engage in different kinds of business than smaller banks, and therefore it needs higher reserves. Requirements for time deposit reserves are also progressive, though much less steeply so than those on demand deposits.

The Federal Reserve System has the legal authority to vary the percentage reserve requirements between 7 and 14 percent on deposits below $400 million, and between 10 and 22 percent on deposits over $400 million. The range of reserve requirements on savings and time deposits is from 3 to 10 percent for all sizes of deposits.

Required Reserves of Nonmember Banks   The required reserves for state-chartered banks that are not members of the Federal Reserve are set by state law and enforced by the banking authorities of the various states. Different arrangements prevail in different states, but, in general, the state laws governing required reserves are less rigorous in either or both of two ways: A state may have lower reserve requirements than the Federal Reserve; and it may permit a wider range of assets to be used to satisfy required reserves. States typically permit correspondent balances to count as required reserves in whole or in part. Additionally, some states permit banks to use United States government securities and even municipal securities as required reserves.

Banks, of course, want to hold as few cash assets as possible since such assets do not earn them any profits in the form of interest. The more rigorous reserve requirements of the Federal Reserve, as compared with state laws, force member banks to hold more cash assets and fewer earning assets. This is easily the main reason why so few state-chartered banks have chosen to join the Federal Reserve System. Both for reasons of equity and for purposes of monetary policy, many people (including officials of the Federal Reserve System) have advocated that Congress pass a law making reserve requirements the same for both member and nonmember banks.

Working Reserves

Working reserves are the cash assets that banks hold even though they are not legally required to do so. These reserves arise out of the nature of the banking business— they "go with the territory." Foremost among the working reserves of a bank are its *cash items in the process of collection,* which are simply checks on other banks that a bank has had deposited with it, and that have been sent on for collection. Since it sometimes takes two or three days to collect these checks, a bank will in the meantime carry them on its books as *cash assets,* that is, money owed to it that earns no interest. For member banks of the Federal Reserve and for some nonmember banks, *correspondent balances* are also working reserves. Banks must hold these balances for a variety of reasons (see Chapter 2) even though they do not formally[3] earn a rate of interest. Finally, some banks will hold *excess reserves.* By *excess* is meant cash reserves over and above those legally required; for example, a member bank may hold larger balances in the Federal Reserve than required by law. In general, big banks hold almost no excess reserves; they figure their nonearning assets with a very sharp pencil indeed. Most excess reserves are held by small banks, where the bankers are harassed by so many different tasks that it is uneconomic for them to engage in the time and expense necessary to adjust their reserve position exactly every week. Even so, with the rise in interest rates in the past few years, the excess reserves of even small banks have fallen substantially.

Size of Primary Reserves

Because primary reserves (with the exceptions noted) do not earn the bank any profit, there is a very simple rule governing the amount a bank should hold: as few as possible.

10-2 SECONDARY RESERVES

The secondary reserves of a commercial bank are a category of assets internal to the bank; that is, they are not a legal requirement and will not be listed separately on a published bank statement. Nevertheless, they are a well-recognized set of assets, familiar to all bankers. Their primary purpose is to provide liquidity to the bank (indeed, they are sometimes called *liquidity reserves*) while at the same time earning the bank a rate of return. They are held in various of the short-term money market instruments, such as Treasury bills, bankers acceptances, commercial paper, and federal funds sold.

Liquidity Defined

It is desirable at this point to define the concept of *liquidity* more precisely than we have done heretofore. By *liquidity* is meant the ability to convert an asset to cash with minimum delay and minimum loss. All assets have some degree of liquidity, including real assets. A house, for example, has some liquidity, but not much. If you want to sell the house quickly, you have to offer it at a very low price; if you want to sell it for a high price, you have to be willing to wait until the right buyer comes

---

[3]As explained in Chapter 2, however, correspondent balances earn a payment in kind in the form of services rendered by the correspondent to the respondent bank.

along. Thus a house has low liquidity, or is *illiquid,* considered as an asset. Demand deposits, in contrast, are almost perfectly liquid; their dollar value doesn't change (no loss), and there is only a very slight delay in spending them (minimum delay).

Money market instruments fall between demand deposits and houses on the liquidity scale, but, in general, they are a lot closer to demand deposits than they are to houses. They score high marks in terms of both minimum delay and minimum loss. Consider a three-month Treasury bill, for example. In the first place, it is traded in what is perhaps the most active market in the world. This means that a bank can easily sell such an asset at any time—there is very little delay in converting it to cash. In the second place, because a Treasury bill is issued by the United States Government, for all practical purposes it is free of default risk. There is no possibility of its not being paid off at maturity and consequently no possibility of the holder suffering a loss due to lack of repayment. Finally, because of its short maturity, the price of a three-month Treasury bill will vary only slightly as market rates of interest change (see Chapter 7). Thus even if a bank decides to sell the bill before it matures, the bank will risk only a minimal loss. It is necessary to emphasize this last point since it is precisely this characteristic that distinguishes (in terms of liquidity) a Treasury bill from a long-term government bond. The bond is also easily marketable and free of the risk of default, but its price will vary markedly as market rates of interest change. In other words, a long-term bond is much less liquid than a bill and hence is not generally considered suitable as a secondary reserve asset.

With some slight modifications, this discussion of the liquidity aspects of Treasury bills could be repeated for the various other money market debt instruments. They are all highly liquid assets, and banks hold them for precisely that reason; they may be sold, or *liquidated,* at any time, and the money realized from their sale can then used by the bank. But the reader may still be a bit puzzled. If the bank needs liquidity so much, why doesn't it just hold the most liquid asset there is—money? The answer, of course, is that if the bank holds money, it doesn't earn any interest. Thus, for a very slight sacrifice of liquidity, the bank can improve its earnings substantially. Figure 10-1 shows the yields on various money market instruments over the past several years.

Size of Secondary Reserves

How much liquidity is enough liquidity? That depends on the individual bank. Some banks find that because of the nature of their customers' business, they experience violent fluctuations in their loan and deposit accounts; other banks have more stable types of customers. There is no simple generalization that will cover all cases. Perhaps the best that can be done here is to indicate the *types* of reasons why banks hold secondary reserve assets.

First and foremost, a bank holds secondary reserves for *seasonal purposes.* By *seasonal* is meant the ebbs and flows of deposits and loans that repeat themselves in a regular pattern year after year. A bank in an agricultural community, for example, will regularly need to make financing available to its customers in the spring; a bank with customers who are predominantly retail merchants will need to provide them with loans in anticipation of holiday spending—Easter and Christmas,

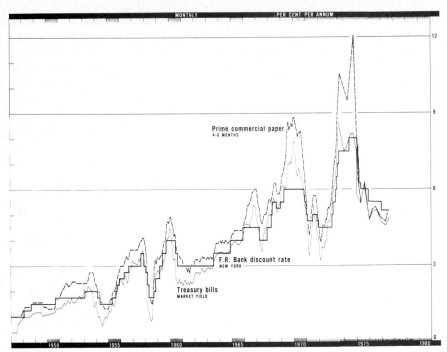

Figure 10-1   Short-term interest rates 1947–1977. *(Source: Board of Governors of the Federal Reserve System,* Historical Chart Book, *1977, p. 98.)*

especially; a bank located in a small college town typically will experience student deposit inflows in September, outflows in June, and a demand for loans from (alas!) the faculty during the summer; and so forth. The possibilities for seasonal patterns are as varied as the American economy itself.

Note that there are two distinct items that the bank must provide for in its seasonal calculations: loans and deposits. That is, the bank must be able to liquidate enough of its secondary reserves to accommodate both deposit withdrawals and an increased demand for loans. In a well-ordered world, these two items would be inversely related so that the bank could use loan repayments to meet depositor withdrawals and vice versa. Unfortunately, it doesn't work that way. In fact, deposit withdrawals and loan demands typically will be *positively* related for the simple reason that people usually draw down their idle balances before requesting loans.

Other short-run factors for which banks hold secondary reserves include random, or unpredictable, fluctuations in loans and deposits; the possibility of an increase in the reserve requirements of Federal Reserve member banks; and "unstable" accounts—accounts of large private or institutional (e.g., state government) customers whose deposits are subject to sudden and sharp fluctuations. Provisions for such contingencies are to some extent a matter of internal bank policy peculiar to the individual bank. As discussed previously, some banks prefer to rely heavily on liability management practices as a source of liquidity, while others have a preference for the more traditional use of secondary reserves. In either case, the goal of the banks is to be able to absorb shocks to the bank without having them disrupt its orderly routine.

Finally, it should be mentioned that many banks will make liquidity provisions for *cyclical* factors. *Cyclical* here refers to the business cycle: alternating periods of recession and economic boom. Banks need to be able to accommodate the loan demands of good customers during periods of economic hyperactivity when money is tight. Because such periods occur at intervals measured in years rather than months, reserve assets held for cyclical purposes typically will carry maturities of up to five years.

10-3 LOANS

After a bank has made adequate provision for liquidity through its primary and secondary reserves, its next priority is to make loans. It is clear that bankers themselves regard their lending activities as lying at the heart of commercial banking. Not only are loans a very profitable type of asset for the bank to hold in terms of sheer earning power, they have the additional advantages of attracting deposits and providing a necessary service to the community. But bank loans also have their disadvantages. On the whole, they are the most risky of bank assets, that is, the most subject to default. Additionally, they are illiquid; they can seldom be converted into cash before maturity. Bankers are understandably cautious in making loans, insisting on high standards of creditworthiness and fixed repayment schedules for long-term loans.

Secured and Unsecured Loans

Many bank loans are *secured* by having borrowers pledge some of their assets against the eventual repayment of the loans. Such assets may be tangible or intangible and would include such things as inventories, real estate, stocks and bonds, and life insurance policies. If a loan is not repaid at maturity, the bank may then obtain legal permission to sell these assets in order to recover its loan. Other bank loans are *unsecured,* which is to say that they involve only the borrowers' promise to pay.

One might think that unsecured loans to businesses would tend to be more risky than secured loans, but this is not the case. Most very large business loans are made on an unsecured basis, depending only on the general credit standing and anticipated income of the borrowers. Secured loans are typically made to small and intermediate-sized businesses.

Classification of Bank Loans According to Purpose

One meaningful way to classify bank loans is according to the purpose for which the loan is made. Banking authorities put loans into six categories: commercial and industrial, or business, loans; agricultural loans; real estate loans; loans to individuals; loans to financial institutions; and other. Table 10-2 gives the dollar amounts and percent of total for each of these categories as of September 30, 1977.

Table 10–2   Loans of Insured Commercial Banks, September 30, 1977
(Millions of Dollars)

Type of loan	Amount	Percent
Commercial and industrial (business)	186,730	32
Agricultural	26,271	5
Real estate	169,334	29
To individuals	134,381	23
To financial institutions*	33,962	6
Other	30,422	5
Total	581,100	100

*Includes loans for purchasing and carrying securities.
Source: Federal Reserve Bulletin, May 1978, p. A18.

Business Loans   As can be seen from Table 10-2, commercial and industrial loans are easily the largest single category of bank loans. As discussed in Chapter 8, under the intellectual stimulus of the real bills doctrine, banks have traditionally been the major supplier of short-term credit to businesses through seasonal loans made for the shipment, processing, and distribution of goods. In the past thirty years, however, reacting to the anticipated income theory of banking, long-term loans have become an increasingly important part of the business loans of commercial banks. Today such *term loans* account for well over half the commercial and industrial loans made by banks.

Term Loans   Bank loans having an orginal maturity in excess of one year are called *term loans.* (The phrase is not very logical. It is an abbreviation of long-term; but since it could just as easily be an abbreviation of short-term, there is no help for it but just to memorize what it means.) From the viewpoint of the business, the advantage of obtaining a term loan from a bank is that, in contrast to borrowing on the capital market, the details of the loan can be tailored to the specific needs of the firm. In particular, the repayment schedule of the loan can be adapted to the cash flows peculiar to an individual business and need not be as standardized as with a bond issue.

Banks make term loans for basically two reasons. The first of these is the obvious one: to finance a capital investment in plant and equipment, which will take several years to pay for itself. The second reason is less obvious but no less important: Many firms use bank loans as a means of interim financing prior to borrowing in the capital market. For example, a firm might use a bank loan of one or two years muturity to finance the initial stages of the construction of a new plant. When the plant nears completion, the firm will refinance this credit by selling bonds in the capital market.

Lines of Credit   Of the various financial arrangements that may exist between a bank and a business, one in particular should be noted because of its popularity: the *line of credit*. With a line of credit, a bank ensures a business in advance that it may borrow up to some stipulated maximum amount at any time. Since the business pays interest only on funds actually borrowed, and since the borrowing may be done with a minimum of fuss, this arrangement has obvious advantages for the business—especially if it has seasonal or unpredictable cash needs. The bank maintains a continuous watch on the credit standing of the business and may revoke its line of credit at any time. With a line of credit, it is customary for the bank to require an *annual cleanup;* that is, the firm must get completely out of debt to the bank at least once during the year. The purpose of this requirement is to ensure the bank that its funds are not being used as permanent capital by the firm.

Compensating Balances Bank loans to businesses frequently require that a business maintain some minimum deposit balance in the bank. This minimum balance is usually defined in terms of either the size of the loan or the size of a line of credit. For example, a bank might require a deposit that is equal to at least 20 percent of a loan or 10 percent of a line of credit. Such a required deposit is called a *compensating balance.* To the extent that it forces the business to hold a larger deposit than it otherwise would, a compensating balance has the consequence of raising the effective rate of interest on bank loans since the business does not have use of the full amount it borrows.

Interest Rates on Business Loans Gross interest rates on bank short-term business loans, classified by geographic region and size of loan, are shown in Table 10-3 for thirty-five financial centers in the United States. Table 10-4 gives the same information for long-term bank loans. It is of interest that there are regional differences in the interest rates charged by banks and that the rates on long-term loans are typically higher than rates on short-term loans. Of even greater interest is the generally inverse relationship that exists between loan rate and loan size; the larger the loan, the lower the rate of interest. This relationship is often interpreted by the unsophisticated as proof that banking is a monopolistic industry that discriminates in favor of large borrowers. In other words, the hypothesis is that banks are fully able to exploit their monopolistic power over small borrowers, who have no alternative sources of loan funds, but are less able to do so with large borrowers, who operate in a national market. But such a conclusion is not warranted by the data.

The data shown in Tables 10-3 and 10-4 are for *gross* rates of interest and are not adjusted for lending costs. And it is clear that making loans is a decreasing cost activity: In terms of credit information, employee time involved, and continuing supervision, it costs very little more to make a $100,000 loan than it does to make

Table 10-3 Interest Rates on Short-Term Business Loans of Commercial Banks, November 30, 1976 (Percent)

Size of loan	New York City	7 Other Northeast	8 North Central	7 South-east	8 South-west	4 West Coast	All 35 centers
$1,000–$9,000	8.56	9.22	8.45	9.13	8.51	8.69	8.83
$10,000–$99,000	7.94	8.34	8.12	8.48	7.82	8.46	8.18
$100,000–$499,000	7.43	7.88	7.69	7.71	7.39	7.88	7.66
$500,000–$999,000	7.24	7.49	7.36	7.04	7.21	7.44	7.31
$1 million and over	6.74	7.34	7.03	7.07	7.12	7.34	7.02
All sizes (weighted average)	6.88	7.62	7.28	7.51	7.33	7.52	7.28

Source: Annual Statistical Digest of the Board of Governors of the Federal Reserve System, 1972–1976, p. 102.

Table 10-4   Interest Rates on Long-Term Business Loans of Commercial Banks,
November 30, 1976 (Percent)

Size of loan	Financial centers						
	New York City	7 Other Northeast	8 North Central	7 South- east	8 South- west	4 West Coast	All 35 centers
$1,000–$9,000	7.19	9.22	9.20	9.87	10.54	8.70	9.39
$10,000–$99,000	8.55	8.44	9.03	9.35	9.05	8.54	8.88
$100,000–$499,000	7.93	7.95	8.35	7.93	8.28	8.31	8.14
$500,000–$999,000	8.06	7.92	8.99	4.00	8.44	7.78	8.13
$1 million and over	7.26	5.73	7.32	7.79	7.20	8.03	7.24
All sizes (weighted average)	7.36	6.64	7.66	7.59	7.73	8.04	7.48

Source: Annual Statistical Digest of the Board of Governors of the Federal Reserve, 1972–1976, p. 104.

a $10,000 loan. Thus an alternative hypothesis, which explains the data equally well, is that the inverse relationship between loan size and rate simply reflects the decreasing cost nature of lending. Much more careful analysis is needed to distinguish between the two hypotheses.

Agricultural Loans   Agricultural loans are just what the name implies—short-term and long-term loans made to farmers for financing crops, buildings, equipment, and land improvements. Although these loans are small relative to other classes of loans, for banks located in predominantly rural areas they are a major source of business. Over two-thirds of such loans are held by banks with less than $10 million of deposits.

Real Estate Loans   Loans secured by real estate—buildings and land—constitute the second largest category of bank loans (the largest category being business loans). Although banks are not the largest lenders in the mortgage market, they are nevertheless a substantial part of it. Direct bank lending accounts for about 17 percent of all mortgages written in the United States.

Loans to Individuals   Bank loans to individuals are generally known as *consumer loans.* These loans are made to people for financing the purchase of durable consumer goods: automobiles especially, but also TVs, refrigerators, washing machines, and home improvements. Such loans are typically made on an installment basis and are a highly profitable business for banks.

Credit-Card Plans   So profitable is consumer lending, indeed, that a number of plans for expanding this type of loan have been developed. Probably the best known of these plans is the *credit card* (e.g., Master Charge and Visa). The use of bank credit cards to finance consumer buying grew very rapidly in the late 1960s and 1970s, with more than half the commercial banks in the country now participating in some type of plan. Even so, credit cards account for only about 15 percent of total bank installment consumer lending.

Loans to Financial Institutions Banks make loans to other banks and to various other financial institutions, such as sales-finance companies, savings and loan associations, and brokers and dealers in securities. Such loans are made primarily by large banks and constitute about 6 percent of total bank loans.

Other Loans This is the catchall category of bank-loan classification. It includes loans to nonprofit organizations, such as churches and educational institutions, overdrafts, and any loan not classifiable into one of the categories listed previously.

10-4 INVESTMENTS FOR INCOME

By *investments* is meant those open market securities held by banks that do not constitute a part of its secondary reserve assets. Bank investments are generally regarded as a residual claimant on bank funds; that is, they are considered to be the lowest priority of bank assets. Only after a bank has taken care of its primary and secondary reserve needs and has met all the legitimate loan demands of its customers does it turn its attention to longer-term investments. Indeed, in some of the tight money episodes of recent years, many large banks had no investments at all; the three categories of primary reserves, secondary reserves, and loans had exhausted their funds.

While banks may hold investments in corporate bonds, only a few banks do so (except for trust-department activities). For all practical purposes, bank investments are held in three types of securities: United States government bonds, municipal securities, and so-called agency bonds.

United States Government Bonds

As noted, bank-held United States government securities maturing within one year should probably be classed as secondary reserves. As indicated in Table 10-5, most other government securities held by banks carry a maturity between one and five years, with only a very small percentage falling due in more than ten years. Between 1950 and 1975, the dollar amount of government securities held by banks stayed about the same, on the average. Beginning in 1975, however, banks began adding

Table 10-5 Bank-owned United States Government Securities, March 1978 (Billions of Dollars)

Maturity	Amount	Percent
1 year or less	25,237	34
1–5 years	41,251	56
5–10 years	5,957	8
10–20 years	611	1
Over 20 years	797	1
Total	73,853	100

Source: Federal Reserve Bulletin, May 1978, p. A33.

substantial amounts to their holdings of government securities. The reason for this upsurge in bank holdings of governments is largely due to a switch in the comparative advantages of government and municipal securities.

Municipal Securities

It will be seen from Figure 10-2 that bank holdings of municipal securities grew enormously between 1950 and 1975, the same period that government securities were holding steady. Since about 1975, however, this situation has reversed: Bank holdings of municipals leveled off, while bank holdings of governments spurted upward. The reason for this reversal has to do with tax laws and interest rates. Before 1975, municipals, because of their tax-exempt status, were a highly attractive investment for banks. After that date, however, interest rates on United States government securities rose very rapidly, and certain tax changes relating to banks occurred. These changes had the effect of reversing the attractiveness of governments and municipals, with the result shown in Figure 10-2. Whether this change is permanent remains to be seen.

Agency Bonds and Other Investments

As noted, banks hold comparatively few corporate bonds. Those they do hold are owned primarily by very large banks because the amount of expertise needed to invest in the issues of private corporations is generally beyond the ability of small and medium-sized banks. Most of the "other" securities held by banks are so-called

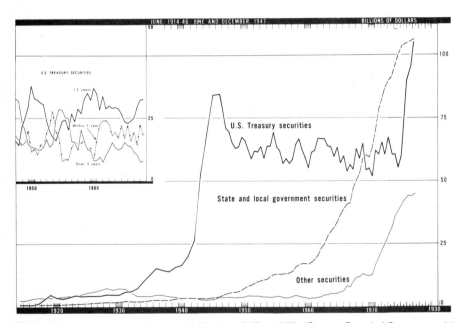

Figure 10-2 Investments of commercial banks, 1947 to 1977. *(Source: Board of Governors of the Federal Reserve System,* Historical Chart Book, *1977, p. 81.)*

agency bonds, that is, bonds issued or guaranteed by various instrumentalities of the federal government, such as the Federal Home Loan Bank Board, the Federal Intermediate Credit Banks, and the Public Housing Administration. As indicated by Figure 10-2, other bank investments are a rapidly growing part of bank investments.

10-5 MANAGING THE BANK'S MONEY POSITION

The economist's interest in commercial banking lies primarily in the fact that banks are the major channel through which monetary policy is conducted. This being the case, the main excuse for taking the reader on a sometimes tedious tour of bank management practices is to develop an intuitive feel for the behavior of banks. The objective of this section is to get it all together—to examine the behavioral response of commercial banks to shifting circumstances. To a considerable extent, all the things we have been discussing come into focus when we consider how a bank *manages its money position,* that is, the various kinds of asset and liability adjustments it makes in order to meet its required reserves.

Seasonal Bank Adjustments: A Case Study

As discussed at the end of Chapter 9, member banks have the privilege of borrowing from the Federal Reserve System. Figure 10-3 was designed to illustrate the reasons why member banks borrow, but it also indicates the variety of other choices open to a bank and the various pressures affecting its reserve ("money") position.

Since Figure 10-3 is a complicated graph, the reader should take a moment or two to become familiar with it. Note, in the first place, that Figure 10-3 shows actual data for a large city bank. The name of the bank is not given, nor is the year to which the data apply. However, we can obtain some idea of the size of the bank by noting that the legend in the upper left-hand corner shows that 10 percent of the required reserves amount to about $3 million. Total required reserves would consequently be about $30 million, and, figuring that required reserves are roughly 10 percent of total (i.e., both time and demand) deposits, it follows that the figure depicts a bank with about $300 million in deposits—certainly not the largest bank in the country, but well above average. Perhaps the only other feature of Figure 10-3 to note particularly is that the data plotted on loans, other securities, and deposits are cumulative changes from the beginning of the year (see the legend in the upper right-hand corner). For example, the peak loan demand of about $11 million that occurred in June does *not* mean that the bank has outstanding loans of only $11 million, but rather that in June loans were $11 million *higher* than they were in December. The other data are self-explanatory.

The dominating aspect of the events shown in Figure 10-3 is the very sizable drop in deposits experienced by the bank at the beginning of the year. During January and February, total deposits fell by some $12 million. During January the deposit withdrawal was more than offset by loan repayments, which, together with the bank's reduction in federal funds sales, permitted the bank to add to its holdings

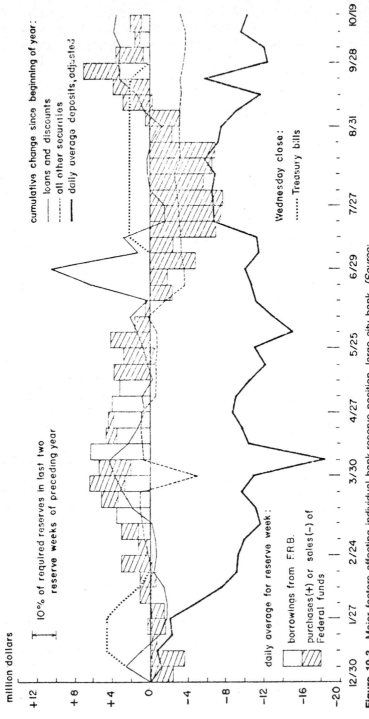

Figure 10-3 Major factors affecting individual bank-reserve position, large city bank. *[Source: Federal Reserve Bank of Chicago, "The Operation of the Federal Reserve Discount Window," September 7, 1960. (Mimeographed.)]*

of Treasury bills. In February, however, the decline in deposits became precipitous and the bank was obliged to make several adjustments: It liquidated its newly bought Treasury bills; it bought federal funds; and, when neither of these proved sufficient to accommodate the deposit outflow, it borrowed from the Federal Reserve System. The bank's situation was further worsened by corporate borrowing needs in March, and the bank was forced into increasingly heavy reliance on the federal funds market and borrowing from the Federal Reserve in order to meet its required reserves. Throughout the late winter and spring months, the bank was regularly acquiring 20 to 25 percent of its reserves from these two sources.

The very sharp drop and recovery in deposits and in "all other securities" that occurred at about April 1 illustrates the sort of things bankers plan for and take in their stride. The state in which this bank does business has a personal property tax that applies to bank deposits but not to holdings of United States government securities. Assessment for the tax is made on April 1. Wealthy people therefore avoid the tax by converting their deposits to government securities just before April 1 and converting them back again shortly afterward. This buying and selling process is very apparent in Figure 10-3, where both deposits and "other securities" (i.e., aside from Treasury bills) fall and rebound by some $6 or $7 million within a two-week period.[4]

In June deposits began to flow back into the bank. To a considerable extent, these funds were invested in the federal funds market, although some of them were also used to accommodate the heavy seasonal loans to business associated with the quarterly payment of corporate income taxes. For the most part, however, this loan demand was met by liquidating other securities. The repayment of those loans in July generated an additional cash flow into the bank, which was invested in Treasury bills and further sales in the federal funds market. The last major influence shown on the bank's operations is the expansion of loans associated with the fall buildup in business inventories. In order to make these loans and meet the concomitant decline in deposits, the bank borrowed federal funds, sold Treasury bills, and borrowed from the Federal Reserve.

The moral of the case history is very easy to understand if the reader will turn back to Chapter 9 and take another look at Table 9-2. What this bank has been doing is to manage changes in its "controllable" items to offset changes in its "uncontrollable" items so that its reserve requirements are met throughout the year.

10-6 REVIEW QUESTIONS

1 What are the goals of bank management?
2 Explain the difference between primary reserves and secondary reserves.
3 Explain the difference between loans and investments.
4 If you were running a bank that had a very sharp increase in its seasonal loan demand, where would you get the funds to meet this demand? Would it matter if it was a small bank or a large bank?

---

[4]In Figure 10-3 the bank's sale of securities appears to occur during the week prior to the deposit decline, but this is misleading. The lag shows up because holdings of securities are measured as of the close of business on Wednesday while the deposit figure is a daily average.

PART 5

THE SUPPLY OF MONEY

The last several chapters have dealt with the *banking* part of this book, that is, with the structure and management of the financial institutions of the United States. Thus, the discussion has so far been confined to only a single stage of Figure 1-1 of Chapter 1: the boxes and arrows labeled "3" on top and "A" below (see Figure V-1). It will be recalled that the number refers to the position of this stage in the logical development of the subject matter of money and banking while the letter refers to the sequence in which it is best to learn the material. Thus to this point the reader has been asked to make a substantial investment in learning about the United States financial apparatus, with only occasional hints concerning its broader implications. This investment will now begin to pay off. With Part Five we begin an inquiry into the *money* part of the book—the process whereby the financial sector affects and is affected by the rest of the economy.

The first step in this inquiry is to investigate the role played by money in the economic life of the nation. Figure V-2, which is again excerpted from Figure 1-1, indicates the scope of Part Five. The next two chapters deal with two primary questions: What is money? and, Where does money come from? Chapter 11 considers the first question, and Chapter 12 begins to answer the second.

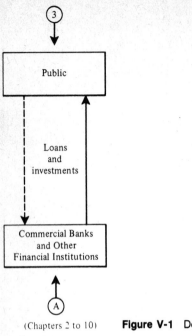

Figure V-1 Detail of Figure 1-1.

(Chapters 2 to 10)

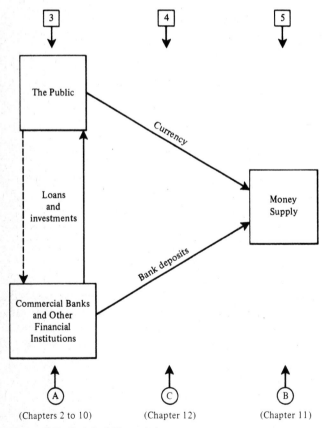

(Chapters 2 to 10)   (Chapter 12)   (Chapter 11)

Figure V-2 Detail of Figure 1-1.

11

Money

If you ask someone what money is, you will most likely get a blank stare. If you persist, you will probably be told that you are asking a dumb question. If you *still* persist, the person you are asking is apt to reach into a pocket with an exaggerated air of impatience, pull out a handful of change, stick it under your nose, and shout, "*That* is money!"[1]

Well . . . yes. Nickels and dimes and quarters are certainly money. But your question hasn't really been answered. You have asked for a general definition and have been given a specific example. Quarters are money, certainly. But so are dollar bills. And so, for that matter, are pounds (in Britain), francs (in France), yen (in Japan), and pesos (in Argentina). Obviously the list could be extended. And this is only an enumeration of modern money. If we were to include historical money, we would also have to add some obvious things, such as gold and silver, and some things that are not so obvious, such as cattle and cigarettes. Clearly, this sort of "definition

---

[1]Further persistence is not recommended unless you are a varsity football player.

by enumeration" is not a very good idea, and not just because it is tedious to do. A more fundamental objection is that it still doesn't tell us what money *is*—why we have put some things on the list and left others off. If cattle can be money, why not giraffes? If dollar bills, why not bubble-gum wrappers?

Money is not a thing like gold or paper. That is, a definition of money cannot reasonably be put in terms of some substance or other. *Money is not what it is but what it does.* This point cannot be made too strongly. A definition of money must be put in functional terms so that we can count as money anything that performs these functions. But what are the functions of money? We can't say that money is anything used to buy hamburgers. That is too narrow. We can't say that money is anything that serves as money. That is circular. We can't say that money is whatever the government says it is. That is untrue. What *are* the functions of money?

11-1 THE FUNCTIONS OF MONEY

It is a curious phenomenon in economics that frequently the best way to understand something is to imagine its opposite. This is certainly true with money. The opposite of a monetary economy is what is called a *barter economy,* that is, an economic system in which no money exists. Markets exist, but not money. Thus in such an economy goods are exchanged directly for other goods—ships for shoes, cabbages for kings. By trying to imagine such an economy—and in particular by trying to imagine its inconveniences and limitations—we can begin to appreciate the various roles played by money in our own economy.

Money as a Unit of Account

Note, in the first place, that in a barter economy there would be no such thing as *price* as we know it. When we ask what the price of something is, it is understood by everyone that what is meant is a dollar price. Indeed, if you were to ask a shoe clerk, "What is the dollar price of that pair?" he would probably think you a bit odd. We are so accustomed to thinking of price in terms of *dollars* that to couple the two words together seems redundant, like calling someone a "rich millionaire." But it doesn't have to be this way, and in a barter economy it wouldn't be this way. In a barter economy, all goods would have to be valued in terms of all other goods. There would have to be a lobster price for books (the number of lobsters given for one book), a matches price for wheat, a wheat price for lobsters, and so forth. In an economy with any sophistication at all, this would obviously be a very clumsy mechanism. Try to imagine walking into a modern department store and finding that the price of a pair of socks is one necktie *or* two packs of cigarettes *or* 1/25 of a tire *or* 15 marbles *or* . . . well, the point is clear. The pricing of goods under such a system would be a nightmare; the keeping of accounting records would be so cumbersome as to be virtually impossible.[2] The existence of money greatly simplifies accounting and pricing practices. The value of all goods can be put in money terms,

[2]The distinction between the unit of account and the numeraire has deliberately been slurred here, though they are conceptually different. An economy could keep books in terms of paper clips (the unit of account) and at the same time express the value of everything in terms of potatoes (the numeraire). But the distinction is not worth making in this context.

and bookkeeping can also be reckoned in the same way. Money becomes a common denominator. Economists call this aspect of money its *unit of account* function.

Although money almost always serves as a unit of account, there have been historical instances in which it has not. In a hyperinflation, for example, when prices are rising almost hourly, merchants may keep their books in terms of a foreign currency with a value that is more stable than that of the local currency even though the local currency continues to circulate. For this reason some economists prefer to think of the unit of account function as a desirable, but not necessary, property of money. But for all practical purposes, money functions as a unit of account.

Money as a Medium of Exchange

Let us return to our barter economy, where goods are exchanged only for other goods. Suppose you are a dentist on vacation and you decide to stop for dinner. How do you pay for it? In a barter economy your only choice would be to hunt (hungrily) for a cook with a toothache. The example sounds absurd, but actually it isn't. For exchange to take place in the absence of money there must be what economists call a *double coincidence of wants.* By this is meant that the wants or needs of two people must coincide; the cook must have a toothache, and the dentist must be hungry.

Money changes all this. Money is generalized purchasing power. Each of us—dentists, cooks, students, and professors—works for money and then uses this money to buy the goods and services everyone else produces. This characteristic of money is called its *medium of exchange* function and is easily the most important function money performs. It permits specialization, not just by job, but also regionally and internationally. It is, in truth, impossible to imagine a complex, modern, industrial economy, with its myriad functional, industrial, and regional interdependencies, without a medium of exchange.

It is necessary to take careful note that money *is* the medium of exchange, not the other way around. That is, we *define* money as anything that performs this function, and we cannot make something into money just by saying it's so. A sow's ear is a sow's ear, not a silk purse. And, as many governments have found to their dismay, legal tender is legal tender, not necessarily money. It may be acceptable for the payment of taxes, but it still may not circulate as a medium of exchange. To perform the medium of exchange function, money must be generally acceptable; that is, virtually everyone must be willing to accept it in payment for goods produced and services rendered. And anything that is so acceptable is money. Historically, many things have served this function—for example, cigarettes in prisoner-of-war camps. And it is necessary to understand that, under such circumstances, cigarettes are money; they don't just perform the same function as money, they *are* money. Money is what it *does,* not what it *is.*

Money as a Store of Value

A third function of money, which is derived largely from its medium-of-exchange function, is that it serves as a *store of value.* What is meant by this, basically, is that money functions as a medium of exchange over time, as well as at an instant of time. Thus, people are willing to be paid only once a week or once a month since they know that the money they are paid today will still be money tomorrow. There is no need to spend money instantly in the fear that something else will shortly be in use as the medium of exchange. The individual is thus enabled to save from his or her present income in order to consume in the future.

Other goods, as well as money, may also serve as a store of value. One can "save" in terms of diamonds, real estate, or rare coins. Thus, while whatever is currently money must perform the function of a store of value, many things that are stores of value are not money. It is first necessary to buy these things (with money), hold them, and then sell them (for money). It is necessary only to hold money. In short, the store-of-value function is a necessary but not sufficient condition for calling something money.

Money as a Standard of Deferred Payment

The fourth and final function of money is that it is a *standard of deferred payment.* This is just a fancy way of saying that debts are expressed in money terms. Of course, it is very convenient to be able to do this because money is generalized purchasing power, expressible in definite and standardized units. It is much more sensible to lend $1,000 for ten years than to lend a cow for ten years. If you lend the money, you know what you'll be repaid; if you lend the cow, the one you get back may be much different from the one you parted with. Thus, while it is possible to conceive of debts being expressed in things other than money, these other things are almost certain to be considerably less convenient.

11-2 THE IMPORTANCE OF MONEY

A discussion of the functions of money does not adequately impart a sense of the importance of money. Such an approach is too detached and "scientific," like analyzing why a joke is funny. It fails to capture the dramatic qualities of money.

The world as we know it could not exist without money. It simply wouldn't work. A world without money could contain only the most crude and primitive economies, could support only a fraction of the people now alive. Contemporary civilization—the arts and sciences as well as trade and commerce—is directly dependent on the human invention called money. Although money is not a factor of production like land, labor, and capital, it is a sine qua non of modern production methods—a permissive factor, in the absence of which land, labor, and capital would be rendered virtually impotent. Adam Smith is noted for his attack on the "mercantilist fallacy," which confused gold and wealth. In his great book, *The Wealth of Nations* (1776), Smith nevertheless listed money as one of the four kinds of "circulating capital," referring to it as the "great wheel of circulation."[3] Smith's judgment has been borne out many times. No matter how badly a currency depreciates in value, it continues to circulate. There is simply no adequate substitute for money, nor can we do without it.

[3]Smith was also careful to point out, however, that it is necessary to subtract money to determine the "neat [net] revenue" of the nation.

11-3 KINDS OF MONEY: COMMODITY STANDARDS

The societies of classical antiquity and primitive societies of modern times tend to use as money whatever is close at hand. What is close at hand is usually a commodity of some sort. When a society uses a commodity for money, it is said to be on a *commodity standard.* If a society is sufficiently undeveloped, just about any useful commodity will do. Salt and cattle, for example, were used as money in ancient Rome; tobacco was used in the early American colonies; and pigs were used in some South Sea islands. All kinds of commodities, ranging from grain to animal skins, have been used as money.[4]

A good currency needs to possess several characteristics, among which are: It must be expressible in standard units so that everyone is talking about the same thing; it must be divisible into very small units so that small purchases can be made; it must be easily transportable so that travelers can carry it with them; and it must be durable so that travelers arrive with the same thing they set out with (dead pigs are not in great demand).

Metallic Standards

It is clear that until recent times metals have proved the most popular form for money to take, chiefly because they possess the desirable characteristics just noted. In ancient times, iron and copper were used, but as mining and smelting techniques improved, these metals lost much of their scarcity value and gold and silver became the predominant form of money.

Bimetallism   Throughout most of modern times, gold and silver have circulated simultaneously as money. Although we are currently accustomed to thinking of gold as the more popular of the two metals, in fact silver was most often used until approximately 150 to 200 years ago. Before that, gold was so scarce and prices and incomes were so low that gold was not a convenient metal for ordinary purchases; it had to be divided into units that were too small to be used easily. Silver, on the contrary, was well adapted to everyday use, and consequently was the metal most commonly used in ordinary transactions. However, the Spanish discovery of gold in the New World and, more especially, the gold strikes in Australia and California in the nineteenth century expanded the world's gold supply sufficiently that gold came into ordinary usage.

Although some countries used either gold or silver exclusively as the basis of their money supply, by far the most common standard was to use both. The use of both gold and silver is called *bimetallism,* or the *bimetallic standard.* Bimetallism involved a governmental definition of the ratio of exchange between gold and silver. For example, between 1792 and 1834 in the United States, the official ratio of silver to gold was 15 : 1; that is, 15 ounces of silver could be exchanged for 1 ounce of gold. Because the coins minted were *full-bodied* (contained their full commodity value of

[4]Commodities possessing no intrinsic value have also been used, for example, feathers, shells, and even woodpecker scalps.

bulk gold or silver), countries on a bimetallic standard were often plagued with problems of regulation.

Gresham's Law   The central regulatory problem of bimetallism was first analyzed by Sir Thomas Gresham in 1558. The traditional statement of *Gresham's law* (as it came to be called) is that "bad money drives out good." Put in this fashion, it is one of those time-honored expressions that sounds good but doesn't really make much sense unless you already know what it means. What Gresham's law means is this: Under a bimetallic standard, gold and silver had both an official ratio of exchange as monetary units and an unofficial ratio of exchange as commodities. When these two ratios were not the same, something had to give. And what gave was the undervalued metal. For example, suppose that the government fixes the silver/gold ratio at 15:1 but that at some later date silver becomes more plentiful and it then takes 16 ounces of silver to buy 1 ounce of gold. Under such circumstances, you could make a profit by trading silver coins for gold coins at a 15:1 ratio and then melting down the gold coins and buying 16 ounces of silver bullion with 1 ounce of gold bullion, thus ending with an ounce more silver than you began with. But since the process is easily understood and simply done, everyone does it and pretty soon there aren't any more gold coins. Bad money (the overvalued silver) has driven out good (the undervalued gold).

The historical importance of Gresham's law is that it explains why a bimetallic standard was so awkward for governments to use. Politics and politicians being what they are, the official ratio of exchange between silver and gold changed much less frequently than their commodity ratio. Countries that were officially on a bimetallic standard therefore often found themselves on a de facto silver (or gold) standard; one metal or the other would periodically disappear from circulation. The only ultimate solution to this problem was to go onto a *monometallic* (single metal) standard, usually gold. Toward the end of the nineteenth century, virtually all major nations were on a gold standard.

The Gold Standard   A complete description of the gold standard would be inappropriate at this point. First, *the* gold standard is not in fact a single thing. It is, rather, variations on a theme, with many shades of meaning and subtleties of distinction. To go into these now would be discursive. Second, the gold standard is really as much (or more) an international monetary standard as a domestic monetary standard, and the necessary background to international financial arrangements has not yet been developed. Consequently, the following discussion of the gold standard will be brief and should not be considered definitive.

In its purest form, the gold standard is a system in which a country defines its monetary unit in terms of gold. For example, when the United States officially went on the gold standard in 1900, the dollar was officially valued at 25.8 grains of gold, 9/10 fine. This means that our gold coins had that much gold in them and that such coins could be converted into gold bullion and vice versa. Money gold was thus convertible into commodity gold, and commodity gold was convertible into money gold. Perhaps the primary advantage of this system was that it gave ordinary citizens complete confidence in their money; the coins they carried in their pockets were worth their full market value as commodities. For everyone taken together, this confidence was misplaced since the demand for gold (and hence its commodity value) was due largely to its use as money. But as long as the country stayed on the gold standard, such considerations were of no concern to the individual citizen; his or her confidence in the value of a twenty-dollar gold piece was well justified.

Nor was this all. Since *all* countries defined their monetary unit in terms of gold, gold served as a common denominator for international financial transactions. That is, if you can convert dollars to gold at a fixed ratio and if you can convert gold to (British) pounds at another fixed ratio, then the ratio of exchange between dollars and pounds is also determined. In this fashion, the rates of exchange of the monetary units of all countries were fixed in relation to one another. Americans going abroad for a European tour would know in advance precisely how many pounds, francs, and marks their dollars would buy.

The great advantage of the gold standard was its stability—the feeling of security that it worked in business people, financiers, and just plain people. But it also had disadvantages, which eventually proved its undoing. Easily the most basic disadvantage of the gold standard was that it insinuated a substantial measure of unevenness into the performance of the domestic economy. If a country had an adverse balance of payments—roughly, if it were buying more goods and services from other countries than it were selling to them—then this excess of foreign expenditures over receipts from abroad had to be paid for with gold. Gold had to be shipped out of the country. While countries maintained *gold reserves* to take care of temporary gold outflows, such reserves clearly could not be sufficient to accommodate long-run outflows. A persistently adverse balance of payments must eventually lead to a complete loss of gold.

Faced with the prospect of long-run gold outflows, a country that wanted to stay on the gold standard had only one real option open to it: It had to deflate its domestic economy. That is, such a country had to adopt policy measures designed to lower its prices. When this happened, foreigners would buy more of its goods and services, and its citizens would buy less abroad. The original source of the problem —the excess of foreign expenditures over foreign receipts—would thus be resolved; expenditures would go down, receipts would go up, and the gold outflow would stop.

The problem was that the cure was frequently more painful than the disease. A deflation of the domestic economy meant more than just falling prices. It also meant a host of other social ills, such as unemployment, falling stock prices, small-business bankruptcies, and labor unrest. During the heyday of laissez faire economics, when governments were widely held to bear no responsibility for such economic misfortunes, this process was politically tolerable. But with the worldwide shift in the 1930s to the welfare-state philosophy, the gold standard in its pure form was largely abandoned.

Representative Money

For clarity and simplicity of exposition, we have been discussing commodity standards under the pretense that only the commodities themselves circulate as money. This is not, of course, true. Virtually any commodity—even gold—becomes too bulky to circulate when large sums are involved. For this reason, many commodities circulate in representative form, which means that the commodity is put on deposit and then some evidence of ownership is circulated in lieu of the commodity itself. For example, between 1900 and 1933 the United States government issued gold certificates. These gold certificates were backed up 100 percent by gold held by the U.S. Treasury and could be converted into gold at any time by presenting the certificates to the Treasury; they were "as good as gold" and a great deal more convenient. Such notes are called *representative money* and do not in any way alter the description or analysis of commodity standards.

11-4 KINDS OF MONEY: FIAT STANDARDS

It is only a short intellectual step from grasping the idea of representative money to understanding *fiat money*. Representative money requires that the full commodity value of a certificate be held on deposit, for example, that gold certificates be backed 100 percent by gold deposits. Suppose, instead, we require that gold certificates be backed only 50 percent by gold. Would this work? The answer, which has been demonstrated over and over again, is yes. The situation is wholly analogous to the deposit-reserve relationship of a commercial bank. Since everybody doesn't want their gold at the same time, the value of the gold actually held on deposit may be substantially less than the value of the certificates in circulation. For example, between 1914 and 1945 in the United States, Federal Reserve Notes were backed only 40 percent by gold certificates.

But the process needn't stop here. If 40 percent will do, why not 25 percent? And if 25 percent, why not 10 percent? And, indeed, why not 0 percent? One feels, of course, that 0 percent is too much—it represents a difference in kind, not just degree. If money has *no* commodity backing, then no one can convert their certificates into gold. But why do they have to? Money is what it does, not what it is. And what money does is to perform the functions discussed in section 11-1. Anything that will function as a unit of account, medium of exchange, store of value, and standard of deferred payment *is* money. If you can take a dollar bill to your neighborhood tavern and buy a beer with it, then that dollar bill is money whether it can be converted into a fixed amount of gold or not.

Money that does not depend on full-value commodity backing is called *fiat money*, or *token money*.[5] In the United States today, all of our hand-to-hand currency—the coins and bills we carry in our pockets, purses, and wallets—is fiat money. This seems to worry some people, but it shouldn't. The important question is not if there is gold backing for your currency somewhere in the vaults of the U.S. Treasury, but if the currency will be accepted by your friendly neighborhood bartender.

---

[5]There is a technical distinction between fiat money and token money: Fiat money has no commodity backing while token money has partial commodity backing. The distinction is not usually operational and hence has not been made in the text. It can be important, however, when the market value of the commodity backing of token money rises. Thus in the 1960s the commodity value of the silver content of some United States coins went above their monetary value. Gresham's law then went into operation, with the result that the old dimes, quarters, and half-dollars disappeared from circulation.

11-5   KINDS OF MONEY: DEPOSIT MONEY

The money we have been discussing so far is obviously money. Pennies, nickels, dimes, quarters, $1 bills, $5 bills, and so on—no one really has any doubt that these are money. What is not so obvious (until it's pointed out) is that these things constitute only a small fraction of the total money supply of the United States— about one-fourth. The other three-fourths is *deposit money*—the demand deposits (checking accounts) held by commercial banks. To see that demand deposits are, in fact, money, run through the checklist of the functions of money:[6] (1) Are demand deposits a medium of exchange? Clearly they are. We are paid by check and we make most of our payments by check, that is, by transferring demand deposits from one person to another. (2) Are demand deposits a store of value? Of course. People and corporations hold wealth in the form of demand deposits. (3) Are demand deposits a standard of deferred payment? Again, the answer is yes. People pay off their debts on automobiles, homes, appliances, and so on, by writing monthly checks to their creditors.

Since the demand deposits of commercial banks perform the functions of money, they must therefore be classified as money. Note that it is the demand deposits *themselves* that are money, not just the checks written against the deposits. Just as a dollar bill is money even though it is tucked away in your billfold, so a demand deposit is money even though it is tucked away in the bank. A check indicates the spending of money, but it is the deposit itself that is the money.

11-6   THE UNITED STATES MONEY SUPPLY

From the preceding discussion, it is apparent that there are three kinds of money currently extant in the United States: coins, circulating notes, and demand deposits. With some minor exceptions (noted in Table 11-1) these components of the money supply are issued by the U.S. Treasury, the Federal Reserve System, and the commercial banking system, respectively. It should be borne in mind that each component of the money supply is fully convertible into each other component. That is, coins may be converted into dollar bills, dollar bills may be converted into demand deposits, demand deposits may be converted into coins, and so on. The interchangeability of the different kinds of money permits the public to hold its money in the most convenient form.

The advantages of coins are obvious: Exact change can be paid and received, and coin-operated machines can be used. The disadvantage, of course, is that coins are bulky and therefore difficult to transport. In general, these advantages and disadvantages are reversed when comparing circulating notes with coins: Notes are easily transported but do not come in denominations of less than $1. The major disadvantage of circulating notes is that they are subject to theft and loss. Particularly where large sums are involved, therefore, most people prefer to use checks

---

[6]Demand deposits are not, of course, a unit of account; however, they are denominated in the unit of account—dollars.

Table 11–1   The Circulating United States Money Supply, March 31, 1978
(Millions of Dollars)

Type of money	Amount	Percent
Coins		
Dollars*	1,024	0.2
Fractional coins*	9,113	2.0
Circulating notes		
United States notes*	315	0.1
Federal Reserve notes†	91,660	20.9
Miscellaneous, in process of retirement	281	0.1
Demand deposits‡	336,300	76.7
Total	438,693	100.0

    * Obligation of the U.S. Treasury.
    † Obligation of the Federal Reserve System.
    ‡ Obligation of the commercial banking system.
    Source: Treasury Bulletin, May 1978, p. 24; and the Federal Reserve Bulletin,
May 1978, p. A16 for demand deposits.

(demand deposits). The disadvantage of checking-account money is that it is sometimes difficult or impossible to spend; many business firms are reluctant to accept
out-of-town checks.

    The various pros and cons of the three different kinds of money are weighed
by individuals when deciding in what form to keep their money. The important point
to note is that the composition (as opposed to the total amount) of the money supply
is determined wholly by the public. If people should find it convenient to hold more
currency and fewer deposits (as is always the case around Christmastime) they need
only go to the commercial banks and convert deposits into currency. If business firms
find themselves with too much till cash (as is always the case right after Christmastime) they need only take this currency to commercial banks and *deposit* it, i.e.,
convert it to demand deposits. The proportions among coins, bills, and deposits are
a matter of the convenience of the public only. Monetary policy consists in controlling the total money stock of the country, not its component parts.

11-7 NEAR MONEY

At the end of Chapter 6, dealing with nonbank financial intermediaries, it was noted
that many economists argue for including certain savings accounts in the definition
of money. While it is not traditional to do so, the lack of tradition is hardly a
persuasive objection, and it is therefore necessary to examine the question more
closely.

    Consider a passbook savings account at a commercial bank. Should this have
been included in Table 11-1 as a fourth component of the United States money
supply, fully comparable to coins, bills, and demand deposits? The traditional way
to approach this problem is to go through the checklist of the functions of money
(as was done with demand deposits). If you do so, you will find that savings accounts
are not a medium of exchange (you don't buy things with them) or a standard of

deferred payment. The only monetary function performed directly by a savings account is that it is a store of value; that is, one can accumulate wealth in this form. But since one can accumulate wealth in many forms, including such real assets as land and antique cars, this does not seem to be a very compelling reason for including savings deposits in our statistics of the money stock of the country.

Advocates for the inclusion of savings accounts in the money supply admit, of course, that the above conclusion follows from the premise. If you define money in functional terms, then you will conclude that demand deposits are money but savings deposits are not; if you begin with a traditional approach, you will get a traditional answer. They therefore argue in favor of a different approach in defining money. Money, they say, is one asset among many assets. These various assets have numerous characteristics: houses may be lived in; insurance policies protect your family under adverse circumstances; savings deposits earn interest; and so forth. From the viewpoint of defining what is meant by *money,* the most relevant characteristic that assets have is *liquidity.* As was discussed in Chapter 10, all assets have some degree of liquidity, but some have more than others. Money has the most liquidity. Indeed, abstractly considered, money is perfectly liquid. But in the real world even what we traditionally and unequivocally call money is not absolutely liquid. Checks cannot always be cashed (we have all seen signs reading "no checks cashed here"), and even currency is not always acceptable, especially large bills. But if we admit that no asset possesses *perfect* liquidity and that all assets possess *some* liquidity, then the obvious question is, Where do we draw the line between money and other assets? In other words, how much liquidity is needed to qualify an asset as money?

Unfortunately, this question does not admit of a ready answer. We cannot analytically specify a point on the liquidity scale above which an asset is money and below which it is just another asset. Using this nontraditional approach, money becomes a matter of degree, not a matter of kind. However, there are two kinds of empirical studies that, although they do not answer the question, can at least be helpful in shedding further light on the issue. The first such approach is to estimate the *cross elasticity of demand.* The cross elasticity of demand between two goods is basically a measure of their substitutability for one another. If, for example, we wished to know to what extent consumers regard apples and pears as substitutes, we would do a study of their cross elasticities. The question we would ask would go like this: If there is a 1 percent change in the price of pears, what will be the percentage change in the quantity of apples demanded? If the answer is 0 percent, then we would say that apples and pears are not substitutes for one another; if the answer is 50 percent, we would say that they are close substitutes. The higher the cross elasticity between two goods, the closer substitutes they are. (Cross elasticities can be estimated with regression analysis, although the actual models used go beyond the scope of this book.)

The substitutability between demand deposits and savings deposits can be estimated by using the cross-elasticity approach. The *price* of a savings deposit is the rate of interest it pays, and the *quantity demanded* of demand deposits is the total amount extant at a point in time. The purpose of such a study is to use the results as an aid in the decision to include or exclude savings deposits as a part of the money supply. If savings deposits are close substitutes for demand deposits, then a good case might be made for their inclusion; if they are poor substitutes, then the traditional definition is strengthened. The studies[7] made on this subject, although certainly not conclusive, seem to indicate generally low cross elasticities, roughly in the 0 to –0.50 range. Since what is meant by a "close" substitute is open to dispute, such results can hardly be considered as settling the matter. But by the same token they do not afford compelling evidence for breaking with tradition and including savings deposits in the statistical definition of the money supply of the United States.

The second approach to the issue of whether to include savings deposits in the money supply comes at the question from a wholly different angle. The basic question posed in this approach is, What difference does it make? Is it simply a compulsive need economists have to classify things into tidy little categories, or is something more fundamental at stake? The answer is that our concern with the proper definition of money is ultimately a concern with the determination of national income. Many economists are persuaded that one of the primary factors in determining national income is changes in the stock of money. If this is what concerns us, they hold, then we should define as *money* any financial asset that gives us a close *statistical* relationship between changes in money (so defined) and national income. The approach is essentially pragmatic; we define as money anything that "works," statistically speaking.

It is tempting to poke fun at this approach. If we should find, e.g., that defining money to include horses improves the statistical relationship between money and national income, should we then do so? But this is a cheap shot. There are appealing theoretical reasons for counting savings deposits as money; there is no reason for counting horses. And it *is* the relationship between money and national income that lies at the heart of the matter.[8]

Empirical studies dealing with this approach have in general been inconclusive. In discussions to come, therefore, when which concept of money is used becomes of critical importance, we shall refer to money both with and without savings deposits. In the meantime, we shall hold the matter in abeyance, recognizing that there is no definite, clearcut answer to the question.

Money: M_1, M_2, M_3, M_4, and M_5

Because the "correct" or "true" definition of money is a matter of controversy among economists, the Federal Reserve System actually computes five statistical series of the money supply. The first of these is the conventional, or traditional, definition of money as the sum of coins, circulating notes, and demand deposits

[7]For an excellent survey of all the work done in this field, see Edgar L. Feige and Douglas K. Pearce, "The Substitutability of Money and Near-Monies: A Survey of the Time-Series Evidence," *Journal of Economic Literature,* June 1977, pp. 439–469.

[8]For a very thoughtful criticism of this approach, however, which is definitely *not* a cheap shot, see Will E. Mason, "The Empirical Definition of Money: A Critique," *Economic Inquiry,* December 1976, pp. 525–538.

adjusted.[9] This data series of the money supply is called M_1 *money*. In contrast, the M_2 supply of money consists of M_1 money plus time deposits (other than large negotiable CDs) at commercial banks. M_3 money is M_2 plus deposits of mutual savings banks, savings and loan shares, and credit union shares. The M_4 and M_5 concepts of money are computed by adding large negotiable certificates of deposit to M_2 and M_3, respectively. It would be comforting if all these different concepts of money moved together at the same time, in the same direction, and by the same amount. Unfortunately, they don't.[10] Especially in the short run (a few weeks or months), they frequently grow at different rates and occasionally even move in opposite directions. Figure 11-1 shows annual movements in all five series since 1959.

The Changing Concept of Money

The United States is currently undergoing sweeping institutional changes that are likely to alter fundamentally what we define as "money." These institutional changes include means of payment alternative to currency and demand deposits at commercial banks. For clearly, such things as NOW accounts at savings and loan associations and share drafts at credit unions perform all the functions of money including, most particularly, the medium-of-exchange function. Additionally, the potentials of the electronic funds transfer system to provide the public with "electronic money" are vast. For the EFTS has the potential, not just to duplicate the checking system electronically, but to create wholly new methods of payment.

So far, these new payments instruments are quantitatively small, amounting to about 1 percent of currency and demand deposits. But they are growing rapidly, and promise to be much more important in the future.[11]

11-8   CREDIT AND MONEY

A common question for students to ask is, Is credit money? What the student usually has in mind is charge accounts and credit cards. If one can "buy" gasoline, dinners, and motel rooms with a credit card, then isn't the credit card money? The question is a sensible one and deserves a careful answer.

The distinction between credit and money can perhaps most readily be made if we begin with the simplest case and work up to more complicated examples. Suppose that you want to buy an automobile and, in order to do so, borrow $3,000 from the bank. When it makes this loan to you, the bank will probably simply

---

[9] *Demand deposits adjusted* are gross demand deposits minus the sum of interbank deposits, United States government deposits, and cash items in the process of collection. The adjustment is made in order to avoid double counting (interbank deposits and CIPC) and eliminate balances on which checks are not actually written (United States government deposits—see Chapter 9).

[10] See Anne Marie Laporte, "Monetary Aggregates Compared," Federal Reserve Bank of Chicago *Business Conditions,* June 1976, pp. 11–15.

[11] For a more extended discussion of these matters, see Carl M. Gambs, "Money-Changing Concept in a Changing World," Federal Reserve Bank of Kansas City *Monthly Review,* January 1977, pp. 3–12.

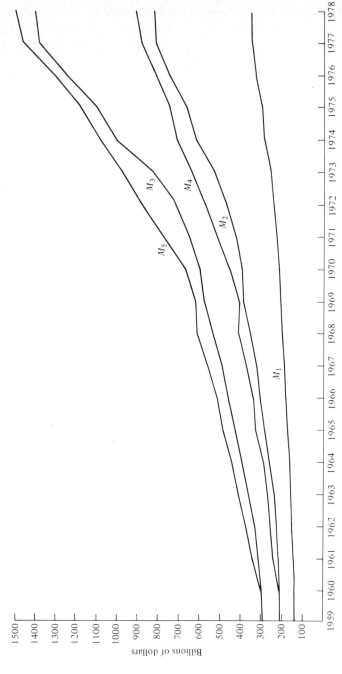

Figure 11-1 M_1, M_2, M_3, M_4 and M_5. (Seasonally adjusted; billions of dollars.) M_1: Net demand deposits plus currency in circulation outside banks; M_2: M_1 plus time and savings deposits at commercial banks, except large negotiable certificates of deposit; M_3: M_2 plus deposits in S&Ls, MSBs, and CUs; M_4: M_2 plus large negotiable CDs; M_5: M_3 plus large negotiable CDs. (*Source:* Federal Reserve Bulletin, *May 1978 for years 1974–1978. Previous years from various issues.*)

increase your demand deposit. The bank's books will then show an increase in its assets (the loan) of $3,000 and an increase in its liabilities (your deposit) of a like amount. Clearly, we cannot count *both* the loan and the deposit as money; if we did so, we would be counting the same thing twice. We therefore count the deposit as money (because it is the deposit that can be spent) and the loan (the bank's asset) as credit.

This same distinction continues to hold under more complicated circumstances. In the preceding example, clearly it would make no difference if you financed the purchase of the automobile through a new car dealer, who, in turn, borrowed the money from the bank. The credit transactions would still be distinct from the money transactions. And, if this is the case when you sign a note on the car, it would still be the case if instead you bought the car with a credit card (which you can't, but the principle is the same).

Credit is not money. The two are analytically distinct. Nevertheless, credit and money are closely related to one another. Indeed, credit is the basis of much of our money, as will be demonstrated in the following chapter.

11-9 REVIEW QUESTIONS

1 What are the four functions of money?
2 Distinguish between a commodity standard and fiat money. Give an example of each.
3 Do you think that a savings deposit in an S&L should be considered as money? Why or why not? Do you think that a better case can be made today for including S&L deposits than could have been made ten years ago? Why?
4 Are money and credit the same thing? Explain.

12

The Supply of Money

Chapter 11 was addressed to the issue of what money is. We now want to ask, Where does money come from? In the case of circulating notes and coins, the answer to this question is relatively simple. In the case of demand deposits, the answer is more complex.

Circulating notes and coins (or, more simply, *currency*) are issued at the convenience of the public. That is, the public may have as many or as few dollar bills as it wants within the limit set by the total amount of money in the economy. The Treasury and the Federal Reserve stand passive in the matter, ready to issue currency in whatever amounts and denominations the public finds useful. Suppose, for example, that the public were suddenly to decide it wanted to hold more currency. It would then go to the commercial banks and convert demand deposits into currency by withdrawing deposits in the form of coins and circulating notes. The immediate impact of this action would be to draw down the vault cash of the banks. In order to replenish their vault cash, the banks would then go to the Federal Reserve and convert their reserves into currency. The Federal Reserve would print and issue Federal Reserve notes in the quantities and denominations asked for by the banks. The process also works in reverse: If the public has more currency than it wants, it "deposits" it (i.e., converts it into demand deposits) in the banking system, which, in turn, exchanges it into demand deposits) in the banking system, which, in turn, exchanges it for additional reserves at the Federal Reserve.

The entire mechanism works smoothly and easily. Indeed, it must work this way, as a moment's reflection will show. If, for example, an attempt were made to restrict the amount of currency in the economy, then it wouldn't be long before currency went to a premium above demand deposits; that is, $1 in currency would be worth more than $1 of deposits. Such a situation would result in a chaotic payments system, which would, in turn, impair the functioning of the economy. The present system avoids this by providing for the full convertibility at par of one kind of money into another.

While in principle the printing and distribution of currency is a simple matter, the source of demand deposits is not. The latter issue requires careful analysis and close attention on the part of the reader. In order to make the discussion as accessible as possible, we shall begin with the simplest case and then move by steps to increasingly complex (and realistic) explanations.

12-1   THE ECONOMICS OF DEPOSIT CREATION

The first step in understanding the process whereby commercial banks create money in the form of demand deposits is to gain a firm, intuitive understanding of the economics involved. Once this understanding is achieved, we can then move on to the compact shorthand of mathematical notation. But the mathematics will be of little value unless there is first an understanding of the economics.

The T Account

It is desirable at this point to make a brief digression in order to introduce and explain a tool of analysis that is frequently helpful in economic theory: the *T account.* A T account is simply an abbreviated form of the balance sheet, showing only the *changes* that have occurred between two points in time. In economic analysis, the T account is most frequently used for showing the consequences of a single transaction on the books of a firm. It is called a *T account* because in form it looks like a large T, with the change in assets being shown in the space under the left-hand side of the crossbar of the T, and the change in liabilities (and capital, if any) being shown on the right.

To illustrate the use of a T account, suppose that someone deposits $1,000 of currency in a bank. The bank then has a $1,000 increase in its deposits (a liability) and a $1,000 increase in its vault cash (an asset). The T account depicting this transaction would be as follows:

Δ Assets		Δ Liabilities	
Vault cash	+$1,000	Demand deposits	+$1,000

It is necessary to emphasize two aspects of the T account: First, it shows only changes in the balance sheet. In the preceding example, the underlying balance sheet may be very detailed and complicated. By showing only changes, we avoid cluttering the sheet with all the items that remain the same. Second, note that the T account must *balance* just as a balance sheet must balance (and for the same reason). That is, either both sides of the T account must change by the same amount and in the same direction, or there must be offsetting changes on the same side so that the net (algebraic) result is zero.

Assumptions of the Simplified Model

In order to understand the nature of the basic economic process underlying the creation of deposits, it is useful to begin by stripping away many of the complicating elements that are operative in the real world. We do this by making certain simplifying assumptions. These assumptions are, of course, unrealistic—indeed, if they were not unrealistic, there would be no point in making them. Once the nature of the simplified process is grasped, then we can proceed to more realistic models by eliminating the assumptions. The initial assumptions are as follows:

Assumption 1. We shall suppose that the commercial banking system is composed of many banks and that each of these banks is required by law to hold *20 percent cash reserves* against its demand deposits. By *cash reserves* is meant that a bank must hold its reserves either as currency in its vaults or as a deposit at the Federal Reserve.

Assumption 2. We shall assume that the public does not change its currency holdings throughout the process to be described. This assumption may be more succinctly expressed by saying that there is *no currency drain* from the banking system.

Assumption 3. We shall assume that each commercial bank in the banking system will put all the money that is legally possible into earning assets (loans and investments). In other words, it is assumed that there are *no excess reserves* in the banking system.

Assumption 4. Finally, we shall assume that the public does not alter its holdings of time deposits throughout the process—that there is *no time deposit drain.*

Summary. The four assumptions may be summarized as follows:

1 20 percent cash reserves
2 No cash drain
3 No excess reserves
4 No time deposit drain

Δ Assets		Δ Liabilities	
Cash Reserves	+$1,000	Borrowings from Fed	+$1,000

Figure 12-1 T Account of member bank after borrowing $1,000 from the Federal Reserve.

The Economic Process

Let us set the model in motion in the following way. At the end of Chapter 9 it was pointed out that member banks have the privilege of borrowing from the Federal Reserve System. Let us suppose that some member bank exercises this privilege, and that the amount borrowed is $1,000. This transaction would result in the balance sheet changes shown in the T account for the member bank in Figure 12-1. Note that the borrowings (a liability) of the bank have risen by $1,000, and in return the member bank has increased its cash reserves (an asset) by $1,000.

Next suppose that the member bank lends out this $1,000 to a customer, who pays it to someone else, who deposits it in another bank, bank I. This transaction increases both the demand deposits and the cash reserves of bank I, with the resulting change in its balance sheet shown by the T account in Figure 12-2a. Note that at this point bank I stands in violation of assumptions 1 and 3. That is, by assumption 1 the bank is required to hold only 20 percent ($200) of this new deposit in its cash reserves; and by assumption 3 the bank will put all of its excess reserves ($800) into earning assets. It is, of course, in the self-interest of the bank to invest this excess cash, since in its present form the cash earns no interest and hence no profits for the stockholders. Let us therefore suppose that the bank lends the $800 of excess reserves to a local haberdasher who borrows the money to finance an

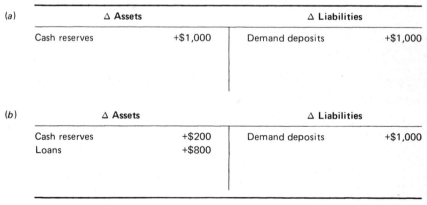

(a)	Δ Assets		Δ Liabilities	
	Cash reserves	+$1,000	Demand deposits	+$1,000

(b)	Δ Assets		Δ Liabilities	
	Cash reserves	+$200	Demand deposits	+$1,000
	Loans	+$800		

Figure 12-2 T Accounts of bank I.

addition to his spring line of men's suits. After the haberdasher has taken the money from the bank, the change in the bank's balance sheet will be as shown by the T account in Figure 12-2b. Note that bank I now conforms to our initial assumptions: It has met the 20 percent legal reserve requirement and is holding no excess reserves.

What happens to the $800? Suppose that the haberdasher pays it over to the clothing manufacturer from whom the suits were bought. By assumption 2, the clothing manufacturer cannot hold the $800 in the form of currency, nor can she (by assumption 4) put it into a time account. She must, that is, put the $800 into a demand deposit in her bank, bank II. Bank II's balance sheet then changes in the manner indicated by the T account in Figure 12-3a.

Note that bank II is now in the same position that bank I was in initially. It has $800 of cash reserve backing up $800 of demand deposits, but it needs only $160 (20 percent of $800) in reserves; it is holding $640 ($800 – $160) of excess reserves and thus is violating assumption 3. Let us suppose that in order to remedy this situation bank II buys Treasury bills in the amount if $640. In this case, the change in the balance sheet of bank II will be as shown in Figure 12-3b. Bank II is now, of course, back in equilibrium and is no longer violating assumption 3.

At the risk of repeating the analysis ad nauseam, let us go through one more round. The $640 worth of Treasury bills bought by bank II were bought from someone, and that someone now has the $640. Again by assumptions 2 and 4, this money must be placed in a demand deposit of a commercial bank—say, bank III. Bank III is now in the same initial position as banks I and II (see Figure 12-4a). And it will, of course, respond in the same way—by drawing down its cash reserves to $128 (20 percent of $640) and expanding its loans and investments by $512 ($640–$128). Figure 12-4b gives the relevant T account.

Obviously, the $512 will be put on deposit at still another bank, and the process will go on and on. But the repetition is tiresome. Rather than tracing the money through successive rounds of deposit-invest-deposit transactions, let us instead pause

(a)

Δ Assets		Δ Liabilities	
Cash reserves	+$800	Demand deposits	+$800

(b)

Δ Assets		Δ Liabilities	
Cash reserves	+$160	Demand deposits	+$800
Investments	+$640		

Figure 12-3   T Accounts of bank II.

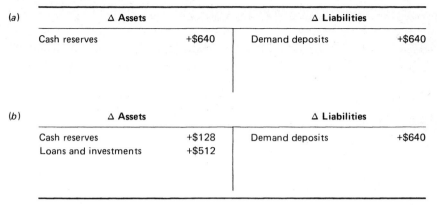

(a)

Δ Assets		Δ Liabilities	
Cash reserves	+$640	Demand deposits	+$640

(b)

Δ Assets		Δ Liabilities	
Cash reserves	+$128	Demand deposits	+$640
Loans and investments	+$512		

Figure 12-4 T Accounts of bank III.

and take stock of what has happened to the banking system by the end of round three. A convenient method for doing this is to *consolidate* the part *(b)* T accounts of banks I, II, and III; that is, we shall add these accounts together and show them in a single, consolidated T account. This is done in Figure 12-5.

The main thing to note about Figure 12-5 is that total demand deposits in these three banks have increased to $2,440. That is, we started with a $1,000 deposit, and we now have $2,440 of demand deposits. Demand deposits have thus been "created" by the banking system. And since demand deposits are money, it is equally accurate to say that the banking system has created money; money has been manufactured by the banking system as a by-product of its lending and investing activities.

There are no tricks—no hidden mirrors or strings—involved in the money-creating process of the commercial banking system. What it comes down to is simply this: Demand deposit money is nothing substantial like gold or silver or even paper notes. Instead, it is a set of bookkeeping entries—ink scratches on the banks' ledgers. And because banks are required to maintain only *fractional reserves* (cash reserves are only a fraction of demand deposits), the bookkeeping arrangements are such that these ledger entries can be expanded by more than a reserve increase. When the banking system obtains new reserves, it can create money by several times that amount.

Δ Assets		Δ Liabilities	
Cash reserves	+$ 488	Demand deposits	+$2,440
Loans and investments	+ 1,952		
Total	+$2,440		+$2,440

Figure 12-5 Consolidated T accounts of banks I, II, and III.

12-2 THE MATHEMATICS OF DEPOSIT CREATION

The question is, Where does the process stop? One way to find this out would be to keep going through the arithmetic of successive rounds. But this would not be very practical for several reasons. For one thing, the process is tiresome; now that the economics of the process are understood, there is nothing more to be gained by generating additional T accounts. For another, an arithmetic example limits us to the particular numbers chosen, and what we would really like is a generalized statement of the problem. Finally, we shall eventually want to relax the initial assumptions, and it is much easier to do this by working with a general formula than with an arithmetic example.

What is desired, therefore, is to set the problem up so that it can be cast in mathematical terms. To see how to do this, consider the $2,440 of deposits in Figure 12-5. This number was obtained, it will be recalled, by summing the deposits of banks I to III. That is, we summed the sequence of numbers

$$1,000$$
$$800$$
$$640$$
$$\cdot$$
$$\cdot$$
$$\cdot$$

But how did we get these numbers? The answer is that each number after the first is 4/5 (80 percent) of the preceding number. That is, the preceding sequence of numbers can also be written as

$$1,000 \quad (= 1,000)$$

$$1,000(4/5) \quad (= 800)$$

$$800(4/5) \quad (= 640)$$
$$\cdot \quad \cdot$$
$$\cdot \quad \cdot$$
$$\cdot \quad \cdot$$

But since the 800 of the third equation is the same as the 800 of the middle equation, we can also write the sequence as

$$1,000 \quad (= 1,000)$$

$$1,000(4/5) \quad (= 800)$$

$$[1,000(4/5)](4/5) \quad (= 640)$$

.   .
.   .
.   .

or

$$1,000 \qquad (= 1,000)$$

$$1,000(4/5) \quad (= 800) \quad 20\%$$

$$1,000(4/5)^2 \quad (= 640)$$

.   .
.   .
.   .

Now we are clearly onto something. This last way of stating the sequence is what is called a *geometric progression,* where the exponent on the fraction (4/5) increases by one each round. With this in mind, let us substitute symbols for the numbers:

ΔB = amount by which the *monetary base* of the banking system has increased ($1,000)

R_D = *reserve requirement* on demand deposits (20%, or 1/5)

$r = 1 - R_D$ (80%, or 4/5)

Thus, the preceding sequence of numbers can be stated symbolically as

$$\Delta B + \Delta Br + \Delta Br^2 + \ldots$$

However, we are interested, not in just the first three rounds, but in what happens to deposits as we go through more rounds. This question can now be put in mathematical terms by asking, What is the sum of a geometric progression? Symbolically, we want to solve the following equation:

$$S = \Delta B + \Delta Br + \Delta Br^2 + \ldots + \Delta Br^{n-1} \tag{1}$$

where S stands for sum and n is any number we choose.

Now multiply both sides of eq. (1) by $1 - r$. Thus

$$(1 - r)S = (1 - r)(\Delta B + \Delta Br + \Delta Br^2 + \ldots + \Delta Br^{n-1}) \tag{2}$$

Performing the indicated multiplication on the right-hand side of eq. (2) gives

$$(1 - r)S = \Delta B + \Delta Br + \Delta Br^2 + \ldots + \Delta Br^{n-1}$$
$$- \Delta Br - \Delta Br^2 - \ldots - \Delta Br^{n-1} - \Delta Br^n$$

Rearranging terms,

$$(1 - r)S = \Delta B + \Delta Br - \Delta Br + \Delta Br^2 - \Delta Br^2$$
$$+ \ldots + \Delta Br^{n-1} - \Delta Br^{n-1} - \Delta Br^n$$

All the intermediate terms on the right-hand side cancel out, so that we are left with

$$(1 - r)S = \Delta B - \Delta Br^n$$

Dividing both sides by $1 - r$ gives

$$S = \frac{\Delta B - \Delta Br^n}{1 - r}$$

or

$$S = \Delta B \frac{1 - r^n}{1 - r}$$

Now we have a general formula that will tell us how many total deposits have been created by the banking system at the end of any given round. To check this, let us see if we can obtain the $2,440 derived from the third round of the T-account analysis. We can do so by letting $\Delta B = \$1,000$, $r = 4/5$, and $n = 3$. Inserting these numbers in eq. (3) gives

$$S = \$1,000 \left(\frac{1 - (4/5)^3}{1 - 4/5} \right)$$

$$= \$1,000 \left(\frac{1 - 64/125}{1/5} \right)$$

$$= \$1,000 \left(\frac{61/125}{25/125} \right)$$

$$= \$1,000(61/25)$$
$$= \$2,440$$

So that's all right; the formula works. But our interest continues to lie in the end result of the process, not just the third (or any other) round. To see where the process stops, consider what happens to the formula of eq. (3) as n becomes very, very large—1 million, 1 billion, and so forth. Since r is less than 1 and greater than

0, as n becomes very large, the expression r^n becomes negligibly small[1] —so small, in fact, that we can simply ignore it. Thus if we were to carry the T-account analysis of section 12-1 to a very large number of rounds, we would find that the total deposits created by the banking system would be equal to $\Delta B\ 1/(1 - r)$.

One further simplifying step can be made: Remember that $r = 1 - R_D$, that is, 1 minus the reserve requirement. But if $r = 1 - R_D$, then clearly $1 - r = 1 - (1 - R_D) = R_D$. Making this substitution, the expansion of demand deposits in the banking system is

$$\Delta D = \Delta B \frac{1}{R_D} \qquad\qquad (4)$$

where ΔD is the change in demand deposits. Returning to the original example, we can now see how much deposit money would be created by the banking system if we continued with the T-account example. Inserting the numbers $\Delta B = \$1,000$ and $R_D = 20$ percent $= 1/5$ in eq. (4), we obtain

$$\begin{aligned} \Delta D &= \$1,000[1/(1/5)] \\ &= \$1,000(5) \\ &= \$5,000 \end{aligned}$$

That is, the end result of the model set in motion in section 12-1 is that the deposits of the banking system would increase by $5,000.

Note that as a by-product of casting the problem in algebraic terms, we have already relaxed assumption 1 of section 12-1. That assumption, it will be recalled, was that reserve requirements are 20 percent or 1/5. But by stating the process in symbolic terms, eq. (4) permits us to substitute any fraction we want for R_D. Thus if $R_D = 1/10$, then ΔD becomes $10,000; if $R_D = 1/4$, then ΔD becomes $4,000. More generally, ΔD and R_D are inversely related; if R_D goes up, ΔD goes down, and conversely.

Equation (4) is very important. It describes the basic process at work in the determination of the money supply. But it is equally important that the student understand the limitations of eq. (4). It is a valid equation only under simplifying assumptions 2 to 4. That is, while eq. (4) describes the fundamentals of the deposit-creating process, it remains unrealistic because it is applicable only to the simplified model of section 12-1.

Contraction of Demand Deposits

One final point needs to be noted: Equation (4) works in both directions; it indicates that the commercial banking system can destroy deposits as well as create them. This is seen most easily by letting ΔB in eq. (4) be a negative number. For example, if the banking system should lose $1,000 of reserves, then $\Delta B = -\$1,000$ and consequently $\Delta D = -\$5,000$. The possibility thus exists that the banking system can

[1]More properly, $\lim\limits_{n \to \infty}\ S = \Delta B/(1 - r)$.

contract the money supply as well as expand it. In fact, the contraction of the money supply because of commercial bank behavior has historically been a very serious economic problem. It has led to (or, at least, worsened) depressions in the past and is the main reason that the Federal Reserve System was established.

12-3 COMPLICATIONS: THE CURRENCY DRAIN

We wish now to see how eq. (4) is modified if assumption 2 (section 12-1) is relaxed by permitting changes in the public's currency holdings. Since our intention in this section is only to assess the general nature of the modification, it will be sufficient for present purposes to replace assumption 2 with an assumption of almost equal simplicity. We therefore assume that when demand deposits change, the public changes its currency holdings by some given proportion of the change in demand deposits—for example, that for every $1 of new demand deposits held by the public, it holds 5 cents more in currency. Algebraically, this relationship can be specified as

$$K = \frac{\Delta C}{\Delta D} \tag{5}$$

where K = currency ratio
  C = amount of currency held by the public
  D = demand deposits

One further relationship needs to be specified at this point: Since it is assumed that the public desires to maintain a given currency ratio, it follows that every time a bank makes a loan or investment the full amount lent or invested is not redeposited in another bank. Instead, some fraction of that amount is "drained" out of the banking system's reserves and converted into hand-to-hand currency. In other words, the initial amount by which reserves are increased [ΔB of eq. (4)] is now divided between currency and bank reserves. Algebraically,

$$\Delta B = \Delta D \ R_D + \Delta C \tag{6}$$

where all the symbols are as previously defined. $\Delta D \ R_D$, the change in deposits times the reserve requirement, is that part of ΔB that stays in the banking system; ΔC is that part of ΔB which is converted into the public's currency holdings. Both of these are dollar amounts, which, taken together, exhaust all of ΔB.

Now it is true that

$$\Delta C = \Delta D \frac{\Delta C}{\Delta D}$$

and from eq. (5), therefore,

$$\Delta C = \Delta D\, K \qquad (7)$$

Substituting eq. (7) into eq. (6) thus gives

$$\Delta B = \Delta D\, R_D + \Delta D\, K$$
$$= \Delta D\, (R_D + K)$$

Dividing both sides by $R_D + K$ then gives

$$\Delta D = \frac{\Delta B}{R_D + K}$$

or

$$\Delta D = \Delta B \frac{1}{R_D + K} \qquad (8)$$

Equations (4) and (8) bear a marked resemblance to one another. The only difference is that eq. (8) has the currency ratio K in the denominator of the right-hand side while eq. (4) does not. Since K is a positive number, it follows that ΔD will be smaller when there is a currency drain than when there is not. To see this, let us repeat the example of section 12-2, adding that $K = 5$ percent $= 1/20$. Then using these numbers with eq. (8) gives

$$\Delta D = \$1,000 \left(\frac{1}{1/5 + 1/20} \right)$$

$$= \$1,000 \left(\frac{1}{5/20} \right)$$

$$= \$1,000 \left(\frac{1}{1/4} \right)$$

$$= \$1,000(4)$$
$$= \$4,000$$

Inclusion of the currency drain has thus reduced the deposit-creating ability of the commercial banking system from $5,000 to $4,000.

It is of some interest to ask what has happened to the original $1,000. Repeating eq. (6),

$$\Delta B = \Delta D \ R_D + \Delta C \tag{6}$$

Since

$$\Delta D \ R_D = \$4,000(1/5)$$
$$= \$800$$

it follows that

$$\Delta C = \$200$$

In other words, of the original $1,000, $800 has gone into the reserves of the banking system and $200 has been drained into the public's hand-to-hand currency. Clearly, the greater the currency ratio, the weaker is the ability of the banking system to create deposits; ΔD is inversely related to K just as it is inversely related to R_D.

The Change in the Money Supply with Currency

One further step remains. Since we are now permitting currency to change, we can no longer assume, as we did in section 12-2, that the change in the money supply and the change in demand deposits are one and the same thing. For now the change in the money supply consists in both the change in demand deposits and the change in currency. That is, letting ΔM be the change in the money supply,

$$\Delta M = \Delta D + \Delta C \tag{9}$$

It would, of course, be convenient to have a formula for ΔM comparable to eq. (8). We can derive such a formula in the following manner. Substituting eq. (7) into eq. (9) yields

$$\Delta M = \Delta D + \Delta D \ K$$
$$= \Delta D \ (1 + K) \tag{10}$$

Now, substituting eq. (8) into eq. (10), we have

$$\Delta M = \frac{\Delta B}{R_D + K}(1 + K)$$
$$= \Delta B \frac{1 + K}{R_D + K} \tag{11}$$

Equation (11), the formula for the expansion of the money supply, may also be illustrated with the previous example. Using the same numbers, we have

$$\Delta M = \$1,000 \left(\frac{1 + 1/20}{1/5 + 1/20} \right)$$

$$= \$1,000 \left(\frac{21/20}{5/20} \right)$$

$$= \$1,000(21/5)$$
$$\Delta M = \$4,200$$

That is, the money supply has expanded by \$4,200–\$4,000 of demand deposits and \$200 of currency. Note that the currency ratio

$$K = \frac{\Delta C}{\Delta D}$$

$$= \frac{\$200}{\$4,000}$$

$$= 1/20$$

12-4   COMPLICATIONS: EXCESS RESERVES

Assumption 3 (section 12-1), that the banking system holds no reserves in excess of those legally required, is not a particularly unrealistic assumption. As we pointed out in Chapter 10, banks do not like to hold more nonearning assets than are necessary. Nevertheless, some banks, especially small banks, feel that the cost of managing their money position so that excess reserves are always zero is prohibitively high. They consequently maintain a certain amount of excess reserves as a "cushion" against the penalty of a reserve deficiency. Additionally, the expansion and contraction of excess reserves has historically been a serious problem for the monetary authorities. For both these reasons, it is worth the effort to see how the introduction of excess reserves into the model modifies the deposit-creating powers of the commercial banking system.

Actually, the introduction of excess reserves into the model is a fairly simple step. In terms of the algebra involved, the mechanics of excess reserves are very similar to those of the cash drain. Therefore, many of the intermediate steps need not be repeated. Only two embellishments to the model of section 12-1 have to be added: First, it is necessary to make some behavioral assumption about the amount of excess reserves the banking system wants to hold. And again, the simplest assumption will be sufficient for our purposes. We shall therefore assume that the banking system holds excess reserves in some given ratio to demand deposits. Algebraically, let

$$X = \frac{\Delta E}{\Delta D} \tag{12}$$

where X = excess reserve ratio
         E = dollar amount of excess reserves held by the banking system
         D = demand deposits

The second modification needed is to realize that ΔB, the amount of new reserves injected into the banking system, now has three places to go instead of just two. Now ΔB can go into required reserves, the public's hand-to-hand currency supply, or excess reserves. Thus

$$\Delta B = \Delta D \ R_D + \Delta C + \Delta E \tag{13}$$

Noting that

$$\Delta E = \Delta D \frac{\Delta E}{\Delta D}$$

and therefore, from eq. (12), that

$$\Delta E = \Delta D \ X \tag{14}$$

we can substitute eqs. (7) and (14) into eq. (13) to obtain

$$\begin{aligned} \Delta B &= \Delta D \ R_D + \Delta D \ K + \Delta D \ X \\ &= \Delta D \ (R_D + K + X) \end{aligned} \tag{15}$$

Dividing both sides of eq. (15) by $R_D + K + X$ then gives

$$\Delta D = \Delta B \frac{1}{R_D + K + X} \tag{16}$$

Equation (16) describes the deposit-creating process of commercial banks when both the currency drain and excess reserves are taken into account. It is very similar to eq. (8), the only difference being that X, the excess reserve ratio, has been added into the denominator. And it should be apparent that X, like K and R_D, is inversely related to ΔD; the larger is X, the smaller will be the change in demand deposits for a given addition to reserves, and conversely.

The Change in the Money Supply with Excess Reserves

Equation (16) gives the formula for the change in demand deposits. As in section 12-3, however, we are equally interested in knowing what the change in the money supply will be as a result of an injection of ΔB dollars into the reserves of the banking system. This question is easily answered. Since excess reserves are not a part of the money supply, we can just carry over eq. (10) from section 12-3. For the convenience of the reader, this equation is repeated here:

$$\Delta M = \Delta D \ (1 + K) \tag{10}$$

Substituting eq. (16) into eq. (10) for ΔD gives

$$\Delta M = \Delta B \frac{1 + K}{R_D + K + X} \tag{17}$$

It may be helpful to extend the arithmetic example of section 12-3 to include excess reserves and then crank these numbers through eq. (17). We can do this by assuming that $X = 5$ percent $= 1/20$. The other numbers, it will be recalled, are $\Delta B = \$1,000$, $R_D = 1/5$, and $K = 1/20$. Inserting these values in eq. (17) gives

$$\Delta M = \$1,000 \frac{1 + 1/20}{1/5 + 1/20 + 1/20}$$

$$= \$1,000 \frac{21/20}{6/20}$$

$$= \$1,000 \left(\frac{21}{6}\right)$$

$$= \$3,500$$

As before, it is also pertinent to ask, Where did the original \$1,000 (that is, ΔB) go? This question can be answered by using these same numbers to solve eq. (16) for ΔD and then substituting this value into eq. (15). Doing so, we find that $\Delta D = \$3,333$ and therefore that \$667 ($\Delta D \, R_D$) go into required reserves; \$166 ($\Delta D \, K$) go into hand-to-hand currency; and \$166 ($\Delta D \, X$) go into the excess reserves of the banking system.

12-5   COMPLICATIONS: TIME DEPOSITS

Finally, we want to eliminate assumption 4—that none of the expanded money supply goes into time deposits. Although the mechanics of relaxing this assumption are similar to those of the other three assumptions, the process will seem a bit more complicated. The difference lies in the following considerations. Stripped to bare essentials, the demand deposit expansion process demonstrates that the banking system can expand by $1/R$ any reserves that are not used for other purposes. The "other purposes" we have considered so far are the currency drain and excess reserves. That is, these two purposes constitute a sort of "leak" in the deposit-creating process; and what remains after the leakages have been satisfied can be used as required reserves by commercial banks to support demand deposits in the ratio $1 : 1/R$. Thus, in the example given at the close of section 12-4, after the leakages were taken care of the banking system had \$667 added to its required reserves. This \$667 was then used to support an increase of \$3,333 in demand deposits, a ratio of required reserves to deposits \$667 : \$3,333, or $1 : 5$.

Viewed in this fashion, the question we need to ask is, What is the leakage from the demand deposit expansion process when time deposits are taken into account? The answer is *not* total time deposits, for the time deposits themselves are based on reserves. Rather, the leakage due to time deposits is the *reserves* that banks hold against time deposits. Note that this is a much smaller number than time deposits. For example, if the public wants to hold time and demand deposits in equal amounts, and if the reserve requirement on time deposits is 5 percent, then a $100 expansion of demand deposits will involve an equal expansion of time deposits but only a $5 leakage (5 percent of $100) from the demand deposit expansion process.

With these principles in mind, we can now proceed to introduce time deposits into the analysis. To do so, let us do away with assumption 4 by replacing it with the assumption that the public wants to hold some given ratio of time deposits to demand deposits. Algebraically, we assume that

$$t = \frac{\Delta T}{\Delta D} \tag{18}$$

where t = time deposit ratio
         T = time deposits
         D = demand deposits

As noted, however, unlike K and X, t does not constitute the drain on the banking system's reserves. Rather, the leakage is the reserves held against time deposits. Let us call this reserve requirement on time deposits R_T (the subscript distinguishes it from R_D, the reserve requirement on demand deposits). Then the reserves held by the banking system against time deposits will be $\Delta T\, R_T$. From eq. (18) we know that $\Delta T = \Delta D t$, and therefore it follows that

$$\Delta T\, R_T = \Delta D\, t R_T \tag{19}$$

The amount by which bank reserves were initially increased, ΔB, now has four uses to which it can be put: reserves on demand deposits, hand-to-hand currency, excess reserves, and reserves on time deposits. That is,

$$\Delta B = \Delta D\, R_D + \Delta C + \Delta E + \Delta T\, R_T \tag{20}$$

Substituting from eqs. (7), (14), and (19) into eq. (20), we have

$$\begin{aligned}\Delta B &= \Delta D\, R_D + \Delta D\, K + \Delta D\, X + \Delta D\, t R_T \\ &= \Delta D\, (R_D + K + X + t R_T)\end{aligned} \tag{21}$$

Dividing both sides of eq. (21) by $R_D + K + X + t R_T$ then gives

$$\Delta D = \Delta B \frac{1}{R_D + K + X + t R_T} \tag{22}$$

Equation (22) is the most sophisticated formula for the expansion of demand deposits that we shall examine. It represents the expansion of demand deposits when the currency ratio, excess reserve ratio, and time deposit ratio are all taken into account. Putting the matter somewhat differently, eq. (22) is the formula for demand deposit expansion when all four assumptions of section 12-1 are relaxed. Note that eq. (22) is, nevertheless, only slightly more complex than eq. (16); only $t R_T$ has been added to the denominator. And note, finally, that ΔD is inversely related to tR_T just as it is to R_D, K, and X.

The Change in the Money Supply with Time Deposits

As in the previous cases, it is also of interest to examine the behavior of the money supply when time deposits are included in the analysis. However, the inclusion of time deposits means that the change in the money supply is no longer as straightforward as it has been because the possibility now exists of defining money in two different ways (see Chapter 11, section 11-7):

$M_1 =$ Demand deposits + currency
$M_2 =$ Demand deposits + currency + time deposits

It is necessary to develop a formula for each of these definitions.

The M_1 Formula   The M_1 definition of money, which excludes time deposits as a part of the money supply, can be derived in a manner comparable to previous cases. Since

$$\Delta M_1 = \Delta D + \Delta C$$

and since

$$\Delta C = \Delta D\, K$$

it follows that

$$\Delta M_1 = \Delta D + \Delta D\, K$$
$$= \Delta D\,(1 + K) \qquad\qquad\qquad (23)$$

Substituting eq. (22) into eq. (23) gives

$$\Delta M_1 = \Delta B \frac{1 + K}{R_D + K + X + tR_T} \qquad\qquad (24)$$

Once again, it may be helpful to the reader to extend the numerical example of previous sections to include enough information to illustrate eq. (24). This can be done by assuming that the ratio of time to demand deposits t is 1, that is, $t = \Delta T/\Delta D = 1$, and that the reserve requirement on time deposits, R_T, is 5 percent $= 1/20$. The other numbers are $\Delta B = \$1{,}000$, $R_D = 1/5$, $K = 1/20$, and $X = 1/20$. Using these numbers, eq. (24) becomes

$$\Delta M_1 = \$1{,}000 \left(\frac{1 + 1/20}{1/5 + 1/20 + 1/20 + 1/20} \right)$$

$$= \$1,000 \left(\frac{21/20}{7/20} \right)$$

$$= \$1,000(21/7)$$
$$= \$3,000$$

Comparing this figure ($3,000) with the results of section 12-4, it will be seen that the inclusion of the time deposit reserve leakage has caused the M_1 money supply to fall from $3,500 to $3,000—that is, when account is taken of time deposits, the ability of the banking system to create money is even further restricted.

It is also of interest to ask, Where has the original $1,000 ($\Delta B$) gone? This question can be answered by solving eq. (22) for ΔD and then inserting this information in eq. (21). When this is done, $\Delta D = \$2,857$, and therefore $571 ($\Delta D\, R_D$) of the original $1,000 has gone into reserves on demand deposits; $143 ($\Delta D\, K$) has gone into hand-to-hand currency; $143 ($\Delta D\, X$) has gone into excess reserves; and $143 ($\Delta D\, tR_T$) has gone into reserves against time deposits. Taken together, these amounts sum to $1,000.

The M_2 Formula   The formula for deriving the M_2 money supply expansion, which by definition includes time deposits as a part of the money supply, can be found by modifying eq. (9) of section 12-3 so that we now have

$$\Delta M_2 = \Delta D + \Delta C + \Delta T \tag{25}$$

Remembering that $\Delta C = \Delta D\, K$, and that $\Delta T = \Delta D\, t$, if follows that

$$\Delta M_2 = \Delta D + \Delta D\, K + \Delta D\, t$$
$$= \Delta D\, (1 + K + t) \tag{26}$$

Substituting the formula for ΔD [eq. (22)] into eq. (26) gives

$$\Delta M_2 = \Delta B \frac{1 + K + t}{R_D + K + X + tR_T} \tag{27}$$

Equation (27) is the formula for the expansion of the money supply when money is defined to include time deposits M_2. Equation (27) will result in a much larger increase in the money supply than did eq. (24) since the former counts time deposits as money while the latter does not. Thus if we use the same numerical example as before with eq. (27), we obtain

$$\Delta M_2 = \$1,000 \left(\frac{1 + 1/20 + 1}{1/5 + 1/20 + 1/20 + 1/20} \right)$$

$$= \$1,000 \left(\frac{41/20}{7/20} \right)$$

$$= \$1,000(41/7)$$
$$= \$5,857$$

Now compare this result with the previous one. When the M_2 money definition is used, the money supply expands to \$5,857; when the M_1 money definition is used, the expansion of the money supply is only \$3,000. The difference between the two is attributable wholly to the inclusion of time deposits in the M_2 definition. That is, by assumption $\Delta T/\Delta D = 1$ and therefore $\Delta T = \Delta D$. But since it has already been shown that $\Delta D = \$2,857$, it must also be true that $\Delta T = \$2,857$. And \$2,857 is, of course, precisely the difference between M_1 and M_2 (that is, \$5,857 – \$3,000 = \$2,857). Putting the matter slightly differently, the examples show that

$$\Delta M_1 = \Delta D + \Delta C$$
$$= \$2,857 + \$143$$
$$= \$3,000$$
$$\Delta M_2 = \Delta M_1 + \Delta T$$
$$= \$3,000 + \$2,857$$
$$= \$5,857$$

The distribution of the initial \$1,000 (ΔB), of course is the same under both the M_1 and M_2 definitions of the money supply.

M_2 Money and the Time Deposit Ratio   While both M_1 and M_2 money will be inversely related to the reserve requirement on time deposits, R_T, the same statement cannot be made about the time deposit ratio t. M_1 money is inversely related to t, but M_2 money is positively related to t. A moment's reflection will show why this is so. The M_1 definition of money does not include time deposits. Consequently, an increase in the public's preference for time deposits over demand deposits adds to the leakages in the money-creating process without adding to money. Under the M_2 definition of money, however, this is not true. M_2 money includes time deposits at commercial banks as part of the money supply, and time deposits have lower required reserves than demand deposits. A shift of funds out of demand deposits and into time deposits therefore actually reduces the leakages in the total deposit-creating process. In a sense, it reduces the average reserve requirement that banks must hold against total (i.e., demand plus time) deposits. And, since M_2 money is defined to include total deposits, a reduction in average reserve requirements increases M_2 money.

12-6   THE MONETARY BASE, THE RESERVE BASE, AND THE MONEY MULTIPLIER

Readers may find themselves a bit hard-pressed at this point, with M_1's and M_2's and K's and X's and whatnot swirling around in their heads. If so, cheer up—things are not so grim as they seem. For while it is always necessary to learn the details of a process in order to understand it, once that understanding has been accomplished it is frequently possible to see things in more general (and therefore simpler) terms. So it is now. Having examined the trees, we now want to step back and see if we can get a clear view of the forest.

Consider again eq. (24), which is repeated here for convenience:

$$\Delta M_1 = \Delta B \frac{1 + K}{R_D + K + X + tR_T} \tag{24}$$

The right-hand side of this equation can in general be divided into two parts: ΔB, which is the amount by which bank reserves were initially increased, and the remainder of the expression, which is what ΔB is multiplied by to obtain the change in the money supply. Let us define the symbol m_B as

$$m_B = \frac{1 + K}{R_D + K + X + tR_T} \tag{28}$$

Next note that ΔB, the *initial* change in reserves, actually ended up in two places: bank reserves and currency holdings of the public. In other words, at the end of the process,

$$\Delta B = \Delta R + \Delta C \tag{29}$$

where ΔR is the change in all bank reserves, including excess reserves. If we now let B stand for *total* bank reserves plus currency holdings of the public (and not just the change in these things, which is what ΔB is), then we can express the determination of the nation's total money supply as

$$M_1 = m_B B \tag{30}$$

In eq. (30), m_B is called the *money multiplier* and B is called the *monetary base* of the banking system. Note that eq. (30) deals with the determination of the total money supply, not just changes in the money supply—i.e., the expression on the left-hand side of eq. (30) is M_1, not ΔM_1.

An Alternative Formulation: The Reserve Base

The B of eq. (30), it will be recalled, is defined to include the public's holdings of currency as well as total bank reserves. Some economists prefer to work with bank reserves only, excluding the public's currency holdings. This concept is called the *reserve base.* The formula for determining the money supply from the reserve base can easily be derived from the formula that makes use of the monetary base, as follows. Combining eqs. (30) and (28) gives the full formula for the monetary-base determination of the money supply. Thus

$$M_1 = B \frac{1 + K}{R_D + K + X + tR_T} \tag{31}$$

Putting the denominator of the money multiplier in ratio form gives

$$M_1 = B\frac{1 + K}{\dfrac{DR_D + C + E + TR_T}{D}}$$

$$= B\frac{1 + K}{\dfrac{R + C}{D}}$$

which, from eq. (29), reduces to

$$M_1 = D(1 + K)$$

Multiplying the right-hand side by R/R $(= 1)$ gives

$$M_1 = R\frac{1 + K}{\dfrac{R}{D}}$$

or

$$M_1 = R\frac{1 + K}{R_D + X + tR_T} \tag{32}$$

The ratio on the right-hand side of eq. (32) is the money multiplier when the reserve base is used, rather than the monetary base. As will be seen by comparing eq. (32) with eq. (31), the two money multipliers are very similar, the only difference being that K, the currency ratio, does not appear in the denominator of the reserve-base money multiplier [eq. (32)]. Thus we can express the determination of the money supply when the reserve base is used as

$$M_1 = m_R R \tag{33}$$

where

$$m_R = \frac{1 + K}{R_D + X + tR_T} \tag{34}$$

Whether one chooses to use the monetary-base approach or the reserve-base approach to money supply theory is largely a matter of convenience, and depends on the problem at hand. The monetary-base approach has the advantage of focusing attention on the *initial* changes that the Federal Reserve can bring about. For example, the ΔB of eq. (4) was the result of an increase in the amount that a member bank borrowed from the Federal Reserve. The reserve-base approach has the advantage of being somewhat less complex (since K appears only in the numerator), and of highlighting the fact that banks and bank reserves play a crucial role in the determination of the money supply. For our purposes, it will usually be convenient to use the reserve-base approach. For this reason, unless otherwise indicated, we will hereafter drop the subscript on m_R and simply use m, which we will refer to as *the* money multiplier.

The Money Multiplier m

A simplified way of thinking about the determination of the money supply of the United States is to ask what determines the two factors of which M_1 is the product: m and R. The explanation of how the reserve base R is determined is quite lengthy; the next four chapters are, in essence, devoted to precisely this issue. For our immediate purpose, it is sufficient simply to note that the reserve base of the banking system is determined primarily by the Federal Reserve System. But while it is necessary to postpone a discussion of the determination of R, the preceding sections of this chapter have put us in an excellent position to discuss the determinants of the money multiplier.

The discussion of the several preceding sections has demonstrated that the money multiplier m is determined when R_D, R_T, K, X, and t are determined [see eq. (34)]. But as will be clear from an examination of eq. (33), it is really more accurate to say that the money multiplier varies with these ratios and that the money supply M_1 is positively related to (varies in the same direction as) the money multiplier. The process can be summarized as follows.[2]

1 The supply of money M_1 is positively related to m.
2 The money multiplier m is inversely related to the:
   Reserve requirement on demand deposits R_D
   Reserve requirement on time deposits R_T
   Excess reserve ratio X (E/D)
   Time deposit ratio t (T/D)
3 The money multiplier m is positively related to the currency ratio K (C/D)[3].

Thus we have broken down the money multiplier into its component parts. But while the theory tells us how a change in each of these components will affect the multiplier (and hence the money supply), it does not tell us why the ratios are what they are. We know, for example, that a decrease in the excess reserve ratio will increases the money multiplier and hence the money supply, other things equal. But the question remains, What determines the excess reserve ratio (and, of course, the other ratios as well)?

Determination of the various components of the money multiplier is basically an empirical issue. That is, money supply theory tells us which variables we need to explain, but the explanation itself is a matter for statistical investigation.[4] Although our knowledge of what determines these ratios is limited, recent research is beginning to provide some tentative answers.

---

[2] The various ratios K, X, and t are now defined as averages instead of changes for consistency with the total money supply concept being discussed.

[3] It is necessary to be clear what is meant here. The money multiplier m, will increase when the currency ratio K increases. However, an increase in currency will normally be accompanied by a decrease in bank reserves R so that the net result will be a decrease in the money supply, M_1.

[4] This is not to say that theory is ignored in the statistical research studies. It continues to tell us which factors are likely candidates as explanatory variables. But whether these variables in fact have an important or negligible influence on, e.g., the excess reserve ratio is basically an empirical question.

Reserve Requirements R_D and R_T   As discussed in Chapter 9, reserve requirements for the demand and time deposits of member banks are set (within specified limits) by the Federal Reserve System. This means that R_D and R_T are *control variables*, i.e., that they are deliberately set by the monetary authority to achieve certain policy goals, such as full employment and price stability. Since these reserve requirements are not determined within the economy but instead are imposed on the economy by the authorities, they cannot in general be explained by behavioral models of the economy.

Different classes of member banks, it will be recalled, have different reserve requirements. Moreover, nonmember banks usually have lower reserve requirements than member banks. These institutional arrangements mean that a movement of deposits from one class of member bank to another or from a member to a nonmember bank will alter the average reserve requirement of the banking system as a whole. One study[5] made of shifts of deposits among member banks indicates that such shifts have very little short-run impact on the money multiplier. And another study[6] of the effect of nonmember bank reserve requirements supports the conclusion that nonmember banks are not a destabilizing influence on the money supply. Notwithstanding such studies, however, many economists advocate an across-the-board, uniform reserve requirement for all banks in order to eliminate potential problems.

The Currency Ratio K   Economic theory tells us that the currency ratio K, the public's ratio of currency to demand deposits, should be related to the substitutability of these two forms of money and the relative cost of holding the one or the other. By *substitutability* is meant that there are some ways that one can use currency where it would be either impossible or inconvenient to use checks, and conversely. One could not, for example, play a pinball machine with a check; and it would be inconvenient (though not impossible) to write a check for a pair of shoelaces. Conversely, using currency to make a downpayment of several thousand dollars on a house would be very awkward. Currency and demand deposits are not perfect substitutes, and the convenience of having one or the other influences the public's currency ratio.

This convenience, however, is tempered by the cost of shifting from one kind of money to the other. By *cost* is here meant, not just explicit costs such as service charges on demand deposits, but also implicit costs such as going by the bank to cash a check. The greater these costs are, the more sluggish will be the public's adjustment of the currency ratio.

Using these general concepts, one recent researcher,[7] William Becker, has

[5]William G. Dewald, "The Required Reserve Ratio for Member Banks," *Bulletin of Business Research (of The Ohio State University)*, September 1972, pp. 1–7.

[6]Dennis R. Starleaf, "Nonmember Banks and Monetary Control," *Journal of Finance*, September 1975, pp. 955–975.

[7]William E. Becker, Jr., "Determinants of the United States Currency-Demand Deposit Ratio," *Journal of Finance*, March 1975, pp. 57–74. See also Alan C. Hess, "An Explanation of Short-Run Fluctuations in the Ratio of Currency to Demand Deposits," *Journal of Money, Credit and Banking*, August 1971, pp. 666–679; and Donald L. Kahn, "Currency Movements in the United States," Federal Reserve Bank of Kansas City *Monthly Review*, April 1976, pp. 3–8.

developed a model that gives very good results in explaining the currency ratio. According to this model, the currency ratio should, first, be *negatively* related to the implicit rate of return on demand deposits, and to the ratio of expenditures to saving. The reasoning is as follows. A higher implicit return on demand deposits will cause people to hold more demand deposits relative to currency, and therefore the ratio C/D will fall. The relationship between the expenditure/saving ratio and the currency ratio is a bit more complicated, but essentially the reasoning is this. If people save more and spend less, then time deposits will rise and currency and demand deposits will fall. But since time deposits and demand deposits are closer substitutes than time deposits and currency, demand deposits are likely to fall more than currency. Consequently, a fall in the ratio of expenditures to saving will cause a rise in the ratio of currency to demand deposits.

Second, the model postulates that the currency ratio should be positively related to the rate of interest on time deposits, the rate of interest on short-term, open market securities, and the volume of retail trade. The positive relationship between the currency ratio and the two rates of interest comes about for approximately the same reason. Consider the rate of interest on time deposits, for example. If this rate rises, other things equal, then people are much more likely to shift demand deposits into time deposits than they are to shift currency into time deposits. This is so because demand deposits and time deposits are closer substitutes than currency and time deposits. Therefore, a rise in the interest rate on time deposits will cause a greater fall in demand deposits than in currency, and the ratio of currency to demand deposits will rise. The same reasoning applies to open market debt instruments, such as commercial paper. Finally, the volume of retail trade is included as a variable on the assumption that more retail trade will cause the public to hold a larger proportion of its money supply in currency, hence raising the currency ratio.

Using quarterly data from 1953 to 1971, the author derived the following regression based on his model.

$$K = .06194 - .00005c - .00879r_d + .00385r_t + .00165r_m$$
$$+ .00038T + .76998K_{t-1}$$
$$r^2 = .89$$

Coefficients on r_d, r_m, and K_{t-1} significant at 1% level
Coefficients on c, r_t, and T significant at 5% level

where K = currency ratio, C/D
     c = ratio of expenditures to saving
    r_d = a measure of the implicit return on demand deposits
    r_t = time deposit interest rate
    r_m = interest rate on 4–6 month commercial paper
    T = volume of retail trade
   K_{t-1} = lagged value of currency ratio

Note that the r^2 is high at .89, all variables have the hypothesized algebraic sign, and all variables are significant at either the 1 percent or 5 percent level of significance. Thus, as remarked at the outset of the discussion, the model does quite a good job of explaining the currency ratio.

The Excess Reserve Ratio X   The demand of commercial banks for excess reserves has received a good deal of attention in the past several years. Interest has grown in the excess reserve ratio X not only because of the importance of this ratio in determining the money supply, but also because it has been a focal point for some disputed issues in monetary policy and theory—issues that will be discussed in later chapters.[8] As a consequence of these disputes, we have a pretty good idea of the factors affecting excess reserves.[9]

In general, the demand by banks for excess reserves is related to the adjustment costs of managing their money position. In other words, it is an expensive process for a bank to be constantly borrowing and lending federal funds, buying and selling Treasury bills, issuing and redeeming certificates of deposit, and so on. Other things equal, a bank will avoid these costs by holding excess reserves as a cushion against a reserve deficiency. But, of course, other things are not equal. Specifically, when a bank holds excess reserves it not only avoids costs but also foregoes returns; that is, excess reserves are nonearning assets, and banks want to earn as much interest as possible.

Taking these two considerations (costs and returns) together, it is evident that the greater the instability of deposit flows, the greater will be adjustments costs and hence the greater the demand for excess reserves; and that the higher are open market interest rates, the greater will be the banks' incentive to invest all available funds and hence the lower will be excess reserves. Using these concepts as his chief explanatory variables, one researcher obtained very satisfactory regression results in a study of the demand for excess reserves.[10]

The Time Deposit Ratio t   The time deposit ratio t has received surprisingly little attention in the empirical literature of economics. What few results we do have must be described as highly tentative both because of their limited number and because of the limited period of time to which they apply. Nevertheless, on the "only game in town" principle, one such study will be described.[11]

It is reasoned, in the first place, that relative to demand deposits time deposits are a luxury good. Demand deposits are the "working" balances of most of us— funds kept in demand deposits are there to be used. Time deposits, on the other hand, are frequently held idle; they are accumulated for such things as savings, retirement, and anticipated major expenditures such as a new car or a trip to Europe. If this

[8]The reference here is to the issue of *free reserves* as an indicator of monetary policy and to the *liquidity trap* concept of John Maynard Keynes. See Chapters 26 and 21, respectively.

[9]See especially Peter A. Frost, "Banks' Demand for Excess Reserves." *Journal of Political Economy,* July/August 1971, pp. 805–825.

[10]Frost, loc. cit.

[11]Dwayne Wrightsman, *An Introduction to Monetary Theory and Policy,* The Free Press, New York, 1971, pp. 60–64. Wrightsman describes his results as "very limited." See also William R. Hosek, "Determinants of the Money Multiplier," *The Quarterly Review of Economics and Business,* Summer 1970, pp. 37–46; and Charlotte E. Ruebling, *An Explanation of the Behavior of the Ratio of Time Deposits to Demand Deposits,* unpublished Ph.D. dissertation, Iowa State University, 1976.

view is valid, it means that time deposits are more responsive to rising incomes than demand deposits; as people's incomes rise, they are likely to increase their holdings of time deposits relative to demand deposits and hence the time deposit ratio will rise.

There is, however, an opposing force that is also at work on time deposits, namely, that there are reasonably good substitutes for time deposits. One might, for example, hold savings in United States government savings bonds or in Treasury bills. The presumption is that people and corporations can be induced to hold their savings in this form if interest rates on such investments are sufficiently above the interest rate paid on time deposits. These open market rates will not have the same effect on demand deposits, however, since Treasury bills (and the like) and demand deposits are *not* close substitutes. Consequently, the higher the open market interest rates relative to time deposit rates, the smaller will be the time deposit ratio.

On the basis of the preceding reasoning, it can be hypothesized that the time deposit ratio t is positively related to income and inversely related to the spread between open market rates and the time deposit rate. This hypothesis may be tested with the use of multiple-regression analysis. One such regression, using monthly data, is as follows:[12]

$$t = -.0025 + .0017Y - .0148TB$$
$$r^2 = .89$$

Coefficients on Y and TB significant at 1% level

where t = time deposit ratio
       Y = personal income, billions of dollars
     TB = Treasury bill rate minus legal maximum rate on savings deposits[13]

It will be noted that the algebraic sign on Y is positive and that the sign on TB is negative, as hypothesized. That is, the time deposit ratio and income move in the same direction while the time deposit ratio and the Treasury bill rate move in opposite directions.

12-7 CONCLUDING REMARKS

To most people it is intuitive that the quantity of money in the economy is an important economic variable. If the size of the United States money stock is doubled or halved, one need not know a great deal about monetary theory to guess that this will somehow affect the pace of economic activity. Consequently, the determination of the United States money supply is a subject of considerable importance, worthy of close and detailed scrutiny. Our aim, however, is not just to understand the process, but also to be able to influence it as a matter of deliberate public policy. That

---

[12]Ibid., (Wrightsman), p. 63.

[13]More accurately, *TB* is the Treasury bill rate minus the legal maximum rate on savings deposits measured in absolute deviations from 3 percent. Personal income is seasonally adjusted; independent variables are lagged one month.

is, we need to be able to understand the role played by the Federal Reserve in the money-creation process.

As we have seen, the money supply of the United States can be thought of as being the product of two factors: m and R. The money multiplier m should not be regarded as a purely mechanical apparatus. Rather, it grows out of the interactions of the public, the banks, and the Federal Reserve—the public when it decides on its currency (K) and time deposit (t) ratios, the banks when they decide on their excess reserve ratio (X), and the Federal Reserve when it sets reserve requirements on demand (R_D) and time (R_T) deposits. Thus, although the Federal Reserve is a major influence in the determination of m, it is certainly not the only influence. The size of the money multiplier is also the result of millions of decisions made by the banking system and the public. While the Federal Reserve may exert a strong influence on m in the long run, it therefore does not and cannot exercise short-run control.

But what of R, the reserve base of the commercial banking system? *In principle* the Federal Reserve could control the money supply even in the short run by offsetting changes in m with changes in R. But this is in principle. To know whether the Federal Reserve can do so *in practice* requires a careful understanding of how banks obtain reserves. This is the subject of the next four chapters.

12-8 REVIEW QUESTIONS

1   In section 12-1, the economics of the demand deposit expansion process was carried through the T accounts of three "rounds" of banks. Carry it through one more round for bank IV. What would the consolidated T accounts of banks I, II, III, and IV look like?

2   Assume that $\Delta B = \$5,000$, $R_D = 1/5$, $K = 0$, $X = 1/10$, and $t = 0$. By how much would demand deposits rise? By how much would the money supply (M_1) rise?

3   Assume that $R_D = 1/5$, $K = 0$, $X = 0$, and $t = 0$, as in section 12-1. Now suppose that a member bank *repays* $1,000 to the Federal Reserve, so that $\Delta B = -\$1,000$. Show the resulting T accounts for two rounds of banks. What is happening to demand deposits?

4   Develop a model to explain *your own* currency ratio K. What are the factors that might (on the average) cause you to hold more currency relative to your checking account? Less? Now put them together into a single model (equation).

PART 6

CENTRAL BANKING

The analysis has progressed to the following point. We know that commercial banks are profit-oriented businesses and that in their dealings with the public, they acquire earning assets (loans and investments). We know further that although it is not part of the banking system's intention, one major consequence of its lending and investing activities is the creation of demand deposits by some multiple of bank reserves. Finally, we know that demand deposits are money. It follows that the banking system is the primary source of the money supply of the United States. Thus, the reader should by now fully understand that part of Figure 1-1 dealing with commercial banks, the public, and the money supply (see Figure VI-1).

The next logical question is, If the banking system can create money on the basis of its reserves, where does it obtain these reserves? This question does not have a simple answer since the reserve base, like the money multiplier, is jointly determined by the interactions of the public, the banks, and the Federal Reserve. But as a very general proposition requiring a number of qualifications, we can think of the process as being dominated by the Federal Reserve System. And since the Federal Reserve supplies reserves to commercial banks and commerical banks use these reserves to create money, it is evident that the Federal Reserve is an extremely important institution deserving our close attention. Accordingly, in Part Six our task is to understand the Federal Reserve both as a political and as an economic institution. That is, we now want to add two additional elements of Figure 1-1 to our under-standing of monetary policy: the box marked "1" above and "D" below, and the arrows marked "2" above and "E" below (see Figure VI-2).

Chapter 13 attempts to show the historical need for the establishment of the Federal Reserve, and Chapter 14 discusses its present-day structure and organiza-tion. Chapter 15 explains the process whereby bank reserves are determined, and Chapter 16 elaborates on the techniques used by the Federal Reserve to dominate this process.

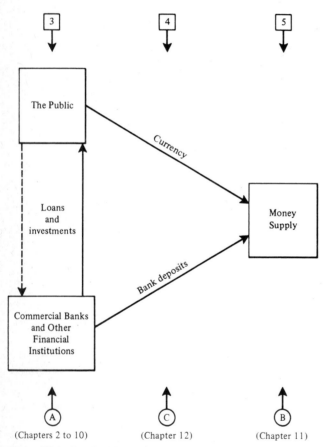

Figure VI-1 Detail of Figure 1-1.

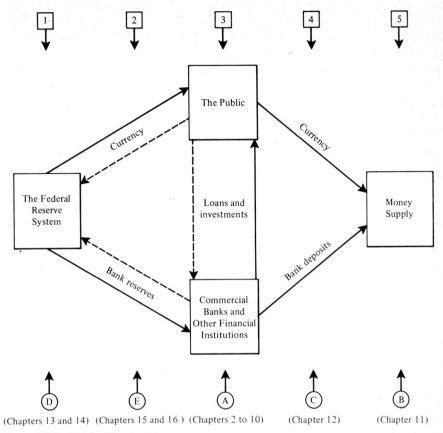

Figure VI-2 Detail of Figure 1-1.

13

The Quest
for Stability

From a historical viewpoint, the most difficult problem faced by Americans in their economic development has been the problem of instability. Throughout the nineteenth century and well into the twentieth, our economic progress was periodically disrupted by massive waves of unemployment and bankruptcy. It is difficult for the contemporary mind, nurtured on thirty-five years of comparative stability, to grasp the full social, political, and psychological impact of these economic catastrophies. True, we still have our business upturns and downturns, our good times and bad, but contemporary recessions are only a faint echo of the depressions of the past. In 1933, for example, national income fell by almost one-half; a full quarter of the labor force had no jobs at all, with most of the remaining employed only part time; business failures were endemic; and farmers were driven from the land. Imagine the despair, the sense of hopelessness, that must have been felt by people who could not support their families, high-school graduates who had no prospect of acquiring jobs, and laid-off workers who were too young to retire and too old ever to work again.

Small wonder that such times bred John Dillingers and Adolph Hitlers. "Hard times" indeed.

One role of the economist is to understand the causes of such economic disasters in order to prevent them. And many economists, both past and present, are persuaded that the historical instability of the *real* sector of the American economy— the instability of sales and employment—can be traced back to the historical instability of our *monetary* sector, our banking system in particular. Whether or not one accepts this viewpoint (and some do not), it is certainly true that in the past the monetary sector of our economy has exhibited a marked tendency to uncontrolled growth and disastrous collapse, a "boom or bust" development unequaled by any other nation in the world. The financial history of the United States is largely a history of attempts to bring this process under control.

From a historical perspective, the American experience with financial instability can be subdivided into two closely related but analytically distinguishable problems: bank failures and control over the money supply. That the two problems are related can be seen immediately by reflecting on the major lesson of Chapter 12: Commercial banks are creators of money. That the two problems are in principle distinct can be understood by noting that (theoretically, at least) the money supply can be controlled even though bank failures are widespread, and that the money supply can be uncontrolled even though the banking system is sound. Nevertheless, historically the two problems fed on one another, and it was not until both the Federal Reserve (1913) and the FDIC (1933) were established that our financial system became reasonably stable.

Our purpose in this chapter is not to present a detailed review of the financial history of the United States. Such a review would require a book in itself. Rather, our purpose is to highlight certain historical episodes in order to show why we must have a central bank and what its purpose is.

13-1 BANKING FROM THE REVOLUTION TO THE CIVIL WAR

Although various rudimentary banking operations were performed by merchants and others prior to the close of the Revolutionary War, our first bank in a modern sense was the Bank of North America, established in Philadelphia in 1782. In the following years a few additional banks were founded, but it was not until after 1800 that large numbers of incorporated banks began to be chartered by the states.

There is one aspect to these early banks that it is important to understand: They were generally note-issuing, rather than deposit-transferring, institutions. We currently think of banks as businesses that hold deposits and transfer them from one person to another. Indeed, as we have seen, today the transfer of deposits constitutes the major part of our payments mechanism. But banks weren't like this in early America. Communities were too isolated and transportation and communication were too slow to make deposit banking feasible. Instead, banks issued debt obligations called *bank notes* that circulated as money. Thus individuals who obtained loans from banks were not given an increase in their deposits, but were instead issued bank notes. These bank notes were redeemable on demand in *specie* (gold and silver), and as long as their convertibility into specie was maintained by the banks, they were a generally accepted medium of exchange. They circulated freely and widely, typically passing through many hands before being presented to the banks for redemption. In short, banks in early America were permitted to issue a type of currency very much like the dollar bills the government issues today.[1]

Like the demand deposits of today, bank notes were issued on the basis of fractional reserves. When it issued bank notes, a bank's only obligation was to be able to redeem them in specie. But since comparatively few note holders asked for redemption, a bank could easily issue notes worth several times the amount of gold and silver it held in its vaults. Moreover, the amount of specie reserves held by a bank was not regulated by law but was instead left to the prudence of the banker. Such a system was obviously subject to severe abuses. A banker who was not "prudent" might *overissue* bank notes, with the result that the bank would fail and the public would be left holding worthless pieces of paper. Additionally, in very prosperous times when great optimism prevailed, *all* banks might overissue notes and a greatly expanded money supply and inflation would result. When the downturn inevitably came, even well-managed banks would be unable to redeem their notes and the entire banking system would *suspend specie payment,* i.e., refuse to redeem their notes in gold and silver.

The First Bank of the United States

With a single exception, all early banks in the United States were chartered by the state governments. The exception was the first Bank of the United States, chartered in 1791 by Congress. This bank, which was chartered for twenty years, was owned in part by the federal government and served as the federal government's fiscal agent by making loans to the government, acting as the government's depository, and so forth. The First Bank was a very large bank for its times, much larger than any other bank in the country. Its head office was in Philadelphia, and it had branches in all the leading cities of the country: Boston, New York, Baltimore, Norfolk, Charleston, Savannah, and New Orleans.

Although the first Bank of the United States was owned largely by private investors and carried on a profitable commercial banking business, it also performed certain functions that we would now recognize as central banking activities. As noted, there was a tendency among the early state banks, both collectively and individually, to overextend loans and consequently overissue bank notes. Because of its very large size, the lending policies of the First Bank greatly affected the lending capacity of the other banks in the system. When the First Bank expanded its loans, for example, it would pay an abnormally large amount of its own bank notes into circulation. These notes would then find their way to other banks, who would either use the notes themselves for reserves or redeem them for specie reserves. Either way, the state banks were enabled to expand loans and hence bank notes and the money

---

[1]Bank notes were not *lawful money,* of course, any more than deposits are lawful money today.

supply. Conversely, if the First Bank contracted its outstanding loans, the state banks would lose reserves to it and would therefore have to curtail their lending activities.

The process can be understood in terms of the money supply equation of Chapter 12: $M_1 = mR$. It will be recalled that M_1 = the money supply, m = the money multiplier, and R = the reserve base of the banking system. As noted previously, there were no required reserves in early American banking, and hence the size of m was determined by the "prudence" of commercial bankers. Additionally, reserves were held largely[2] against bank notes rather than deposits. But the formula can be modified by thinking of the money supply M_1 as being composed predominantly of bank notes and of m as being inversely related to the average reserve ratio of the banking system. Given this interpretation, the First Bank influenced the money supply in two ways: First, it could issue more or less of its own notes, thereby expanding or contracting R and hence M_1. Second, by building up or drawing down its own specie reserves, the First Bank could change the average reserve ratio of the banking system and hence change m and therefore M_1.

Of course, it required a bank that was very large relative to the other banks in the system to appreciably affect the average reserve ratio, but as we have seen, the First Bank was very large. Even so, the central banking powers of the First Bank were quite limited; it could alter the reserve base and the average reserve ratio only marginally, and could consequently have only a limited effect on the total amount of bank notes in circulation.

Not only did the first Bank of the United States exercise central banking powers over the money supply, it also had indirect, extralegal powers over individual banks. Recall that the First Bank had branches in all the major cities of the country. If the First Bank came to believe that a state bank was making questionable loans or overissuing bank notes relative to its specie reserves, the First Bank would instruct its branches to present such notes promptly to the state bank for redemption. The offending state bank was thus obliged to hold larger specie reserves than other banks, with the consequence that it rapidly corrected those policies which the First Bank found offensive. State banks that behaved in a prudent manner were not disciplined; the First Bank would either hold their notes or pay them back into circulation. Thus, by picking and choosing which state bank notes to redeem and which not to redeem, the First Bank was able to exercise regulatory powers over the banks of its time similar to the regulatory powers that are vested in the FDIC today.

The charter of the First Bank came up for renewal in 1811 and received substantial opposition in Congress. The opposition presented a variety of objections: The Bank was owned by foreigners; it was unconstitutional; and it was involved in politics. Perhaps the strongest opposition came from the state banks, who resented the discipline forced on them by the First Bank. Whatever the cause, the effect was that in 1811 Congress refused to renew the charter of the first Bank of the United States, and for the next five years (during the War of 1812) even an informal federal banking authority did not exist.

---

[2]Some deposits were used even then, but they were probably much smaller in amount than bank notes (good statistics do not exist).

The Second Bank of the United States

In the five years following the demise of the first Bank of the United States, state banking burgeoned. Freed of the discipline of the First Bank and spurred on by the inflationary financing of the war, the number of state banks rose from less than 100 in 1811 to almost 250 in 1816; the note issues of state banks more than doubled; and suspension of specie payment by all banks was virtually continuous throughout the War of 1812. The financial condition of the country was, in fine, chaotic. In belated recognition of this state of affairs, Congress in 1816 chartered the second Bank of the United States.

The second Bank of the United States resembled the First Bank in broad outline, but there were also some important differences. For one thing, the Second Bank was much larger than the First. Its capital was fixed at $35 million, and it was permitted to hold a maximum of $55 million of property—a huge amount by the standards of the time. The Second Bank, with some twenty-five branches throughout the country, was almost certainly the nation's largest corporation. Another important difference between the First and Second Bank was the clear recognition of the quasi-public nature of the latter. Not only did the federal government subscribe one-fifth of the Bank's capital (other investors were limited to $300,000), but five of the Bank's twenty-five directors were appointed by the President of the United States.

The Second Bank operated in much the same style as the First. It carried on the normal commercial banking functions: lending, investing, issuing notes, and accepting deposits. It acted as fiscal agent for the federal government. Most important, from our point of view, it continued and to some extent expanded the role of the Bank of the United States as the country's central bank. It regulated the issuing of state bank notes by selectively presenting such notes promptly for redemption in specie, and it exercised a limited influence over total bank credit.

Like its predecessor, the Second Bank was chartered for twenty years. And, again like its predecessor, it ran into increasing political opposition as the time approached for its charter to be renewed. Despite some apparent mismanagement in its early years, financial historians are in substantial agreement that the Second Bank was a successful institution. It brought order out of chaos and had a generally benign influence on the banking system of its day. However, the same forces that opposed the rechartering of the First Bank also opposed the rechartering of the Second: The state banks still found its policies too constraining; the antifederalists still questioned the constitutional right of Congress to charter a bank; and the Bank continued in its unwise course of political involvement. Added to these forces of opposition were two strange (and contradictory) political bedfellows: the advocates of "easy money," who favored the comparatively lax lending and note-issuing policies of the state banks; and the "hard money" advocates, who opposed paper money of any kind and advocated the exclusive use of gold and silver coins.

Andrew Jackson—"Old Hickory"—was President of the United States in the early 1830s. A tough and able politician with a mercurial temper, Jackson was a dedicated hard money advocate. Nicholas Biddle was president of the Second Bank of the United States in the 1830s. An able but autocratic administrator, Biddle was adamant in his opposition to Andrew Jackson. In 1831 when Jackson vetoed a congressional bill providing for the rechartering of the Second Bank, the dye was cast; the clash between these two stubborn and willful men became inevitable. Biddle openly but vainly opposed Jackson's reelection in 1832, and in 1836 Jackson was successful in blocking all attempts to recharter the Bank. As a consequence, the Second Bank's charter was allowed to expire. It obtained a charter from the State of Pennsylvania in the same year, suspended specie payment in 1839, and was liquidated in 1841.

The "Bank War" between Nicholas Biddle and Andrew Jackson is one of the most significant and colorful episodes in our monetary history. Many historians feel that had the outcome been different, the entire course of our banking history would have been changed. But such speculation is idle. The Second Bank's charter was *not* renewed, and for the twenty-seven years between 1836 and 1863 there were no federally chartered banks in the United States.

State Banking before the Civil War

For most of the period between the chartering of the Bank of North America in 1782 and the expiration of the charter of the second Bank of the United States in 1836, there was only one federal bank in the country. After 1836 and until 1863 there was none. By 1836 the number of state-chartered banks had grown to approximately 700, and by the outbreak of the Civil War this figure had more than doubled. Additionally, there were probably an equal number of "private" banks,[3] that is, banks owned and operated by individuals and partnerships, without benefit of corporate charter of any kind. Our interest in the central banking aspects of the First and Second Banks should not obscure the fundamental reality that early American banking was overwhelmingly a state banking system.

As can be imagined, the state banking system was a very mixed bag. The charters, functions, and control over the state banks varied widely. Banks were frequently chartered for the purpose of financing some special enterprise—a turnpike, a canal, or a toll bridge—and the state government itself was often the sole or major stockholder of one or more banks. With a few notable exceptions, bank regulation by the state governments was at best haphazard and at worst nonexistent. To add to the confusion, the bulk of the nation's currency consisted of the bank notes of the various state banks, with the federal government exercising no jurisdiction and itself issuing only coins.

It is difficult for the contemporary mind, used to a well-regulated banking system and an orderly currency, to grasp the full extent of the monetary disorders of those times. About 2,000 private institutions each had the authority to print money in whatever denominations they chose. Even legitimate bank notes often circulated at less than their face value, the amount of the discount depending on the financial status of the bank and its geographical location relative to the point of circulation. The situation was counterfeiter's paradise. Bank notes were easily duplicated and "raised" (changed in face value). Furthermore, many notes were overtly

[3]Accurate data do not exist.

fraudulent, that is, issued against banks that were wholly fictitious. Add to this the slow and cumbersome transportation and communication system of the early nineteenth century in a basically frontier society, where news of a bank failure in one part of the country might take weeks to reach another part, and you may begin to get some idea of the fundamentally chaotic condition of the country's payments' mechanism. Trade and commerce, never easy, became doubly difficult. No one could possibly keep track of which note was worth how much. Somehow order had to be restored.

The Suffolk Banking System   In 1818 a group of merchants in Boston organized the Suffolk Bank, which would accept and pay out the notes of only those interior New England banks that were willing to maintain redemption balances with it. In 1824 the Suffolk Bank announced a plan known as the *Suffolk Banking System* where each country bank was required to keep a redemption fund with it sufficient to redeem at par all the country bank's notes received by the Suffolk Bank.

Many of the interior banks refused to join the plan at first, but when the other seven Boston banks agreed to participate, most of the country banks were forced to join. (A bank that did not join would have its notes accumulated in Boston and then presented in large batches for redemption in specie.) The Suffolk Banking System was very successful. By 1825 virtually all New England banks were members of the System, and their notes continued to circulate at par up to the time of the Civil War.

The New York Safety Fund System   In 1829 the legislature of New York adopted a plan for protecting note holders and depositors. This plan, called the *Safety Fund System,* is generally regarded as a forerunner of the present-day FDIC. The Safety Fund System required the banks of New York to make periodic payments into a centralized fund up to a maximum of 3 percent of the bank's capital. The fund was then to be used to reimburse the note holders and depositors of those banks that failed.

The Safety Fund System was only moderately successful. Its resources were severely strained in the wave of bank failures (1837–1842) that followed the demise of the second Bank of the United States. The System was subsequently altered by legislative amendment to limit its liability to bank notes only (not deposits) and to certain banks. But the limitation placed on its liability also limited the System's effectiveness, and it died a natural death in 1866.

The Free Banking System   During the entire period from 1782 to 1837–1838, a special legislative act was required to charter a bank. That is, a bank could be chartered only if a bill was passed by the legislature providing for the chartering of that bank and that bank alone. Such a system was subject to considerable political abuse: Bank charters went to the friends of the party in power, and bribery of legislators was rampant. Moreover, the system gave quasi-monopolistic powers to banks already in business, and such banks used these powers to vigorously oppose the chartering of any new banks. Not only was this system contrary to the democratic spirit of the times, but also many people felt that it resulted in too few banks and hence an amount of bank credit that was inadequate for a rapidly growing country.

During the panic of 1837, which followed the nonrenewal of the charter of the second Bank of the United States, the country suffered widespread bank failures and banks generally fell into public disfavor. Partly as a consequence of this and partly because of the abuses noted previously, in 1838 the New York legislature passed the *Free Banking Act.* [4] This act provided that the state would grant a banking charter to anyone, providing only that certain minimum requirements were met. "Free" entry into the banking business was thus ensured to all, subject only to compliance with the general bank incorporation law. Among the requirements that had to be met was the provision that banks secure their notes with specified securities, which were held by the state comptroller. In the event that a bank failed, these securities would then be sold to redeem the notes of that bank.

Wildcat Banking   The Free Banking System worked very well in New York State, where it was implemented with examination, supervision, and other safeguards. The idea of free banking spread rapidly to other states, however, where the law was either inadequate to protect the public from fraud or emasculated by lack of governmental control. In the western states particularly, free banking degenerated into so-called *wildcat banking.* Banks of very dubious soundness would be set up in remote and inaccessible places "where only the wildcats throve." Bank notes would then be printed, transported to nearby population centers, and circulated at par. Since the issuing bank was difficult and often dangerous to find, redemption of bank notes was in this manner minimized. These and similar abuses made banking frequently little more than a legal swindle. Banking fell into such disrepute that some states prohibited banking altogether while others made it a state monopoly.

The Forestall System   One of the primary defects of the state banking system was that in general banks were not required to maintain reserves. Many banks did so, of course, simply out of prudence. But prior to the Civil War, only two states, Massachusetts and Louisiana, had mandatory reserve requirements applicable to both bank notes and deposits. The provisions of the Louisiana system are particularly noteworthy.

The Louisiana Bank Act of 1842, better known as the *Forestall System* (after Edmond J. Forestall, a New Orleans banker and author of the act), provided that the banks of that state had to maintain one-third specie reserves against their outstanding bank note and deposit liabilities. Furthermore, these banks had also to cover the remaining two-thirds of such liabilities with commercial paper assets having a maturity of not more than ninety days, which could not be renewed. Banks were forbidden by law to pay the notes of other banks back into circulation and instead had to present them at the issuing bank for redemption in specie. The act

---

[4]Michigan passed such a law in 1837, but the New York Act is usually considered the pivotal act, partly because the Michigan law was copied from the New York Act while the passage of the latter was still pending.

made no provision for the chartering of new banks, and an effective system of bank examination was instituted.

The Forestall System gave Louisiana what was probably the strongest banking system in the country at that time. In the panic of 1857, when virtually all other banks in the country suspended specie payment, New Orleans banks continued to redeem their notes in gold. The concept of protective bank reserves received a good deal of favorable notice because of this incident and subsequently was incorporated into the National Bank Act (1863).

The Independent Treasury   The United States government, like other note holders and depositors, had suffered losses from bank failures. In 1846 Congress set up the *Independent Treasury System,* which established a number of subtreasuries around the country for the purpose of holding all United States government funds.[5] The idea behind the Independent Treasury was to avoid losses by making governmental fiscal operations independent of commercial banks. However, the constant physical transfer of cash that this policy entailed ultimately proved too costly and too inconvenient. Within a few years the complete divorce between government finance and commercial banks was abandoned, although a modified system of subtreasuries continued in existence until the 1920s.

Summary of Banking before the Civil War

In reviewing the highlights of the early development of banking in the United States, two fundamental defects of the system should stand out in the reader's mind: First, our money lacked *integrity.* The holder of a bank note had no real assurance that it was not simply a worthless piece of paper; the owner of a bank deposit could wake up any morning to find that what has been thought of as "money in the bank" was now simply a creditor's claim on a bankrupt corporation. Today we smile at recluses who are reputed to have money hidden under their mattresses, thinking them eccentric if not downright mad. But for much of our history many mattresses have been a good deal safer than many banks.

The second defect of the early banking system is that during these times there was no control over the total money supply. Especially after the shutting down of the Second Bank, the expansion and contraction of the money supply occurred haphazardly—a by-product of the profit-seeking activities of gamblers, swindlers, and cheats, as well as prudent people of finance. No attempt was made to use the country's total stock of money as a deliberate tool of public policy.

13-2   BANKING FROM THE CIVIL WAR TO WORLD WAR I

Although today we recognize that the maintenance of the integrity of our money involves both currency and deposits and their interchangeability, no such general recognition existed at the time of the Civil War. Rather, the overriding issue was

---

[5]An abortive attempt to establish an Independent Treasury was made in 1840.

currency reform. In part, this was a result of the comparatively small role that deposits played in the payments mechanism of the country. But even more important was the near anarchy of the currency supply. As noted previously, each state bank was authorized to print and issue bank notes; there were no federal notes; and counterfeit notes, raised notes, and notes on nonexistent banks were plentiful. In 1863 Congress passed the National Currency Act, subsequently known as the *National Bank Act,* which was "An Act to provide a national currency, secured by a pledge of United States Stocks, and to provide for the Circulation and Redemption thereof." As subsequently amended in 1864 and 1865, this act accomplished its purpose very well. Within a few years state bank notes had disappeared and a uniform national currency was circulating at par. In the process of accomplishing this currency reform, the National Banking System[6] was created and dual banking[7] became a permanent feature of American finance.

The National Banking System

The National Bank Act sought to incorporate into a system of national banks most of the bank reforms that had proved successful in previous state banking legislation. These included currency reform, reserve requirements against deposits, and rigorous (for the time) standards of chartering and supervision.

Currency Reform   The National Bank Act (as amended) launched a two-pronged attack on the currency situation. The first of these was to establish a system of uniform, high-quality bank notes that would be acceptable at par in all parts of the country. To accomplish this, the act provided that national banks could issue bank notes only to the extent that they deposited federal bonds with the Comptroller of the Currency (the chief administrative office of the National Banking System). The amount of national bank notes that a bank could have outstanding was limited to 90 percent of the bonds deposited, where the value of the bonds was either their market price or their par value, whichever was lower. The bank's notes were a first lien against the assets of the issuing bank, which meant that the bonds used as collateral could be sold to repay noteholders in the event of bank failure. Additionally, an upper limit was set on the amount of notes any one bank could issue, the limit being the paid-in capital of the bank. Finally, a national bank was required to maintain with the Comptroller a redemption fund equal to 5 percent of its notes outstanding. In short, elaborate precautions were taken to ensure the integrity of national bank notes. These precautions were highly successful; national bank notes were circulated at par in all parts of the country, with most noteholders neither knowing nor caring which particular national bank had issued the note.[8]

The second prong of the attack on the "currency mess" was to eliminate the bank notes of state-chartered banks. In 1866 a 10 percent tax on state bank notes became effective, and such notes disappeared from circulation after that time. It

[6]The organization of the present-day National Banking System is described in Chapter 3.
[7]Dual banking is discussed in Chapter 2.
[8]The note-issuing privilege of national banks was revoked in 1933.

Table 13-1   Incorporated Commercial Banks in the United States, 1834–1900

Year	State bank	National banks	Year	State bank	National banks
1834	506	.....	1868	247	1,640
1835	704	.....	1869	259	1,619
1836	713	.....	1870	325	1,612
1837	788	.....	1871	452	1,723
1838	829	.....	1872	566	1,853
1839	840	.....	1873	277	1,968
1840	901	.....	1874	368	1,983
1841	784	.....	1875	586	2,076
1842	692	.....	1876	671	2,091
1843	691	.....	1877	631	2,078
1844	696	.....	1878	510	2,056
1845	707	.....	1879	648	2,048
1846	707	.....	1880	650	2,076
1847	715	.....	1881	683	2,115
1848	751	.....	1882	704	2,239
1849	782	.....	1883	788	2,417
1850	824	.....	1884	852	2,625
1851	879	.....	1885	1,015	2,689
1852	815	.....	1886	891	2,809
1853	750	.....	1887	1,471	3,014
1854	1,208	.....	1888	1,523	3,120
1855	1,307	.....	1889	1,791	3,239
1856	1,398	.....	1890	2,250	3,484
1857	1,416	.....	1891	2,743	3,652
1858	1,422	.....	1892	3,773	3,759
1859	1,476	.....	1893	4,188	3,807
1860	1,562	.....	1894	4,188	3,770
1861	1,601	.....	1895	4,369	3,715
1862	1,492	.....	1896	4,279	3,689
1863	1,466	66	1897	4,420	3,610
1864	1,089	467	1898	4,486	3,581
1865	349	1,294	1899	4,738	3,582
1866	297	1,634	1900	5,007	3,731
1867	272	1,636			

Source: Board of Governors of the Federal Reserve System, Banking Studies, Waverly Press, Baltimore, Md., 1941, p. 418.

seems clear that the tax on state bank notes was, in fact, designed to eliminate, not only the bank notes, but also the state banks themselves. It was felt that the state banks could not survive without the note-issuing privilege, and that as a consequence of the tax they would be either liquidated or reorganized as national banks. In fact, there was a very substantial drop in the number of state-chartered banks after the passage of the National Bank Act. In 1863 there were about 1,500 state banks in the country; by 1868 the number had decreased to about 250, with a commensurate rise in national banks. (Table 13-1 gives the data.) After 1868, however, state banks began to increase in numbers, and by 1892 they were once again more numerous than national banks.

There were basically three reasons for the resurgence of state banking after the 1860s. First, the total number of banks in the country, both state and national, grew rapidly in the latter half of the nineteenth century; the country was being settled and developed at an unparalleled pace, and more banks were needed. Second, the attraction of a state, as opposed to a national, bank charter was very great. In terms of capital requirements, reserve requirements, and rigor of supervision and regulation, state-chartered banks were generally more attractive. But neither of these factors would have been decisive had it not been for the third reason, easily the most basic of all: Beginning about 1855, demand deposits in commercial banks in the United States became larger than bank notes in total amount. Table 13-2 gives the data. After the Civil War, the volume of bank notes remained virtually unchanged at about $300 million to $350 million while the dollar volume of deposits spurted upward. This upsurge in deposit banking reflected the nation's increasing homogeneity. A truly national payments mechanism was needed, and deposit banking met this need. But deposit banking was, of course, something that state banks

Table 13-2 Bank Notes and Deposits, 1834–1890 (Millions of Dollars)

Year	Bank notes	Deposits	Year	Bank notes	Deposits
1834	95	76	1863	239	394
1835	104	83	1864	210	427
1836	140	115	1865	289	547
1837	149	127	1866	296	657
1838	116	85	1867	291	657
1839	135	90	1868	298	689
1840	107	76	1869	294	673
1841	107	65	1870	291	679
1842	84	62	1871	313	817
1843	59	56	1872	331	875
1844	75	85	1873	340	908
1845	90	88	1874	341	886
1846	106	97	1875	342	948
1847	106	92	1876	317	898
1848	129	103	1877	302	958
1849	115	91	1878	313	863
1850	131	110	1879	321	1,144
1851	155	129	1880	337	1,143
1852	161	137	1881	350	1,417
1853	146	146	1882	352	1,506
1854	205	188	1883	348	1,557
1855	187	190	1884	331	1,507
1856	196	213	1885	309	1,653
1857	215	230	1886	308	1,688
1858	155	186	1887	277	1,995
1859	193	260	1888	245	2,019
1860	207	254	1889	207	2,296
1861	202	257	1890	182	2,442
1862	184	296			

Source: Board of Governors of the Federal Reserve System, *Banking Studies*, Waverly Press, Baltimore, Md., 1941, p. 417.

could do despite the tax on their bank notes. As a result, while the attack on the issuance of bank notes by state-chartered banks was successful, it was an empty victory. State banks simply shifted to deposit banking, which was increasingly profitable. Thus, by the end of the nineteenth century the National Banking System had ensured the integrity of a part of the money supply—currency—but by that time bank-issued currency had dwindled to a small fraction of the total money created by the banking system. The integrity of deposit money remained seriously in doubt.

Reserve Requirements The National Bank Act (as amended) required that national banks hold reserves against their deposit liabilities. For reserve purposes, national banks were classified into three categories: *central reserve city banks,* which were required to hold 25 percent reserves in lawful money; *reserve city banks,* which were also required to hold 25 percent reserves, but where half of these could be held in the form of correspondent balances in central reserve city banks; and *country banks,* which were required to hold 15 percent reserves, three-fifths of which could be held in the form of correspondent balances at central reserve city and reserve city banks.

The requirement that national banks hold reserves against deposit liabilities was clearly a major improvement in banking, which resulted in much stronger and safer banks. But the provision that national banks could *pyramid* their reserves, that is, use correspondent balances to satisfy their reserve requirements, proved to be one of the major defects of the National Banking System. The trouble with pyramiding was that it made national bank reserves appear to be much larger than they really were because the same currency could be used to support deposits at different banks. Suppose, for example, that country banks received an increase of $150 in their currency reserves. This $150 could then be used to support $1,000 of deposits in the country banks since their required reserves were 15 percent. However, the country banks had to keep only $60 in their vaults; the other $90 could be sent to city correspondents. The $90 received by the reserve city banks could be used to support $360 of deposits because their required reserves were 25 percent. But again, the reserve city banks had to keep only one-half of this ($45) in their vaults; the remaining $45 could be deposited in central reserve city banks, where the 25 percent reserve requirement made it capable of supporting $180 of deposits. The original $150 was thus actually supporting $1,540 ($1,000 + $360 + $180) of deposits, which is less than a 10 percent reserve, although reserves *appeared* to be 15, 25, and 25 percent at country, reserve city, and central reserve city banks, respectively.

The system worked, of course, as long as the public was content with its currency ratio. But when, as frequently happened, the public grew uneasy about the soundness of the banking system and tried to increase its currency holdings, country banks would demand currency from their reserve city correspondents, the reserve city banks would in turn draw down their balances in central reserve cities (New York and Chicago), and the central reserve city banks would find themselves unable to meet these currency demands. The result was often a financial panic in the New York money market, which would precipitate a panic in the stock exchanges (via call loans). Bankruptcies, unemployment, and hard times generally followed.

Chartering and Supervision One object of the National Banking Act was to establish a system of banks that was substantially safer than state banks. In this, the act must be judged successful. Several features of the act are worthy of note: (1) The capital requirements for national banks were higher than those on comparable state-chartered banks. (2) National bank stockholders were subject to *double liability;* that is, stockholders of banks could not only lose their investment, but could also be made to pay an additional amount equal to the par value of the stock (this feature has since been repealed). (3) National banks originally were not permitted to make real estate loans or engage in trust activities. (4) Standards of supervision and examination of national banks were a good deal more exacting than those applied to most state banks. And so forth. The record of failures among national banks, while not good, has nevertheless been considerably better than that of state banks.

Inadequacies of the National Banking System The National Bank Act accomplished its primary objective of currency reform, but even so it suffered from certain inadequacies. Two of these have already been discussed: the pyramiding of reserves and the failure to guarantee the deposit component of the money supply. Two additional weaknesses of the National Banking System should also be considered: the complaint that the national banks provided an inelastic currency and the lack of any formal mechanism for supplying additional reserves to the banking system in times of crisis.

Inelastic Currency When the National Monetary Commission was established following the panic of 1907, perhaps its most severe criticism of the National Banking System was that the currency supplied by these banks was *inelastic.* Although the meaning of *inelastic* was not always clear, what in general it meant was that there was no method built into the National Banking System for varying bank notes according to seasonal and cyclical needs. Seasonally, the public demanded a larger currency ratio at particular times of the year, especially in the early autumn and at Christmas, and yet the volume of national bank notes remained roughly constant throughout the year. Critics complained that the seasonal demands for currency resulted in a loss of reserves from the banking system, with a consequent periodic tightening of credit that was unrelated to the needs of business.

The cyclical aspect of an inelastic currency was held to be even more serious. Recall that the national banks could issue bank notes only up to 90 percent of the value of government bonds deposited with the Comptroller, and that the value of these bonds was based on either their market value or their par value, whichever was the lower. Since interest rates and bond prices vary inversely (see Chapter 7), this provision meant that the volume of bank notes had to go down during tight money periods when interest rates were rising, and could rise (though not commensurately) during easy money periods when interest rates fell. Suppose, for example, that a bank bought a government bond for $100 and, on this basis, issued $90 in national bank notes. Then if interest rates rose so that bond prices fell to $90, the bank was obliged to recall $9 of bank notes (= $90 − $81, which is 90 percent of $90). In the opposite case, that of falling interest rates and rising bond prices, banks could expand the issuance of national bank notes only up to the maximum 90 percent of par value. As a consequence, bank notes were expanded and contracted according to the state of the bond market, not according to the needs of trade. It was in this sense that the National Banking System was held to provide an inelastic currency.

No Control over Reserves   The second inadequacy of the National Banking System was that it provided no method for expanding total bank reserves during times of crisis. We have already seen that a rise in the public's desired currency ratio would lead to extraordinary pressures on the reserves of the central reserve city banks because of the pyramiding of reserves. In fact, full-fledged banking panics occurred in 1873, 1884, 1893, and 1907; and very tight credit situations occurred more often. Banks frequently suspended currency payments at such times. What was needed was some institution that stood outside the commercial banking system, untouched by the panics but having the capacity to create massive amounts of new reserves. In short, what was needed was a central bank. Such an institution was not established until 1914 (the Federal Reserve System); before that, since the need existed, various makeshift attempts at performing the central banking function were undertaken.

Central Banking Functions under the National Banking System

Although arrangements for controlling bank reserves prior to 1914 were generally weak and of limited usefulness, it is nevertheless instructive to describe two such arrangements briefly: the Independent Treasury and bank clearinghouses.

The Independent Treasury   As was discussed in section 13-1, in 1846 the federal government set up a number of subtreasuries around the country for the purpose of sequestering government funds—holding them outside the commercial banking system. While the fiscal affairs of the government soon proved to be too closely related to commercial banks to permit a complete divorce of their activities, the system of subtreasuries nevertheless persisted. Some (not all) Secretaries of the Treasury took advantage of the continued existence of the *Independent Treasury System* to exert a measure of control over total bank reserves. If the Secretary felt that the banks were in the process of overexpanding credit, he or she could order that government funds be transferred out of the banking system and stockpiled in the subtreasuries. Such an action would drain reserves from the banks and curtail a credit boom before it got out of hand. Contrariwise, if the Secretary wanted to promote easier credit conditions, he could order funds transferred from the subtreasuries to the commercial banks, thereby expanding the reserves of the latter. The entire process can be understood in terms of the money supply equation $M_1 = mR$. By sequestering or not sequestering funds in the subtreasuries, the Secretary was affecting the size of R, the reserve base of the banking system.

Bank Clearinghouses   A *clearinghouse* is a voluntary association of banks, usually in the same city, for the purpose of exchanging local checks with one another. Suppose, for example, a city has ten banks in it, where each bank is receiving checks drawn against deposits in the other nine banks. Rather than each bank having bilateral exchanges of checks with every other bank, it is much more efficient to have a central clearinghouse where all checks are sent and where only *net* amounts are either paid to or collected from the clearinghouse.[9] The first clearinghouse in the United States was established in New York City in 1853 and thereafter was routinely used for transferring the reserves of some banks to other banks.

However, in times of panic a *general* shortage of reserves would arise. A general reserve shortage was an altogether different matter from the routine clearing of checks. Because of the currency demands of their country respondent banks and the public, many of the clearinghouse members would find themselves unable or unwilling to meet their clearinghouse obligations. When this happened, the clearinghouse would issue certificates that could be used to settle balances among the local banks. Although until 1908 these certificates could not be used as legal reserves, they conserved on legal reserves. From 1908 to 1914 clearinghouse certificates were legalized and sometimes even circulated as currency. Again a makeshift system had been found to expand the reserve base of the banking system during emergencies.

13-3 BANKING FROM WORLD WAR I TO WORLD WAR II

The Panic of 1907, which clearly seemed to have originated in the financial sector of the economy, resulted in a sharp but short-lived depression—work stoppages and business failures. The public decided it had had enough. In 1908 Congress created the National Monetary Commission to investigate the entire question of banks and money in the United States. The Commission's report proposed the establishment of a central bank, and after a number of modifications had been made in the Commission's proposal, the Federal Reserve Act was passed in 1913. The Federal Reserve System, which was actually set up in 1914, had as its major purposes "to furnish an elastic currency, to afford means of rediscounting commercial paper, [and] to establish a more effective supervision of banking in the United States. . . ."

The Federal Reserve System

Since Chapters 14 and 15 will be devoted to the structure of the Federal Reserve and the extent to which it controls the money supply, very little will be said here about these two subjects. What is of primary interest in an historical context is that the Federal Reserve Act, while certainly one of the great landmarks in American banking history, nevertheless failed to produce the stability in our monetary affairs that its framers had hoped for. Specifically, the Federal Reserve System did not deal with the issue of the integrity of the deposit component of the money supply. Indeed, bank failures were exceptionally high even during the relatively prosperous period of the 1920s, averaging about 600 banks per year. Table 13-3 gives the data. The common expression at the time was that the country "had too many banks and not enough bankers," and there is some truth to this.

[9]The clearinghouse function is discussed more fully in Chapter 14.

Table 13-3   Suspensions of Incorporated Commercial Banks in the United States, 1920–1939

Year	State banks	National banks	Total
1920	136	7	143
1921	409	52	461
1922	294	49	343
1923	533	90	623
1924	616	122	738
1925	461	118	579
1926	801	123	924
1927	545	91	636
1928	422	57	479
1929	564	64	628
1930	1,131	161	1,292
1931	1,804	409	2,213
1932	1,140	276	1,416
1933	2,790	1,101	3,891
1934	43	1	44
1935	30	4	34
1936	42	1	43
1937	54	4	58
1938	51	1	52
1939	37	4	41

Source: Board of Governors of the Federal Reserve System, *Banking Studies*, Waverly Press, Baltimore, Md., 1941, p. 419.

It had been hoped that most state banks would voluntarily choose to join the Federal Reserve (membership is mandatory for national banks), but few did. As a consequence, lax examination and regulation of many state banks continued, with the results shown in Table 13-3. When the economy turned downward in 1929, bank failures turned upward. The first of the banking panics occurred in 1931 when over 2,000 banks failed; the second panic occurred in the spring of 1933 when an unbelievable 4,000 banks suspended operations. One of the first acts of Franklin Roosevelt, on assuming the Presidency, was to declare a "banking holiday," that is, he closed down every bank in the country and permitted only those judged "sound" by examiners to reopen for business. Roosevelt felt that such a drastic measure was needed to restore public confidence in the banking system. Between 1921 and 1933, some 11,000 banks suspended operations.

The behavior of the Federal Reserve System during these times remains a matter of controversy. One of the purposes of establishing the System had been to provide a method whereby newly created reserves could be made available to the commercial banks. The Federal Reserve accomplished this task adequately during the 1920s. But during the early years of the 1930s it was put to a severe test and found wanting. Huge injections of additional reserves were needed, and the Federal Reserve did not provide these reserves because of a technical defect in the law (which we shall not discuss here). Some critics maintain that this law was never a binding constraint on Federal Reserve activities,[10] although others disagree.[11] In either case, given the extraordinary nature of the times, it seems reasonably clear that had the Federal Reserve been predisposed to bolder action it could either have gotten Congress to change the law or else have ignored the law with impunity. But it did neither, and as a consequence the money supply shrank, the depression worsened, and thousands of banks failed.

The Federal Deposit Insurance Corporation

After the banking debacle of 1933 it was clear that the United States needed some method of guaranteeing the integrity of bank deposits, just as the National Banking System had guaranteed the integrity of the currency. To this end, the Federal Deposit Insurance Corporation was first established on a temporary basis in 1933 and then made permanent in 1935. The system of deposit insurance instituted by the FDIC has already been described in Chapter 3 and will not be repeated here. Its stabilizing influence on the banking system can be inferred from Table 13-3; after 1933 the number of bank failures in the country dropped dramatically. Not only did the FDIC provide security for small depositors by insuring their deposits, but (perhaps equally important) it finally accomplished what the Federal Reserve Act had not: It brought virtually all the banks in the country under a single, rigorous system of examination and supervision.

13-4 REVIEW QUESTIONS

1   In what ways did the First and Second Banks of the United States behave like a modern central bank?
2   What part of the money supply did the national banking system impart integrity to? What part did it ignore?
3   Why was our banking system so unstable throughout the nineteenth century?
4   Of the two main defects in our monetary system in the nineteenth century, the lack of integrity of the money supply and the lack of control over the total money supply, which was corrected by the FDIC? Which by the Federal Reserve System?

[10]See Milton Friedman and Anna J. Schwartz, *A Monetary History of the United States 1867–1960*, Princeton University Press, Princeton, N.J., 1963, pp. 399–406.
[11]See Josephine M. McElhone, "Free Gold as a Constraint on Monetary Policy During the Early Stages of the Great Depression," unpublished doctoral dissertation, Iowa State University, Ames, 1970.

14

The Federal Reserve System

The Federal Reserve System is the central bank of the United States. In common with other central banks throughout the world, its most basic function is to manage the nation's money supply. But the Federal Reserve does a great many other things as well, ranging from clearing and collecting checks to approving bank holding-company applications. All these functions, monetary and nonmonetary alike, are matters of consequence, and it is important that we examine the political base of the Federal Reserve. It is all too easy to get caught up in the technical aspects of money supply theory and forget that the Federal Reserve System is fundamentally a political organization.

The political organization of the *Fed* (as it is often called) has been shaped by history, accident, and our unit banking system. It is unique among the major central banks of the world. Where central banks in other countries are typically centralized, the Fed sprawls across the United States with a head office in Washington, twelve district banks, and twenty-four branches. Where central banks in other countries deal with all the banks in that country, substantially less than half the banks in the United States are members of the Federal Reserve System. Where central banks in other countries are a part of the government, the Fed is an independent agency.

The structure of the Federal Reserve is largely a compromise between the advocates of states rights, who felt that a centralized banking authority would threaten the dual banking system and put too much power in Washington, and the advocates of a strong central bank, who felt that a centralization of power was a necessity if the country was ever to escape the periodic financial panics of the nineteenth century. As a result of the compromise, the Federal Reserve became a curious mixture of local, regional, and national decision-making powers. In the banking acts of 1933 and 1935, after the debacle of the early Depression years, most of the real authority in the Federal Reserve System was transferred to Washington. But the form, if not the substance, of the early structure remained, and it is this divergence between form and substance that largely accounts for the apparent complexity of the Federal Reserve System as it is currently constituted.

14-1 STRUCTURE OF THE FEDERAL RESERVE SYSTEM

The bureaucratic structure of the Federal Reserve System may be visualized as a triangle (Figure 14-1) with the chief administrative group, the Board of Governors, at the top of the triangle and the member banks at its base. Occupying the middle of the triangle are the twelve district banks. Additionally, attached to the outside of the triangle and connected to both the Board of Governors and the district banks are two committees: the Federal Advisory Council, which is not very important, and the Federal Open Market Committee, which is extremely important. We shall consider each of these parts of the Federal Reserve System (Figure 14-1) in turn.

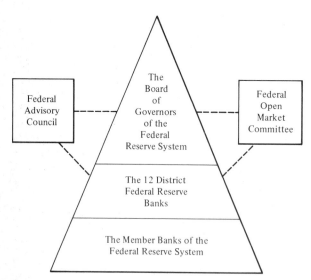

Figure 14-1 Structure of the Federal Reserve System.

The Board of Governors of the Federal Reserve System

The central controlling authority in the Federal Reserve System is the *Board of Governors.* Either by direct authority or by having veto powers, virtually all the important administrative decisions for the System are made by the Board. The Board is composed of seven members who are appointed by the President with the advice and consent of the Senate. However, it should not be inferred that because membership on the Board is obtained by Presidential appointment, the Board of Governors is therefore under the control of the President. Each member of the Board is appointed for a very long term, fourteen years, and an appointment may be neither renewed nor terminated by the President. Since a new member is appointed every two years, this means that if there are no resignations, the President will be able to appoint only two of the seven members of the Board during his first term of office, and will be able to have appointed a majority of the Board only during the last year of his last term of office. Additionally, Congress has made it very clear that it regards the Federal Reserve as its own creature, not as a part of the executive branch of government. Indeed, in recent years some of the most colorful political disagreements over the proper conduct of monetary policy have been between the Secretary of the Treasury (representing the executive branch) and the Chairman of the Board of Governors. The purpose of making the Board independent of the executive branch of government is to make it nonpartisan—"above" party politics.

The powers of the Board of Governors are wide-ranging and will be best understood as we consider the various other parts of the System. Briefly, they include: (1) serving as a majority on the Federal Open Market Committee, where monetary policy is fundamentally made; (2) approving the discount rate, that is, the rate of interest at which member banks may borrow; and (3) setting reserve requirements for member banks. Additionally, a great many day-to-day administrative decisions, internal to the System, are made by the Board.

Member Banks of the Federal Reserve System

Easily the most basic reason why banks join the Federal Reserve System is that they have federal charters. By law all national banks must be members of the Fed; state-chartered banks may join if they are willing to meet certain requirements and if they wish. About 90 percent of the state banks do not belong to the Federal Reserve. There are many factors that make membership in the Fed unattractive to state banks. As noted in Chapter 3, the reserve and capital requirement of member banks are generally tougher than those required by the states. For example, a multiple-regression analysis of member and nonmember banks in Illinois found that member banks tended to hold smaller amounts of earning assets than nonmember banks and to be comparatively less profitable.[1]

Although the reserve and capital requirements are probably the most important barriers to membership, various other obstacles also exist. Historically, one of the most important of these obstacles has been the *par clearance* provision that is

[1]Lucile S. Mayne, *The Cost of Federal Reserve System Membership,* The American Banker's Association, New York, 1967.

mandatory for all member banks. To *clear at par* means that a bank must pay the full amount of a check written against one of its accounts and deposited in a bank in another town.[2] In the early years of the Federal Reserve, these *clearing charges* (remitting less than the face value of the check) were an important source of income for many small banks, and consequently these banks refused to join the System. However, there are now fewer than 40 banks in the United States that do not clear at par. Other factors that make Federal Reserve membership unattractive to state banks involve various technical regulations dealing with loans, assets, affiliates, and so on, which are generally more restrictive for member than for nonmember banks. Finally, it should be noted that most of the services provided by the Federal Reserve to member banks are also available to nonmember banks, so that not only are the barriers to joining costly, but the incentives to join are weak.[3]

The member banks of the Federal Reserve System are technically its owners. When a bank joins the System, it is required to buy stock in the System in the amount of 3 percent of the member bank's capital and surplus.[4] (This requirement is not an obstacle to membership since Federal Reserve stock pays an annual dividend of 6 percent and is completely riskless.) It must be emphasized, however, that this stock "ownership" is strictly technical. It does not carry with it the usual connotation of control, nor do the member banks receive a share of the System's "profits" (except for the fixed 6 percent noted previously). As with so many aspects of the Federal Reserve's structure, stock ownership by the member banks is largely of historical origin. It represents a compromise between those who thought the Federal Reserve should be controlled by the commercial banking system and those who regarded such a position as absurd and instead argued that the Fed should be a governmental agency whose member banks did as they were told. The compromise consisted in member bank ownership[5] of the System and Presidential appointment of the Board of Governors.

The District Federal Reserve Banks

The Board of Governors does not, for the most part, administer directly to the member banks. Instead, its rules and regulations and its examinations and supervisions are carried out through the intermediation of the district Federal Reserve Banks. For administrative purposes, the United States is divided into the twelve districts shown in Figure 14-2. These districts do not follow state boundaries but are intended to appoximate (in an admittedly rough fashion) economically homogeneous areas of the country. As the reader has no doubt anticipated, partitioning the

---

[2]Students frequently confuse par clearance with service charges on out-of-town checks, but the two are not the same. Par clearance requires that a bank remit the full face value of its own checks to other banks. Service charges are a small charge that a bank makes for cashing a check drawn on an account in *another bank*. The latter is a fairly common practice, particularly in college towns, and does not violate Federal Reserve regulations.

[3]Section 14-3 discusses the declining membership of the Federal Reserve System.

[4]An additional 3 percent may be requested by the Federal Reserve, but this has never been done and it is very unlikely that it ever will be.

[5]Prior to the centralization of authority in the System in 1935, "ownership" by member banks was a bit more substantive than it is now. At that time the district banks had greater freedom to make decisions and the member banks elected (as they still do) a majority of the board of directors of the district banks.

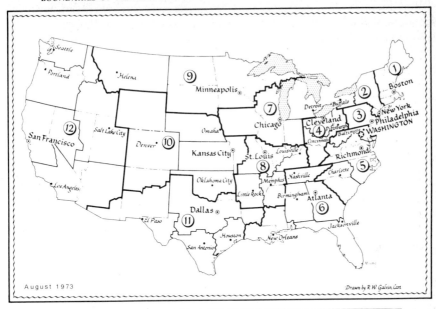

THE FEDERAL RESERVE SYSTEM

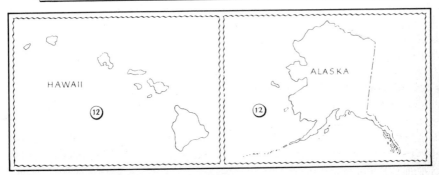

Legend

—— Boundaries of Federal Reserve Districts ——Boundaries of Federal Reserve Branch Territories

✪ Board of Governors of the Federal Reserve System

◉ Federal Reserve Bank Cities • Federal Reserve Branch Cities

· Federal Reserve Bank Facilities

Figure 14-2 Districts, district banks, and branches of the Federal Reserve System. (*Source: Federal Reserve Bulletin, any issue.*)

country into twelve districts was the result of a compromise by the framers of the Federal Reserve Act. The states-rights advocates were fearful that a single, centralized authority in Washington would have too much power and too little knowledge of the particular needs of different parts of the country. As a consequence, the Federal Reserve Act provided that the country should be divided into not less than eight or more than twelve districts, each with a district bank. The choice was made at the outset to set up the maximum number. Each district has a district bank named after the city in which it is located, for example, the Federal Reserve Bank of New York and the Federal Reserve Bank of Minneapolis. Additionally, some of the district banks have established a total of twenty-four branches for administrative purposes. Although the original district banks had a good deal of autonomous decision-making authority, for the most part this power was transferred to the Board of Governors by the Banking Act of 1935. The district banks are now most validly regarded as subordinate extensions of the Board, whose purpose is to carry out the Board's decisions at a regional level.

Each district bank has a nine-member board of directors. Six of the nine are elected by the member banks of the district, and of these six, three must be bankers and three must have no banking connections. The three members who are not elected by the member banks are appointed by the Board of Governors and are supposed to represent the interests of the public. The two primary duties of the board of directors are to set the discount rate, that is, the rate of interest at which the district bank will make loans to the member banks of that district, and to appoint the president and first vice president of the district bank. In each of these cases, however, the decision of the board of directors is subject to the approval of the Board of Governors. This requirement has in effect emasculated the original powers of the board of directors of the district banks since in practice the Board of Governors simply refuses to approve any decision that they themselves have not made. This is particularly true in setting the discount rate, with the consequence that the discount rate moves up and down uniformly for all twelve district banks.

The chief administrative officer of each district bank is its president. The president of the bank is responsible for its day-to-day operation and for carrying out the regulations promulgated by the Board of Governors. Additionally, five of the twelve district bank presidents are voting members of the Federal Open Market Committee (FOMC), and the remaining seven regularly attend the meetings of the FOMC and participate in its discussions. Since the decisions of the FOMC lie at the heart of the monetary policy process, this means that the district bank presidents help formulate monetary policy. They must therefore be well informed on current economic affairs, as well as on the daily routine of their banks and the problems of the member banks in their district. It is a highly responsible job.

The Federal Advisory Council

As the name implies, the Federal Advisory Council has no powers other than its powers of persuasion. It is advisory to the Board of Governors. One member is appointed from each Federal Reserve District by the board of directors of each district bank. The Federal Advisory Council is required to meet in Washington a minimum of four times a year and to make representations to the Board of Governors concerning banking matters and credit policy.

The Federal Open Market Committee

From the viewpoint of monetary policy, the most important group of people in the Federal Reserve System is the Federal Open Market Committee (FOMC). Whenever you read in the newspaper, for example, that interest rates are increasing (or decreasing), it is almost certainly the ultimate consequence of a decision made by the FOMC. How this decision is made and the techniques whereby it is carried out are major topics in Chapters 15 and 16 that follow and will not be described in detail at this point. For present purposes it is sufficient simply to note that the FOMC decides for the Federal Reserve System how many government securities to buy or sell in the open market; that these decisions directly affect the reserve base R of the commercial banking system; and that changes in the reserve base, working through the money supply equation $M_1 = mR$, influence the quantity of money in the country. In short, decisions of the FOMC are a major factor in determining how much money there will be in the country. The importance of these decisions and hence the importance of the Federal Open Market Committee can hardly be exaggerated.

The FOMC is composed of twelve members. Of these, seven are the members of the Board of Governors and the remaining five are presidents (or sometimes vice presidents) of the twelve district banks. Because of his prominence in the System and because his bank is the district bank that actually carries out the policies of the FOMC, the president of the Federal Reserve Bank of New York is always a member of the Committee. The other four president memberships of the FOMC are rotated annually among the other eleven district bank presidents as follows.

One from the Federal Reserve Bank of either Cleveland or Chicago
One from the Federal Reserve Bank of either Boston, Philadelphia, or Richmond
One from the Federal Reserve Bank of either Atlanta, Dallas, or St. Louis
One from the Federal Reserve Bank of either Minneapolis, Kansas City, or San Francisco

Profits of the Federal Reserve System

The Federal Reserve is not a profit-oriented institution; it is not a business firm, and it is not motivated by a desire to maximize profits. Nevertheless, the process of carrying out monetary policy results in the System's annual income being substantially greater than its expenses. In other words, the System in fact earns a profit even though this is not one of its objectives. The Federal Reserve's expenses are the usual ones of any organization: the payment of employees, utilities, maintenance of facilities, and so on. Its primary source of income is that, in the course of conducting the open market operations of the FOMC, it has acquired over $100 billion worth of United States government securities. For legal purposes the Federal Reserve is the owner of these securities, and hence like any other owner it is entitled to the interest that such securities pay. In recent years these interest payments have been running at the rate of over $6 billion annually. Since the System's expenses, including dividend payments to member banks, amount only to about 10 percent of this, it is evident that the Federal Reserve makes very substantial profits. What happens to these profits? Ever since 1947 they have been transferred back to the United States Treasury. In 1978 this transfer amounted to about $5.9 billion.

14-2   FUNCTIONS OF THE FEDERAL RESERVE SYSTEM

While the economist's interest in the Federal Reserve System naturally centers on its political organization and money control functions, in fact the vast bulk of the people who work for the System have nothing to do with either of these matters. Rather, they are engaged in the routine, day-to-day activities of the Federal Reserve —what are usually called its *chores*. [6] These activities include the supervision, examination, and regulation of member banks; the clearing and collecting of checks; acting as fiscal agent for the United States government; and engaging in extensive economic research.

Supervision, Examination, and Regulation of Member Banks

The supervision, examination, and regulation of the commercial banking system and the amount of overlap and coordination among the various agencies responsible for these tasks has already been discussed in Chapter 3. The discussion will not be repeated. It is perhaps sufficient to remind the reader that the district banks of the Federal Reserve examine only the state-chartered member banks (the examination of national banks being left to the Comptroller of the Currency), and that the Board of Governors is involved in many decisions concerning holding companies, bank mergers, monopoly in banking, and so on. Both the Board and the district banks employ large numbers of lawyers, economists, and examiners to conduct analyses and make recommendations about these matters.

The Clearing and Collection of Checks

One of the major achievements of the Federal Reserve System has been to set up an efficient nationwide mechanism for the *clearing and collection of checks.* Properly speaking, when a check is *collected,* it is presented to the bank against which it is drawn and that bank pays it. The *clearing* of checks is different. When checks are cleared through the banking system, the mutual amounts that two or more banks owe to one another are simply offset so that no currency actually changes hands. The *clearing and collection* of checks therefore refers to a system wherein reciprocal amounts of checks are offset against one another, or *cleared,* and where only the net

---

[6]Calling these activities *chores* is an unfortunate bit of snobbery on the part of economists. The word is meant to indicate that these jobs are dull and uninteresting, but what is interesting or uninteresting is a matter of individual taste. Certainly the chores are vital to the proper functioning of the financial sector of the economy.

differences are paid, or *collected.* Prior to the establishment of the Federal Reserve, only local checks were cleared; out-of-town checks were collected through correspondent banks. This mechanism was badly inefficient. In effect, the Federal Reserve set itself up as a nationwide clearinghouse for the banking system.

Local Check Clearing While the clearing and collecting of checks among banks located in the same city usually does not directly involve the Federal Reserve, it is nevertheless instructive to consider such local clearing. In principle, at least, the system used by the Federal Reserve for clearing and collecting checks on a district-wide and nationwide basis is no different than the system used by banks locally.

Imagine a city with four banks in it, banks A, B, C, and D. Each bank in this city is, of course, daily receiving checks that are drawn against the three other banks in the city. If each bank were required to collect (properly so-called) these checks, then every day there would have to occur twelve transactions among these banks:[7] Bank A would have to collect from the other three banks, bank B would also have to collect from the other three banks, and so forth. But it would obviously be foolish for each bank to collect from each other bank—e.g., for bank A to collect currency from bank B *and* for bank B to collect currency from bank A. At a minimum, therefore, we would expect the banks to arrange for *bilateral clearing,* that is, for each pair of banks to arrange to offset their mutual amounts of checks and then collect only the net difference in currency. If such bilateral clearing agreements were made among all twelve banks, Bank A would clear with banks B, C, and D; bank B with C and D; and bank C with D only.[8] But it would also be foolish for the banks to limit themselves to bilateral clearing. It would be more efficient (in terms of the number of transactions involved) for the banks to arrange for *multilateral clearing,* where mutual amounts involving more than two banks are cleared. For example, if bank A owes bank B, bank B owes bank C, and bank C owes bank A, then all three debts can be cancelled simultaneously. A local clearinghouse is simply a multilateral clearing arrangement among banks in the same city.[9]

To illustrate the use of a clearinghouse transaction, consider Table 14-1. In this table, we assume that there are four banks in town and that each bank has received checks in varying amounts drawn against deposits in every other bank. These checks are taken to the clearinghouse, where they are entered in the body of the table (the individual bank entries). For example, reading down the first column (from the left), bank A has received $750 worth of checks drawn against bank B, $200 worth against

[7]More generally, the number of separate transactions would be $n^2 - n$, where n is the number of banks in town. Note that the number of transactions increases more rapidly than the number of banks. For example, a city with ten banks would have to have $100 - 10 = 90$ daily transactions.

[8]More generally, the number of separate transactions would be $\Sigma_{i=1}^{n-1} i$, where n is the number of banks. Note that the number of transactions still rises more rapidly than the number of banks. For example, a city with ten banks would have to have $1 + 2 + 3 + 4 + 5 + 6 + 7 + 8 + 9 = 45$ daily transactions.

[9]The story (probably not true) goes that the clearinghouse was invented by the bank messengerboys in London who, rather than each making a separate trip to each bank in the city, arranged to meet at a coffeehouse every day and get all their business taken care of at once.

Table 14-1 A Clearinghouse Transaction

	Bank A is owed by	Bank B is owed by	Bank C is owed by	Bank D is owed by	Total debits	Net debits
Bank A owes to	. . . . . .	$ 100	$350	$150	$ 600	
Bank B owes to	$ 750	. . . . . .	$ 50	$200	$1,000	
Bank C owes to	$ 200	$ 400	. . . .	$100	$ 700	$ 200
Bank D owes to	$ 250	$1,000	$100	. . . .	$1,350	$ 900
Total credits	$1,200	$1,500	$500	$450	$3,650	
Net credits	$ 600	$ 500	. . . .	. . . .	. . . . . .	$1,100

bank C, and so forth. Each column is to be interpreted in the same way; the rows are simply the reverse of the columns. If bank A is owed $750 by bank B, then it must also be true that bank B owes $750 to bank A; bank B also owes $50 to bank C and $200 to bank D. Each row is to be interpreted similarly. If, now, we add all the numbers in a row, we will get the total amount that any one bank owes to the other three banks ("Total Debits"). Thus bank A owes a total of $600 to banks B, C, and D. Similarly, each column shows how much each bank is owed ("Total Credits"). Thus bank A, for example, is owed $1,200 by the other three banks.

The next step is to net out the credits and debits for each bank ("Net Debits" and "Net Credits" in Table 14-1). Thus bank A has total credits of $1,200 and total debits of $600, and so bank A receives a net credit with the clearinghouse for $600 ($1,200 – $600). Similarly, bank B has a net credit of $500, and banks C and D have net debits of $200 and $900, respectively. Now all that is necessary is for each bank to either *pay* its net debit *to* the clearinghouse or *collect* its net credit *from* the clearinghouse. Thus, banks C and D would pay $200 and $900, respectively, to the clearinghouse; and banks A and B would collect $600 and $500, respectively, from the clearinghouse. The entire process takes only a few minutes and is obviously more efficient than separate bilateral clearing agreements, especially if the number of banks is very large.

Intradistrict Check Clearing and Collection In principle, check clearing and collection within a Federal Reserve district is as simple as it is with a local clearing-house association. All the banks in the district could send their out-of-town checks to the district bank, which would then arrange the net debits and credits in the manner illustrated in Table 14-1. While in general it does work this way, the institutional framework of the Federal Reserve and the geographic distances involved require some modifications:

1 Since member banks are holding reserve balances at the district bank, it is not necessary that actual currency change hands. After calculating the net credits or debits, the district bank simply makes a bookkeeping transfer of reserves from debit banks to credit banks.
2 All banks in the district are not member banks of the Federal Reserve. This problem is overcome in either of two ways. Nonmember banks in areas

served by Regional Check Processing Centers of the Federal Reserve (which includes most areas of the country) are permitted to deposit checks drawn on other banks in their region. Nonmember banks that are not in such an area, or who do not want to use the Federal Reserve's facilities directly, may clear checks through their correspondents, who in turn clear through the Federal Reserve. The only restrictions on this arrangement is that *nonpar* banks (banks that do not remit checks at par) cannot clear through the Federal Reserve. (As previously noted, the number of nonpar banks is quite small—less than 40—and growing smaller.)

3   Because of the need to transport checks over substantial distances, it may not be possible to clear checks on a same-day basis, as it is with most local clearinghouses. To make the clearing process function smoothly, the district bank sets up a *deferred availability schedule* based on the location of the bank against which the check is drawn. This schedule specifies the number of days a bank must wait before it receives credit for a check sent to the Fed. For example, suppose a bank in Chicago receives a check drawn against a bank in Des Moines, Iowa. The Chicago bank will then dispatch this check to the Federal Reserve Bank of Chicago. But the Chicago Fed will not give the Chicago bank immediate credit for the check because Des Moines is so far away. Instead, it will give the Chicago bank credit after one day; i.e., the *availability* of the funds to the Chicago bank is *deferred* by one day. But after one day the Chicago bank will have the money credited to its reserve account. Since it may actually take more than one day to present the check to the Des Moines bank, the method of using a deferred availability schedule frequently gives rise to an extension of credit by the Federal Reserve to the bank sending in the check. In other words, the Chicago bank may receive an increase in its reserves before there is a decrease in the reserves of the Des Moines bank. This extension of credit by the Fed is known as the *float* and will be discussed in more detail in Chapter 15.

Interdistrict Check Clearing and Collection   When checks are cleared between commercial banks in two different Federal Reserve Districts, the clearing process is only slightly more complicated than it is within a single district. To illustrate the process, suppose that a check written on a bank in Boston is deposited in a bank in San Francisco. Then the San Francisco bank will send the check to the San Francisco Fed, the San Francisco Fed will send the check to the Boston Fed, and the Boston Fed will collect it from the Boston bank. The net result is that the reserve account of the San Francisco bank has increased and the reserve account of the Boston bank has decreased. The only loose thread is that the Boston Fed now owes the San Francisco Fed the amount of the check. These debts among district banks are settled through the *Interdistrict Settlement Fund* in Washington, which is essentially a clearinghouse for the district Federal Reserve Banks.

Size of the Federal Reserve Check-Clearing Operations   The amount of and number of checks cleared annually by the Federal Reserve System is huge. In 1977 the System handled more than thirteen billion items, amounting to more than $5.5 *trillion.*

Wire Transfer Service   In addition to its check-clearing operation, the Federal Reserve also transfers money and government securities by *wire,* which consists of a series of linked computers at each of the district banks. The transfer of funds through these computers is similar to check clearing, except that the "check" is an electronic message. The process is practically instantaneous. Unlike check clearing, however, the Federal Reserve charges a small fee for this service and will not handle amounts below a specified minimum.

Fiscal Agent for the Treasury

One of the major jobs of the Federal Reserve System is to serve as the *fiscal agent* for the United States Treasury. That is, the Federal Reserve acts for and advises the Treasury on a wide variety of financial matters.

The Federal Reserve acts as the Treasury's bank. That is, just as business firms hold deposits in commercial banks, the Treasury holds a deposit in the Federal Reserve against which it writes checks. As described in Chapter 9 (and as will be analyzed in greater detail in Chapter 15), only a small part of the Treasury's funds are held in its account at the Federal Reserve at any one time. The bulk of its funds are held in the *tax and loan* deposits of commercial banks and are transferred to the Federal Reserve prior to spending. The purpose of handling Treasury funds in this manner is to have as little impact on commercial bank reserves as possible.

Another important fiscal function of the Federal Reserve is to aid the Treasury in its (public) debt-management operations. The Federal Reserve is involved in all stages of this process. It advises the Treasury on the terms of new security offerings, publicizes the issues, receives bids, and collects money for the issues when they are sold. The Federal Reserve also makes interest payments and redeems matured government securities for the Treasury and handles the trust accounts of various other government agencies.

Finally, the Federal Reserve acts as the fiscal agent of the Treasury in many matters involving foreign exchange operations. In particular, the Federal Reserve Bank of New York deals in foreign currencies both for the System and for the Treasury.

Economic Research

The Federal Reserve System conducts what is probably the largest and best known program of economic research within the United States government. Although the System's research efforts are focused primarily on financial matters, the conduct of monetary policy leads it into all phases of economics. Huge amounts of data are collected on a regular basis by the System (some of which are published in the *Federal Reserve Bulletin*), and a great many specialized surveys are made each year. These data are analyzed both for purposes of current economic intelligence and for more basic research purposes. One of the most interesting innovations in economic research in the past few years has been the development of a very large simulation model of the United States economy, which the Federal Reserve has developed in conjunction with various universities.

14-3 THE DECLINING MEMBERSHIP OF THE FEDERAL RESERVE SYSTEM

One problem that is currently of considerable concern to Federal Reserve officials is the dwindling importance of member banks in our commercial banking system. This decline has occurred both in terms of bank members and bank deposits. Table 14-2 shows how dramatic this decline has been in the past several years. The decline has occurred largely among smaller banks, although a few large banks have also chosen to withdraw from the System.

The main reason why many member banks have chosen to withdraw from the System, and why many new banks have chosen not to join, is clear. The nature of the legal reserve requirements of member banks is such that membership in the Federal Reserve System is quite costly.[10] One study, for example, concludes that, if a nonmember bank joined the Federal Reserve System, its earning assets would fall by about 4 percent, thereby reducing its profits. Of course, joining the Federal Reserve would provide certain free services to the bank, but these services are apparently not sufficient to cover the added expense, especially for small banks.[11]

It is not wholly clear whether the membership attrition in the Federal Reserve System is a genuine problem of public policy, or merely a bureaucratic problem. That is, it is not clear if the conduct of monetary policy would be materially hampered by fewer banks being members of the System, or if the concern of the Federal Reserve officials is simply the loss of membership per se. One study,[12] at

Table 14-2 Declining Federal Reserve Membership (Percentage of All Commercial Banks)

Year	Number of member banks	Deposits held by member banks
1965	45.1	82.9
1966	44.7	82.6
1967	44.2	82.5
1968	43.7	81.9
1969	43.0	80.3
1970	42.1	80.0
1971	41.6	79.1
1972	41.0	78.3
1973	40.5	77.3
1974	40.0	77.0
1975	39.6	75.1
1976	39.3	73.8
1977	38.6	72.7

Source: Federal Reserve Bulletin, May 1978, p. A16 and previous issues.

[10]Lawrence G. Goldberg and John T. Rose, "The Effect on Nonmember Banks of the Imposition of Member Bank Reserve Requirements—with and without Federal Reserve Services," *Journal of Finance,* December 1976, pp. 1457–1469. See also Chris Joseph Prestopino, "Do Higher Reserve Requirements Discourage Federal Reserve Membership?", *Journal of Finance,* December 1976, pp. 1471–1480.

[11]R. Alton Gilbert, "Utilization of Federal Reserve Bank Services by Member Banks: Implications for the Costs and Benefits of Membership," Federal Reserve Bank of St. Louis *Review,* August 1977, pp. 2–15.

[12]Dennis R. Starleaf, "Nonmember Banks and Monetary Control," *Journal of Finance,* September 1975, pp. 955–975.

least, suggests that nonmember banks are *not* a problem so far as control of the money supply is concerned. In any case, the Federal Reserve has made two proposals to Congress, either of which would almost certainly result in the reversal of the membership trend. One proposal is to require uniform reserve requirements of *all* banks, member and nonmember alike, which would virtually eliminate the advantage of nonmember status. The other proposal is to permit the Federal Reserve to pay a rate of interest on member bank reserves, which would provide a substantial incentive for banks to join the System.

14-4 THE INDEPENDENCE OF THE FEDERAL RESERVE SYSTEM

At the the beginning of this chapter, it was noted that the Federal Reserve System is fundamentally a political organization. It is, in fact, that agency of the government responsible for the conduct of monetary policy, a function that many believe is as important as our foreign policy. The difference is that if we, as citizens, don't like our foreign policy, we know who to blame and what we can do about it: We can blame the President and vote against him. But if we don't like our monetary policy, who do we blame and what do we do about it? In other words, who controls the Federal Reserve? To whom is it politically responsible?

The Federal Reserve is what is called an *independent agency.* This is not to say that it is somehow outside the government, like a private corporation. It is firmly embedded in our political system. But within that context, and in the short run, the Federal Reserve does not take orders from anyone. Its decisions about monetary policy are made independently of the President, Congress, and partisan politics.

The independent status of the Federal Reserve stems largely from two aspects of its structure. First, recall that each member of the Board of Governors is appointed for a fourteen-year term and may be neither removed from nor reappointed to office. This feature of the Federal Reserve Act means (as was intended) that the Board of Governors is independent of the President. Once appointed, a member of the Board is beholden to no one; he or she needn't fear being fired because of an unpopular decision, nor need he or she curry favor in hope of reappointment. A new member is, in effect, removed from the political process for the next fourteen years.

Second, the independence of the Federal Reserve from Congress is derived from its profitability. Remember that the System's annual income is far greater than its expenses and that, in fact, it annually transfers billions of dollars of "profits" to the Treasury. Congressional influence over the policies of most government agencies stems from control over the purse strings. Most agencies must request annual appropriations from Congress, and Congress can be more or less generous with its appropriations, depending on its approval or disapproval of the policies followed by the agency. Not so with the Federal Reserve. Whether Congress approves or disapproves of current monetary policy, the Federal Reserve is ensured of an income that is more than adequate to continue its present scale of operation.

It should be emphasized, however, that the independence of the Federal Reserve is of a short-run nature only. In the long run, Congress can pass laws that the Fed must obey, and the President can bring enormous pressure to bear. The System

is fully aware of these possibilities and behaves accordingly. It seems a fair generalization to say that the Federal Reserve accepts the social and economic goals of the
President and Congress but retains its independence in the methods it chooses to
achieve these goals.

The question arises as to whether the Federal Reserve *should* be independent.
This is a very controversial issue, with strong arguments to be made on both sides.
Many people feel that just as "war is too important to be left to generals," monetary
policy is too important to be left to economists. As matters stand, they complain,
the President is given the blame for an unpopular monetary policy but no power to
change it. In campaign oratory, for example, it is common to hear that the party
in power has "caused high interest rates." But the truth is that no elected official
has much influence over interest rates and that the Federal Reserve has a great deal
of influence. The logic of such arguments, therefore, is that the Federal Reserve
should somehow be made responsible to the elected representatives of the people,
either by making it subordinate to the Treasury or by eliminating its profitability and
thus making it dependent on annual congressional appropriations.

The argument favoring Federal Reserve independence is basically historical. In
the past, there seems always to have been a tendency for governments to abuse the
monetary system, with inflationary results. In olden days, this conflict worked itself
out when kings would *debase* the "coin of the realm." That is, a king would alloy
gold coin with some base metal such as lead and would then try to spend the new
coins at the old prices. It didn't take merchants and shopkeepers very long to figure
out what was happening, of course, and so they simply raised their prices (inflation)
to compensate for the debased coins. In more modern times, when the money supply
was composed mainly of paper currency, governments would simply print more
money and try to spend it at current prices. Both the Continental Congress during
the Revolutionary War and the Confederacy during the Civil War engaged in this
practice. And, again, the result was inflation. The more money the government
printed, the more worthless it became. Business people simply raised their prices.

As we have seen, our money supply is now composed mostly of deposits in
commercial banks. The contemporary method of debasing the monetary unit is
correspondingly more complicated, but the principle is the same. The central bank
can create deposits for the Treasury by lending to them, that is, by writing up (in
a bookkeeping sense) the Treasury deposit at the Federal Reserve. This money—and
that is exactly what it is—would then be available for the government to spend. And
if this were done on a large enough scale, the result would again be inflation.

The argument for an independent Federal Reserve can thus be summarized as
follows: There is a fundamental conflict of interest between the government and the
central bank. The government loves to spend but hates to tax. One way out of this
dilemma is to create new money to spend, and the creation of new money in large
amounts results in inflation. But the central bank (Federal Reserve) is charged with
the responsibility of preventing inflations, and it can do this only by limiting the
quantity of money in the economy. To attempt to combine both the government and
the central bank into a single organization is thus to court disaster in the form of
severe inflation.

Various measures have been proposed for making the Federal Reserve more

---

Responsibility of the Monetary Authority to Congress

For years the monetary authority has acted as if it were independent not only of the Executive, but of the Congress to which it is legally responsible. The Federal Reserve Board members are appointed for a term of 14 years, a period nearly twice as long as any President can normally hold office. Financing of Board operations is obtained largely from interest paid on its holdings of U.S. Government bonds. Thus, the Board enjoys complete financial independence not only from the Executive, but from the Congress, even to the point of refusing to allow the General Accounting Office to audit the System's books, a unique exception among Federal agencies.

To improve and modernize the central banking system, the Congress should enact legislation which would:

- **Vest open market operations in the Federal Reserve Board and eliminate the Open Market Committee. This would serve the purpose of maintaining the monetary powers vested in the Congress by the Constitution in a body that is exclusively public rather than in a mixed committee like the Open Market Committee.**

- **Require the Federal Reserve to pay into the Treasury all of its revenues, to come before the Congress for appropriations as other agencies do, and provide for audit of the Board and regional bank accounts by the Comptroller General. These provisions are designed to insure public control.**

- **Retire existing Federal Reserve stock, thereby eliminating the spurious notion that the member banks own the Federal Reserve System.**

Figure 14-3 Legislative proposals of the Joint Economic Committee concerning the structure of the Federal Reserve System. (*Source: Joint Economic Committee, Congress of the United States, The 1973 Joint Economic Report, Washington, 1973, p. 29.*)

responsible to the Congress or the President. Figure 14-3, for example, is taken from the *Joint Economic Report,* which is published annually by a congressional committee. At this point the reader should have no difficulty in understanding the gist of the legislation being proposed by this committee.

14-5 REVIEW QUESTIONS

1 Turn back to Figure 14-1 (page 254) and see if you can explain the function of each of the five parts of the Federal Reserve System.
2 Imagine a town with three banks in it. Draw up a clearinghouse transaction for this town, making up your own numbers.
3 Why has there been a decline in Federal Reserve membership in recent years?
4 Do you think the Federal Reserve should be an independent agency? Why or why not?

15

Controlling
Bank Reserves

The Federal Reserve System was not originally meant to exercise control over the money supply on a continuing basis. Rather, the intent was to prevent financial panics—to establish a *lender of last resort* where *all* commercial banks could turn when they were *all* in need of reserves. It may seem just a short intellectual step from the defensive posture of sometimes influencing bank reserves in order to prevent panics, to the dynamic policy of influencing them continually to promote economic stability. In fact, the intellectual step *is* a short one. But politically it was a long journey. In 1913 the economic philosophy of the United States was predominantly that of laissez faire; the "business of America" was, as President Calvin Coolidge later put it, "business." But the Great Depression of the 1930s changed all that. Implicit in the New Deal of President Franklin Roosevelt was the assumption that the federal government was responsible for the economic welfare of the people. And as these changes occurred in our political philosophy, a similar change occurred in the role of the Federal Reserve. No longer was it expected to confine itself to being the lender of last resort. To this function was added the dynamic use of its central banking powers to achieve the goals of full employment, price level stability, economic growth, and equilibrium in the balance of payments.

Our goal in this chapter is to begin to understand how the Federal Reserve System attempts to achieve these goals; that is, we want to understand the precise nature of the powers the Federal Reserve possesses and the limitations on these powers. In essence, the message of this chapter is that the Federal Reserve's monetary powers are derived largely from the degree of control it exerts over member bank reserves. We therefore need to begin the discussion by establishing a link between the Federal Reserve System and member bank reserves.

15-1 THE FEDERAL RESERVE'S BALANCE SHEET

The first step in our analysis is to be clear about what is being explained. What we want to explain are those reserves of member banks that are held as deposits in the Federal Reserve System. To put the matter negatively, we are *not* explaining the reserves of nonmember banks or the vault cash of member banks. However, the omission of nonmember reserves from our analysis is a relatively minor matter; if the Federal Reserve can control the reserves of member banks, then for all practical purposes it can control the reserve base of the commercial banking system. The omission of member bank vault cash is also not serious; if the Fed can control those reserves deposited with it, then it can offset variations in vault cash reserves and thus make the *total* member bank reserves what it wishes.

Our immediate task is to explain the complex of forces determining member bank reserves held in the Federal Reserve. Beyond this, our ultimate goal is to understand how the Federal Reserve is able to dominate this process. It therefore seems logical to begin our analysis with a framework that combines both the Federal Reserve and member bank reserves. Such a framework exists in the balance sheet of the Federal Reserve System—what is more formally called the *Consolidated Statement of Conditions of All Federal Reserve Banks*. This balance sheet, which contains member bank reserves as a liability item, is shown in Table 15-1.

For convenience, each of the entries in Table 15-1 has been assigned a symbol (indicated in parentheses to the right of the entry): thus gold certificates are denoted by GC, cash by C, and so on. The three parts of the balance sheet may thus be expressed symbolically as

$$\text{Assets} = GC + SDR + C + D\&A + USGS + CIPC + OA$$
$$\text{Liabilities} = N + R + T + F + OD + DAI + OL$$
$$\text{Capital} = CAP$$

Because of the fundamental accounting identity that liabilities plus capital equal assets, Table 15-1 may also be written as an equation using these symbols. Thus

$$N + R + T + F + OD + DAI + OL + CAP$$
$$= GC + SDR + C + D\&A + USGS + CIPC + OA \quad (1)$$

Table 15-1 The Balance Sheet of the Federal Reserve System, March 31, 1978 (Millions of Dollars)

Assets		Liabilities and capital	
Gold certificates (GC)	11,718	Liabilities	
Special drawing		Federal Reserve notes (N)	91,666
rights (SDR)	1,250	Member bank reserves (R)	27,900
Cash (C)	323	Treasury deposits (T)	4,705
Discounts and		Foreign deposits (F)	352
advances (D&A)	9,295	Other deposits (OD)	740
United States government		Deferred availability	
securities (USGS)	101,577	item (DAI)	5,622
Cash items in process of		Other liabilities (OL)	1,234
collection (CIPC)	8,354	Total liabilities	132,219
Other assets (OA)	2,328	Capital (CAP)	2,626
Total assets	134,845	Total liabilities and capital	134,845

Source: Federal Reserve Bulletin, May 1978, p. A12.

Since our interest lies in explaining the reserves of member banks R, we can solve eq. (1) for R:

$$R = GC + SDR + C + D\&A + USGS + CIPC + OA$$
$$- N - T - F - OD - DAI - OL - CAP \quad (2)$$

In principle, eq. (2) gives a complete explanation of the determinants of member bank reserves held at the Federal Reserve. If any one of the items on the right-hand side of the equation that has a plus sign in front of it goes up, and if none of the other items changes, then member bank reserves must go up. Similarly, an increase in any of the minus items must, all other items remaining the same, cause a decrease in R. Thus we *could* proceed to explain member bank reserves by analyzing the behavior of each item on the right-hand side of eq. (2).

However, eq. (2) is not very convenient to work with. For one thing, it contains fourteen separate symbols in addition to R, and working with so many items is messy and awkward. One feels that at the very least some of these items should be lumped together. Beyond this, and even more important, is that all the items in eq. (2) are not necessarily meaningful for *economic* analysis. Equation (2) is derived from Table 15-1, and Table 15-1 is a balance sheet drawn up by accountants for accounting purposes. But what is analytically meaningful for accountants may not be meaningful for economists. We consequently want to simplify eq. (2) and improve it as a tool of analysis.

Transforming the Federal Reserve's Balance Sheet

As a first step, let us rearrange the terms in eq. (2) by grouping some of them together in parentheses:

$$R = SDR + D\&A + USGS - T + (OA - F - OD - OL - CAP)$$
$$+ (CIPC - DAI) + (GC + C - N) \quad (3)$$

The first four terms in eq. (3), *SDR, D&A, USGS,* and *T,* will be maintained as they appear in Table 15-1; these are significant concepts and are useful just as they are for our purposes. Our interest lies, rather, in changing the three expressions in parentheses.

Consider the first parenthetical expression $(OA - F - OD - OL - CAP)$. These symbols stand for other assets, foreign deposits, other deposits, other liabilities, and capital, respectively. In general, we may think of these as a group of small and miscellaneous accounts that can be lumped together with a single symbol to simplify the equation. Let us call this symbol *OTHER* and define it as the negative of $(OA - F - OD - OL - CAP)$. Thus

$$OTHER = F + OD + OL + CAP - OA \quad (4)$$

Substituting eq. (4) into eq. (3), we now have

$$R = SDR + D\&A + USGS - T - OTHER$$
$$+ (CIPC - DAI) + (GC + C - N) \quad (5)$$

Consider next the second parenthetical expression in eq. (3), $(CIPC - DAI)$, that is, *cash items in the process of collection* minus *deferred availability items.* These terms are grouped together because they both arise in the check-clearing and check-collecting activities of the Federal Reserve. Their precise role in determining bank reserves will be analyzed more fully in section 15-2, but their general nature can be indicated briefly at this point. *Cash items in the process of collection* is the dollar value of all the checks the Federal Reserve has received but not yet collected. *Deferred availability items* is the dollar amount of these same checks that the Federal Reserve has *not* paid. When you subtract the amount of checks the Federal Reserve has not paid from the amount it has received but not yet collected, you obtain the value of the checks the Federal Reserve *has* paid but not collected. In other words, sometimes the Fed will pay a bank for a check before it is collected. When this happens, it is called a *float.* Thus, we can define

$$FLOAT = CIPC - DAI \quad (6)$$

Substituting eq. (6) into eq. (5), we have

$$R = SDR + D\&A + USGS - T - OTHER$$
$$+ FLOAT + (GC + C - N) \quad (7)$$

The previous two changes were made solely for the purpose of simplifying the basic equation (3). However, the change we wish to make in the third parenthetical expression $(GC + C - N)$ is for the purpose of making the data analytically more meaningful. That is, our aim here is to transform the information found on the Federal Reserve's balance sheet in such a fashion that it becomes more useful to us. We can do this by combining it with information contained in the accounts of the U.S. Treasury, and by making some fairly simple definitions.

Consider, first, the symbol GC in the expression $(GC + C - N)$. GC stands for the gold certificates owned by the Federal Reserve. These gold certificates are issued to the Fed by the Treasury and are backed 100 percent by gold; that is, they are a sort of currency that is used exclusively between the Federal Reserve and the Treasury. When the Treasury buys gold, it *may* print gold certificates and sell these to the Federal Reserve. However, the Treasury is not required to do this; instead, it may simply buy the gold and hold it. Thus the Treasury may, and in fact does, own more gold than the Federal Reserve owns gold certificates. The total amount of gold owned by the Treasury is called the *gold stock* and is a more meaningful concept than gold certificates because it reflects the country's international financial position. It would therefore be useful to include the gold stock in the member bank reserve equation. We can do this be defining *free gold* as gold owned by the Treasury against which no gold certificates have been issued. Then,

$$\text{Gold stock} = \text{gold certificates} + \text{free gold} \tag{8}$$

or, letting GS stand for gold stock and FG stand for free gold,

$$GS = GC + FG$$

Rearranging terms gives

$$GC = GS - FG$$

Let us put eq. (8) to one side for a moment and concern ourselves next with the final two terms of the expression $(GC + C - N)$. C is the cash (currency) holdings of the Federal Reserve and consists of the coins and bills held by the district Federal Reserve Banks from which currency is supplied to member banks. N is *all* Federal Reserve notes that the Federal Reserve has issued, including those held by the Federal Reserve itself. C and N clearly have something to do with the country's currency supply, and we consider them together for that reason. But they constitute only a part of our currency and include some currency held by the Fed itself. It would be much more meaningful if we could somehow change these items so that we could see how the total amount of currency held by the public affects member bank reserves. Moreover, it would also be useful to know how the Treasury's behavior with respect to its issuance and holding of currency affects bank reserves. We can accomplish both these objectives by again (as with gold stock) making use of some information provided by the Treasury and some simple definitions.

First we define *Treasury currency outstanding* as all currency (primarily coins) issued by the Treasury, regardless of where it is held. Next we define *Treasury cash* as currency held by the Treasury itself *plus free gold*. Free gold is included in

Treasury cash because, from the Treasury's viewpoint, it can be sold to the Federal Reserve in the form of gold certificates and then spent. Thus it is *cash* to the Treasury (although note that it is *not* a part of Treasury currency outstanding).

With these definitions in mind, we can now derive the amount of currency held by the public, called *currency in circulation,* which is the total amount of currency issued by the Treasury and the Federal Reserve minus Federal Reserve cash and Treasury cash after the latter has been adjusted for free gold. Symbolically, we write

$$CinC = TCO - (TC - FG) + N - C \qquad (9)$$

where $CinC =$ currency in circulation
$\quad\quad\ TCO =$ Treasury currency outstanding
$\quad\quad\ \ \ TC =$ Treasury cash
$\quad\quad\ \ \ FG =$ free gold
$\quad\quad\ \ \ \ \ N =$ Federal Reserve notes outstanding
$\quad\quad\ \ \ \ \ C =$ Federal Reserve cash

Clearing the parentheses in eq. (9) gives

$$CinC = TCO - TC + FG + N - C$$

Solving for $N - C$ then gives

$$N - C = CinC - TCO + TC - FG$$

and multiplying both sides of this equation by -1 results in

$$C - N = TCO + FG - CinC - TC \qquad (10)$$

Now let us return to the original expression $(GC + C - N)$. From eq. (8), we have that $GC = GS - FG$; and from eq. (10), we have that

$$C - N = TCO + FG - CinC - TC$$

Making these two substitutions into $(GC + C - N)$ gives

$$GC + C - N = GS - FG + TCO + FG - CinC - TC$$

The *FG*s cancel out, leaving

$$GC + C - N = GS + TCO - CinC - TC \qquad (11)$$

Substituting eq. (11) into the reserve eq. (7) results in

$$R = SDR + D\&A + USGS - T - OTHER + FLOAT$$
$$+ GS + TCO - CinC - TC \quad (12)$$

The terms on the right-hand side of eq. (12) are usually rearranged in order to group related items. Thus the *member bank reserve equation* more commonly appears in the form

$$R = GS + SDR + USGS + D\&A + FLOAT + TCO$$
$$- CinC - TC - T - OTHER \quad (13)$$

Equation (13) is very important. It is published weekly by the Federal Reserve System and read avidly by financial analysts all over the country. We shall analyze this equation carefully in section 15-2. What is necessary at this point is that the reader understand that eq. (13) *must* be true. It is not merely hocus pocus about algebra. It is derived from the fundamental balance-sheet identity that assets = liabilities + capital, plus a few definitions. Any change in member bank reserves held at the Federal Reserve must show up somewhere on the right-hand side of eq. (13).

15-2   THE MEMBER BANK RESERVE EQUATION

Since it is difficult to keep in mind the definitions of all the symbols used in section 15-1, let us rewrite eq. (13) using words:

		Sources: factor supplying reserve funds	Uses: factors absorbing reserve funds
Member bank reserves at the Federal Reserve System	=	+ Gold stock + Special Drawing Rights certificates + United States government securities held by the Federal Reserve + Discounts and advances + Float + Treasury currency outstanding	− Currency in circulation − Treasury cash − Treasury deposits at the Federal Reserve − Other Federal Reserve accounts and capital

This is known as the *member bank reserve equation.* Note that, in very general terms, the right-hand side of the equation consists of two parts: those terms having a plus sign and those having a minus sign. The plus terms are called the *sources* of member bank reserves, or, more formally, the *factors supplying reserve funds.* By this is meant that if nothing else changes, an increase in one of these items will cause an equal increase in member bank reserves. Note that the opposite is also true: A decrease in a source will cause a decrease in member bank reserves. In other words, sources and member bank reserves move in the same direction. The minus terms are called the *uses* of member bank reserves, or the *factors absorbing reserve funds.* Uses and member bank reserves move in opposite directions: When one of the uses items increases, member bank deposits at the Fed decrease and vice versa.

In section 15-1 it was demonstrated that the member bank reserve equation is necessarily true. But this demonstration was largely algebraic. Many terms remain undefined, and we have not inquired at all into the *economic* process whereby each of the items in the equation affects bank reserves. Accordingly, in this section we shall analyze the economics of the reserve-creating process. Only in this way shall we gain a sophisticated understanding of the power of the Federal Reserve to influence the money supply.

Sources of Member Bank Reserves

The sources of member bank reserves may generally be grouped into three categories: (1) gold stock and Special Drawing Rights certificates, both of which have to do with the international sector of the economy; (2) United States government securities held by the Federal Reserve, discounts and advances of member banks, and float, all three of which involve an extension of credit by the Federal Reserve System; and (3) Treasury currency outstanding, which reflects decisions made by the U.S. Treasury.

International Factors   Changes in the gold stock and in SDR certificates involve very similar economic analyses. We shall consequently go thoroughly into the economics of a change in the gold stock, and indicate only briefly the modifications necessary to analyze a change in *SDR* certificates.

Gold Stock   The gold stock is the monetary gold of the United States. It is owned exclusively by the U.S. Treasury; since 1934 it may not circulate as part of the country's money supply. The Treasury uses it in its financial dealings with other countries. These international financial relationships are quite complicated and are in a continual state of change. To discuss them at this point would take us too far afield. For present purposes, it is sufficient to provide an answer to the question, What happens to member bank reserves *if* the gold stock changes?

Changes in the gold stock stem basically from either of two underlying causes: domestic gold-mining operations and our international economic relations with other countries. The effect on member bank reserves is the same no matter which of these two forces causes gold stock to change. Since the amount of domestic gold mining in the United States is negligible, we shall confine the discussion to changes in the gold stock arising from international causes.

The effect of a change in gold stock on bank reserves can be explained best by using an example. Suppose that the U.S. Treasury buys $1 of gold from a foreign central bank, say, the Bank of England. The Treasury will pay for this gold purchase by instructing the Federal Reserve to transfer $1 from its (the Treasury's) account to the deposit of the Bank of England at the Federal Reserve. The relevant T

Treasury		Federal Reserve		Member bank	
Δ Assets	Δ Liabilities	Δ Assets	Δ Liabilities	Δ Assets	Δ Liabilities
Gold stock + $1			Treasury deposit − $1	No change	No change
Deposit at the Federal Reserve − $1			Deposit of the Bank of England + $1		

Figure 15-1a

Treasury		Federal Reserve		Member bank	
Δ Assets	Δ Liabilities	Δ Assets	Δ Liabilities	Δ Assets	Δ Liabilities
Deposit at the Federal Reserve +$1	Gold certificates +$1	Gold certificates +$1	Treasury deposit +$1	No change	No change

Figure 15-1b

accounts are shown in Figure 15-1a. At this point, member bank reserves have not changed. However, this does not invalidate the original statement that an increase in gold stock will increase member bank reserves, other things being equal. For the other things are not yet equal, that is, not as they were before we began the example. In particular, the Treasury and Bank of England deposits at the Federal Reserve have changed from their original levels.[1] It is thus necessary to reverse these two changes in order to analyze the effect of an isolated increase in gold stock. This can easily be done.

With respect to the Treasury, let us suppose that it issues gold certificates to the Federal Reserve in exchange for an increase in its deposit there.[2] (The Treasury almost always does this when it buys gold.) The T accounts showing this transaction are given in Figure 15-1b. Next assume that the Bank of England decides that it does not want to keep idle balances in the Federal Reserve and consequently invests its $1 in U.S. Treasury bills. The Bank of England will pay for these bills by writing a check against its account at the Fed, and whoever sells it the bills will then deposit this check in a member bank.[3] The member bank will then present this check to the Federal Reserve, and the Fed will pay it by decreasing the deposit of the Bank of England and increasing the member bank's reserves. While all of this may sound complicated, in fact it is quite simple, as can be seen by looking at Figure 15-1c.

[1] In terms of the member bank reserve equation, at this point four offsetting changes have occurred:

Gold stock (a source)	+$1
Treasury deposit at the Federal Reserve (a use)	−$1
Treasury cash (a use)	+$1
Other accounts and capital at the Federal Reserve (a use)	+$1

Thus the net change in sources minus the net change in uses is $1 − $1 = 0, and member bank reserves have not changed. The change in Treasury cash and the "other" item require further explanation. Recall that Treasury cash includes free gold. Since the increase in the gold stock has not been accompanied by an increase in gold certificates, it represents a change in free gold and hence in Treasury cash. The increase in the "other" item reflects the increase in the Bank of England's deposit since the other accounts and capital include the deposits of foreign central banks.

[2] In terms of the reserve equation, this would have two offsetting effects among the uses: Treasury cash would decrease because of the decrease in free gold (see footnote 1); and the Treasury deposit at the Federal Reserve would increase.

[3] Throughout this section it will be assumed that all commercial banks are member banks of the Federal Reserve System. This assumption is made solely for ease of exposition; the analysis is in no way dependent on it. In our example, if the Bank of England's check were deposited in a nonmember bank, the Federal Reserve would add $1 to nonmember bank balances. Since such balances are included in the "other" category, it would then be necessary to make further assumptions in order to make "other" things equal to what they were before.

The "other things" are now back to equal. We have restored the Treasury and Bank of England deposits at the Federal Reserve to their original amounts (i.e., there is a zero net change in these entries in the T accounts), and hence we have isolated the consequence of an increase in the gold stock. This consequence can be seen clearly in Figure 15-1*d,* which consolidates the T accounts of Figures 15-1*a* to *c.* Thus, the figures show that an increase in the gold stock causes an increase in member bank reserves. Additionally, the reader will find it instructive to compare the T account of the member bank in Figure 15-1*d* with the T account of the bank shown in Figure 12-2 (Chapter 12). They are, in fact, identical. That is, Figure 15-1*d* shows the beginning point of the process whereby the banking system creates money.

One additional point may be made about the relationship between gold stock and member bank reserves: The relationship is reversible. In other words, a *decrease* in the gold stock will cause a *decrease* in member bank reserves, other things being equal. It would be too tedious to demonstrate this process, but the reader can easily work it out by assuming a Treasury sale of gold and reversing all the algebraic signs of Figures 15-1*a* to *c.*

SDR Certificates   Like gold, *Special Drawing Rights* are used in the settlement of debts among nations. They are created by the International Monetary Fund and are sometimes referred to as *paper gold.* When the Treasury decides to "monetize" its Special Drawing Rights, it issues SDR certificates to the Federal Reserve and receives in payment an increase in its deposit at the Federal Reserve. This operation is strictly between the Federal Reserve and the Treasury and at this point does not involve any change in member bank reserves.[4] However, when the Treasury spends this money, the check it writes will eventually be deposited in a member bank, which will send the check to the Fed for collection. The Federal Reserve will then collect the check by reducing the Treasury's deposit to its original level and increasing the member bank's reserve account. Thus at the end of the process, the net change will be that SDR certificates have gone up and member bank reserves have gone up by

Treasury		Federal Reserve		Member bank	
Δ Assets	Δ Liabilities	Δ Assets	Δ Liabilities	Δ Assets	Δ Liabilities
No change	No change		Deposit of the Bank of England – $1	Reserves at the Federal Reserve + $1	Deposits + $1
			Member bank reserves + $1		

Figure 15-1c

[4]In terms of the reserve equation, the increase in SDR certificates (a source) is offset by the increase in the Treasury's account at the Federal Reserve (a use). To isolate the effects of the increase in SDR certificates, it is necessary to reduce the Treasury deposit to its original level, which is the next step in the text discussion.

Treasury		Federal Reserve		Member bank	
Δ Assets	Δ Liabilities	Δ Assets	Δ Liabilities	Δ Assets	Δ Liabilities
Gold stock + $1	Gold certificates + $1	Gold certificates + $1	Member bank reserves + $1	Reserves at the Federal Reserve + $1	Deposits + $1

Figure 15-1d

an equal amount. The reverse is also true: A decrease in SDR certificates will lead to a decrease in member bank reserves, other things being equal.

Federal Reserve Credit Outstanding   Whenever the Federal Reserve acquires assets, member bank reserves will rise. With some minor exceptions (included in the "other" account in the reserve equation), Federal Reserve assets are the result of an extension of credit (loans) by the System. They are known collectively as *Federal Reserve credit outstanding* and are the sum of three items in the member bank reserve equation: United States government securities held by the Federal Reserve; the discounts and advances made to member banks; and float.

United States Government Securities Held by the Federal Reserve   Like any other investor, the Federal Reserve System is free to buy and sell United States government securities on the open market. The decisions to buy or sell such securities are made by the Federal Open Market Committee (described in Chapter 14), and their actual purchase or sale is known as *open market operations.* Since open market operations are easily the most important means available to the Federal Reserve for controlling bank reserves, we must consider them carefully. Happily, in principle they are not at all complicated.

When the Federal Reserve buys government securities in the open market, there are two possible sellers: a member bank or anyone else. If the seller is a member bank, the effect on member bank reserves is straightforward. The Federal Reserve receives the securities and pays for them by increasing the member bank's reserves. The member bank gives up the securities and receives in payment an increase in its reserves at the Fed. The T accounts showing these transactions are given in Figure 15-2. Clearly, the increase in United States government securities held by the Federal Reserve has resulted in an increase in member bank reserves.

But suppose the Fed buys the securities from someone other than a member bank—you, for instance. Then what? Actually, in this case the process is only slightly more complicated. When the Federal Reserve buys the securities from you, it will pay you with a check drawn against itself. You will then deposit the check in your bank, and the bank will forward the check to the Federal Reserve for payment. The Federal Reserve will pay the check by increasing the bank's reserves. The transactions involved are shown in the T accounts of Figure 15-3. Again, an increase in United States government securities held by the Federal Reserve has resulted in an increase in member bank reserves.

The process also works in reverse, of course. If the Federal Reserve *sells* United

Federal Reserve		Member bank	
Δ Assets	Δ Liabilities	Δ Assets	Δ Liabilities
United States government securities + $1	Member bank reserves + $1	United States government securities − $1	
		Reserves at the Federal Reserve + $1	

Figure 15-2

States government securities in the open market, then the reserves of member banks will go down. The T-account transactions would be identical to those shown in Figures 15-2 and 15-3, except that all the algebraic signs would be reversed.

Two additional points should be made about the open market operations of the Federal Reserve. Note first that the Federal Reserve is in the enviable position of being able to acquire assets simply by writing up liabilities against itself. In this specific case, for example, the Federal Reserve buys government securities (assets) and pays for them by increasing member bank reserves (liabilities). All of us do this, of course, whenever we buy anything on credit. The difference between us and the Federal Reserve is that *we* shall eventually have to pay our debts. Not so with the Federal Reserve. Its liabilities are permanent. While any member bank may draw down its reserves at the Fed, these reserves will be transferred to some other bank so that in total the reserves stay the same. It is for this reason that, under present institutional arrangements, the Federal Reserve cannot suffer a liquidity crisis. It cannot run out of money because its liabilities are indefinitely expandable.

The second point to note about open market operations is that they are completely under the control of the Federal Reserve; that is, the Federal Reserve can buy or sell exactly the amount of government securities it wishes. Recall from Chapter 7 that the market for United States government securities is perhaps the

Federal Reserve		Member bank		You	
Δ Assets	Δ Liabilities	Δ Assets	Δ Liabilities	Δ Assets	Δ Liabilities
United States government securities + $1	Member bank reserves + $1	Reserves at the Federal Reserve + $1	Deposits + $1	United States government securities − $1	
				Deposit at member bank + $1	

Figure 15-3

most active market of any kind in the world; literally hundreds of millions of dollars worth of these securities change hands daily. If the Federal Reserve wishes to buy a certain amount of securities, therefore, it need only offer to pay a price that is slightly higher than market price; if it wishes to make a large sale, it need only offer to sell the securities at a slightly lower price. In short, the open market operations of the Federal Reserve are both precise and quick.

Discounts and Advances   As mentioned previously, member banks of the Federal Reserve System have the privilege of borrowing from the Federal Reserve. The borrowings of these member banks are called *discounts and advances.* Properly speaking, when a member bank makes a discount, it sells some of its assets (e.g., a banker's acceptance) to the Fed. An advance, alternatively, is a direct loan from the Federal Reserve to the member bank secured by a pledge of United States government securities. In practice, discounts are seldom made anymore, and virtually all member bank borrowing consists of advances. Advances are typically of short maturity, seldom exceeding two weeks. Member bank borrowing from the Federal Reserve results very directly in an increase in member bank reserves. When a member bank borrows, the Federal Reserve makes a loan to it by increasing its reserve deposit. That's all there is to it. The relevant T accounts are shown in Figure 15-4.

The Federal Reserve's control over member bank borrowing is much less complete than the control it exercises over its open market operations. Its primary method of altering member bank borrowing is by changing the *discount rate,* that is, the rate of interest charged member banks for advances. In principle, when the Federal Reserve raises the discount rate, member banks will borrow less than they otherwise would, and vice versa when the Federal Reserve lowers the discount rate. However, a number of other variables besides the discount rate enter into the borrowing decisions of member banks, so that the responses of member banks to changes in the discount rate are not wholly predictable. It is, perhaps, fair to say that the Federal Reserve influences but does not control member bank borrowing.

Float   It will be recalled from the previous section[5] that *float* arises from the check-clearing activities of the Federal Reserve System and is defined as the difference between cash items in the process of collection and deferred availability items on the Federal Reserve's balance sheet. Although float has already been discussed

Federal Reserve			Member bank		
Δ Assets		Δ Liabilities	Δ Assets		Δ Liabilities
Discounts and advances	+ $1	Member bank reserves + $1	Reserves at the Federal Reserve	+ $1	Borrowings + $1

Figure 15-4

[5]See also Chapter 14, section 14-2.

Bank A		Federal Reserve		Bank B	
Δ Assets	Δ Liabilities	Δ Assets	Δ Liabilities	Δ Assets	Δ Liabilities
Cash items in the process of collection + $1	Deposits + $1	Cash items in the process of collection + $1	Deferred avail- ability + $1	No change	No change

Figure 15-5a

in general terms, it is now desirable to discuss it in detail. We can do this best by using an example.

Suppose that banks A and B are located in two different cities in the same Federal Reserve district. A customer of Bank A receives a check drawn against an account in bank B. Bank A's customer then endorses the check and deposits it in her account at bank A. Bank A credits the account for the amount of the check and forwards the check to the Federal Reserve district bank. Upon receipt of the check, the district bank will process it and send it on to bank B so that bank B can acknowledge its validity. The accounting procedure at the Federal Reserve is to give bank A a *deferred availability* credit for the check, which means that the check will not be added to bank A's reserves immediately. Instead, the addition to bank A's reserves will be deferred for a day or two, depending on a fixed schedule maintained by the Federal Reserve. *Deferred availability* is a liability of the Federal Reserve, that is, funds it owes to bank A. The offsetting asset entry on the Federal Reserve's books is to *cash items in the process of collection.* These *cash items* are checks that have been received by the district bank but which it has not as yet collected. These bookkeeping entries are actually easier to show than to describe. Figure 15-5a depicts them.

At this point in the procedure, no increase has occurred in the float since cash items in the process of collection and deferred availability items have each increased by an equal amount. However, it frequently happens that the number of days for which check payment is deferred is less than the number of days it actually takes the Federal Reserve to collect the check. Thus, suppose that bank A is given credit for the check after one day but that it actually takes three days for the Federal Reserve to collect the check from bank B. At the end of one day, therefore, the district bank will transfer the amount of the check from its deferred availability account to the reserves of bank A, as shown in Figure 15-5b. Note, however, that the amount of the check has not yet been subtracted from bank B's reserves and, in fact, won't be subtracted for another two days. During those two days, consequently, the reserves of bank A will have increased but the reserves of bank B will have remained unchanged. Consequently, *total* bank reserves will have increased. Putting the matter somewhat differently, during those two days the Federal Reserve's cash items in the process of collection will be greater than its deferred availability items. By definition, this is the float, and it has resulted in an increase

Bank A		Federal Reserve		Bank B	
Δ Assets	Δ Liabilities	Δ Assets	Δ Liabilities	Δ Assets	Δ Liabilities
Cash items in the process of collection − $1			Deferred availability − $1	No change	No change
Reserves at the Federal Reserve + $1			Member bank reserves + $1		

Figure 15-5*b*

in member bank reserves. This result is shown in Figure 15-5*c,* which is a consolidation of the T accounts of Figure 15-5*a* and *b.*

The float is, in effect, an interest-free loan from the Federal Reserve to the commercial banking system. Nor is this loan a trivial amount. During the past few years, it has been averaging about $5 billion annually. This being the case, the question naturally arises as to why the Federal Reserve operates in this manner. There would be two possible ways to eliminate the float: First, the Federal Reserve might defer payment on all checks it receives until it actually collects them. The Fed feels, however, that to do so would worsen the country's payments mechanism. One great advantage of the float is that it provides a measure of certainty about the future to banks sending checks to the Fed; the float acts as a sort of shock absorber when the check-clearing system becomes clogged with too many items (for example, at Christmastime), or when the weather makes the physical transportation of checks slow and difficult.

The second way in which the float might be eliminated would be to set a more realistic schedule for the deferred availability items. The schedule could be extended to include three-day, four-day, and five-day deferrals, for example. In this case, the float would sometimes be positive (as it always is now) and sometimes negative, averaging out to about zero for the year. The Federal Reserve rejects this course of action, however, in order to encourage the banking system to clear through them rather than through correspondent banks. Although it may be admitted that a quick

Bank A		Federal Reserve		Bank B	
Δ Assets	Δ Liabilities	Δ Assets	Δ Liabilities	Δ Assets	Δ Liabilities
Reserves at the Federal Reserve + $1	Deposits + $1	Cash items in the process of collection + $1	Member bank reserves + $1	No change	No change

Figure 15-5*c*

and smooth clearing system was one of the original purposes for which the Federal Reserve was established, it remains a nice question whether a $5 billion annual subsidy to the commercial banking system is a socially desirable way to accomplish this goal.

Treasury Currency Outstanding   Although most of the notes that circulate as currency among the public are issued by the Federal Reserve, there are about $320 million worth of United States notes outstanding that are an obligation of the United States Treasury. Additionally, the Treasury is responsible for issuing all United States coins. Together, these components of our currency supply—United States notes and coins—constitute what is known as *Treasury currency outstanding.* [6] It includes *all* currency obligations of the Treasury, regardless of where this currency is held; in particular, it includes Treasury obligations held by the Treasury itself and by the Federal Reserve System.

An increase in Treasury currency outstanding will result in an increase in member bank reserves, other things being equal. Actually, Treasury currency outstanding is so closely interdependent with Treasury cash, Treasury deposits at the Fed, and currency in circulation that other things are almost never equal. That is, it is difficult to devise a realistic example in which Treasury currency outstanding increases in isolation from the other elements in the member bank reserve equation. However, the following simple example (admittedly contrived) will serve well enough to illustrate the general nature of the case.

Suppose that the Treasury sells $1 in coins to the Federal Reserve. The Federal Reserve will pay for these coins by increasing the Treasury's deposit. Up to this point bank reserves are unaffected, but when the Treasury spends the addition to its deposit at the Fed, member bank reserves will increase.

Uses of Member Bank Reserves

The various sources of member bank reserves may be thought of as a number of creeks that empty into a lake. The *uses* of member bank reserves are the outlets from the lake. And, just as the size of the lake is determined by the difference between the amount of water going into it and the amount being drained out, so the size of member bank reserves is determined by the difference between sources and uses. As we have seen, there are four such uses: currency in circulation, Treasury cash, Treasury deposits at the Federal Reserve, and other accounts and capital.

Currency in Circulation   The total amount of coins and notes held by the public—our hand-to-hand currency—is called *currency in circulation.* It *excludes* all currency held by the Treasury and the Federal Reserve, but it *includes* the vault cash of member banks. All other items in the bank reserve equation remaining unchanged, when currency in circulation increases, member bank deposits at the Fed will decrease by an equal amount (and vice versa). The way this works is quite

[6]Additionally, Treasury currency outstanding includes a small amount of various kinds of notes (e.g., national bank notes) that are still being retired.

simple. Suppose that in June the public finds it convenient to increase its currency holdings for vacationing purposes. People will then go to their banks and "withdraw money" (i.e., convert demand deposits to currency). The banks, finding themselves with a depleted vault cash position, will go to the Federal Reserve and convert their reserve deposits to currency. The net result is that currency in circulation will have increased and the reserves of member banks will have decreased.

Treasury Cash   The amount of currency held by the Treasury, plus the Treasury's free gold, is called *Treasury cash.* As with Treasury currency outstanding, a change in Treasury cash will typically be associated with a change in one of the other items in the reserve equation, especially currency in circulation, the Treasury deposit at the Fed, Treasury currency outstanding, or gold stock. The following rather artificial example will suffice to explain how an increase in Treasury cash will cause a decrease in member bank reserves, other things being equal.

The Treasury, like a business firm, sometimes buys things for currency and therefore must have a stock of bills and coins on hand. Suppose that the Treasury decides to replenish this stock by buying Federal Reserve notes from the Federal Reserve. To pay for these, the Treasury will draw on its account at the Fed; i.e., the immediate impact of this transaction will be that Treasury cash goes up and the Treasury deposit at the Fed goes down. Since both of these items are uses, the changes in them will be offsetting and hence bank reserves will be unaffected at this point. But now suppose that in order to replenish its account at the Federal Reserve, the Treasury borrows a like amount of money from the public. It will borrow this money by selling, say, a Treasury bill, and will be paid for the Treasury bill with a check drawn against a member bank. The Treasury could[7] then deposit the check with the Federal Reserve, and the Federal Reserve would collect the check by increasing the Treasury's account and decreasing the member bank's reserve deposit. Since the two changes in the Treasury's account at the Federal Reserve cancel one another, the net result of this series of transactions is that Treasury cash has increased and member bank reserves have decreased.

Treasury Deposits at the Federal Reserve   One way of thinking about the United States government is that it is a huge business employing millions of people, buying and selling goods and services, and spending and receiving billions of dollars annually. And, like any other business concern, it is necessary for the government to maintain an *operating balance* in the bank because the money coming in (revenue) is not exactly and at all times equal to the money going out (expenditures). The operating balance of the United States government is called the *general fund,* and it is held in the form of the *Treasury deposit at the Federal Reserve.* Other things being equal, when this deposit goes up, member bank reserves will fall; and when

---

[7]The word "could" should be stressed, perhaps, since in practice the check would first be deposited in a tax-and-loan deposit at a commercial bank and only later transferred to the Treasury's account at the Federal Reserve. The net effect of this transaction would be the same as that described in the text, of course. For a description and analysis of the tax-and-loan (T&L) accounts of the Treasury, see the subsection immediately following.

Treasury		Federal Reserve		Member bank	
Δ Assets	Δ Liabilities	Δ Assets	Δ Liabilities	Δ Assets	Δ Liabilities
Taxes due − $1		No change	No change		Deposits − $1
Tax-and-loan accounts + $1					Tax-and-loan accounts + $1

Figure 15-6a

it goes down, member bank reserves will rise. Since the Treasury's management practices with respect to the general fund give it potential central banking powers, it is necessary to consider this item carefully.

Let us begin by outlining the method currently used by the Treasury for handling its tax receipts and loan revenues. When a corporation sends the money it withholds from its employees' wages to the Treasury, the money is sent in the form of a check drawn against the corporation's deposit in a member bank. Upon receipt of this check, the Treasury will redeposit it in the *same* bank the check was drawn on. That is, the Treasury maintains deposits, called *tax-and-loan (T&L) accounts*, in most of the banks in the country. When it receives a check drawn against one of these banks, it simply returns the check to the bank for a credit to the T&L account. From the commercial bank's viewpoint, all that has happened is that a deposit has been transferred from one customer to another. Figure 15-6a shows the transaction. Receipts from Treasury borrowing are handled in approximately the same way.

It is necessary to emphasize that at this point member bank reserves have not changed at all. In fact, it is for precisely this reason that the Treasury handles its receipts through the T&L accounts. The Treasury does not want its taxation, borrowing, and spending activities to affect bank reserves and the money supply. If they did affect reserves, it would constitute a sort of accidental monetary policy.

The Treasury does not spend funds directly out of its T&L accounts. Instead, it first transfers these funds to its deposits at the Federal Reserve and then writes checks against this deposit. It is this process of transferral that affects bank reserves. When the Treasury takes funds from its T&L account and adds them to its deposit at the Fed, the accounting transaction at the Federal Reserve is simply to deduct

Treasury		Federal Reserve		Member bank	
Δ Assets	Δ Liabilities	Δ Assets	Δ Liabilities	Δ Assets	Δ Liabilities
Tax-and-loan account − $1		Member bank reserves − $1	Reserves at the Federal Reserve − $1		Tax-and-loan account − $1
Deposit at the Federal Reserve + $1		Treasury deposit + $1			

Figure 15-6b

Treasury		Federal Reserve		Member bank	
Δ Assets	Δ Liabilities	Δ Assets	Δ Liabilities	Δ Assets	Δ Liabilities
Taxes due − $1			Member bank reserves − $1	Reserves at the Federal Reserve − $1	Deposits − $1
Deposit at the Federal Reserve + $1			Treasury deposit + $1		

Figure 15-6c

that amount from the member bank's reserves and add it to the Treasury's deposit. The process can be illustrated by continuing the example of Figure 15-6a. This is done in Figure 15-6b, and the net result, i.e., the consolidated T accounts, is shown in Figure 15-6c. This result is that an increase in the Treasury deposit at the Federal Reserve will cause a decrease in member bank reserve deposits, other things being equal. The opposite is also true. If the Treasury decreases its deposit at the Fed without replenishing it from its commercial bank T&L accounts, then bank reserves will increase.

It is, perhaps, worth making the point explicitly that the Treasury thus potentially possesses central banking powers. That is, by a deliberate manipulation of its deposit at the Federal Reserve, the Treasury *could* regulate the reserve base of the banking system and hence influence the money supply. In fact, the Treasury does not do so, preferring instead to leave all central banking responsibilities to the Federal Reserve. As a consequence, the Treasury tries to manage the general fund so that it varies as little as possible. But the flow of funds through the U.S. Treasury is so large and the timing of receipts and expenditures sufficiently uncertain that the general fund will nevertheless vary considerably from week to week.

Other Federal Reserve Accounts and Capital   As described in section 15-1, the Federal Reserve balance sheet contains a hodgepodge of small asset, liability, and capital accounts, ranging from the buildings and fixtures of the district banks to the deposits of foreign central banks. These accounts are grouped together in the member bank reserve equation under the miscellaneous item "Other Federal Reserve accounts and capital." It is not worthwhile analyzing this item in detail. In general terms, it affects bank reserves in much the same way as the Treasury's deposit does. That is, if the deposits of foreign central banks rise or if nonmember bank balances go up, then member bank reserves go down (and vice versa).

15-3 GENERAL INSTRUMENTS OF FEDERAL RESERVE CONTROL

Table 15-2 shows the actual figures for the member bank reserve equation for March 1978. Since the data are continuously changing, the specific numbers in the table are not of particular importance. Instead, what is desirable is that the reader acquire some idea of the relative magnitude of the various items and some feel for their behavior. Among the sources of reserves, note that the amount of government securities held by the Federal Reserve is easily the largest item, accounting for about three-fourths of total sources. Also of interest is float. Although float does not appear very large relative to the other amounts, it is perhaps the most volatile item in the entire equation; because of the weather or other conditions, float can change by literally hundreds of millions of dollars within a matter of hours.

Currency in circulation is the largest single factor absorbing reserve funds. Notwithstanding its size, currency in circulation tends to move in a fairly well-defined seasonal pattern, like a river moving within the confines of its banks. However, again like a river, it sometimes does the unexpected—floods, dries up, or cuts new channels. Of the other uses, Treasury cash is almost negligibly small; the various components of the "other" category tend to move in offsetting amounts, making it

Table 15-2 Factors Affecting Member Bank Reserves, March 1978 (End-of-Month Figures; Millions of Dollars)

Sources: Factors supplying reserve funds	
Gold stock	11,718
SDR certificates	1,250
Federal Reserve credit outstanding	
United States Government securities*	109,770 ← ①
Discounts and advances	1,102 ← ②
Float	2,732
Treasury currency outstanding	11,441
Other Federal Reserve assets	2,328
Total sources	140,341
Uses: Factors absorbing Reserve funds	
Currency in circulation	102,392
Treasury cash	393
Treasury deposit at the Federal Reserve	4,705
Other Federal Reserve accounts and capital	4,952
Total uses	112,442
Member bank reserves at Federal Reserves	
(Sources — uses)	27,900
Memoranda	
Plus: Vault cash†	8,797
Equals: Total member bank reserves	36,697
Of which	
Required reserves are	36,660 ← ③
Excess reserves are	37

*Includes Federal Agency Securities of $8,193 million.
†Based on weekly averages of daily figures for reserve period one week previous to report date.
   Source: Federal Reserve Bulletin, May 1978, pp. A4–A6 (details may not sum due to rounding).

reasonably stable; and, as noted previously, the Treasury attempts (not always successfully) to maintain its deposit at the Federal Reserve at a constant size.

We are now in position to appreciate the task faced by the money managers of the Federal Reserve System. In simple terms, their job is to manage the reserve base of the commercial banking system in order to manage the nation's money supply. If they feel that we should have more money in the country, then they will expand bank reserves; if they feel the country has too much money, then they will contract bank reserves. But as should by now be clear to the reader, there are many factors that affect bank reserves—float, treasury cash, and so on—other than the deliberate decisions of the Fed. What the Federal Reserve must do, therefore, is to offset or reinforce the net effects of all these other factors. Suppose, for example, that (other things being equal) currency in circulation should increase by $1 billion, thereby causing bank reserves to decrease by an equal amount. If the Federal Reserve wanted reserves to decrease by $1 billion, then it would do nothing; if it wanted them to decrease by more or less than that amount, then it would take action to reinforce or offset the change in currency in circulation.

The points of entry of the Federal Reserve into the reserve-creating (and hence money-creating) process are shown by the circled numbers on the right-hand side of Table 15-2. These are the so-called *general,* or quantitative, *instruments of monetary policy.* ① is the amount of United States government securities owned by the Fed. Changes in this figure are the result of *open market operations.* As noted, the Federal Reserve has absolute control over this figure; it may buy or sell exactly that amount of securities it wishes and on a continuous basis. Open market operations are the main device used by the Federal Reserve for carrying out monetary policy. ② reflects member bank borrowing from the Federal Reserve. By setting the rate of interest at which member banks may obtain discounts and advances, the Federal Reserve can influence the size of this variable. The setting of this interest rate is called *discount rate policy.* ③ affects, not the size of member bank reserves, but rather the amount of deposits a given amount of bank reserves can support (the money multiplier). Although the Federal Reserve has absolute control (within legal limits) over percentage reserve requirements, for administrative reasons they are not changed very often. This policy instrument is called *variations in reserve requirements.*

To summarize, the general instruments of Federal Reserve control are: (1) open market operations, (2) discount rate policy, and (3) variations in reserve requirements. A great many issues are involved in the actual, day-to-day use of these instruments, and these issues will be discussed in Chapter 16. For the moment, the reader need only understand in principle how and why each of the instruments can be used to affect the country's money supply.

15-4 CAN THE FEDERAL RESERVE CONTROL THE MONEY SUPPLY?

As we have stressed repeatedly in the last several chapters, the money supply M_1 of the American economy is determined according to the equation $M_1 = mR$. Moreover, both the money multiplier m and the reserve base of the banking system

R are determined through the interactions of the public, commercial banks, and the Federal Reserve System. But if this is the case—that is, if M_1 is the result of decisions made in three separate sectors of the economy—then in what sense do we have a monetary *policy?* For the word "policy" suggests a deliberate and purposeful control over some economic variable—in this case, money. Thus if the phrase *monetary policy* is to have operational content, there must be some sense in which the Federal Reserve is the dominant influence in the money supply process. That is, there must be some sense in which the Federal Reserve can "control" the quantity of money in the economy.

The traditional argument that the Federal Reserve is able to control the money supply generally rests on the assumptions that (1) the money multiplier m is stable and (2) the Federal Reserve is able to determine the reserve base R. Then with m stable and R under the control of the Fed, the Fed can clearly control M_1 in the equation $M_1 = mR$. But this is true only to the extent that assumptions 1 and 2 are true. In other words, the money multiplier could be so powerful in its effects and so erratic in its movements, that its real world behavior could swamp the effects of R on M_1. If so, being able to control the reserve base could still leave the Federal Reserve unable to control the money supply. Alternatively, the effects of factors over which the Fed has no control in the bank reserve equation could be so powerful and so erratic that open market operations would not be sufficiently large or quick to allow the Fed to control the reserve base. In this case also, the Federal Reserve would be helpless to control the country's money stock.

Both assumptions 1 and 2 are empirical issues; that is, logic (theory) cannot tell us if they are true or false because they deal with magnitudes, not logical relations. They raise the question, How much? not, Why? For this reason, we must turn to the evidence to answer the question of whether the Federal Reserve can control the United States money supply.

The Stability of the Money Multiplier

Since what is at issue is the *stability* (and not the size) of the money multiplier, it is sufficient for our purposes to examine only the month-to-month changes in m. This is done in Figure 15-7 for the period January 1973 to March 1978. As will be seen

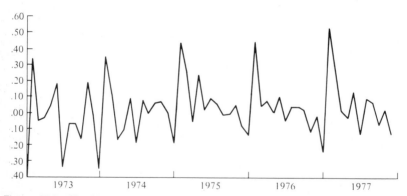

Figure 15-7   Monthly changes in the money multiplier Δm, 1973–1977.

from this figure, monthly changes in the money multiplier are typically quite small. Consequently, the conclusion that most observers draw from evidence such as that shown in Figure 15-7 is that the money multiplier is stable enough for the Federal Reserve to control the money supply within reasonable limits. This is not to say, of course, that the multiplier is so stable that the Fed could determine M_1 exactly at any time. But in the longer run (3 to 6 months) and on the average, changes in the money multiplier should not prove a serious obstacle to effective Federal Reserve control over the money supply.

Open Market Operations and the Reserve Base

Can the Federal Reserve control the reserve base? This question is a bit more difficult to answer and requires some preliminary explanation. First, there is the matter of timing. In order to use open market operations to control the reserve base absolutely, hour by hour and day by day, the Federal Reserve would have to be instantly aware of all changes in the bank reserve equation and in the vault cash of member banks. In fact, this information is available on a preliminary basis only after a time lag in some cases of several days, and accurate information may be available only after several weeks. As a consequence, the Federal Reserve attempts to make weekly statistical projections of all factors affecting bank reserves other than its own holdings of United States government securities and then uses these projections as a basis for its open market operations. These projections are not of unerring accuracy, however, and as a consequence the Federal Reserve cannot precisely control the reserve base of member banks in the very short run. What it does, instead, is to "hunt" for the desired level of reserves by compensating this week for errors made last week. In other words, the Federal Reserve aims at controlling the reserve base in terms of a long-run average of the figures.

Second, it is necessary to distinguish between *dynamic* and *defensive* monetary policy. Dynamic monetary policy is the pursual of certain national goals, such as full employment and price stability. Defensive monetary policy is just what we have been discussing in this section: the use of open market operations to offset the net effect of the uncontrolled items in the member bank reserve equation. The purpose of making this distinction between dynamic and defensive open market operations is to put the reader on guard that a high r^2 is not to be expected in a statistical investigation of defensive policy alone. That is, defensive policy can at best explain only a part of open market operations.

With the foregoing matters in mind, let us now return to the original question, Can the Federal Reserve control the reserve base of member banks? To put the question into testable form, let us rephrase it as the following hypothesis: Changes in the Federal Reserve's holdings of United States government securities move in such a way as to offset changes in the uncontrolled items in the member bank reserve equation. Two researchers,[8] using monthly data, obtained the following results from a regression analysis of this question:

---

[8]Michael W. Keran and Christopher T. Babb, "An Explanation of Federal Reserve Actions (1933–68)," *Federal Reserve Bank of St. Louis Review,* July 1969, pp. 7–20. For more complex models dealing with this same issue, and arriving at approximately the same conclusion, see the following two

$$\Delta USGS = .132 - .81 \, \Delta D\&A - .49 \, \epsilon F - 1.02 \, \Delta GS + .50 \, \Delta TCO + .91 \, \Delta O$$
$$r^2 = .52$$

Coefficients on all variables except ΔTCO significant at the 5% level

where

$\Delta USGS =$ change in the Federal Reserve's holdings of United States government securities, adjusted for reserve requirement changes and shifts in deposits between classes of banks

$\Delta D\&A =$ change in the discounts and advances of member banks

$\Delta F =$ change in float

$\Delta GS =$ change in gold stock, including foreign currency held by the Federal Reserve

$\Delta TCO =$ change in Treasury currency outstanding

$\Delta O =$ change in all other factors

Note that, with the exception of Treasury currency outstanding (which is not significantly different from zero), all the terms in this equation have the correct algebraic sign. For example, since it is a source, if the float increases, then Federal Reserve holdings of governments would have to go down to offset this. Hence the minus sign. By the same token, the coefficient on the "other" items has a plus sign in front of it since this is a use of reserve funds. The somewhat low r^2 (.52) was expected; defensive open market operations explain only about half of Federal Reserve policy action. The remainder are presumably undertaken as a part of dynamic monetary policy.

Conclusion   The preceding results strongly suggest that the Federal Reserve has control over the reserve base of the banking system but that this control is not absolute. In other words, during very short periods of time, the reserve base may move in ways that are contrary to the Federal Reserve's intention. But in the long run, the Fed can compensate for these erratic fluctuations and on the average achieve a fairly high degree of control over the reserve base.

Can the Federal Reserve Control the Money Supply?

We thus return to our original question: Can the Federal Reserve System control the nation's money supply? As should be apparent by now, this question does not have a simple yes or no answer. It depends, first, on what period of time is being considered. If we are talking about a week, the answer is clearly no. If we are talking about six months, the answer is a qualified yes.

Given the longer time period, the answer depends, secondly, on what we mean by *control.* If by this word we mean the ability to specify the nation's money stock exactly, with no imprecision, then again the answer is no. But if instead we mean

articles: William G. Dewald and William E. Gibson, "Sources of Variation in Member Bank Reserves," *Review of Economics and Statistics,* May 1969, pp. 143–150; and Leonall C. Andersen, "Federal Reserve Defensive Operations and Short-run Control of the Money Stock," *Journal of Political Economy,* March-/April 1968, pp. 275–288.

Table 15-3 Difference between Annual Growth Rates of the Monetary Base and the Money Supply, 1954–1973

	One month	Three months	Six months	Nine months	Twelve months	Eighteen months	Twenty-four months
Mean	0.090%	0.124%	0.123%	0.134%	0.141%	0.160%	0.182%
Standard deviation	3.975	2.117	1.475	1.233	1.092	0.890	0.774

Source: Based on Table 1 in Albert E. Burger, "The Relationship Between Monetary Base and Money: How Close?" Federal Reserve Bank of St. Louis *Review*, October 1975, p. 4.

the ability to determine the order of magnitude of the money supply—to achieve a "ball-park" figure—then the answer is yes.

This general conclusion is illustrated very nicely by the data given in Table 15-3. This table shows the mean (average) and standard deviation (see Appendix to Chapter 1) of the difference between the growth rates of the monetary base[9] and the M_1 money supply for different periods of time. An example will help to clarify this. Suppose that we were to calculate the percentage growth rate in the monetary base for some one month, and then make the same calculation for the M_1 growth rate for that month. Then we subtract this M_1 growth rate from the monetary base growth rate, which tells us how much faster the former grew than the latter. If we did this for all months in a period and then took the mean (average) of these figures, we would know the average differential monthly growth rates of money and the monetary base. This is how the uppermost figure in the first column was reckoned. However, as is always true of the mean, this figure is apt to be misleading. For example, if the difference between the two growth rates was +16 percent in one month and –16 percent in another month, then the mean of the two months would be zero percent, which would give the appearance of exactly the same growth rates when in fact there had been large differences. For this reason, the standard deviation of the different growth rates has also been calculated. The standard deviation tells us how tightly the data are grouped about their means. Finally, note that, when performing these calculations, there is no need to confine ourselves to *one-month* growth rates; the same set of calculations can be done for three-month growth rates, six-month growth rates, and so forth. This is the meaning of the other six columns.

The economic significance of Table 15-3 is to be found by reading across the rows. Note, first, that the differences in the monetary base and money supply growth rates are quite small—less than 0.2 percent in all cases. Second, note that these differences do not change much as the period of time increases; for example, the average *monthly* difference in growth rates is 0.90 percent, while the same figure for a 24-month growth rate is 0.182 percent. The main thing to note about Table 15-3, however, is the steady decline in the standard deviation as the time period gets longer. The standard deviation for a one-month growth rate, for example, is 3.975, while the standard deviation for a 24-month growth rate is only 0.774. What this means is that the variability of the differences in the two growth rates declines as

[9]Note that the monetary base, and not the reserve base, is used in this study. The monetary base, recall, is defined as member bank reserves plus currency in circulation. It is obtained by moving currency in circulation *(CinC)* from the right-hand side to the left-hand side of eq. (13).

the period involved gets longer. In other words, the Federal Reserve's control over the money supply is much more accurate in the long run than in the short run.[10]

Concluding Comment

In the preceding discussion the conclusion was reached that the Federal Reserve can dominate the money-creating process over a period of months. It can, that is, determine the *average* quantity of money in the economy with a *reasonable* degree of accuracy. But a warning is in order. For to say that (with appropriate qualifications) the Federal Reserve *can* control the money supply is not to say that the Federal Reserve *does* control the money supply. The two statements are not the same. At certain times and under certain circumstances, the Fed may deliberately choose to give up some part of its money stock control in order to achieve other operating objectives. This is particularly true with respect to money market interest rates. In other words, the Federal Reserve may choose to try to establish a certain level of interest rates in the economy rather than a certain level of money.

15-5 REVIEW QUESTIONS

1 Suppose that the Federal Reserve's holdings of United States government securities goes up by $1 billion, and that currency in circulation also goes up by $1 billion. What is the net effect on member bank reserves? Explain.

2 Show the T accounts for a Federal Reserve *sale* of government securities to a member bank.

3 What are the three *general controls* of the Federal Reserve? Which affect the reserve base? Which affects the money multiplier?

4 Can the Federal Reserve control the money supply of the United States week by week? month by month? year by year? How do you explain the difference in your answers?

[10]See also Jack L. Rutner, "The Federal Reserve's Impact on Several Reserve Aggregates," Federal Reserve Bank of Kansas City *Monthly Review,* May 1977, pp. 14–22.

16

Techniques
of Monetary
Management

The Federal Reserve System dominates the money supply process through open market operations, discount rate policy, and variations in reserve requirements. The reader should now understand in principle how each of these general controls works. But understanding them "in principle" is not sufficient. Too many questions remain unanswered: Who decides how many securities to buy? Where are they bought? How are the actual purchases made? Why does the Fed use one instrument at one time and another at another? What changes in the instruments have been proposed? And so forth. In this chapter we shall inquire into these and similar questions concerning the technical aspects of the instruments of monetary control. It should, perhaps, be reiterated that our concern here lies only in the *technical* issues surrounding these instruments. That is, we still are not ready to launch into a full-scale discussion of monetary policy. Nevertheless, many of the matters we shall deal with are quite controversial, at least among those who follow monetary affairs closely.

A second point needs to be noted. So far only the general, or quantitative, policy instruments of the Federal Reserve have been mentioned. But in fact the powers of the Federal Reserve System go beyond this. In addition to its *general* instruments, the Fed possesses the authority to vary, by administrative action, certain key financial variables in the credit markets. These are called its *selective,* or *qualitative,* controls. Their purpose is to permit the Federal Reserve to select a particular financial market (e.g., the stock market) and alter credit conditions in that market in isolation from what is happening in the rest of the economy. These selective controls will also be described and discussed in this chapter.

Finally, the monetary powers of the U.S. Treasury will be examined. While the Treasury seldom uses its monetary powers, preferring to leave central banking to the central bank, it nevertheless possesses a potential for influencing credit conditions by the way it handles its tax and loan receipts and manages the public debt. We shall inquire briefly into these matters at the end of the chapter.

16-1 GENERAL INSTRUMENTS OF MONETARY CONTROL

The techniques used by the Federal Reserve to determine the country's total money supply are called its *general controls* because they affect financial conditions in general. That is, the use of these instruments does not discriminate among the various financial submarkets, such as consumer finance, real estate finance, and business finance. Rather, changes in these instruments establish an overall framework of monetary ease or tightness for the economy as a whole, and individuals in the economy are then left free to adjust to this framework in the manner most suited to their own circumstances.

Open Market Operations

As analyzed in Chapter 15, when the Federal Reserve buys government securities, member bank reserves increase by an amount equal to the value of the securities bought. Conversely, when the Federal Reserve sells government securities, member bank reserves decrease. The purchase and sale of government securities by the Federal Reserve is known as *open market operations.* Open market operations are the most fundamental of all the monetary tools available to the Federal Reserve.

Setting Open Market Policy   The open market policies of the Federal Reserve System are established by the Federal Open Market Committee, whose membership includes all seven members of the Board of Governors and five of the twelve presidents of the district banks (see Chapter 14). The FOMC meets about once a month in Washington. Present at these meetings, in addition to the twelve voting members of the Committee, are the seven nonvoting district bank presidents plus a variety of staff economists from the district banks and the Board. Before monetary policy is finally decided upon, there is a (sometimes heated) discussion of the appropriate policy to follow for the next month. During the discussion, everyone is encouraged to air his or her views, including the seven nonvoting district bank presidents. It is perhaps worth noting that differences of opinion do not appear to follow any special pattern; in particular, neither the Board members nor the president members of the Committee seem to group into voting blocs.

The actual procedure that the FOMC uses in setting monetary policy is as follows.[1] In the weeks prior to the meeting, the staff economists at the Board have made two types of economic forecasts. One of these, called a *judgmental forecast,* is put together by various staff members who are experts on different areas of the economy—consumption, investment, international trade, financial markets, and so forth. As the name implies, this judgmental forecast is based on the judgment of these experts about what is going to happen in their particular sector of the economy over the next year or so. The second kind of forecast that is made is based on a very large and very elaborate mathematical and statistical model of the United States economy. This is called the *model forecast.* After these two forecasts have been made, they are compared and the differences between them studied. Adjustments are then made in both forecasts so that they agree in basic respects. Finally, the adjusted model forecast is then used to try to predict the consequences of alternative monetary policy actions (this process is called *simulation*).

The staff then presents the predictions of the adjusted model to the Federal Open Market Committee. It is then that the heated discussion begins. Some members may disagree with the assumptions underlying the model, and argue that something different will happen. Probably the greatest source of disagreement, however, stems from the different value judgments of the various members. Some, for example, may argue that inflation is the number one problem, and the Fed should try to stop it even at the cost of a rise in unemployment. Others may argue the opposite. Still others may want to focus on the value of the dollar in the international exchanges. And so forth. The issues will finally come to a vote among the twelve voting members of the FOMC, with the majority prevailing. This vote will establish the *domestic policy directive* of the FOMC.

The domestic policy directive establishes a *range of tolerance* for the annual growth rate in the money supply. By "range of tolerance" is meant that the Committee wants open market operations to be carried out in such a way that the growth rate of the money supply will fall within this range. However, since there is some ambiguity as to what is meant by "money" in this context, the FOMC actually specifies a range of tolerance for three monetary concepts—M_1 (currency plus demand deposits); M_2 (M_1 plus savings and time deposits at commercial banks, except for large negotiable certificates of deposit); and M_3 (M_2 plus deposits at MSBs, S&Ls, and CUs). Table 16-1 shows the range of tolerance of the FOMC for early 1978.

Along with the adoption of the range of tolerance for the growth rates of money, the FOMC also adopts a written *qualitative* statement that is supposed to reflect its collective thinking about what monetary policy should be over the following weeks. Unfortunately, this qualitative statement is couched in terms of such vague generality that it is of very little help (and is sometimes an object of ridicule) to outside

---

[1]For a more detailed description, together with some criticisms and suggestions for change, see William Poole, "The Making of Monetary Policy: Description and Analysis," *Economic Inquiry,* June 1975, pp. 253–265.

Table 16-1   Range of Tolerance for FOMC Objectives, March 21, 1978

Variable	Range of tolerance, %
M_1	$4-6\frac{1}{2}$
M_2	$6\frac{1}{2}-9$
M_3	$7\frac{1}{2}-10$
Federal funds rate	$6\frac{1}{2}-7$

Source: Federal Reserve Bulletin, May 1978, p. 392.

observers. For example, the qualitative statement adopted by the FOMC in its March 1978, meeting stated that it was FOMC policy to "encourage continued economic expansion and help resist inflationary pressures, while contributing to a sustainable pattern of international transactions." The reader's guess is as good as anyone's as to what this means (if anything).

There is one final step to the FOMC decision-making process. As explained in the preceding chapter, Chapter 15, the Federal Reserve's control over the money supply is very imprecise in the short run. Open market operations, however, must be carried out on a day-to-day (and, indeed, minute-to-minute) basis. And the FOMC cannot realistically expect open market operations to be conducted during such short periods of time with the only objective being to control the money supply. In fact, the amount of money in the economy is known accurately only after a lag of several weeks. What the FOMC does, consequently, is to specify an *operating target* for open market operations that is thought to be consistent with the range of tolerance of the money supply growth rates. This operating target is put in terms of the rate of interest on federal funds. Thus the FOMC might specify that, in order to achieve a monetary growth rate between 4 and 6 percent, the federal funds rate should not go below 6 nor above 7 percent. Since the federal funds rate is known continuously, and since open market operations are a major influence on this rate, such an operating goal is easily achieved. Table 16-1 shows the range of tolerance for the federal funds rate thought to be consistent with the money supply objectives of the FMOC.

One question remains: How does the FOMC know that a particular federal funds rate will be consistent with a particular growth rate of the money supply. Once again, the answer is—a model. In this case, the model is a monthly financial model developed by the staff economists at the Board of Governors. The output of the model is a forecast of what federal funds rates will emerge in the market if bank reserves and the money supply grow at particular rates.[2]

Concurrent Resolution 133   A few years ago, monetary policy was made in secret, with the current intentions of the FOMC becoming known only several months after a decision had actually been made. The rationale behind this procedure was to avoid giving bond traders tips that would lead to speculative profits on

---

[2]Perhaps the moral of the FOMC decision-making process is that readers who wish to become professional economists should learn as much as they can about constructing and estimating econometric models.

"inside" information. To explain, recall from Chapter 7 that bond prices and interest rates vary inversely—i.e., when one goes up the other goes down, and conversely. Then if one knew that the FOMC had decided to pursue, for example, an easy money policy (lower interest rates) then one would also know that bond prices would necessarily rise. Obviously, profits could be made on the basis of such information.

The difficulty with the secrecy surrounding the FOMC meetings was that it left Congress as much in the dark as everyone else. But Congress felt that monetary policy was a powerful influence on the economy, and that they should have some input into the decision-making process. Consequently, in 1975 the Congress approved *House Concurrent Resolution 133*. This requires that the Federal Reserve consult with the appropriate Congressional committees four times per year. These hearings, the resolution said, should concern FOMC "objectives and plans with respect to the ranges of growth or diminution of monetary and credit aggregates in the upcoming twelve months." However, the resolution goes on to stipulate that the FOMC is not bound by these stated intentions, and is free to change them if economic conditions seem to warrant it. Thus Congress can now debate current monetary policy with Federal Reserve officials, although the Fed is not obliged to act on Congressional suggestions.

Executing Open Market Policy Because of its strategic location, all purchases and sales of United States government securities for the Federal Reserve System are made by the Federal Reserve Bank of New York. The department within the New York Bank that makes these securities transactions is known as the *trading desk*. The person in charge of the trading desk is called the *federal open market committee account manager* (or, more simply, the *account manager*), and is typically a senior vice president of the Bank. It is his responsibility to put into practice the current economic policy directive adopted at the latest meeting of the FOMC. As an aid in this job, the account manager is subject to a constant flow of information. He attends all meetings of the FOMC, where he reports on the recent activities of the trading desk, gives his views on the current state of the financial markets, and listens carefully to the discussion preceding the adoption of the FOMC's policy directive. Between the FOMC meetings, the account manager is in daily telephone contact with one or more Committee members. He also receives daily (and in some cases hourly) reports and projections on the various factors in the member bank reserve equation, and every day discusses current market developments with at least one dealer in government securities.

"Straight" Trades and Repurchase Agreements All Federal Reserve transactions in government securities are made through twenty government security dealers (discussed in Chapter 7). Each of these dealers is connected by direct telephone line with the trading desk. Transactions between the dealers and the trading desk may be either of two types: *straight trade* or *repurchase agreement*. A straight trade is just what it sounds like—an ordinary purchase or sale of some specified government security at a quoted ask or bid price.

A repurchase agreement occurs when the Federal Reserve enters into an arrangement to buy a security from a dealer and then have the dealer buy it back ("repurchase" it) at some specified price and on some specified future date (usually fifteen days or less). Repurchase agreements are, in effect, a secured loan from the New York Fed to the government securities dealer. They are made at the request of the dealer but only when the FOMC approves the transaction. Their purpose is to provide the financing necessary for the dealer to maintain an inventory of government securities when obtaining such financing through other channels (e.g., loans from commercial banks) would prove too disruptive to the market. Quantitatively, repurchase agreements are relatively unimportant; less than 1 percent of the government securities owned by the Federal Reserve are held under repurchase agreements.

Effects of Open Market Operations   Open market transactions of the Federal Reserve System have two direct financial effects. One of these, the effect on member bank reserves, has already been discussed at length. But there is also another direct effect of open market operations that it is important to understand: the effect on interest rates. Recall from Chapter 7 that market interest rates and security prices vary inversely; when interest rates increase, security prices decrease, and conversely. Security prices, in the short run at least, are determined by supply and demand like any other price. Thus when the Federal Reserve buys a particular government security, it adds to the demand for that security and hence bids its price up. But the increase in price also and necessarily means a decrease in the yield of the security because of the inverse relationship between yield and price. Thus an open market purchase by the Fed will have the immediate consequence that the market yields on government securities will be lower than they would otherwise have been; an open market sale will result in higher interest rates.

The importance of the bank reserve and interest rate effects of open market operations lies in the following consideration. In using its open market operations, the Federal Reserve can control bank reserves *or* it can control interest rates, *but it cannot do both.* To understand why this is so, consider the following example.[3] Suppose the Federal Reserve were to decide to fix the market yield on three-month Treasury bills at 6 percent. It could *not* do this by administrative decree (the Fed has no such power), but it *could* do this by offering either to buy or sell unlimited quantities of this security at such a price that its yield would be 6 percent. If it did this, then no one would *sell* at a lower price, since they could sell to the Fed at a higher price; and no one would *buy* at a higher price since they could buy from the Fed at a lower price. The price would thus be fixed; and since the price couldn't vary, neither could the yield. Consequently, the Federal Reserve would have effectively determined the market yield on three-month Treasury bills at 6 percent. But note that in doing so it has lost its control over bank reserves. Anytime the Fed buys a bill, bank reserves go up; anytime it sells a bill, bank reserves go down. And it must buy or sell *at the initiative of the public;* it cannot determine the volume or even the direction of its open market transactions.

The contrary case would also hold true. If the Federal Reserve wishes to achieve

[3]The example describes, in essence, the open market policy followed by the Federal Reserve System from 1941 to 1951 (the "pegging" period). It is put in the form of an example in the text to avoid all the descriptive clutter and qualifications a historical account would entail.

some given level of member bank reserves, then it must buy or sell a certain amount of securities irrespective of what happens to market rates of interest because of these purchases or sales. It follows that the Fed can control either yields or reserves, but not both. The importance of this point cannot yet be made fully apparent to the reader, but its essence can be indicated briefly. Two competing monetary theories are currently being debated in academic, governmental, and business circles. One of these, the *neo-Keynesian* theory, emphasizes the role played by interest rates in our economic system; the other, the *monetarist* theory, emphasizes the role played by the quantity of money and hence by bank reserves. Because the Federal Reserve cannot control both bank reserves and interest rates simultaneously, it also cannot satisfy both the neo-Keynesians and the monetarists simultaneously. Thus, the Federal Reserve's current operating procedure of specifying a range of tolerance for *both* money supply and interest rates (the federal funds rate) is really something of a compromise. Where single-valued goals for each of these variables might be inconsistent with one another, getting both of them to fall within a specified range is much more feasible. Moreover, remember that the federal funds rate range chosen as an operating target is deliberately selected as one that will be consistent with the more basic money supply objectives of the Fed.

Discount Rate Policy

When member banks borrow from the Federal Reserve System, the reserves of the banking system are increased by an amount equal to the borrowings; when they repay previous borrowings, bank reserves go down. The Federal Reserve can affect the total volume of such borrowings by raising or lowering the rate of interest charged member banks, that is, the *discount rate*. While the board of directors of each district bank is given the legal authority to set the discount rate applicable to the member banks of that district, actions taken under this authority are subject to the approval of the Board of Governors in Washington. In practice, this has meant that the Board of Governors sets the discount rate for the entire System. For example, in 1972 the Board of Governors disapproved a total of twenty-two proposed changes in the discount rate.

For a long time the Federal Reserve System has taken the position that discounting is a privilege, not a right, of member banks. In other words, the System holds that it is under no obligation to lend to a member bank simply because that bank is willing to pay the current discount rate. Instead, the Federal Reserve contends that it may, it if so chooses, refuse to lend to a member bank. This aspect of the discount mechanism should not be misunderstood, however. The Federal Reserve does not administer the discount window arbitrarily by playing favorites. Rather, it has fostered the "privilege" view of discounting in two ways: (1) The Federal Reserve has encouraged the attitude among member banks that they should be *reluctant borrowers* and make use of their discounting privilege only as a last resort. As a result, many member banks never borrow from the Fed, and many others borrow only rarely. (2) For those banks that do borrow, the Federal Reserve engages in what it calls *surveillance,* which works like this: The first time a bank requests a loan, the loan is granted almost automatically. But if the bank continues to request extensions of the loan, the Fed will begin a series of administrative maneuvers that have the effect of harassing the bank. For example, the Fed may begin by requesting detailed information justifying the loan, then request personal discussions with the member bank's president, and then ask for meetings with the bank's board of directors. A very persistent bank ultimately may be refused a loan, but matters seldom progress that far.

Theories of Discounting   There are two persistent theories as to why member banks borrow from the Fed: the *need theory* and the *profit theory*. According to the need theory, banks borrow from the Federal Reserve primarily because of some emergency, i.e., because a bank "needs" to borrow. For example, an unexpectedly large deposit withdrawal might force a bank into the discount window for temporary accommodation. Or a local disaster such as a crop failure or the shutting down of a plant might require short-run assistance from the Fed. The Federal Reserve encourages member banks to borrow for need.

The profit theory holds that banks borrow when it is in their self-interest to do so, i.e., when it is profitable. Suppose, for example, that the going rate on federal funds is 6 percent and that the discount rate is 5 percent. A member bank faced with a deposit withdrawal can use either channel to adjust its reserve position; that is, it can either buy federal funds, or it can borrow from the Fed. The profit theory holds that the bank will choose that channel of adjustment which minimizes its costs (maximizes its profits). Thus, in this example, the bank will borrow from the Fed at 5 percent in preference to buying federal funds that cost it 6 percent. Of course, the opposite is also true. If the discount rate is above the federal funds rate, then the bank will buy federal funds in preference to borrowing.

Reform of the Discount Mechanism   One way or another, the various changes in the discounting mechanism that have been proposed turn on the question of whether banks follow the need or profit theory of borrowing. Those who feel that member banks borrow for profit generally also feel that the discount mechanism constitutes a sort of escape hatch that member banks can use to shield themselves from a restrictive monetary policy. The argument goes like this: Suppose that in its open market operations the Fed is (other things equal) pursuing a tight money policy by selling government securities. This will cause bank reserves to fall and market rates of interest to rise. The discount rate, being set by administrative decree rather than market pressures, generally lags behind movements in open market rates. Thus, in the situation described, the discount rate will frequently be lower than the Treasury bill rate and banks will find it profitable to adjust their reserve positions by borrowing from the Fed. But note that if they do so, this will at least partially offset the Federal Reserve's open market policy. The Federal Reserve will be reducing reserves by selling securities and simultaneously increasing reserves by lending to member banks; it will be taking money in through the front door and paying it out through the back door. Reasoning along these lines, some students of monetary policy have advocated that Federal Reserve discounting be abolished.[4] The discount window, it is held, is an anachronism, a holdover from the discredited commercial loan theory of banking. If it were harmless, it wouldn't matter. But it isn't harmless. Discounting reduces the precision of Federal Reserve control over bank reserves; it makes open market operations a mushy tool of policy. Therefore, they say, let us get rid of it.

In response, officials of the Federal Reserve System have in essence urged the needs view of member bank borrowing. There are, they say, two reasons for retaining the discount rate policy: First, the appropriate analogy for the relationship of discounting to open market operations is not that of an "escape hatch" but that of a "safety valve." Open market operations, the argument runs, have their *initial* impact on a few large money market banks. When the Fed undertakes security sales on a very large scale, these banks lose large amounts of reserves. They therefore need some mechanism that will give them time to adjust to this reserve loss. Discounting is such a mechanism. It permits these banks a temporary source of reserves until they can make more fundamental adjustments in their secondary reserve assets. In the absence of the discount window, it is held, the Federal Reserve would be inhibited in its open market operations; if there were no discount window, open market operations would have to be undertaken in smaller amounts than is sometimes desirable.

The second reason for retaining the discount rate policy proposed by Federal Reserve officials is a very straightforward needs argument. Some banks, they say, especially small banks, occasionally find themselves in emergency situations. A flood, drought, or strike can result in severe inroads being made on a small bank's liquidity. Such a bank does not have ready access to the federal funds market and may not be able to make fundamental asset adjustments (e.g., contracting loans) without causing serious damage to the local economy. The surest and best course for such a bank to follow is to borrow from the Fed. To abolish member bank borrowing because of the advantages taken of it by large banks is to leave the small banks stranded; it is to throw the baby out with the bath water.

The Federal Reserve has recently changed the discounting procedure to make it more suitable to the requirements of contemporary commercial banking. Under present arrangements, member banks may be accommodated at the discount window for three reasons: (1) a *basic borrowing privilege,* which permits member banks to borrow limited amounts for limited periods on virtually an automatic basis; (2) a *seasonal credit accommodation,* which permits those banks with demonstrable seasonal needs to exceed their basic borrowing privileges during certain times of the year; and (3) *emergency credit assistance,* which provides loans to member banks and, in an extreme emergency, other financial institutions as well.

Setting the Discount Rate   Notwithstanding the recent changes made in the administration of member bank borrowing, the Board of Governors has apparently

---

[4]Milton Friedman, *A Program for Monetary Stability,* Fordham University Press, New York, 1960, pp. 35–45.

been discouraging member banks from borrowing for "profit" in recent years. They have been doing this by moving the discount rate frequently so that it closely follows movements in the federal funds rate. For example, two researchers,[5] using monthly data from 1968–1974, found the following statistical relationships to hold between the discount rate and the spread between the federal funds rate and the discount rate.

$$FRD = 0.34(RFF - FRD)$$
(constant term not given)
$$R^2 = .98$$
          Coefficient on $RFF - FRD$ significant at 1 percent level

where FRD =   the discount rate at the Federal Reserve Bank of New York.
          RFF =   interest rate on federal funds.

In this regression, note that the r^2 is very high and that the coefficient on the independent variable (the federal funds rate minus the discount rate) is highly significant. Given that the statistical "fit" is quite good, note in particular that the algebraic sign on the independent variable is positive (+). Thus, the regression is to be interpreted to mean that when the spread between the federal funds rate and the discount rate increases, the discount rate will be raised, and conversely for a narrowing spread.[6] The economic significance is basically this: The Federal Reserve determines the federal funds rate through its open market operations and then sets the discount rate accordingly. In other words, open market operations are the basic tool of monetary policy and member banks discounting a subsidiary tool.

Variations in Reserve Requirements

Although their original purpose was to protect depositors by ensuring some minimum level of bank liquidity, reserve requirements are now regarded by nearly all economists primarily as a monetary policy tool. Unlike the other two general controls of the Federal Reserve, *variations in reserve requirements* work on the money supply by changing the money multiplier m rather than the reserve base R. As discussed previously, if the Federal Reserve raises reserve requirements, the money multiplier (and hence the money supply) will go down; if reserve requirements are lowered, the money supply will go up. The Board of Governors has the authority to change reserve requirements within specified limits, as described in Chapter 9.

Variations in reserve requirements are the least used of the Federal Reserve's three general instruments of monetary control. While in principle reserve require-

[5]Raymond E. Lombra and Raymond G. Torto, "Discount Rate Changes and Announcement Effects," *Quarterly Journal of Economics,* February 1977, pp. 171–176. See also Richard T. Froyen, "The Determinants of Federal Reserve Discount Rate Policy," *Southern Economic Journal,* October 1975, pp. 193–200.

[6]In fact, the independent variable is a distributed four-month lag, where the weights on the lagged terms have been determined by the Almon technique. The Almon distributed lag procedure goes well beyond the elementary statistical techniques used in this book. Notwithstanding this technical discrepancy between the text and the study, the interpretation given in the text is accurate.

ments could be changed by small fractions of a percent, the Fed has always held that such changes would be administratively very difficult to make. Member banks, they suggest, would have trouble coping with hundredths or even tenths of a percentage point. As a consequence, the Fed does not make reserve requirement changes of less than ½ percent. But since an across-the-board decrease of, say, ½ percent would have the initial effect of creating very substantial *excess* reserves in the banking system and the ultimate effect of creating very substantial increases in the money supply, the Federal Reserve uses reserve requirement changes only infrequently. They are the blunt instrument of monetary policy, used only when powerful measures seem called for.

Reform of Reserve Requirements   A number of proposals have been put forward from time to time calling for a revision of reserve requirements as presently constituted. For example a number of people have suggested that the reserve requirements of *all* banks in the country—small and large, member and nonmember—be made uniform. The purpose of this proposal is to give the Federal Reserve better control over the money supply by eliminating changes that occur because of shifts of reserves among different classes of banks. (It would also have the effect of eliminating the primary barrier to wider Federal Reserve membership—higher reserve requirements for member banks). Others have proposed that reserves be held against bank assets rather than against deposit liabilities, as is now the case. Thus a bank would hold different amounts of reserves against its government securities, against various kinds of loans, and so on. The advantage claimed for this scheme is that by a judicious varying of the reserves against different types of assets, the Federal Reserve could encourage banks to extend credit into particular sectors of the economy. Many people, however, find such detailed intervention into the economy politically objectionable.

100 Percent Reserve Requirement Plan   One proposed plan for changing reserve requirements that was quite popular several years ago is worthy of special (though brief) note. This plan calls for banks to hold 100 percent cash reserves against their deposit liabilities. If adopted, such a scheme would completely alter the nature of American commercial banking. Banks as we know them would disappear and would be replaced by deposit-transferring institutions that would obtain profits exclusively from service charges. The lending functions of banks would be taken over by savings intermediaries whose liabilities would not be money. The advantages claimed for this scheme are twofold: It would eliminate, once and for all, the problem of bank failures (banks with 100 percent cash reserves against deposits cannot fail), and it would give the monetary authorities absolute control over the money supply.

There are a great many pros and cons of the 100 percent reserve plan that will not be discussed here.[7] The political possibility of such a plan actually being enacted into legislation is remote.

[7]The interested reader should consult George Tolley, "100 Percent Reserve Banking," in Leland B. Yeager (ed.), *In Search of a Monetary Constitution,* Harvard University Press, Cambridge, Mass., 1962, pp. 275–304. See also Chapter 27 for a more complete discussion of this proposal.

Lagged Reserve Accounting   A very technical issue of reserve requirements, but one which is nevertheless quite controversial, concerns what is called *lagged reserve accounting*. As currently administered, the reserve requirements of the Federal Reserve System do not require member banks to hold legal reserves against their *current* deposit liabilities. Instead, their present legal reserve requirements are based on deposits as they were two weeks previously. In other words, a member bank's average reserves *this* week must legally be a certain percentage of average deposits *two weeks ago.* This arrangement, many economists charge, results in a good deal of mischief. Why? To understand this, recall the simplest demand deposit equation of Chapter 12: $\Delta D = \Delta B(1/R_D)$, where ΔD is the change in deposits, ΔB is the initial increase in bank reserves, and R_D is the reserve requirement on deposits. One way to view this equation is that legal reserve requirements put a limit on the ability of the banking system to create deposits. For example, if $\Delta B = \$1,000$ and $R_D = 1/5$, then the increase in demand deposits (ΔD) is limited to $5,000. The main thing to note is that as R_D goes down, the ability of the commercial banks to create deposits goes up. And at the limit, as R_D approaches zero, the amount of deposits that banks can create becomes infinite. What has this to do with lagged reserve accounting? Just this: the reserve requirement against *newly created* demand deposits is zero. In other words, if the banking system gets new reserves today, then for the next two weeks it can create (theoretically) an infinite amount of deposits. Naturally, since bankers are prudent business people, and since the day of reckoning is only two weeks off, they don't do so. But the main point is that the Federal Reserve has no control over *current* deposits. That is, lagged reserve accounting has created yet another element of imprecision to the Federal Reserve's control of the money supply.

One economist, William Poole,[8] has recently proposed that lagged reserve accounting be turned completely around, and that 100 percent reserve requirements be placed on changes in deposits that have occurred within the past two weeks. In other words, where lagged reserve accounting now places *zero* reserve requirements against new deposits, Poole would have the Fed require member banks to hold *100 percent* reserves against such deposits. The advantage of such a scheme, Poole argues, is that would enhance Federal Reserve control over the money supply. An open market purchase of securities today, for example, would create new deposits on a dollar-for-dollar basis; if the Fed bought $1 million of treasury bills, then the money supply would go up by $1 million, neither more nor less. Of course, after two weeks the reserve requirement would fall to its present level, thus freeing additional reserves for the banking system's use. But this two-week interim would, according to Poole, give both Federal Reserve officials and bankers adequate time to plan how to respond to a development that they would know of beforehand.

Poole's plan has a great deal to recommend it. It is a sort of hybrid between the fractional reserve system and the 100 percent reserve plan, retaining many of the advantages of the latter without requiring the sweeping institutional changes of

---

[8]William Poole, "A Proposal for Reforming Bank Reserve Requirements in the United States," *Journal of Money, Credit and Banking,* May 1976, pp. 167–180.

eliminating the former. Perhaps the main barrier to its adoption is that, under present institutional arrangements, it would apply only to member banks of the Federal Reserve System. Thus member banks would have even more stringent reserve requirements, which would undoubtedly worsen the problem of declining bank membership in the Fed.

Secular Increase in the Money Supply   One of the most hotly debated issues concerning the technical aspects of central banking involves the method whereby the money supply is increased on a *secular,* or long-run, basis. In the long run (decades, say), as the economy grows, the money supply must grow with it. In general, the Federal Reserve may choose either of two methods for accomplishing the secular expansion of the money supply: open market purchases of government securities or a gradual lowering of reserve requirements. If the Fed chooses the former method, then over the years it will greatly add to its holdings of government securities. As previously explained, a large part of the income earned on these securities is returned to the United States Treasury. Thus the ultimate beneficiary of expanding the money supply through open market operations is the United States taxpayer. If, alternatively, the Federal Reserve chooses to expand the money supply by lowering the reserve requirements of member banks, then these banks are enabled to acquire additional earning assets, which increases their profits; the banks, that is, are the ultimate beneficiary of the second method. Query: Which method should the Fed use?

The answer is not as obvious as it may seem. Note, in the first place, that banks pay corporate income taxes, so that the benefits from using reserve requirements for a secular expansion of the money supply do not accrue wholly to the banking system. Secondly, banking is not as profitable as many other American industries, and some observers feel that there would be advantages to increasing bank profits. Finally, a lowering of reserve requirements would encourage greater membership in the Federal Reserve System, which many people feel would be socially desirable. Notwithstanding these arguments, however, a great many students of monetary affairs continue to feel that the primary source of a secular growth in the money supply should be open market purchases by the Federal Reserve System.

Coordinating the General Instruments of Monetary Control

Each of the general controls of the Federal Reserve has its weaknesses and strengths. They are not perfect substitutes for one another. The Federal Reserve therefore can choose to use one instrument rather than another, or to use some combination of the instruments, in order to achieve a given goal.

Strengths and Weaknesses   Open market operations have three strengths of considerable importance: flexibility, precision, and size. By *flexibility* is meant that any given open market policy can be revised or even reversed on any hour of any day; the Fed can buy on Monday, sell on Tuesday, and buy again on Wednesday. By *precision* is meant that the Federal Reserve can buy or sell exactly the amount of securities it wishes and, since bank reserves are changed on a dollar-for-dollar basis with such transactions, the Fed can therefore add or subtract precise amounts to or from the reserve base. Finally, by *size* is meant that open market operations can be conducted on any scale, from massive to minute. These three strengths of open market operations make it the favorite tool of the Federal Reserve for the day-to-day conduct of monetary policy.

However, open market operations also have weaknesses. For one thing, they have no *announcement effects.* Because they are not well understood by the public and because they are engaged in routinely for both dynamic and defensive policy purposes, they lack the headline-catching appeal of changes in the discount rate or reserve requirements. There are times when Federal Reserve officials feel it desirable to give a clear signal of their intentions to the public, and open market operations are poorly suited to this purpose. Another weakness of open market operations is that their effects may take some time—about a month—to permeate the banking system. Open market operations are conducted through the money market in New York City, and their initial effects are felt on banks there. As these banks adjust, their actions will affect banks in other geographic areas, which, in turn, will make adjustments, and so forth. But there are times when it is important to make immediate and instantaneous changes in all parts of the country simultaneously, and open market operations are poorly designed for this task.

Compared to open market operations, changes in the discount rate are lacking in both precision and size. The Federal Reserve can never be certain how much bank borrowing will change in response to a change in the discount rate. But it does know that such responses will be small relative to open market operations or changes in reserve requirements. However, changes in the discount rate do receive substantial publicity on the front pages of newspapers and on television; they are generally considered an admirable vehicle for underscoring current monetary policy. Moreover, the discounting mechanism is capable of adding quickly to the reserves of member banks throughout the country on an "as needed" and selective basis.

Variations in reserve requirements also lack flexibility and precision. A decision to change them is not easily reversed. And, although the Federal Reserve can calculate closely by how much excess reserves will be changed in response to a given change in requirements, as long as the Fed confines such changes to ½ percent steps, they will lack precision. The strength of reserve requirement variations is that they have the potential for powerfully affecting the reserve positions of all member banks instantaneously.

The Appropriate Mix   One aspect of central banking in the United States is thus to find the *appropriate mix,* or blend, of the general instruments of control. What is appropriate or inappropriate depends, of course, on the particular circumstances of the economy, the financial markets, and the commercial banking system. The art of central banking lies in the skillful orchestration of the powers that it commands.

16-2   SELECTIVE INSTRUMENTS OF MONETARY CONTROL

In addition to its general instruments, the Federal Reserve also has other powers at its disposal, called its *selective instruments*. Where the purpose of the general instruments is to set the monetary tone (easy or tight) for the economy as a whole, the selective instruments are meant to give the Federal Reserve an ability to affect particular sectors of the economy on a selective basis. They may be used either to reinforce a more general policy or to shield a particular sector from the Fed's general policy.

Stock Market Credit

The Federal Reserve System has the authority to set minimum margin requirements on the purchase of stock. A *margin requirement* is the downpayment a purchaser of stock must pay to buy the stock on credit. An example of a margin requirement is as follows: Suppose you wanted to buy $1,000 worth of stock. If the margin requirement is 70 percent, this means that you can pay $700 of your own money and borrow $300 to buy the stock. The $1,000 worth of stock is then used as collateral against the $300 loan. Clearly, if the margin requirement is lowered to 40 percent, it becomes easier to buy stock; and if the margin is raised to 90 percent it becomes more difficult. The Federal Reserve has the legal authority to vary the margin requirement from 25 to 100 percent. Moreover, this authority applies to *all* lenders—securities brokers, commercial banks, and others—not just to member banks of the Federal Reserve.[9]

The reason why the Federal Reserve was given the authority to set margin requirements illustrates nicely the broad purpose of selective controls. In the spring of 1929 the United States economy switched from prosperity to recession. But despite the recession, stock prices rose at an extraordinary clip throughout the summer months of 1929. It was clear to some observers, including Federal Reserve officials, that the rise in stock prices was "unhealthy," the result of a purely speculative boom. But the Fed was on the horns of a dilemma: If it used its general controls to make money tight in the hope of choking off the credit pouring into the stock market, then it ran the risk of worsening the recession. Alternatively, if it made money easier in order to counteract the recession, then it ran the risk of adding even more credit to the already unhealthy conditions in the stock markets. What the Federal Reserve needed (but did not have at the time) was some method of making credit generally easy in the economy but selectively tight in the stock market; it needed a shotgun for the economy and a rifle for the stock market. As is too frequently the case, the barn door was locked after the horse had been stolen; the Fed was given regulatory authority over margin requirements in 1934 and has utilized this selective policy many times since then.

Even so, it is not clear that control over margin requirements is particularly

[9]Although there are some exceptions to this. For a fuller explanation, see Ann P. Ulrey, "The Structure of Margin Credit," *Federal Reserve Bulletin,* April 1975, pp. 209–220.

effective. Empirical studies on the matter seem to indicate that the effects of changing margin requirements are largely psychological[10] and in the long run do not substantially limit the excessive use of credit for stock purchases.[11]

Moral Suasion

A second type of selective control sometimes used by the Federal Reserve System is what is called *moral suasion*. (One sometimes wonders what bureaucratic genius thinks up such names.) Moral suasion is a general term describing a variety of informal or nonlegal methods used by the Federal Reserve to persuade its member banks to behave in a particular manner. The methods employed range from well-publicized speeches given by members of the Board of Governors, to letters sent to all member banks, to voluntary programs of credit restraints, replete with conferences, guidelines, and committees. The objectives of moral suasion are typically to restrain the growth of bank credit (loans) going into particular sectors of the market. For example, the Fed might come to feel that consumer spending is putting too much inflationary pressure on the economy and ask its member banks to curtail consumer loans. Or it might feel that too many banks are using the discount window for "profit" rather than "need" and issue warnings that profit-type borrowing will be closely watched. The possible uses of the Federal Reserve's moral powers to be "suasive" are endless.

The effectiveness of moral suasion depends on the method used, the objective, and the period of time under consideration. A speech given by a high-ranking Federal Reserve official probably would have little immediate and no long-run influence on bank behavior. A strongly worded letter sent to member banks may elicit a good deal of immediate voluntary compliance, but as it becomes increasingly apparent that some banks are ignoring it, enthusiasm may wane as time goes on. Under the proper circumstances, however, moral suasion can be quite effective. A good example of this was the Voluntary Foreign Credit Restraint Program instituted by the Federal Reserve in 1965. The purpose of the Program was to reduce capital outflows from the United States in order to help correct our international balance of payments deficit. Since a comparatively small number of very large banks accounted for the vast bulk of such outflows, the Federal Reserve was able to establish guidelines and elicit full cooperation over a prolonged period of time. Indeed, it seems likely that in large part the voluntary nature of this program accounted for its success.

Consumer and Real Estate Credit Controls

The Federal Reserve System does not now have selective controls designed to regulate the volume of credit being channeled into the consumption goods and real estate markets. But about thirty years ago the Federal Reserve did have such controls, and there remains a good deal of support for reinstating them on a standby

[10]See Jules I. Bogen and Herman E. Krooss, *Security Credit: Its Economic Role and Regulation,* Prentice-Hall, Inc., Englewood Cliffs, N.J., 1960.

[11]Thomas Moore, "Stock Market Margin Requirements," *Journal of Political Economy,* April 1966, pp. 158–167.

basis (i.e., to be used only when needed). For this reason it is worthwhile considering them briefly.

Consumer Credit Controls   With the exception of two brief periods in 1947–1948 and 1949–1950, the Federal Reserve was authorized to control the flow of installment credit for the purchase of consumer durable goods from 1941 to 1952. By *consumer durable goods* is meant such things as furniture, refrigerators, washer-dryers, and especially automobiles. The form taken by the controls was twofold: The Federal Reserve was given the authority to vary the minimum downpayment required for the purchase of such goods; additionally, the Federal Reserve was authorized to limit the maximum number of months over which an installment contract could run.

The purpose of the consumer credit controls was to stop an existing price inflation. One cause of an inflation is excessive demand for certain goods; when producers find that they cannot fill all their orders, they raise their prices to make more profits. One way to slow down an inflation, therefore, is to eliminate the excess demand so that producers do not have unfilled orders. A higher downpayment means that some people can't afford certain goods. For example, if a refrigerator costs $1,000 and the downpayment is 10 percent, a lot of people will have the necessary $100 to begin buying it. But if the downpayment were raised to 25 percent, fewer people would be able to afford the resulting $250 initial outlay. By raising the required downpayment the Federal Reserve was thus able to decrease the demand for refrigerators (and other consumer durables). The same type of reasoning applied to the limit on the maximum payment period. Ignoring interest costs, if you owe $1,200 on something and can repay it over a two-year period, then your cost per month is $50. But if the payment period is shortened to one year, then your monthly payment rises to $100—too high for many people to afford. Thus the Federal Reserve could also shorten the maximum payment period for consumer installment loans in order to decrease excess demand.

There were (and are) two main objections to the consumer credit controls. The first was ideological: Many people felt that these controls were an unwarranted governmental intervention into the private economy. Business people, it was argued, should be allowed to make their own decisions about the specific terms of installment purchases—the government shouldn't interfere. A less theoretical argument was that the consumer credit controls were very difficult to enforce.[12] Try to imagine the difficulties involved in checking up on over 200,000 retail outlets for consumer durable goods to make sure that each sale conformed to regulations. Then add to this commercial banks, personal loan companies, and so forth, which also make loans to consumers. The result, as you would expect, was that the controls were widely violated. The job was just too big for an organization such as the Federal Reserve to handle.

[12]For an analysis of this problem with respect to selective credit controls generally, see Edward J. Kane, "Good Intentions and Unintended Evil: The Case Against Selective Credit Allocation," *Journal of Money, Credit and Banking,* February 1977 (Part 1), pp. 55–69.

Real Estate Controls   Between October 1950 and June 1953 the Federal Reserve was also given authority to set minimum downpayments and maximum payment periods for credit extended to finance the building of new houses. The purpose of this control was to prevent inflation in the housing market by limiting the demand for housing. As with consumer credit controls, serious problems of enforcement were encountered.

Interest Rate Ceilings on Time Deposits (Regulation Q)

The selective controls discussed so far are definitely selective controls. They were designed and have been used as measures to control the flow of credit going to specific sectors of the economy. There is one additional control that the Federal Reserve has, which, while not originally intended as a selective control, has on a couple of occasions been used by the Federal Reserve for that purpose. This is the authority given the Federal Reserve to set the maximum interest rate that commercial banks[13] may pay on time deposits, known as *Regulation Q*.[14] The original purpose of Regulation Q was to limit price competition among banks so that the high cost of attracting deposits would not tempt them to make risky loans. However, in 1966 and again in 1969 the Federal Reserve used its authority over time deposit rates to try to divert credit flows from one channel to another. To this extent many economists regard rate ceilings as a species of selective control.

Both 1966 and 1969 were years of strong inflationary pressures in the United States economy. Business demand for loans was exceptionally heavy, and business expenditures were contributing materially to the inflationary pressures. Open market interest rates were very high; indeed, they hadn't been as high since the Civil War. As open market rates moved above the ceiling rates established under Regulation Q, the Federal Reserve was put under considerable pressure to raise the ceiling so that the rate that banks could pay on their negotiable CDs would be competitive with market rates on Treasury bills, commercial paper, and so forth. The Federal Reserve refused to do this, with the result that in both cases (1966 and 1969) there was a very substantial drop in the volume of outstanding CDs as investors shifted out of them and into other short-term–debt instruments. During 1969, for example, the volume of CDs fell by about $12 billion, a drop of more than 50 percent from their 1968 level.

The purpose of the Fed's refusal to raise ceilings on time deposit rates was twofold: First, by not raising the ceiling in line with the rise in competitive rates, the Fed forced a drop in the volume of CDs. This loss in time deposits strained the commercial banking system's liquidity, with a consequent curtailment in the expansion of bank loans to businesses. Since it was felt that it was precisely these loans that were a major factor contributing to the inflation, this curtailment was regarded

[13]Actually, the Federal Reserve may set rate ceilings on time deposits only for member banks. However, the FDIC has the same authority over nonmember banks and follows the Fed's lead in this matter. The Federal Home Loan Bank Board sets ceiling rates for savings and loan associations.

[14]When it began operation, the Federal Reserve issued a series of lettered "regulations" dealing with its administrative powers. Thus Regulation A deals with discounting, Regulations T, U, and G with margin requirements, Regulation Q with ceiling rates on time deposits, and so forth.

as a good thing. The second purpose of holding the line on rate ceilings had to do with the relationship between commercial banks and other savings institutions. It was felt that if banks were permitted to raise time deposit rates, they would attract large amounts of deposits away from savings and loan associations. Not only would this have threatened the financial stability of the S&L industry, but it would also have substantially decreased the funds available for home building since more than 80 percent of S&L assets are in home mortgages. Why not also raise the rates that S&Ls were paying their depositors? It was felt that S&Ls could not afford to pay higher rates. When S&Ls raise deposit rates, they are raised on *all* deposits and consequently their cost of doing business rises tremendously. But their income depends largely on mortgages made in the past, and is to this extent fixed. Thus had S&Ls raised their deposit rates, many of them would likely have been caught in a "crunch" between rising costs and a relatively fixed income. Alternatively, if the Fed had raised the ceiling on commercial bank time deposit rates without a similar rise in S&L rates, the S&Ls would have been caught in a crunch between deposit withdrawals and illiquid assets (mortgages).[15] Under the circumstances, the Federal Reserve felt that it could both slow down the growth of bank loans to business and shelter the residential construction market by not raising ceiling rates on time deposits.

A number of economists have criticized the Federal Reserve's use of Regulation Q as a weapon of selective credit control in 1966 and 1969. First, it is felt that putting a damper on bank loans to business is best left to the general credit controls, such as open market operations. Second it is argued that if sheltering the home loan market from the consequences of tight money is a socially desirable goal, then some more forthright method of accomplishing this goal should be found (e.g., a direct subsidy).

16-3 CENTRAL BANKING POWERS OF THE TREASURY

In Chapter 15, dealing with the member bank reserve equation, it was pointed out that actions of the U.S. Treasury affect bank reserves in a number of ways. Principal among these is the manner in which the Treasury handles the money it collects from taxes and borrowing. To the extent that these funds are held in the Treasury's (tax and loan) accounts at commercial banks, bank reserves increase; to the extent they are held in the Treasury's deposit at the Federal Reserve, bank reserves decrease. There is another aspect to the financial operations of the Treasury, not yet mentioned, which some observers feel give it powers *comparable* to those of the central bank. This is *debt management,* that is, the way in which the Treasury chooses to manage the outstanding public debt. It is necessary to emphasize that debt manage-

---

[15]The reader may wonder why S&L depositors didn't shift their savings to open market investments, such as Treasury bills. One answer is that many did. The result was a serious slowdown in the flow of funds going into S&Ls and a consequent large volume of loans being made from the FHLBB to individual associations. Another answer, however, is that open market debt is not nearly as good a substitute for an S&L deposit as a savings account at a bank. A rise in bank rates, unaccompanied by a rise in S&L rates, would almost surely have resulted in net withdrawals from the latter.

ment does *not* affect the money supply. But it does do something that seems quite similar.

Debt Management

One way to view the effect on the economy of a change in the money supply is that it changes total liquidity. Money is a perfectly liquid asset, and therefore an increase in the money supply increases the economy's liquidity and vice versa. But money is not the *only* liquid asset. All other financial instruments possess some liquidity —not as much as money, perhaps, but nevertheless *some* liquidity. Moreover, different financial instruments have different degrees of liquidity. In particular, short-term debt is generally regarded as being more liquid than long-term debt (see Chapter 10). Thus if we could increase the amount of short-term debt and decrease the amount of long-term debt, the liquidity of the economy would be increased. Conversely, decreasing short-term and increasing long-term debt would decrease liquidity. In this view, then, changing the maturity structure of the economy's outstanding debt has effects similar to (though not so powerful as) changing the money supply.

We do not, of course, have any control over the maturity of most of the total debt outstanding; most debt is contracted among individuals and corporations, and its maturity is a matter of private negotiation. There is, however, a part of the total debt that we *do* have control over. This is the *public debt.* The public debt is managed by the Treasury, and in performing this management function the Treasury can and does decide on the debt's maturity structure. That is, the Treasury can and does decide whether to issue short-term Treasury bills or long-term government bonds. In making such decisions, some economists believe that the Treasury is willy nilly exercising a sort of second-class monetary policy.

The potential influence of Treasury debt management policies on the behavior of the economy remains obscure. The best evidence, though not conclusive, indicates that the influence is probably quite weak.[16] However this may be, two points need to be noted: First, the Treasury does not now use its debt management powers as a macroeconomic stabilization weapon; the maturity structure of the debt is managed with a view to keeping the interest charges on the public debt as low as possible, nothing more. Second, it is very doubtful that debt management can do anything that monetary policy, properly so-called, cannot do faster, better, and cheaper.

16-4 REVIEW QUESTIONS

1 Explain why open market operations are the *major* tool of monetary policy, instead of discount rate policy or variations in reserve requirements.

---

[16]See James E. Van Horn and David A. Bowers, "Liquidity Impact of Debt Management," *Southern Economic Journal,* April 1968, pp. 526–537.

2   What is lagged reserve accounting? Why does it cause problems for Federal Reserve control of the money supply?
3   Explain how margin requirements might make credit tight in the stock markets even though it was easy in the rest of the economy. Describe a situation where such a state of affairs might be a good thing.
4   Explain the theory of debt management. Do you think it should be used to help stabilize the economy? Why or why not?

PART 7

MONETARY THEORY

The United States does not have a centrally planned economy as does, for example, the Soviet Union. We make no collective attempt to coordinate the economic activities of the millions of individuals who comprise our labor force or the hundreds of thousands of business firms where these people work. Instead, the production, distribution, and consumption of goods and services in our economy is left to the interplay of supply and demand in the marketplace. Most people seem to prefer this type of economic system, apparently feeling that it combines both freedom and efficiency. Nevertheless, such a system almost inevitably results in total economic activity being carried on at an irregular pace. Since business people are free to set their own prices, a general rise in prices—inflation—sometimes occurs. Since business people are not told how many workers they must employ, a general wave of unemployment—recession—sometimes occurs. We would naturally like to reduce the magnitude of these swings in prices and employment, since a great many people get hurt when they happen. The problem is how to do it.

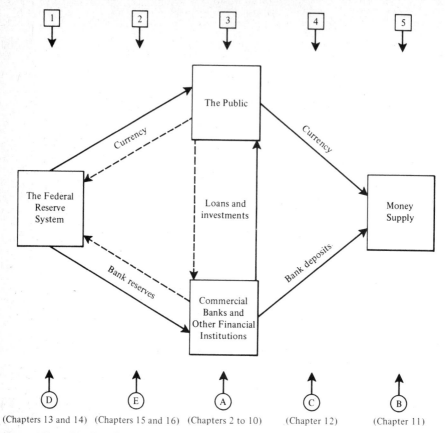

Figure VII-1   Detail of Figure 1-1.

What we need to achieve this goal is some macroeconomic stabilization mechanism with three characteristics: (1) It must be socially controllable; that is, it must be susceptible to deliberate and positive manipulation by the federal government. (2) It must be consistent with a market-guided economic system. And (3) it must work —must be powerful enough to slow down the upward thrust of prices during an inflation and to check the decline in employment during a recession. It should come as no surprise to the reader that monetary policy is widely regarded as such a mechanism. Consider Figure VII-1. This figure, which is taken from Figure 1-1 of Chapter 1, indicates in broad outline how monetary policy is carried out: By controlling the reserve base of the banking system, the Federal Reserve is able to control (within limits) the total money supply of the United States. Clearly, this mechanism fits admirably well the first two of the three characteristics noted previously. The determination of the money supply (monetary policy) is subject to social control; that is, monetary policy is conducted by an agency of the federal government, the Federal Reserve System. Moreover, monetary policy is ideally suited to a free-enterprise economy. Fundamentally, monetary policy consists only in having the

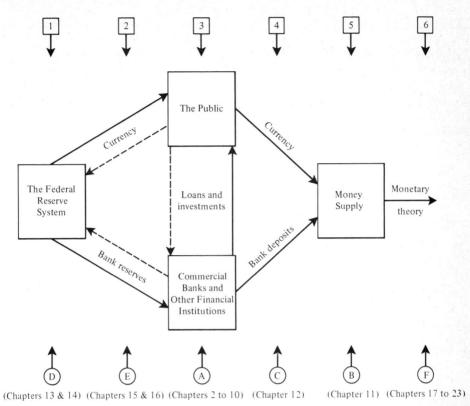

Figure VII-2   Detail of Figure 1-1.

Federal Reserve buy and sell government securities in the open market—something anyone else may do, too. No coercion is involved; no one is forced to do anything they don't want to do.

But what about the third required characteristic? Is monetary policy powerful enough to stabilize the economy? Will it work? It is this question that we shall now begin to consider. It is essential that the reader keep in mind, however, that a simple answer to this question does not exist. For note that what we are asking, basically, is this: What role do changes in the size of the money supply play in the determination of our national income? This is a very big question indeed. It quite literally involves millions of economic decisions made by consumers, industrialists, financiers, government officials, and so on. We cannot query each of these people about each decision he or she has made, nor can we conduct a controlled, laboratory experiment of the economy. In other words, the answer to our question is not directly observable.

But if the question is important and if we cannot answer it by direct observation, what other choice do we have? The answer is that it is necessary to construct a *theory* of the role played by the money supply in the functioning of our economic system. This is what Chapters 17 through 23 are about. In terms of Figure 1-1, we now add an additional step to our understanding of the monetary process of the United States. This can be seen by comparing Figures VII-2 and VII-1. The added element is the arrow on the right marked "6" above and "F" below: monetary theory.

A final warning is in order. Monetary theory is currently a matter of intense controversy among professional economists. People who consider themselves "practical" are frequently inclined to turn a deaf ear to such "academic" debates. But do not be misled by the abstract nature of the arguments. A great deal depends on who is right and who is wrong. In the entire field of monetary economics, there is perhaps no more "practical" subject than monetary theory.

17

Some Preliminaries

The purpose of this chapter is threefold: First, it is necessary to define certain aggregate economic concepts and indicate how they are measured. This discussion will be brief. The second purpose of the chapter is to contrast, in nontechnical terms, the two foremost theories of the role played by the quantity of money in our economy. It is necessary to emphasize the *nontechnical* nature of this discussion. The intent is not to explain the theories themselves, but to show the reader what to be on the lookout for when the theories *are* discussed in later chapters. Finally, the third purpose of this chapter is to give some indication of why the controversy is important.

17-1 SOME SOCIAL STATISTICS

Monetary theory is concerned with the role played by money in the determination of certain key, overall measures of how well the economy is performing. Among these measures, the three that are referred to most frequently are: unemployment; national income, or gross national product; and the general price level.

The Rate of Unemployment

Every month the Bureau of Labor Statistics of the U.S. Department of Labor collects and publishes data on labor-force participation. Although the data collected are broken down by age, sex, race, and so on, from our viewpoint the most important statistic published is the overall *unemployment rate,* which is expressed as a percentage of the total labor force. Thus when it is reported in the newspapers that the unemployment rate is, say, 5.3 percent, this means that 5.3 percent of our total labor force was unemployed last month.

To be considered unemployed, an individual must not only be unemployed, but also able to work, looking for work, and willing to work. Thus people who are sick or retired or who have voluntarily withdrawn from the labor force (such as students and housewives) are not included in the statistics. Additionally, anyone who is employed at all, even part time, is considered employed; that is, no distinction is made between part-time and full-time employment.

The only other point we need take note of is the idea of *full employment.* By full employment is *not* meant zero unemployment. At any given time there will be a certain number of people who are between jobs, that is, who have either quit or been laid off one job and have not yet started another. Thus to have *everyone* employed would require that workers could not move from job to job in order to better themselves, and that employers could not dismiss workers because of individual incompetence or technological change. Consequently, some positive amount of unemployment is generally considered both necessary and desirable—a concomitant of the free-enterprise economy. The question is, How much unemployment can we have and still regard the work force as fully employed? There is no good answer to this question. By custom, more than anything else, economists have come to regard an unemployment rate of 5 percent as "full" employment. This definition is admittedly arbitrary.

Gross National Product and All That

A second indicator of our aggregate economic well being is *gross national product* (GNP). Intuitively, GNP is the nation's total income. Definitionally, GNP is the country's total output of currently produced goods and services valued at current market prices. Data on GNP are published every three months and are expressed in annual terms, seasonally adjusted. In other words, a reported GNP of, say, $1,500 billion means that if the country produced goods and services for the whole year at the rate that they were produced for the past quarter, then it would produce $1,500 billion worth of goods and services. Note that GNP is a measure of *current* output only; it is *not* a measure of all market activity. The sale of a used car, for example, would not be included in GNP since by definition a used car has not been currently produced. By the same token, most financial transactions are excluded from GNP. The purchase of a common stock, e.g., simply represents the transfer of ownership of an already existing asset, not the production of a new asset. Finally, it is necessary to mention that in order to avoid counting the same thing more than once, only the *final* sales of goods and services are recorded in GNP accounts. Suppose, for example, that a tire manufacturer sells tires to an automobile manufacturer, which puts them on the automobiles it sells to consumers. Since the price of the tires is included in the final sale price of the automobile, to count both these sales would be to overstate the value of current output. Only one set of tires was produced, and they cannot logically be counted in GNP *both* when they are sold to the automobile manufacturer *and* when they are sold to the consumer.

A market transaction necessarily involves two people: a buyer and a seller. Since the money paid by the buyer is equal to the money received by the seller, it follows that GNP can be calculated in either of two ways: When calculated from the seller's viewpoint, GNP may be thought of as *income;* when calculated from the buyer's viewpoint, it may be thought of as *expenditures.* Both these aspects of GNP are used in measuring the following concepts, with which we shall be concerned in Chapters 18 to 23.

1 *Consumption Expenditures* These are the expenditures made by consumers for consumer goods and services. They include such intangibles as concerts and brokerage fees as well as such tangibles as new cars and overcoats. Note that the *motive* behind consumption expenditures is pleasure and that they are limited by consumer income. That is, people spend money on consumer goods in order to make their lives more comfortable, and because they can afford to.

2 *Investment Expenditures* These are the expenditures on plant and equipment made by business firms. It is important that the reader keep firmly in mind that the word "investment" is not here being used in its popular sense of any expenditure on an income-producing asset. While the purchase of a share in a mutual fund may be an investment for the individual, from the viewpoint of the economy as a whole it does not add to our productive capacity. Putting the matter somewhat differently, when an individual makes an investment by buying a mutual-fund share, someone else makes a disinvestment by selling that share. Aggregating over everyone in the economy, these financial investments and disinvestments cancel out, leaving us with only additions to our productive capacity. Note that the *motive* lying behind investment is profit; new additions are made to our capital stock because business people believe it will be profitable to do so.

3 *Government Expenditures on Goods and Services* These are, of course, just what they sound like—the expenditures made by federal, state, and local governments for highways, schools, parks, armies, and so on. Note that the *motive* behind government expenditures is political; that is, it is not a function of other economic factors, such as profit and income.

4 *Taxes* These are funds collected involuntarily from individuals and corporations by the government. Although their purpose is to finance the government, note that total taxes may be less than, equal to, or greater than government expenditures since the government may also finance itself by borrowing.

5 *Personal Income* This is the total income receipts of individuals (as opposed to corporations). It includes wages, interest, rent, and profit.

6 *Personal Disposable Income* This is the income that individuals have avail-

able after they pay their income taxes. By definition, it is equal to personal income minus personal income taxes.

7 *Personal Savings* Personal disposable income may be either spent on consumption or saved. Thus, by definition, personal savings are equal to personal disposable income minus consumption expenditures. Once income has been saved, it may then be invested, either directly or indirectly.

The General Price Level

Everyone has heard the TV comedian make a joke, or the conservative business person make a complaint, that today's dollar is only worth 50 cents (or some such). Have you ever wondered exactly what was meant by this? The first step in understanding it is, of course, easy enough. To say that the dollar is only worth 50 cents is simply to say that $1 will today buy only half as much as it used to. But how do we know how much $1 will buy, both then and now? And what do we mean by "then," anyhow?

Statements about the declining value of the dollar are really indirect ways of talking about inflation. By inflation is meant a general rise in prices. Thus, to say that $1 is only worth half as much as it was ten years ago is also to say that the price level has doubled in the past ten years. Rather than talking about the value of the dollar, therefore, it is more straightforward to talk about inflation. The question is, How do we measure it? How do we know if, since 1970, prices have gone up by 100 percent, 43 percent, or by some other percent? Changes in the general price level are measured by using a *price index.* While there are a number of price indexes published regularly, we shall briefly describe only two: the *consumer price index* and the *GNP deflator.*

Consumer Price Index The price index that is best known among the general public is the *consumer price index.* This index is computed monthly by the Department of Labor, and during times of rapidly rising prices it is frequently the subject of front-page stories in the newspapers. The consumer price index attempts to measure the cost of a typical market basket of goods and services to middle-class urban families. It does this by collecting prices on several hundred consumer goods, weighting each good by its importance in the typical consumer budget, and then computing a weighted average of these prices. To illustrate the procedure, assume the following hypothetical market basket of three consumer goods:

Consumer good	Percentage of consumer budget spent	1970 Prices	1980 Prices
Food	30	$200	$400
Clothing	20	$100	$100
Housing	50	$300	$400

Our interest lies in comparing the 1980 price level with the 1970 price level. To do this, we shall let 1970 be the *base year* and express the price level in 1980 relative to this base. The weighted price level for 1970 is found by multiplying each price by its weight, adding these products together, and then dividing the whole thing by the sum of weights. Thus,

$$\text{Price level in 1970} = \frac{(30)(200) + (20)(100) + (50)(300)}{100}$$

$$= 230$$

Doing the same thing for 1980 gives

$$\text{Price level in 1980} = \frac{(30)(400) + (20)(100) + (50)(400)}{100}$$

$$= 340$$

Expressing the 1980 price level as a percent the 1970 price level gives

$$\frac{\text{Price level in 1980}}{\text{Price level in 1970}} = \frac{340}{230}$$

$$= 1.48 \text{ or } 148\%$$

Thus, on this basis, we would say that between 1970 and 1980 prices rose by 48 percent.

There are several conceptual difficulties with the consumer price index. Perhaps the one most easily seen from the example just given is that the measured change in prices depends as much on the weights used as it does on prices. As consumer tastes change over time, the weights used become increasingly unrealistic; at the same time, severe difficulties of continuity are encountered when the weights are changed. Another serious problem is that of qualitative change. Technological improvements in goods may cause some prices to increase, but such improvements are not captured by the consumer price index. For these and other reasons, most economists feel that the consumer price index is most accurate when measuring large price movements during short periods of time.

The GNP Deflator   For statistical work in analyzing the aggregate behavior of the United States economy, most economists prefer to use the *gross national product deflator* as their measure of price movements. The GNP deflator is calculated in the following manner: First, the current-year GNP is calculated using current-year prices. Next, the current-year GNP is calculated using base-year prices. The ratio of these two GNPs implies a price level change, which is called the GNP deflator.

To illustrate, assume an economy in which only three goods are produced: automobiles, houses, and potatoes. The quantity of production and relevant prices are as follows:

1980 Production	1980 Prices	1970 Prices
4 million automobiles	$ 5,000	$ 4,000
10 million bushels of potatoes	$ 10	$ 5
200,000 houses	$20,000	$15,000

The gross national product in 1980 is thus

1980 GNP = (4 million)($5,000) + (10 million)($10) + (200,000)($20,000)
         = $24,100 million

Next, we may calculate what the value of GNP in 1980 *would have been* if 1970 prices had still prevailed:

1980 GNP in 1970 prices = (4 million)($4,000) + (10 million)($5)
                              + (200,000)($15,000)
        = $19,050 billion

Taking the ratio of the two, we obtain

$$\frac{1980 \text{ GNP}}{1980 \text{ GNP in 1970 prices}} = \frac{\$24,100 \text{ billion}}{\$19,050 \text{ billion}}$$

$$= 1.27 \quad \text{or } 127\%$$

On this basis, we would say that between 1970 and 1980 prices rose by 27 percent.

The GNP deflator is preferred by economists as an index of price movements largely because of its comprehensiveness. Where the consumer price index is based on price changes in a limited number of goods, the GNP deflator reflects the price changes of all goods and services entering into GNP. Nevertheless, many of the same problems arise with both indexes, especially that of qualitative improvements. Additionally, the GNP deflator is available only on a quarterly (three-month) basis, which limits its usefulness for short-term analysis.

Nominal and Real   Two words the student should get used to because they will be used frequently are "nominal" and "real." By *nominal* is meant the change in some economic variable measured in *current* prices. For example, we might speak of the change in nominal wages, or nominal income. In so doing we would mean the actual dollar change in wages or income between two periods. In contrast, a change in *real* wages or income would be the change after correcting for changes in the price level. Suppose, for example, that the wage rate for plumbers was $15 an hour in 1975 and $20 an hour in 1980. We would then say that the *nominal* wages of plumbers had risen from $15 to $20. However, suppose also that during this same time prices had risen by 20 percent. We would then say that the *real* wages of plumbers had risen from $15 to $16.66. This latter figure is derived by dividing the 1980 wage rate by the 1980 price index; that is,

$$\frac{\$20}{1.2} = \$16.66$$

The purpose of making the distinction between nominal and real changes is to distinguish changes that reflect merely higher prices from changes that reflect our economic well-being.

17-2 THE KEYNESIAN AND QUANTITY THEORIES OF MONEY: A NONTECHNICAL COMPARISON

As discussed in the introduction to Part Seven, monetary theory is an attempt to understand the role played by the quantity of money in the functioning of our economy. More specifically, we wish to know the answer to the following question: If the Federal Reserve changes the quantity of money, how will this affect the unemployment rate, national income (GNP), and the general price level? Since this question is too big to be answered by direct observation, it is necessary to develop a theory to deal with it. The purpose of such a theory is twofold: First, we want to explain something big with something small. That is, we want to explain a highly complicated set of phenomena (income, prices, and employment) by reference to a comparatively limited set of variables. We want, in short, to reduce the problem to manageable proportions by abstracting from a host of minor complications. Second, we want the theory to be able to generate testable hypotheses. It is not sufficient merely to *assert* that when the quantity of money is altered a particular chain of events occurs that leads ultimately to a change in national income. Each link in this chain must be scrutinized closely in the light of available evidence. Our interest lies not only in establishing if each such link exists, but also in how strong it is. Many issues in monetary theory ultimately turn on empirical questions—the size of a particular coefficient, for example.

It should come as no surprise to the reader to learn that there currently exist two competing theories of the role of money in the economy. Such disputes are not at all uncommon. Liberals and conservatives, for example, have different theories of politics; scientists have different theories of the origin of the universe; accountants have different theories of the proper way to value convertible debentures; and so forth. Economics would be a dull subject indeed if all economists always agreed on everything. The two monetary theories are called by different names by different people, but the most commonly used names are the *Keynesian theory*[1] and the *quantity theory*. Needless to say, each theory has its subgroups, and it is not always clear where certain people should be classified. The following discussion should therefore be regarded only as an impressionistic attempt to explain the major issues that divide the Keynesians and quantity theorists.

Modern Keynesian Monetary Theory

Keynesian monetary theory, as viewed by contemporary Keynesians, can be explained with the aid of Figure 17-1. The first thing to note about this figure is that

[1] Named after the British economist John Maynard Keynes (1883–1946).

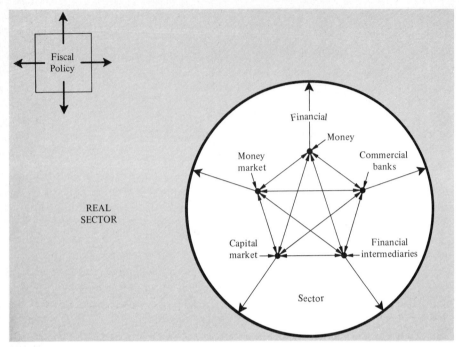

Figure 17-1 Modern Keynesian monetary theory: a schematic.

it divides the economy into two parts: the *financial sector* and the *real sector.* The financial sector (inside the large white circle) contains purely monetary phenomena: financial institutions, such as commercial banks and the various nonbank financial intermediaries, and financial assets such as short-term and long-term debt, common stocks, and money. The real sector (the shaded area) contains the tangible goods and services of the economy. It is the real sector that defines our standard of living. Overcoats and drill presses are real; jobs are real; relative income distribution is real. The real sector, that is, matters. If we increase the number of consumer goods available, then we are better off. But the same cannot be said of the financial sector. Doubling the quantity of money, debt, or common stocks makes no difference *unless it somehow affects the real sector.* The fundamental question of monetary theory is, therefore, How do changes in the financial sector affect the real sector?

Contemporary Keynesians have a complicated answer to this question. In the first place, note that the dot representing money in Figure 17-1 is the same size as all the other dots in the financial sector. The figure has been deliberately drawn this way to emphasize the fact that modern Keynesians regard money as one financial asset among many. They acknowledge, of course, that money is important. For one thing, there is the purely practical consideration that the quantity of money is controllable and that other financial assets are not. Additionally, money is perfectly liquid, in contrast with other assets. But while the Keynesians regard money as important, it is not thought of as dominating the financial sector of the economy; other financial instruments and institutions are important too.

Now suppose that there is a change in the quantity of money in the economy. Modern Keynesians see the consequences of this change as first setting up a complicated series of interactions within the financial sector. An increase in the quantity of money, for example, may make the public feel excessively liquid. People therefore attempt to switch from money to short-term debt instruments, which, in turn, lowers the short-term rate of interest. The change in the short-term interest rate will then affect long-term interest rates and the stock market, which will affect the behavior of savings and loan associations, insurance companies, and so forth. This series of events is known as *portfolio theory.* Modern Keynesians are very big on portfolio theory, believing that it is a key piece in the puzzle of monetary theory.

The portfolio adjustments that occur in the financial sector then spread to the real sector through the activities of all the various financial institutions. Note that Figure 17-1 has a definite boundary (the heavy line) separating the financial and real sectors. This boundary line indicates that contemporary Keynesians see the transmission of disturbances from the financial sector to the real sector as one of the major problems that monetary theory must analyze. That is, they think it is important that we understand the precise nature of the *transmission mechanism* linking the financial and real sectors—how it works and whether it is powerful or weak. In general, the Keynesian analysis of the transmission mechanism runs in terms of rates of return, that is, interest rates, profit rates, and the like. For example, a business person thinking about constructing a new apartment building may decide to do so only if cheap financing is available—that is, if interest rates are low. Thus a change in the financial sector (interest rates) has been transmitted to the real sector (apartment-building construction).

Now the thing to note about the modern Keynesian view of the role played by money in the economy is that it *may* be erratic, or weak, or both. There are two crucial points in the analysis: *portfolio adjustments* and the *transmission mechanism.* With respect to portfolio adjustments, Keynesians suggest that a change in the quantity of money may have different effects at different times, depending on the nature of the portfolio adjustments that are carried out. For example, an increase in the quantity of money may have one effect if there is a lot of long-term debt outstanding and very little short-term debt, and quite a different effect if the proportions of short-term and long-term debt are reversed. Additionally, other spontaneous changes may occur in the financial sector that affect the real sector but have nothing to do with the quantity of money. A stock-market crash, for example, or a change in the laws governing savings and loan associations may affect the real sector in the same way that money does. Therefore we need to know a great deal more about the nature of these portfolio adjustments, say the Keynesians, before we can predict the exact consequences of monetary policy. With respect to the transmission mechanism, Keynesians also tend to be somewhat skeptical as to its effects on the real sector. A major disturbance in the financial sector *may* be transmitted clearly and directly to the real sector, but then again it may not. Before we can say for certain, it is necessary to formulate and test many hypotheses.

Because of these reservations, modern Keynesians are reluctant to place exclusive reliance for economic stabilization on monetary policy. The quantity of money in the economy is important, they say, but not so important that we can afford to scrap all other macroeconomic stabilization devices. In particular, Keynesians advocate the vigorous use of *fiscal policy,* by which is meant the deliberate use of the federal government's powers to tax and spend to stabilize the economy. Fiscal policy operates *directly* on the real sector of the economy (see the box in the upper-left-hand corner of Figure 17-1). For example, a reduction in personal income taxes will directly affect personal disposable income; and consumers, having more take-home pay, will buy more consumer goods and thus stimulate the economy. Or a massive governmental program of highway construction will obviously stimulate the construction industry, the automobile industry, the petroleum industry, and so forth. Because of their insistence that economic stabilization requires the use of *both* fiscal and monetary policy, modern Keynesians are sometimes called *fiscalists.*

The Modern Quantity Theory of Money

Although there are a number of minor points of contention, contemporary proponents of the *quantity theory of money* tend to see the economy in terms of the same set of variables as the Keynesians. The quantity theorists, that is, do not totally reject the Keynesian analysis and set up an entirely different way of viewing the world. The differences that divide the two groups are more subtle than that. Indeed, the distinction between the two theories is very largely a matter of emphasis—a difference in degree rather than kind. But do not be misled by these analytical similarities into thinking that it therefore doesn't matter which theory is correct. The *consequences* of the two theories, especially the political consequences, are quite dissimilar and quite profound.

The general nature of the modern quantity theory and its major points of contrast with the Keynesian theory can be understood with the aid of Figure 17-2. The first thing to note about this figure is that it contains the same ingredients as Figure 17-1: the distinction between the real and financial sectors, the institutions and instruments of the financial sector, and fiscal policy (in the upper left-hand corner). Note also, however, that the arrangement of these ingredients is different than in Figure 17-1. The first point of difference is that the quantity of money now occupies the central position in the figure and is represented by a dot that is substantially larger than any other element in the financial sector. The purpose of drawing the figure this way is to give the impression that quantity theorists regard money as the driving force in the financial sector, an asset that totally dominates all other financial instruments. As a consequence of this view of money as a variable of overriding importance, modern quantity theorists tend to be much less concerned than Keynesians about the portfolio adjustments taking place throughout the rest of the financial sector. Of course, quantity theorists do not ignore these adjustments or even think them unimportant. But the pulse beat, so to speak, of changes in the quantity of money is so strong, and the resistances offered it by other variables so weak, that portfolio adjustments are relegated to a position of secondary importance by the quantity theorists.

A second point of contrast between the quantity theorists and the Keynesians lies in the nature of the transmission mechanism, the mechanism that transmits impulses from the financial sector to the real sector. Unlike the Keynesians, the

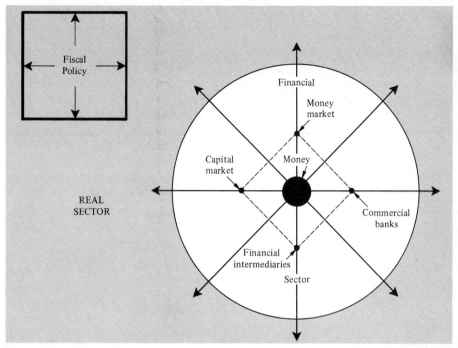

Figure 17-2 The modern quantity theory of money: a schematic.

quantity theorists see no particular difficulty about this mechanism. This point is made in the Figures 17-1 and 17-2 in two ways: First, the heavy boundary line between the financial and real sectors in Figure 17-1 is omitted in Figure 17-2, indicating that the quantity theorists do not see the transmission mechanism as a major analytic problem. Second, note that in Figure 17-1 money is not connected directly with the real sector. Rather, for Keynesians the changes in the quantity of money are transmitted to the real sector only indirectly through the various financial institutions. In contrast, Figure 17-2 has arrows running straight from the quantity of money to the real sector. Quantity theorists, that is, argue that the quantity of money has a *direct* effect on the real sector in addition to its indirect effects via portfolio adjustments. Fundamentally, the quantity theory holds that if people are given larger money balances, they will spend more and this spending will affect nominal income.

Finally, note that Figure 17-2 has a heavy border around fiscal policy. Quantity theorists tend to have relatively little faith in fiscal policy. First, they feel that fiscal policy is unnecessary; they suggest that monetary policy alone is quite adequate to do the job of stabilizing the economy and hence there is little need for fiscal policy. Second, quantity theorists have serious reservations about how effective fiscal policy really is. They would argue, for example, that an increase in government spending will cause a decrease in private spending, with the result that total spending will rise very little. Because of their emphasis on monetary policy as the primary method of economic stabilization, modern quantity theorists are sometimes called *monetarists*.

Summary

To summarize, modern quantity theorists believe that the quantity of money is the dominant variable in the financial sector, that changes in the quantity of money directly affect the real sector, and that monetary policy alone is sufficient to stabilize the economy. In contrast, modern Keynesians believe that money is only one financial asset among many, that changes in the quantity of money affect the real sector only indirectly via portfolio adjustments, and that economic stabilization requires the use of fiscal policy as well as monetary policy.

17-3 WHO CARES?

At this point the reader may be inclined to shrug his or her shoulders and ask what difference it all makes. The impassioned debates between the Keynesian and quantity theorists may seem terribly abstract, a mere technical squabble among professional economists. But in fact a great deal turns on who is correct in this matter. The debate has profound implications for the proper conduct of monetary policy and profound political implications. While a discussion of the implications for monetary policy would be premature at this point, a brief discussion of the political implications may help the reader understand the importance of the controversy between the Keynesians and the quantity theorists.

Recall from the introduction to Part Seven that there are three characteristics of a macroeconomic stabilization mechanism: It must be socially controllable; it must be consistent with a market-guided economic system; and it must work. Monetary economists, of course, are concerned primarily with the last of these characteristics: Is monetary policy an effective method of stabilizing the economy? But how this question is answered necessarily has implications for the second characteristic, and it is the second characteristic that has embedded in it the seeds of political controversy. To be specific, if monetary policy is judged to be ineffective, then some other means of economic stabilization must be found. But this "other means" is likely to involve more direct governmental intervention into the private economy than monetary policy. Thus monetary theory, though seemingly an abstract and severely intellectual discipline, nevertheless contains much of the passion and color of the political arena.

The quantity theory view of the role played by money in the economy is fundamentally conservative in its political consequences. This is not to say that the quantity theory is deliberately designed to lend support to a conservative politics. But the theory is conservatively oriented in its *implications*. For monetary policy is generally the least obtrusive of stabilization devices; it blends easily into the background of a market economy. If it can be demonstrated that monetary policy alone is sufficient to ensure us full employment without inflation, then conservative politics will have been strengthened substantially.

In contrast, the implications of Keynesian monetary theory tend to support a liberal approach to political issues. The Keynesian theory, it will be recalled, places less reliance on monetary policy for economic stabilization, insisting that fiscal policy is needed also. But fiscal policy, which utilizes the government's powers to tax and spend, tends to be more interventionist than monetary policy. When taxes are reduced, for example, some people are more likely to benefit than others—taxes can be cut for the poor or the rich, corporations or individuals, elderly or young. In the same fashion, increased government spending can be directed toward specific areas, specific industries, and the needs of specific groups (urban renewal, for example). Thus fiscal policy brings economic stabilization more clearly into the political spotlight and makes market decisions more subject to the political process. Conservatives tend to see this as a threat, liberals as an opportunity.

It should be emphasized again that monetary theory is not politically motivated. The problems that monetary economists wrestle with are how monetary policy works and how effective it is. Insofar as most economists are concerned, the political chips will have to fall where they may. But the reader should nevertheless be aware that a good deal is at issue in the controversy between the Keynesians and the quantity theorists.

17-4 THE NEXT SIX CHAPTERS

In Chapters 18 and 19 we shall discuss the development of the quantity theory of money, beginning with its traditional origins (Chapter 18) and carrying it through to its current state (Chapter 19). In Chapters 20 to 22 we shall do the same for the Keynesian theory. Finally, in Chapter 23 we shall compare the two theories, both theoretically and empirically.

17-5 REVIEW QUESTIONS

1 Are you employed or unemployed according to the Department of Labor's definition?
2 If Americans were suddenly to switch from automobiles to motor scooters as their primary means of transportation, what would be the implications for the accuracy of the consumer price index?
3 If you were to buy an antique car for $15,000, would this transaction enter into Gross National Product?
4 Which of the government's stabilization policies, monetary policy or fiscal policy, is the more interventionist?

18

The Traditional Quantity Theory of Money

In about 1734 Richard Cantillon, an Irish-born banker living in Paris, wrote: "In general, I estimate that an effective increase of money in the State causes a proportional increase of consumption, which gradually produces price increases."[1] Cantillon was a quantity theorist.

The quantity theory of money is a very old and very persistent theoretical explanation of the macroeconomic role of money in an economy. The persistence of this theory from classical times to the present day is probably due to its strong common-sense appeal. In its traditional version, the quantity theory simply asserts the two propositions implicit in Cantillon's statement: (1) An increase in the quantity of money in a country will cause people to spend more; and (2) this greater spending will cause an increase in nominal national income (GNP). Most people find

[1] Richard Cantillon, *Essai sur la nature du Commerce en général* [1755], Geo. H. Ellis, Boston, Mass., 1892, p. 215.

both propositions straightforward and intuitively satisfying. They feel that they themselves behave as the first proposition asserts, and they can understand that if everyone else behaves as they do, then more goods will be produced, or prices will rise, or both.

While modern quantity theorists do not put the matter into such simple terms, they nevertheless see the role played by money as straightforward. According to their view, the Federal Reserve controls the supply of money and the public controls the demand for money. In this way, monetary theory is cast in the familiar mold of economic analysis: supply and demand. And, just as supply and demand jointly determine price and quantity in microeconomic analysis, so also price and quantity are jointly determined by supply and demand in the quantity theory of money. The difference in this case is that by *price* is meant the *price level* and by *quantity* is meant *real national income*. The product of the two, of course, is nominal national income, i.e., GNP expressed in current market prices.

We have already discussed at length (Chapters 2 to 16) the mechanics whereby the Federal Reserve System dominates the money supply. Although there is some slippage, or imprecision, in this mechanism, there is very little doubt that on the average the Fed can control the quantity of money within fairly narrow limits. (Whether it *does* is another question.) Since the determinants of the supply of money are known, quantity theorists therefore argue that monetary theory reduces to a theory of the *demand* for money. Thus, according to the quantity theorists, the fundamental question of monetary theory is, very simply, What are the determinants of the demand for money? Because this question is so basic, it is necessary to be clear about what it means. In ordinary usage, the words "money" and "income" are frequently interchanged. Thus, when speaking of someone who is well-to-do, it is common practice to say that the person "has a lot of money" when in fact what is meant is that the person earns a lot of income. Don't confuse money and income. When we ask why people demand money, we do *not* mean income. Rather, we are talking about money in the sense of *money balances*. Why do people and corporations hold a certain amount of money in the bank?

There have been a number of answers to this question. For the sake of clarity, it will be best to develop the subject historically. In this chapter, consequently, we shall discuss the early formulations of the quantity theory. In Chapter 19 we shall discuss the modern quantity theory.

18-1 THE TRANSACTIONS-VELOCITY APPROACH

As noted, the classical theory of money held that the more money people have, the more they will spend; and the more they spend, the greater nominal national income will be. This view of the role of money in the economy was given its most definitive statement in the writings of the great American economist Irving Fisher about seventy years ago.[2] Because Fisher, like the classical writers before him, focused

[2]Irving Fisher, *The Purchasing Power of Money,* The Macmillan Company, New York, 1911, especially chap. 8.

attention on the reasons why people *spend* money, his theory is usually referred to as the *transactions-velocity approach* to monetary theory.

The Equation of Exchange

The centerpiece of the transaction-velocity approach to monetary theory is the *equation of exchange.* The equation of exchange is, in fact, an identity; that is, it is necessarily true by definition at all times and under all circumstances. To see that this is so, and to help the reader in understanding the nature of the equation of exchange, it is best to begin by putting the matter in its most tautological (circular) form. To do so, consider the simplest possible market transaction—buying a loaf of bread in a grocery store, say. If the loaf of bread costs 50 cents, then when you buy it you will *spend* 50 cents and the grocer will *receive* 50 cents. That is, the amount of money you spend is necessarily equal to the amount of money the grocer receives. But this same statement holds equally well for all market transactions. Thus we can write that in the aggregate

Total money expenditures for goods and services
= total money receipts from the sale of goods and services (1)

Equation (1) is merely an identity; in itself it tells us nothing that we didn't already know. But don't dismiss it on that account. Remember, for example, that a balance sheet is also an identity, but it is certainly a useful business device. What is needed to make eq. (1) a useful tool for economic analysis is a classification of each side of the equation in meaningful terms, that is, a classification in terms of those variables that we are interested in.

First, consider the right-hand side of eq. (1), total money receipts from the sale of goods and services. This is the exchange transaction when viewed from the seller's side, and therefore it immediately suggests that prices are somehow involved. We can lend concreteness to this idea in the following fashion. Let us suppose that we have the ability to count each and every market transaction in the economy during a given period of time, say, one year. Keep in mind that what we are counting are transactions, not the goods themselves. Thus, when an automobile is sold, that is one transaction, and when a pencil is sold, that also is one transaction. At the end of the year we would therefore have an accurate count of the total number of transactions that took place during the past twelve months. Now suppose that in addition to keeping count of the number of transactions, we also keep an accurate record of the price at which each transaction is made. At the end of the year we could add up all these prices and then take their mean, or average, which would give us the *average price* at which all transactions occurred. Finally, by multiplying these two magnitudes together, we obtain the total money receipts from the sale of goods and services during the year. That is,

Total money receipts from the sale of goods and services
= average price of transaction X total number of transactions (2)

Next consider the left-hand side of eq. (1), total money expenditures for goods and services. Since we are trying to construct a theory of money, it seems sensible to have one component of our breakdown of total expenditures be the quantity of money in the economy. The question then becomes, What can we multiply the quantity of money by so that the product of the two equals total expenditures? But to ask the question is virtually to answer it. Consider a dollar bill, for example. During the course of one year, this dollar bill may be spent, say, ten times. If we then multiply this dollar bill by the number of times it was spent, we obtain the total expenditures carried out by that piece of money—in this case $10. To obtain the total expenditures for the entire economy, we *could* do this for each piece of money. But it is easier and logically amounts to the same thing to multiply the *total* quantity of money by its *average* rate of turnover, or *velocity.* Thus we can write, again as an identity,

Total money expenditures on goods and services
$$= \text{money supply} \times \text{velocity of money} \quad (3)$$

Substituting eqs. (2) and (3) into eq. (1) then gives

Money supply $\times$ velocity of money
$$= \text{average price of transaction} \times \text{total number of transactions} \quad (4)$$

Letting M = money, V = velocity, P = average price level, and T = transactions, eq. (4) can then be written as

$$MV = PT \quad (5)$$

Equation (5) is the *equation of exchange.* As indicated, it is an identity; that is, there is no possibility of its not being true. It is, in fact, simply a restatement of eq. (1). The equation of exchange is therefore *not* a theory, any more than a balance sheet is a theory. But the equation of exchange is nevertheless a good deal more useful than eq. (1) because it permits us to *develop* a theory of the role of money in the economy. We can do this by developing behavioral explanations for each of the four variables in eq. (5).

Money The determinants of the quantity of money in the economy should by now be thoroughly familiar. It is necessary to note only that the quantity of money is our control variable; that is, it is the one element in the equation of exchange that is determined by a deliberate act of public policy.

Prices The price level in the equation of exchange is viewed as a residual; it is seen as being wholly determined by the interactions of the other three variables: M, V, and T. This view of prices as being determinate is attributable in part, at least, to the classical assumption that all prices (including wage rates) are completely flexible in both an upward and downward direction.

Transactions   The behavior of transactions in the traditional quantity theory of money is more complex than the behavior of either money or prices.[3] It is most easily understood by distinguishing between the long and short run.

Transactions in the Long Run   In the long run—a period of time measured in years—the classical economists reasoned that a capitalist economy has as its natural point of equilibrium the full employment level of national income. Although the economy may temporarily (in the short run) move away from full employment, when it does so forces are generated within the economy that eventually move it back to full employment equilibrium. The classical argument for full employment equilibrium rested on a doctrine known as *Say's law of markets*. [4] It would take us too far afield to go thoroughly into Say's law, but the general idea is that if wages are flexible, then any sizable amount of unemployment in the economy will force wage rates down as workers compete for jobs. These lower wage rates will then stimulate the demand for more workers, and eventually the result will be a restoration of full employment (though at a lower wage rate).

Now the point to note is that full employment necessarily sets a maximum on the number of transactions taking place in the economy. If the work force is fully employed, then by definition it is producing all the goods and services it can: It cannot produce more. But if transactions cannot rise above the maximum imposed by full employment, and if Say's law will not (in the long run) let transactions fall below this same maximum, then transactions must move along the growth path of the economy, like a balloon bumping along a slanted ceiling.

In the long run, therefore, the classical quantity theorists thought of transactions as gradually becoming larger and larger as economic growth occurred. The consequence of this view can be readily seen if we hold M and V constant and solve the equation of exchange for P:

$$P = \frac{\overline{MV}}{T}$$

where the bars over M and V indicate that we are treating them as constants. In this case, the price level will fall as T rises because of economic development. Alternatively, if we treat only V as a constant, so that

$$P = \frac{M\overline{V}}{T}$$

then the price level P can remain unchanged in the long run only if the quantity of money M grows at the same rate as T. If M grows faster than T, there will be a secular (long-run) rise in prices—that is, an inflation.

---

[3]In fact, modern quantity theorists still regard the division of a change in nominal income between a change in prices and a change in real income as a major theoretical problem. See Milton Friedman, "A Theoretical Framework for Monetary Analysis," *Journal of Political Economy,* March/April 1970, p. 222.

[4]After the French economist Jean Baptiste Say (1767–1832).

It is worth calling to the reader's attention that we have now moved from a mere identity in eq. (1) to a full-fledged theory of money. In other words, now we can begin to see some of the consequences of changing the quantity of money and some of the possible policy choices open to us.

Transactions in the Short Run   It was recognized by the early quantity theorists that the economy does not always operate at full employment. The full employment level of national income was thought of as a point of *equilibrium* toward which the economy tends to move in the long run, but in the short run, a state of *disequilibrium* is possible. It takes time for wages to change and for employers to respond to the changes. Thus, in what Irving Fisher called the *transition*—the period between two points of long-run equilibrium—a change in the money supply might affect *both* the price level and the volume of transactions.

Suppose, for example, that for some reason there is a sharp decrease in the quantity of money. Assuming again that velocity is constant, it is apparent from the equation of exchange

$$M\overline{V} = PT$$

that if M falls, PT must also somehow fall. But the adjustment need not occur immediately in prices only. Instead, the early quantity theorists held that approximately the following sequence of events would occur: The decrease in the quantity of money would result in a smaller amount of money expenditures, and hence a smaller number of sales (transactions) would be made by business firms. This decreased volume of business transactions would cause workers to be laid off, and the unemployment rate would rise. The rise in unemployment, however, would bring wages down, and the lower wages would cause other prices to fall too. Eventually, wages and prices would fall by enough to restore full employment. Thus, although in the long run the effect of a decrease in the money supply would be a lower price level, in the short run the effect would be unemployment and a business recession.

In the opposite case, that of an increase in the quantity of money, transactions might also be affected in the short run. Thus, an expansion of the money supply during a recession might stimulate business and restore full employment more quickly than the natural forces of the marketplace.

Velocity   The behavior of velocity was the most crucial and most difficult theoretical problem faced by the early quantity theorists. And their most fundamental assumption, in this respect, was that velocity and money were independent of one another. By *independent* is meant that one does not change *because* the other does —in particular, that changes in velocity are not caused by changes in the quantity of money. It is easy to understand the necessity for this assumption by direct inspection of the equation of exchange $MV = PT$. Clearly, if a rise in M causes a like fall in V, then the two changes will offset each other and nothing will happen on the right-hand side of the equation *(PT)*. As Irving Fisher put it, if M and V vary inversely, then an "increase in the quantity of money would exhaust all its effects in reducing the velocity of circulation, and could not produce any effect on prices."

As we shall see, the assumption of independence between velocity and money was one of the major points on which John Maynard Keynes attacked the quantity theorists, and it remains an issue of contention between modern Keynesians and quantity theorists. Our immediate concern, however, is with the historical quantity theory, and we shall therefore accept (temporarily) the assumption of independence.

What determines velocity? Velocity, recall, is the average rate at which people spend their money, and so the question can be put alternatively as, What determines the rate at which people spend money? The early quantity theorists felt that there are primarily two aspects to the answer to this question: the payments mechanism and spending habits. The term *payments mechanism* refers to how often people are paid. To see how this affects velocity, consider the following very simple example: Imagine an individual whose annual salary is $12,000 and who is paid this $12,000 in a lump sum at the beginning of each year. Imagaine, further, that this person spends her money at a constant rate (i.e., an equal amount each day) in such a fashion that on the last day of the year her cash holdings drop to zero. The average cash balance of this person would then be one-half of $12,000, or $6,000; in the early part of the year she would be holding more than this amount, and in the last half of the year she would be holding less. Now the point to note is that if this person *receives* $12,000 and *holds* (on the average) $6,000, then the rate of turnover of her "money supply" is 2, which is to say that the velocity is 2. This can most readily be seen by reference to the equation of exchange. Think of PT as the value of the goods and services this individual has bought throughout the year, that is, the average price paid for them (P) times the number of things bought (T). Clearly PT = $12,000; that is, this person has purchased $12,000 worth of goods and services throughout the year. Her money supply (M) is $6,000—her average cash balance for the year. Then solving the equation of exchange $MV = PT$ for V gives

$$V = \frac{PT}{M}$$

and inserting the previous numbers into this equation gives

$$V = \frac{\$12,000}{\$6,000}$$

$$= 2$$

Next let us suppose that the payments mechanism changes so that this same individual is now paid $1,000 at the beginning of each month. She continues to spend her money at a constant rate, but now she draws her balance down to zero on the last day of every month rather than only on the last day of the year. Her average balance M will in this case be $500 each month and therefore $500 for the year. Since she will still buy $12,000 worth of goods and services throughout the year, her PT

will continue to equal $12,000. The velocity of circulation will therefore be 24; that is,

$$V = \frac{PT}{M}$$

$$= \frac{\$12,000}{\$500}$$

$$= 24$$

The point of the exercise is that by increasing the frequency with which this person is paid, we have caused velocity to rise. This will be true in general: The more often the payments mechanism causes people to be paid, the higher will be velocity.

But what about spending habits? The effect of spending habits on velocity can also be illustrated with the preceding example. Suppose that instead of spending $1,000 at a constant rate throughout the month, the individual spends $600 in the first half of the month and $400 in the second half. How will this affect her average cash balance? For the *first half* of the month the average cash balance will be $700; that is, between the first and the fifteenth of the month the balance drops from $1,000 to $400, and the mean of these two numbers is $700 ($1,000 + $400/2).[5] The average cash balance during the *second half* of the month is $200; that is, between the fifteenth and the thirtieth, the balance falls from $400 to $0. Taking the month as a whole, the average cash balance is simply the average of these two amounts, or $450 ($700 + $200/2). The changed spending pattern of this individual has therefore caused her average cash balance to fall from $500 to $450. This, in turn, will cause velocity to rise, as can be seen by solving the new equation of exchange. Thus, letting $PT = \$12,000$ (as before) and $M = \$450$,

$$V = \frac{PT}{M}$$

$$= \frac{\$12,000}{\$450}$$

$$= 26.6$$

so that where before the velocity was 24, now it is 26.6.

The early quantity theorists did not confine their analysis of velocity exclusively to the payments mechanism and spending habits. Various other factors, such as population density and the physical means of transporting money (e.g., trains and airplanes), were also seen as determining factors. But the analysis of the payments mechanism and spending habits is sufficient to illustrate the major conclusion the

---

[5]This assumes that the $600 spent in the first half-month is spent at a constant rate; the same assumption is made regarding the $400 spent in the second half-month.

early quantity theorists arrived at with respect to velocity: By and large, the velocity of money circulation is stable. In other words, velocity does not make large and erratic jumps from one year to the next—3 this year, 27 next year, 12 the following year, and so on. The basis of this conclusion lies in the nature of the determinants of velocity. Consider the payments mechanism. This is something that evolves slowly over time. Employers do not pay their workers weekly this year, annually next year, semimonthly the following year, and so on. The payments mechanism may change, of course, but it does so gradually and with a definite trend in one direction or the other. Thus, there is nothing inherent in the payments mechanism that would lead us to expect it to behave erratically. The same is true of spending habits. Indeed, *habits* are by definition actions that are repeated over and over again; if they are not repeated, then they aren't habits. Reasoning along these lines, the early quantity theorists deduced that velocity next year would be pretty much the same as it was this year. Not exactly the same, of course. That would be too much to ask of any economic relationship. But pretty much the same—predictable within a fairly narrow margin of error.

The consequence of this analysis of velocity for early monetary theory was profound. If (1) velocity is reasonably stable and predictable; (2) money and velocity are independent; (3) Say's law of markets results in full employment equilibrium in the long run; and (4) prices are determined by the other factors—if these things are true, then it follows that the price level and the quantity of money will tend to move in the same direction. It should not be inferred, however, that money and prices are necessarily proportional—for example, that a 10 percent increase in the money supply will necessarily bring about a 10 percent increase in the price level. Even in the long run, as we have seen, the volume of transactions T will grow because of economic development, and velocity V is likely to drift in one direction or another owing to changes in the payments mechanism, changes in spending habits, and so forth. And in the short run especially, both V and T are likely to wobble around a good deal. So the early quantity theorists did not argue that the relationship between money and prices is precise (except perhaps in the context of a very formal and static model). But they did argue that money and prices tend to move together in the same direction and that the primary cause of changes in the price level is changes in the quantity of money in the economy.

What does all this mean? It means that, beginning with the simple identity of eq. (1), we have now moved to a theory of monetary policy. That is, we have now developed a theoretical construct that tells us how the Federal Reserve should behave in order to cure some of the country's economic ills. Consider, for example, what appears likely to be one of the major economic problems of the decade of the 1980s: *inflation,* or a period of rapidly rising prices. But the quantity theory tells us that prices and the money supply tend to move in the same direction. It follows that the appropriate cure for inflation is to decrease the quantity of money (or, in an expanding economy, to slow down the growth rate of the money supply). The opposite conclusion also follows: In a period of deflation (falling prices) or recession (falling real income) the appropriate policy for the Federal Reserve to follow is to increase the money supply; an expansionary monetary policy will stimulate the economy. In short, the central bank can control movements in the price level by controlling movements in the money supply.

Sound simple? It *is* simple—too simple, perhaps. Certainly the modern Keynesians think so, and even contemporary quantity theorists would regard these conclusions as a simplistic statement of a more complex relationship. But at the very least, early versions of the quantity theory give us two things: a rule of thumb for understanding why gross swings in monetary policy occur and a set of empirical hypothesis that are subject to statistical investigation. We shall eventually discuss this latter point, but before doing so it will be helpful to take up an alternative formulation of the early quantity theory: the *cash-balance approach.*

18-2   THE CASH-BALANCE APPROACH

The early development of the cash-balance approach to the quantity theory of money is generally associated with the name of the English economist A. C. Pigou (1877–1959). Although Pigou published his most fundamental paper on the theory of money[6] only six years after Irving Fisher's major work appeared, in many ways Pigou was ahead of his time and is generally considered a bridge between traditional and contemporary quantity theorists. Pigou's theoretical research differs in a variety of ways from that of Fisher, but, as has become customary, we shall focus on only one of these differences.

Just as the centerpiece of the transactions-velocity approach to the quantity theory is the equation of exchange, so the centerpiece of the cash-balance approach is the so-called *Cambridge equation.* (Pigou, a Professor of Economics at Cambridge, was highly influential in shaping the way his colleagues thought about money.) Like the equation of exchange, the Cambridge equation is also an identity. Indeed, in a strictly mathematical sense it is the same identity. Because this is so, we need not go back to basics but can instead begin with eq. (5); that is, we need not demonstrate again the validity of the equation of exchange, but instead we shall simply use this as our point of departure.

The equation of exchange is, remember,

$$MV = PT \tag{5}$$

Now let us solve this equation for M. Thus,

$$M = \frac{PT}{V} \tag{6}$$

and we rewrite eq. (6) in the following form:

$$M = \frac{1}{V}\ (PT) \tag{7}$$

[6]A. C. Pigou, "The Value of Money," *Quarterly Journal of Economics,* November 1917, pp. 38–65.

Next let us define a symbol k such that

$$k = \frac{1}{V} \tag{8}$$

and then substitute k into eq. (7), which gives

$$M = kPT \tag{9}$$

Equation (9) is the Cambridge equation.

Mathematically sophisticated readers (and some who are not so sophisticated) may consider the foregoing bit of algebraic legerdemain absolutely trivial, a mere substitution of one symbol for another. If that's what you think, it only proves that (so far, at least) you're a better mathematician than you are an economist. Mathematically, of course, eqs. (6) to (9) *are* trivial. In fact, they are *meant* to be trivial. Their whole point is to demonstrate that if the equation of exchange is an identity, then so also is the Cambridge equation; the Cambridge equation, that is, must also be true under all conditions of time, place, and circumstance. But in terms of economic analysis, there are two substantial differences between these equations.

First, the most obvious difference between eqs. (5) and (9) is that the latter equation is expressed in terms of k, which is the reciprocal of velocity (that is, $k = 1/V$). But the word "reciprocal" expresses a mathematical relationship. The real question is, Does k have an *economic* interpretation? The answer, of course, is yes. Think about it a moment. If by *velocity* is meant how many times per year the money supply turns over in order to accommodate the economy's annual volume of sales, then k must be that fraction of the annual sales volume which is held in the form of *cash balances.* An example may help clarify this. Suppose that the annual dollar volume of sales PT in the economy is $1,500 billion and the money supply M is $300 billion. Then from these figures we would deduce that velocity is 5; that is,

$$MV = PT$$

$$V = \frac{PT}{M}$$

$$= \frac{\$1,500 \text{ billion}}{\$300 \text{ billion}}$$

$$= 5$$

But we can say equally well that cash balances are 1/5—that is, that people are, on the average, holding one-fifth of the annual sales volume in the form of cash balances. Thus, from the Cambridge equation

$$M = kPT$$

$$k = \frac{M}{PT}$$

$$= \frac{\$300 \text{ billion}}{\$1,500 \text{ billion}}$$

$$= 1/5$$

The difference between the two approaches involves more than mere mathematics. Each raises a substantially different set of questions. Where the transactions-velocity approach asks the question, Why do people *spend* money? the cash-balance approach asks the question, Why do people *hold* money? Milton Friedman, generally acknowledged as the leading contemporary quantity theorist, puts the matter this way:

> The essential feature of a money economy is that it enables the act of purchase to be separated from the act of sale. An individual who has something to exchange need not seek out the double coincidence—someone who both wants what he has and offers to exchange what he wants. He need only find someone who wants what he has, sell it to him for general purchasing power [money] and then find someone who has what he wants and buy it with general purchasing power [money].
>
> In order for the act of purchase to be separated from the act of sale, there must be something which everybody will accept as "general purchasing power"—this is the aspect of money emphasized in the transactions [-velocity] approach. But there must also be something which can serve as a temporary abode of purchasing power in the interim between sale and purchase. This is the aspect of money emphasized in the cash-balance approach.[7]

The second significant economic difference between the equation of exchange and the Cambridge equation is that where V is on the left-hand side of the former equation, k is on the right-hand side of the latter. Mathematically, of course, this is no difference at all; we may put anything anywhere as long as we observe the rules of algebra. But in terms of economic analysis, the Cambridge version of the quantity theory is highly suggestive of a wholly different approach. Take another look at eq. (9), which is repeated here for convenience:

$$M = kPT \tag{9}$$

The left-hand side of this equation is open to direct interpretation: It is simply the *supply* of money. But the right-hand side is also readily interpreted: It is that fraction of the annual sales volume of the economy which people are holding in the form of cash balances. In other words, it is the *demand* for money. The Cambridge equation

[7]Milton Friedman, *A Theoretical Framework for Monetary Analysis,* National Bureau of Economic Research, New York, 1971, NBER Occasional Paper 112, pp. 8–9.

thus has the happy property of casting monetary theory in a mold familiar to all students of economics: supply and demand.

To see how the Cambridge equation can be used to analyze the role played by the quantity of money in the economy, let us assume (as before) that the economy is in equilibrium with M = $300 billion, k = 1/5, and PT = $1,500 billion. Then, according to the Cambridge equation, $300 billion = 1/5 ($1,500 billion). People are holding just that quantity of cash balances which they want to hold; the supply of money is equal to the demand for money. Now suppose that, for whatever reason, the Federal Reserve increases the quantity of money in the economy from $300 billion to $400 billion. What is the response to this change on the right-hand side of the equation? To see the answer to this question, note that people now have larger cash balances than they want to hold. They only *want* to hold $1/5PT$ as cash balances, but now they have cash balances equal to $4/15PT$ (that is, $k = M/PT =$ $400 billion/$1,500 billion = 4/15). The supply of money, that is, exceeds the demand for money. People and business will therefore attempt to reduce their cash balances. They will do this by buying things—by spending their excess money balances on all the myriad things our economy offers: stocks, bonds, shirts, machines, and so on. But note that while *one* person can decrease the amount of cash balances he is holding, *everyone* taken together cannot—the money simply gets passed from hand to hand, like the game of "hot potato" children play. The result is a great churning of expenditures in the economy, and these expendituress cause PT to rise.

If transactions T are at or near their maximum because of full employment, then most of the rise in PT will be caused by a rising price level. In other words, in their efforts to reduce their cash balances, people will bid against one another for the things they buy, with the result that prices will be bid up—the classic case of demand-pull inflation where "too much money is chasing too few goods." Equilibrium will be restored only when prices have risen sufficiently that PT equals $2,000 billion. For when PT equals $2,000 billion, then people will once more be holding $1/5PT$ in the form of cash balances; that is, $400 billion/$2,000 billion = 1/5. The supply of money will once more be equal to the demand for money, and the system will be back in equilibrium.

The process also works in reverse. If the Federal Reserve should decrease the supply of money from $300 billion to $200 billion, then the public will have less money than it wants to hold; that is, the demand for money will exceed the supply. As a result, people will try to increase their cash balances by holding onto their money. But as in the previous case, these efforts will be frustrated in the aggregate. There is only so much money to go around, and not *everyone* can get more. But in its efforts to increase its cash balances, the public will decrease its expenditures, with the result that prices will fall. Prices will continue to fall until PT drops to $1,000 billion. At that point k will once again equal 1/5; that is, $k = M/PT$ = $200 billion/$1,000 billion = 1/5. The economy will then be back in equilibrium, with the supply of money equal to the demand for money.

18-3 THE INCOME VERSION OF THE CAMBRIDGE EQUATION

While the Cambridge equation $M = kPT$ seemed to contain considerable analytic power, it was nevertheless stated in an unsatisfactory form. Basically, there were two difficulties: First, there were severe problems of measurement. Remember that T refers to *all* transactions in the economy taking place during a given time period and that P is the average price at which all these transactions take place. The task of trying to measure concepts of such sweeping generality was formidable indeed. Second, it was not clear that P and T were what *should* be measured. T, for example, included such transactions as the purchase and sale of used houses. But the transfer of title to a house from one person to another does not make our society any wealthier; it is only the production of *new* goods and services that we are interested in. These and other considerations led economists to restate the Cambridge equation in terms of the gross national product accounts in the following manner. Let

Y = nominal national income
y = real national income
P = implicit GNP price deflator

By definition,

$$Y = Py$$

that is, nominal income equals real income times the price index. To lend concreteness to these definitions, suppose that *nominal* income (i.e., measured in current prices) is $800 billion in 1970 and $1,500 billion in 1980. Suppose, also, that the price index shows that 1970 = 100 and 1980 = 150. Then, noting that

$$y = \frac{Y}{P}$$

we would say that *real* income in 1980 was $1,000 billion. That is, real income in 1980 = $1,500 billion/1.5 = $1,000 billion.

Next we can restate the Cambridge equation in income terms:

$$M = kY \tag{10}$$

or

$$M = kPy \tag{11}$$

Note that k is now defined differently than it was before. k now expresses that fraction of its annual *income* (not transactions) which the public wants to hold in the form of cash balances.

This form of the Cambridge equation, called the *income version,* gives two additional insights into the traditional quantity theory of money: First, from eq. (10) it is apparent that the demand for money is regarded as proportional to nominal national income. In other words, if nominal income Y rises by 10 percent, so also will the demand for cash balances. k is the constant of proportionality, the coefficient that defines the relationship between the quantity of money in the economy and nominal national income.[8]

To see the second insight into the traditional quantity theory of money, rewrite eq. (11) in the form

$$\frac{M}{P} = ky \tag{12}$$

The left-hand side of this equation, M/P, is called *real cash balances,* which define the purchasing power value of a given stock of money. For example, if the nominal stock of money M in the economy remains the same and if prices P double, then real cash balances M/P will be halved. This concept of real cash balances is regarded as highly significant by modern quantity theorists. Its significance lies in the observation that although the Federal Reserve may be able to control the *nominal* amount of money M in the economy, it cannot control the *real* amount of money M/P because it cannot control the price level P. It is the public that controls the *real* amount of money by bidding prices up or down.

18-4 CRITICISMS OF THE TRADITIONAL QUANTITY THEORY

The traditional statement of the quantity theory of money came under severe criticism in the decades following the publication of J. M. Keynes's *General Theory of Employment, Interest, and Money* in 1936. The criticisms generally focused on three issues: the empirical behavior of k (or V); the assumption of full employment; and the assumed independence of M and k (or V).

The Empirical Behavior of k (or V)

It will be recalled that the early quantity theorists generally concluded that V would be relatively stable since it depends on such things as the payments mechanism and spending habits, factors that do not change rapidly. The same reasoning was applicable to k, of course, since k was the reciprocal of V ($k = 1/V$).[9] With the development of the income version of the quantity theory, it became possible to subject this conclusion about the stability of k (or V) to empirical testing. In the income version of the quantity theory, $k = M/Y$ and both the money supply M and the national income Y are observable phenomena. Thus, a measure of k is shown in Figure 18-1. Since this series is patently not stable, critics of the quantity theory charged that the whole theoretical apparatus was invalid.

[8]That is, from eq. (10), $dM/dY = k$.
[9]Although A. C. Pigou suggested a number of reasons why k might change in the short run, his analytical insights were not generally followed up until the development of the modern quantity theory.

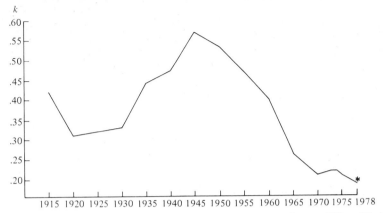

Figure 18-1 The Behavior of K, 1915–1977. *Quarter 1. (*Source: Milton Friedman and Anna J. Schwartz*, A Monetary History of the United States, 1867–1960, *New York, National Bureau of Economic Research, 1963, table A-5 for data to 1960; 1975–1978,* Federal Reserve Bulletin, *May 1978, A14 for M, and A52–A53 for NNP. 1973–1975,* Federal Reserve Bulletin, *March 1976, A12 for M, and A55 for NNP. Money is M_1; income is net national product.*)

The Assumption of Full Employment

Remember that the traditional quantity theory assumed that wage rates were flexible and therefore (because of Say's law of markets) a capitalist economy had its long-run equilibrium at the full employment level of national income. On the basis of this analysis, it was concluded that a change in the quantity of money would have its primary effect on the price level. Two things happened: First, the Great Depression of the 1930s ground on and on, with no apparent end in sight. The assertion that the economy had a *tendency* to full employment, like a cork rising to the top of a pond, seemed less and less relevant to real world problems. Second, J. M. Keynes's *General Theory* denied the validity of Say's law and reached the theoretical conclusion that a capitalist economy could be in complete equilibrium at *less* than full employment. Both of these events, the depression and the *General Theory,* suggested that the quantity theory, if not invalid, was certainly irrelevant.

The Independence of *M* and *k* (or *V*)

Perhaps the most devastating criticism of all, however, came from an unexpected quarter: Keynes's analysis of the rate of interest. Since the Keynesian theory of the determination of national income will be treated in detail in Chapters 20 to 22, we shall not discuss it at length now. But the general nature of Keynes's theory of interest as it applies to the traditional quantity theory can be indicated briefly.

Keynes's theory of the rate of interest, as originally developed in his *General Theory,* asserted that the rate of interest in the economy is determined by the supply of and demand for money. Since the ability of the central bank to fix the supply of money was not in dispute, the novel feature of his theory, and the primary point of contention, was his assertion that the quantity of money demanded by the public and the prevailing interest rate are inversely related to one another. Just as people

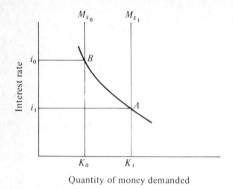

Figure 18-2   The Keynesian relationship between the rate of interest and the demand for money.

will demand larger quantities of beefsteak the lower its price, said Keynes, so also will they demand larger cash balances the lower the rate of interest. Thus we are entitled to draw a demand-for-money curve, as in Figure 18-2, which shows the quantity of money demanded (quantity) as a function of the rate of interest (price).

Two questions arise: Why did Keynes argue that the demand for money is a function of the rate of interest? and, What difference does it make? The answer to the first question is rather complicated, but briefly Keynes argued as follows: At a very low rate of interest (such as point A in Figure 18-2) people will come to believe that the interest rate will rise in the future. But when the interest rate goes up, bond prices go down. Thus, if the interest rate is very low, people will prefer to hold money, where their return is zero, rather than bonds, where they will suffer losses. Therefore, at a low rate of interest there will be a high demand for cash balances. The opposite case also applies. If the interest rate is very high (as at point B in Figure 18-2), then people will believe that it is likely to fall in the future. But a falling interest rate means rising bond prices. People will thus prefer to hold bonds, where they will receive a positive rate of return, instead of money, where they will receive a zero rate of return. At a high rate of interest, therefore, there will be a low demand for cash balances. Keeping in mind that not everyone has the same expectation about the future, we can then fill in the in-between cases and generate a demand-for-money function such as that shown in Figure 18-2.

But the question remains, What difference does it make in the traditional quantity theory of money? The answer to this question is best understood by looking again at (the income version of) the Cambridge equation:

$$M = kY$$

If the quantity of money M is increased and if k is thought of as a constant, then the economy will adjust to the larger quantity of money by expanding nominal income Y largely through an increase in the price level. Nominal income, that is, is the mechanism that adjusts the supply of money to the demand for money; it keeps the two in equilibrium. Not so for Keynes. For Keynes, an increase in the money supply will cause k to increase. For example, in Figure 18-2 if the money supply increases from Ms_0 to Ms_1, then the quantity of money demanded will increase from K_0 to K_1. What *is* true in the Keynesian analysis is that the rate of interest will fall —from i_0 to i_1. It *may* be true that the fall in the rate of interest will affect nominal income Y. But then again it may not. At the very least, said Keynes, further analysis is needed of the relationshop between the rate of interest and nominal income. In the event that no such relationship exists, or only a very weak relationship exists, then changes in money will largely be absorbed by offsetting changes in k, and Y will be unaffected.

These issues, in a modified form, continued to divide the modern quantity theorists and the modern Keynesians. As noted in Chapter 17, modern quantity theorists continue to view changes in the quantity of money as having a *direct* effect on nominal income. Modern Keynesians, on the contrary, insist that a change in the money supply affects the real sector of the economy only *indirectly* through some transmission mechanism such as the rate of interest.

A Word of Caution

It is a common mistake for beginning students to confuse criticisms of the quantity theory with criticisms of the equation of exchange (or the Cambridge equation). This is not correct. The equation of exchange is an identity; it must be true. The quantity theory, properly so called, deals with the *behavior* of the various elements that make up the equation of exchange, and it is these behavioral postulates that constitute the points of contention.

18-5 REVIEW QUESTIONS

1 Explain why the equation of exchange, $MV = PT$, is an identity (i.e., *must* be true).
2 In what two significant ways does the Cambridge equation differ from the equation of exchange?
3 What are the main advantages of stating the Cambridge equation in its income version?
4 What was Keynes's main criticism of the quantity theory of money? Can you name the other criticisms?

19

The Modern
Quantity Theory
of Money

It is one of the paradoxes of monetary theory, in which the subject so richly abounds, that the early Keynesian criticisms of the traditional quantity theory pointed out the trail that the modern quantity theorists were to explore. For what the Keynesian criticism came to, when all was said and done, was that the demand for money was a function of the rate of interest. More specifically, and putting the matter into mathematical notation, Keynes had said that

$$k = f(i) \tag{1}$$

where k is as defined in Chapter 18, i is the rate of interest, and f is the functional notation [that is, eq. (1) is to be read as "k is a function of i," meaning that a change in i will cause a change in k].[1] The significance of this statement lies, perhaps, as

[1]In fact, Keynes had also included a *transaction demand for money,* which meant that k was of function of both i and $Y;$ however, the point being made in the text is the same in either case. The complete Keynesian system is discussed in Chapters 20 to 22.

much in expressing an attitude, or way of viewing the matter, as it does in expressing a precise mathematical relationship. For what eq. (1) says, in very general terms, is that k is a *variable to be explained.* And once this general attitude is adopted, it is not a very big step to regarding k as a function of *more than one* variable; that is, from writing eq. (1) it is not a very big step to writing

$$k = f(i; x, y, z) \tag{2}$$

where x, y, and z in eq. (2) are still other variables (besides the rate of interest) that can reasonably be supposed to determine the value of k. Probably the single most distinctive feature of the modern quantity theorists—the one that separates them from the traditional quantity theorists more than anything else—is that they regard k, not as fixed, but as a relationship that changes in a regular manner as other factors in the economy change. As Milton Friedman has put it, "k is to be regarded not as a numerical constant but as . . . a function of still other variables."

Why is this important? There are two reasons: First, as is apparent from eq. (2), this way of stating the problem raises the possibility of empirical estimation; that is, regression analysis can be used to "explain" the demand for money. As we shall see, statistical researches into the demand-for-money function typically are not put in the *form* of eq. (2), but nevertheless the point remains valid: For modern quantity theorists, the determinants of the demand for money are largely an empirical question. The second and more fundamental reason for the importance of regarding k as a variable to be explained is this: *If,* say the modern quantity theorists, we know what determines the demand for money, and *if* the demand-for-money function is stable (does not shift about unexpectedly), *then* we can predict the consequences of a given change in the money supply. The situation is wholly comparable to, say, that of beef. If we know all the things that determine the demand function for beef, then we can predict what will happen to the price and quantity of beef sold if there is a change in supply. The same is true of the demand for and supply of money, except in this case we are predicting *total* prices and quantities, i.e., nominal national income.

The appropriate arguments that go into the demand-for-money function— essentially, the x, y, and z of eq. (2)—are thus matters of considerable importance to modern quantity theorists. As is to be expected, different people have somewhat different views on the question. The following is one such view.

19-1 THE QUANTITY THEORY OF MILTON FRIEDMAN

Milton Friedman, Nobelist in economics, columnist for *Newsweek* magazine, and originator of several path-breaking ideas in economic theory and policy, is easily the leading contemporary quantity theorist. No serious student of monetary affairs can afford to be unacquainted with his work. While much of Friedman's theoretical work is carried on at such a high level of abstraction as to make it unsuitable for beginning courses in monetary economics, he has upon occasion stated his theory of money in less rigorous terms.[2] It is these less rigorous statements that will be summarized here.

Friedman's approach to the question of why people demand money is to regard money as a good like other goods and therefore to analyze the demand for money in terms of the theory of consumer choice. When we ask why people demand automobiles, for example, we generally organize our thoughts by noting: (1) people want automobiles because of the convenience, or *utility,* that automobiles give them; (2) people are *constrained* in the number of things they can buy by the size of their *incomes;* and (3) given people's incomes, the *cost* of buying a car relative to the cost of buying other things will influence how many cars a person wants to own. These same three ingredients, says Friedman, also enter into the demand for money: the *utility* of holding money, the *income constraint,* and the *cost* of holding money.

Like all other goods, the utility of owning a cash balance is not directly observable; it is a subjective feeling found only in the emotions of the consumer. But it is clear, nevertheless, that holding money does provide utility for individuals and business firms. For individuals, it provides a buffer against unexpected emergencies, such as a sickness, and also a bridge between the monthly paycheck and continuous expenditures. For businesses, *operating balances* additionally permit the exploitation of sudden profit-making opportunities and in this sense can be regarded as a factor of production. While such utilities rendered by money cannot be measured directly, these feelings are sufficiently common to us all that we know they exist.

In order to understand Friedman's views on the relationship between income and the demand for money, it is necessary to remind the reader of the identity $Y = Py;$ that is, nominal income is equal to the product of the price level and real income. Friedman chooses to treat P and y separately rather than in their combined form of nominal income Y. Insofar as the price level P is concerned, Friedman, in common with traditional quantity theory, regards prices and the demand for money as directly and proportionally related to one another. In other words, a 1 percent increase in the price level will cause a 1 percent increase in the quantity of money demanded. For real income y, the relationship is different. Here, Friedman argues that a change in real income will cause a *more than proportional* change in the demand for money. For example, a 1 percent increase in real income might cause a 2 percent increase in the demand for money. Friedman reasons, in this respect, that money balances are a luxury good like education and recreation: People's demand for them will rise more rapidly than their real incomes.

Finally, let us consider the costs of holding money balances. Basically, Friedman sees two costs involved here: First, there is the *opportunity cost* of holding money, by which is meant the income that would have been earned if the money had been invested rather than held. Thus, the opportunity cost of holding money is the rate of interest in the economy. If you hold $1,000 in a demand deposit for one year when instead you could have invested that $1,000 at 7 percent, then it has

---

[2]See especially Milton Friedman, "The Supply of Money and Changes in Prices and Output," *The Relationship of Prices to Economic Stability and Growth: Compendium of Papers Submitted by Panelists,* U.S. Congress, Joint Economic Committee, 1958, pp. 241–256.

cost you $70 [(0.07) ($1,000)] to hold the money. Clearly, the higher the interest rate, the greater the opportunity cost of holding money. It follows that the demand for money and the rate of interest will vary inversely; that is, the higher the cost, the smaller will be the quantity demanded.

The second cost of holding money is the loss in purchasing power if prices rise. Suppose, for example, that you hold $1,000 in the bank for one year and that during the year prices rise 10 percent. Then at the end of the year, the $1,000 will buy only about 90 percent of the same goods and services that it could have bought at the beginning of the year. The purchasing power value of the money has decreased, and to that extent you have suffered a loss, that is, a cost of holding the money. Friedman thus argues that in periods of rapidly rising prices (inflation) people will tend to reduce their money balances. And the more rapidly prices rise (the higher the cost), the smaller will be the quantity of money demanded.

In summary, Friedman sees five factors as determining the demand for money: (1) utility of money balances, (2) price level, (3) level of real income, (4) rate of interest, and (5) rate of change in the price level. These five factors can be stated even more compactly by putting them in the form of a functional equation, i.e., in a form similar to eq. (2). Thus, Friedman's theory may be written as

$$M^D = f(U, P, y, i, \dot{P}) \tag{3}$$

where
$U =$ utility of money balances
$P =$ price level
$y =$ level of real income
$i =$ rate of interest
$\dot{P} =$ rate of change in the price level

Equation (3) may be simplified on the basis of the following two observations: First, it may generally be assumed that the utility of money balances U is stable— does not shift around erratically. Since our interest centers in explaining why the demand for money *changes,* we may thus drop U from further consideration. Second, the evidence we have on the matter from other countries suggests that the rate of change in the price level $\dot{P}$ must be very large and prolonged before it appreciably affects the demand for money. Since, in general, the United States has not been plagued with long periods of hyperinflation, we may also disregard the variable $\dot{P}$. Making these two adjustments in eq. (3) leaves us with the simplified demand-for-money function

$$M^D = f(P, y, i) \tag{3}$$

where the symbols are defined as in eq. (4).

Testing the Hypothesis

When put into a specific form, eq. (4) is clearly an hypothesis that may be subjected to empirical testing, i.e., it may be investigated with the tools of regression analysis.

In fact, a great many empirical studies on the nature of the demand-for-money function have been conducted in recent years. Before considering the results of these studies, however, it is necessary to make a few observations about the nature of logarithms. These observations will be offered without proof. (The reader who is already acquainted with the mathematical rules governing logarithms may skip the following section.)

A Digression on Logarithms   The logarithm of a number is the power some preselected number must be raised to so that it equals that number. This sounds complicated, but it really isn't. For example, suppose the preselected number, called the *base,* is 10 and the number we are interested in is 247. Then it is true that

$$10^{2.3927} = 247$$

That is, 10 raised to the 2.3927 power equals 247. In this case, 2.3927 is said to be the *logarithm* of 247. Mathematically, this would be written as

$$\log 247 = 2.3927$$

It is necessary to note two rules about logarithms.

1   The logarithm of the product of two numbers equals the sum of the logarithms of each number when considered separately. For example, suppose we want to know the logarithm of 7 times 16. This logarithm will be equal to the logarithm of 7 plus the logarithm of 16. That is,

$$\log [(7)(16)] = \log 7 + \log 16$$

More generally,

$$\log aX = \log a + \log X$$

where a and X are any two numbers.

2   The logarithm of a number raised to some power is equal to the power times the logarithm of the number. For example, suppose we want to know the logarithm of 14^2. This logarithm will be equal to 2 times the logarithm of 14. That is,

$$\log 14^2 = 2(\log 14)$$

More generally,

$$\log X^a = a(\log X)$$

where a and X are any two numbers.

In addition to these two rules of logarithms, it is necessary to note two properties of logarithms that make them particularly useful for empirical work in economics.

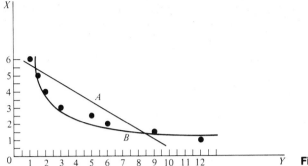

Figure 19-1

1 Many relationships in economics are better described by a curve than by a straight line. A demand function, for example, which relates price and quantity demanded, will typically be curved. The difficulty lies in trying to estimate a curve with regression analysis, since the type of regression equation most easily fitted to data is a straight line. One way around this difficulty is to first take the logarithms of the original data and then fit a straight-line regression to these logarithms. The reason this works is that a logarithmic transformation of many curves will turn out to be a straight line.

An example may help the reader understand this property. Suppose we are interested in the relationship between two economic variables X and Y. We collect data on both these variables and then plot our observations as the data shown in Figure 19-1. A straight line, such as the line marked A in Figure 19-1, would not describe the data very well. What *would* describe the data would be a curved line such as that labeled B. But a curved line is difficult to derive with regression analysis. A way out of this difficulty is to take the logarithms of X and the logarithms of Y and then calculate a straightforward (linear) regression between the two series of numbers. Figure 19-2, for example, shows the logarithms of the dots in Figure 19-1. It is apparent that a straight line, such as that marked C in Figure 19-2, fits these transformed data very well.[3]

2 The second and final property of logarithms we shall mention has to do with the economic concept of elasticity. By *elasticity* is meant the percentage change in one thing relative to (divided by) the percentage change in something else. For example, suppose that a 1 percent increase in the price of shoes resulted in a ½ percent decrease in the quantity of shoes demanded. Then we would say that the price elasticity of the demand for shoes is–½ percent/1 percent = –0.5. Ignoring the algebraic sign, it is customary in economics to call an elasticity greater than 1 *elastic,* equal to 1 *unitary elastic,* and less than 1 *inelastic* (these terms should be familiar to the student from the principles of economics course). One happy property of a logarithmic equation is that it gives us elasticities directly, without further calculation.[4] For the elasticity, in such an equation, is simply the coefficient

---

[3]To be a bit more mathematical, the reader may recognize that the equation $Y = 4X^3$ describes a curve. By taking the logarithms of both sides of this equation we obtain $\log Y = \log 4 + 3(\log X)$, which describes a straight line.

[4]To be precise, this is true of equations expressed in *natural* logarithms, i.e., where the logarithmic base is $e = 2.71828$.

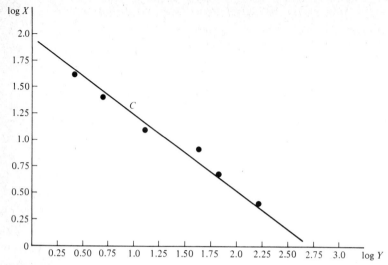

Figure 19-2

on the logarithm of the explanatory variable. For example, in the logarithmic equation

$$\log Y = 1,000 + 2(\log X)$$

2 is the elasticity of Y with respect to X; that is, a 1 percent change in X will cause a 2 percent change in Y.

This completes our digression on logarithms. With these principles in mind, we shall now return to a discussion of the empirical tests of Friedman's demand-for-money hypothesis.

The Demand-for-Money Equation Equation (4), it will be recalled, written in functional form, is

$$M^D = f(P, y, i) \tag{4}$$

where P is price level, y is real income, and i is rate of interest. It is customary to write eq. (4) in the specific form

$$M^D = aPy^b i^c \tag{5}$$

where a, b, and c are the constants to be determined (by regression analysis). The next step is to assume that the economy adjusts quickly to a disequilibrium in the supply of and demand for money; that is, we assume that when there is a change in the quantity of money supplied, the quantity of money demanded quickly changes in a like manner to restore equilibrium. Algebraically, we assume that

$$M^D = M^S \tag{6}$$

where M^S is the money supply. Then, substituting eq. (6) into eq. (5), we have

$$M^S = aPy^b i^c \tag{7}$$

or, dropping the superscripts for simplicity,

$$M = aPy^b i^c \tag{8}$$

Next, we divide both sides of eq. (8) by P, which gives

$$\frac{M}{P} = ay^b i^c \tag{9}$$

Note that the term on the left-hand side of eq. (9), M/P, is real money balances. Treating real balances as a single variable, we can then take logarithms of both sides of eq. (9) to give

$$\log \frac{M}{P} = \log a + b(\log y) + c(\log i) \tag{10}$$

Equation (10) is the basic form taken by most empirical demand-for-money studies done by quantity theorists in recent years. The reader should recognize it as being in a form suitable for testing with the use of multiple-regression analysis. That is, each of the variables M/P, y, and i is an observable, real world phenomenon for which we have data. It is only necessary to calculate the logarithms of these data and then apply the standard technique of regression analysis to the resulting numbers. The regression equation will then give us the estimated values of b, c, and $\log a$. These values, plus the usual regression concepts of r^2 and significance, will then be either consistent or inconsistent with Milton Friedman's hypothesis about the nature of the demand for cash balances.

It may occur to the reader to wonder why, if the testing of Friedman's hypothesis is as straightforward as this, more than one such study is needed. The answer to this question is that there are a variety of data which will satisfy eq. (10). For example: We could use either the M_1 definition of money (currency plus demand deposits) or the M_2 definition (M_1 plus time deposits); we could use either short-term or long-term interest rates on either government securities or corporate securities; we could use different time periods; we could use data from other countries; and so forth. It is only after a great many such studies have been done, all giving generally similar results, that we can begin to have confidence in an hypothesis.

The Regression Results The following is an estimated regression equation of Friedman's demand-for-money hypothesis. This equation has been selected from several similar equations presented in the same study[5] and is generally typical of the statistical findings, not only of this study, but of other studies as well. (The regression is based on annual United States data for the period 1892–1960.)

$$\log \frac{M}{P} = -3.003 + 1.394(\log y) - 0.155(\log i)$$

$r^2 = .99$

Coefficients on $\log y$ and $\log i$ both significant at the 1% level

where M/P = real per capita money stock, where *money* is defined to include time deposits (that is, M_2).

  y = real per capita permanent[6] income

  i = rate of interest on four-month to six-month commercial paper

These results are impressive. First, note that r^2 is very high (.99) and that the coefficients on income and interest are very significant. Second, note that the algebraic signs on these coefficients are as Friedman hypothesized them to be—positive (+) for real income and negative (–) for the rate of interest. Finally, consider the numerical values of the coefficients, keeping in mind that in a logarithmic equation these values are elasticity estimates. The coefficient on $\log y$ (1.394) is thus to be interpreted as the elasticity of the demand for real money balances with respect to real income. It says that if real income rises by 1 percent, the demand for real money balances will rise by 1.394 percent. This is just what Friedman hypothesized—that cash balances were a luxury good, elastic with respect to income.[7] On the other hand, the coefficient on $\log i$ (–0.155) is quite low. This coefficient says that the demand for real money balances is inelastic with respect to the rate of interest—specifically, that a 1 percent increase in the interest rate (e.g., from 5 to 5.05 percent) will cause a decrease of only 0.155 percent in the demand for real money balances. Other studies tend to confirm this, having obtained estimates of the interest elasticity of the demand for money in the range of –0.1 to –1.0.

This last finding in particular—that the demand for money is interest inelastic —is regarded as very significant by modern quantity theorists. They feel that it suggests that the demand for money is not very responsive to changes in the rate of interest, contrary to the criticisms of the quantity theory made by J. M. Keynes. We shall return to this point in Chapter 23, where the Keynesian and quantity theories will be compared.

[5]David Laidler, "The Rate of Interest and the Demand for Money—Some Empirical Evidence," *The Journal of Political Economy,* December 1966, pp. 543–555. The regression is taken from table 2.
  [6]*Permanent* income is a weighted average of present and past values of income.
  [7]More recent studies, however, cast doubt on this conclusion, suggesting that the income elasticity of the demand for money may be less than 1. See, for example, Philip E. Graves, "Wealth and Cash Asset Proportions," *Journal of Money, Credit and Banking,* November 1976, pp. 487–496.

Friedman's Transmission Mechanism   Even though the demand-for-money studies just described appear to lend substantial support to Friedman's view of the role of money in the functioning of the economy, the question nevertheless arises as to how monetary policy works. What is the mechanism, that is, whereby a change in the quantity of money in the financial sector is transmitted to the real sector? As indicated in Chapter 17, modern quantity theorists are not overly concerned with this issue, feeling that the process is very subtle, and therefore difficult to pin down statistically. They therefore generally take the position that it is sufficient to demonstrate a direct statistical connection between changes in the quantity of money and national income. Nevertheless, Friedman has on occasion described the process in what he calls "impressionistic" terms. It is worthwhile considering his views briefly.[8]

Suppose a situation in which the monetary sector is in equilibrium, that is, where the supply of money is exactly equal to the demand for money. Specifically, let us assume that the supply of money is $100 billion, so that the economy is in equilibrium with

$$M^S = \$100 \text{ billion} = M^D$$

Now suppose that for some reason the Federal Reserve decides to increase the money stock by 10 percent to $110 billion. What happens next?

The banking system will be the first to be affected. For as we have seen, the usual way for the Federal Reserve to increase the money supply is through open market operations, which add to the reserve base of the commercial banking system. The commercial banks are thus thrown into a state of disequilibrium, suddenly finding themselves with excess reserves. They will seek to rid themselves of these nonearning assets by expanding their loans and investments. This process will restore the banks to equilibrium but will leave the nonbank public in a state of disequilibrium: The actions of the banking system will create money (demand deposits), and some members of the public will now find themselves with larger cash balances than they care to hold at the prevailing levels of prices, real income, and interest rates.

The nature of the public's disequilibrium needs to be described more closely. Basically, it is a disequilibrium in the public's balance sheet. Think of an individual who has various assets, such as money, common stocks, a house, and a car; and various liabilities, such as a mortgage, car payments, and insurance premiums due. He now finds himself with the wrong *proportions* in these things. In particular, the percentage of his assets that he is holding in the form of money may be too high relative to his other assets and the nature of his liabilities. He will therefore attempt to readjust his balance sheet so that it suits him better. He may, for example, attempt

[8]Milton Friedman and Anna J. Schwartz, "Money and Business Cycles," *The Review of Economics and Statistics,* February 1963 (supplement), pp. 32–64. See also Milton Friedman and David Meisselman, "The Relative Stability of Monetary Velocity and the Investment Multiplier in the United States, 1897–1958," in Commission on Money and Credit, *Stabilization Policies,* Prentice-Hall, Inc., Englewood Cliffs, N.J., 1963, pp. 165–268.

to reduce his excess money holdings by using them to buy bonds. But if he does so, he will simply shift the redundant money balances to the person he buys the bonds from. This person, in turn, may then decide to invest in apartment buildings, a European vacation, or whatever. And someone else, of course, will always receive the money and thus have her balance sheet disturbed. In this fashion the initial increase in the quantity of money will spread throughout the economy in little ripples of spending, like a handful of pebbles thrown into a still pond.

Where will the process end? It will end when the economy is returned to a state of equilibrium—that is, when the *demand* for money has risen by 10 percent—so that now

$$M^S = \$110 \text{ billion} = M^D$$

What causes the demand for money to rise by the \$10 billion needed to restore equilibrium are the adjustments that take place in prices, real income, and interest rates. We can obtain some idea of these adjustments by referring back to the estimated demand-for-money function described previously. This regression equation, it will be recalled, was

$$\log \frac{M}{P} = -3.003 + 1.394(\log y) - 0.155(\log i)$$

From this equation we can derive the following elasticity estimates: The elasticity of *nominal* money balances with respect to

$$
\begin{aligned}
\text{Prices } P &= 1.0 \\
\text{Real income } y &= 1.394 \\
\text{Interest } i &= -0.155
\end{aligned}
$$

These elasticity estimates can be used to tell us by what percent that variable must change (the other variables remaining constant) in order to produce a 10 percent increase in the demand for nominal money balances. To understand this, consider the following sequence of events: The economy is in equilibrium with $M^S = \$100 \text{ billion} = M^D$. Now the Federal Reserve increases the money supply by \$10 billion, or 10 percent. At this point, therefore, the supply of money exceeds the demand for money by 10 percent. What must happen to restore equilibrium is that the demand for money must also somehow rise by 10 percent. The unitary elasticity (1.0) of the price level tells us that one way for this to happen would be for prices to rise by 10 percent; that is, a 10 percent increase in prices, *if real income and interest rates remain constant,* will cause an increase in the demand for nominal money balances of 10 percent.

Suppose, alternatively, that prices and interest rates remain constant and that the entire adjustment in the demand for money occurs through real income. By how much must real income increase in order to produce a 10 percent increase in the demand for money? Since the elasticity of the demand for money with respect to real income is 1.394, we know that a 10 percent increase in real income will cause a 13.94 percent increase in the demand for money. It follows that an increase in real income of

$$10\% \ \left(\frac{10\%}{13.94\%}\right) \ = \ 7.1\%$$

will produce a 10 percent rise in the demand for money, other things being equal.

Finally, consider what must happen if the full adjustment in the demand for money occurs through interest rates alone. Since the interest elasticity of the demand for money is −0.155, we know by the definition of elasticity that a 10 percent decrease in the rate of interest will cause only a 1.55 percent increase in the demand for money. The interest rate must therefore decrease by

$$10\% \ \left(\frac{10\%}{1.55\%}\right) \ = \ 64.5\%$$

to produce a 10 percent increase in the demand for money. Thus if, for example, the interest rate was initially 6 percent, it would have to decrease to 2.13 percent to restore equilibrium, prices and real income remaining constant.

The quantity theorists suggest that it is unlikely that only one of these three factors would be involved in the adjustment process. Rather, they believe that all three would have a part to play. Thus, in practice, equilibrium would be restored by some combination of rising prices, rising real income, and lower interest rates.

19-2   THE WEALTH EFFECT

An alternative formulation of the quantity theory of money focuses on the amount of wealth in the economy as a constraint on the demand for money, rather than income. This approach, which is generally associated with two economists named Karl Brunner and Allan Meltzer, is called the *wealth effect.* To explain the nature of the wealth effect, recall that the estimated demand-for-money equation described in section 19-1 uses income as the *constraint* on money holdings. By "constraint" is meant that people are constrained from holding larger money balances by the size of their incomes, just as they are constrained from buying large and expensive cars by the size of their income. Proponents of the wealth effect, however, argue that this is an incorrect specification of the demand-for-money function. What constrains people in the holding of assets is not income, they say, but wealth. Thus, for example, a retired person living off the interest from an S&L deposit could convert such a deposit to an expensive automobile even though her income might be low. The same reasoning, they say, applies to the amount of cash balances people decide to hold; the constraint on the size of these balances is determined by the proportion of their wealth that people want to hold as money.

The wealth effect raises many subtle and complex issues in monetary theory.[9] It suggests that the appropriate approach to macroeconomic theory is from the view-point of the public's balance sheet, rather than its income statement. Empirically, however, whether the wealth constraint or the income constraint is used seems to make very little difference in demand-for-money studies. The reason for this seems to be that wealth and income are highly correlated with one another, so that approximately the same statistical results are achieved whichever variable is used.

19-3 THE CROWDING-OUT EFFECT

It will be recalled from Chapter 17 that one of the most basic issues that divides the monetarists and the Keynesians is the effectiveness (or lack thereof) of fiscal policy. While a formal explanation of the theory of fiscal policy must be postponed until Chapter 21, the general idea, and the basis of the disagreement between the monetarists and the Keynesians, can be described at this point.

The fundamental idea underlying fiscal policy is really quite simple. Viewed as an economic entity, the government has two basic powers: to tax and to spend. When the government taxes people, it takes income away from them, thus leaving them with *less* to spend in the private sector of the economy. When the government spends, it adds to people's incomes, thus giving them *more* to spend in the private sector. Clearly, if the government takes (taxes) more than it gives (spends), then *net* spending in the private sector goes down. Contrariwise, if the government spends more than it taxes, net spending in the private sector goes up. Thus, the theory goes, the government can, by a judicious use of its taxing and spending powers, dampen or stimulate the pace of economic activity in the private sector of the economy.

Monetarists take a dim view of this theory. What it fails to take into account, they say, is the *crowding-out effect.* To understand the crowding-out effect, it is first necessary to understand what monetarists mean by a *pure* fiscal policy. When the government increases its level of expenditures, it has three choices in the way it finances this: It may tax, it may borrow, or it may create new money. Only the first two of these, say the monetarists, are cases of "pure" fiscal policy. In the third case, that of money creation, fiscal policy is actually a sort of disguised monetary policy and cannot be analyzed by itself. For this reason, monetarists confine their analysis of the crowding-out effect to pure fiscal policy.

Let us first examine the case where the government raises its level of spending and finances the increased spending by raising taxes by the same amount. In this case, contrary to what most people would guess, there will be some stimulus to the economy, because a part of the income that is taxed away would otherwise have been saved, and hence would not have contributed to total expenditures. But, of course, the government spends it all, and the *net* effect on total expenditures is therefore positive.[10] But while there is thus *some* effect if increased government expenditures

---

[9]See Karl Brunner and Allan H. Meltzer, "Money, Debt, and Economic Activity," *Journal of Political Economy,* September/October 1972, pp. 951–977.

[10]This is the so-called *balanced-budget multiplier,* a more rigorous analysis of which may be found in any macroeconomic theory textbook.

are financed by an equivalent increase in taxes, this effect is likely to be slight. Most of the government's increased spending has simply "crowded out" private spending. Indeed, so slight will the net effect be, say the monetarists, that massive swings in the government's budget would be necessary to have any appreciable effect on the economy.

But what about the second case, where increased government expenditures are financed by government borrowing? Here too, say the monetarists, the net effect, while positive, is likely to be weak. To understand why, consider the following example. Suppose that the government increases its expenditures by $10 billion and, in order to do this, borrows $10 billion by selling bonds to the public. In order to sell its debt, the government will have to compete in the bond market with private borrowers. But since the only way that the government can compete is by offering higher interest rates to investors, interest rates will have to rise. In fact, interest rates will have to rise by just enough that enough private borrowers get discouraged by the higher interest rates and decide not to borrow (and spend) $10 billion. Thus, in this case too, the increased spending by the government has crowded out private spending. The positive effect of this operation comes, not from government spending, but from what happens to the demand for money. For the higher rate of interest will cause people to want to hold smaller cash balances, with the consequence that *some* increase in spending occurs. How much of an increase? That depends on the interest elasticity of the demand for money. If this elasticity is very low, as the monetarists say, then the rise in interest rates will have very little effect on the demand for money. Again, the conclusion is that huge changes in government spending policy would be needed for economic stabilization.

19-4 RATIONAL EXPECTATIONS

One of the most interesting developments in monetarist thinking in recent years has been the theory of *rational expectations*. While a formal definition of rational expectations would take us too far afield, it is possible to explain the general idea informally. Rational expectation theory argues that the general public formulates expectations about the future on the basis of all relevant information available currently. By "relevant information" is meant, not just statistical data, but also a knowledge of the cause-and-effect economic relationships involved. Most particularly, the rational expectations hypothesis argues that the public knows just as much about the nature of the economy as policy makers do. If this view is correct, the implications for economic policy in general, and monetary policy in particular, are profound. For what it implies is that no economic policy can work that relies for its success on policy makers knowing more than the public. And if this is true, it follows (in a manner to be explained) that the monetary authorities cannot affect any of the real variables in the economy, such as employment and interest rates. Putting the matter positively, the only thing the authorities can influence is nominal values (prices). To illustrate how this conclusion is derived from rational expectations, we will consider two cases: the determination of interest rates, and the Phillips curve.

Interest Rates and Rational Expectations

For many years macroeconomic theory has held that, other things equal, an increase in the quantity of money will cause interest rates to fall, and a decrease in the money stock will cause interest rates to rise. The reason for this relationship, which was explained in the final section of Chapter 18, is that an increase in the supply of any commodity will normally cause its price to fall, and money is no exception. The price of money (i.e., of borrowing money), however, is the rate of interest. Therefore an increase in the supply of money will cause interest rates to go down, and conversely for a decrease in the supply of money.

Monetarists disagree with this analysis and, in fact, arrive at exactly the opposite conclusion. An increase in the quantity of money, they say, will *eventually* result in a *higher* rate of interest; a decrease in the quantity of money will eventually cause a lower rate of interest. To understand the nature of this argument, let us suppose that the Federal Reserve suddenly and unexpectedly raises the growth rate of the money stock from 5 to 10 percent. The *immediate* effect of this change is that interest rates will fall; people will find that they have more money than they want, and hence will spend their excess money balances. One of the things they will buy will be bonds, and the price of bond will therefore rise. And since rising bond prices mean falling bond yields, interest rates will fall.

But this is only the immediate effect. In the longer run, the higher growth rate in the money supply will mean a higher rate of inflation, with the consequence that interest rates will not only go back up to where they were before, but will actually go to higher levels. Why? Because lenders' expectations about future inflation will have changed, and they will demand a higher interest rate to compensate them for the greater expected decline in the value of the dollar. For example, if you want to earn 5 percent on the money you lend and the inflation rate is also 5 percent, then you will have to earn 10 percent on your money to get a *real* rate of return of 5 percent. Thus in this view, the *nominal,* or market, rate of interest is composed of two parts: the real rate of interest and the expected rate of inflation. That is,

$$i = r + p^e \tag{11}$$

where i is the market rate of interest, r is the real rate of interest, and p^e is the expected rate of price inflation. Clearly, if the p^e of eq. (11) increases, i will go up by an equal amount. Hence the increase in the money supply will raise p^e, which will raise i: an easier monetary policy will cause *higher* market rates of interest, not lower.

But where do rational expectations come in? They enter the process in the following manner. In the model just described, we began with the assumption that the Federal Reserve *suddenly and unexpectedly* raised the growth rate of the money supply. Let us drop this assumption and assume instead that the Fed follows some consistent pattern in deciding on monetary policy. This pattern could be almost anything, so long as it is *consistent.* For example, the Fed might decide to increase the growth rate of money by 1 percent every year, or the Fed might decide to raise the monetary growth rate by a certain amount whenever the unemployment rate rose to a certain level, or the Fed might decide to behave according to some other, more complicated rule. The point is that whatever decision rule the Fed decides upon will be quickly learned by the public and incorporated into its expectations about inflation. Not to do so would be irrational. It would imply that the public is stupid and incapable of recognizing a behavioral pattern that is repeated over and over. But if the public knows what the Fed is going to do and acts accordingly, then even the *temporary* decline in interest rates will be eliminated. In terms of eq. (11), monetary policy will be *immediately* incorporated into the public's price expectations p^e, with the result that nominal interest rates i will *immediately* go higher. But note that this means that the real rate of interest r is unaffected. This is the meaning of the statement at the beginning of this section that the implication of rational expectations for monetary policy is that the monetary authorities cannot affect the real variables in the economy, only nominal variables.

But the reader may still have a puzzlement. Why, it may be asked, can't the Federal Reserve change its mind? That is, even if the Fed behaves according to some rule today, it doesn't necessarily follow that it will behave according to the same rule next month, or next year. And if this is the case, then why can't the Fed affect real interest rates by frequently changing its mind? There are two answers to this question. First, the rational expectations hypothesis does not claim that the public's expectations are always, or even usually, correct. The only claim made is that the public's expectations are based on the best *available* information, including a knowledge of the decision-making process of the Federal Reserve. Naturally, if the monetary authorities change their decision-making process, then the public's expectations will be wrong, at least for a time. But note that it must be a genuine change of mind on the part of the Fed, not one that was thought out beforehand, because if it was thought out beforehand then the public will quickly catch on to that, too. The second answer is that, if the Federal Reserve does change its decision rule frequently and genuinely, then to all intents and purposes it will have abandoned setting monetary policy. For a frequent change of mind is operationally indistinguishable from a policy of *random* decision making, which is no policy at all.

Rational Expectations and the Phillips Curve

It is a common belief among the public that there is an inverse relationship between the rate of unemployment and the rate of increase in the price level. That is, it is widely believed that when unemployment goes up, the inflation rate does down, and vice versa. Among economists, this relationship is known as the *Phillips curve* (after the English economist A. W. Phillips, who first estimated the relationship).[11] Economists usually show this theoretical relationship graphically, as in Figure 19-3. In this figure, the curve marked "PP" is the Phillips curve. It shows how much inflation will be associated with each level of unemployment. For example, according to Figure 19-3, if unemployment is 6 percent, then prices will rise at a rate of 5 percent per year; similarly, an unemployment rate of 5 percent is associated with a price rise

[11]A. W. Phillips, "The Relationship Between Unemployment and the Rate of Change of Money Wages in the United Kingdom, 1861–1957," *Economica* (N.S.), November 1958, pp. 283–299.

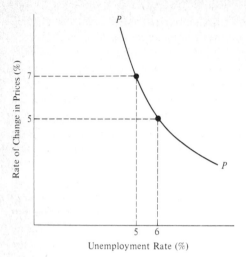

Figure 19-3 Hypothetical Phillips Curve.

of 7 percent; and so forth. Thus, the Phillips curve says that there is some trade-off between inflation and unemployment such that the closer the economy comes to full employment, the faster prices will rise.

The policy implications of the Phillips curve, as shown in Figure 19-3, are that we cannot both have our cake and eat it too: We can have stable prices *only* if we are willing to accept a high level of unemployment, or, alternatively, we can have full employment *only if* we are willing to accept a high rate of inflation. Or, of course, we can have some combination of the two. In any case, policy makers are thrown into a dilemma: Whatever they do will be wrong, since whatever choice they make will result in someone getting hurt.

Monetarists deny that the Phillips curve analysis is correct, basing this denial on the theory of rational expectations. The argument runs as follows. The Phillips-curve relationship will prevail, say the monetarists, only so long as, and to the extent that, the inflation rate is *unexpected.* For if people expect inflation, then this expected rate of inflation will be taken into account in determining wages. For example, if a union wants a 4 percent increase in real wages and expects the inflation rate to be 6 percent, then it will insist on a 10 percent wage increase. Corporations, who also expect a 6 percent inflation rate, will be willing to grant the 10 percent wage increase because they know that the prices of their products will be rising at the same rate as inflation, and hence that they will be able to pay their workers at the inflation rate (6%) plus the worker's increase in productivity (4%).

If this analysis is correct, a *fully anticipated inflation* cannot lower the unemployment rate; if everyone knows that it is going to happen, then they will take this into account in their present calculations, with the result that it will have no effect on real variables such as how many people corporations hire. Putting the matter the other way around, it is only *unanticipated inflation* that can affect the level of unemployment. For if unions and corporations sign a contract based on an *expected* inflation rate of 6 percent, and the *actual* inflation rate turns out to be 10 percent, then the corporations will be willing to hire more people because labor is cheap (the real wage rate is low).

What this means, then, is that the Phillips-curve relationship will prevail only so long as the monetary authorities are able to fool the public by causing unexpectedly high rates of inflation. And this, of course, is where rational expectations come in. For the rational expectations hypothesis says that you can't fool people for very long. And this means that unemployment can be reduced only if the authorities are prepared to accept higher and higher rates of inflation. Suppose, for example, that the inflation rate is 1 percent, and that everyone comes to expect it. Then unemployment will be reduced only if the inflation rate is raised to 2 percent. But people will catch onto this quickly, and unemployment will go back up. Then the authorities will have to raise the inflation rate to 3 percent. This too may work for awhile, but eventually the public will figure out that when unemployment rises to a certain level, the authorities will increase the inflation rate by 1 percent. When this happens, the authorities will then have to raise the inflation rate by 2 percent each time; and when the public figures that out, the Fed will have to up the ante to 3-percent jumps. And so forth. In the long run, all that will have happened is that the economy will be experiencing a runaway inflation; the unemployment rate will be what it was at the outset. Thus, as with the analysis of interest rates, monetary policy will have affected only nominal values (prices) in the economy. Real variables (unemployment and production) will not have changed.

Rational Expectations and Stabilizing Prices   If the preceding analysis of the relationship between the Phillips curve and rational expectations is correct, it presents policy makers with a particularly difficult decision in halting an ongoing inflation. For what the analysis suggests is that, once an inflation is underway, it may take either a substantial or a prolonged rise in unemployment to stabilize prices. Suppose, for example, that the inflation rate has been running at 10 percent, and that everyone has gotten used to this rate and adjusted accordingly. Then if the authorities suddenly put on the monetary brakes, so that the inflation rate drops to zero, there will very likely be a large increase in unemployment as employers find that pay raises granted in anticipation of a 10 percent inflation were resulting in a very large rise in real wages. Of course, once expectations had adjusted to a zero inflation rate, and union contracts adjusted accordingly, then unemployment would fall. But in the meantime it might go quite high. Alternatively, the authorities might decide to reduce the inflation rate gradually—by 1 percent per year, say. This would result in a smaller rise in unemployment than in the previous case, but the unemployment would last over a longer period of time since inflationary expectations would decline only gradually. Most monetarists would choose this latter course as being the more humane, but such a judgment is, of course, outside the realm of economics.

Concluding Comment on Rational Expectations

The rational expectations hypothesis is too recent a development in economic theory for it to have been accepted by most, or even a majority of, economists. Its great appeal is that it puts the formulation of the public's expectations on the same assumption of rationality as is used in other areas of economic decision making. There have, however, been a number of criticisms[12] of rational expectations—for example, that the public's cost of gathering and processing information is too high for it to make frequent and costly changes in expectations; that rational expectations would require public access to very large and complex econometric models; that rational expectations necessitate the public's having a complete model of governmental decision-making processes; and so forth. Whether the rational expectations hypothesis is incorporated into macroeconomic theory will eventually turn on how useful it is for understanding *empirical* relationships. So far, the returns are not all in.

19-5 REVIEW QUESTIONS

1 If the quantity of money supplied exceeds the quantity of money demanded by 10 percent, by how much (other things equal) would interest rates have to fall to restore equilibrium if the interest elasticity of the demand for money is –0.5?

2 In what sense will a government deficit financed by government borrowing "crowd out" private expenditures?

3 In 1978, the inflation rate was about 8 percent. At the same time, the interest rate on home mortgages was about 10 percent. Was this a high or a low rate of interest? (Be careful how you answer this; it is trickier than it looks.)

4 If the rational expectations hypothesis is correct, then what would a long-run Phillips curve look like?

[12]For a balanced and thoughtful critique of the rational expectations hypothesis, see William Poole, "Rational Expectations in the Macro Model," *Brookings Papers on Economic Activity,* **2:** 1976, pp. 463–505.

20

Traditional Keynesian
Theory:
Analysis
of the Real Sector

In 1936 the British economist John Maynard Keynes published a book on economic theory, *The General Theory of Employment, Interest, and Money.* In the forty-five years since it was first published, this book has had a tremendous impact on public policy—comparable, probably, to that of Adam Smith's *Wealth of Nations* or Karl Marx's *Capital.* It is doubtful that there is any country in the noncommunist world that does not follow, to a considerable extent, the stabilization policies advocated by Keynes. As Keynes himself wrote: "The ideas of economists and political philosophers, both when they are right and when they are wrong, are more powerful than is commonly understood. Indeed the world is ruled by little else. Practical men, who believe themselves to be quite exempt from any intellectual influences, are usually the slaves of some defunct economist."

The system of economic thought set forth by Keynes has, of course, been modified considerably over the past several decades. Some of his ideas were incomplete, some have not withstood the test of empirical investigation, and some were simply wrong. Nevertheless, Keynes's fundamental view of the world—his "vision" of economic reality—persists to the present day in what has come to be called *post Keynesian,* or *traditional Keynesian, economic theory.* Traditional Keynesianism is a well-developed, logically consistent system of economic thought. It includes, but is not limited to, monetary theory. We shall discuss traditional Keynesianism in this chapter and in Chapter 21.

20-1 METHOD OF THE KEYNESIAN THEORY

The reader may remember Figures 17-1 and 17-2 showing the economy divided into two sectors: the *real* sector and the *financial,* or *monetary,* sector. Keynesian economic theory proceeds by first analyzing these sectors in isolation from each other and then combining them into a single theory of the entire economy wherein each sector interacts with the other. In all three analyses—that of the real sector, the monetary sector, and the combination of the two—the method used is the same. It is what is called *static equilibrium analysis.* A static theory is essentially a timeless (i.e., nonhistorical) analysis. By *equilibrium* is meant a situation in which all the forces in the economy are exactly counterbalanced against one another, like weights on a jeweler's scale.

The procedure we shall follow is first to determine the conditions necessary for equilibrium to occur in the real sector, which is the subject of this chapter. Then, in Chapter 21 we shall inquire into the equilibrium conditions of the monetary sector. Finally, also in Chapter 21, we shall determine equilibrium in the whole economy by discovering under what circumstances both the real and the monetary sectors will be in equilibrium at the same time.

20-2 EQUILIBRIUM IN THE REAL SECTOR: AN INTUITIVE EXPLANATION

The real sector of the economy will be in equilibrium when investment is equal to saving. That is, letting I stand for investment and S for saving, the real sector equilibrium condition is

$$I = S$$

Since this conclusion is by no means obvious, it will be best to begin with an intuitive explanation of it.

Imagine an economy in which there is no foreign trade and no government. (The government will be introduced shortly, but foreign trade complications will be postponed until Chapter 24.) In this economy there are then only two kinds of economic agents: (1) households, which have the function of consuming the goods and services the economy produces and furnishing the labor and other services needed to produce this output; and (2) business firms, which have the function of producing the goods and services that the households consume and hiring the labor and other services of the households. How such an economy would work can be visualized with the aid of Figure 20-1.

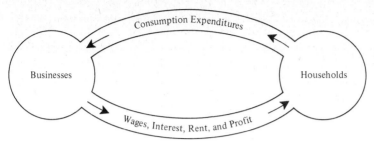

Figure 20-1 The circular flow of income.

To understand Figure 20-1, it is necessary to keep in mind that just about every family in our economy functions in two roles—that of producer and that of consumer. The most common way that people function as producers is by working at jobs for which they receive wages. But people also furnish other productive services for which they are paid: They lend money for interest and furnish property for profits and rent. The sum of these various payments represents the total income households have available for spending. When they spend this income, households function in their role as consumers, buying back all of the things that they themselves have produced. Thus the process of "getting and spending" can be visualized as a great circular pipeline through which money flows. Figure 20-1 shows this pipeline. Households, on the right-hand side of the figure, spend money with business firms, on the left. This is shown by the arrow running from households to businesses at the top of the figure. The arrow at the bottom of the figure shows the payments of wages, interest, profit, and rent made by business firms to households.

If the economy worked as simply as shown in Figure 20-1, then there would never be any reason for national income (GNP) to change. But the economy is not this simple for two reasons: First, household spending will usually be less than household income because households *save*. Second, business spending typically will be greater than sales receipts because businesses borrow and *invest*.

Figure 20-2 is similar to Figure 20-1 except that saving and investing are included. Note that saving represents a *drain* out of the flow of income and that investment represents an *injection* into it. It should be clear by looking at Figure 20-2 that the total flow of income will not change as long as *investment is equal to saving.* For in that case, what is drained out through saving is added back in through business investment, and the total income flow is therefore stable, or unchanging. The economy is then said to be in equilibrium. It is in this sense that the equilibrium condition for the real sector of the economy is that investment equals saving, that is, $I = S$.

It will be instructive to consider what happens to the economy if saving and investment are not equal. Suppose, for example, that in Figure 20-2 the amount of saving is less than the amount of investment. Then the amount being injected into the income stream is bigger than the amount being drained out. The income stream will thus be flooded with additional business spending, which, in turn, will swell household income receipts. Out of these larger incomes people will be able to save

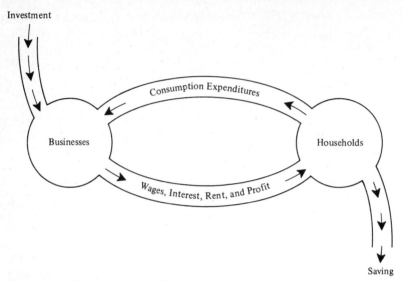

Figure 20-2 The circular flow of income.

more, and hence saving will begin to rise. Saving will continue to rise as long as household incomes rise, and household income will rise as long as investment is greater than saving. Thus equilibrium will be restored only when the flow of income has expanded enough to generate sufficient new saving such that $I = S$.

Now suppose the opposite case, that saving is greater than investment. Then more is being taken out of the income stream through household saving than is being put into it by business investment. Business firms then find themselves unable to sell all they produce, and inventory accumulates on their shelves. Businesses will not continue to produce still more goods under such circumstances, and so they will cut back on production. But when businesses do this, they will hire fewer factors of production and household incomes will fall. And as their incomes fall, households will save less. Saving then begins to shrink, and it will continue to shrink as long as income falls. And income will continue to fall as long as investment is greater than saving. The fall in income will come to a halt, and equilibrium will be restored, only when saving has shrunk to the point where it is once more true that $I = S$.

It is important to note explicitly that in the Keynesian view it is through changes in income that saving is ultimately brought into balance with investment. When saving and investment are *not* equal, forces are generated in the economy that cause national income to change until they *are* equal. Thus changes in saving and investment are typically regarded by Keynesians as the immediate cause of changes in national income—of inflations and unemployment.

The Algebra of Equilibrium

The foregoing explanation of the $I = S$ equilibrium condition for the real sector was intuitive. The matter can also be stated very easily in algebraic terms. Basically, what the model does is to recognize that income may be looked at in either of two ways: First, we may view national income Y as the sum of all *expenditures* on current production in the economy. Classifying expenditures into consumption spending C and investment spending I, we may thus write

$$Y = C + I \qquad (1)$$

Alternatively, we may think of income as the *receipt* of wages, interest, profit, and rent. Once this income is received, there are only two things the household can do with it: spend it on consumption goods and services or save it. Thus, from this viewpoint, we may write

$$Y = C + S \qquad (2)$$

where S is saving, and Y and C have already been defined. Substituting the definition of income in eq. (1) into eq. (2), we have

$$C + I = C + S$$

or, canceling out the Cs,

$$I = S \qquad (3)$$

Investment and Saving Schedules

The foregoing bit of algebra can be confusing because it seems to suggest that by definition saving and investment are *always* equal. Although this is not correct, it is a difficult point that should be clarified.

The difficulty is a matter of words rather than substance. As an explanation, look at Figure 20-3, which is a simple supply and demand graph. By *supply* in this graph is meant the entire line, or *schedule*, marked *SS*; similarly, by *demand* is meant the entire schedule marked *DD*. Supply is equal to demand at only one point in this graph: the point marked *A*, where the two schedules cross. At point *A*, this

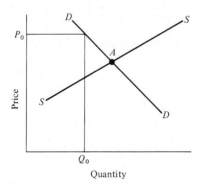

Figure 20-3 Supply and demand disequilibrium.

market is thus said to be in equilibrium because supply equals demand. Suppose, however, that the market is *not* in equilibrium. Suppose instead that the price is P_0. At this price the quantity bought and the quantity sold will both be Q_0 even though the market is in disequilibrium. In describing this situation, we would say that supply is not equal to demand but that the quantity bought *is* equal to the quantity sold.

This same distinction can be made with respect to investment and saving. In equilibrium, saving equals investment in the sense that the saving *schedule* equals the investment *schedule*. In *disequilibrium,* the quantity of saving will equal the quantity of investment, but the two schedules will not cross at that point. Equation (3), $I = S$, is thus to be interpreted in the schedule sense to mean that the real sector is in equilibrium when this condition holds.

20-3 DETERMINANTS OF THE SAVING SCHEDULE

In the Keynesian view, the household is seen as first receiving a certain amount of income and then deciding how much of this income to spend on consumption goods and services. What is left is saving. Thus the *basic* decision the individual makes is how much of current income to spend on consumption; once this decision has been made, saving is necessarily determined as the difference between income and consumption. In order to understand what determines saving, therefore, it is necessary to turn the question around and ask, What determines consumption expenditures?

The traditional Keynesian answer to this question is both simple and straightforward: Consumption, it is held, is determined primarily by income. When we ask, for example, why one person drives a Ford and another a Cadillac, the most obvious answer is that the latter can afford a high-priced car and the former cannot. Thus the greater a person's income, the higher his or her standard of living is likely to be. Since this will be true in general, we can hypothesize that consumption is a *function* of income. This functional relationship can be expressed as

$$C = f(Y) \tag{4}$$

meaning that consumption C is a function of income Y; when income changes, consumption will change in the same direction. Equation (4) is called the *consumption function* in traditional Keynesian economics.

A very important hypothesis about the nature of the consumption function is that

$$0 < \frac{\Delta C}{\Delta Y} < 1 \tag{5}$$

where the symbol Δ (delta) means *a change in* and the symbol $<$ expresses an inequality. Inequality (5) thus says that the ratio of a change in consumption to a change in income is greater than 0 and less than 1. This ratio $\Delta C / \Delta Y$ is called the *marginal propensity to consume.*

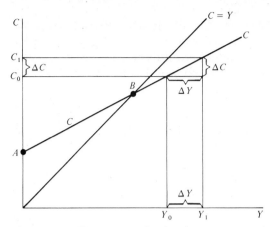

Figure 20-4 The consumption function.

It will be helpful, in terms of our subsequent development of the Keynesian theory, to illustrate graphically the consumption function and the marginal propensity to consume. This is done in Figure 20-4. On the vertical axis is shown consumption expenditures C measured in dollars. Income Y is shown along the horizontal axis and it also is measured in dollars. The line marked $C = Y$, which bisects the right angle formed by the two axes, shows all points where consumption expenditures are equal to income, that is, where all income received is spent on consumption. The line $C = Y$ is included in the figure as a geometric aid to the reader; it is not an economic concept. Any point above this line indicates a situation where consumption is greater than income; any point below it indicates that consumption is less than income.

The consumption function in Figure 20-4 is shown by the line marked CC, which slopes upward to the right. This line says that consumption is positively related to income—that as income increases along the horizontal axis, consumption increases along the vertical axis. There are two things to notice about the consumption function as drawn in Figure 20-4: In the first place, note that it begins at a positive level of consumption when income is 0 (point A) and it is not until after point B is reached that consumption expenditures become less than income. This part of the consumption function, the line segment AB, may be puzzling to the reader. Since it lies above the $C = Y$ line, it implies that at low levels of income, consumption expenditures are greater than income, i.e., that people are spending more than they are earning. How can this be? In fact, the answer is comparatively simple. At very low levels of income people will tend to live off past saving rather than reduce their living standards further. Thus, they will draw down their savings accounts, sell their stocks and bonds, and borrow against their insurance policies.

The second thing to note about the consumption function shown in Figure 20-4 is that, as drawn, it depicts a marginal propensity to consume that is greater than 0 and less than 1. This can be seen by considering what happens to consumption as income increases from income level Y_0 to income level Y_1. At income level Y_0, consumption expenditures are C_0; when income rises to Y_1, consumption rises to C_1. Now the line segment from Y_0 to Y_1 on the horizontal axis measures the *change* in income that has occurred, and by definition the change in income is ΔY. Similarly, the line segment from C_0 to C_1 on the vertical axis measures the *change* in consumption, or ΔC. For convenience of interpretation, these magnitudes, ΔY and of ΔC, have been transferred inward in the figure so that they form the two legs of the small triangle that has the consumption function as its hypotenuse. It is apparent from direct inspection of this triangle that the ratio $\Delta C/\Delta Y$ is greater than 0 and less than 1, that is, that the marginal propensity to consume lies between 0 and 1.

One further point should be noted: From Figure 20-4 it can be seen that the closer the ratio $\Delta C/\Delta Y$ is to 1, the steeper is the consumption function; and, conversely, the closer $\Delta C/\Delta Y$ is to 0, the flatter is the consumption function. The marginal propensity to consume is thus measured by the *slope* of the consumption function.[1]

The saving function is derived from the consumption function. Figure 20-4, without all the clutter, is reproduced afresh as the top half of Figure 20-5. The

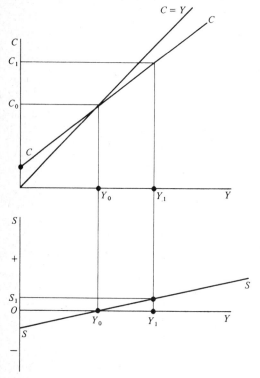

Figure 20-5 The consumption function and the saving function.

[1]Mathematically, let $C = a + bY$. Then $dC/dY = b$, and by definition b is the slope of the line described by the equation. $\Delta C/\Delta Y$ is a linear approximation of dC/dY.

bottom half of Figure 20-5 is the saving schedule. Note that with the saving schedule the horizontal axis continues to measure income Y but the vertical axis measures saving S. The saving schedule is derived in the following manner: Consider income level Y_0. The consumption function (in the top half of Figure 20-5) indicates that at income level Y_0 all income is spent on consumption. But since all income is spent on consumption, it follows that at this level of income saving must be 0. Therefore in the bottom half of Figure 20-5 we record saving as 0 at income level Y_0. Consider next income level Y_1. Since at this level of income the consumption function lies below the line $C = Y$, it follows that consumption is less than income. But from eq. (2), $S = Y - C$, and consequently saving must be equal to the distance between the consumption function and the line $C = Y$. We therefore record this amount of saving, S_1, at income level Y_1 in the lower half of Figure 20-5.

We could repeat the preceding steps over and over again for still other levels of income. If we did so, we would eventually generate the entire savings schedule, as shown by the line marked SS in the lower half of Figure 20-5. One geometric property of the savings schedule is apparent from Figure 20-5: The steeper the consumption function, the flatter will be the savings schedule, and conversely. This property of the savings schedule can be stated algebraically. Recall from Figure 20-4 that the marginal propensity to consume is defined as $\Delta C/\Delta Y$ and is measured by the slope of the consumption function. In a similar manner, we may define the *marginal propensity to save* as

$$0 < \frac{\Delta S}{\Delta Y} < 1 \tag{6}$$

The marginal propensity to save is measured by the *slope* of the saving function. In fact, the marginal propensities to consume and save are bound together in a definite mathematical relationship, as follows: Since any change in income must either be spent on consumption or saved, it follows that

$$\Delta Y = \Delta C + \Delta S \tag{7}$$

Dividing both sides of eq. (7) by ΔY gives

$$1 = \frac{\Delta C}{\Delta Y} + \frac{\Delta S}{\Delta Y}$$

or $\quad \dfrac{\Delta S}{\Delta Y} = 1 - \dfrac{\Delta C}{\Delta Y} \tag{8}$

In words, eq. (8) says that the marginal propensity to save equals 1 minus the marginal propensity to consume.

An Estimated Consumption Function

To give the reader some confidence in the validity of the concepts just discussed, we shall estimate a consumption function with the use of regression analysis:[2]

$$C = 3.5 + .9 Y_d$$
$$r^2 = .99$$

Coefficient on Y_d significant at the 1% level

where C is personal consumption expenditures and Y_d is disposable (i.e., after-tax) personal income. The figures are annual, in billions of dollars, and cover the period 1954–1977. Note that the constant term is positive and that the marginal propensity to consume is greater than 0 and less than 1. Both relationships are as hypothesized.

20-4   DETERMINANTS OF THE INVESTMENT SCHEDULE

Why do businesses invest? The answer given by Keynesian economics is quite straightforward: Investment is made for *expected profit*. When we use the word "investment" here, we are talking about the actual construction of physical plant and equipment. We do *not* mean financial investment, that is, buying common stocks, bonds, or the like. As explained previously, from the viewpoint of the entire economy, investment is the annual addition to our productive facilities, or capital stock. And in a capitalist economy, this capital formation depends on the profit motive.

In very general terms, we may think of a business person as calculating expected profits by first reckoning the total expected sales receipts from an investment and then subtracting expected costs from this amount. Traditional Keynesianism focuses primarily on only one of these costs: *interest*. Thus, the argument runs, the lower the interest costs, the more investment that will be undertaken; and, conversely, the higher the interest costs, the more business people will be discouraged from investing.

The reason Keynesians emphasize the rate of interest in the economy is its pervasiveness. By *pervasive* is meant that *all* business firms must pay interest costs, either explicitly or implicitly. Firms that have to borrow money in order to make an investment are paying interest explicitly on the borrowed funds. But even businesses that have their own funds to invest in the form of retained earnings have to pay an implicit cost for the funds. After all, such businesses could instead have lent the money out at the current interest rate. If they choose to invest rather than lend, then they are foregoing the interest they could have received and hence are implicitly paying that cost.

The inverse relationship between the rate of interest and the amount of invest-

---

[2]This consumption function should be considered as more illustrative than literal. In practice, estimating consumption functions is much more complicated than this. For a discussion of why this is so, see any recent textbook on macroeconomic theory.

ment in the economy may be explained in the following way: At any given time, there are a variety of profitable investment opportunities in the economy. Even after an adjustment is made for the risk involved, some of these investments will carry a very high expected rate of profit—100 percent or more. Others, more plentiful, will entail much lower expected profits—say, in the neighborhood of 5 or 6 percent. And, of course, in-between cases will also exist. What keeps everyone from investing at the higher expected profit and no one from investing at the lower expected profit is imperfect information. If everyone had perfect, or complete, information, then no low-profit opportunities would be made until all high-profit opportunities had been exhausted. But since we do not live in a world where complete information is available to everyone, all these investment opportunities will be available simultaneously.

In deciding whether to undertake a particular investment, a businessman is seen as first calculating his expected profits net of interest costs. That is, he figures out what the expected profit rate would be if he didn't have to pay any interest. He then compares this profit rate with the current rate of interest. If the profit rate is above the interest rate, he will then go ahead with the investment. For example, if the businessman can borrow the funds needed to make the investment for 6 percent and then invest them at 10 percent, he will do so. But in the contrary case, where the rate of interest is above his expected profit rate, he will not do so. For example, he will not borrow money at 8 percent in order to invest it at an expected 5 percent profit rate. Thus the cutoff point for investment in the economy will be the going rate of interest. The higher the interest rate, the fewer investments that will be undertaken; and the lower the interest rate, the more investments that will be undertaken.

From these considerations we can develop an investment schedule showing investment to be inversely related to the rate of interest. This is done in Figure 20-6. The vertical axis measures the rate of interest i, and the horizontal axis measures investment expenditures I. (Note that the lower the interest rate, the greater will be investment, and conversely.) The investment schedule shown in Figure 20-6 is called (somewhat unfortunately) the *marginal efficiency of investment,* or MEI, *schedule.* By *marginal* is meant the *new* investment going on in the economy; *efficiency* is used in the economic sense to mean *profitable.* Hence *marginal efficiency of investment* is to be understood as referring to the expected profitability of new investment expenditures. Hereafter, we shall use the terms *investment schedule, marginal efficiency of investment,* and MEI interchangeably.

20-5   EQUILIBRIUM IN THE REAL SECTOR: THE *IS* SCHEDULE

We are now in a position to analyze the underlying conditions necessary for equilibrium to occur in the real sector of the economy. It will be recalled that the requirement for equilibrium is that investment be equal to saving ($I = S$). We now know that investment is determined by the rate of interest and that saving is determined by income. It follows that some combination of interest and income will result in saving and investment being equal. In fact, there are a variety of such combina-

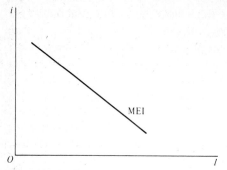

Figure 20-6   The marginal efficiency of investment schedule.

tions. We can derive these combinations from the investment and saving schedules
with the aid of Figure 20-7, as follows.

Look, first, at the top half of Figure 20-7. The right-hand side of the top half,
it will be noted, is simply the saving schedule; it is identical to the saving schedule
shown in Figure 20-5. The left-hand side of the top half of Figure 20-7, however,
is a little different from the MEI schedule shown in Figure 20-6. Actually, all that
has been done here is to interchange the axes of the MEI schedule. The reader can
easily see this by giving the book a quarter turn clockwise; then investment will be
on the horizontal axis and interest on the vertical axis, as usual. The change in the
axes has been made for the visual convenience of the reader. Since both saving and
investment are measured in dollar amounts, we can calibrate both the saving axis
on the right and the investment axis on the left identically (i.e., a given distance on

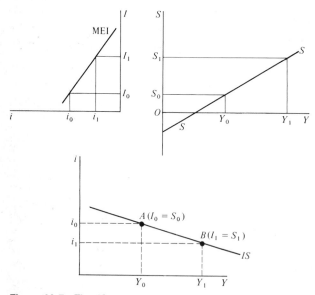

Figure 20-7   The *IS* schedule.

either axis represents the same number of dollars). By direct inspection of Figure 20-7, it is then easy to see when investment equals saving.

Consider the level of investment I_0 in the top half of Figure 20-7. Following the guideline leftward to the MEI schedule and then downward to the horizontal axis, it is apparent that the interest rate necessary to bring about this amount of investment is i_0; that is, when the interest rate is i_0, investment will be I_0. Now go back to the investment level I_0 on the vertical axis. From the way the figure is constructed, the dollar amount of investment I_0 is equal to the dollar amount of saving S_0. Since we are interested in the conditions necessary to bring about an equality between saving and investment, we want to know under what circumstances the saving level S_0 will prevail. Following the guidelines rightward and down, it is clear that saving will be S_0 when income is Y_0. It follows that when interest is i_0 and income is Y_0, saving will equal investment (that is, $S_0 = I_0$).

We record this finding in the lower half of Figure 20-7. This part of the figure shows interest rates on the vertical axis and income on the horizontal axis. The purpose of this graph is to show all combinations of interest rates and income levels where investment equals saving, and hence where the real sector of the economy is in equilibrium. We have just found one such combination: i_0, Y_0. This combination is indicated as point A on the graph; that is, at point A, $I_0 = S_0$.

We can repeat the analysis for other combinations of interest and income. For example, when interest is i_1 and income is Y_1, investment I_1 will equal saving S_1, which is shown as point B on the graph in the lower half of Figure 20-7. And so forth. By finding all possible combinations of i and Y that result in $I = S$, we generate the entire line in the lower half of Figure 20-7 labeled IS (meaning $I = S$).

An understanding of the IS schedule is essential. It shows all possible combinations of interest and income where investment equals saving, and hence shows all possible points of equilibrium in the real sector.

20-6 THE GOVERNMENTAL SECTOR

The macroeconomic role of the government can be explained most readily with the aid of Figure 20-8, which bears a strong resemblance to Figure 20-2. The difference between Figures 20-2 and 20-8 is that in Figure 20-8 the drain out of the income stream consists of saving and *taxes*. That is, when we include the government in our model of the real sector, individuals can do three things with their income: spend it on consumption goods and services, save it, and pay taxes with it. Thus, we now rewrite eq. (2) as:

$$Y = C + S + T \tag{9}$$

where T is taxes and the other symbols are as previously defined.

The injections into the income stream in Figure 20-8 consist of two sources: investment (as before) and government spending. Since, from an expenditures view-

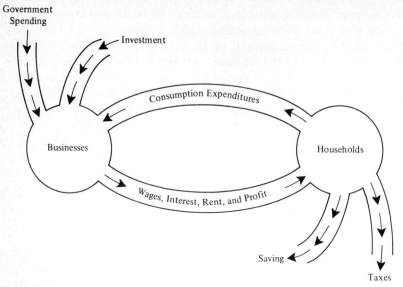

Figure 20-8 The circular flow of income.

point, income is now the sum of consumption, investment, and government expenditures, we must replace eq. (1) with

$$Y = C + I + G \tag{10}$$

where G is government spending.

It is important to understand that the inclusion in the model of governmental economic activity does *not* require government spending to be equal to taxes. Government spending may be larger than taxes if the government decides to finance some of its spending by borrowing; or it may be smaller than taxes if the government decides to repay previous borrowing. What *is* true is that for equilibrium to occur in the real sector now, it is necessary that the sum of investment and government spending equal the sum of saving and taxes. This is readily seen by substituting eq. (10) into eq. (9), which gives

$$C + I + G = C + S + T$$

or, canceling the Cs,

$$I + G = S + T \tag{11}$$

Equation (11), the necessary condition for equilibrium to occur in the real sector when the government is included in the Keynesian model, is to be interpreted in the same *schedule* sense as was the equation $I = S$.

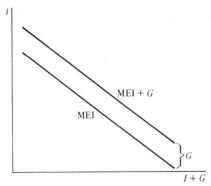

Figure 20-9 The MEI + *G* schedule.

The modification of the model to include the government requires that we adjust the way we think about the investment and saving schedules. These schedules are now to be interpreted as inclusive of government spending and taxation. Consider, for example, Figure 20-9. The MEI schedule shown in this figure is the same as that shown in Figures 20-6 and 20-7. To these investment expenditures we must now add the expenditures of the government *G*. Recall, however, that *G* is assumed to be *imposed* on the economy. Geometrically, this means that we obtain an *upward shift* in the MEI schedule; that is, the MEI + *G* line differs from the MEI line by the constant *G*.

The saving schedule of Figures 20-5 and 20-7 must also be modified to include the governmental sector. Since taxes *T* are assumed to be imposed on the economy in a lump-sum amount, the saving function is shifted upward by the amount of the tax. As shown in Figure 20-10, this results in the line parallel to the saving schedule, that is, the line marked *S* + *T*.

20-7 THE MULTIPLIER

A geometric (or mathematical) property of the Keynesian analysis of the real sector is that a given change in investment, government spending, or taxation will lead to

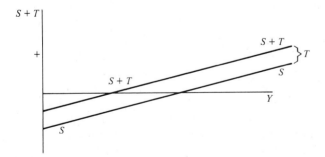

Figure 20-10 The *S* + *T* schedule.

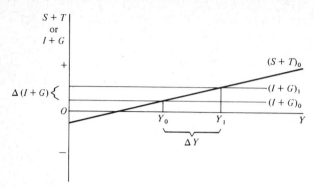

Figure 20-11   Geometrical representation of the expenditures multiplier.

a larger change in national income. This concept is called the *multiplier,* and it can be illustrated with the aid of Figure 20-11.

The horizontal axis in Figure 20-11 measures income Y. The vertical axis, scaled in dollars, measures either investment and government spending, $I + G$, or saving and taxes, $S + T$, depending on which we are interested in at the moment. The usual saving schedule is shown in Figure 20-11 as $(S + T)_0$. The usual investment schedule, however, is not shown. Instead, the amount of investment and government spending is measured by the horizontal line labeled $(I + G)_0$. This line is horizontal to indicate that both I and G are invariant with respect to income. The reader should be sure to understand the $(I + G)_0$ line. The line does *not* say that neither I nor G can change; it *does* say that neither one will change *because* income changes.

From eq. (11) the equilibrium requirement for the real sector, including the government, is that $I + G = S + T$. In Figure 20-11, with the saving schedule $(S + T)_0$ and the horizontal $(I + G)_0$ line, this requirement will be satisfied at income level Y_0. We shall therefore refer to Y_0 as the equilibrium level of income, given the $(S + T)_0$ schedule and the $(I + G)_0$ line. Now suppose that the $I + G$ line shifts upward from $(I + G)_0$ to $(I + G)_1$ while the $S + T$ schedule remains the same at $(S + T)_0$. Such a shift in the $I + G$ line could occur for three reasons: First, there could be a sudden increase in the level of government spending; second, a major new invention (like the computer) could open up a lot of profit opportunities for investment in the economy; and third, a fall in the rate of interest would make previously unprofitable investment profitable. Whatever causes the shift from $(I + G)_0$ to $(I + G)_1$, the question we are interested in is, What effect does this have on the equilibrium level of income Y_0?

To see the answer to this question, note that at the new level of investment and government spending, $(I + G)_1$, saving and taxes will have to increase until it is once more true that $I + G = S + T$. But according to the saving schedule $S + T$ will rise to the level $(I + G)_1$ only if income rises from Y_0 to Y_1. The income level Y_1 is therefore the new equilibrium level of income. The important point to note is that the *change* in income from Y_0 to Y_1 is greater than the change in $I + G$ from

$(I + G)_0$ to $(I + G)_1$. In other words, the ratio $\Delta Y/\Delta(I + G)$ is greater than 1. This is the multiplier.

How can this be? How is it possible that, for example, a $1 million increase in investment will lead to a $4 million increase in income? The *geometry* leads to this conclusion, but it does not tell us anything about the *economics* involved. To understand the economics of the multiplier, take the following example: Suppose that a business woman decides to build a new plant costing $1 million. When she builds this plant, she will spend the $1 million on material and labor, and consequently the people who receive this money will experience an immediate increase in their income of $1 million. Now assume that the marginal propensity to consume, $\Delta C/\Delta Y$, is 3/4. This marginal propensity to consume says that when people's income rise by a $1 million, they will increase their consumption expenditures by $750,000 [3/4 ($1 million)]. They will therefore buy an extra $750,000 worth of TV sets, new cars, vacations, and so forth. This $750,000 then accrues as additional income to the people who sold them these goods and who, in turn, then spend 3/4 of it, or $562,500. This amount then becomes other people's income, and so forth.

The increase in total income at this point is $1 million + $750,000 + 562,500 = $2,312,500. And the process is not yet completed. To see what the end result will be, consider how we obtained these numbers: They were obtained by taking $1 million + 4/5 ($1 million) + (4/5)^2($1 million). This is a geometric progression, mathematically the same as the one obtained for the bank deposit expansion process described in Chapter 12.[3] The sum of this geometric progression will eventually be

$$\Delta Y = \frac{\$1 \text{ million}}{1 - 3/4}$$

$$= \$4 \text{ million}$$

That is, the initial increase in investment of $1 million will eventually lead to an increase in income of $4 million.

These results, obtained from an arithmetic example, can be generalized by noting that the fraction 3/4 is the marginal propensity to consume and that $1 million is the change in investment. Letting (as usual) $\Delta C/\Delta Y$ stand for the marginal propensity to consume and ΔI stand for the change in investment,

$$\Delta Y = \Delta I \frac{1}{1 - \Delta C/\Delta Y} \tag{12}$$

Dividing both sides of eq. (12) by ΔI gives

$$\frac{\Delta Y}{\Delta I} = \frac{1}{1 - \Delta C/\Delta Y} \tag{13}$$

[3]See pages 208 to 211.

Equation (13) can be simplified further by recalling eq. (8), which says that the marginal propensity to save is equal to 1 minus the marginal propensity to consume. Symbolically,

$$\frac{\Delta S}{\Delta Y} = 1 - \frac{\Delta C}{\Delta Y} \tag{8}$$

But the right-hand side of eq. (8) is the denominator of the right-hand side of eq. (13). Thus we can write eq. (13) equivalently as

$$\frac{\Delta Y}{\Delta I} = \frac{1}{\Delta S/\Delta Y} \tag{14}$$

In words, the multiplier is equal to the reciprocal of the marginal propensity to save.

We have discussed the multiplier only in terms of changes in investment and government spending. But the same type of phenomenon can also occur because of shifts in the $S + T$ schedule, that is, because of changes in either saving or taxes. A geometric representation of this is shown in Figure 20-12, which is fundamentally the same as Figure 20-11 in that the same quantities are measured on the axes and once again the $S + T$ schedule and $I + G$ line are shown. In this case, however, our interest centers on the $S + T$ schedule rather than on the $I + G$ line.

Consider, first, the saving schedule $(S + T)_0$. This saving schedule, taken together with the $(I + G)_0$ line, will result in the equilibrium level of income Y_0. At income level Y_0, that is, it will be true that $I + G = S + T$, the condition necessary for equilibrium in the real sector. Now suppose that, for whatever reason, the saving schedule shifts downward from $(S + T)_0$ to $(S + T)_1$. Then at this new, lower $S + T$ schedule, income will have to rise from Y_0 to Y_1 before it is once again true that $S + T = I + G$. But the *change* in income from Y_0 to Y_1 is greater than the *change* in the $S + T$ schedule [measured by the vertical distance between $(S + T)_0$ and $(S + T)_1$]. Thus the downward shift in the saving schedule has caused a multiple expansion in the level of income just as in the previous case.

A downward shift in the $S + T$ schedule could result either from a change in the public's desire to save or from a cut in government taxes. Since in general the

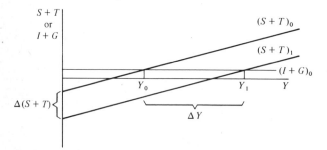

Figure 20-12 Geometrical representation of the tax multiplier.

consumption function (and hence saving) is considered a stable economic relationship, let us concentrate on a cut in taxes. Suppose, then, that the government reduces taxes by the lump-sum amount of $1 million. What effect will this have on people's behavior? The first thing to note is that people will now have $1 million more to spend than they previously did. They will therefore spend this money according to their marginal propensity to consume $\Delta C/\Delta Y$. If the marginal propensity to consume is 3/4, then a $1 million cut in their taxes will cause them to spend an extra $750,000. This money will then become other people's income, and they, in turn, will spend three-fourths of it, or $562,500; and so forth. The money will continue to change hands, through round after round, until national income has grown by enough so that it is once more true that $I + G = S + T$. As before, the size of the increase will depend on the value of the marginal propensity to consume (or, alternatively, the marginal propensity to save).[4]

One final point should be made about the multiplier process. Until now the discussion has been cast in terms that eventually lead to increases in national income. But the multiplier process is fully symmetrical; that is, a multiple *decrease* in national income will result from a decrease in government spending and investment and from higher taxes. This can be seen from Figure 20-11 and 20-12 simply by beginning at income level Y_1 and assuming a downward shift from $(I + G)_1$ to $(I + G)_0$ in Figure 20-11 or an upward shift from $(S + T)_1$ to $(S + T)_0$ in Figure 20-12. The economics involved is also the same, except in reverse. A decrease in investment or government spending or an increase in taxes will mean that income that people would otherwise have received is now withheld from them. They will consequently reduce their consumption expenditures, and this, in turn, will cause other people's income to fall, and so forth. The end result will be a contraction in national income equal to some multiple of the contraction in I or G or the increase in T.

20-8 CONCLUDING COMMENT

The traditional Keynesian analysis of the real sector of the economy emphasizes the investment and saving schedules. Any actions that affect investment, government spending, taxes, or the consumption function, working through the multiplier, will affect national income. Thus, from the Keynesian viewpoint, if we wish to design public policies to stabilize the real sector—to avoid unemployment and inflation— it is necessary somehow to operate through one of these four aspects of the real sector (I, G, T, and C or S).

[4]However, the value of the tax multiplier will be less than the value of the investment or government spending multiplier because the first-round effect of the $I + G$ multiplier is missing from the tax multiplier. For example, an increase of $1 million in government spending immediately increases income by $1 million, but the first-round effect of a $1 million decrease in taxes is the $750,000 increase in consumption expenditures (if $\Delta C/\Delta Y = 3/4$). Thus, the tax multiplier "skips over" the first round of the $I + G$ multiplier and begins with the second round. Although this means that the tax multiplier is less powerful than the $I + G$ multiplier, it need not concern us in the present context. In principle, there is some change in taxes that will provide the same effect on national income as any given change in I or G.

Generally speaking, Keynesians feel that it is not possible to affect the consumption decisions made by the public. The *public* decides what proportions of its after-tax income to spend on consumption and what proportion to save. With the possible exception of consumer-goods rationing during wartime, there does not appear to be any feasible way to alter the consumption function as a matter of deliberate public policy. This leaves investment, government spending, and taxes as the channels through which stabilization policy must operate.

Government spending and taxing (G and T) are clearly and directly under the control of the government. Abstracting from the political difficulties involved, the government can, for example, change its total expenditures by building more or fewer dams, highways, schools, and so forth. The government can also change its tax policies so that the consuming public is left with a greater or lesser disposable income. Government spending and taxing policies designed to stimulate or cool down the pace of economic activity are called *fiscal policy*. Fiscal policy operates directly on the real sector of the economy by shifting G and T. This leaves investment I as the sole remaining channel through which the real sector of the economy might be affected by monetary policy.

In the Keynesian view, the expenditures made by business firms for new investment can be influenced by *monetary policy*. Recall that investment is a function of the rate of interest: When the rate of interest rises, investment expenditures will fall, and conversely. But for the Keynesians the rate of interest is determined in the *monetary sector* of the economy. We shall examine the traditional Keynesian view of the monetary sector in Chapter 21.

20-9 REVIEW QUESTIONS

1 Explain, in common-sense terms, why the real sector will be in equilibrium when saving is equal to investment. Now suppose that saving is less than investment. How will the economy get back to equilibrium?
2 What is the main determinant of the amount you save? of the amount you invest?
3 Suppose the government spends $1 billion to build a new dam. Will this add $1 billion to national income, or more than $1 billion? How? What is the main name of the economic process you have just described?
4 In what way is government spending similar to investment? In what way is it different?

21

Traditional Keynesian Theory: Analysis of the Monetary Sector and Overall Equilibrium

As discussed in Chapter 20, traditional Keynesian theory proceeds by first analyzing the conditions necessary for the real sector of the economy to be in equilibrium, then doing the same for the monetary sector, and finally combining the two analyses into a single overall theory. Our inquiry into the real sector led to the *IS* schedule of Figure 20-7, which is repeated as Figure 21-1. It will be recalled that this *IS* schedule shows all equilibrium combinations of interest and income in the real sector. Our next task is to derive a similar schedule for the monetary sector of the economy.

21-1 EQUILIBRIUM IN THE MONETARY SECTOR

The monetary sector of the economy will be in equilibrium when the demand for money is equal to the supply of money. Since the determination of the money supply by the central banking authorities has already been discussed, we shall concentrate on the demand for money.

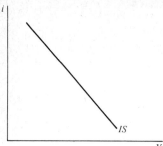

Figure 21-1   The *IS* schedule.

The Demand for Money

The traditional Keynesian analysis of the demand for money identifies three *motives* for holding cash balances: the precautionary, transactions, and speculative motives.

The Precautionary Motive   People and business firms hold cash balances as a bulwark against future emergencies and opportunities. Sickness, a fire, an unexpected business opportunity—all these things require a cushion of cash balances to fall back on. We shall use the symbol M^P for the precautionary demand for money. For our purposes, it will be sufficient to regard M^P as a constant.

The Transactions Motive   The second motive for holding cash balances is to take care of commercial transactions arising in the day-to-day process of living. Individuals need to buy things more or less continuously even though they receive income in lump-sum amounts at regular intervals. Similarly, receipts and expenditures of business firms are not perfectly coordinated, and they, too, need to maintain an operating balance to bridge this gap. The symbol M^T will be used for the transactions demand for money. Since these balances are held for transactions purposes, it is hypothesized that they will vary directly with the level of national income Y. For our purposes, it will be sufficient to regard transactions balances as a constant proportion of income. Thus we may write

$$M^T = kY \tag{1}$$

where M^T = transaction demand for money
Y = national income
k = constant of proportionality, $0 < k < 1$

The M_A Demand for Money   It is customary to combine the precautionary and transactions demand for money into a single demand schedule called the *demand for active balances*. Letting M_A stand for the demand for active balances, we may therefore write

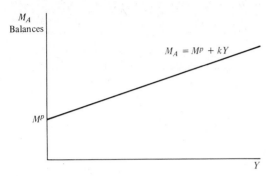

Figure 21-2   The M_A demand-for-money function.

$$M_A = M^P + M^T \tag{2}$$

Substituting eq. (1) into eq. (2), we then have

$$M_A = M^P + kY \tag{3}$$

A plot of eq. (3) is a straight line; that is, the M_A demand for money is equal to a constant M^P plus a coefficient k times a variable Y, and such an equation describes a straight line. This line is graphed in Figure 21-2.

The Speculative Motive   The third motive for holding cash balances, and the one that is uniquely Keynesian in origin, is called the *speculative motive,* or the *speculative demand for money.* This aspect of the demand for money, unlike the two motives just discussed, is neither straightforward nor obvious. Nevertheless, it is a crucial part of the traditional Keynesian analysis and therefore must be considered carefully.

To understand the speculative demand for money, it is necessary to make explicit something that has been only implicit so far. The analysis of the real sector in Chapter 20 was developed in terms of *the* rate of interest. There is, of course, no such thing as *the* rate of interest; instead, there are many interest rates in the economy, depending on such things as term to maturity, creditworthiness of the bond issuer, tax features of the bond, and so on. The traditional Keynesian model abstracts from these complications and makes the simplifying assumption that there are only two kinds of financial assets in the economy: *money* and *bonds. Money* is assumed to be a financial asset that is perfectly liquid but that bears no rate of interest. By *bonds* is meant long-term debt that is illiquid and that does bear a rate of interest. In such a simplified world, the entire portfolio adjustment of the monetary sector consists in a choice between money and bonds.

How is such a choice made? The basic principle is that the investor chooses between the utility to be derived from the liquidity of money and the utility to be derived from the yield on bonds. But the *yield on bonds* is not so simple a concept as it may at first seem. For the *yield* on a bond consists of two parts: (1) the number of dollars the bond pays annually (coupon payments) and (2) the change in the price of the bond between when it is bought and when it is sold. And this second part of the yield, the change in the bond price, depends on *future* movements in the market rate of interest. If interest rates fall, bond prices will rise, and vice versa. Of course, there is no way to know what is going to happen in the future. But even though bond investors do not know for sure what is going to happen to the market rate, they must nevertheless formulate some expectation about it and then act on the basis of this expectation. The question then becomes, How do bond investors formulate such expectations?

The answer given by the traditional Keynesian analysis is that bond investors make judgments about the future by comparing the present with the past. Suppose, for example, that at present the interest rate is higher than it has been at any time in the past twenty-five years. Then the assumption is that bond investors will feel, on the whole, that the rate of interest is more likely to fall than it is to rise still higher. But if the interest rate falls, then bond investors will stand to make substantial profits because a falling interest rate means a rising bond price. They will therefore prefer holding bonds, where they make a very high rate of return, to holding money, where their rate of return is zero. Thus at a very high rate of interest, the quantity of money demanded will be quite low.

Alternatively, suppose the opposite case—that at present the interest rate is *lower* than it has been for the past twenty-five years. In this case, it is assumed that bond investors will expect that the interest rate will most probably rise in the future. But if the rate of interest rises, then the price of bonds will fall. Thus, anyone who buys a bond today would expect to lose money on it during the following year. Under such circumstances, the typical investor will prefer holding money, where the return is zero, to holding bonds, where the return is negative. It follows that when the market rate is very low, the quantity of money demanded will be very large. Money balances will, in the given case, be held as a *speculative investment* (hence the phrase *speculative motive*).

The M_I Demand for Money   The preceding analysis leads to the conclusion that the quantity of money balances demanded will be high at a low rate of interest and low at a high rate of interest. We can easily imagine that intermediate interest rates will produce intermediate quantities of money demanded because expectations will be mixed. The speculative demand for money therefore can be represented by a continuous curve showing an inverse relationship between the rate of interest and the demand for cash balances. This curve is shown in Figure 21-3. It is called by various names: Sometimes it is referred to as the *demand for "idle" balances* to distinguish it from the *demand for "active" balances.* Probably the most common name for the curve shown in Figure 21-3, however, is the *liquidity preference schedule.* This name is derived from Keynes's *General Theory* and is meant to indicate that the public *prefers* to be *liquid* and hence that it will hold money unless induced not to do so by a high interest rate. We shall label the horizontal axis of Figure 21-3 "M_I balances" (for *idle money*), and label the curve "LP" (for *liquidity preference*).

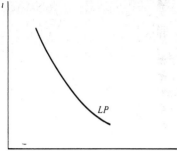

M_I balances   **Figure 21-3** The M_I demand-for-money function.

Figures 21-2 and 21-3, taken together, constitute the total demand for money in the traditional Keynesian model. Letting L stand for the total demand for money, we can thus write

$$L = M_A + M_I \qquad (4)$$

The Supply of Money

As explained previously, the traditional Keynesian model assumes that the supply of money is an *exogenous* variable, meaning that it is determined outside the theoretical system (in contrast with an *endogenous* variable, such as interest or income, which is determined within the theoretical system). The exogenous nature of the money supply in the theory means that we shall treat it as a given quantity, responsive to neither the interest rate nor the level of income. Notwithstanding this, it will be convenient to show the (fixed) quantity of money in a graph that divides the money supply into two parts: that part being held in M_A balances and that part being held in M_I balances. This is done in Figure 21-4.

In Figure 21-4, M_A balances are measured along the vertical axis and M_I balances are measured along the horizontal axis. Because both axes are scaled in

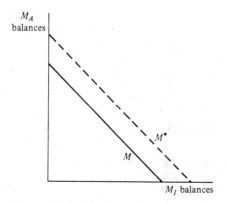

Figure 21-4 A fixed quantity of money divided between M_A and M_I balances.

dollars, we can calibrate them equally; that is, a given distance measures the same number of dollars on either axis. By constructing Figure 21-4 in this manner, we can show the (fixed) quantity of money as the downward sloping line marked M. This line forms a 45-degree angle with both axes, and any point on this line will show the same *total* of $M_A + M_I$. An increase in the money supply will be shown by an outward shift in this curve (for example, to the line marked M^*). A decrease in the money supply is represented by an inward shift (for example, from M^* to M). To repeat, any point *on* the line M indicates the same total supply of money.

Equilibrium in the Monetary Sector: The *LM* Schedule

We are now in position to derive the conditions necessary for equilibrium to occur in the monetary sector of the economy. We can do this by combining the information given in Figures 21-2 to 21-4. This is done in Figure 21-5. Figure 21-5 looks very complicated. In fact, it isn't, as a bit of study will show. There are two things to note about Figure 21-5 that will help make it intelligible: In the first place, note that you are already familiar with three of the four graphs shown. The graph in Figure 21-5d is the M_A demand-for-money function; the graph in Figure 21-5a is the liquidity preference schedule; and the graph in Figure 21-5c is the fixed money supply depicted in Figure 21-4. Thus the only graph that has not already been explained is the one in Figure 21-5b. It is this graph, and this graph only, that we wish to explain; we shall use the other three graphs to do so.

The second thing to note about Figure 21-5 is that as you move up, down, or sideways from one graph to another, you will encounter the same axis. For example,

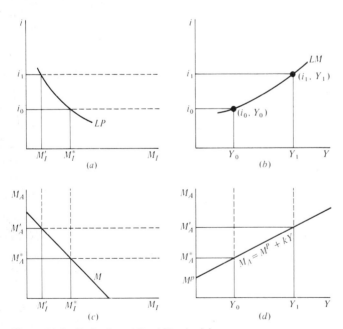

Figure 21-5 Derivation of the *LM* schedule.

the horizontal axis in Figure 21-5b is identical to the horizontal axis directly below it in Figure 21-5d; both measure income. Similarly, the vertical axis in Figure 21-5d is the same as the vertical axis in Figure 21-5c; both measure M_A balances; and so forth. All side-by-side or above-and-below axes are the same. This characteristic permits us to move "around" Figure 21-5 from one part to another in a manner that will become apparent in a moment.

The immediate, or proximate, condition for equilibrium to occur in the monetary sector of the economy is that the demand for money be equal to the supply of money, i.e., that

$$L = M \tag{5}$$

where L is the demand for money and M is the supply of money. Our purpose now is to discover the circumstances under which eq. (5) will hold true. We shall do this with the aid of Figure 21-5. As a first step, let us arbitrarily choose some level of income on the horizontal axis of Figure 21-5b, say, income level Y_0. We can take this level of income and transfer it directly downward to the horizontal axis of Figure 21-5d; that is, the income level Y_0 in Figure 21-5b is the same as the income level Y_0 in Figure 21-5d, which is the graph of M_A money balances. It tells us that if the level of income is Y_0, then the amount of M_A balances the public will want to hold will be M^*_A, which is shown on the vertical axis of Figure 21-5d. Next take this amount of M_A balances, M^*_A, and transfer it directly leftward to Figure 21-5c, which shows all possible combinations of M_A and M_I balances that will result in a fixed supply of money. It follows, from Figure 21-5c, that if the public demands M^*_A balances, then it must also demand M^*_I of M_I balances if the supply of money is to be equal to the demand for money. The question is, thus, Under what circumstances will the public be willing to hold an amount of M_I balances equal to M^*_I —no more and no less?

This question can be answered by transferring the M^*_I on the horizontal axis of Figure 21-5c directly upward to the horizontal axis of Figure 21-5a, which is the liquidity preference schedule of Figure 21-4. It tells us that the public will be willing to hold M^*_I of M_I balances—no more and no less—only if the rate of interest is i_0 (measured on the vertical axis of Figure 21-5a). Then we can take this rate of interest i_0 and transfer it directly rightward to the vertical axis of Figure 21-5b.

We now have one combination of income and interest (Y_0, i_0) at which it is true that the demand for money is equal to the supply of money ($L = M$) and hence where the monetary sector is in equilibrium. Since the axes of Figure 21-5b measure interest and income, this combination can be shown in the interior of that graph. Specifically, the point labeled (Y_0, i_0) in Figure 21-5b shows one possible point of equilibrium in the monetary sector. But this is only one such combination; there are others. For example, suppose that instead of beginning at income level Y_0, we had chosen to begin at Y_1. Then, from Figure 21-5d, the M_A demand for money would be M'_A. Moving next to Figure 21-5c, we see that if $M_A = M'_A$, money supply will equal money demand only if the public wants to hold M'_I of M_I balances. Figure 21-5a tells us that the public will want this amount of M_I balances only if the rate of interest is i_1; and transferring i_1 to Figure 21-5b then gives us the income-interest combination (Y_1, i_1) as a second possible point of equilibrium in the monetary sector.

If we were to repeat this analysis for all possible levels of income, we would eventually generate the curve shown in Figure 21-5b. This curve is known as the *LM schedule* (short for $L = M$); it shows *all possible* points of equilibrium in the monetary sector. Any point *not* on this curve will not be a point of monetary equilibrium; and, conversely, any point that *is* on the *LM* schedule *will* be a point of monetary equilibrium.

21-2 OVERALL EQUILIBRIUM: *IS* AND *LM*

It remains only to take the final step and derive the overall equilibrium conditions for both sectors simultaneously. This is easily done. The *IS* schedule (Figure 21-1) measures the rate of interest on the vertical axis and income on the horizontal axis. Similarly, the *LM* schedule (Figure 21-5b) measures the same variables on *its* axes. Since both graphs measure the same thing, it is therefore permissable to show them both on a single graph, that is, to superimpose one graph on the other. This is done in Figure 21-6.

To understand Figure 21-6, it is necessary to keep the following point in mind: The *IS* schedule shows all interest-income combinations where investment equals saving $(I = S)$ and therefore where the real sector is in equilibrium. The *LM* schedule shows all interest-income combinations where the demand for money equals the supply of money $(L = M)$ and therefore where the monetary sector is in equilibrium. What is necessary for overall equilibrium in the economy is that the economy be on both the *IS* and *LM* schedules *at the same time.* But this condition is met at only a single point in Figure 21-6: the point marked *E,* where the two schedules cross. And point *E* will be attained only when the rate of interest is i_e and the level of income is Y_e. Any other interest-income combination will represent a disequilibrium in the economy.

Only one other aspect of Figure 21-6 needs to be discussed: The income level Y_e should *not* be interpreted as being the full employment level of income. Full

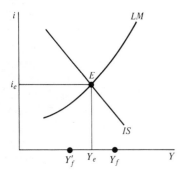

Figure 21-6 Overall equilibrium: the *IS–LM* graph.

employment may occur at an income level either greater or less than Y_e. If full employment income is greater than Y_e—for example, at Y_f—then the economy will be in a recession; if it is less than Y_e—for example, at Y'_f—then the economy will have an inflation.

21-3 MONETARY POLICY

The purpose of monetary theory goes beyond the mere analytics of the role played by the quantity of money in the functioning of the economy. A more fundamental purpose is to develop a theoretical guide to monetary policy. It is this issue—the implications of the Keynesian theory for monetary policy—that will be examined in this section.

Monetary Policy in a Recession

To understand the monetary policy inherent in the Keynesian analysis of the economy, let us look again briefly at Figure 21-6. Suppose that, in terms of this figure, the economy is in equilibrium at income level Y_e. Suppose, further, that the full employment level of income is Y_f (to the right of Y_e on the income axis of the figure). As discussed previously, the relative positions of these two levels of income indicate that the economy is operating at less than full employment—that it is in a recession. The appropriate course of action for the monetary authorities is therefore to try to increase the equilibrium level of income, that is, to shift Y_e to the right so that it is closer to Y_f. The question is, How (in the context of the Keynesian theory) can the central banking authorities accomplish this goal?

To see the answer to this question, consider Figure 21-7. This figure is similar to Figure 21-5 in that it shows the four-part derivation of the LM curve. However, Figure 21-7 also shows what happens if the supply of money is increased: Suppose, first, that the money supply labeled M' in Figure 21-7c is the quantity of money outstanding in the economy. Then, as explained previously, we can begin at income level Y_0 in Figure 21-7b and "move around" all of Figure 21-7 to find the rate of interest that must prevail in order for the monetary sector of the economy to be in equilibrium. For visual convenience, this movement from one part of Figure 21-7 to another has been marked with a heavy line, and each point of intersection with a function has been marked as ①. As will be seen, the equilibrium rate of interest consisent with Y_0 is i_0. If we were to construct similar guidelines for all levels of income, we would then generate the LM' schedule.

Now suppose that the Federal Reserve System increases the money supply. How can this be shown in Figure 21-7? As we have seen, a larger stock of money can be shown by shifting the 45-degree line of Figure 21-7c outward. This new, larger money supply is shown as the dashed line in Figure 21-7c and is labeled M^*. Now let us repeat the previous analysis, except using the money supply M^*. Beginning (as before) at income level Y_0 on the horizontal axis of Figure 19-7b, we follow the same guideline downward and then leftward. This time, however, with the money supply M^*, we stop at the point marked ② and then proceed upward and rightward along the dashed guidelines. It will seen that, in this case, the equilibrium interest rate is i_1. In other words, the point marked ② in Figure 21-7 is now a point of equilibrium in the monetary sector. But the point ② lies off the LM' schedule. This will be true in general. If we were to begin with other levels of income (not shown) and work around Figure 21-7 using the money supply M^*, we would generate an entirely new LM schedule such as that shown by the dashed line marked LM^*. Thus, an increase in the quantity of money, everything else remaining the same, *shifts the LM schedule to the right.*

It should now be apparent how the Federal Reserve can overcome a recession. Suppose that the Federal Reserve buys government securities, lowers the discount rate, or reduces reserve requirements for member banks. These actions, taken individually or in combination, will increase the supply of money in the economy. The increase in the money supply will shift the LM schedule of Figure 21-8 rightward from LM' to a new LM schedule such as the dashed line marked LM^*. With this new schedule LM^*, the new equilibrium level of income will be Y^*_e, which, of course, is equal to Y_f. By increasing the money supply, the Federal Reserve has overcome the recession by changing the situation from $Y'_e < Y_f$ to $Y^*_e = Y_f$.

One difficulty with the preceding analysis is that it is very formal and may leave the false impression that monetary policy is a purely mechanical affair: The Federal Reserve simply pulls the correct level and—presto!—full employment is restored. But the mechanical impression is, of course, a property of the model itself, not of the economic process it is attempting to describe. A less formal, more impressionis-

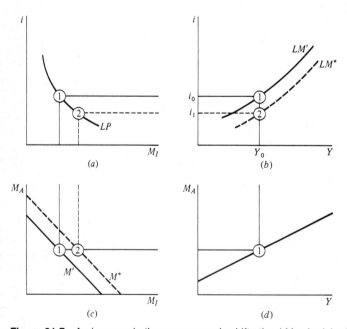

Figure 21-7 An increase in the money supply shifts the *LM* schedule rightward.

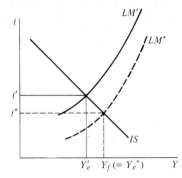

Figure 21-8   An antirecession monetary policy.

tic, description of the traditional Keynesian view of the monetary policy process would be the following.

The economy is in a recession. The Federal Reserve therefore adopts an easy money policy; that is, it expands the money supply more rapidly than it had previously been doing. The more rapid expansion of the money supply has the immediate consequence of lowering interest rates. (Note in Figure 21-8 that the full-employment–equilibrium interest rate $i*$ is lower than the less than full employment interest rate i'.) This decrease in interest rates will then stimulate investment spending in the economy. Business people will find that, with the cheaper financing available, previously unprofitable investments will become profitable. Investment therefore increases. The people who receive the money spent by the business people will buy consumer goods with it, and the people who sell them these consumer goods will, in turn, experience an increase in income and hence buy even more consumer goods, and so on. The result is that national income rises. Hopefully, it rises by just enough (and no more) to restore full employment.

Monetary Policy in an Inflation

The implications of the Keynesian model for an antiinflationary monetary policy are more difficult to show, geometrically speaking, than those for an antirecession policy. This difficulty reflects a fundamental assumption in the Keynesian model. This assumption—perhaps "empirical judgment" would be a better term—is that prices and especially wage rates are *inflexible downward but flexible upward.* In other words, the Keynesian view of economic reality is that business firms and labor unions are much more reluctant to permit prices and wages to fall than they are to allow them to rise. From the viewpoint of the individual business firm, a reduction in its employees' wages might result in a disastrous strike, whereas higher wages can be passed on to the consumer in the form of higher prices. Similarly, labor leaders negotiating a union contract would soon find themselves in deep trouble with their membership if they were to accept a wage reduction, whereas an inflationary wage increase would be accepted without question. Thus, in general, Keynesians feel that the actual behavior of prices in the economy is that they can increase with ease but decrease only with great difficulty. In terms of the formal model, this viewpoint is translated into the more rigid statement that although prices can adjust upward quickly, they cannot go downward at all.[1]

This asymmetrical assumption about prices, that they can go up but not down, means that the full employment income level cannot legitimately be held fixed if the equilibrium level of income lies to the right of it on an *IS-LM* graph. Such a situation is a theoretical representation of inflation, and inflation *can* occur in the Keynesian system even though deflation (falling prices) cannot. Within the context of the *IS-LM* framework, the analysis of monetary policy for an inflation accordingly becomes slightly more complex.

To understand the inflationary process in Keynesian analysis, consider Figure 21-9. Our immediate interest centers on the two heavy lines *IS* and *LM'* (ignore the dashed line *LM** for the moment). With these two schedules, the equilibrium income level will be Y'_e. However, Y'_e represents a larger amount of national income than Y_f, the full employment level of income. The first question is, How are we to interpret such a situation?

To see the answer to this question, suppose we have the following situation: Let full employment income Y_f be $1,500 billion and equilibrium income Y'_e be $1,700 billion, *both expressed in current prices.* Now the equilibrium income of $1,700 billion means that consumers and businesses want to buy $1,700 billion of consumption and investment goods. The $1,500 billion full employment income, however, means that *measured in current prices* the economy is capable of producing only $1,500 billion of consumption and investment goods, that is, $200 billion less than people want to buy. How can this difference be reconciled? What must happen is that *prices rise* (inflation). People will attempt to buy more goods than are available, and businesses, unable to fill all their orders, will raise prices to clear the market.

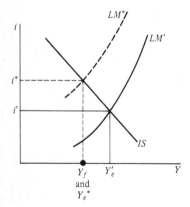

Figure 21-9 An antiinflation monetary policy.

This inflationary process will continue until prices have risen by 13 percent, that is, until full employment income rises from $1,500 billion to $1,700 billion. The economy will then be in equilibrium: People will want to buy $1,700 billion of goods, and the economy will be producing $1,700 billion of goods.

Geometrically, in terms of Figure 21-9, the process just described can be represented by a rightward shift in Y_f. The reader is thus asked to imagine that if the government takes no action, the point Y_f on the horizontal axis of Figure 21-9 will move steadily to the right until it equals Y'_e. At $Y_f = Y'_e$ the economy will be at full employment equilibrium, but it will have arrived there through a process of inflation. But it would clearly be much more desirable to shift Y'_e leftward to achieve equilibrium so that the social evil of inflation could be avoided. The question is, How can we do it?

An alternative to letting Y_f move up to Y'_e through inflation would be to decrease the money supply, which will shift the LM schedule leftward from LM' to LM^* (the dashed line). With LM^* the relevant LM schedule, it will be seen that the new equilibrium in the economy will be Y^*_e. Of course Y^*_e is equal to Y_f. Thus, by decreasing the money supply, monetary policy has been able to achieve full employment equilibrium *without inflation.* One feature of this antiinflationary monetary policy should be noted in particular: It involves a higher rate of interest. In terms of Figure 21-9, the rate of interest has risen from i' to i^*. (This rise in interest rates during inflation has political consequences that will be discussed later.)

To avoid giving too mechanistic an impression, it will be best to describe the economic process underlying an antiinflationary monetary policy. Suppose, therefore, that the economy is undergoing inflationary pressures in the sense that the dollar value of spending is greater than the dollar value of goods and services the economy can produce, measured in current prices. What is then necessary is to decrease total spending. To do this, the Federal Reserve will slow down the rate of increase in the money supply. This will cause interest rates to rise, which will discourage businesses from making investments. The volume of investment expenditures will therefore decline, and this decline, working through the multiplier, will cause a slackening in the demand for consumer goods. The result will be a slowdown in aggregate demand, hopefully by just enough to eliminate the inflationary pressures in the economy.

Two Key Issues

The monetary aspects of the traditional Keynesian model may be described in broad terms as follows: A change in the quantity of money causes portfolio adjustments in the monetary sector that result ultimately in a changed rate of interest; the changed rate of interest then transmits this disturbance in the monetary sector to the real sector by changing investment expenditures. The point to note about these two processes is that they describe *empirical* relationships, which may be strong, weak, or even nonexistent. For example, the portfolio adjustments caused by a change in the quantity of money may or may not result in the desired change in the rate of interest. And even if the rate of interest does change, this may or may not have the desired effect on investment expenditures. Whether these relationships are

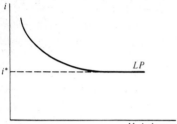

M_I balances   **Figure 21-10** The liquidity trap.

powerful or weak is therefore a critical issue in Keynesian economics. If they are powerful relationships, then monetary policy will be a powerful tool for economic stabilization; if, however, they are very weak relationships, then Keynesians argue that monetary policy will be an unreliable instrument for curing the social ills of inflation and unemployment. Accordingly, a great deal of research has dealt with investigating the nature of these two relationships.

The Liquidity Trap Issue The theoretical possibility that the public's portfolio response to a change in the quantity of money may fail to elicit the desired change in the interest rate can be explained best with the aid of Figure 21-10, which shows the liquidity preference schedule. Figure 21-10 is the same as Figure 21-3, with one exception: It will be noted that the liquidity preference schedule in Figure 21-10

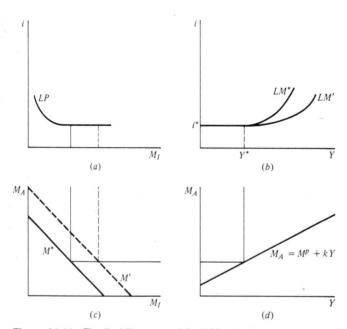

Figure 21-11 The liquidity trap and the *LM* schedule.

turns horizontal at very low rates of interest. Technically, when this happens, it is said that the interest elasticity of the demand for money is infinite. Practically, what is meant is that the interest rate cannot fall below a given minimum (i^* in Figure 21-10) no matter how large the increase in the money supply.

To see that this is so, let us take the liquidity preference schedule of Figure 21-10 and insert it into the four-part diagram of Figure 21-5. This is done in Figure 21-11, where the LP curve in Figure 21-11a is horizontal at the interest rate i^*. Beginning at income level Y^* in Figure 21-11b and using the money supply M^* in Figure 21-11c, we can then "go around" Figure 21-11 in the usual way and derive the interest-income equilibrium combination (i^*, Y^*). This combination (i^*, Y^*) lies on the schedule LM^* in Figure 21-11b. Now suppose that the money supply is increased from M^* to M' in Figure 21-11c. If we once more begin with income Y^* Figure 21-11b and go around the figure (but this time using money supply M'), it will be seen that the interest-income combination (i^*, Y^*) is still an equilibrium point. In this case, however, the point (i^*, Y^*) lies on the LM' schedule instead of the LM^* schedule. What has happened, geometrically, is that the LM schedule has shifted rightward; but because the lower left-hand "tail" of LM^* and LM' are both horizontal at the same rate of interest, this part of the two schedules coincides, or overlaps. When this happens, the monetary sector is said to be in a *liquidity trap.*

The result of a liquidity trap situation is that monetary policy becomes powerless to change the level of national income. Any increase in the money supply is simply absorbed into M_I balances, and interest rates remain the same. But since interest rates cannot fall, investment cannot be stimulated and hence national income cannot rise. The situation is illustrated in Figure 21-12. Here the IS schedule crosses the LM^* schedule in its horizontal portion, with the result that equilibrium income is Y_e. An increase in the money supply will shift the LM schedule from LM^* to LM', but the intersection of IS and LM' continues to give equilibrium income Y_e. Thus, because monetary policy is unable to cause portfolio adjustments that result in a lower interest rate, investment and hence income are unchanged. Monetary policy is wholly ineffective to move Y_e toward Y_f, the full employment level of income.

Empirical Studies of the Liquidity Trap   In the late 1930s, when interest rates were extremely low and the excess reserves of the commercial banking system were

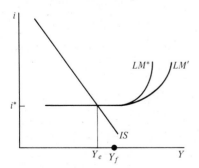

Figure 21-12 Monetary policy is ineffective in a liquidity trap.

extremely high, it was widely believed among Keynesian economists that the United States economy was in a liquidity trap situation. It was therefore argued that monetary policy was incapable of curing the severe unemployment of the times, and that other means of accomplishing this goal had to be found. Because the issue is important, several empirical studies of the behavior of the demand for money during the late 1930s have subsequently been made. These studies give little, if any, support to the liquidity trap idea.[2] Instead, they indicate overwhelmingly that even at very low rates of interest, the interest elasticity of the demand for money is relatively low, certainly not infinite. We may consequently dismiss the liquidity trap, properly so called,[3] as a possible cause of the ineffectiveness of monetary policy.

The Interest Elasticity of Investment   The theoretical possibility of a breakdown in the transmission mechanism can be explained with the aid of Figure 21-13 (shown below) which gives the MEI schedule of Figure 20-6. In this case, however, the MEI schedule is vertical (straight up and down). Technically, such an MEI schedule is said to have a *zero interest elasticity of investment.* Practically, what Figure 21-13 says is that business people do not base investment decisions on the rate of interest; whatever the rate of interest, business people will make the same amount of investment. This can be seen in Figure 21-13. Whether the rate of interest is i^* or i', the amount of investment remains the same at I^*.

The consequence of such an MEI schedule can be seen in Figure 21-14, which repeats the derivation of the *IS* schedule in Figure 20-7. In this case, however, we use the MEI schedule of Figure 21-13. Our interest lies in determining how this type of MEI schedule will affect the shape of the *IS* schedule. In fact, the answer to this problem is comparatively simple. Since the investment schedule in Figure 21-14 is horizontal, there is only a single level of income that will satisfy the equilibrium requirement that $I = S$: This is income level Y^*, where $I^* = S^*$. Now the thing to notice in particular is that the equilibrium level of income Y^* is consistent with *any* rate of interest. It follows that the vertical MEI schedule of Figure 21-13 implies

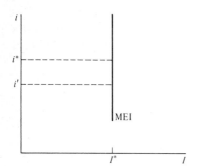

Figure 21-13   An interest-inelastic MEI schedule.

[2]See especially George R. Morrison, *Liquidity Preferences of Commercial Banks,* The University of Chicago Press, Chicago, 1966.

[3]The interest elasticity of the demand for money nevertheless remains a point of contention between the modern quantity theorists and the modern Keynesians. This issue will be discussed in Chapter 23.

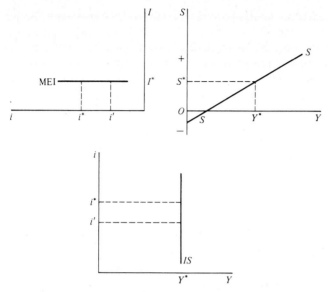

Figure 21-14   An interest-inelastic MEI schedule causes an interest-inelastic *IS* schedule.

a vertical *IS* schedule such as that shown in the lower half of Figure 21-14. More-over, although we have illustrated the situation with an extreme example, the following statement is also correct: For a given saving schedule, the steeper the MEI schedule, the steeper will be the *IS* schedule.

A vertical *IS* schedule, as in Figure 21-14, implies that monetary policy is an ineffective tool for economic stabilization. This can most readily be seen from Figure 21-15, which shows the usual *IS–LM* analysis, except that in this case the *IS* schedule is the vertical one of Figure 21-14. The equilibrium level of income, of course, is Y_e, where the two schedules cross. Now suppose that the full employment level of income is Y^*_f, to the right of Y_e. As we know, this is a theoretical description of a recession. The appropriate monetary policy therefore is to increase the quantity of money in the economy. Let us suppose the Federal Reserve does this and as a consequence the *LM* schedule shifts rightward from LM^* to LM'. Such a shift in

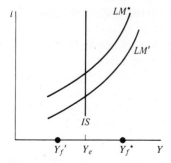

Figure 21-15   Monetary policy is ineffective with an interest-inelastic *IS* schedule.

the LM schedule has no effect on the equilibrium level of income; it remains the same at Y_e. Alternatively, suppose that Y'_f, to the left of Y_e, represents full employment income. This is an inflationary situation, and the appropriate monetary policy would be to decrease the money supply. If this is done, the LM schedule will shift leftward, as from LM' to LM^*. But again this makes no difference in terms of the equilibrium level of income Y_e. Y_e remains the same whichever LM schedule is used.

The economics of the graphic analysis may be described in general terms as follows: The Federal Reserve changes the money supply in order to try to achieve full employment equilibrium. The change in the money supply elicits the hoped-for portfolio adjustments among the public, and the rate of interest consequently changes in the desired direction. At this point, however, the process breaks down because of a failure in the transmission mechanism. The change in the rate of interest in the monetary sector fails to produce any change in the real sector. Specifically, investment expenditures do not change, and consequently income does not change.

Although the preceding analysis has been stated in terms of the limiting case of a vertical IS schedule, it should be apparent that the steeper the IS schedule, the less effect will a given change in the quantity of money have on economic activity. The nature of the real world relationship between interest rates and investment expenditures thus becomes a crucial question in Keynesian analysis.

The Empirical Relationship between Interest and Investment   In the quarter century following the publication of Keynes's *General Theory* in 1936, a great deal of effort was expended by the economics profession in trying to estimate the interest elasticity of investment. Mail surveys were sent to businesses, in-depth interviews carried out, and regression equations estimated. In general, the results of these studies were disappointing. They seemed to indicate that the effect of interest rates on investment expenditures ranged from small to negligible. If this was the case, then the logical consequence of the Keynesian theory was that monetary policy could not be entrusted with the formidable task of economic stabilization; it simply was not powerful enough to carry this burden. As a result, many Keynesian economists became disenchanted with monetary policy. "Money doesn't matter" was essentially the attitude that many of the early Keynesians came to adopt.

Measuring the determinants of the investment decision, especially the role played by interest rates, is a tricky business. By now, most early studies of this question have been reexamined and found to contain serious statistical biases. Additionally, more recent studies employing more sophisticated statistical techniques have been carried out. These studies have in general reversed earlier findings and have concluded that investment is fairly responsive to changes in interest rates. We shall discuss these findings under four headings: business plant and equipment expenditures; business inventories; residential construction; and state and local government expenditures.

Business Plant and Equipment Expenditures   The theoretical explanation for an inverse relationship between interest rates and investment expenditures on plant and equipment, it will be recalled, rests on the idea of interest as a cost. An easy money policy lowers interest rates, thus reducing production costs; a tight money policy works in the opposite manner to decrease investment expenditures.

Recent studies of the relationship between fixed business investment and interest rates indicate an elasticity in the range of –0.2 to –0.6. Such a range of elasticities suggests that interest rates play a reasonably important role in the determination of business investment. Suppose, for example, that the elasticity is –0.4. Then a rise in the rate of interest from 4 to 5 percent (which is a relative increase of 25 *percent*) will cause fixed investment expenditures to decrease by 10 percent (that is, 25 percent of 0.4). If business spending on plant and equipment is $150 billion, this means that a rise in the interest rate from 4 to 5 percent will cause expenditures to fall by $15 billion (10 percent of $150 billion). In absolute terms, $15 billion is a substantial amount of expenditures, especially since its effects on the economy will be exaggerated through the operation of the multiplier.

Business Inventories Theoretically, the relationship between the rate of interest and business inventory investment is similar to that for plant and equipment. A business firm with too little inventory on its shelves will suffer profit losses through not being able to fill orders; alternatively, if it has too much inventory, it will also suffer profit losses because of high storage and other carrying costs. In principle, therefore, there is some optimal size of inventory for a business firm, one that is neither too small nor too large. Without going into detail, this optimal inventory size will vary positively with the costs of maintaining the inventory, and one element of these costs is the rate of interest. It theoretically follows that higher interest rates should lead firms to hold smaller inventories, and lower interest rates lead them to hold larger inventories. Do they?

The studies that have been made on the subject seem to indicate that there is little or no relationship between interest and inventory.[4] A common interpretation of these negative findings is that business expectations about future price and demand changes are so powerful that they swamp interest rate effects.

Residential Construction Monetary conditions have a substantial impact on residential construction (housing), as has been shown in a variety of studies. When money is tight and interest rates high, new housing declines; when money is easy and interest rates low, new housing picks up. But while the result is clear, the reasons for it are not so obvious. One explanation is the standard one, that the demand for housing is interest elastic. According to this view, the purchase of a house is the largest expenditure most families ever make, and most houses are financed through a mortgage. Even a small rise in mortgage rates can result in raising the total amount spent on a house over a period of years by several thousand dollars. Accordingly, consumers will tend to postpone buying houses during periods of tight money and speed up house buying during periods of easy money.

Alternatively, many researchers in this area feel that the responsiveness of residential construction to credit conditions is largely a supply phenomenon. The theory is that because FHA and VA mortgage rates are determined administratively rather than by market forces, they tend to lag behind other interest rates in the economy. Consequently, when interest rates rise, these mortgages become compara-

[4]For a summary view, see Michael J. Hamberger, *The Impact of Monetary Variables: A Selected Survey of the Recent Empirical Literature,* Staff Economic Study 34, Board of Governors of the Federal Reserve System, 1967.

tively unattractive to lenders, who put their money into other kinds of securities. Contrariwise, when interest rates fall, FHA and VA mortgages become extremely attractive compared with other kinds of loans, and the supply of mortgage funds increases.

State and Local Government Expenditures   The expenditures of state and local governments seem also to be sensitive to interest rate changes. The reason for this, apparently, is that many of the capital expenditures on such things as schools, sewer systems, and highways are financed by bonds rather than taxes. Many states have laws that place an upper limit on the rate of interest municipalities may pay on such bonds. And even in the absence of this, municipal bond flotations are frequently so large and extend over such a long period of time that just a small change in the rate of interest may result in a difference in hundreds of thousands of dollars in interest payments over the life of the bond issue. As a result, many state and local bond issues will be postponed during periods of tight money, only to be resumed again when credit conditions ease.[5]

21-4 FISCAL POLICY

While the preceding discussion indicates that interest rates are a significant determinant of much investment expenditure in the United States, many Keynesian economists continue to doubt that monetary policy *alone* is a sufficiently powerful stabilization device that we can afford to rely on it exclusively. It seems a fair statement to say that the attitude of most Keynesian economists has shifted from the "money doesn't matter" position of the early Keynesians to a "money matters but so do other things" position of the modern Keynesians. Those economists who are unwilling to rely exclusively on monetary policy to stabilize the economy generally advocate *fiscal policy* as a second powerful means of achieving full employment without inflation.

The theory of fiscal policy and the role it plays in Keynesian economics can be illustrated with the use of Figure 21-16. The reader will recognize Figure 21-16 as the standard one showing the derivation of the *IS* schedule. It will be recalled that the MEI schedule in the upper left-hand corner of Figure 21-16 includes government expenditures and that the saving schedule in the upper right-hand corner includes taxes. Let us therefore pose the following question: If the government raises its expenditures while holding taxes constant, what effect will this have on the *IS* schedule?

This question can be answered by noting that the solid schedule marked *IS** in the lower half of Figure 21-16 is derived from the $(I + G)^*$ and $(S + T)^*$ schedules in the upper half. If, now, the government raises expenditures without changing taxes, the $(I + G)^*$ schedule increases to $(I + G)'$, where the latter is indicated by the dashed line. This will shift the *IS** schedule rightward to *IS'* (the

[5]Paul F. McGouldrick and John E. Peterson, "Monetary Restraint and Borrowing and Spending by Large State and Local Governments in 1966," *Federal Reserve Bulletin,* July 1968, pp. 552–581.

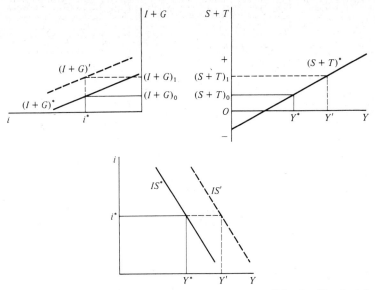

Figure 21-16 An increase in government expenditures shifts the *IS* schedule rightward.

dashed *IS* schedule). Although it is not shown, the reader should by now be able to discover that a decrease in taxes will have the same effect, i.e., will shift the *IS* schedule rightward. And, of course, the opposite is also true; a decrease in government expenditures or an increase in taxes will shift the *IS* schedule leftward. Thus, fiscal policy—changes in the government's spending and taxing policies—can be represented theoretically in the Keynesian model by shifts in the *IS* schedule.

To see how fiscal policy can be used to complement monetary policy, consider Figure 21-17. Note in particular that the *IS** schedule is quite steep in Figure 21-17. (As discussed previously, the empirical basis for such an *IS* schedule is a low interest elasticity of investment expenditures.) With *IS** and *LM** the relevant schedules, we know that equilibrium will occur at income level Y^*_e. Since Y_f, the full employment level of income, lies to the right of Y^*_e, we know also that Figure 21-17 is a theoretical representation of a recession. The appropriate monetary policy, therefore, is to expand the money supply, which will shift the *LM* schedule rightward to, say, *LM'*. But this shift in the *LM* schedule, *taken by itself,* is insufficient to move equilibrium income up to full employment. This can be seen by noting that the *IS** and *LM'* schedules intersect at income level Y_e. Although Y_e is larger than Y^*_e, it is nevertheless not as large as Y_f. In fact, it can be seen from Figure 21-17 that there is *no realistic* shift in the *LM* schedule that will move equilibrium income up to full employment. To accomplish this would require an increase in the money supply so large that interest rates would have to become negative. It follows that, in the situation described, monetary policy can be helpful in moving the economy *toward* equilibrium but cannot by itself get the economy all the way there. This is where fiscal policy comes in.

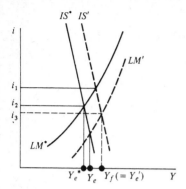

Figure 21-17 The combined use of monetary and fiscal policy.

Let us suppose that the government either increases its spending and/or decreases taxes. The *IS* schedule will therefore shift rightward from IS^* to IS'. Then the intersection of IS' and LM' occurs at the full employment level of income Y_f $(= Y'_e)$. Thus, what monetary policy alone has been unable to accomplish, monetary and fiscal policy working together have been able to do.

The argument is of course symmetrical—i.e., it also applies to an inflationary situation. The only difference is that in this case the constraint on monetary policy may be a rate of interest that is *politically* unacceptable. In other words, as long as the *IS* schedule has *some* elasticity (is not perfectly vertical), then theoretically there is *some* decrease in the money supply that will shift the *LM* schedule leftward by enough to prevent inflation. But such a drastic decrease in the money supply might involve an interest rate so high as to be politically infeasible (even though it is technically possible).

To illustrate, consider Figure 21-17 once again. Now, however, suppose that we begin with the dashed *IS* and *LM* functions IS' and LM' and that we want to move this equilibrium leftward. One way to do so would be to decrease the money supply, which would have the effect of shifting the *LM* schedule leftward to LM^*. Note that this will cause the interest rate to rise from i_3 to i_1. Now, suppose that the interest rate i_1 is so high that it is very unpopular. People complain that bankers are getting rich, that they can't afford to buy houses, and so on, and write their Congressional representatives about it. Then it may not be judged politically feasible[6] to *further* decrease the money supply (which would result in still higher interest rates). What can be done, instead, is to cause the *IS* schedule to shift leftward by raising taxes or decreasing government expenditures, which would shift the *IS* schedule leftward from IS' to IS^*. In this case, equilibrium income will fall to Y^*_e and interest rates will fall from i_1 to i_2. Once again, a combination of monetary and fiscal policy will have accomplished what monetary policy alone could not do.

---

[6]Although the Federal Reserve may be an independent agency, it is not wholly insensitive to the political consequences of its actions.

Concluding Comment

Since our concern is primarily with monetary policy, we have skipped over many of the theoretical niceties and practical difficulties of fiscal policy. Some of these matters will be touched on in later chapters; others will not be discussed at all. But the small amount of space devoted to fiscal policy should not lead the reader to the mistaken belief that this is all there is to it—there is much more.

21-5 REVIEW QUESTIONS

1 Explain why there is an inverse relationship between the interest rate and the demand for money (i.e., the liquidity preference schedule).
2 Pick a point off the *LM* schedule of Figure 21-5*b* and explain why this is a point of disequilibrium in the monetary sector. What forces would be generated in the monetary sector to restore equilibrium?
3 In common-sense terms, explain how an antirecession monetary policy works.
4 Derive the *IS* schedule using a very steep (but not vertical) MEI schedule. What does this tell you?

22

Modern Keynesian Economics

The traditional Keynesian theory is complicated. And as with any complex subject, there is some tendency to become so enmeshed in detail that one fails to see its overall structure. Yet it is precisely in this overall structure that the connection between traditional and modern Keynesianism is to be found. At the risk of some repetition, therefore, let us try to disentangle ourselves from the underbrush of the theory and get a broader view of the Keynesian landscape.

Basically, the traditional Keynesian macroeconomic theory may be classified into three parts: First, there are the *portfolio adjustments* that occur in the monetary sector when the quantity of money is changed; these portfolio adjustments are analyzed in terms of the liquidity preference theory of interest. Second, there is the *transmission mechanism* linking the monetary and real sectors of the economy; this function is performed by the MEI schedule, relating the rate of interest to investment expenditures. Third, there is the *adjustment mechanism* of the real sector, which describes the equilibrium adjustments that take place in the real sector when investment changes; this is the multiplier of the traditional Keynesian theory and the assumption of upward flexible but downward inflexible prices.

Modern Keynesian theory continues to accept this threefold scheme of classification as meaningful. And, to a considerable extent, it is the continued acceptance of this scheme that marks modern Keynesians as the direct descendants of traditional Keynesianism. But while the organizing principles of portfolio adjustments, a transmission mechanism, and an adjustment mechanism continue to be accepted as the major issues to be explained, modern Keynesians regard the earlier analyses of these issues as crude. This is not to say that modern Keynesians *reject* the traditional analyses; it *is* to say, rather, that they regard them only as first approximations—a good place to start but seriously lacking in descriptive validity. Thus, modern Keynesians have expended a good deal of effort in extending the original Keynesian analysis. In this chapter we shall describe some recent theoretical developments that have the effect of generalizing traditional Keynesian analysis.

22-1 PORTFOLIO ADJUSTMENTS IN THE FINANCIAL SECTOR

The traditional Keynesian analysis of the public's portfolio adjustments is unsatisfactory in two respects. To understand the first of these recall that the traditional Keynesian analysis makes the simplifying assumption that the monetary sector of the economy contains only two assets: money and long-term bonds. Such an assumption can only be regarded as drastic, an extreme oversimplification of the actual variety and complexity of the real world. Modern Keynesian analysis recognizes how limiting this assumption is. Not only do assets other than money and long-term bonds exist, but there are also financial institutions other than commercial banks. Consequently, modern Keynesians have sought to extend the analysis of the monetary sector to include other types of financial instruments and institutions; they have sought to develop a theory of finance, rather than merely a theory of money. (In recognition of this, we shall hereafter refer to *financial sector* rather than the *monetary sector.*)

The second unsatisfactory aspect of the portfolio adjustment mechanism of traditional Keynesianism also has to do with the divergence between that theory and observed, real-world behavior. Recall that the liquidity preference theory is based on individual investor expectations about the future course of interest rates. Thus, e.g., if the investor believes that rates are likely to rise in the future, he or she will hold money rather than bonds because the expected rise in interest implies a fall in the price of bonds. The point to note especially about this theoretical construct is that the investor is assumed to hold *either* money *or* bonds but not both. In other words, it is implicit in the liquidity preference theory that only nondiversified portfolios are held by individuals. The liquidity preference *schedule* is derived from the assumption that at any given time different investors have different expectations, so that some are in bonds and some are in money, but each individual portfolio is pure. This is an unsatisfactory assumption, being contrary to observed fact. For, obviously, virtually all investors hold *diversified portfolios*—portfolios that contain a variety of assets, including (but not limited to) *both* money and bonds.

Both of these unsatisfactory aspects of traditional Keynesian liquidity preference theory have been resolved in modern Keynesianism by replacing the traditional
liquidity preference theory with the modern theory of portfolio selection.

Portfolio Theory and the Demand for Money

The modern theory of portfolio selection was discussed extensively in Chapter 5.
This discussion, it will be recalled, concluded with Figure 5-4, which is reproduced
here as Figure 22-1. This figure shows the investor's expected return (measured as
the mean of past returns) on the vertical axis, and the investor's anticipated risk
(measured as the standard deviation of past returns) on the horizontal axis. The
interior of the graph is composed, basically, of two elements: (1) the investor's
indifference curves (I_1, I_2, and I_3), which show the investor's subjective trade-offs
between different levels of risk and expected return. Since a higher indifference curve
will always be preferred to a lower one, the objective of the investor is to reach the
highest indifference curve that is attainable given the amount of money at her
disposal. (2) The second element in the interior of the graph depicted in Figure 22-1
is the curve labeled $S3$ only–N–$S1$ only, known as the *efficient portfolio.* This curve,
recall, shows all possible risk-return combinations of stocks $S1$ and $S3$. It is "efficient" in the sense that all points to the left of the curve are unattainable; and that
any point to the right of the curve will be inferior to any point *on* the curve. That
is, any point to the right of the curve will either give more risk with the same return,
or less return with the same risk. Combining the indifference curves and the efficient
portfolio into a single analysis, the investor is thought of as moving along the $S1$
only–N–$S3$ only curve until she reaches the highest indifference curve possible. This
is accomplished at point P in Figure 22-1. At point P, that is, the investor is investing
her money in the wisest possible way, given her subjective preferences for risk and
return. (The reader who has not followed this brief review of portfolio theory may
wish to review section 5-1 of Chapter 5 at this point.)

What has all this to do with monetary theory? The answer is simple: Since
money is an asset, we can use portfolio theory to explain why people hold money

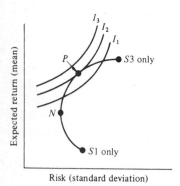

Figure 22-1 Asset choice in a mixed portfolio.

as part of a mixed, or diversified, portfolio. In other words, we can use portfolio theory to explain the demand for money.

Let us suppose that an investor is confronted with a choice between two assets, one of which we shall call *bonds* and the other *money. Bonds,* which in fact can be any asset, have the characteristic of a positive expected return and a positive amount of risk. *Money,* we suppose, also has a positive amount of risk because the investor feels that the general price level might change (which, of course, would change the real value of his money holdings). However, we shall suppose also that the investor thinks it equally likely that prices will fall or rise, so that his expected average return from holding money balances is zero. The question we want to answer is, Will the investor hold money as part of a diversified portfolio even though its expected return is zero?

This question can be answered within the framework of the theory of portfolio selection. In Figure 22-2 the point marked B represents the pure bond portfolio and the point marked M (on the horizontal axis) represents a portfolio composed only of money. The curve *BPM* represents the risk-return possibilities of all combinations of money and bonds. The risk-return indifference curves of the investor indicate that he will prefer the diversified portfolio P beyond all others open to him. But point P includes money in the investor's portfolio. Thus, a rational investor will hold money as part of his investment portfolio even though money has a zero expected rate of return. The reason he will do so is that by holding money he can vary the risk-return characteristics of his *entire* portfolio to obtain the best (to him) possible combination. And note that this theoretical result is general; that is, if we were to expand the asset choices open to the investor to include several assets (instead of just two), he would probably continue to hold money as one ingredient of his diversified portfolio.

Let us now take one final step before concluding our discussion of the relationship between monetary theory and portfolio theory. Let us suppose that the rate of interest (and hence the expected return) on bonds rises but that the risk of bonds remains the same. In terms of Figure 22-2, this means that the point B shifts directly

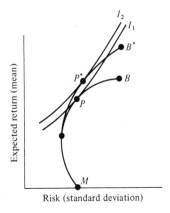

Figure 22-2 Portfolio theory and the demand for money.

upward to the point B^*; that is, a portfolio composed entirely of bonds will now have a greater expected return and the same risk. Our interest lies in determining what this does to the demand for money.

The first thing to notice is that with the higher interest rate on bonds, the investor now has a different risk-return possibility curve, namely, the curve labeled "B^*P^*M." In the relevant range, this curve will everywhere lie above the old curve (BPM). Thus the investor can now reach a higher indifference curve, namely, the curve marked "I_2." The investor will consequently choose the new portfolio combination of bonds and money represented by the risk-return combinaiton P^*, where the curve B^*P^*M is just tangent to the indifference curve I_2. But note that the point P^* lies to the right of point P, indicating that the investor has decided now on a new portfolio involving more risk than the old one. The reason he has done this, essentially, is that the higher expected return on bonds has induced him to give up some safety in return for more yield. But note, also, that since the risks of both bonds and money are just the same as they originally were, a greater risk in the total portfolio must mean that the investor has moved away from money and toward bonds; that is, the rise in the bond rate has caused the investor to reshuffle his portfolio so that he prefers to hold more bonds and less money.

What does all this mean? It means that we now have a much sounder theoretical basis for arguing that there is an inverse relationship between interest rates and the demand for money. In the traditional Keynesian analysis, this relationship was hypothesized on the basis of the liquidity preference schedule, which, in turn, was based on the assumption of a two-asset world and nondiversified portfolios. But portfolio theory, as we have seen, is based on diversified portfolios and can be extended to encompass any number of assets. Moreover, it leads to the same conclusion: At high rates of interest the quantity of money demanded will be small, and at low rates of interest the quantity of money demanded will be large. But note, finally, that this relationship is not especially robust. Money is only one asset among many, and changes in the quantities of these other assets may also lead to changes in the composition of investor portfolios. Thus modern Keynesians feel that the demand for money may be unstable; that is, it may shift about as conditions and circumstances change.

The Management of the Public Debt

The Treasury's power to control the maturity structure of the outstanding public debt, discussed briefly at the end of Chapter 16, takes on new meaning in light of the theory of portfolio selection. If money is to be regarded simply as one asset among many, then changes in the public's holdings of these other assets should have effects comparable to changes in the quantity of money. In other words, a rollover of the public debt from, say, mostly long term to mostly short term should cause substantial readjustments in investor portfolio holdings. If this is so, the debt management activities of the Treasury take on many of the same characteristics as monetary policy for modern Keynesians. Indeed, some contemporary Keynesian economists regard monetary policy and debt management policy as essentially the same thing and argue that (theoretically) the two should be treated as a single policy instrument.[1] Thus, in this view, money is that debt of the government which has zero return and maturity but is not different in kind from other types of government debt. The government therefore should control the size and mix of its *total* (including money) outstanding debt as a method of economic stabilization.

Empirical studies suggest that moderate changes in the maturity composition of the public debt have very weak effects on the economy. And while it is possible that massive refundings from short to long term (or vice versa) might affect the economy appreciably, such refundings would almost certainly prove disruptive to the capital markets. Nevertheless, it should be kept in mind that the economic consequences of changing the maturity composition of the debt are very difficult to pin down, empirically speaking. To give only a single example of these difficulties, we have virtually no information on the maturities of outstanding *private* debt. And if the maturity of private debt changes in such a way that it offsets the effects of similar but opposite changes in the public debt, then it will appear that public debt management is inconsequential when, in fact, it is not. Thus, the weak results obtained in such studies should not be interpreted as an absolute denial of the potential usefulness of debt management or as a contradiction of portfolio theory.

The Theory of Financial Intermediaries

Just as many modern Keynesians tend to question the viewpoint that money is a unique and dominant asset, regarding it instead as simply "one asset among many," so also they question the viewpoint that commercial banks are unique and dominant financial institutions. Modern Keynesians suggest, instead, that commercial banks are simply "one financial institution among many"—a very important institution, to be sure, but not different in kind from savings and loan associations, mutual savings banks, credit unions, and the like. This argument runs as follows.

Stripped to its bare essentials, what a commercial bank does is to collect money from one group of people and lend it to another group of people. Viewed in this light, the question naturally arises as to why the first group doesn't just lend directly to the second group. Who needs the bank? The answer is that the first group of people —the bank's depositors—does not want to buy what the second group has to offer —loans and investments. The depositors want their money where they can get it back at any time; and the bank's loan customers want to have the use of the funds over some definite period of time. The bank is thus said to *intermediate* between the two groups. It is able to do this because the withdrawals of one customer typically will be offset by the deposits of another customer, so that the *total* amount of funds in the bank will be comparatively constant. The bank can thus risk making loan commitments for definite periods of time. But note that the bank is certainly not unique in this respect. There are many other financial institutions that also intermediate between different groups of people, that is, are able to do for each group collectively what no individual of either group could do alone. A savings and loan association, for example, borrows by accepting savings deposits and then lends by

---

[1]See James Tobin, "An Essay on the Principles of Debt Management," in Commission on Money and Credit, *Fiscal and Debt Management Policies,* Prentice-Hall, Englewood Cliffs, N.J., 1963.

investing in home mortgages. In principle, though not in detail, it is doing just what a commercial bank is doing: intermediating between two different groups of people.

Consistent with their position that monetary theory must encompass all adjustments in the financial sector, modern Keynesians argue that the role of nonbank financial institutions must be included in any realistic analysis of the effects of monetary policy. Such institutions, of course, do not create "money" in the sense of a medium of exchange, as banks do. But from the viewpoint of portfolio theory, they do something that perhaps is equally important: They create highly liquid financial assets. To understand this, consider Figure 22-3, which shows a series of T-account transactions between a commercial bank and a savings and loan association.

In Figure 22-3a we suppose that a depositor of the bank, Ms. Jones, decides to withdraw $10,000 from her demand deposit and open a savings account with it at the S&L. Initially, the S&L simply adds this amount to its own account at the bank, so that from the bank's viewpoint it has just transferred the money from one depositor (Ms. Jones) to another (the S&L). Next, suppose that the S&L decides to invest $9,500 of this money in a home mortgage and keep the remaining $500 on

	Commercial bank		S & L	
(a) Assets	**Liabilities**	**Assets**	**Liabilities**
	− $10,000 demand deposit of Ms. Jones	+ $10,000 deposit at bank	+ $10,000 savings deposit of Ms. Jones
	+ $10,000 S & L deposit		

	Commercial bank		S & L	
(b) Assets	**Liabilities**	**Assets**	**Liabilities**
	− $9,500 S & L deposit	− $9,500 deposit at bank	
	+ $9,500 deposit of home builder	+ $9,500 mortgage	

	Commercial bank		S & L	
(c) Assets	**Liabilities**	**Assets**	**Liabilities**
	+ $500 S & L deposit	+ $500 deposit at bank	+ $10,000 savings deposit of Ms. Jones
	+ $9,500 deposit of home builder	+ $9,500 mortgage	
	− $10,000 deposit of Ms. Jones		

Figure 22-3

deposit at the bank as a liquidity reserve. To simplify matters, we shall suppose further that the home builder who receives the $9,500 deposits it in the same bank. This series of transactions is shown in Figure 22-3b. Once again the commercial bank has just transferred funds from one deposit (the S&L) to another (the home builder). The S&L has simply switched its assets from one form (cash) to another (the mortgage).

Now consider the net result of this series of transactions, shown in Figure 22-3c. The commercial bank has lost the $10,000 deposit of Ms. Jones but has gained it back again in the combined deposits of the S&L ($500) and home builder ($9,500). The net change in the bank's demand deposit liabilities is therefore zero. But the S&L has acquired a net increase in its savings account liabilities of $10,000 and has financed a $9,500 home mortgage. Consequently the transactions shown have expanded the assets of the nonfinancial public by $10,000. In other words, the total amount of money (demand deposits) in the economy has not changed, but Ms. Jones is now the proud owner of a $10,000 savings account.

The question is, of course, What effect does the creation of this savings deposit have on the functioning of the economy? The answer to this question can be approached within the context of portfolio theory. Using this approach, it seems likely that the proliferation of near money financial assets will affect the optimum portfolios of the public. Furthermore, since such near monies as S&L accounts have about the same risk and higher return than demand deposits, the changes that occur in the public's portfolios are likely to be away from money and toward near money assets. Thus, the general effect of nonbank financial intermediaries will be to decrease the demand for money balances.

Summary

There are two primary conclusions to be reached from the various aspects of the financial sector just described: One is that the demand for money is an (inverse) function of the rate of interest. This theoretical conclusion, while a key piece of the traditional Keynesian analysis, has been considerably strengthened by the development of portfolio theory. The second and more controversial conclusion reached by modern Keynesian analysis is that the demand for money may be unstable. Changed expectations, which change optimal portfolios, changes in the maturity structure of both public and private debt outstanding, the growth of nonbank intermediaries in both size and variety—all these will affect the public's demand for money balances. Modern Keynesians thus tend to regard the demand for money as a potentially unstable economic relationship, an uncertain foundation on which to build anything so important as stabilization policy.

22-2 THE TRANSMISSION MECHANISM

In traditional Keynesian monetary theory it is the marginal efficiency of investment (MEI) schedule that links the real sector to the monetary sector. This schedule, it will be recalled, hypothesizes a functional relationship between investment expenditures and the rate of interest. Since the MEI schedule is the mechanism that transmits impulses from the monetary sector to the real sector, it is sometimes called the *transmission mechanism.*

Modern Keynesians regard the MEI schedule as a crude first approximation to the realities of how monetary policy actually affects national income. In place of this simple and rather mechanical concept, they have therefore substituted three analyses, commonly called the three *channels of monetary policy:* the cost-of-capital effect, the wealth effect, and the credit rationing effect.

Cost-of-Capital Effect

The *cost-of-capital effect* is a straightforward extension of the theory of portfolio selection discussed previously. In that discussion, the analysis was confined to the process of choosing an efficient set of *financial* assets from among those available, but there is no need to confine the discussion to financial assets only. One may also hold *physical* goods as part of an asset portfolio. For example, one could (and many do) hold a portfolio consisting of money, bonds, and apartment buildings. The apartment buildings would be held for exactly the same reason as the financial assets: their risk and return characteristics. Since this is the case, it follows that portfolio theory can be extended to include an analysis of the relationship between money and physical capital.

To illustrate such an analysis, let us suppose that the asset portfolio of the public is initially in equilibrium—that people and institutions are holding just those amounts of financial (including money) and physical assets that they desire to hold under prevailing conditions of risk and return. Now suppose that, for whatever reason, the Federal Reserve decides to expand the money supply. This increase in the money supply, as we have seen, will mean that the public's portfolio is no longer in equilibrium. At prevailing interest rates, people will attempt to spend their excess money balances to acquire bonds. As a result, a downward pressure will be exerted on interest rates and interest rates will fall.

The fall in interest rates will throw the public out of equilibrium with respect to the desired proportion of physical capital it is holding in its asset portfolio. The return on physical capital will now be high relative to the return on bonds, and consequently the public will attempt to add more units of physical capital to its portfolio. But unlike financial assets, which can be expanded or contracted quickly, physical capital must be produced and this takes time to do. A gap will therefore develop between the *desired* amount of physical capital and the amount that *actually* exists in the economy; the demand for capital will be greater than the supply. As with any other good, this excess demand will cause the market price of physical capital to rise. And since the cost of producing capital will be initially unchanged and its market price will have risen, the production of new capital goods (investment) will be stimulated. Investment expenditures will consequently rise. Equilibrium will be restored slowly as the gap between the desired and actual capital stock is closed by new investment.

The theoretical conclusion reached by the cost-of-capital effect is thus similar to that reached by the traditional Keynesian concept of the MEI schedule: An increase in the quantity of money will lower interest rates and stimulate investment expenditures. But even though the conclusion is similar, the cost-of-capital analysis is much more satisfactory. It brings the transmission mechanism into the same portfolio theoretical framework as the demand for money.

Wealth Effect

The cost-of-capital effect just described affected the economy through the rearrangement of the public's asset portfolio. There is another aspect of the public's portfolio, not yet mentioned, which also may have major consequences for spending decisions. This is the *wealth effect* of monetary policy. To understand the wealth effect, consider again briefly the sequence of events just described: (1) The money supply goes up; (2) interest rates fall; and (3) the market price of capital rises. Note in particular that (2) and (3) have increased the value of the public's total asset holdings without a corresponding increase in its liabilities. For when interest rates fall, as we have seen, the market price of outstanding bonds rises; and, similarly, the increase in the market price of physical capital will increase the total value of the assets of capital owners. In short, the public is indirectly made *wealthier* by the expansion in the money supply.

Modern Keynesians hypothesize that the increase in the public's wealth resulting from an expansionary monetary policy may have powerful consequences for spending decisions. Most especially, they feel, an increase in the value of the public's equity claims (common stocks) against physical capital may stimulate consumption expenditures. For example, a household that owns some mutual-fund shares may feel much more like buying a new color TV if the value of these shares has been rising than if it hasn't. In some Keynesian models of the economy, the wealth effect of monetary policy substantially influences consumer behavior.

Credit Rationing Effect

Most of our theorizing about the possible consequences of monetary policy assumes that what keeps the quantity of loans supplied equal to the quantity demanded is the market rate of interest. But in fact loan agreements between lenders and borrowers involve a number of other factors, and these other factors may also be used to move the market to equilibrium. For example, a commercial bank might be willing to make short-term but not long-term loans. Or a savings and loan association might change the loan/value ratio it requires for mortgage lending. When financial institutions use nonprice (i.e., noninterest rate) terms to bring a market into equilibrium, they are said to be engaged in *credit rationing*. Many contemporary Keynesians believe that credit rationing is an important channel through which monetary policy works.

While credit rationing affects all loan markets in some degree, most studies of this phenomenon have concentrated on the home mortgage market. Here, it is argued, flood or drought conditions typically prevail with respect to the availability of funds. When interest rates rise, the rates paid on open market securities generally rise much more quickly than the rates paid on savings accounts at S&Ls and commercial banks. As a result, a process called *disintermediation* may occur; that is, people may withdraw their money from savings accounts and instead buy the higher-yield, open market securities. This process reduces, in particular, the funds available to S&Ls, who are major lenders in the home mortgage market. Additionally, in times of tight money commercial banks are likely to favor short-term (and therefore liquid) business loans over long-term (and therefore illiquid) home mortgages.

Summary

Before concluding this section, it is desirable to note explicitly that modern Keynesian monetary theory, like its traditional forebearer, continues to see monetary policy as affecting the economy *indirectly*. This stands in contrast with the modern quantity theorists, who hypothesize a direct link between money and spending through the demand for money. As James Tobin, probably the leading contemporary American Keynesian, has stated, "By open market operations, the monetary authority varies the supply of . . . bonds relative to cash, and thus affects the bond rate and *indirectly* the willingness of wealth owners to hold [physical capital]. The power of open market operations depends on the strength of this *indirect* effect."[2]

22-3 ADJUSTMENTS IN THE REAL SECTOR

Keynesian monetary theory is embedded in a more general theory of the macro-economy. That is, Keynesians regard it as the main task of economic theory to explain how the economy works—how income, employment, and the price level are determined. The task of monetary theory is to explain the role played by money within this more general framework. Thus while adjustments that occur in the real sector are not, strictly speaking, a part of monetary theory, it is nevertheless necessary to round out our survey of modern Keynesian economics by considering briefly contemporary theorizing about these adjustments.

It will be remembered that the traditional Keynesian *IS–LM* analysis contains one process and one assumption describing real sector adjustments. The process is the multiplier theory, which says that a change in investment will cause a larger change in national income. The assumption is that prices are flexible upward but not downward, so that inflation occurs only after full employment has been reached. Both the multiplier process and the assumption about prices have been modified by modern Keynesianism. We shall consider each in turn.

The Multiplier-Accelerator Process

The Keynesian theory described in Chapters 20 and 21 was a *static* theory in which two points of equilibrium were compared. Within this static framework, the multiplier process was used to explain how an autonomous change in investment expenditures would cause a (larger) change in national income. In the present context, the

[2]James Tobin, "The Theory of Portfolio Selection," in E. H. Hahn and F. P. R. Brechling (eds.), *The Theory of Interest Rates,* Macmillan & Co., Ltd., London, 1965, pp. 36–37. Italics supplied.

point to note about this process is that causation runs in one direction only. Changes in investment cause changes in income, but the reverse is not true. But this is clearly unreasonable. In order to produce more real income, for example, business people will need more plant and equipment, and this means more investment. Thus, causation runs in both directions: Changes in investment cause income to change, and changes in income cause investment to change. There is thus a *looped,* or *feedback,* mechanism at work in the economy that cannot be described adequately by the one-way causation of the multiplier. Keynesian economists have consequently developed the *multiplier-accelerator theory* to describe this process.

The multiplier-accelerator theory is what is called a *dynamic* (as distinct from static) theory. By "dynamic" is meant that it describes how national income will change over time—period by period. To understand how this works, let us make the following assumptions: (1) that there is a fixed capital/output ratio in the economy, for example, that it takes $2 of capital equipment to produce $1 of real income; and (2) that *current* expenditures depend on *past* expenditures, for example, that this year's consumption expenditures are a function of last year's income. On the basis of these two assumptions, we can construct a dynamic multiplier-accelerator model.

To do so, let us begin with the familiar identity that income is the sum of consumption plus investment; that is, that $Y = C + I$. In this case, however, we want to date these terms. Thus, we write

$$Y_{1980} = C_{1980} + I_{1980} \tag{1}$$

where the subscripts indicate the year we are concerned with (that is, C_{1980} means *consumption in 1980*). Next, in line with the second assumption, let us suppose that consumption expenditures in any given year are proportional to income in the previous year. This gives

$$C_{1980} = aY_{1979} \tag{2}$$

where a is the marginal propensity to consume and, in this case, is a constant of proportionality.

Investment I must still be explained. To do so, we shall also need the first assumption, that there is a fixed capital/output ratio in the economy. The capital (or capital stock) of an economy is its *total* productive facilities, that is, the total amount of plant and equipment in existence. Investment is the *addition* to plant and equipment. The relationship between capital and investment, therefore, is that investment is the *change* in the capital stock. Combining this definition with assumptions 1 and 2, we can therefore write

$$I_{1980} = b(Y_{1979} - Y_{1978}) \tag{3}$$

where b is the capital/output ratio. The idea behind eq. (3) is simply that the change in the capital stock (investment) this year depends on how much income (output) changed last year, and on the capital/output ratio b.

Substituting eqs. (2) and (3) into eq. (1) gives

$$Y_{1980} = aY_{1979} + b(Y_{1979} - Y_{1978}) \tag{4}$$

Equation (4) has some very interesting properties.[3] In the first place, it is dynamic in the following sense: If we know the values of a and b, and if we know the income level in 1979 and 1978, then we can solve eq. (4) to predict the 1980 income level Y_{1980}. But then we can take this predicted 1980 income level and use it to predict income in 1981; that is, we can use the solution to eq. (4) to solve the equation

$$Y_{1981} = aY_{1980} + b(Y_{1980} - Y_{1979}) \tag{5}$$

We can then use the 1981 income level of eq. (5) to predict income in 1982, and so forth. In this fashion, we can generate an entire time path for income in future years.

Of even greater interest is that the time path of income generated by eq. (4) will not in general be linear; that is, as we move into the future, income will not necessarily grow along a straight line. Instead, it may rise and fall cyclically.[4] What such a cycle looks like depends on the values of a and b (the marginal propensity to consume and the capital/output ratio, respectively). For example, if $a = 0.5$ and $b = 0.5$, then we will get a *damped* cycle such as that shown in Figure 22-4a. Alternatively, if $a = 0.6$ and $b = 2.0$, we will get an *explosive* cycle such as that shown in Figure 22-4b. Other combinations of a and b are possible, and these will determine the nature, amplitude, and periodicity of the resulting cycle.

The significance of the multiplier-accelerator analysis in modern Keynesian theory lies in what it says about the *source* of economic instability. Where modern quantity theorists see variations in the money supply as the primary cause of inflations and recessions, contemporary Keynesians, on the contrary, feel that the real sector of the economy is inherently unstable. They point to the dynamic multiplier-accelerator theory in support of their position. Any shock to the economy, say the Keynesians, which causes autonomous changes in spending, will be translated into business fluctuations.

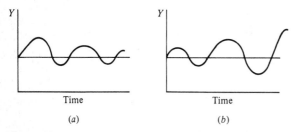

Time	Time
(a)	(b)

Figure 22-4   Income cycles generated by a multiplier-accelerator model.

[3]Equation (4) is what mathematicians call a *second-order difference equation with constant coefficients.* There are general methods for solving it, which we shall not discuss.
[4]Noncyclical time paths are also possible, but we shall not discuss these.

Who is right and who is wrong in this matter has profound implications for the conduct of monetary policy. If the quantity theorists are right and money is the primary source of economic instability, then most (not all) such instability can be eliminated by stabilizing the money supply. Quantity theorists therefore recommend a steady increase in the nation's monetary stock, come what may. But if the Keynesians are right and most economic instability originates in the real sector, then the proper role of monetary policy is to offset swings in economic activity. Keynesians therefore advocate a variable monetary policy, that is, increasing the money supply rapidly during recessions and slowly during inflations.

The Phillips Curve

The traditional Keynesian model makes the simplifying assumption that prices are flexible upward but not downward. On the basis of this assumption, the model performs in the following manner: Up to the point of full employment, all increases in nominal income occur because *real* income rises; i.e., prices are constant. Beyond the point of full employment, all increases in nominal income occur because *prices* rise; i.e., real income is constant. This is not realistic, of course. Prices do rise before the full employment point is reached, and increases in real GNP occur after that point. The traditional analysis is couched in these terms as a strictly formal matter and is not meant to be taken literally.

Modern Keynesian theory has accordingly developed the analysis of the relationship between price increases and unemployment so that questions of inflation can be handled at a more realistic level. This has been done in terms of what is called the *Phillips curve.* The general nature of the Phillips curve can be understood by looking at Figure 22-5, which measures the unemployment rate on the horizontal axis and the *rate of change* of prices on the vertical axis.[5] (It is necessary to emphasize that the vertical axis is a *rate* of change, not the price *level.*) The curve marked "PP" is the Phillips curve; it shows how much inflation will be associated with each level of unemployment. For example, according to Figure 22-5, if unem-

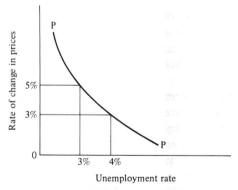

Figure 22-5 Hypothetical Phillips curve.

[5]The Phillips curve is also discussed in Chapter 19, Section 19-4.

ployment is 4 percent, then prices will rise at a rate of 3 percent per year; similarly, an unemployment rate of 3 percent is associated with a price rise of 5 percent; and so forth. Thus, the Phillips curve says that there is some trade-off between inflation and unemployment such that the closer the economy comes to full employment, the faster prices will rise.

Causes of the Phillips Curve   Various explanations of the Phillips curve have been put forth from time to time. By far the most common explanation has to do with the noncompetitive nature of American industry and labor. According to this view, many key industries in the United States are oligopolistic in nature; that is, they are able, within limits, to set the prices for their products rather than having prices determined for them by competition in the market. Similarly, labor unions are able to force higher than competitive wages by threatening work stoppages. Thus, during periods of economic boom (low unemployment), unions demand substantial wage increases, which are then passed on to consumers by oligopolistic industries. As a consequence, the closer the economy gets to capacity output (full employment), the greater are the inflationary pressures.

Stability of the Phillips Curve   A great many economists, especially quantity theorists but also a growing number of Keynesians, have come to the conclusion that the Phillips curve is an unstable economic relationship. In other words, it is suggested that there is a tendency for the curve to shift outward over time so that a given level of unemployment becomes associated with increasingly larger rates of inflation. The basis for these shifts in the Phillips curve, it is held, is expectations about future prices. Thus, if the economy has been inflating over the past few years, unions and corporations may begin to anticipate this in negotiating wages and setting prices. For example, if a union wants a 6 percent increase in real wages and expects the inflation rate to be 3 percent, it may insist on a 9 percent wage increase. If this increase has the consequence of increasing the rate of inflation from 3 to (say) 4 percent, the Phillips curve will shift outward. Thus, according to this view, the cost of maintaining full employment is not just inflation but an *accelerating rate* of inflation. Inflation grows steadily worse, and the only way to stop it is to put the economy through a prolonged period of unemployment so that expectations are changed.

The empirical basis for such a shift in the Phillips curve is shown in Figure 22-6, which plots the relationship between price changes and the unemployment rate over the past several years. It will be seen that a single curve would fit these data poorly but that three curves seem to fit the data reasonably well. A great many empirical studies[6] of the Phillips-curve relationship have been undertaken in recent years, and the conclusions of these studies seem to confirm the impression given by Figure 22-6: While there may be some short-run trade off between inflation and unemployment, in the long run the Phillips curve is probably vertical.

[6]See Anthony M. Santomero and John J. Seater, "The Inflation-Unemployment Trade-off: A Critique of the Literature," *Journal of Economic Literature,* June 1978, pp. 499–544.

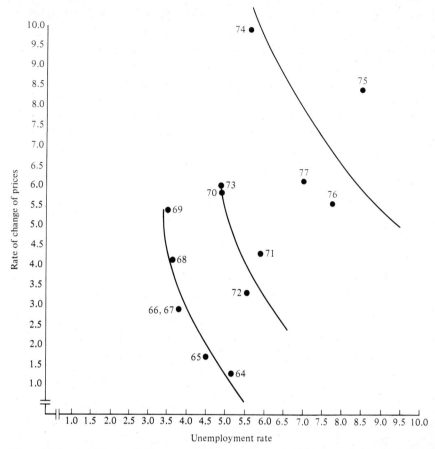

Figure 22-6   A shift in the Phillips curve? (*Source:* Economic Indicators, *March 1978, pp. 12, 14.*)

22-4   REVIEW QUESTIONS

1 What assumptions does liquidity preference theory depend on that portfolio theory does not?

2 List three reasons why modern Keynesians might regard the demand for money as an unstable economic relationship.

3 What is credit rationing? Do you think this is a realistic channel through which monetary policy might affect the economy?

4 If the real sector of the economy is unstable, as the multiplier-accelerator theory suggests, what are the implications for the conduct of monetary policy?

23

Issues and Evidence: The Theories Compared

In the past several years a considerable number of empirical studies have been undertaken in the hope of settling some of the issues that divide the quantity and Keynesian theories—or, at least, narrowing the areas of disagreement between them. In general, it seems fair to say that some convergence has occurred, i.e., that each group has acknowledged the validity of some of the points made by the other and that both groups have come to accept the factual evidence on the nature of certain relationships. Thus, progress is being made. But "progress," of course, is not "final truth," and there remain many areas of substantial disagreement. Thus, the proper frame of mind in which to approach the remainder of the chapter is not that you are now going to "learn what the answer is", but rather that you are going to participate in some of the research issues that continue to excite monetary economists.

23-1 A BRIEF REVIEW

Because the quantity theory of money was discussed in Chapters 18 and 19, the reader may by this time have forgotten what it was all about and consequently may be having some trouble keeping track of the issues that divide the quantity and Keynesian theories. If so, a brief review of the impressionistic sketch of the two theories given in Chapter 17 may prove helpful at this point. (If not, skip to section 23-2.)

Figures 23-1 and 23-2 were first presented in Chapter 17 and are reproduced here without change. Both figures, it will be recalled, make use of the same ingredients—both are built from the same raw materials, so to speak. It is as though two architects, both using mortar and bricks, had designed two quite different houses. The first "house"—the quantity theory shown in Figure 23-1—is a comparatively simple and uncluttered structure. The quantity of money is connected directly to the real sector via the demand for money. And this demand for money is a stable and dominant force in the economy: Given an increase in the money supply, the real sector adjusts largely by increased spending, which has the primary effect of raising prices or real GNP or both. No major barriers exist in the transmission of the monetary impulse to the real sector of the economy. And while the existence of financial institutions and instruments other than banks and money is acknowledged,

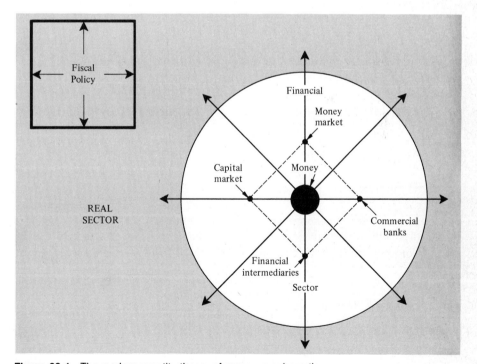

Figure 23-1 The modern quantity theory of money: a schematic.

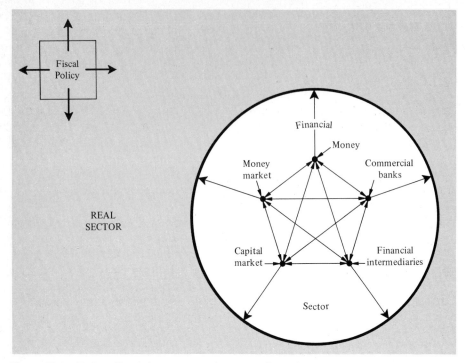

Figure 23-2 Modern Keynesian monetary theory: a schematic.

these do not have any important effect on the demand for money; money is *the* dominant asset. Fiscal policy, on the contrary, has comparatively little effect on the real sector.

The house that Keynes built (Figure 23-2) looks altogether different. It is more complex. Money is one asset among many, and the demand for money is determined within a web of interdependencies that includes all other assets (portfolio theory). Additionally, the mechanism that transmits disturbances in the financial sector to the real sector poses major analytic problems (the cost of capital, the wealth effect, and credit rationing). The real sector adjusts to these disturbances within the context of sluggish price movements, so that employment and real GNP are the primary equilibrating forces (the multiplier-accelerator). Finally, fiscal policy is seen as a powerful policy instrument for stabilizing the economy. In the Keynesian theory, monetary theory and policy are embedded in a broad theory of the macroeconomy.

23-2 THE DEMAND FOR MONEY

It will be recalled that early formulations of the cash-balance approach to the quantity theory of money regarded the demand for money as proportional to nominal national income. Thus, to review the matter briefly, the income version of the Cambridge equation is

$$M = kPy$$

where $M =$ money supply
         $P =$ price level
         $y =$ real income
         $k =$ that fraction of its nominal annual income that the public wants
             to hold in the form of cash balances

Since the product of prices P and real income y is equal to nominal income Y, that is, since $Py = Y$, it follows that *if k is a constant,* the demand for money is a fixed proportion of nominal income. Consequently, changes in the quantity of money were viewed by the early quantity theorists as having their primary effect on the price level, particularly in the long run.

Keynes, it will be recalled, challenged this view. Keynes argued that the demand for money was, among other things, a function of the rate of interest. If this view were correct, then k could no longer be regarded as a constant. In other words, k could take on *various* values for any *given* level of Py (or Y), depending on what the rate of interest happened to be. The role played by money in the economy became correspondingly more complex. Thus, one of the first issues to be addressed by statistical investigators was whether the demand for money was a function of the rate of interest.

Is the Demand for Money a Function of Interest?

Of the many empirical studies that have been carried out concerning the demand for money and the rate of interest, only one has failed to uncover a significant statistical relationship. This single exception was a study done by Milton Friedman[1] (whose modern quantity theory of money was described previously.) Friedman examined the period 1869–1957 and reported that while the evidence indicated the demand for money was functionally related to real income and prices, this same evidence seemed to show that the relationship between the demand for money and the rate of interest was weak to nonexistent. Since this was one of the first such studies done, and because of Friedman's professional stature, it raised serious doubts about the matter.

Subsequent investigations, however, noted flaws in Friedman's method. To mention only one such flaw, Friedman had defined money to include the time deposits of commercial banks. In and of itself, there is nothing remarkable about this; as discussed previously, it is a moot point whether the M_1 or the M_2 definition of money is the correct one. But in this particular case, it did matter. For although the rate of interest is a *cost* (i.e., an opportunity cost) of holding currency and demand deposits, it is a *return* on time deposits. A general rise in all rates of interest, including those paid on time deposits, will therefore tend to decrease the demand for currency and demand deposits but increase the demand for time deposits. Conse-

---

[1]Milton Friedman, "The Demand for Money—Some Theoretical and Empirical Results," *Journal of Political Economy,* June 1959, pp. 327–352.

quently, by lumping time deposits in with demand deposits and currency, Friedman was limiting the responsiveness of the *total* series to changes in the rate of interest.

Virtually all studies since Friedman's have shown that the rate of interest is a significant determinant of the demand for money. There is, indeed, probably no issue in monetary economics that can be regarded as more firmly settled than this one. Thus, on the basis of the evidence, the traditional Keynesian criticism of the traditional quantity theory of money has been shown to be valid.

The Interest Elasticity of the Demand for Money

The question of whether the interest rate and the demand for money are functionally related is a crude one. It is a simple yes-or-no-type question, admitting of no subtleties of distinction or shades of difference. It is, as indicated, a question dividing the *traditional* Keynesians and *traditional* quantity theorist. But *modern* quantity theorists accept the proposition that the demand for money is a function of the rate of interest and base their case instead on how powerful this relationship is. According to this view, a low interest elasticity of the demand for money supports the quantity theory while a high interest elasticity supports the Keynesian theory.

The importance attached to the numerical value of this elasticity can most clearly (though somewhat misleadingly) be explained by looking at extreme cases. Suppose that the interest elasticity of the demand for money is zero. This means that a 1 percent change in the rate of interest will cause a 0 percent change in the quantity of money demanded, which, in turn, means that there is no relationship between the two. In other words, a zero elasticity is the *traditional* quantity theory assumption, the extreme case where the full impact of a change in the money supply is absorbed by a change in nominal income. But suppose, alternatively, that the interest elasticity of the demand for money is infinite. This means that a 1 percent (or any other percent, for that matter) change in the rate of interest will result in an unlimited change in the quantity of money demanded. This is the extreme Keynesian case of the *liquidity trap*, where the liquidity preference schedule turns horizontal. Under such circumstances, monetary policy becomes impotent; it cannot affect the real sector of the economy because it cannot affect the rate of interest.

From a consideration of the extreme quantity theory and the extreme Keynesian cases it seems to follow that a small interest elasticity of the demand for money supports the quantity theory and a large elasticity supports the Keynesian theory. Although this is correct in principle, it can be quite misleading to the unwary. For what is meant by *small* and *large* in this context is not as obvious as it may seem at first. Thus, the extreme cases suggest a range of elasticities from zero to minus infinity, and when one is told that the estimated elasticities range from about –0.1 to –1.0, it seems to provide strong support for the quantity theory. But this is not so. An interest elasticity of the demand for money of –1.0 is well within the Keynesian range (although it is not, certainly, the extreme Keynesian case). To see why this is so, let us examine two estimated demand-for-money functions, one of which is simply repeated from Chapter 19.

The estimated demand-for-money function given in Chapter 19, it will be recalled, was

$$\log \frac{M}{P} = -3.003 + 1.394(\log y) - 0.155(\log i)$$

where M/P is the real per capita money stock, y is real per capita permanent income, and i is the rate of interest on four-month to six-month commercial paper. Since this regression was discussed at length in Chapter 19, it will not be discussed again beyond repeating that the coefficient on $\log i$, -0.155, is the estimated interest elasticity of the demand for money.

Now let us consider a second estimated demand-for-money function, this one specified somewhat differently than the one just given. To understand this regression, recall that Milton Friedman's modern quantity theory regards money balances as a commodity like other commodities and therefore capable of being analyzed within the theory of consumer behavior. In particular, the rate of interest is a *cost* of holding money balances, and the level of real GNP (y) is the *income constraint*. However, if instead of thinking of money balances as a consumer good we think of them as part of a total portfolio of assets, it may be more sensible to use a measure of the economy's *wealth* (rather than income) as the appropriate constraint. A variant of the quantity theory, therefore, is to view the demand for real money balances as a function of interest and wealth. One researcher,[2] pursuing this line of inquiry, estimated the following regression using United States data for the period 1900–1958:

$$\log \frac{M}{P} = -1.48 - 0.949(\log i) + 1.11(\log W)$$

$r^2 = .98$

Coefficients on i and W significant at the 1% level

where M/P = real money stock, with money defined as currency plus demand deposits (that is, M_1)

i = interest rate on twenty-year corporate bonds

W = measure of the real wealth of the economy

The first thing to note about this regression equation is that, statistically speaking, it is just as "good" as the previous one; that is, the coefficient of determination r^2 is equally high, and the coefficients on the two variables are also very significant. Nevertheless, it turns out that when we use (1) the M_1 money definition (rather than M_2), (2) the long-term rate of interest (rather than the short-term rate), and (3) a wealth constraint (rather than income), the interest elasticity of the demand for money rises. In the first regression, the interest elasticity was $-.155$; in this regression, the interest elasticity (the coefficient on $\log i$) is $-.949$. At first this may not seem like much of a difference; both elasticity estimates are, after all, smaller than

[2]Allan H. Meltzer, "The Demand for Money: The Evidence from the Time Series," *Journal of Political Economy*, June 1963, pp. 219–246.

1 in absolute value. But that this *is* a substantial difference will be seen when it is realized that .949 is *more than six times larger* than .155.

To see that these two estimates of the interest elasticity of the demand for money may lead to quite different attitudes about how powerful monetary policy is, let us take the following example. Suppose that the economy is in equilibrium with the supply of money equal to the demand for money at $100 billion; that is,

$$M^S = \$100 \text{ billion} = M^D$$

Now suppose that the Federal Reserve increases the money stock by 10 percent to $110 billion. This increase will mean that the economy is initially thrown into disequilibrium; the supply of money will be greater than the demand for money. Somehow, therefore, the demand for money will also have to increase by 10 percent, or $10 billion, in order to restore equilibrium. The question we want to ask is this: If the full adjustment in the demand for money is borne by interest rates alone, by how much will they have to fall to restore equilibrium?

Let us answer this question first on the basis of the regression equation that estimated the interest elasticity of the demand for money at −.155. It will be recalled that this elasticity is to be interpreted in the following way: If prices and real income remain constant, then a 1.0 percent decrease in the rate of interest will cause a 0.155 percent increase in the demand for money. Thus, in order for the demand for money to rise by the needed 10 percent, the interest rate would have to fall by

$$10\% \left(\frac{1.0\%}{0.155\%} \right) = 64.5\%$$

A 64.5 percent fall in the rate of interest would mean, for example, that the interest rate would have to fall from 6.0 to 2.13 percent to restore equilibrium in the economy. Modern quantity theorists regard this as an unreasonable conclusion. Interest rates, even short-term interest rates, do not fall by such huge amounts in brief periods of time. Consequently, they argue, a substantial part of the 10 percent change in the demand for money needed to restore equilibrium must come about because of changes in the other two variables: prices and real income.

Now let us consider the consequence of a 10 percent increase in the money supply if the interest elasticity of the demand for money is −.949, as given by the second regression equation. This elasticity is to be interpreted in the customary way: a 1 percent decrease in the rate of interest will cause a 0.949 percent increase in the demand for money (prices and wealth remaining constant). Consequently, for an increase of 10 percent in the demand for money to occur, the rate of interest would have to fall by

$$10\% \left(\frac{1.0\%}{0.949\%} \right) = 10.54\%$$

This result is much more feasible than the one based on the first regression. If, for example, the interest rate was initially 6 percent, then it would have to fall to only 5.37 percent in order to increase the demand for money by 10 percent (prices and wealth remaining unchanged). In contrast with the previous case, such a decrease is entirely feasible, even for the long-term interest rate. Thus, Keynesian economists feel that they can reasonably argue that the *immediate* and *direct* effect of an increase in the money supply is to decrease the rate of interest and that only later and indirectly (via the fall in the interest rate) will income be affected.

The conclusion to be derived is that, so far at least, empirical demand-for-money studies have not settled the controversy between the quantity theorists and the Keynesians. What these studies *have* done, and which is no small matter, is to narrow the area of disagreement. Modern quantity theorists do not now accept the judgment of their traditional forebearers that the interest elasticity of the demand for money is zero. And modern Keynesians, similarly, now reject the liquidity trap hypothesis that the interest elasticity is some very large number, possibly even approaching a value of minus infinity. Both sides, that is, accept the empirical verdict that the interest elasticity of the demand for money almost certainly lies somewhere in the range –0.1 to –1.0. But this range is nevertheless broad enough to accommodate both theories. Hopefully, progress will continue to be made, and future studies will continue to narrow the area of disagreement.

The Stability of the Demand-for-Money Function

It will be recalled that many of the theoretical developments in modern Keynesian economics lead to the conclusion that the demand for money is a potentially unstable economic relationship. Modern quantity theorists most emphatically deny this and argue that the demand for money is perhaps the most stable of all economic functions. Who is right and who is wrong about this issue is a matter of considerable importance. If the demand function for money is stable, and if other conditions are right, then monetary policy becomes a very potent policy instrument for economic stabilization. But if the demand for money is unstable, then monetary policy is a tool whose effects are erratic, and additional stabilization devices are needed—most notably, fiscal policy.

The difficulty, of course, lies in knowing just what is meant by the word "stable." Stable is a word like "high" or "long"—meaningful only when it is understood in context. Thus we might be willing to use some criterion to say that "this function is *more* stable than that function" or that a given relationship is stable in the sense that it can be used to predict economic activity within some specified margin of error, but we cannot use the word in a contextual vacuum.

The Brunner-Meltzer Study   One of the first studies of the stability of the demand-for-money function was carried out by Karl Brunner and Allan Meltzer, two well-known quantity theorists. The Brunner-Meltzer study[3] defined stability in terms of *predictability*. According to this test, a stable economic relationship is one that can be predicted by using past data. Thus, we should regard a relationship as stable if by using past data we can forecast future values of it with some reasonable

---

[3] Karl Brunner and Allan H. Meltzer, "Predicting Velocity: Implications for Theory and Policy," *Journal of Finance,* May 1963, pp. 319–359.

degree of accuracy. An unstable relationship, in contrast, would result in inaccurate predictions.

The Brunner-Meltzer test of stability of the demand-for-money function is approximately as follows: Let us arbitrarily choose some year—say, 1958—and estimate a demand-for-money function based on the *previous* ten years. In other words, we estimate this function on the basis of the data for the period 1948–1957 (but we do *not* use 1958 data). It will be recalled that such an estimated relationship will give us estimates of the interest and income elasticities of the demand for money. Next, we combine these elasticity estimates with money supply, interest rates, and income as they actually were *in 1958* and, on this basis, predict what velocity should have been in 1958. Then we compare this *predicted* velocity with the *actual* velocity of 1958. The point is to see how close the predicted and the actual velocities are. If they are close together, then we would conclude that the demand for money in 1958 was similar to the demand for money in 1948–1957, i.e., that the coefficients in the regression equation based on 1948–1957 data continued to describe the relationship in 1958. Aternatively, if actual and predicted velocity are markedly different, we would say that the demand for money was unstable—that the demand for money was different in 1958 than in the period 1948–1957.

Although the explanation in the previous paragraph was, for simplicity, described in terms of a single year (1958), it should be apparent that it could be done for any year for which the necessary data exist. The period used by Brunner and Meltzer was 1910–1958, excluding 1941–1950, which gave them forty-nine pairs of actual and predicted values. Their absolute average (mean) prediction error was 4.2 percent (that is, on the average, predicted velocity differed from actual velocity by 4.2 percent). Whether these results warrant applying the adjective *stable* to the demand-for-money function is a matter of judgment, of course. Just as there is no absolute basis on which to say whether a function is *stable,* so also there is no absolute basis for saying how "close" actual and predicted values of velocity are. Nevertheless, it seems fair to say that the Brunner-Meltzer study impressed a large number of monetary economists. While not in itself conclusive, this study has frequently been cited as a piece of evidence strongly supporting the hypothesis that the demand-for-money function is a stable economic relationship.

Stability and Statistical Significance   Another definition of the word "stable" should be discussed: This definition equates *stable* with the statistical concept of *significance.* When we say that a coefficient in a regression equation is significant, recall, we mean the probability that such a relationship actually exists. For example, the statement that a coefficient is "significant at the 1 percent level" means that (according to the mathematics of probability) there is only one chance in a hundred that the true coefficient is zero. (At this point the reader may wish to review the discussion on statistical significance in the Appendix to Chapter 1.)

What does significance have to do with stability? The general idea is this: If the demand-for-money function is unstable, then money, real income, prices, and interest rates should be found to be historically associated with one another in many different ways. For example, even if we hold prices and real income constant, an unstable demand-for-money function would nevertheless mean that the relationship between interest and money would change depending on circumstances (e.g., the riskiness of bonds). This, in turn, would lead to a low level of significance for the coefficient of interest in the regression equation. Alternatively, a stable relationship between interest and the demand for money would mean that there is a one-to-one relationship between the level of interest rates and the quantity of money demanded (other things being equal); in *this* case, a high level of significance would result. Thus, one test of stability in demand-for-money studies is to examine the statistical significance of the coefficients in the regression equations.

Because it is standard practice to do significance tests when estimating regression equations, we have a great many tests of the stability hypothesis using the significance criterion. Virtually all studies done of the demand-for-money function using data prior to 1974 indicated that (using the significance criterion) the function was stable. In 1974, however, one of those things happened that make the study of economics simultaneously frustrating and challenging: Regression equations that had previously worked quite well in predicting the demand for money suddenly began to go awry and to seriously overestimate the public's demand for cash balances.[4] Because the public demanded less money than the regressions predicted it would, this development has come to be called the *case of the missing money*.[5]

The Case of the Missing Money   The apparent shift in the demand-for-money function that began in about 1974 can best be explained with the aid of Table 23-1. This table shows both the actual and the forecasted demand for money for each quarter from the first quarter of 1974 through the second quarter of 1976. The *actual* demand for money is, of course, the average money stock that existed in the indicated quarter. The *forecasted* demand for money is based on a regression equation of the general type that we have been studying,[6] and which predicted quite well (i.e., with a small error) prior to 1974. The final column of Table 23-1 is simply the difference between the actual and the forecasted demand for money. This column shows, for example, that a regression based on 1952–1973 data would, if extrapolated to the second quarter of 1976, have predicted that the public would want to hold $22.3 billion more than they actually did—an error of almost 10 percent. Moreover, when the money supply is broken down into its component parts (currency and demand deposits), the prediction error for demand deposits alone is a whopping 14.3 percent for 1976:2.

[4]The reader might pause and reflect on the methodological implications of this. It is one of the major differences between the physical sciences and the social sciences. Physicists, for example, having once discovered that a body in a vacuum falls at the rate of 16 feet per second squared, can then reasonably assume that this physical law will continue to hold true in the future. But economists, having discovered what appears to be a social law of human behavior, cannot reasonably make the same assumption; human beings and human institutions are a good deal more contrary than falling bodies. This is one reason that economists are better at explaining the past than they are at predicting the future.

[5]See especially Stephen M. Goldfeld, "The Case of the Missing Money," *Brookings Papers on Economic Activity,* **3**: 1976, pp. 683–739. See also Jared Enzler, Lewis Johnson, and John Paulus, "Some Problems of Money Demand," *Brookings Papers on Economic Activity,* **1**: 1976, pp. 261–282.

[6]In addition to income and money-market interest rate variables, the regression also contained the time deposit rate at commercial banks. See Goldfeld, *op. cit.,* p. 685.

Table 23-1   Actual and Forecast Values for Money-Demand Equation, 1974:1–1976:2
(Billions of 1972 Dollars)

| Year | Money demand (M_1) | | |
and quarter	Actual	Forecast	Error
1974			
1st Quarter	244.4	245.6	−1.2
2nd Quarter	241.2	244.1	−3.0
3rd Quarter	236.7	242.5	−5.8
4th Quarter	232.3	241.8	−9.5
1975			
1st Quarter	226.9	241.6	−14.7
2nd Quarter	228.6	242.6	−14.0
3rd Quarter	228.7	243.8	−15.1
4th Quarter	226.1	245.4	−19.4
1976			
1st Quarter	225.9	248.2	−22.3
2nd Quarter	227.9	250.3	−22.3

Source: Based on Stephen M. Goldfeld, "The Case of the Missing Money," *Brookings Papers on Economic Activity*, 3: 1976, Table 2, p. 687.

The question that naturally arises is why, if regression equations worked well (statistically speaking) prior to 1974, they did not continue to do so after 1974. The author of the paper from which Table 23-1 is taken, Stephen Goldfeld, made a massive effort to find ways to reduce the forecasting error, including using different statistical techniques and alternative explanatory variables. And while Goldfeld was able to make some progress in this respect, the basic problem nevertheless remained: Regression equations that predicted well before 1974 did poorly afterward, and regressions that did well after 1974 did poorly for previous years. Thus we are left with the tentative conclusion that some sort of structural shift occurred in the public's demand for money function, beginning in about 1974. What this structural shift (if any) may have been is, of course, impossible to say. It may well have been something of a nonmeasurable nature, such as the public's newly granted ability to transfer funds from savings accounts to checking accounts via telephone, an ability which makes it much easier to hold a bare minimum of demand deposits. The main point is not so much *why* the shift occurred, but that it *did* occur—unexpectedly.

Monetary Policy and the Stability Issue   At first blush it may seem that unpredictable shifts in the demand-for-money function would make it very difficult, if not impossible, to use monetary policy to stabilize the economy. Basically, this argument would be that, even though the Federal Reserve can control the quantity of money (M), it cannot control velocity (V), so that changes in total expenditures (PT) can still occur to disrupt the smooth functioning of the economy. While this is not an unreasonable conclusion, the matter is actually more complicated than this. To understand why, look again at Table 23-1. The point to note in particular is that the error column of this table requires, at the extreme, the regression equation to forecast *2 ½ years into the future*. Most economic forecasts, however, are much

Table 23-2 Actual and Forecast Values for Money-Demand Equation Including Lagged Value of Money, 1974:1–1976:2 (Billions of 1972 Dollars)

Year and quarter	Error
1974	
1st Quarter	−1.2
2nd Quarter	−1.8
3rd Quarter	−3.1
4th Quarter	−4.2
1975	
1st Quarter	−6.3
2nd Quarter	−1.0
3rd Quarter	−4.1
4th Quarter	−7.0
1976	
1st Quarter	−5.7
2nd Quarter	−3.7

Source: Stephen M. Goldfeld, "The Case of the Missing Money," Brookings Papers on Economic Activity, 3: 1976, Table 2, p. 687.

nearer term than that. And, this being the case, the consequences of an occasional structural shift in the demand-for-money function may not be nearly so devastating for monetary policy as may appear at first glance. To understand why, consider Table 23-2. This table shows the forecasting errors of the same regression equation as Table 23-1, except that the money stock of the previous quarter is also used. For example, the forecast for the second quarter of 1976 is based on the values of income, interest rates, and money supply of the first quarter of 1976. Comparing Tables 23-1 and 23-2, it is apparent that the forecasting errors are substantially reduced when the previous quarter's money stock is included in the regression.[7] A moment's thought will show why this is so: To include the previous quarter's money stock is to "correct" the error every quarter; in a sense, what the equation does is to "start over" each quarter. But of course the Federal Reserve has money-supply data in any given quarter for the previous quarter. Consequently, the Federal Reserve should be much closer to the size of errors shown in Table 23-2 than in Table 23-1.

Summary of the Stability Issue   What does all this mean? It suggests that the demand-for-money function is a fairly stable economic phenomenon for long periods of time, but which occasionally[8] shifts due to structural changes in the financial institutions of the economy. While the demand-for-money function is apparently not

[7]This conclusion is buttressed by a study done by Laumas and Mehra. Using an advanced statistical technique that tests directly for stability, these researchers found that the demand-for-money function (1900–1974) was unstable when a lagged money supply variable was excluded, and stable when such a variable was included. See G. S. Laumas and Y. P. Mehra, "The Stability of the Demand for Money Function, 1900–1974," The Journal of Finance, June 1977, pp. 911–916.

[8]One study concludes that there was a similar shift in the demand-for-money function in the early 1960s. See Myron B. Slovin and Marie Elizabeth Sushka, "The Structural Shift in the Demand for Money," The Journal of Finance, June 1975, pp. 721–731.

so stable as the quantity theory would suggest, neither is it so erratic as to make the quantity theory useless as a guide to monetary policy.[9]

23-3 MODELS OF THE ECONOMY

The purpose of monetary theory is to explain the link that connects monetary policy with the real sector of the economy. The practical value of monetary theory, therefore, lies in its ability to explain and predict various measures of aggregate economic activity. In this spirit, various attempts have been made to develop models of the economy that incorporate monetary policy as one of the chief features of the model. In this section we shall describe and contrast two such models, one of which is basically monetarist (quantity theory) while the other is fundamentally Keynesian. Since even the simplest of these models would require too much space to describe in detail, the descriptions will be put in general terms.

The St. Louis Model

In recent years a group of economists at the district Federal Reserve Bank of St. Louis have been very active in developing and testing an economic model based on the quantity theory of money. Because the quantity theory establishes a direct and immediate connection between money and national income, this model of the economy is comparatively small. Even so, the model contains eight equations and eight variables, making it too lengthy to present here. One of the equations of the model, however, is of particular interest since it purports to test the relative strength of monetary and fiscal policy and hence figures prominently in the Keynesian versus quantity theory controversy. Before discussing the St. Louis equation (as it is usually called), however, it is necessary to discuss briefly *lags* in economic relationships.

Lags in Economic Relationships   The relationship among many economic events is sequential. For example, if the wages of automobile workers are raised today, it may take several months before the full impact of this wage raise is felt by the merchants selling consumer goods in Detroit. People simply do not adjust instantaneously to changed economic circumstances. It is, of course, necessary to take these lags into account in empirical studies. There are various statistical techniques available for doing this, many of them quite sophisticated. For our purposes, it is sufficient to know how to interpret lagged relationships within the context of regression analysis.

Suppose that we believe that changes in the quantity of money are the primary determinant of changes in national income. Suppose further, however, that we do not believe that the impact of a change in the quantity of money is felt fully and immediately on national income, but instead is spread out over several quarters. Then a change in the money supply made today might have, say, 20 percent of its

---

[9]Although occasional shifts in the demand-for-money function do raise serious questions about a monetary policy of steadily increasing the quantity of money. For more discussion of this point, see pages 523–526.

impact on national income this quarter, 25 percent next quarter, 35 percent the following quarter, 20 percent in the next quarter, and no effect thereafter. Now if this is the case, we can say equivalently that 20 percent of the change in income this quarter is caused by the change in the money supply this quarter; 25 percent is caused by the change in the money supply that occurred one quarter ago; 35 percent is caused by the change in the money supply that occurred two quarters ago; and 20 percent is caused by the change in the money supply that occurred three quarters ago. Algebraically, we can write this as

$$\Delta Y_t = .20\Delta M_t + .25\Delta M_{t-1} + .35\Delta M_{t-2} + .20\Delta M_{t-3}$$

where ΔY = change in income and ΔM = change in the money supply. The subscripts t, $t - 1$, $t - 2$, and $t - 3$ in this equation are to be interpreted in the following way: t (time) is the current quarter; $t - 1$ is one quarter ago; $t - 2$ is two quarters ago; and so on. Thus, the symbol ΔM_{t-3}, for example, means "the change in the money supply that occurred three quarters ago." In a regression equation, the coefficients (.20, .25, .35, and .20) are not given but are determined by the data. With these principles in mind, we shall now return to the St. Louis equation.

The St. Louis Equation   As noted previously, the St. Louis model of the economy attempts to assess the relative impact of monetary and fiscal policy on national income. The key equation in this model is a regression equation where current income is the dependent variable and current and lagged values of money supply and fiscal policy are the independent variables. Because the lag goes back by three quarters, there are eight independent variables in the equation (the current plus three lagged quarters both for money and for fiscal policy). This many variables make the equation difficult to read, and it will consequently be convenient to display the regression results differently than we have done so far. The *form* of the regression, written in functional notation, is

$$\Delta Y_t = f(\Delta M_t, \ldots, \Delta M_{t-3}, \Delta F_t, \ldots, \Delta F_{t-3}) \tag{1}$$

where ΔY_t = change in current income
  ΔM = change in the M_1 money supply (in the quarter indicated by the subscript)
  ΔF = change in fiscal policy (in the quarter indicated by the subscript)

The fiscal policy variable is the *high-employment surplus,* i.e., the federal government's tax receipts minus its expenditures as they would have been if the economy were operating at full employment. The coefficients for this regression are given in Table 23-3. The data are in billions of dollars, and the period covered is from the first quarter of 1952 to the second quarter of 1968.

The results shown in Table 23-3, if valid, have profound implications for public policy. For what they suggest is that *monetary* policy plays a major role in the

Table 23-3   Estimated Coefficients of Eq. (1)

Period	Coefficient on	
	ΔM	ΔF
t	1.57*	-.15
$t-1$	1.94*	-.20
$t-2$	1.80*	.10
$t-3$	1.38	.47*

*Coefficient significant at 5 percent level; $r^2 = .56$; constant term is 1.99.

Source: Leonall C. Andersen and Jerry L. Jordan, "Monetary and Fiscal Actions: A Test of Their Relative Importance in Economic Stabilization," *Federal Reserve Bank of St. Louis Review*, November 1968, pp. 11–24.

determination of national income and that *fiscal* policy plays almost none. To see that these *are* the implications of the regression equation, note that the coefficients on ΔM are large, of the correct algebraic sign (+), and statistically significant (except for $t - 3$). The coefficients on ΔF, on the contrary, are small and generally insignificant. Moreover, the algebraic sign on ΔF should be negative because ΔF is defined as tax receipts minus government expenditures, and when the government takes in more in taxes than it spends, this will (theoretically) have a depressing effect on national income. But it will be seen in Table 23-3 that the algebraic signs of the ΔF coefficients are mixed: two negative and two positive. The implication is that fiscal policy has little to do with determining changes in national income.

The Quantity Theory View of Fiscal Policy   The question naturally arises as to how such a weak fiscal policy as that implied by Table 23-3 can be explained. The theory of fiscal policy, after all, seems straightforward and sensible: If the government spends money (expenditures), national income rises; if the government takes in money (taxes), national income falls. The net result of these two activities (taxes minus expenditures) should therefore have a powerful influence on national income, or so it would seem. Yet according to Table 23-3, it doesn't. Why?

Quantity theorists answer this question by arguing that government expenditures crowd out private expenditures. There are, they say, a number of reasons for this *crowding-out effect*. [10] For one thing, an increase in government expenditures not financed by taxes will have to be financed by bond sales to the public; but bond sales will raise interest rates, which, in turn, will discourage private investment expenditures. Thus, government expenditures will be substituted for private expenditures, with little net increase in the total. Additionally, it is held, government spending programs may sometimes compete directly with private business, and when this happens, fiscal policy will be ineffective. For example, if the federal government builds a swimming pool in a park when private enterprise would have built one across the street, then no *net* increase in spending will occur.

For these and other reasons, modern quantity theorists are skeptical about the effectiveness of fiscal policy as a method of economic stabilization, and instead

[10]For a more complete explanation of the crowding-out effect, see Chapter 19, section 19–3.

suggest placing major reliance on monetary policy. They point to such studies as the one summarized in Table 23-3 to support this contention. Keynesians, of course, disagree.

Criticisms of the St. Louis Equation   The policy conclusions drawn from the St. Louis equation have not gone unchallenged. In general, the criticisms have centered on three issues: that the variables used in the equation have been *misspecified;* the so-called *reverse-causation* criticism; and the propriety of using a *reduced-form* equation. We shall discuss each of these criticisms in turn.

Misspecification of Variables   One frequent criticism of the St. Louis equation is that its results, at least insofar as they apply to fiscal policy, are not robust. By "robust," in this context, is meant that a somewhat different specification of the variables used in the equation alters the nature of the conclusions to be derived from it. To illustrate the nature of this criticism, we will describe a study where the money-supply variable has been specified differently.

Recall that modern Keynesian macroeconomic theory regards money as simply one financial asset among many that possess some degree of liquidity. Pursuing this line of thought, some economists have argued that "money" should be defined as a *weighted average* of various financial assets. For example, we might develop a statistical series where a dollar of currency is added in as a dollar, but where a dollar of time deposits is added in only as 50¢. This would imply that the appropriate weight for currency is 1, and that the appropriate weight (or degree of liquidity) for time deposits is 0.5. One recent researcher, Ronald Koot,[11] developed such a series using six financial assets: currency, demand deposits, time deposits, mutual savings bank shares, savings and loan deposits, and United States savings bonds. In this statistical series, the weights attached to the various financial assets are not chosen arbitrarily, but instead are determined by an advanced statistical technique called factor analysis. Koot then used this series, which he called M_w, rather than the conventional definition of money (M_1) in the St. Louis equation for the period 1953–1974. The results of making this substitution are shown in Table 23-4.

Looking at Table 23-4, what is immediately apparent is that the fiscal policy variable ΔF is generally significant and generally has the correct algebraic sign ($+$). This is particularly apparent when the coefficients are summed over the four-quarter lag. But note also that the monetary-policy variable ΔM_w is also significant and also has the correct sign ($+$). Thus, from the results shown in Table 23-4, one would conclude that *both* monetary and fiscal policy have an important influence on national income.

Taken by itself, the Koot study is not, of course, conclusive. But similar studies, which respecified the fiscal-policy variable,[12] the time period covered,[13] and so forth,

[11]Ronald S. Koot, "On the St. Louis Equation and an Alternative Definition of the Money Supply," *The Journal of Finance,* June 1977, pp. 917–920.

[12]E. Gerald Corrigan, "The Measurement and Importance of Fiscal Policy Changes," *Federal Reserve Bank of New York Monthly Review,* June 1970, pp. 133–145.

[13]See Benjamin M. Friedman, "Even the St. Louis Model Now Believes in Fiscal Policy," *Journal of Money, Credit and Banking,* May 1977, pp. 365–367.

Table 23-4   The St. Louis Equation with M_w

Period	Coefficient on	
	ΔM_w	ΔF
t	1.16	0.58*
$t-1$	2.41*	0.41*
$t-2$	2.42*	0.03
$t-3$	1.14	-0.20
Sum of coefficients	7.09*	0.82*

*Coefficient significant at 5 percent level; r^2 = .59; constant term not given.
   Source: Based on Ronald S. Koot, "On the St. Louis Equation and an Alternative Definition of the Money Supply," *The Journal of Finance*, June 1977, Table 1, p. 918.

have arrived at approximately the same conclusion: Money matters, and so does fiscal policy. Such a conclusion is, of course, fully consistent with modern Keynesian theory.

The Reverse-Causation Criticism   In Chapter 12 we derived a formula for the determination of the money supply in the United States. To refresh the reader's memory, this formula is summarized as

$$M = mR \tag{2}$$

where M = money supply
         R = reserve base of the commercial banking system
         m = money multiplier

In subsequent chapters it was argued that in the long run the Federal Reserve System, through its various policy instruments, can control the reserve base R and that consequently it can control the money supply whatever the money multiplier may be. Because of this, the monetary theory discussed so far has taken the money supply as an *exogenous* variable, that is, a variable imposed on the economy from outside, not determined by forces within the economy. While this general description of the money creating process is valid, it may nevertheless be misleading for two reasons.

In the first place, the value of the money multiplier is not determined by the Federal Reserve authorities. Instead, it is determined largely by decisions of the public and commercial banks. Thus, to again refresh the reader's memory, the formula for the money multiplier is

$$m = \frac{1 + K}{R_D + X + tR_T} \tag{3}$$

where K = currency ratio
         R_D = demand deposit reserve ratio
         X = excess reserve ratio

$t =$ time deposit ratio
$R_T =$ time deposit reserve ratio

Clearly, such things as the public's currency ratio, the division between time and demand deposits, and the excess reserves that banks decide to maintain are outside the control of the Federal Reserve. Thus, although it is true that in the long run the Federal Reserve can control the reserve base R in such a manner as to offset any spontaneous changes in the money multiplier m, it is also true that *at any given time* the money supply is determined in part by decisions of the public and commercial banks.

In the second place, note that in the short run the reserve base itself can be determined in part by factors other than Federal Reserve policy. Member bank borrowings from the Fed, for example, are only loosely influenced by the discount rate. Additionally, other elements in the bank reserve equation (such as float and treasury balance at the Fed) may suddenly change, and it will take time for the Federal Reserve to realize these changes and take corrective action. Thus, at any given time even the reserve base may be determined in part by the decisions of the public and the commercial banking system.

Now what all this means, say the Keynesians, is that the money supply may have a substantial *endogenous* component, that is, a part of it is determined by forces within the economy, not (exogenously) imposed on the economy from outside. Moreover, there is a good reason to suppose that this endogenous component is positively related to income. For example, when income rises and interest rates increase, then it is likely that banks will draw down their excess reserves and increase their borrowings from the Fed. Both of these actions will expand the money supply. Similarly, a higher national income may cause the public to decrease the proportion of its money balances that it is holding in the form of currency and to correspondingly increase its demand deposits. These actions will also cause the money supply to increase. But if all this is so—if the money supply is even in part endogenous and positively related to national income—then there are feedbacks, or *loops*, to the monetary process: An increase in the money supply will cause an increase in national income, but an increase in national income will also cause an increase in the money supply.

This is the *reverse-causation* criticism of the St. Louis equation. Very simply, the criticism says that to some extent changes in income cause changes in the money supply, not the other way around, as eq. (1) asserts. If this is the case, say the Keynesians, it is small wonder that there is a significant *statistical* relationship between money and income; the wonder would be if there weren't. But such a statistical relationship, taken by itself, can hardly be offered as proof of the overriding importance of monetary policy.

A very interesting test of the direction of causation between money and income has been devised by an economist named Christopher Sims. Although the *Sims test* (as it is called) involves some advanced statistical techniques, the essence of the test can be explained simply. Suppose that we have two statistical time series, X and Y, and that we have reason to believe that they are causally related but we do not know which way the causation runs. In other words, we do not know if X is causing Y or if Y is causing X. Then what we can do, says Sims, is to regress current values of one variable on past, current, *and future* values of the other variable. Suppose, for example, that we wanted to test the hypothesis that X causes Y. Then to test this hypothesis we would set up a regression equation of the following form:

$$Y_t = f(X_{t+4}, \ldots X_{t+1}, X_t, X_{t-1}, \ldots X_{t-4}) \tag{4}$$

Note that, in eq. (4), current values of Y (Y_t) are shown as a function of future values of X (X_{t+4}, etc.), current values of X (X_t), and past values of X (X_{t-1}, and so on). Now the *test* for causality is simply this: If X is causing Y, then the coefficients on the *future* values of X should have no effect on the current values of Y, and hence should not be statistically significant. Coefficients on current and past values of X, on the other hand, should be statistically significant. Naturally, we could use the same method to test the hypothesis that Y is causing X.

Using this test, Sims found that the direction of causality runs from money to income, and not the other way around.[14] In other words, the test showed that changes in money cause changes in national income, but that changes in national income do not cause changes in money. Subsequent studies have applied the Sims test directly to the St. Louis equation and have come to the same conclusion.[15] Thus on the basis of our present knowledge, the best evidence says that money causes income. (Score one for the folks at the St. Louis Fed!)

The Reduced-Form Criticism   Perhaps the most fundamental criticism of the St. Louis equation made by the Keynesians is that it says nothing at all about the mechanics of *how* money affects the economy. Thus, it is said, the St. Louis equation is a *reduced-form model* of the economy that may hide more than it reveals. What is meant by a *reduced-form model* is rather technical, but the general idea can be made clear through the use of an illustration. Let us suppose that we have the following very simple three-equation model of the economy:

$$\Delta Y = \Delta C + \overline{\Delta I} + \overline{\Delta G} \tag{5}$$
$$\Delta C = b(\Delta Y - \Delta T) \tag{6}$$
$$\Delta T = t(\Delta Y) \tag{7}$$

where Y = national income
C = consumption
I = investment
G = government spending
T = taxes

The deltas, of course, mean "a change in," and the bars over $\overline{\Delta I}$ and $\overline{\Delta G}$ indicate that we are treating these as exogenous variables (i.e., as "givens"). Equation (5) says

[14]Christopher A. Sims, "Money, Income and Causality," *American Economic Review,* September 1972, pp. 540–552.
[15]J. W. Elliott, "The Influence of Monetary and Fiscal Actions on Total Spending: The St. Louis Total Spending Equation Revisited," *Journal of Money, Credit and Banking,* May 1975, pp. 181–192.

that a change in national income is the sum of the changes in consumption, investment, and government expenditures. Equation (6) says that changes in consumption
expenditures are proportional to changes in after-tax income, $\Delta Y - \Delta T$. Finally,
eq. (7) states that changes in taxes are proportional to changes in national income.

There are two methods of estimating this simple model. The first method is to
find its reduced form and estimate that. To obtain the reduced form, note that the
model has three equations and three unknowns: Y, C, and T (remember that G and
I are given). We can therefore solve this system of equations for any one of these
variables. In particular, since we are interested in income, let us solve it for ΔY. To
do so, we begin by substituting eq. (7) into eq. (6), which gives

$$\Delta C = b(\Delta Y - t \Delta Y) \tag{8}$$

Next, we substitute *this* equation, eq. (8), into eq. (5), which gives

$$\Delta Y = b(\Delta Y - t \Delta Y) + \overline{\Delta I} + \overline{\Delta G} \tag{9}$$

Since eq. (9) contains only one unknown ΔY, it can be solved to give

$$\Delta Y = \frac{1}{1 - b - bt} (\overline{\Delta I} + \overline{\Delta G}) \tag{10}$$

Equation (10) is the reduced form of the model. It says that if you multiply changes
in investment and government spending by $1/(1 - b - bt)$, you will obtain changes
in national income.

Now suppose that we wanted to estimate the model [eqs. (5) to (7)] by using
only the reduced form [eq. (10)]. We could do so by lumping ΔI and ΔG together
and calling them *autonomous expenditures*, or ΔA (that is, $\Delta G + \Delta I = \Delta A$). Then
we could use regression analysis to test the hypothesis that

$$\Delta Y = c + d \, \Delta A \tag{11}$$

where c and d are the estimated coefficients of the regression and theoretically c
should equal zero and d should equal $1/(1 - b - bt)$. The trouble with estimating
eq. (11)—which is the equivalent of eq. (10), the reduced form of the model—is that
it tells us very little about the validity of the original model. In other words, our
original model hypothesized that changes in consumption were a function of changes
in after-tax income and that changes in tax revenues were a function of changes in
national income. But eq. (11) tells us nothing about these hypotheses. All eq (11)
says is that there is some (statistical) relationship between ΔA and ΔY. Such a
relationship, if valid, *might* be due to the hypotheses contained in the model, but
then again it might not; there is no way to tell from the reduced form.

The second method of estimating the model [eqs. (5) to (7)] would be to do a
regression study of each equation separately.[16] This is called a *structural model.*

---

[16]Equation (5) is an identity—true by definition—and so in practice there would be no need to
estimate it.

Such a study *would* tell us if our underlying hypotheses about the way the economy works are statistically acceptable. Additionally it would give us the values of b and t separately rather than lumping them together in the single coefficient d of eq. (11).

What does all this have to do with the St. Louis equation? The answer is that the St. Louis equation is a reduced-form model and therefore subject to the same criticisms as those made of eq. (11). All it says is that there is some (statistical) relationship between ΔM and ΔY, but it does not tell us the detailed nature of this relationship. Moreover, the set of hypotheses from which the St. Louis equation is presumably derived are not even given. The Keynesians consequently argue that, in the absence of a structural model which lays out the underlying relationships, the St. Louis equation proves very little. It *may* be valid, they say, but then again it may not. There is no way to tell from the reduced form, especially if you don't even know what system of equations the reduced form is reduced from.

The MPS Model

From the immediately preceding discussions of *reverse causation* and *reduced-form versus structural models,* the reader might reasonably infer that Keynesians tend to build elaborate models of the economy, replete with many sectors and feedback mechanisms. This is correct. The proliferation of good and detailed data about the economy, the development of sophisticated statistical techniques for handling such problems as lagged relationships and seasonal variations, and the availability of high-speed computers have made the construction of such models feasible. Contemporary Keynesians regard complex models as the only sensible way to understand a complex economy, and tend to take a dim view of single-equation tests of aggregate economic relationships. It is for this reason, incidentally, that Keynesians at times may seem on the defensive with respect to such controversies as the St. Louis equation. Modern Keynesians do not regard such studies as very meaningful and typically do not engage in them except in response to a challenge from quantity theorists.

Several elaborate and basically Keynesian econometric models of the economy have been developed during the last decade or so. Because such models *are* elaborate, usually involving fifty or more equations, it is not possible to describe them here in detail (for which the reader should be duly thankful). But one such model, which focuses in particular on the consequences of monetary and fiscal policy actions, can be described in very general terms. This model was first developed during the mid-1960s by a group of economists at the Massachusetts Institute of Technology and the Social Science Research Council. They were joined later by another group of economists at the University of Pennsylvania, and the model has subsequently come to be known as the *MPS model.*

The MPS model is not a set "thing." Instead, it is constantly evolving as new ideas are developed and new hypotheses are tested and included in the model. It contains well over 100 equations and about 200 variables (counting both endogenous and exogenous variables). These equations and variables are used to describe ten major spending, pricing, and employment sectors. For example, equations analyzing expenditures on plant and equipment, inventory, consumption, housing, and state and local government expenditures are all included in the model. Each of these sectors is analyzed separately, and then they are tied together through an interconnecting algebraic system of actions and reactions.

The model is distinctly neo-Keynesian. Included in it are equations describing the channels through which Keynesians see monetary policy working: the cost-of-capital, wealth, and credit rationing effects described in Chapter 22. Included also are the effects of government taxation and spending policies, which vary depending on what part of the economy they affect first. The model is based on the neo-Keynesian accelerator-multiplier principle, and prices are determined by a Phillips-curve-type relationship (both described in Chapter 22). A number of looped, or feedback, relationships are included. The coefficients used in the model have been estimated on the basis of regression analysis.

The MPS model is used in two ways: First, it is used to try to *predict* economic events, such as inflations and recessions. This is done by using past data to establish statistical relationships and then running the model a few quarters into the future. Although such attempts at prediction have not been overwhelmingly successful, they do seem to be better than the "seat-of-the-pants"-type prediction used by many forecasters. The second way the model is used is to *simulate* policy changes, by which it is meant that in any particular quarter the model can be made to behave as *though* a particular policy action had been taken and then run into the future to see what the consequences of this policy action would be. For example, the consequences of a $1 billion open market sale or a $5 billion tax reduction can be simulated. By using such simulation runs, policy makers can be forewarned of the consequences of many of their actions, not just in terms of the ultimate effect on income and prices, but also in terms of the impact on such things as interest rates, housing, and state and local finance.

Econometric model building on the scale of the MPS model is still in its infancy, but it seems fair to say that it has a promising future. The model is adaptable enough to incorporate new ideas and new discoveries as they are made, and the potential of such models for predicting economic events and simulating policy actions is very great.

23-4 CONSEQUENCES OF THE TWO THEORIES

The debate between modern quantity theorists and modern Keynesians is far from settled. Each side continues to score off the other, raise crucial issues, and develop evidence in support of their own position. But progress is being made, and it seems possible that some day the two theories will converge sufficiently so that only a few empty slogans separate them. In the meantime, however, the monetary authorities must make do with what they have, and each of the theories leads to distinctly different conclusions about the conduct of stabilization policy. Although a thorough discussion of these matters must be postponed until after we consider the international aspects of the economy (a topic not yet touched on), a brief indication of the nature of the policy consequences of the two theories can be indicated.

The most obvious difference between the two theories, and one that has been mentioned several times, is the relative emphasis placed on fiscal and monetary policy. Quantity theorists tend to believe that monetary policy is all that is needed to stabilize the economy and that fiscal policy isn't very effective anyhow. Keynesians feel that fiscal policy is a powerful force in the economy and that both monetary and fiscal policy are needed to avoid inflations and recessions.

A second important difference between the quantity and Keynesian theories has to do with the way in which monetary policy is conducted. In the quantity theory, it will be recalled, the quantity of money impinges *directly* on spending decisions of all types. If this is true, then the appropriate variable for the Federal Reserve to control is the quantity of money in the economy. Keynesians, alternatively, see monetary policy as influencing the economy *indirectly,* to some extent through credit rationing, but primarily through interest rates (cost-of-capital and wealth effects). In the Keynesian view, therefore, the appropriate variable for the Federal Reserve to control is interest rates. The trouble is that the Federal Reserve cannot do both; it cannot control both the quantity of money *and* interest rates. It must do one or the other.

The situation is comparable to that of a monopoly: A monopoly can determine what quantity of a good it wants to produce and then passively set a price that will clear the market, or it can establish a market price and then passively produce that quantity of its product which will clear the market. But it cannot simultaneously determine both price and quantity. The Federal Reserve is a sort of monopolist in the production of money. As such, it can, if it chooses, determine to a very close degree the quantity of money in the economy. But if it does so, interest rates (the price of money) will move passively to whatever level clears the market. Alternatively, it can decide to determine interest rates (price) and passively furnish whatever quantity of money will clear the market. But it cannot do both—it cannot simultaneously determine both interest rates and the quantity of money. (See Chapter 16, section 16-1, for a more detailed explanation of this point.) The Federal Reserve therefore cannot conduct monetary policy as both the Keynesians and quantity theorists say they should.

A third very important difference between the two theories, perhaps the most fundamental of all, is that quantity theorists see major disturbances in the economy as arising in the monetary sector while Keynesians see them as arising in the real sector. In other words, the quantity theorists argue that the *causes* of inflations and recessions are to be found largely in changes in the quantity of money. Keynesians, on the contrary, argue that the causes of inflations and recessions are to be found for the most part in shifts in autonomous expenditures, especially in private business investment. The implications of these two views for the conduct of monetary policy are profound. If the quantity theorists are correct, then the best way for the Federal Reserve to behave is to increase the money supply smoothly and steadily. Many quantity theorists, most especially Milton Friedman, therefore argue that monetary policy should be conducted according to a fixed *rule,* for example, that the quantity of money in the economy should be increased by 4 percent per year, come what may. By following such a rule, they argue, most of the instability in the economy can be eliminated.

The Keynesian view is quite different. Keynesians argue that the economy is unstable, not because the quantity of money is unstable, but because private business investment expenditures are unstable. If this is the case, then the appropriate conduct of monetary policy is to influence investment in the hope of smoothing it out, that is, to lop off the peaks and fill in the valleys of investment cycles by making interest rates high or low. But this requires that monetary policy be conducted in a discretionary fashion, that is, that the appropriate policy be decided according to the circumstances of the moment, not according to some fixed rule.

Clearly, the Federal Reserve cannot do both; it cannot behave both according to a rule and at its own discretion. And when one considers that all recent studies, Keynesian and quantity theory alike, indicate that monetary policy has a major influence on how well the economy operates, then one begins to grasp the importance of this debate. It is literally true that the economic well being of millions of Americans will be affected by who is right, who is wrong, and the choice made by the Federal Reserve.

23-5 REVIEW QUESTIONS

1 Try to explain why a shift in the demand for money function might have occurred around 1974.
2 Read back through pages 447–448 and show how you would construct a Sim's test for the hypothesis that Y causes X. Suppose that the only statistically significant coefficient in this test turned out to be that on Y_t. What would you conclude?
3 What is the reduced form of the following model (solve the model for C)?

$$C = aY_d$$
$$Y_d = Y - T$$
$$T = bY$$

where C = consumption
  Y_d = disposable personal income
  T = taxes
  Y = national income

4 Why is it important to know whether economic disturbances originate in the real sector or the financial sector?

PART 8

INTERNATIONAL MONETARY RELATIONS

The behavior of the United States economy affects other nations, and the behavior of other nations affects the United States economy. Thus far, we have ignored this fact and have treated our domestic monetary system as though it were isolated from the rest of the world. But we can no longer afford to maintain this fiction. A complete understanding of the monetary process requires that its international aspects be taken into account.

Every part of the domestic monetary system contains an international element. Commercial banks and other institutions finance international trade and investment; the Federal Reserve System deals with its foreign counterparts; and what happens to the international value of the dollar will affect income, employment, and the price level. Thus, in terms of Figure 1-1 of Chapter 1, each of the elements A to F in some measure will have its international aspect. Rather than describing these aspects piecemeal by scattering them throughout Chapters 2 to 23, they are grouped together in the following two chapters so that the reader can better understand how they are connected to one another and to the domestic economy.

Chapter 24 deals with international financial arrangements stemming basically from transactions among individuals: international finance, the foreign exchange market, and the balance of payments. Chapter 25 deals with monetary arrangements among nations—past, present, and future possibilities.

24

International Monetary Relations among People

A dollar earned in Dallas and spent in New York is still a dollar, but 1 dollar earned in Dallas and spent in Paris is 5 francs. This is not a minor difference. Any time an economic transaction crosses an international border, it becomes involved in two distinct sets of laws, currencies, customs, and (probably) languages. To facilitate international transactions, despite these national differences, a great many specialized financial institutions, instruments, and markets have been developed.

24-1 THE STRUCTURE OF INTERNATIONAL BANKING

Before 1965, American commercial banks paid comparatively little attention to the international aspects of their business. At that time, the international sector of our economy accounted for only about 6 percent of the Gross National Product, and banks were generally content to make arrangements for the international affairs of their customers through foreign correspondents. Only about three American banks had extensive overseas operations.

Matters have changed dramatically in the past fifteen years. For one thing, our international sector has grown substantially, and Americans have become highly conscious of such things as the "strength" of the dollar abroad. For another, our industrial dependence on imported petroleum has been highlighted by the energy crisis. Most fundamental of all, however, is that United States banks, as they have responded to these events, have found offshore business to be highly profitable. Today, well over a hundred of our largest banks have an extensive network of foreign correspondents, branches, and subsidiaries.

Foreign Correspondent Banking

Domestic correspondent banking was described in Chapter 2. As will be recalled from that discussion, correspondent banking is a system whereby banks hold deposits with one another and perform various services in return for these deposits. Essentially the same type of arrangement may be made with banks in other countries. This is called *foreign correspondent banking.*

Foreign correspondent banking is a good deal more complicated than its domestic counterpart. The major reason for this is that the foreign correspondent will very likely be operating within a wholly different institutional framework—different laws, customs, and banking structure. Naturally, the foreign institutions take precedent, so that quite a bit of confusion may result over what the American respondent bank wants done, and what *can* be done by the foreign correspondent bank. Beyond this, foreign banks understandably give priority to their own affairs and customers. For both these reasons, exclusive reliance on foreign correspondents has proven increasingly unsatisfactory for many American banks. Although correspondent relationships continue to be an important and, indeed, essential part of international banking, many banks have chosen to supplement these relationships with a more direct, and more active, international involvement.

Foreign Branches of United States Banks

United States banks now have well over 700 *branches* in foreign countries. Establishment of these branches has evidently proven quite profitable. A substantial part of the total assets of U.S. banks are held abroad; some banks obtain half or more of their profits from foreign activities; and a few banks have over half their employees on foreign soil.

Overseas branches of an American bank are a part of that bank, just as is a domestic branch. For example, legal reserves are calculated against total deposits, including those in foreign branches; or again, foreign branches are subject to examination by the appropriate U.S. banking authorities. Nevertheless, and as might be expected, foreign branches have some unique characteristics. For example, foreign branches are permitted to engage in some (but not all) of the banking activities "usual" to banks in the country in which the branch is domiciled, even where those activities may not be permitted to banks in the United States. And, of course, they must abide by the laws of the host country, where such laws are more restrictive than U.S. banking laws.

The advantages to a large U.S. bank of having a foreign branch are considerable.

Foremost among these is that the bank's customers can conduct their foreign business operations through a known quantity—the U.S. bank—whose attention is focused on the peculiar needs of that customer. Additionally, the foreign branch can advise the head office about profitable investment opportunities abroad, about foreign money markets, about political developments that may affect the bank's holdings of foreign currencies, and the like. Probably the major disadvantages are the costs of establishing a foreign branch, and the amount of expertise needed to operate simultaneously within the confines of two different sets of laws and customs.

Branches of Foreign Banks in the United States Just as U.S. banks have established branches in foreign countries, so a number of foreign banks have located branches in our country. Originally intended simply to follow their corporate customers into U.S. markets and thereby facilitate credit transactions, the operations of these foreign branches have now expanded to the point where they offer a full range of banking services—not only to foreign customers, but to strictly American customers as well. They operate predominantly in Illinois, New York, and California, and their activities are generally regulated by the laws of those states.

Foreign Affiliates of United States Banks

The bank holding-company movement, described in Chapter 2, has resulted in what is certainly the newest, and probably the most dynamic, development of U.S. international banking in recent years. A bank holding company, it will be recalled, is a corporation formed for the purpose of owning the controlling amount of stock in at least one bank, and in other bank-related businesses. There is, of course, no reason for bank holding companies to confine their activities to the United States, and many do not. Citibank of New York, for example, has affiliate companies in more than fifteen countries (in addition to branches in almost sixty countries).

Two aspects of overseas bank holding-company activity are of particular interest. Note, in the first place, that a foreign bank owned by an American bank holding company is independently incorporated under the laws of that country. This means that it may engage in certain business activities that are accepted banking practice in the host country, but are illegal under the laws of the United States. For example, many foreign countries permit banks to underwrite the issuance of new securities —an activity which, with certain exceptions, they are strictly prohibited from doing in the United States. The second point to note is that bank holding-company affiliates need not be banks at all. They need be only "bank related"—for example, a data-processing company, or a mortgage loan company.

Both these aspects of overseas holding-company activity present special problems for the bank regulatory agencies, especially the Federal Reserve System, which is charged with the responsibility of supervising bank holding companies. The problems arise from the fact that the overseas operations of American bank holding companies could threaten the stability of the parent corporation, hence of some (usually very large) domestic banks, hence of our entire banking system. As a consequence, the Federal Reserve has had a tendency to scrutinize these international activities carefully. In general terms, the Fed is required to weigh three considerations: (1) the effect the acquisition of a new affiliate will have on the solvency of affiliated U.S. banks; (2) the monopolistic implications for U.S. banking; and (3) the competitive position of U.S. banks and nonbanking corporations in foreign markets. While the international expansion of bank holding companies is too recent for firm guidelines to have been established as yet, it seems fair to say that so far the Fed's regulatory approach has been characterized by considerable caution.

Edge Act Subsidiaries A type of international banking that dates back a long time in the United States is the *Edge Act Corporation.* The purpose of the Edge Act, passed in 1919, was to permit American banks to operate overseas and to engage in certain activities that were prohibited to them domestically. The corporations resulting from the Edge Act may engage only in international banking and related activities. They are of many forms. Some do not accept deposits, for example, while others engage in the full range of international banking activities.

An interesting aspect of Edge Act corporations, and one which has kept them a viable corporate structure despite more recent developments in international branching and holding-company affiliates, is that an Edge Act corporation is permitted to establish as many as five "offices" within the United States. Since these offices need not be in the same city or state as the head office, they frequently give the parent banking corporation nationwide outlets for its international business affairs. These offices can offer international banking services and advise large corporate customers concerning such matters as exchange rate movements, international money and capital markets, and tax laws in foreign countries.

24-2 INTERNATIONAL BANKING ACTIVITIES

With the growth of American banking into the international sphere, the international banking departments of banks have become correspondingly more important. Where a few years ago these departments were largely service departments, designed only to attract and hold certain corporate accounts, today they are frequently one of the most important and profitable departments in the bank.

The international banking department of a commercial bank is, in a sense, simply a microcosm of the bank as a whole. That is, with few exceptions, they do not do anything which in principle is not duplicated elsewhere in the purely domestic departments of the bank: they extend credit, and they handle payments from debtors to creditors by transferring deposits. However, in practice, the amount of risk involved in an international transaction is considerably higher than in a domestic transaction. The need to reduce this risk has led to a number of specialized financial instruments, which require the expertise of an international banking department. Two such instruments, the letter of credit and the bill of exchange, will be described briefly.

The Letter of Credit

Because exporters and importers may have only the vaguest notion of one another's creditworthiness, most of the financial instruments of foreign trade somehow involve the guarantee of a commercial bank. One such instrument, the *letter of credit,* is issued by the importer's bank; it guarantees payment to the exporter up to some specified amount of money. In this fashion, the exporter is protected by a substitution of the bank's good faith and credit for that of the importer. The importer is also protected, since the letter of credit typically specifies in close detail all the things an exporter must do to receive payment.

There are a great many different kinds of letters of credit. Two of these are particularly noteworthy in the present context: the *import letter of credit* and the *export letter of credit.* The distinction between these turns on what currency is to be used in making payment. An import letter of credit requires that payment be made in the importer's currency, and an export letter of credit requires that it be made in the exporter's currency. For example, if an American firm imports Scottish woolens under an import letter of credit, it would make payment for these in dollars; if an export letter of credit is used instead, payment would be made in pounds sterling.

The reason that the distinction between import and export letters of credit is important is that the choice of one or the other will determine which party bears the *exchange risk,* or the risk of converting one currency to another. Since the terms of most business deals are agreed upon far in advance of actual payment, there is always the risk that the price of one currency will change in terms of the other. And when this happens, either the exporter or the importer will suffer a loss. If payment is made in the importer's currency, then the exporter bears the risk; if it is made in the exporter's currency, then the importer bears the risk. To illustrate, suppose we have the following situation. On January 1 an American export firm sells machinery valued at $2 million to an English importer. The terms of the sale are that the machinery is to be delivered on April 1 and payment is to be made at that time. Furthermore, the sales contract specifies that an import letter of credit is to be used. If, when the contract is made, £1 (1 pound) is worth $2, the use of the import letter of credit means that the total obligation of the English firm is to pay £1 million, which is worth $2 million under the exchange rate prevailing on January 1. But suppose that by April 1 the exchange rate has changed so that £1 = $1.95. Then, when the English firm pays the American firm, the £1 million will be worth only $1.95 million. The American firm will therefore receive $50,000 less than it thought it would—that is, it will have borne the exchange risk.[1] Alternatively, if an export letter of credit had been specified, then the American firm would have received the full $2 million—that is, the English firm would have borne the exchange risk.

---

[1]The discussion in the text is cast in terms of exchange *risk,* since it is typically the avoidance of an adverse movement in the foreign exchange rate that motivates the decision of whether to use an import or an export letter of credit. Note, however, that there is also an opportunity for gain. Thus, in the above example, if the exchange rate had moved to £1 = $2.05, and if an import letter of credit had been used, the American firm would have *gained* $50,000. However, for the American firm to specify an import letter of credit in the expectation of a favorable move in the exchange rate is to cast itself in the role of speculator. Most firms prefer to leave such speculation to professionals.

The Bill of Exchange

Once the importer's bank has issued a letter of credit, the exporter can (typically) be paid only by complying with the specified terms. These terms include acquiring the necessary documents showing that the goods have been shipped—invoices, bills of lading, insurance, and so on. The exporter will then attach these documents to a *bill of exchange,* which is sent to the importer's bank. The bill of exchange orders the bank to make payment to some specified party, usually either the exporter or the exporter's bank. If the documents are drawn correctly and the other terms of the letter of credit have been met, the importer's bank will then comply with this order.

The two main types of bills of exchange are the *sight draft* and the *time draft.* A sight draft, as the name implies, is payable on demand, that is, as soon as the importer's bank receives it. A time draft is payable on some future date. In this latter case, the importer's bank typically will accept the obligation to pay the draft in the future, making it a *bankers acceptance* (see Chapter 7), which then becomes a highly liquid money market instrument that may be sold by the exporter.

24-3 THE INTERNATIONAL MONEY AND CAPITAL MARKETS

It is by no means new for the citizens of one country to be able to lend funds in another country. In the nineteenth century, for example, a New York financier could convert dollars to pounds sterling and then lend the pounds so acquired in the London money or capital markets. Even though such activities became fairly extensive in some of the world's leading financial centers, such centers still could not truly be called *international* markets because loans were always made in the currency of the host country—pounds in London, dollars in New York, and so forth. During the late 1950s, however, financial markets developed that could genuinely be called international. The central feature of such a market is that it makes possible the lending and borrowing of funds in a currency outside the country of origin. For example, it became possible for an Englishman, in London, to lend dollars to another Englishman in London. The money market (short-term) aspect of such a market is called the *Eurodollar market.* The capital market (long-term) aspect is called the *Eurobond market.*

The Eurodollar Market

The Eurodollar market, properly so-called, is actually a part of a larger market. Narrowly used, the term denotes dollar-denominated deposits in European banks. However, the broader market includes banks in non-European financial centers, such as Singapore and Tokyo, and deposits denominated in currencies other than the dollar (this latter is sometimes called the *Eurocurrency market*). However, since European banks (including European branches of American banks) and dollars continue to dominate the market, we will here concentrate on this aspect.

The mechanics of the Eurodollar can become quite complex. For our limited purposes, however, a fairly simple, and fairly typical, example will suffice to explain its general nature. Suppose that an American car dealer imports $1 million worth of English automobiles, with the terms of the deal being an import letter of credit and a sight draft. Then, as we have just seen, the English exporter will immediately come into possession of a $1 million deposit in an American bank. For a variety of reasons, the English exporter may wish to continue to hold dollars rather than converting them to pounds. For example, she may have another business deal coming up in a few weeks that will require dollars, and rather than undergo the trouble, expense, and risk of selling the dollars for pounds now and then reversing the transaction shortly thereafter, she may prefer simply to hold the dollars straight through. One way she might do this, of course, is to buy a time deposit (certificate of deposit, or CD) in a New York bank. Again, however, there are a number of reasons why she might not want to do this. She might, for example, be unfamiliar with the New York bank and the New York CD market, and prefer to deal with a bank and market in London that she is familiar with. A more likely, and more compelling, reason, however, would be that short-term interest rates in London were higher than in New York. Naturally, she would like to earn as much interest on the funds as possible while she is not using them. For whatever reason, the English exporter temporarily holding dollars has the option of shifting them from the New York bank to one of the London banks that accepts Eurodollar deposits. Note that her time deposit in London is denominated in dollars—that is, no conversion to pounds has occurred.

So far as the New York bank is concerned, the above set of transactions has left its *total* deposit liabilities unaffected. All that has happened is that the ownership of an account has shifted, first from the American importer to the English exporter, then from the English exporter to the English bank. The English bank, however, is in a much different position. It is now holding a million-dollar deposit in the New York bank, and it has its customer's guarantee (in the form of a CD) that these funds will not be withdrawn for a stipulated period of time. During this period of time, the funds can be lent out. The English bank might, for example, lend them to a Paris bank, which in turn lends them to a French importer of Italian shoes.

Uses of the Eurodollar market are quite varied. It is used, for example, by foreign central banks to make temporary deposits of excess dollar holdings. It is also used by foreign commercial banks to make interbank transfers of funds. And, of course, it is used by large corporations (and, occasionally, governments) in need of dollars for financing international trade. One of the most interesting uses of the Eurodollar market is as a source of loan funds for commercial banks of the United States. In this case, the U.S. bank borrows dollars (frequently through its foreign branch office) in the Eurodollar market, then lends them out domestically. Since Eurodollars thus borrowed are nondeposit liabilities, they are not subject to ordinary reserve requirements. The Federal Reserve System has, however, imposed special reserve requirements on such borrowings.

Two final points should be made about the Eurodollar loan market. First, interest rates paid on Eurodollar deposits (and hence on loans) are generally higher than comparable interest rates in the United States. The second noteworthy point is that, although we have described the Eurodollar market as a money market, this is not entirely correct. Eurodollar *deposits* are largely short term, but Eurodollar *loans* may be, and frequently are, made at effective maturities in excess of one year.[2] Thus, in the case of Eurodollars, as in other commercial banking activities, the banks intermediate by borrowing short and lending long, although such intermediation is less pronounced with Eurobanks than with domestic banks.

The Eurobond Market

Just as a truly international money market in the form of Eurodollars came into existence in the 1950s, so a truly international capital market emerged in the 1960s. This market, probably because of its similarities with the Eurodollar market, has come to be called the *Eurobond market.*

As the name implies, the Eurobond market is a market where bonds are denominated in a currency other than that of the country in which they are issued. While strictly speaking this is all that is necessary to designate a bond a Eurobond, the actual market is considerably more complex than this. For example, a French firm may engage a German investment-banking syndicate to sell dollar-denominated bonds, and Italian and English investors may be the principal buyers of such bonds. It is particularly in this broader sense that the Eurobond market is international in character.

It may reasonably be asked why it is desirable to issue and market bonds in such a complex manner. Why, that is, doesn't the French firm simply engage a French investment banker to issue franc-denominated bonds to be sold to French investors? The answer is that the world is frequently more complicated than that. The French corporation may need to borrow dollars for overseas investments, but be discouraged from floating this loan in the United States either by its own government or by the stringent disclosure rules of the U.S. Securities and Exchange Commission. It may engage the underwriting services of the German investment bankers because of more favorable regulations in West Germany, or because of cheaper underwriting costs. The English and Italian investors may prefer dollar-denominated bonds because of the high inflation rates in their own countries, because of interest rate differentials, or for reasons of tax evasion. The complexities of the modern world thus give rise to complex institutions.

One final note about Eurobonds. While the bulk of these bonds are denominated in dollars, they are also denominated in the currencies of other countries—German Deutsche marks, particularly. Indeed, a few, called *multiple currency bonds,* are denominated in a weighted average of many currencies, with strict rules detailing how their value is to be determined.

24-4   THE FOREIGN EXCHANGE MARKET

Notwithstanding the development of the international money and capital markets, most of the huge amount of importing, exporting, and foreign investment that goes

---

[2]These long-term loans are frequently made in the form of a series of short-term loans that are automatically renewed. The purpose of this arrangement is that it permits the interest rate on the loan to be adjusted periodically, so that it reflects current money market conditions.

on throughout the world involves at some point the conversion of one currency into another. The market in which these conversions occur, which has no domestic counterpart, is known as the *foreign exchange market.*

The Spot Market for Foreign Exchange

When foreign currency is bought or sold for immediate delivery, it is said to be traded spot, and the market for carrying on such trades is known as the *spot market.* Many of the financial arrangements for carrying on international trade involve commercial banks, and it is logical, therefore, that the spot market for foreign exchange is centered in the world's banking system. Although relatively few United States banks actively engage in foreign exchange trading, these banks are quite literally connected with all other banks through a worldwide network of correspondent, branch, and affiliate relationships. Thus, what is bought and sold in the foreign exchange market (typically) is not actually foreign *currency* but rather bank deposits denominated in foreign currencies.

Any one of the United States banks actively engaged in the foreign exchange market will have both buy and sell orders on any given day; thus, each of these banks, to some extent, can function internally as its own "market" for foreign exchange. For example, a United States importer may have required £1,000, which he wants to trade for dollars, and at the same time a United States importer may need £1,000 to pay for some English goods she has bought. If both are customers of the same bank, the bank can simply function as a intermediary, simultaneously buying the exporter's pounds and selling them to the importer.

But, of course, there is no reason why the purchases and sales of a particular currency should exactly "wash," or be equal, on a given day for a given bank. Thus, a bank may find itself with either too much or too little of some foreign currency. When this happens, banks will trade among themselves, and those banks with too much of one currency will sell it to banks having too little. In New York, this trading among banks is carried on through nine foreign exchange brokers. These foreign exchange brokers are linked with other foreign exchange brokers in other financial centers throughout the world: London, Zurich, Tokyo, Bonn, and so forth. In this fashion, the spot foreign exchange market is a truly worldwide market linking each individual citizen of each individual nation.

The Foreign Exchange Rate   But what happens if there is a worldwide shortage or surplus of a particular currency? Then the price of that currency in terms of other currencies will change. This price is known as the *foreign exchange rate.* To illustrate the nature of the foreign exchange rate, look at Figure 24-1. This figure shows the quantity of British pounds supplied and demanded on the horizontal axis. On the vertical axis is shown the price of British pounds expressed in terms of United States dollars—for example, £1 = $2 (or whatever the price may be).

The demand schedule, labeled *DD* in Figure 24-1, slopes downward and to the right to indicate that the lower the price of pounds, the more will be demanded. This increase in the quality of pounds demanded as the foreign exchange rate falls occurs

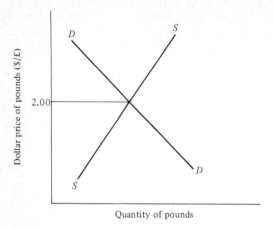

Figure 24-1 Determination of the foreign exchange rate.

for a variety of reasons. Probably the most readily understood of these is in terms of international trade. Thus, suppose that a case of Scotch whiskey sells for £25 in England. Then, if the (dollar) price of 1 pound is 2 dollars, the price of a case of Scotch to Americans will be $50 (25 × $2). If the foreign exchange rate were to fall from $2 to $1.95 per pound, then the price of Scotch to Americans would fall from $50 to $48.75 (25 × $1.95). Since the price of Scotch is lower, Americans will buy more of it, thus increasing the demand for British pounds.

The upward slope of the supply schedule *SS* in Figure 24-1 occurs for the opposite reason (in terms of international trade). An increase in the dollar price of pounds means that American goods will be cheaper to the English, and consequently they will buy more American goods. Thus, the quantity of British pounds supplied will be greater the higher is the exchange rate.[3]

It is important to keep in mind, however, that foreign exchange rates may change in response to a great many circumstances besides foreign trade. Thus, for example, higher interest rates in New York may cause foreign lenders to move (and convert) funds into the United States, and American lenders to repatriate funds from abroad. Or again, cheaper production costs abroad may cause American manufacturing firms to set up plants in foreign countries. Indeed, many movements in foreign exchange rates are due to speculative activity based on expectations about price movements in such things as common stocks, bonds, and the foreign exchange rates themselves. Thus, in practice, the determination of the foreign exchange rate is considerably more complicated than is suggested by Figure 24-1.

Spot Arbitrage The preceding discussion of the determination of the foreign exchange rate involved only two currencies: pounds and dollars. But, of course, we could analyze the relationship between any two currencies in the same way. The difficulty with such an approach is that it limits the explanation of exchange rate

---

[3]This assumes that the English elasticity of demand for United States export goods is greater than unity.

determination to two currencies at a time. We now want to carry the analysis one step further and show how a consistent price structure for all currencies is determined simultaneously in the foreign exchange markets. This is done through a process known as *arbitrage*.

To understand the mechanics of arbitrage, it is necessary to realize that in a market economy it is frequently possible to accomplish the same goal in more than one way. Suppose, for example, that you wanted to take a month's vacation in Mexico and therefore wanted to buy Mexican pesos with dollars. The most obvious way to do this would be directly, that is, sell dollars for pesos. But another, less direct, way would be to sell dollars for Belgian francs and then sell the Belgian francs for Mexican pesos. Either way you would have started with dollars and ended with pesos, but it is possible that one way could be cheaper than the other. To illustrate this possibility, suppose the following exchange rates prevail among the three currencies:[4]

> 1 dollar = 60 francs
> 3 francs = 1 peso
> 10 pesos = 1 dollar

In this case, if you converted a dollar directly into pesos, you would get 10 pesos. But if instead you sold your dollar for 60 Belgian francs and then sold these francs for pesos, you would get 20 pesos. Thus, the indirect method is cheaper; it will get you 20 pesos for your dollar rather than 10.

The arbitrage process makes use of *both* the direct and indirect paths, one path from dollars to pesos and the other path from pesos back to dollars. With the preceding foreign exchange rates, for example, you could sell 1 dollar for 60 Belgian francs, then sell the 60 francs for 20 Mexican pesos, and *then* sell the 20 pesos for 2 dollars. In this way you would start out with 1 dollar and end up with 2 dollars. Moreover, if you made all your purchases and sales simultaneously in a single foreign exchange market, such as New York, there could be no risk involved.

Spot arbitrage transactions in the foreign exchange markets may thus sound like a capitalist's paradise: risk-free profits. But like most market transactions, they also serve a definite economic function. For what the system of arbitrage does is to bring about a consistent determination of all foreign exchange rates—that is, it integrates the foreign exchanges so that they are truly a single market for all currencies. To see how this works, consider again the dollar-franc-peso illustration. As we have seen, the system of exchange rates given above would cause people to sell dollars for francs, francs for pesos, and pesos for dollars. But these sales would change the supply and demand schedules that determine the three exchange rates. Thus, the sale of dollars for francs would increase the supply of dollars relative to francs and make francs comparatively more expensive. After the rate changed, for example, 1 dollar might buy only 50 rather than 60 francs. Similarly, the sale of

---

[4]The following discussion ignores transactions costs. Thus, in practice, there would be a *spread*, or difference, between buying and selling prices.

francs for pesos would make pesos more expensive relative to francs, and the sale of pesos for dollars would make dollars more expensive to the Mexicans. The result of these arbitrage transactions would thus be to change the exchange rates, and they would continue to change until arbitrage was no longer profitable. For example, they might change to something like this:

1 dollar = 50 francs
4 francs = 1 peso
12½ pesos = 1 dollar

Then you could sell a dollar for 50 francs, sell the 50 francs for 12½ pesos, and sell the 12½ pesos for 1 dollar. You start with 1 dollar and you end with 1 dollar—no profit. Arbitrage has thus integrated the separate foreign exchange rates into a single, worldwide market for the currencies of all nations.[5]

Spot Speculation   It is possible to speculate in the spot foreign exchange market, just as in any other market. And the principle is the same: Buy at a low price and sell at a high price. If, for example, the price of a Mexican peso today is 10 cents and you believe that next week it will be 11 cents, then you could do the following: Buy 10 pesos today for 1 dollar, hold them for one week, and then sell them for $1.10 (10 X 11 cents). If you guess correctly, you will have made a dime for each dollar you invest.

The Forward Market in Foreign Exchange

If an importer who buys goods today has to pay for the goods in a foreign currency one month from today, it may be convenient to buy the currency now for delivery in a month. Similarly, an investor in foreign securities who has money coming due in a fortnight may find it convenient to sell that currency for delivery in two weeks. Buy and sell orders of foreign currency for future delivery occur in the *forward market* for foreign exchange.

The economic function of the forward market is to permit foreign traders and investors to *hedge.* Hedging is a means of shifting the risk of a possible movement in the exchange rate to someone else. For example, suppose that you're an American exporter of machinery and that you know you will be paid £1 million in twenty-three days. You also know that the spot dollar-pound rate of exchange is £1 = $2, making your £1 million worth $2 million on today's foreign exchange market. But what you *don't* know is what the exchange rate will be twenty-three days from now. If, over the twenty-three-day period, the exchange rate should move from £1 = $2 to £1 = $1.95, then your £1 million would be worth only $1.95 million—a loss of $50,000 because the exchange rate changed. To eliminate this risk, and ensure yourself a certain future price, you could hedge by selling the £1 million forward against dollars, delivery to be made in twenty-three days. By doing so, you would have

---

[5]In fact, three-point, or triangular, arbitrage is quite rare because one of the jobs of foreign exchange dealers is to quote consistent crossrates so that arbitrage opportunities do not open up in the first place.

shifted the risk of a dollar-pound price change to whoever bought your £1 million. The same principle, of course, applies to financial investors who hedge their investments.

Speculation in the Forward Market   Speculation is, of course, possible in the forward exchanges. The process involved is simply to bet that the spot rate of exchange will change in the future by more or less than the forward rate indicates. For example, suppose that the spot rate for pounds is $2 and you believe that in thirty days it will be $2.05. Then, if the thirty-day forward rate on pounds is $2.01, you could buy pounds forward at this price and then sell them for $2.05 on the day they were delivered (assuming you had guessed correctly).

24-5   THE BALANCE OF PAYMENTS

A part of international finance is closely related to international trade: the purchase of goods and services by the citizens of one country from the citizens of another country. And, as we have just seen, international finance also has its purely financial aspects: arbitrage, speculation, and long-term and short-term lending and investing. It is desirable for a nation to know where it stands with respect to the *whole* of its citizens' international financial dealings with the citizens other countries, and to have a meaningful scheme for classifying various parts of this whole. The *balance of payments* is the device economists and government officials use to accomplish this task.

Balance of Payments Accounting: Sources and Uses of Funds

The balance of payments is an accounting device similar to, but not the same as, the balance sheet of a business firm. It is similar to a balance sheet in that it is based on a system of double-entry bookkeeping. It is different from a balance sheet in that it records the *flows* of various items over a period of time instead of at a single point in time; it is like a motion picture rather than a snapshot.

The formal rules of balance of payments accounting can be mind boggling to anyone except an accounting major.[6] Fortunately, it is possible to explain the nature of a balance of payments in less formal (though also less rigorous) terms. This approach uses the concept of *sources* and *uses* of funds—an approach which, as explained on page 154, is closely related to the balance sheet. To review the matter briefly, recall that a balance sheet makes use of the identity that

$$\text{Assets} = \text{liabilities} + \text{capital} \qquad (1)$$

Now since eq. (1) is true, it must also be true that *changes* in assets, liabilities, and capital must be equal. That is, it must also be true that

---

[6]And even for accounting majors, there are some difficulties. Thus, balance of payments accounting records credits and debits with algebraic signs that are the opposite of normal accounting procedures. Credits are pluses, and debits are minuses. (If you're not an accounting major and you don't understand this footnote, don't worry about it.)

$$\Delta \text{ assets} = \Delta \text{ liabilities} + \Delta \text{ capital} \tag{2}$$

Note that since eq. (2) deals with changes, it is basically a *flow* concept. That is, eq. (2) shows changes that have occurred *between two points in time.* Now think of the right-hand side of eq. (2) as the *sources* of funds that the citizens of a country use in their international financial dealings, and the left-hand side as the uses of those funds. Then an equivalent form of eq. (2) is

$$\text{Uses} = \text{Sources} \tag{3}$$

Equation (3) is the basic identity underlying a balance of payments statement, except that, rather than being displayed as two sides of a ledger, the balance of payments is usually put into a single column with algebraic signs (+ and –) before each entry. That is, in balance of payments accounting, eq. (3) is typically written in the equivalent form

$$\text{Sources} - \text{Uses} = 0 \tag{4}$$

Note that, in this sense (but *only* in this sense) the balance of payments must balance —that is, the algebraic sum of all entries must net to zero.

Some Illustrations   Because the balance of payments is based on the principles of double-entry bookkeeping, each international transaction that an individual or corporation makes involves *both* a change in sources *and* a change in uses.[7] If you are not familiar with the rules of accounting, however, this point can be quite puzzling. We shall therefore go through three examples in order to illustrate the nature of balance of payments accounting. The three examples are:

Transaction 1   A United States exporter sells $1,000 worth of goods abroad and is paid in foreign currency, which he holds. The export of the goods abroad is a *source* of foreign exchange to a citizen of the United States, and hence is recorded with a positive algebraic sign (+) in the balance of payments. The acquisition of the foreign exchange and the subsequent holding of it is use of these funds, and hence is recorded as a minus item.

Transaction 2   A United States importer buys $10,000 worth of foreign goods and pays for them in dollars. Here the importation of the foreign goods is a *use* of funds (–), and is so recorded. The willingness of the foreigner to accept payment in dollars is a source (+) of funds.

Transaction 3   A recent immigrant to the United States sends $200 home to her mother. This is a bit trickier than transactions 1 and 2. Probably the easiest way to think of it is that the immigrant is importing her mother's happiness and is paying for it by remitting $200. Then the import is a use (–) of funds, and the willingness of the mother (a foreigner) to accept payment in dollars is a source (+) of funds, as in transaction 2.

---

[7]Or equal but offsetting changes in sources, and the same for uses.

A Simple Formula Even with the preceding examples as a rough guide, the reader will still be having difficulty in keeping the sources and uses of foreign exchange clearly in mind. If so, the following formula may prove helpful as a ready reference:

$$\text{Exports} - \text{imports} + \text{net services} - \text{net transfers} - \text{net private capital outflow}$$
$$- \text{net governmental capital outflow} = 0$$

Surplus and Deficit in the Balance of Payments

At some time or other, you have probably heard or read that the United States is running a deficit in its balance of payments. Since you have just been put to a good deal of trouble learning that balance of payments accounting necessarily requires the sum of all transactions to be zero (i.e., sources – uses = 0), you may be understandably puzzled by what is meant by a *deficit* (or *surplus*) in this context. Actually, the United States no longer computes deficit and surplus data on the balance of payments, but the concept is nevertheless an important one, well worth taking a few moments to understand.

Suppose we were to list all the sources and uses of funds arising from international transactions in a single column. Then, as we have seen, the algebraic sum of this column would necessarily equal zero. But now suppose, instead of first listing all the sources of funds and then all the uses of funds, we were to mix the sources and uses together in order to contrast related items. For example, we might want to show exports and imports together because these have to do with international trade, and we might want to show various financial transactions together because they too are similar. Now clearly, the algebraic sum of *all* transactions would continue to be zero, just as when we separated sources and uses. But if we were to draw a line somewhere in the middle of the column and then take the algebraic sum of only the numbers *above the line,* we would very likely get a plus or a minus figure. This is what is meant by a deficit or surplus in the balance of payments. If the numbers above the line sum to a negative figure, then we call this a *deficit;* if they sum to a positive figure, we call it a *surplus.*

Obviously, the question is, where do we draw the line? The answer is, wherever we please. This is not to say that what is meant by a deficit (or surplus) is random or arbitrary. It *is* to say, rather, that where we draw the line depends on the particular problem we are interested in. For example, if we were interested only in how many goods we sold to foreigners compared to how many they sold us, we would draw the line so that only exports and imports were above it (this is called the *balance of trade*). Or if we were interested in whether our debt obligations to foreigners had increased or decreased, we would draw the line below "capital assets." Indeed, since we are interested in many different problems having to do with the balance of payments, there is no reason why we can't draw many lines. And, in fact, this has been done in the recent past. There are thus many different definitions of a surplus or deficit in the balance of payments.

As previously mentioned, the United States government no longer computes many of the balance of payment surplus and deficit concepts that it used to. (The government does, however, publish—in great detail—the underlying data, so that

Table 24-1   United States International Transactions, 1977 (Millions of Dollars)

Merchandise exports		120,585
Merchandise imports		151,644
Balance of trade	-31,059	
Military transactions, net		1,334
Investment income, net		17,507
Other service transactions, net		1,705
Balance on goods and services	-10,514	
Remittances, pensions, and other transfers		-1,932
United States government grants, nonmilitary		-2,776
Balance on current account	-15,221	
Private capital flows		
Change in United States private assets abroad (increase, -)		-30,740
Change in foreign private assets in the United States (increase, +)		13,746
Governmental capital flows		
Change in United States government assets, other than official		
reserve assets, net (increase, -)		-3,679
Change in United States official reserve assets (increase, -)		-231
Change in foreign official assets in the United States (increase, +)		37,124
Statistical discrepancy		-999
Total		0

Source: Federal Reserve Bulletin, July 1978, p. A54. Individual items have been rearranged for comparisons.

if you are *very* patient you can figure them out for yourself.) The reason that this change was made is a bit complicated, and depends on material covered in Chapter 25. Briefly, the United States went from a fixed to a floating exchange rate system in 1973, and this move made many of the surplus and deficit concepts, especially those involving capital flows, of dubious merit.[8] The Department of Commerce, which collects and publishes the data, consequently decided that computing the surplus and deficit balances was apt to do more harm than good. It is for this reason, incidentally, that virtually all newspaper accounts you now see will discuss only our balance of trade (and not our balance of payments).

The United States Balance of Payments

At this point you may have the uneasy feeling that the balance of payments is like a panda bear: You know what it is, but you've never actually seen one. If so, look quickly at Table 24-1—there it is, in living black and white!

Actually, Table 24-1 is not officially known as the "balance of payments." Rather, reflecting the previously mentioned changes made in the way the data are presented, it is now officially called "United States International Transactions." But a rose by any other name is still a rose, and most people continue to call it the balance of payments. We shall too.

---

[8]For a good explanation of this change, see Janice M. Westerfield, "A Lower Profile of the U.S. Balance of Payments," Federal Reserve Bank of Philadelphia, *Business Review,* November/December 1976, pp. 11–17.

Two points about Table 24-1 should be noticed at the outset. Notice first that the grand total of all the figures in the extreme right-hand column is zero. This, as we have just seen, is a necessary consequence of the way the data are recorded. Notice second that some of the row entries are clustered together, with a gap between one cluster and the next. This has been done so that similar items can be compared. For example, the first two rows deal with exports from, and imports into, the United States. These are clearly items that are related to one another, which it is desirable to compare. We shall discuss each of these clusters in turn.

Balance of Trade   The first two items of Table 24-1, merchandise imports and merchandise exports, make up what is known as the *balance of trade*. This balance is probably the oldest concept in international finance, dating back to at least the sixteenth century. It is computed by subtracting merchandise imports from merchandise exports, and it is intended to be a measure of how well United States' goods are selling abroad relative to the sale of foreign goods in the United States. As shown in Table 24-1, in 1977 the United States imported about $31 billion more goods than it exported—a very substantial, and very worrisome, trade deficit.

Balance on Goods and Services   In addition to merchandise exports and imports, countries provide services to one another. Perhaps the most obvious of these is tourist travel; when Americans tour abroad, or when foreigners tour the United States, they are essentially buying the "service" of foreign scenery. Additionally, the stationing of United States troops abroad, the income Americans earn on past foreign investments, and the use of foreign vessels for shipping our goods, are all considered services. Clearly, we are interested in the purchase and sale of services as well as goods, and hence we compute the *balance on goods and services*. Generally speaking, in 1977 we sold more services abroad than we purchased, with income on past investments being by far the largest single service item. This partially offset our trade deficit, so that our balance on goods and services was a deficit of "only" about $10 billion.

Balance on Current Account   The phrase *current account* is generally used to distinguish those transactions that are being conducted in the present (as distinct from debt, or *capital account,* transactions). The balance on current account is derived by adding transfers to the balance on goods and services. These transfers are of two kinds: private and governmental. Private transfers consist mostly of remittances from United States residents to relatives living abroad, and the payment of pension funds to United States citizens living abroad. Governmental transfers are primarily economic aid to foreign governments. Since both kinds of transfers are, on balance, typically going *from* the United States *to* other countries, the balance on current account will be less (more negative) than the balance on goods and services. Thus, from Table 24-1, in 1977 the United States balance on current account was about –$15.2 billion, or about $5 billion less than the balance on goods and services.

It is worth noting that since the sum of the items below any given entry is of an equal amount but opposite algebraic sign as the items above that point, the lower items can be thought of as *financing* the items above, that is, as being the financial counterpart of the transactions previously recorded. Thus, the current account is financed by the various short-term and long-term capital movements listed below it, and by the change in our government's financial relationship to foreign governments.

Private Capital Movements The two-item cluster immediately below the balance on current account is not a "balance" in the sense of the three balances just discussed. That is, these two items are to be contrasted with one another, and do not represent a cumulative subtotal, as in the previous cases. These two items, taken together, show the movement of *private* capital out of and into the United States. The first of these, "changes in United States private assets abroad," shows the net amount of foreign investments made by United States citizens and corporations. These investments may be of two kinds: *financial* investments, where debt and equity securities are acquired; and *direct* investments, where physical assets are acquired—for example, the construction of a new branch office of a United States bank. Note that an *increase* in U.S. private foreign investment carries a minus sign in the balance of payments. This is because it is a *use* of our funds, since it requires a payment to foreigners.

The second item in this cluster is the foreign counterpart of the item just described. It shows the net movement of private foreign capital into the United States. It too represents both financial and direct investment, this time by private foreign citizens and corporations in American financial and real assets. An increase in it is entered with a positive (+) algebraic sign because it is a *source* to funds of the United States.

Comparing these private capital flows, note that the volume of foreign private investment made by Americans abroad has been about twice as large as the amount of investments made by foreigners in the United States—$30 billion as compared to $13 billion. The reason for this movement of American capital out of the United States, and foreign reluctance to invest in the United States, undoubtedly is the result of a complex of forces. But one such force seems clear: expectations of a declining value of the dollar in the foreign exchanges. Thus Americans could make a profit, and foreigners avoid a loss, by investing in non-American securities as the exchange value of the dollar depreciates. Note, of course, that this movement of capital out of the United States is a contributing factor to the decline in the value of the dollar.

Governmental Capital Movements Like private citizens, governments also spend money abroad to acquire assets. The cluster of three items just below the private capital movements cluster in Table 24-1 shows these *government capital movements* in 1977.

The first of these items shows the assets acquired abroad by the United States government that were not undertaken for the purpose of influencing the value of the dollar vis-a-vis other currencies, for example, supporting U. S. military installations abroad. Note that, just like private capital flows, an increase in this item is recorded with a minus sign since it is a use of funds. The second item in this cluster, "change in United States official reserve assets," *does* represent actions taken by our government in support of the exchange value of the dollar. This item is the sum of a number of other items (not shown separately), such as our gold stock, but mostly it represents changes in the Federal Reserve's holding of foreign currencies. Note that this figure, –$231 million, is entered into the balance of payments as a negative (–) amount. This means that it is a *use* of funds to United States citizens.

The final item in the governmental capital movements group is the change in foreign official asset holdings in the United States. This figure indicates that in 1977, foreign governments increased their holdings of dollars, United States government obligations, and the like, by more than $37 billion. The meaning of this item is that the bulk of our deficit on current account was financed by the willingness of foreign governments to buy up excess dollars and hold them in the form of investments in the United States.

Statistical Discrepancy   The final item in the balance of payments shown in Table 24-1 is the *statistical discrepancy*. In order to understand this item, it is necessary to understand a bit about how the data are collected for calculating the balance of payments. In the first place, many of the data are reckoned on a sampling basis—for example, some (not all) returning tourists might be asked how much money they spent abroad, and then total tourist expenditures would be estimated from this sample. Second, the government does not necessarily obtain both sources and uses data for any given transaction. It may, for example, know that goods of a certain value were exported but may not know how those particular goods were paid for. For both these reasons, balance of payments data contain both errors (incorrect data) and omissions (transactions that were missed completely). However, since the balance of payments is constructed according to the rules of double-entry bookkeeping, where for every source there *must* be a use, we *know* that it must logically sum to zero. If it doesn't, we therefore add the entry "statistical discrepancy" to *force* it to sum to zero. It is important to note that the errors and omissions are *net;* that is, both sources (+) and uses (–) have been missed in collecting the data. The statistical discrepancy entry is therefore *not* a measure of the accuracy of the balance of payments.

Recent Behavior of the United States Balance of Payments

Figure 24-2 shows the data for some of the balance of payments concepts just discussed: merchandise exports and imports (the difference between these is the balance of trade); the balance on goods and services; and the balance on current account. Two points about Figure 24-2 are of interest. Note, first, the very substantial growth over the past ten years in both our imports and exports. This reflects the increasing importance of the international sector in our economy. Second, note that our trade deficit has been persistent in the past five years, and seems to be growing larger. The causes and consequences of this deficit are matters of considerable official concern. To understand the nature of this concern, it is first necessary to develop an understanding of how sovereign nations deal with one another in the realm of international economics. This is the subject of Chapter 25.

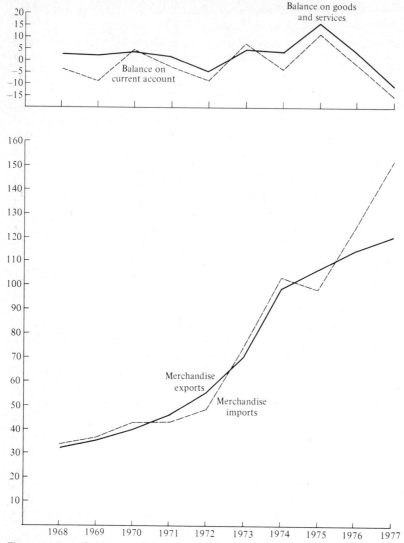

Figure 24-2 U.S. balance of payments, 1976–1977 (billions of dollars).

24-6 REVIEW QUESTIONS

1. Name the three different types of overseas banking engaged in by American commercial banks. Why do you think overseas banking has grown so rapidly in the past fifteen years?
2. Why are the risks of international finance greater than those of domestic finance? Name and explain two financial instruments commonly used in international finance. How do these instruments reduce the risks associated with foreign trade?
3. Why is the Eurodollar market *international* in character? How can American banks use Eurodollars?

4 Explain how one could engage in profitable spot arbitrage if the following exchange rates prevail:

1 pound = 2 dollars
1 pound = 12 francs
1 dollar = 5 francs

Now explain how the exchange rates of these currencies would move, under the supply and demand pressures of spot arbitrage, to eliminate the possibility of profitable arbitrage.

5 If the United States is running a deficit on current account, what are the ways in which this deficit can be financed?

25

International Monetary Relations among Nations

If you read the newspaper regularly, especially the business news, you have probably noticed stories about the "movement" of the dollar "against" some other currency such as the West German mark or the Japanese yen. For example, the news story might begin something like this: "The dollar fell against the yen yesterday for the third straight day, closing at 198 yen to the dollar, down from 201 on Monday." Such a sentence may understandably puzzle you, raising more questions than it answers. What does it *mean?* What difference does it make? Why doesn't the government *do* something about it?

The first of these questions is fairly easily answered, though the answer can be a bit confusing to the unwary. What the statement means is that the number of yen you can buy for one dollar has decreased. This in turn means that the price of the yen has gone up, that is, has become more expensive. Why? Look at it this way. Suppose you were to hear someone say that a year ago you could buy a dozen eggs for $1.50, but that now they cost $2 per dozen. What the person who made that statement has done is to vary the number of dollars (from 1.5 to 2) but hold the quantity of eggs (one dozen) constant. But it could equally well be put the other way around. That is, we could say exactly the same thing by holding the number of dollars constant and varying the number of eggs. In this latter case we would say that, where a year ago you could buy a dozen eggs for $1.50, now you can only get nine eggs for $1.50. Whichever way we put it, we would be describing a case where the price of eggs went up. So also with yen (or any other currency). If three days ago you could buy 201 yen for a dollar and today you can only buy 198 yen for a dollar, then the price of yen has gone up.

The second question—why it matters—is also fairly easy to answer. Imagine that you have scrimped and saved for a long time so that you can take a vacation in Japan. You have gotten together the price of airfare plus, say, $1,000. You figure that, considering the prices of lodging, food, and travel in Japan, you can spend a week there sightseeing. So far, so good. But *now* suppose that (just to make it dramatic) the dollar "falls" against the yen from 1 dollar = 250 yen to 1 dollar = 200 yen. Then all your calculations have to be redone. For where at the old (1 dollar = 250 yen) exchange rate your dollar would buy 250,000 yen, at the new (1 dollar = 200 yen) exchange rate, it will buy only 200,000 yen. Since this will keep you there only about five days, you may decide it isn't worth it and go to Philadelphia instead.

In the example just given, note two things. Note first that the prices of most Japanese goods and services have not changed *to the Japanese.* That is, the price of a night's lodging is still 2,500 yen, the price of a railway ticket from Tokyo to Sendai still 10,000 yen, and so forth. But while these prices haven't changed for the Japanese, the prices of most Japanese goods and services *to Americans* have gone up.[1] This means not just the price of vacationing in Japan, but the prices of most things we buy from them—automobiles, cameras, TVs, and so forth. And next note that the process works in reverse. The prices of American goods have generally become cheaper to the Japanese, which is likely to induce them to spend their yen on United States goods, and to take their vacations here. Moreover, this same phenomenon, that American goods have become less expensive relative to Japanese goods, is likely to occur in third countries as well, so that Japanese companies find themselves at a competitive disadvantage in world markets.

These events have repercussions on the economies of Japan, the United States, and, to a lesser extent, other countries. Employment may go up in the United States, for example, and go down in Japan. Mexico, whose exchange rate fluctuates with (is "tied" to) the dollar, may find itself importing fewer Japanese TVs and more American-built automobiles, and this may affect its price level. Clearly, these are the sorts of things that are matters of great concern to national governments. Thus we

---

[1]The price of some Japanese goods to Americans may not rise. This case would occur where the United States dominates world markets. For example, if the United States is the major producer of some good X, and Japan only a minor producer, then the price of X may be determined by the value of the dollar. In this case, the price of that part of X produced in Japan would not rise to Americans.

come to the third question: Why doesn't the government *do* something about it? The simple answer is that it does. But a more realistic answer is that the international payments mechanism is a highly complicated affair, where governments have only limited choices, and where all choices may have some disagreeable aspects. The remainder of this chapter is devoted to discussing these choices.

25-1 THE THREE CHOICES

In general terms, there are three types of policies a nation can use to correct an exchange rate disequilibrium. The nature of these policies can best be understood by referring to Figure 25-1, where the existing rate of exchange between the dollar and the pound is assumed to be $1.95 = £1.[2] Note, however, that the foreign exchange market is not in equilibrium at this rate: The quantity of pounds demanded *OB* is greater than the quantity being supplied *OA*. To attain long-run equilibrium, the United States[3] has three choices:

1 It can hold the rate of exchange fixed at $1.95 = £1 and try to shift the supply and demand schedules by making adjustments in its domestic economy. For example, it might adopt deflationary monetary and fiscal policies, which would lower its price level and real national income. For reasons to be explained presently, this would increase exports and decrease imports and hence shift supply rightward and demand leftward until the equilibrium rate was $1.95 = £1. This is called a policy of *fixed exchange rates.*
2 It can use nonprice rationing methods to allocate its existing supply of pounds *OA* among the larger demand for pounds *OB*. The use of such nonprice rationing methods is known as *exchange controls.*
3 It can, very simply, let the dollar-pound exchange rate move upward to $2 = £1, thereby attaining equilibrium through the price mechanism. This is called a policy of *floating exchange rates.*

The world payments mechanism is currently on a variant of choice number 3, called a *managed float.* Before discussing this, however, it will be instructive to consider briefly the other two choices—fixed exchange rates and exchange controls.

---

[2] The observant reader will notice that we have here shifted the way the dollar/foreign currency ratio is expressed. In the previous example in the text, that of the yen, the foreign exchange rate was quoted as the number of yen 1 dollar would buy. In Figure 25-1 and the subsequent text, the exchange rate is given in terms of the number of dollars required to buy 1 pound. This change has been made deliberately, because that is the way popular newspaper accounts are written. That is, newspaper accounts quote all currencies *except the pound* in terms of the number of units needed to buy a dollar, but the pound is quoted in terms of the number of dollars needed to buy it. Logically, of course, it makes no difference, since one ratio is the reciprocal of the other. But note that a rise in the £ ratio means that the pound has become more expensive.

[3] The illustration implicitly assumes a two-country world. In other words, Great Britain is being used as a proxy for the rest of the world.

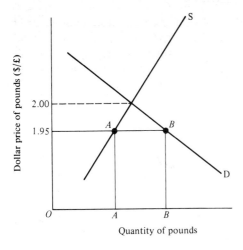

Figure 25-1

Adjustments under fixed and fluctuating exchange rates, and exchange controls.

25-2   RELATIVELY FIXED EXCHANGE RATES

The term *fixed exchange rates* is something of a misnomer. It describes a theoretically pure case rather than historical reality. Even in the heyday of the gold standard before World War I, foreign exchange rates rose and fell within a limited range. The title of this section is therefore "*Relatively* Fixed Exchange Rates," where the emphasis is on the adverb. Such a phrase is tiresome to read, however, and the system of relatively fixed exchange rates will hereafter be called *fixed exchange rates.*

   To understand the system of fixed exchange rates as it has operated in the past (and may operate in the future), it is necessary to distinguish analytically between two different kinds of exchange rate disequilibria. First, there is the temporary, or *transitory,* disequilibrium, which occurs in the short run but reverses itself later on. Such a transitory disequilibrium might be caused, for example, by a crop failure or by a movement of liquid capital attracted elsewhere by higher interest rates. Second, there is the permanent, or *persistent,* disequilibrium, which continues on indefinitely unless corrective action is taken. The cause of a persistent disequilibrium is some deep-seated economic phenomenon—for example, profit opportunities, price structures, or patterns of world trade.

   Although in practice it is often very difficult for the authorities to distinguish between transitory and persistent disequilibria, the fixed exchange rate system is more readily understood if the discussion is organized around these two concepts.

Adjustments to Transitory Disequilibrium

If a nation feels that a disequilibrium will not continue for very long, then quite naturally it wants such a disequilibrium to cause a minimum of disturbance to its domestic economic policy. The nation need only be in international equilibrium *on the average,* with short periods of deficits being counterbalanced by short periods of surpluses. To cope with temporary disequilibria, two expedients have been developed: limited movements in exchange rates, and international monetary reserves.

Limited Movements in Exchange Rates As indicated, all systems of fixed exchange rates have historically permitted some limited leeway for the automatic realignment of currency prices. The situation can best be described with the aid of Figure 25-2, where both the supply and demand schedules *SS* and *DD* turn horizontally at the foreign exchange rates £1 = $1.95 and £1 = $2.05. The schedules are drawn this way to make the following point: Within the range between $1.95 and $2.05 a free market is permitted. For example, a shift in the private demand for pounds from *DD* to *D' D'* will simply raise the cost of pounds to Americans; no official intervention in the market will occur. A more substantial shift, however, such as that from *DD* to *D" D"* will cause the Federal Reserve to intervene. What Figure 25-2 says is that at the price of £1 = $2.05, the Federal Reserve will furnish the market with an unlimited supply of pounds. The reverse is also true; at a price of £1 = $1.95, the Federal Reserve will demand an unlimited number of pounds. Under such circumstances, the price of pounds can fluctuate freely between $1.95 and $2.05 but cannot move outside that range.

The free movement of exchange rates, even within a limited range, will help adjust a nation's payments imbalance. For example, in Figure 25-2 a shift in the demand for pounds from *DD* to *D' D'* will cause pounds to become relatively more expensive to Americans. Our imports from England consequently will decline. At the same time, the cost of dollars to the English has become relatively cheaper, and our exports to England will therefore increase. As a result of both these circumstances, our balance on current account will become larger.

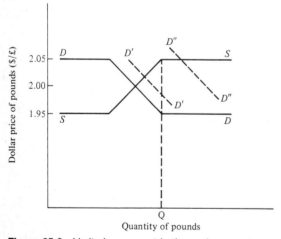

Figure 25-2 Limited movement in the exchange rate.

International Monetary Reserves Limited movements in exchange rates are not sufficient in themselves to accommodate large, temporary fluctuations in a nation's exchange rate. This can be seen by referring again to Figure 25-2. If the demand for pounds shifts from *DD* to *D" D"*, official intervention into the market is required. The Federal Reserve (or the Bank of England) must therefore be prepared, under a fixed exchange rate system, to supply whatever amount of pounds the market demands beyond Q, in order to keep the price of pounds from rising above £1 = \$2.05. To do so, the Federal Reserve must *have* the pounds to sell, or else somehow be able to obtain them. How much foreign currency (or its equivalent) a nation's government holds is known as its *international monetary reserves.*

A nation may hold international monetary reserves in a variety of forms. In order for the Federal Reserve to support the dollar price of pounds, for example, it is not necessary for it to have pounds. Some other asset that can readily be converted into pounds will do as well. This other, nonpound, asset can logically take on almost any form as long as it is broadly acceptable by other central banks around the world. Historically, central banks have used gold to perform this function. Over about the past thirty years, gold has been joined by so-called key currencies, by special drawing rights (SDRs) of the International Monetary Fund, and by swap agreements among central banks. Since the managed float system that the world now uses for international payments also requires international monetary reserves, we shall describe these arrangements in section 25-4.

Adjustments to Persistent Disequilibrium

Limited exchange rate movements and international reserves are measures designed to deal with situations where exchange surpluses and deficits alternate over some (unspecified) period of time. But clearly they are not sufficient to remedy a permanent disequilibrium, since eventually a nation must exhaust its international reserves. What then *are* the remedies open to a country if it wants both to maintain a fixed exchange rate without exchange controls, and to correct a persistent downward pressure on its currency?

The most fundamental answer to this question is that such a country must subordinate its domestic stabilization policies to maintaining an equilibrium in its exchange rate. In other words, a nation typically faces a distinct choice between (1) maintaining high employment and reasonable price stability at home, and (2) maintaining fixed exchange rates in its dealings with other countries. It can choose *either* (1) *or* (2), but it cannot choose *both*. To understand why this is so, it is necessary to understand the economic relationships among imports, exports, income, prices, interest rates, and capital flows.

Imports, Exports, and Income   Generally speaking, a nation's volume of imports is a positive function of its real income. That is, as its income (GNP) rises, so will its imports, and as its income falls, its imports will also fall. This relationship is made intuitively apparent by considering the two great components of income in the private economy: investment and consumption. An increase in income means that both investment and consumption increase. But an increase in investment, i.e., the addition of plant and equipment to our capital stock, means that we must increase our imports. If nothing else, we must buy from abroad a number of raw materials, such as oil and tin, that we ourselves do not possess in sufficient quantities.

Similarly with consumption goods. As people's real incomes rise, they will buy more and more goods, and some of these will be imported (automobiles and foreign vacations are good examples).

Exports, on the contrary, can be thought of as autonomous, that is, unaffected by the level of our domestic income. This is not wholly accurate, since as our imports rise other countries will be able to buy more of our goods, but it is close enough for our limited purposes here. To repeat: Exports are largely unresponsive to our domestic level of real income.

Exports, Imports, and the Price Level   A second factor affecting our exports and imports is the level of prices in the United States relative to other countries—or, more realistically, comparative rates of inflation. To see how this works, suppose that our price level is rising more rapidly than prices throughout the rest of the world. In this case, our exports will be priced out of world markets; that is, they will become too expensive for foreigners to buy. By the same token, foreign goods will become increasingly attractive to Americans. If the prices of United States automobiles rise while foreign car prices remain the same, for example, Americans will switch to foreign makes and imports will therefore rise. The reverse is also true. If foreign price levels increase more rapidly than ours, then our exports will rise as American goods become more attractive to foreigners and our imports will fall as foreign goods become less attractive to Americans (assuming a fixed exchange rate).

Short-Term Capital Flows and Expected Rates of Return   Short-term capital will tend to gravitate to those financial centers where expected rates of return are highest and leave the centers where these rates are lowest. For example, if the rate of interest in London is 10 percent while in New York it is only 6 percent, then (other things equal) corporations with temporary funds at their disposal will tend to lend them out in the London money market.

The Adjustment Process   What has all this to do with the problem of eliminating a persistent downward pressure on the dollar under a system of fixed exchange rates? The answer to this question will be apparent if the reader will reflect on the main lesson to be learned from our study of monetary theory: Monetary and fiscal policy affect real income, the price level, and interest rates. Since these are precisely the variables that affect imports, exports, and capital flows, it follows that monetary and fiscal policy should somehow be useful in dealing with an exchange rate disequilibrium. It remains only to describe how.

Let us suppose that there is a persistent tendency for the international value of the dollar to fall, and that this tendency stems from two sources: Our imports are greater than our exports (deficit on current account), and short-term capital is moving out of the United States (deficit on capital account). Now suppose that the Federal Reserve decides to pursue a tight money policy, which, as we have seen, will lower our real income, lower our price level, and raise our interest rates. The fall in real income will decrease our imports while leaving our exports unaffected; the fall in our prices (or the slowdown in our inflation rate) will increase our exports and decrease our imports. Now note that these two things (lower income and prices) have the effect of eliminating our deficit on current account. This deficit was by definition *too many* imports and *too few* exports. But the tight money policy has *decreased* imports and *increased* exports. The current account deficit is therefore corrected. Similarly, the higher interest rates in the United States will tend to stem the outflow of short-term capital and consequently correct the deficit on capital account. *Moral:* A tight money (and fiscal) policy can be used to eliminate a persistent downward pressure on the dollar.

But there is a kicker to all this. For note that in order to restore an equilibrium in our exchange rate, the Federal Reserve has had to depress and deflate the economy, i.e., has had to pursue a policy that caused real income and prices to fall. This is the meaning of the statement made at the beginning of this discussion: A nation that wants both to maintain fixed exchange rates and to correct a persistent payments deficit must subordinate its domestic policy goals to its international policy goals. It must deliberately deflate its economy to overcome a deficit and inflate its economy to overcome a surplus. Of course, sometimes the national and international objectives coincide, as when a country is undergoing a runaway inflation and also has a payments deficit. Then the correct policy on both scores is tight money. But the original point nevertheless remains valid: With a fixed exchange rate regime, the *fundamental* reason for the tight money policy is the payments deficit, not inflation.

The potential conflict between domestic and international monetary policies under a fixed exchange rate system is a bitter pill for most people to swallow. To deliberately provoke such personal disasters as unemployment and bankruptcies for something so seemingly abstract as a fixed exchange rate is to cure the disease by killing the patient. Or so, at least, most industrial nations have apparently concluded since that great watershed in world economic history, the depression of the 1930s. It is small wonder, then, that the world has searched diligently in the past four decades for some workable alternative.

Currency Devaluation   A possible "solution" to the dilemma faced by a nation with the conflicting goals of domestic stability and a fixed exchange rate should be mentioned briefly. This is the possibility of a *currency devaluation.* In this case, what the country does is to hold on to its old rate of exchange until its international reserves are nearly exhausted, and then change to a new rate of exchange all at once and by a large amount. In terms of Figure 25-1, for example, the United States would maintain the exchange rate of £1 = \$1.95 for as long as it could, then announce one Sunday morning that the new exchange rate was £1= \$2. In doing so, the United States would have devalued the dollar.

The discerning reader (an admittedly redundant phrase) will immediately note that a currency devaluation is not really consistent with a policy of fixed exchange rates. Fixed exchange rates mean just that —*fixed.* Currency devaluation, on the contrary, means a *change* in the exchange rate. Thus the "solution" of currency devaluation is not really a solution at all. Rather, it is a violation of the underlying assumptions of a fixed exchange rate regime. In other words, it is really a movement away from fixed exchange rates and toward floating exchange rates, a sort of halfway house. Nevertheless, it was widely used before the world moved to floating rates in

1973. The advantage of a devaluation, as opposed to a pure float, is that *between* devaluations there may be relatively long periods of exchange rate stability. The disadvantages are that the new exchange rate, after the devaluation, is determined by administrative decree and hence is only by accident an equilibrium rate; and that a devaluation nearly always occurs as the result of a crisis situation.

25-3   EXCHANGE CONTROLS

If a nation is committed to fixed exchange rates and is undergoing a persistent balance of payments deficit and downward pressure on its exchange rate, then one alternative open to it is to depress its domestic economy. But as you can readily imagine, such a course of action is extremely distasteful. Especially in democratic countries, it is virtually impossible for the administration to persuade unemployed workers that their joblessness is a lesser evil than a fall in the international value of the nation's currency. In consequence, nations have sought for a way out of this dilemma. One such way is to impose *exchange controls.*

Broadly conceived, an exchange control is any *direct* governmental device that has the aim of making a nation's supply of foreign exchange equal to the demand for it by nonprice methods. The word "direct" needs to be emphasized here since deflationary monetary and fiscal policies accomplish this same goal indirectly. We *can* include import tariffs and quotas, however, as long as their objective is to correct a payments deficit (and not, e.g., to encourage an infant industry or make a nation self-sufficient for military purposes). Governmental regulation of the foreign exchange market is also used.

Tariffs and Quotas

A nation may limit the amount of foreign exchange its citizens demand by limiting the quantity of foreign goods they can buy. This may be done in either of two ways: First, the government may impose a heavy tax (an import duty, or *tariff*) on all or some foreign goods, which will make these goods so expensive that people either switch to domestic substitutes or do without. Second, the government may impose quantitative restrictions on the number of goods of a particular type that can be imported; once this *quota* is filled, no more of that good can be imported until the following year.

There are many objections to tariffs and quotas. Easily the most fundamental is that they interfere with the international specialization of production and hence lessen total world welfare. Less fundamental, but still very important, is that tariffs and quotas are administratively difficult and probably not very effective anyhow. The administrative difficulty with a tariff is that if the duty is set too low, it may not have much effect in discouraging imports, and if set too high, it will encourage smuggling. The enforcement problems are formidable. A quota system is, if anything, even worse. It involves passing out import licenses to certain favored importers, discriminating against particular foreign countries who may otherwise be classified as friendly, and frequently promoting market gluts early in the year and market short-ages later on. The potential ineffectiveness of import restrictions can be realized by noting that they touch only the balance of goods and services and leave capital flows unaffected. Thus exporters, for example, may invest their earnings in foreign coun-tries, and what is gained on current account is lost on capital account. Economists are virtually universal in their condemnation of the use of trade barriers to correct payments deficits. They are widely used.[4]

Exchange Regulation

Because direct restrictions on foreign trade tend to be both unpopular and ineffec-tive, a number of nations have adopted direct regulations over the foreign exchanges. These tend to be of two general types: quantitative restrictions and cost restrictions.

Quantitative Restrictions   A country faced with a chronic shortage of foreign exchange may correct it by using the method of government exchange rationing. Under this method, all citizens receiving foreign currency are required to surrender it to the government and all those who wish to use foreign currency are required to apply to the government for it. The government, of course, sells only as much as it buys (or can borrow abroad), and the supply of and demand for foreign exchange are in this fashion kept equal to one another.

Quantitative restrictions on the foreign exchange market are an administrative nightmare. The government must somehow enforce the regulation that all foreign exchange be turned over to it, and this is very difficult. Black markets flourish. And when it sells the foreign exchange, the government must decide to whom it should be sold, what types of imports should be permitted, where these imports should come from, and so on. Such decisions lead almost inevitably to bribery and corruption.

Cost Restrictions   The second method of exchange regulation rations foreign exchange through cost considerations, but in a very special way. Under this method, different exchange rates are established, depending on the type of transaction. In an underdeveloped country, for example, tractors might be imported at a very favorable rate of exchange, while Cadillacs are imported at a very unfavorable rate, or exports that have an inelastic foreign demand (e.g., petroleum) might be assigned a different exchange rate than those that have an elastic demand.

These *multiple-currency practices,* as they are called, are administratively clumsy. They are, in effect, a substitute for tariffs and subsidies and involve many of the same disadvantages. They are used primarily by underdeveloped countries that are attempting to encourage the process of industrialization, but it is doubtful that they are very effective.

---

[4]The political pressures for the use of trade barriers are often strong. The reasons for this probably have more to do with the effects of trade barriers on the domestic distribution of income than with their effects on the balance of payments.

25-4 FLOATING EXCHANGE RATES

If fixed exchange rates are politically unacceptable and exchange controls are economically undesirable, how are nations to adjust to a persistent shortage of foreign
exchange? The third possibility is that suggested in the discussion of Figure 25-1:
Let the exchange rate move to an equilibrium price. Although such a system may
seem both simple and obvious, there are a number of objections to it. Foremost
among these is the fear that exchange rate movements will disrupt world trade and
lead to a loss in world welfare. Thus, the fear is that exchange rates will not move
slowly and sedately toward their equilibrium value, but will instead gyrate wildly
and erratically. If such gyrations occur, it is feared that they will sharply increase
the risks of foreign trade, and consequently that the amount of foreign trade will fall
and, with it, total world welfare.

The system of floating exchange rates has two main variants: the *clean float,*
where foreign exchange rates respond only to the market forces of supply and
demand without government interference; and the *managed float* (sometimes also
called a *dirty float*), where central banks intervene in the exchange markets to iron
out temporary and meaningless fluctuations. Of the two, the clean float is the
theoretically pure case, and it will be instructive to examine it first even though it
is not the actual system in use today.

The Clean Float

As indicated, the clean float would simply treat the foreign exchange market like any
other competitive market where price is determined by supply and demand. No
official (i.e., governmental) intervention would occur.

There are two main advantages claimed for the clean float: First, it would
eliminate the need for international monetary reserves and exchange controls. The
price system would be used instead. Second, the conflict between domestic stabilization and international equilibrium, which is the main objection to the fixed exchange
rate system, would be resolved. Domestic policies designed to foster full employment, price stability, and economic growth would be pursued without regard to their
implications for the foreign exchange rate; the foreign exchange market would
automatically equilibrate itself. This is not to say that the domestic and international
economies would be unrelated to one another. It would still be true that a depreciation of the exchange rate would hurt export industries. But the varying fortunes of
these industries would no longer be a matter of special concern to the government.
They would have to learn to cope with uncertainty in the price of foreign exchange
in the same way they now cope with uncertainty in other market prices.

Many economists argue that these advantages of a clean float would be more
than outweighed by its disadvantages. The main concern, in this respect, centers
around the issue of stabilizing and destabilizing speculation. Stabilizing speculation
occurs when movements away from an equilibrium immediately cause speculators
to take a small gain and, by doing so, force the price back to equilibrium. For
example, suppose that the dollar-pound equilibrium rate were £1 = \$2 but that the
actual rate had moved temporarily to £1 = \$1.95. Then speculators could buy

pounds at the latter price in the expectation that the exchange rate would quickly return to £1 = $2 and that they could therefore make a 5-cent profit on each pound they bought. In doing so, speculators would increase the demand for pounds and increase the supply of dollars, and in this fashion would actually cause equilibrium to be restored. Thus, speculation would have stabilized the market. Destabilizing speculation is just the opposite. It is a situation where speculative activity drives the exchange rate away from equilibrium and causes wider price fluctuations than would otherwise occur. Such destablizing speculation might occur on the basis of unfounded rumors, for example.

The concern over whether the activities of speculators would be stabilizing or destabilizing is ultimately a concern over the volume of world trade and the international specialization of production. There is little doubt that a highly unstable market increases the risks of international trading and hence reduces the amount. Consequently, if speculation under a clean float system should prove to be destabilizing, many economists feel that such a system would do more harm than good. Advocates of the clean float make three counterarguments, which will be mentioned briefly.

Purchasing-Power Parity   The issue here is whether there *is* such a thing as a fundamental equilibrium relationship between two currencies. The doctrine of *purchasing-power parity* argues that, in theory at least, there is. This doctrine holds that the natural relationship between the currencies of two countries depends on the price levels of each. Thus, if it takes three units of the currency of country A to buy the same market basket of goods that one unit of the currency of country B will buy, then one unit of B's currency should exchange for three units of A's currency. The doctrine of purchasing-power parity asserts that a free market exchange rate will gravitate toward this equilibrium.[5]

Profitability of Speculation   It is frequently argued that speculation must either be stabilizing or unprofitable. The idea is that profitable speculation requires the speculator to buy at a low price and sell at a high price. Thus, if the exchange rate is below equilibrium, speculators will buy and thereby drive the price back up. Contrariwise, if the foreign exchange rate is above its equilibrium, speculators will sell, driving the price down. If they behave differently than this, it is held, speculators will lose money and hence not remain speculators very long.

This argument is not very persuasive. It assumes that speculative activity occurs only at the peaks and troughs of market fluctuations and only in response to movements away from equilibrium. But, in fact, speculators may buy profitably even though the price is above equilibrium if they believe the price will go still higher, and conversely for selling. The purchases and sales of speculators may thus feed on one another, causing exchange rates to fluctuate more sharply than they otherwise would.

[5]For some empirical evidence that supports the purchasing-power parity theory, see Henry J. Gailliot, "Purchasing Power Parity as an Explanation of Long-Term Changes in Exchange Rates," *Journal of Money, Credit and Banking,* August 1970, pp. 348–357.

Hedging in the Forward Market   Finally, proponents of a clean float argue that importers and exporters can eliminate exchange risks by using forward contracts. For example, an importer who knows she will need foreign exchange in a month can buy the needed exchange in the forward market. Although the forward contract adds to her costs, at least they are definite costs that can be included in her profit calculations. This point is well taken; forward contracts can shift exchange risk from business people to professional speculators. The only shortcoming of the argument is that forward cover typically is not available for long-term investments.

The Managed Float

The world's international monetary system, as it currently functions, can most accurately be described as a managed float system. While there are a number of exceptions, and a wide variety of arrangements, at present most of the world's major currencies adhere to this system. By a *managed float* (or *dirty float*) is meant a system wherein the foreign exchange markets are allowed to seek their own equilibrium prices—that is, to "float"—but where official central bank intervention is carried on to prevent disorderly markets. A *disorderly market* is one in which sharp, temporary, and meaningless price fluctuations occur.

To illustrate the idea of a managed float, suppose that in Figure 25-3 the curve market *B* is the exchange rate as it would move over time if it were determined solely by market forces—i.e., if the country involved were on a clean float. It is to be noted that curve *B* does not change, however, only because of fundamental forces. It might go up or down, for example, because of temporary short-term capital movements, or because of the activities of speculators. The curve marked *A* shows how the exchange rate *would* move if it responded only to such fundamental forces as shifts in world trade patterns, comparative rates of growth and inflation in different countries, and so forth. The idea behind a managed float is thus, very simply, to have the government intervene in the foreign exchange market for the purpose of converting curve *B* to curve *A*—to iron out the wobbles in curve *B* by selling and buying foreign exchange at the appropriate time and in the right amounts. If the system works as it is supposed to, then no nation would ever have a *persistent* deficit or surplus of foreign exchange, although at any given time several nations might have transient disequilibria.

There are two primary difficulties with a dirty float. The first is that it requires an almost inhuman degree of expertise on the part of the authorities. At any given

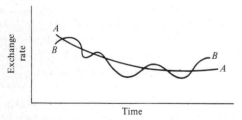

Figure 25-3   The principle behind the dirty float.

time they must know where curve *A* is relative to curve *B*. That is, they must have such a sure and detailed knowledge of their payments position that they are able to sort out which parts of it are *persistent,* reflecting fundamental economic forces, and which are *transient.* If the authorities do not have such knowledge (and they don't), then they are likely to make costly mistakes. Furthermore, they will be subject to political pressure from those domestic industries whose profits can be improved by moving the exchange rate one way or the other.

The second difficulty with a dirty float is that, just like fixed exchange rates, it requires an enormous international bureaucratic network of various kinds of international monetary reserves. For clearly, if a central bank is to intervene in the foreign exchange market for stabilization purposes, it first must *have* the foreign exchange. To facilitate the managed float system, therefore, central banks have maintained the international reserve system developed under the regime of fixed exchange rates. These reserves take many forms, but the most common are: Gold, key currencies, Special Drawing Rights (SDRs), and swap agreements among central banks.

Gold   Although gold has historically been the premiere international reserve asset, since 1973 its role in that capacity has been in doubt. In the olden days, before 1973, the world was on a fixed exchange rate regime, and it frequently happened that central banks used gold to settle debts among themselves. Thus, a nation needing foreign currency to support its exchange rate would buy such currency in exchange for a promise to pay gold. In 1971, however, the United States declared that it would no longer sell gold to foreign central banks, and two years later the world abandoned fixed exchange rates. While the U.S. Treasury does occasionally now sell gold on the free market, it does not seem to use these sales primarily for the purpose of acquiring foreign exchange. Thus, although our gold holdings (about $50 billion at market prices in 1978) *could* be used as an international reserve asset, they apparently *are* not. It is entirely possible, however, that gold may regain its time-honored place in the future.

Key Currencies   A *key currency* is the currency of one nation that comes to be generally acceptable for settling debts among all governments. For example, if the dollar is generally regarded as a key currency, then it is not necessary for England to have, say, francs in order to support the price of the pound relative to the franc. Instead, England can sell its dollar reserves to the French government for francs and then use these francs to support the market.

The use of a key currency as an international reserve asset depends on the willingness of those countries with strong foreign exchange positions to accept this currency, and this willingness depends to a considerable extent on the economic strength of the key-currency country. Unfortunately, the shifting sands of economic fortune leave a great deal to be desired in this respect. Thus, the British pound sterling ceased to be a key currency when the British empire waned. In the past three decades, the United States dollar has been the most commonly used key currency throughout the world. Whether it will continue to be so, despite our weakening international economic position, remains to be seen.

Cooperative Agreements Among Central Banks   A third method for dealing with a transient deficit is for central banks to make certain financial arrangements among themselves, usually on a bilateral basis. These arrangements may take on several forms, but the most common is a *swap agreement.*

To understand the nature of a swap agreement, it is necessary to expand the discussion to consider the problem of a *surplus* country, that is, a country with upward pressure on its foreign exchange rate. Just as a deficit draws down a country's reserves, a surplus builds them up. In accumulating reserves, a surplus country runs a risk: It may suffer a substantial loss on the foreign exchange it is holding. To understand this possibility, consider the following example. Suppose the United States is the deficit country, West Germany is the surplus country, and the rate of exchange between the dollar and the mark is 1 dollar = 3 marks. Now suppose that in its efforts to support this exchange rate, the Bundesbank (the German central bank) buys dollars for marks and therefore builds up its dollar reserves. Suppose, next, that the United States government decides to stop supporting the dollar against the mark. Then the dollar price of marks will rise—that is, Americans will be able to buy *fewer* marks with a dollar. For example, the exchange rate on the dollar might move to 1 dollar = 2 marks. The question is, Where does this leave the Bundesbank? The answer is, Holding the bag. For when the Bundesbank *bought* the dollars, it had to pay 3 marks for each dollar. But now each dollar is worth only 2 marks, and therefore the Bundesbank has suffered a loss of 1 mark for every dollar it bought —bought, moreover, in an effort to help the United States support its unrealistic exchange rate. (Nice guys finish last, *especially* in international finance.)

Naturally, the Bundesbank is not very pleased at this prospect, and it would therefore like to find some way to support the dollar that would not entail a potential loss. One way it can do so is by entering into an agreement with the Federal Reserve whereby each central bank agrees to "swap" (exchange) some amount of its currency for some amount of the other's currency and then swap back again at some future date. Since both swaps are made at a predetermined rate of exchange, the Bundesbank runs no risk of a loss (although the Federal Reserve does). In the meantime, the Bundesbank has the use of the dollars to intervene in the market.

Swap agreements are particularly useful in speculative movements against a currency. In the example just given, the pressure on the dollar might be caused by speculators. Their reasoning would be that they can now (i.e., before the exchange rate change) buy 3 marks for 1 dollar; then if the dollar falls to 1 dollar = 2 marks, they can obtain $1.50 for every 3 marks they buy, making a 50 percent profit on the deal. They therefore "run" the dollar, that is, try to convert as many dollars as they can into other currencies. If the exchange rate movement can be held off long enough, however, the speculators may eventually get tired of this unproductive use of their money and bring it back home. The swap agreement, like currency reserves, provides the means for doing this.

Swap aggreements among central banks are substantial. Although the amount varies from year to year, the agreements entered into by the Federal Reserve have been running in excess of $20 billion.

Special Drawing Rights   The most recently developed type of international reserve asset is the *Special Drawing Right* issued by the International Monetary Fund (IMF). The IMF, which is described in section 25-5, is an international agency. Since 1970 it has been granted the authority to create SDRs. These SDRs, sometimes called "paper gold," serve as international monetary reserves among the member nations of the IMF. They are described more fully in section 25-5.

Pegged Rates and Joint Floats

Although the nations of the world moved to a floating exchange rate system as a result of the international monetary crisis of 1973, there is room within this system for certain special arrangements to be made by particular countries, and by groups of countries. Two such arrangements will be described briefly: the *pegged rate* and the *joint float.*

Pegged Exchange Rates   A smaller country that has very strong economic ties to a larger country may decide to *peg,* or fix, the value of its currency to that of the larger country in order to stabilize the price of goods traded with the larger country. Since the currency of the larger country will be floating against the world's other major currencies, this means that the smaller country will have a combination fixed and floating exchange rate—fixed against the larger country and floating against the rest of the world. For example, the Mexican peso in 1978 was pegged to the dollar at about 1 peso = 4.4 cents. This exchange rate was fixed, but when the dollar changed value (floated) against the French franc, for example, so did the Mexican peso. Note that this kind of arrangement means that when the Federal Reserve intervenes in the foreign exchange market to alter the value of the dollar, it is willy-nilly also altering the value of the peso. Thus the responsibilities of the Federal Reserve, when it "manages" our float, extend substantially beyond the narrow self-interest of the United States. Approximately fifty currencies are pegged to the dollar.

Joint Floats   Several Western European countries have banded together in what is known as a *joint float.* Under this arrangement, these currencies are permitted to float against one another only within a limited range (about 4 percent), but to float against other currencies without official limits. Thus the Belgian franc and the German mark, for example, might be permitted to change value relative to one another only slightly, but to jointly change value relative to the dollar by a great deal. The purpose of a joint float is to enhance the economic integration of the countries involved by making their currencies interchangeable within narrow limits of value. However, joint floats have not been particularly successful; they possess many of the same weaknesses as fixed exchange rates.

25-5   THE INTERNATIONAL MONETARY FUND

The *International Monetary Fund* (IMF) was established in 1944 to attempt to restore some semblance of order to the international monetary economy, which had been reduced to chaos first by the Great Depression and then by World War II. The IMF's purposes were threefold: to promote stable exchange rates among member nations; to work for the free convertibility of currencies (i.e., to eliminate exchange controls); and to be a source of foreign exchange for countries with a temporary shortage of foreign exchange. Although a number of significant changes have occurred in the IMF since its inception thirty-five years ago, its goals remain approximately the same.

The IMF and Floating Exchange Rates

As originally set up, one of the primary goals of the IMF was to work toward an international payments system that was based on fixed exchange rates. The IMF pursued this goal with fixity of purpose (no pun intended) for more than thirty years. However, the collapse of the fixed exchange rate system in 1973 resulted in a de facto system of floating exchange rates, and this left the IMF practically alone in its defense of the old regime. In 1976, at what has come to be known as the *Jamaican Agreement,* the member nations of the IMF changed its charter and accepted floating exchange rates. This change in the charter of the IMF was ratified in 1978.

Two aspects of the IMF's acceptance of the floating exchange rate system should be noted. The first is that the IMF has not gone all the way and endorsed a clean float. Rather, the amended IMF charter provides for central bank intervention into the foreign exchanges, i.e., a managed float. Thus the IMF continues to pursue its original goal of "stable" exchange rates.

The second noteworthy point is that the IMF is supposed to engage in *surveillance* of central bank intervention in the foreign exchange market to attempt to make sure that one country does not use such intervention to gain artificial trade and monetary advantages over other nations. To explain, suppose that the United States is suffering from widespread unemployment and therefore decides to try to stimulate its export industries. One way of doing so would be to *undervalue* its currency. For example, it might try to hold an exchange rate with the Japanese yen of 1 dollar = 200 yen, when the equilibrium rate was 1 dollar = 250 yen. Then Japanese citizens would find American goods inexpensive; they could buy a dollar's worth for only 200 yen, whereas if the equilibrium rate prevailed, a dollar's worth of goods would cost 250 yen. The Japanese would therefore turn from home-produced goods to American imports. By the same token, Americans would find Japanese goods expensive, and would therefore tend to buy more domestically produced goods. The net result, of course, would be to stimulate American industry and hence to reduce our unemployment. But note that it would do so only at the cost of raising the level of unemployment in Japan. In other words, the United States would have "exported" its unemployment. Such policies are called *beggar-thy-neighbor* policies. They are considered undesirable not only because they are morally reprehensible, but also for the very practical reason that they frequently result in competitive currency undervaluations by *all* countries, so that no one gains and everyone loses.

There can be little doubt that the managed float system is subject to the kind of abuse just described. What is doubtful is that IMF surveillance can be very effective in preventing it, since the IMF has very few sanctions it can impose on an offending, but sovereign, nation.

The IMF and International Monetary Reserves

The International Monetary Fund is also a source of international monetary reserves for its member nations. These reserves, which are intended to tide nations over a temporary disequilibrium in its foreign exchange market, are of two kinds: *Regular Drawing Rights* and *Special Drawing Rights.*

Regular Drawing Rights When it joins the IMF, each nation is assigned a currency *quota,* which is determined by a variety of factors such as the size and economic strength of the country. This quota is filled, approximately, by having the nation pay over to the IMF 25 percent of its quota in gold and the other 75 percent in its own currency. Having met its quota, the member nation is then entitled to "draw" foreign currencies from the Fund up to 25 percent of its quota in any one year by paying in an equivalent amount of its own currency. When a nation exercises these *Regular Drawing Rights,* as they are called, it must eventually reverse the transaction, usually within three to five years. Regular Drawing Rights are not automatic (although they are virtually so the first time) and must be accompanied by an explanation of the steps being taken to correct the deficit that caused the draft. The quota system and the Regular Drawing Rights of the IMF are thus designed to be a sort of "credit line" to help nations deal with transient exchange rate difficulties.

International Liquidity and SDRs As indicated, international reserve assets are for the purpose of tiding a country over transient movements in its foreign exchange rate. In a sense, international reserves are similar to the reserve assets of a commercial bank: When a bank experiences an adverse clearing balance, it needs primary and secondary reserves to give it time to make more fundamental adjustments. International monetary reserves perform a similar function for a nation. Indeed, we can carry the analogy with a bank one step further by noting that we would not expect a bank that had tripled in size during the last thirty years to continue to hold the same amount of reserves. The same reasoning applies to nations. As world trade expands and price levels generally rise, nations must perforce hold a larger amount of international reserves. The question is, Where are these additional reserves to come from?

Both gold and key currencies are poorly suited to provide an answer to this question. The expansion of the world's gold supply is dependent on gold discoveries and the development of more economical gold-refining methods. But both of these are hit-or-miss propositions; they cannot be counted on to expand the world's gold supply smoothly and in just the right amount. The same is true of key currencies. To expand international liquidity with a growing amount of key currencies requires that the key-currency countries run continuous deficits—deficits that are, moreover, of just the right size to furnish the world with just the right additional amount of international reserves. Not only is it very unlikely that this will happen, but it is also open to the objection that it provides a subsidy to those countries that least need it. Suppose, for example, that the United States dollar is a key currency. Then this means, approximately, that the United States can *permanently* import more goods than it exports. Many underdeveloped countries, starved for capital, argue that this is the reverse of justice. They suggest, instead, that it is the poor countries that should be able to have an excess of imports and the rich countries that should furnish these goods.

In 1970, after several years of negotiations, the IMF began creating *Special Drawing Rights,* which are a net addition to the world's supply of international monetary reserves. Thus, for the first time in history nations achieved a degree of international cooperation that permitted the creation of reserves as a deliberate act of public policy rather than as the by-product of such accidents as gold discoveries.

SDRs are created at irregular intervals by the IMF and are allocated among the member nations on the basis of each nation's quota. In practice, they work very much like gold used to (and are, indeed, sometimes called *paper gold*), although the rules surrounding their use and acceptance are more complex. Generally speaking, and without going into detail, a nation wanting to exchange SDRs for the currency of another country notifies the IMF, and the IMF notifies the other country. If everything goes smoothly, the deficit country receives the foreign currency it requested and the other country receives the first nation's SDR holdings. The only other points that might be noted are: The amount of its SDR allotment a deficit country may use is limited, and the amount of SDRs a surplus country is obliged to accept is also limited.

The use of SDRs to expand world liquidity overcomes most of the disadvantages of gold and key currencies but carries with it some disadvantages of its own. Since SDRs can be created at will, they are not dependent on such irrelevant events as gold discoveries or deficits in particular countries. In principle, at least, they can be increased in relation to the needs of world trade. But this is in principle. In practice, an increase in SDRs is a political matter, requiring a very high degree of cooperation among sovereign nations.

25-6 EVALUATION OF THE FLOATING EXCHANGE RATE SYSTEM

The world began the decade of the 1970s with a system of fixed exchange rates— a system that, with only a few exceptions, had been in existence for centuries. The world is ending the decade of the 1970s with a system of floating exchange rates. This dramatic change in the nature of what may well be the most important market in the world did not come about as a result of rational and cooperative decision making among sovereign nations. Instead, it was the consequence of a series of international monetary crises that ended in the collapse of the fixed-rate system in March 1973. Thus the new system was born in the midst of chaos, and many people prophesied that it would not prove viable in the long run—that world trade and finance could not withstand the uncertainty of flexible exchange rates. It therefore seems sensible to ask, How is the new system doing? Have exchange rates become the target of international speculation to the point where world welfare is seriously threatened, as critics of the new regime charged they would? Or have floating rates proved a workable alternative to fixed exchange rates and exchange controls, as its defenders hoped?

These questions can be restated, less colorfully but more carefully, as follows: (1) Are foreign exchange rates more volatile under the new system? and (2) If so, is this due to the activities of speculators or to fundamental economic forces?

Stability of Fixed and Floating Exchange Rates

When we ask if foreign exchange rates have become more unstable under the floating rate system, the necessary first step would seem to be to specify what it is we mean by "unstable." A natural statistic to use, in this connection, is the *standard deviation.* The standard deviation, it will be recalled, is the square root of the variance, and is a measure of the dispersion of a series of numbers about their mean (see the Appendix to Chapter 1). Thus it would seem reasonable to conclude that foreign exchange rates have become more unstable if the standard deviations of changes in them are greater in the years following the shift to the floating rate system, than they were in the years immediately preceding that shift. One researcher, using this approach, derived the data shown in Table 25-1. This table shows the standard deviation of the daily percentage changes in nine currencies relative to the dollar in the three years before and after March 1973. It is apparent from the table that foreign exchange markets *have* become more unstable. In only two of the currencies shown has the standard deviation gone down, and the mean standard deviation for all nine currencies almost doubled. Data such as these, together with impressionistic accounts of market participants, leave virtually no doubt that the shift to the floating rate system has resulted in bigger day-to-day changes in foreign exchange rates.

Speculation or Fundamental Economics?

It is hardly suprising that daily movements in foreign exchange rates have become more variable since 1973. That is, after all, just what is meant by "fixed" and "floating": By definition, fixed rates are not supposed to move, and floating rates are.

Table 25-1 Standard Deviation of Daily Percentage Changes in Exchange Rates Between the U.S. Dollar and the Currencies of Nine Major Trading Partners

Currency	June 1, 1970, to February 28, 1973	March 2, 1973, to June 30, 1976
Belgium	0.301	0.654
Canada	0.208	0.148
France	0.342	0.658
Germany	0.373	0.662
Italy	0.195	0.597
Japan	0.488	0.408
Netherlands	0.295	0.583
Switzerland	0.301	0.744
United Kingdom	0.245	0.474
Mean standard deviation	0.305	0.548

Source: Adapted from Donald S. Kemp, "The U.S. Dollar in International Markets: Mid-1970 to Mid-1976," Federal Reserve Bank of St. Louis *Review*, August 1976, Table II, p. 10.

A more fundamental question than the comparative variability of the rates is therefore as follows: Do long-run exchange rate movements seem to have occurred largely because of destabilizing speculation, or because of fundamental economic forces?

This is, of course, a difficult question to give a definite answer to. But one researcher, Donald Kemp,[6] has offered some very interesting statistical analysis that seems to suggest that exchange rate movements, in the long run at least, are due largely to fundamental economic forces.

By "fundamental" forces, Kemp means comparative rates of inflation in different countries. The theory here is quite straightforward. Suppose two countries, A and B, where 2 units of A's currency = 1 unit of B's currency. Now suppose that the price level in country A rises rapidly, while that of B remains constant. Then the citizens of country A will switch from buying their own, high-priced goods, to buying the comparatively cheap goods of country B. This will mean that the citizens of A demand a lot more of B's currency, and therefore the value of B's currency will *appreciate,* or rise, relative to A's currency. For example, the new rate of exchange might move to: 4 units of A's currency = 1 unit of B's currency. Then the citizens of country A will have to spend 4 units of their currency to buy something of unitary value in B, whereas before the inflation they could buy it for 2 units of A's currency.

On the basis of the above theory, we can hypothesize that there should be a negative statistical relationship between changes in exchange rates and changes in prices in different countries—that is, the higher the rate of inflation, the lower the value of the currency. This hypothesis can be tested by using regression analysis for the period 1973–1976. Doing so, Kemp found the following relationship:

$$\% \ \Delta ER = 6.765 - .936(\% \ \Delta CPI_f - \% \ \Delta CPI_{U.S.})$$
$$r^2 = .85$$

Coefficient on $(\% \ \Delta CPI_f - \% \ \Delta CPI_{U.S.})$ significant at 1% level

where $\% \ \Delta ER =$ the quarterly percentage change in the exchange rate
$\% \ \Delta CPI_f =$ the quarterly percentage change in the consumer price index for nine foreign countries that are major trading partners of the United States (the nine countries are those given in Table 25-1)
$\% \ \Delta CPI_{U.S.} =$ the quarterly percentage change in the consumer price index of the United States

Note that the r^2 in this regression is high at .85, and that the coefficient on the independent variable (the inflation rate in foreign countries minus the inflation rate in the United States) is highly significant. Note also that the coefficient on the independent variable is negative, as hypothesized. It would thus seem that a good

[6]Donald S. Kemp, "The U.S. Dollar in International Markets: Mid-1970 to Mid-1976," *Federal Reserve Bank of St. Louis Review,* August 1976, pp. 7–14. Note that Table 25-1 is taken from Kemp's paper also.

case can be made for the view that floating exchange rates do respond to fundamental economic forces, and are not just pushed around haphazardly by speculators.

Conclusion

As compared to our centuries-long experience with fixed exchange rates, the world has had only a brief experience with floating exchange rates. It is, perhaps, still too early to make a final judgment about them; our experience is too short to include all the possible things that might go wrong. But is does seem fair to conclude the following: So far, so good.

25-7 REVIEW QUESTIONS

1   What are the three basic choices open to a country with a disequilibrium in the foreign exchange market for its currency?
2   How can a country on a fixed exchange rate system adjust to a temporary deficit in its foreign exchange rate? to a permanent disequilibrium?
3   What are the main objections that economists have to exchange controls?
4   What is the difference between a "clean float" and a "dirty float" (managed float)? Which of these systems is now used by most industrial nations? What are the most common types of international reserves used for official intervention with a managed float?
5   What are Special Drawing Rights? Who issues them? What is their purpose?
6   So far, what does the evidence seem to indicate about the managed float system? Are exchange rates more or less stable? Does speculation dominate exchange rate movements?

PART 9

ISSUES IN MONETARY POLICY

Monetary policy, the translation of theory into practice, can be divided into two fairly distinct parts: First, there is the question of how monetary policy *should* be conducted. This question is considered in Chapter 26 under the assumption that the current institutional framework of the Fed is maintained intact. In Chapter 27, more basic reform proposals are considered. Second, there is the question of how monetary policy *has* been carried out in recent years. This is the subject of Chapter 28.

Thus we come, finally, to the last element of Figure 1-1 in Chapter 1 (shown as Figure IX-1): monetary policy and the behavior of the macroeconomy. Our concern in this part of the book will be with the formulation and execution of monetary policy.

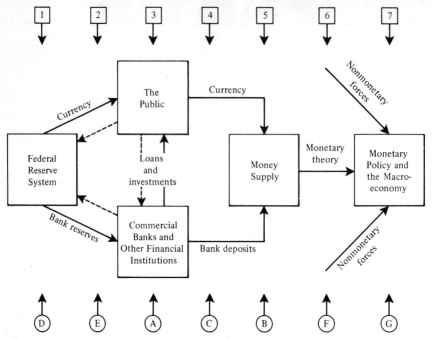

Figure IX-1 A schematic of monetary policy.

26

Strategies
of Monetary Policy

Imagine a person making a business trip from Houston to Dallas. She needs to know where she is going and how she is going to get there. The Federal Reserve, in implementing monetary policy, faces much the same set of problems: It must have a *goal,* and it must choose a monetary policy *instrument* for getting there. Unfortunately, the analogy stops there. The goals of monetary policy are a good deal more complicated than "Dallas," and the choice of a policy instrument more subtle than whether to drive or fly. Nevertheless, the trip must be made. That is what this chapter is about.

26-1 GOALS OF MONETARY POLICY

By the *goals* of monetary policy are meant its ultimate aims or objectives. Three such goals have been explored in some depth so far: full employment, price level stability, and stability in the international exchange value of the dollar. To this set of three, it is now necessary to add a fourth: economic growth. And, like the other three, economic growth is best seen out of the corner of one's eye: When viewed directly, it is apt to prove elusive.

The most common definition of economic growth is a per capita increase in real net national product (NNP). *Net* national product, GNP minus depreciated capital equipment, is used because the wearing out of capital is a cost of economic growth. *Real, per capita* NNP expresses the judgment that economic growth should somehow measure the standard of living, or economic welfare, of the population. The difficulty with this definition is that it implicitly contains a number of concepts to which everyone would not spontaneously agree. The most obvious of these is that capital depreciation is hardly an adequate measure of the cost of growth. There are many other costs of a social nature: air and water pollution, for example, or the extermination of certain species of wildlife. Beyond this, the measure says nothing about the distribution of income. Should a rising real NNP in which benefits accrue only to a small group of very wealthy people *really* be considered economic growth?

Even granted the definition of economic growth, there is still the problem of deciding what *rate* of growth is desirable. The ultimate causes of economic growth are matters about which there is a good deal of dispute, but the proximate causes are generally held to be such things as the productivity of the labor force, the availability of natural resources, and the accumulation of capital goods. From a public policy viewpoint, there is little that can be done about the first two causes, but capital accumulation depends on the willingness of a society to save and invest. And saving and investing *can* be influenced by public policy—by monetary and fiscal policy—as we have seen. But saving and investing are by definition the foregoing of present for future consumption, and how much of this decision should be a matter of public policy and how much should be left to individuals is a nice question. There is no good answer. By tradition, more than anything else, a growth rate of around 4 percent has come to be considered "adequate." But a warning is in order: There is even less consensus about this figure than there is about similarly arbitrary definitions of "full" employment, price level "stability," and "equilibrium" in the exchange value of the dollar.

Conflicts in the Goals of Monetary Policy

Defining the goals of macroeconomic policy is slippery but not impossible. All that is needed is a willingness to live with a certain amount of vagueness. Much more severe is the problem of potential conflicts among these goals. By *conflicts* is meant whether all the goals can be achieved simultaneously. Thus, for example, suppose that the American public could agree unanimously that monetary policy should be set in pursuit of the following goals:

1   5 percent rate of unemployment
2   2 percent rate of change in the price level
3   0 change in the foreign exchange rate
4   4 percent rate of increase in per capita real NNP

Considered individually, each of these goals is realistic, but achieving all of them at the same time is quite another matter. The reason for this is that reaching one goal may make it impossible to reach another. Two such situations have already been considered: The Phillips curve, which says that the closer the economy is to full employment, the faster prices will rise; and balance of payments equilibrium under a system of fixed exchange rates, which requires that the domestic economy be systematically deflated and inflated.[1] Additionally, the goal of economic growth may conflict with any of the other three goals.

To understand the nature of the potential conflict between growth and the other three goals, we must distinguish between a *necessary* conflict and a *policy* conflict. A necessary conflict is a situation where the achievement of one goal necessarily means the nonachievement of another. The best example of this is the Phillips curve. A policy conflict is a situation where there is no necessary conflict between two goals but where monetary policy cannot pursue both goals simultaneously. The conflict between growth and price stability, for example, is a policy conflict. Historically any rate of price increase is consistent with any rate of growth. But in a situation where the economy is experiencing a high rate of inflation and a slow growth rate, the authorities are thrown into a dilemma. If they try to curb the inflation through tight money, the higher interest rates will retard investment and hence economic growth. If they pursue an easy money policy to stimulate growth, the low interest rates will spur the inflation. Similar potential policy conflicts exist between growth and full employment or the exchange stability of the dollar.

Reconciling the Goals

The Federal Reserve thus has a problem. It is charged with the responsibility of achieving multiple goals that either necessarily or potentially conflict with one another. It must therefore make a choice among these goals. Three questions arise: What does the law require that the Fed *should* do? What does the Fed *say* it does? and, What does the Fed *actually* do?

The Employment Act of 1946   The Federal Reserve System receives little, if any, guidance from the law about the problem of conflicting objectives. The basic legal document in the area of macroeconomic objectives is the Employment Act of 1946 . This Act, which marks the government's official acceptance of responsibility for the state of the economy, reads in part: "It is the continuing policy . . . of the Federal Government . . . to promote maximum employment, production, and purchasing power." Clearly, this isn't very helpful. Not only are the goals defined ambiguously (what is "maximum" purchasing power?) and incompletely (where is the foreign exchange rate?), but not even a hint is given about how to reconcile conflicts among these goals.

A number of people have from time to time proposed that the Employment Act be amended to specify precise goals and a system of priorities in the event of conflicts

[1]In the absence of exchange controls; see Chapter 25.

among these goals. But such precision is fraught with difficulties, not the least of which are political. Such proposals have met with a notable lack of enthusiasm.

What the Fed Says   But even if the law doesn't say what to do, still the Fed must do something. Why not, then, just ask the Fed what it does when its goals are in conflict? Several people have tried this, ranging from United States Senators to ordinary people. And what does the Fed reply? What any sensible bureaucrat would reply when faced with a question which, however answered, is sure to make someone mad: It denies the problem exists.

The (more or less) official position of the Federal Reserve is that the goals of full employment, price stability, payments equilibrium, and economic growth are mutually consistent. But there is a catch here. For Fed officials usually modify these goals with adjectives like *sustainable* and *maintainable*. Thus, for example, we have statements like "Price stability is necessary for *maintainable* full employment and *sustainable* economic growth." The implication seems to be that although an inflation might increase employment briefly, in the longer run it would lead to economic maladjustments that would cause a recession. How long is the long run? And what evidence is there for such statements? No one, apparently, is saying.

Analyzing Fed Behavior   Since neither the law nor the Federal Reserve is very informative about the priorities used in resolving conflicts among economic goals, several economists have attempted to shed light on this issue by using the method of regression analysis. The first such study to make use of United States data covered the period 1952–1961.[2] Although this period is now out of date, a consideration of the study will serve to explain the method used.

The main assumption of this study is that the authorities formulate monetary policy in response to the various economic goals just described. Accepting this assumption, then, in general terms we may write[3]

$$\text{Monetary policy} = f \text{ (unemployment, prices, growth)} \tag{1}$$

The next step is to quantify eq. (1). Letting the money supply M serve as the proxy for monetary policy, the unemployment rate U for unemployment, the consumer price index P for prices, and real GNP y for economic growth, eq. (1) can be written as

$$M_t = a + bM_{t-1} + cU_t + dy_t + eP_t \tag{2}$$

Notice in particular that the right-hand side of eq. (2) includes the money supply

[2]William G. Dewald and Harry G. Johnson, "An Objective Analysis of the Objectives of American Monetary Policy," in Deane Carson (ed.), *Banking and Monetary Studies,* Richard D. Irwin, Inc., Homewood, Ill., 1963, pp. 171–189. The method was first developed and applied to Canadian data by G. L. Reuber, "The Objectives of Canadian Monetary Policy, 1949–61," *Journal of Political Economy,* April 1964, pp. 109–132.

[3]The balance of payments goal is left out here. Dewald and Johnson did not find it statistically significant, presumably because it was not of much concern during the period covered.

lagged one-quarter (M_{t-1}). The reason for this[4] will become apparent soon. Running the regression for the indicated period gives

$$M_t = 26.9 + .75M_{t-1} + .46U_t + .04y_t - .09P_t$$
$$r^2 = .99$$

Coefficients on M_{t-1}, U_t, and Y_t *significant at 5% level*
Coefficient on P_t not significant

With this regression in hand, let us now pose the following question: Holding any one goal constant, how would the remaining two goals have to change so that the authorities would take no action? In other words, if one goal is held constant, then theoretically it is possible for the remaining two goals to change in such a fashion that they exactly *offset* one another in the minds of the authorities. If we can find out what changes are considered offsetting, then we can obtain some idea of the trade-offs used by Federal Reserve officials.

First, move $.75M_{t-1}$ to the left-hand side of the regression. This gives

$$M_t - .75M_{t-1} = 26.9 + .46U_t + .04y_t - .09P_t \tag{3}$$

Now since we are interested in the case where there is *no change* in monetary policy (i.e., where no action is taken), this means we are interested in the case where

$$M_t - M_{t-1} = 0$$

or

$$M_t = M_{t-1}$$

But if $M_t = M_{t-1}$, then eq. (3) can be written

$$(1 - .75)M = 26.9 + .46U + .04y - .09P \tag{4}$$

where the subscripts have been dropped for convenience. Dividing both sides of eq. (4) by $(1 - .75)$ gives

$$M = 109.2 + 1.9U + .15y - .36P \tag{5}$$

Now treating M as a constant, what will happen to y and U if P rises by 1 percent? The answer is that U will rise by 0.19 percent (y constant) and that y will rise by \$2.34 billion (U constant). In other words, if the price level rises by 1 percent and the unemployment rate also rises by 0.19 percent, real GNP remaining the same, then the authorities will do nothing. They will be willing to "trade" a 1 percent rate

---

[4]An additional reason for including M_{t-1} in the regression was to estimate the lag in monetary policy.

of inflation for a 0.19 percent increase in the unemployment rate. Similarly, they will "trade" a 1 percent increase in the price level for a $2.34 billion increase in real GNP (U constant).

The precise numbers obtained in the preceding study need to be taken with a large grain of salt. For one thing, the coefficient obtained on the price level variable P is not statistically significant, and the balance of payments goal is not even included. Additionally, more recent followup studies seem to indicate that the monetary authorities assign different priorities at different times.[5] But what this and similar studies *do* seem to suggest is this: No matter what the monetary authorities may *say* about the "mutual consistency" of policy goals, they *act* as though these goals are conflicting.

26-2 LAGS IN MONETARY POLICY

In the past few years several economists have raised the possibility that monetary policy may affect the economy only after a long and variable time lag. Should such a charge be substantiated empirically, the implications for monetary policy would be profound. It could mean that monetary policy, as presently conducted, is perverse —that it can make matters worse rather than better.

The Problem of Lags

The purpose of monetary policy is to help stabilize the economy. The traditional interpretation of this statement is that monetary policy should stimulate the economy when business is slack and tranquilize it when business is brisk. A lengthy lag in the effect of monetary policy could mean that it does just the opposite: stimulates the economy during an inflation and further depresses it during a recession.

To understand this, suppose that monetary policy has only a single, unambiguous goal—to eliminate the business cycle—and that monetary policy is sufficiently powerful to achieve this goal. But suppose also that a change in monetary policy made today will not affect the economy until eighteen months from now. Consider what would happen under these circumstances if the monetary authorities based their decisions on the state of *current* economic conditions. If the economy is currently in a recession, then the appropriate monetary policy would be easy money. But eighteen months from now, when the easy money policy finally took effect, the economy might be into its prosperity phase. In that case, the easy money decision taken today would stimulate the economy a year and a half later during prosperity, thereby causing an inflation. The opposite case also holds: If the economy is currently undergoing prosperity, the policy decision would be for tight money. But in eighteen months the economy might be in a recession and the tight money policy would further depress it, causing unemployment to be greater than it otherwise would have been. Thus, the possibility of a long lag in monetary policy raises the

[5]See Glenn T. Potts and Dudley G. Luckett, "Policy Objectives of the Federal Reserve System," *Quarterly Journal of Economics,* August 1978, pp. 525–534.

specter that it might be destabilizing; that is, it might make swings in the business cycle bigger rather than smaller.

If, in fact, there is a long lag in the effectiveness of monetary policy, then the monetary authorities should properly make decisions based, not on what is happening today, but on what they believe *is going to* happen in the future. But this is a shaky business at best. Our present ability to forecast economic events is not great. Nevertheless, considerable progress has already been made in the development of models of the economy, such as those described in Chapter 23, and further progress may be expected. It is thus possible, at least, that the monetary authorities will some day be able to cope with the problem of a delayed impact of monetary policy.

But the problem doesn't stop there. For the problem of monetary lags is not just that they are lengthy but also that they are *variable,* which in this context must be understood to mean "of uncertain length." Thus, a given change in monetary policy at one time may require a lag of sixteen months before its full impact is felt while at another time it may require only six months. The point is not so much that the lag may be of different lengths at different times but that the length of the lag is *uncertain.* If this is the case, then the lag problem cannot be resolved by accurate economic forecasts alone, for the state of the economy may be quite different sixteen months from now than it will be six months from now, and the authorities must know on which period to base their current decisions.

Types of Lag

The importance of the lag problem for the proper conduct of monetary policy makes it mandatory that this issue be studied carefully. As an aid in such studies, the lags of monetary policy are usually classified into two types: *inside* and *outside lags.*

Inside Lags   The inside lag of monetary policy is the amount of time that elapses between the need for action and the actual taking of that action. For example, if the economy turns from prosperity to recession in May but monetary policy does not turn from tight to easy money until September, then we would say that the inside lag was four months long. The inside lag may be subclassified into the *recognition* and *action lags.*

Recognition Lag   The recognition lag is the amount of time it takes between the need for action and the recognition of that need. For example, the economy may experience a downturn in May, but this fact may go unremarked until July. The recognition lag exists for many reasons. First, economic data cannot be collected, processed, and assimilated instantaneously; the latest data available even to key decision makers may describe events that occurred a month or more previously. Second, the interpretation of economic data is not yet reducible to a mechanical rule. At any given time some economic series will be moving in one direction, others in another. And it frequently happens that a particular observation in a series of data will be spuriously high or low. Even several months after the event, with all the data available, it is sometimes impossible to fix the exact month of an economic turning point.

Action Lag   The action lag is the time that elapses between when the need for action is recognized and when the action is in fact taken. For example, it might be well understood by July that the economy has reached a turning point, but corrective measures are still not undertaken until September. Action lags occur in any bureaucratic organization. Certain key people may not be available, for example, and matters are allowed to drift. Or it may be that everyone recognizes that something must be done but cannot agree on exactly what.

Outside Lags   The outside lag of monetary policy (sometimes also called the *impact lag*) is the time between when a particular action is taken and when the effects of that action have some substantial impact on the goals of monetary policy. For example, the Federal Reserve might switch from a tight to an easy money policy in September, but this action might still not affect the unemployment rate until the following August. The length of the outside lag depends, in part, on the structure of the economy—for example, the precise nature of the interdependencies among various industries. But it may also depend on such intangibles as consumer and producer expectations or even political events.

Measurement of Lags

Empirical attempts to estimate the length of monetary policy lags have not been very successful. Although a number of studies have been made, the results are markedly contradictory, and their findings appear to depend to an unusual degree on the research method used. Estimates of the inside lag are probably the most satisfactory, although they necessarily depend to some extent on the subjective judgment of the investigator. The investigator must decide, first, at what point a shift in monetary policy was needed and, second, at what point a shift in monetary policy was actually made. Neither of these points is obvious; the latter, especially, depends to a considerable extent on an interpretation of what was said at a particular meeting of the Federal Open Market Committee. Nevertheless, the studies made[6] seem to indicate that the inside lag is relatively short—almost certainly not longer than six months and probably more like two or three months.

Estimates of the outside lag of monetary policy are highly controversial. Some studies show it to be relatively brief—five or six months— while others indicate that it exceeds eighteen months. Probably the most honest summary of these studies is simply to state that we don't yet know what the length of the lag is. Most likely it lies somewhere between six months and two years, but such a range is entirely too broad to be meaningful.

There are a number of difficulties involved in trying to estimate the length of monetary policy lags. Foremost among these is that the effects of monetary policy are not concentrated at a single point in time but are spread out over time; some effects are direct and immediate while others are indirect and delayed. Researchers inquiring into this question consequently use some arbitrary benchmark in estimating the length of the lag, for example, how long it takes for 90 percent of the effect

---

[6]A convenient summary of these studies may be found in Dwayne Wrightsman, *An Introduction to Monetary Theory and Policy,* The Free Press, New York, 1971, p. 227.

to be felt. But this is not a wholly satisfactory procedure. Another difficulty is that because the structure of the economy is not fully known, spurious statistical relationships between policy changes and goal changes may crop up. A fall in unemployment today may or may not be due to an easy money action taken a year previously.

Lags in Fiscal Policy

Since fiscal policy is to some extent an alternative to monetary policy, the question arises as to which has the shorter lag. As with monetary policy, researches into the lag structure of fiscal policy have yielded conflicting estimates. The weight of the evidence suggests that the outside lag of fiscal policy is shorter than that for monetary policy, but this conclusion is highly tenuous. One thing does seem clear, however: The *inside* lag for fiscal policy is quite long. The reason for this is that fiscal policy is made by Congress, and that august body is not noted for its hasty actions.

26-3   CHOICE OF POLICY INSTRUMENTS UNDER UNCERTAIN CONDITIONS

The discussion of both the Keynesian and quantity theories of money in Chapters 18 to 23 implicitly assumed that monetary policy is conducted in an atmosphere of certainty. That is, it was implicitly assumed that the monetary authorities had a sure and detailed knowledge of how our economic system works. If such an assumption were accurate, the problems that beset the Federal Reserve would be greatly reduced. Unfortunately, however, monetary policy must be carried on in an uncertain world—uncertain not only in terms of conflicting goals and variable lags, but also in terms of precise knowledge of very fundamental economic relationships. Thus, for example, although we know their general nature, we do not know the *exact* parameters of the money supply function, the money demand function, the consumption function, or the marginal efficiency of investment function. In other words, we do not know exactly either the position or slope of the *IS* and *LM* functions of the Keynesian model. And our inexact knowledge of these matters has a profound effect on whether the Federal Reserve should try to stabilize the economy by controlling interest rates or by controlling the quantity of money. To explain the nature of this statement, we shall consider three cases: (1) The Federal Reserve is certain of the *IS* function, but uncertain of the *LM* function; (2) the Federal Reserve is certain of the *LM* function but uncertain of the *IS* function; and (3) the Federal Reserve is uncertain of both the *IS* and *LM* functions.[7]

Case I: Uncertainty in the *LM* Function

Recall that the *LM* function shows all points of equilibrium in the monetary sector, that is, all points where it is true that the demand for money is equal to the supply of money. Underlying these points of equilibrium are such economic relationships

[7]The analysis is based on the path-breaking article by William Poole, "Optimal Choice of Monetary Policy Instruments in a Simple Stochastic Macro Model," *Quarterly Journal of Economics,* May 1970, pp. 197–216.

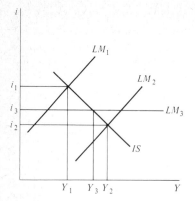

Figure 26-1 Uncertainty in the *LM* schedule.

as the money multiplier, the reserve base of the banking system, the transactions demand for money, and the liquidity preference schedule. Clearly, any or all of these relationships may change in a dynamic economy, thus shifting the *LM* schedule. Thus, consider Figure 26-1. In this figure, only a single *IS* schedule is shown, reflecting our assumption that the *IS* schedule is known with certainty. However, two upward-sloping *LM* schedules are show, LM_1 and LM_2 (for the moment, ignore the horizontal *LM* schedule, LM_3). The purpose of showing two *LM* schedules is to indicate that we are uncertain as to where, *precisely,* the *LM* schedule is. It could be LM_1 or LM_2, or anywhere in between.

Now suppose that you are an official of the Federal Reserve, and that it is your job to try to achieve income level Y_3 (full employment) in the economy. The question you ask yourself is this: Am I better off trying to get to income level Y_3 by controlling the quantity of money, or by controlling interest rates? The answer is as follows. If you try to get to income level Y_3 by controlling the money supply, then the *actual* level of income you will achieve will lie somewhere between Y_1 and Y_2. In other words, by choosing the money supply as your monetary policy instrument you run the risk of missing your goal of Y_3 and causing either an inflation (e.g., Y_2) or unemployment (e.g., Y_1). The reason for this is that, by choosing the money supply as your policy instrument, you have left it uncertain as to what the *LM* schedule will be, and hence uncertain as to what income level prevails.

But now suppose that you decide instead to use the rate of interest as your policy instrument. In this case, the *LM* schedule will be the horizontal line LM_3. The reason LM_3 becomes the appropriate *LM* schedule is that the Federal Reserve can always achieve a target rate of interest by "pegging" the government securities market. What the Fed does is, very simply, to offer to buy or sell unlimited quantities of government bonds at a fixed price. Then the price of the bonds won't change, since no one will sell at a lower price or buy at a higher price. And since the bond price can't change, neither can its yield. In this way, the Federal Reserve makes the money supply perfectly elastic at a given rate of interest, which results in a horizontal *LM* curve. But note that with LM_3, the relevant *LM* curve, you can achieve income level

Y_3 precisely (assuming you know exactly where the *IS* curve is). That is, by using an interest rate policy instead of a money supply policy, you have eliminated the random response of income.

The moral of the analysis is consequently this: If the nature of the *LM* curve is uncertain and the nature of the *IS* curve is certain, then the Federal Reserve should use interest rates as its instrument variable in the conduct of monetary policy.

Case II: Uncertainty in the *IS* Function

Now let us consider the opposite case, where there is uncertainty about the *IS* curve, but where the nature of the *LM* function is known for sure. This case can be analyzed with the aid of Figure 26-2. In this figure, notice that we now have two *IS* curves, IS_1 and IS_2, but only one upward-sloping *LM* curve, LM_1. (Again, ignore the horizontal *LM* curve, LM_2, for the moment.) Analogous to case I, we assume that the *IS* curve can fall (randomly) anywhere between IS_1 and IS_2. Recall that the *IS* curve shows all points of real sector equilibrium, where investment equals saving. The reason for this uncertainty about the exact location of the *IS* curve, therefore, stems from uncertainty about the nature of the relationship between interest and business investment (the MEI curve), the public's desire to consume (the consumption function), and the government's spending and taxing policies. Again, we want to ask the following question: If it is the Federal Reserve's goal to achieve full employment (Y_f in Figure 26-2), should it choose to control the money supply or interest rates?

This question can be answered by looking at Figure 26-2. If the Federal Reserve decides to use the money supply as its policy instrument, then LM_1 is the relevant *LM* curve. Since LM_1 cuts the *IS* curves between Y_2 and Y_3, it is apparent that national income must lie somewhere in between. Alternatively, if the Federal Reserve chooses to use the interest rate as its policy instrument, then, as explained in case I, LM_2 becomes the relevant *LM* function. In *this* case, where LM_2 is the relevant *LM* curve, national income will lie anywhere between Y_1 and Y_4. Thus, although neither policy instrument will necessarily result in full-employment income (Y_f) exactly, controlling the money supply will come closer in the sense that the range around Y_f is narrower. In contrast to case I, therefore, this analysis leads to

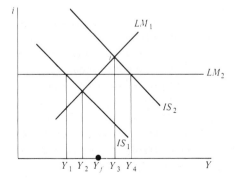

Figure 26-2 Uncertainty in the *IS* schedule.

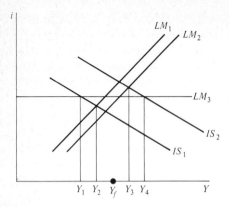

Figure 26-3 Uncertainty in both *IS* and *LM*.

the following conclusion: If the nature of the *IS* curve is uncertain, and the nature of the *LM* curve is certain, then the Federal Reserve should use the money supply as its instrument variable in the conduct of monetary policy.

Case III: Uncertainty about both the *IS* and *LM* Curves

It should be apparent that our knowledge of the American economy is sufficiently tenuous that we do not know the precise nature of *either* the *IS* or *LM* curve. In other words, the most realistic case is the case where there is uncertainty about *both* the *IS* and *LM* curves. This case can be analyzed by combining Figures 26-1 and 26-2. This is done in Figures 26-3 and 26-4, both of which show two *IS* schedules and two upward-sloping *LM* schedules. In the case of uncertainty in both schedules, as one would expect, whether the Fed should use interest rates or money supply as its policy instrument depends on which schedule is *more* stable. Figure 26-3 assumes that the *LM* schedule is the more stable. In this case, the Federal Reserve should use the money supply as its policy instrument. This can be seen by noting that, if the Fed uses the money supply instrument, income will vary between Y_2 and Y_3, whereas if it uses the interest rate (LM_3) income will vary between Y_1 and Y_4 —a much broader range. The opposite case is shown in Figure 26-4. In this case,

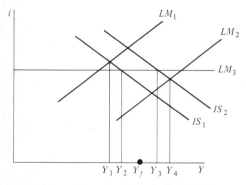

Figure 26-4 Uncertainty in both *IS* and *LM*.

the *IS* schedule is the more stable function, and the appropriate policy instrument is the rate of interest (LM_3). Thus in the case of Figure 26-4, it is apparent that using the rate of interest as the policy variable leads to a narrower range of national income.

Conclusion

The analysis of the choice of monetary policy instruments has considerable relevance for the Keynesian-monetarist debate. The focal point of this debate, at least so far as monetary policy is concerned, centers on whether to use interest rates or money supply as the policy instrument in the conduct of monetary policy. It will be recalled that the monetarists argue that the demand-for-money function is a highly stable economic relationship, and hence that the *LM* curve is similarly stable. Consistent with this view, they argue that monetary policy should be carried out by controlling the growth rate of the money supply (the case shown in Figure 23-3). Keynesians, on the other hand, tend to regard the money demand function as a potentially unstable economic relationship, and argue that the Federal Reserve should focus its policy efforts on controlling interest rates. Meanwhile, the Federal Reserve, in an uneasy compromise, continues to use both interest rates and money supply as policy instruments.[8]

26-4 REVIEW QUESTIONS

1 How might the goals of price stability and economic growth conflict?
2 What are some of the difficulties in quantifying what is meant by "full" employment?
3 Explain how a long lag in monetary policy might mean that it could make the economic situation worse instead of better.
4 If there are no uncertainties in either the *IS* or *LM* curve, does it matter if the Fed uses the interest rate or the money supply as its policy instrument? Explain your answer, using a graph.

[8]See the discussion of open market operations in Chapter 16, section 16-1.

27

Alternative
Monetary Policies

If monetary policy affects the economy only after a lag, as seems likely, then the Federal Reserve has essentially two choices. One choice is to leave the formulation of monetary policy basically unchanged but develop a strategy for its conduct; this was the subject of Chapter 26.

But there is a second choice: It is possible to undertake such a fundamental change in the way monetary policy is formulated that the whole question of strategy becomes irrelevant. For example, it would be possible to instruct the Federal Reserve to expand the money supply by a fixed percentage every year, irrespective of what was going on elsewhere in the economy. In this case, there would be no concern about goals or instruments. Once the decisions had been made as to what definition of money to use and its appropriate annual increase, monetary policy would be fixed forever.

This chapter deals with alternative monetary policies that have been proposed from time to time. We shall begin with a discussion of *discretionary* monetary policy

—basically the system now in use—because this is one of the alternatives open to us. Then we shall discuss (section 27-2) a permanent policy of easy money. Next, we shall consider the proposal for a fixed rate of change in the money supply, mentioned previously. Finally, in the last section we discuss a proposal for changing the fundamental character of commercial banks by requiring them to hold 100 percent cash reserves. While this final proposal does not, strictly speaking, deal with monetary policy, it is closely akin to the rule proposal.

27-1 DISCRETIONARY MONETARY POLICY

The type of monetary policy that is now in existence in the United States is what is usually called *discretionary monetary policy,* or monetary policy that is made at the discretion of the Board of Governors of the Federal Reserve System. Sometimes (as during an inflation) the Board will decide that the state of the economy requires a tight money policy and will take the steps necessary to ensure that money is tight. At other times (as during a recession) it will decide that an easy money policy is required. Because discretionary monetary policy means that the Fed tries to offset the business cycle, it is sometimes referred to as *countercyclical monetary policy,* or a policy of *leaning against the wind.*

Most economists and virtually all Federal Reserve officials favor a discretionary monetary policy. There are two fundamental reasons for this: First, the majority opinion holds that the sources of major disturbances in the economy are to be found in the real sector. This is basically the Keynesian (both traditional and modern) view. According to this view, the economy is inherently unstable. Certain expenditures categories, especially investment, behave erratically, and this erratic behavior then spreads to the rest of the economy. The result is the business cycle. (A formal analysis of this viewpoint is the multiplier-accelerator process described in Chapter 22.)

If the economy is inherently unstable, and if the source of this instability lies in the real sector of the economy, then it follows that monetary policy should be discretionary. Or so, at least, it seems to the majority of economists. In this case, monetary policy is most appropriately used to limit the range of swings in real output, and the erratic nature of these swings means that no absolute rule for the conduct of monetary policy will prove adequate to the task of stabilizing the economy. Human judgment is required.

The second reason for advocating discretionary monetary policy is that the economic system is too complex, our knowledge of how it works too limited, and the consequences of a malfunction too important to rely exclusively on a rule. A simple rule cannot hope to deal with the complex of interactions among all the varied institutions and markets of the financial sector, on the one hand, and the myriad economic decisions of the real sector, on the other. Even a very complicated rule, such as might conceivably be programmed for a computer, would be inadequate. Decisions must be made and conflicts resolved, and only human intelligence is up to the job.

Critics of the discretionary approach to monetary policy (and there are many) acknowledge that under ideal conditions such an approach would be at least as good as a rule. At worst, the authorities could follow the rule; at best, they could improve on it. But, say the critics, conditions are never ideal. The economy *is* complex—so complex, indeed, that no one person or group of persons can hope to grasp it in its entirety. Moreover, human judgment means human error. Consequently, discretionary monetary policy frequently makes matters worse rather than better. The existence of long and variable lags, confusion over goals, and the imperfect state of our knowledge of these matters almost inevitably lead to judgmental errors.

27-2 PERMANENT EASY MONEY

To judge by newspaper accounts, a policy of easy money is very popular among politicians and everyday people. This, at least, seems to be the implication of the frequent complaints one reads about high interest rates. "People can't afford to buy houses anymore" and "Bankers are getting rich" are statements familiar to us all. To a considerable extent, such statements probably reflect ignorance of the monetary policy process. Everyone wants low prices, and the price of borrowing money is no exception. The connection between interest rates and the pace of economic activity is not generally understood.

Notwithstanding that the *breadth* of the support for easy money probably rests on ignorance, some people advocate it after having given the matter considerable study and thought. The reasoning behind the advocacy of a fixed easy money policy rests on three arguments: (1) High interest rates are a cost of production and hence actually contribute to inflation; (2) tight money causes resources to be reallocated in a socially undesirable way; and (3) inflation is preferable to unemployment. Each of these arguments will be considered in turn.

High Interest Rates as a Cause of Inflation

One common view of the cause of inflation is that it is cost induced, that is, a so-called *cost-push inflation.* According to this theory, which is very popular with the man in the street, rising prices are caused by rising costs of production. Business people generally put the primary blame on rising wage rates, while labor unions blame excessive profit margins. In either case, once the cost-push theoretical framework is adopted, it can be argued that any increased cost is passed on to the consumer in the form of higher prices. And since they are a cost, this argument can be applied to interest rates. Thus a tight money policy, it is sometimes held, is actually inflationary. Tight money means high interest rates; high interest rates mean higher production costs; and higher production costs mean higher consumer prices.

This view of tight money as a cause of inflation is almost universally condemned by economists.[1] It runs directly contrary to both the quantity and Keynesian theories. Thus suppose that the economy is in equilibrium with stable prices and full

---

[1]See George Horwich, "Tight Money, Monetary Restraint and the Price Level," *Journal of Finance,* March 1966, pp. 15–33. However, for a contrary view see John A. Hotson, "Comment," *Journal of Finance,* March 1971, pp. 152–155.

employment. If the cost-push view of interest rates is correct, then it must be argued that in this equilibrium situation a *decrease* in the quantity of money would cause prices to *rise*. But from the quantity theory viewpoint, a decrease in the money supply would result directly in a decrease in nominal income; and from a Keynesian viewpoint, it would cause higher interest rates, discourage investment, and therefore cause a fall in real income. In neither case would a decrease in the money supply cause higher prices.

High interest rates and inflation are probably associated in the popular mind because they occur together so frequently. But because two things happen at the same time, it does not follow that they are causally related; and, if they are causally related, it doesn't follow that the direction of causality runs one way rather than the other. In this case, the explanation is probably that the Federal Reserve will pursue a tight money policy during an inflation, thereby causing interest rates to rise, and that inflationary expectations lead to higher *nominal* interest rates.

The Differential Effects of Monetary Policy

While acknowledging that tight money is to some extent effective in combatting inflation, some people nevertheless argue that it reallocates resources in a socially undesirable manner. Tight money, this argument runs, does not press down evenly on all sectors of the economy. Rather, some industries are substantially depressed during tight money episodes while others are affected hardly at all; and the hardest-hit industries are the most socially desirable ones. To take a single example, the United States government has a number of programs and agencies designed specifically to encourage the construction of new housing, and yet new housing construction is very adversely affected by tight money. Since this same state of affairs exists in other industries, some people argue that the side effects of tight money are too high a price to pay for economic stability. They therefore advocate that monetary policy should never exceed some moderate degree of restraint.

The *differential effects* of tight money—that is, the apparent fact that tight money affects various sectors of the economy differently—can generally be classified into two kinds: those that involve a differential response to high rates of interest and those that occur because of nonprice rationing by lenders.

Response to High Interest Rates   Just as the price elasticity of the demand for liver may vary markedly from one person to the next, so different industries will have different interest elasticities in their demands for borrowing money. Industries that are highly sensitive to interest rate changes (high elasticity) will tend to be depressed during tight money periods; industries that are insensitive to interest rates (low elasticity) will not be affected very much. Those industries most frequently mentioned as having both high elasticity and high social priority are the savings industry, housing, and state and local governments.

The Savings Industry   The savings industry—S&Ls, credit unions, insurance companies, and so on—is frequently harmed by periods of tight money. It is harmed in two ways: First, some savings institutions may become caught in a severe price squeeze because the rate of interest they must pay on their liabilities rises more rapidly than the rate of return on their assets. To illustrate, consider a savings and loan association during a period of rising interest rates. The rate of interest paid by the S&L to its depositors will generally rise as other interest rates rise. But most of the assets of the S&L are invested in long-term mortgages that were written in previous years when interest rates were low. These mortgage rates were fixed when the mortgage contract was originally written, and consequently they cannot rise as money becomes tighter. The S&L is thus squeezed between the rising cost of attracting and holding deposits and the relatively fixed income it receives from its previous investments.

The second way that the savings industry is harmed by periods of tight money is through a process known as *disintermediation,* in which the usual intermediating function of savings institutions is reversed. Instead of collecting small amounts of money from a lot of people and then making large loans in the capital market, the intermediary may find itself doing just the opposite: borrowing in the capital market and making loans to its customers. To see how the process of disintermediation works, let us use the example of life insurance companies in the period 1965–1970. Most life insurance policies contain a provision whereby the policyholder may borrow money at some stipulated rate of interest. During the latter part of the 1960s, this rate of interest was typically 5 percent. When money became tight, many policyholders found it cheaper and easier to borrow from their insurance companies than through normal borrowing channels. The insurance companies thus found themselves engaged in a substantial small-loan business. One research study[2] of this period, for example, derived the following regression equation:

$$\Delta PL = -70 + 28(\Delta i) - 16(\Delta M_1)$$
$$r^2 = .96$$

Coefficients significant at 5% level

where $\Delta PL =$ net change in policy loans at fifteen large life insurance companies (millions of dollars)
   $\Delta i =$ change in the six-month commercial paper rate
   $\Delta M_1 =$ percentage change in the M_1 money supply

The data are for quarterly observations and cover the period 1965–1970.

The main thing to note about the preceding regression is that the algebraic signs on the coefficients are as hypothesized; that is, as interest rates Δi rise, so do policy loans at insurance companies. Similarly, the smaller the percentage change in the money supply, the larger will be the amount of policy loans demanded. Thus, tight money (high interest rates and a slow growth rate in the money supply) results in disintermediation at life insurance companies. A related process also occurs at other thrift institutions. When open market interest rates rise above the deposit-rate

[2]Francis H. Schott, "Disintermediation Through Policy Loans at Life Insurance Companies," *Journal of Finance,* June 1971, pp. 719–729.

ceilings set by Regulation Q, for example, S&L depositors will tend to withdraw their savings and invest them instead in such things as U.S. Treasury bills.

There are two reasons to be concerned about the effects of tight money on the savings industry. First, there is the sheer question of instability. A severe cost-price squeeze or a massive disintermediation conceivably could result in widespread bankruptcies throughout the industry. The social and political, as well as economic, implications of such a catastrophe are patent. Second, even in the absence of such severe consequences, many people hold that the effects of tight money on the savings industry are highly undesirable because the savings industry is so intimately connected to the construction industry, especially the construction of housing. S&Ls and insurance companies hold large quantities of home mortgages, and to the extent that these institutions find funds unavailable, the construction of new housing is slowed. Since practically everyone gives new housing high marks as a socially desirable goal, it is argued by advocates of easy money that the side effects of tight money are undesirable.

The Housing Industry   The inverse relationship between housing construction and monetary policy is well documented. One reason for this relationship has just been described, and a further analysis may be found in Chapter 21. Only one other point need be added: It is sometimes argued that although housing construction moves countercyclically, *on the average* it is not retarded by monetary policy. Thus, the argument runs, although it is true that housing construction will be depressed during tight money, it is equally true that it will be prosperous during easy money. Over the long run, therefore, housing suffers no harm from monetary policy. The difficulty with this argument is that it seems to assume that the credit cycle is regular, with tight and easy money periods of equal length. But, in recent years, at least, tight money has been more common than easy money.

State and Local Government Financing   The effect of monetary policy on state and local government expenditures was discussed in Chapter 21. The conclusion of that discussion was that although tight money apparently has a substantial effect on government borrowing, the effect on government spending is less pronounced. To the extent that tight money does depress spending in the public sector, many people find this policy very undesirable. Such people (usually on the political left) argue that the public sector of our society (not economy) is starved for capital. The needs of the public sector, they say, are urgent. We need more schools, hospitals, pollution control, recreational areas, and urban mass transportation, to name only a few. As with housing, tight money should not be permitted to subvert these goals. These people therefore advocate a policy of low interest rates and easy money.

Nonprice Credit Rationing   Some evidence exists to suggest that the effects of monetary policy are not limited to differences in the interest elasticities of *borrowers*. According to this view, *lenders* will choose among various potential borrowers and then make their choice effective by nonprice means. For example, a commercial bank might simply refuse to lend to someone even though that person was willing to pay the going rate of interest. When this occurs, it is known as *nonprice credit rationing* (or, more simply, credit rationing).

The outright refusal of a loan application is not the only way that credit can be rationed. There are many others. Lenders may shorten the requested maturity of the loan, for example, or require higher than normal collateral. Whatever form credit rationing may take, it inevitably appears as an arbitrary decision to the borrower. For this reason, many people feel that credit rationing discriminates against certain classes of borrowers. While the word "discriminate" is probably misleading[3] in this context, it is nevertheless widely used. In particular, it is commonly believed that during periods of tight money, lenders discriminate against small-business borrowers.

Studies made of bank lending practices during periods of tight money give mixed results on the issue of discrimination against small businesses. One early study,[4] based on an extensive Federal Reserve survey of bank lending practices in 1955 and 1957, concluded that small businesses were not discriminated against. A later study,[5] however, using the same data source but a different model, came to the opposite conclusion. The issue thus remains in doubt. To the extent that a consensus exists on the matter, it is that during periods of tight money, small businesses per se are probably not discriminated against but that less creditworthy businesses are.[6] In other words, when money is tight, lenders will raise their minimum standards for acceptable borrowers. And since small businesses tend, on the average, to be financially weaker than big businesses, the result is that a disproportionately high number of small businesses are denied loans.

If the preceding analysis is correct (and there is evidence to support it), then tight money probably does have an adverse effect on the growth of small business. Once again, the advocates of easy money charge that this runs contrary to socially desirable goals; that is, it is an explicit objective of the United States government —as exemplified in the Small Business Administration—to encourage small business.

Inflation versus Unemployment

A third argument used by advocates of easy money simply makes the value judgment that inflation is preferable to unemployment. This argument accepts the Phillips curve analysis (see Chapters 19 and 22) that full employment and price stability are mutually exclusive goals—we can have one or the other but not both. It is consequently necessary to choose between them. While acknowledging that inflation is bad, advocates of easy money maintain that widespread unemployment is even worse. Most people, they say, can somehow hedge against inflation. Contracts

---

[3]To *discriminate* is to base a decision on an irrelevant consideration, e.g., whether the loan applicant is male or female, black or white. But the nonprice rationing of loans probably is for the most part based on relevant (i.e., economic) considerations. For an elaboration of this point, see Manak C. Gupta, "Differential Effects of Tight Money: An Economic Rationale," *Journal of Finance,* September 1972, pp. 825–838.

[4]G. L. Bach and C. J. Huizenga, "The Differential Effects of Tight Money," *American Economic Review,* March 1961, pp. 52–80.

[5]William L. Silber and Murray E. Polakoff, "The Differential Effects of Tight Money: An Econometric Study," *Journal of Finance,* March 1970, pp. 83–97.

[6]See Gupta, loc. cit. See also Dudley G. Luckett, "Credit Standards and Tight Money," *Journal of Money, Credit and Banking,* November 1970, pp. 420–434.

(including wage contracts) can be written in such a manner that payments vary according to the price index. In this fashion, the social tensions created by inflation can be substantially eased if not eliminated altogether. Not so with unemployment. Widespread joblessness falls with particular severity on certain groups—the black, the young, the poor. Arbitrarily excluding these people from the promise of economic security enjoyed by other Americans puts a strain on the fabric of our society that can be neither compromised nor eliminated. If choose we must, say the easy money advocates, then let us choose full employment and inflation.

Since this viewpoint expresses (for the most part) a straightforward value judgment, not much can be said about it either pro or con. However, one point may be repeated from the discussion of the Phillips curve in Chapter 19: There is evidence to suggest that the Phillips curve is shifting outward. If this should prove to be the case, then the choice that must be made is not between given rates of unemployment and inflation, but between unemployment and an *accelerating* rate of inflation. This latter choice may be much more difficult to make.

Summary of the Easy Money Position

Advocates of easy money should not be thought of as inflationists in the sense that they believe a rising price level to be a desirable economic goal for its own sake. Instead, they feel that the social costs of achieving price level stability are too high. Tight money subverts so many other policy goals, they hold, that the game is not worth the candle. Easy money and mild inflation are the least of several social evils.

27-3 A MONETARY RULE

As mentioned previously, another alternative to the current system of discretionary monetary policy would be to establish a fixed rule for the behavior of the Federal Reserve. The proposal for a monetary rule dates back at least to the 1930s[7] and has a number of variants. Probably the best known of these is the rule proposed by Professor Milton Friedman. Friedman argues that the Federal Reserve should be instructed to expand the United States money supply by a fixed percentage every month. His definition of "money" is the M_2 definition (M_1 plus time deposits), and his proposed rate of increase is anywhere in the 3 to 5 percent range. However, neither of these empirical judgments is crucial to his proposal; that is, he does not object strenuously to a narrow M_1 definition of money or to some percentage increase outside the indicated range. The heart of Friedman's proposal lies in having a *constant* rate of increase in the money supply, however defined.

The case that Friedman makes for a fixed growth rate in the money supply can be classified generally into two categories: First, there is the positive advantage to be derived from it: namely, the economy would function better. Second, there is the negative advantage of preventing the Federal Reserve from making things worse.

[7]Henry Simons, "Rules Versus Authorities in Monetary Policy," *Journal of Political Economy,* February 1936, pp. 1–30.

Positive Advantages of a Monetary Rule

As a quantity theorist, Friedman is persuaded that fluctuations in the GNP are caused primarily by fluctuations in the growth rate of the money supply. It follows that if the money supply is made to move along a smooth growth path, then the GNP will tend to do the same. Friedman acknowledges that not all instability in the macroeconomy will be eliminated by his rule. Some will remain. But Friedman feels that the real sector of the economy is in the main stable, and that in the absence of monetary disturbances the business cycle would have only very shallow peaks and troughs.

A further advantage claimed by Friedman for a monetary rule is that it would tend to eliminate destabilizing expectations. As matters stand, he says, business people must cope, not only with the uncertainties of their own companies' affairs, but also with the uncertainties of general and erratic movements in the price level. A great deal of economic energy goes into trying to anticipate the future. Expectations about prices are formulated and acted upon, and when they are wrong, the economic consequences can be severe. With a constant growth rate in the money supply, at least this source of instability can be minimized. People engaged in business will not be forced into speculative activities.

It is primarily because of the beneficial effects of stable expectations that Friedman is not overly concerned with the specific percentage by which money grows. If the percentage of increase is set too high, then a *steady* rise in prices will result. But one can adjust to an anticipated inflation. Similarly, if the percentage is set too low, the economy will deflate at a constant rate. But again, as long as the fall in prices can be anticipated, no great harm will result. On the whole, Friedman believes that a constant price level is most desirable, but the really important thing is that the business community knows what to expect in the future.

A third positive benefit claimed for Friedman's monetary rule is that it would reduce the amount of government intervention in the economy. Federal Reserve officials would be relieved of their present need to make judgments about the ultimate goals of society and instead would be told to function merely as technicians in expanding the money supply. Friedman attaches a good deal of importance to limiting the role of government in the economy.

Negative Advantages of a Monetary Rule

But if the growth rate of money has a powerful influence on the GNP, would it not be best to use monetary policy to eliminate *all* instability in the economy? Friedman's answer to this question is pragmatic: In theory, he says, a discretionary monetary policy is to be preferred to a rule. But this is in theory. *In practice,* Federal Reserve officials are presented with conflicting goals, and their tendency is to switch from one goal to another according to shifting political circumstances. *In practice,* monetary policy takes effect only after a lag of variable and uncertain length and consequently may make the economy less rather than more stable. *In practice,* the historical record supports the view that the Federal Reserve has made and continues to make significant errors of judgment. Thus, Friedman's position is not that his rule would work perfectly, but only that it would work better than discretionary monetary policy. At a minimum, a rule would have the negative advantage of being less bad than what we have now. As Friedman has said:

> Like other academicians, I am accustomed to being met with the refrain, "It's all right in theory but it won't work in practice." Aside from the questionable logic of the remark in general, in this instance almost the reverse of what is intended is true. There is little to be said in theory for the rule that the money supply should grow at a constant rate. The case for it is entirely that it would work in practice. . . .[8]

Criticisms of a Monetary Rule

Most economists do not agree with Friedman's monetary rule proposal. There are many reasons for this: First and foremost, probably, is the Keynesian analysis of the macroeconomy, which views the real sector of the economy as inherently unstable. If this is the case, then a monetary rule would leave the economy helpless, i.e., unable to defend itself against the extremes of the business cycle. Boom and bust would be treated identically under Friedman's rule; the authorities would expand the money supply by the same percentage in either case. Friedman, of course, denies that major swings in the business cycle would occur if this rule were adopted. But this conclusion, his critics charge, rests on his analysis of the relationship between money and national income. And neither his theory nor his evidence is sufficiently strong to warrant our giving up monetary policy as a flexible tool of economic stabilization. The case for a causal link between changes in money and changes in income is far from proved.

Related to the preceding argument is the criticism that blind adherence to a fixed rule of monetary policy would leave the economy vulnerable to changes in velocity. A strict limit set on the growth rate of currency and demand deposits might encourage the substitution of near money assets in the public's financial portfolio, and to the extent that people make such substitutions, velocity will rise. If, for example, the public suddenly began using S&L savings deposits to satisfy its precautionary demand for money, then the velocity of money would rise.

The possibility of major swings in velocity creates, in turn, the possibility of major swings in the GNP even though the growth rate of the money supply does not change. This can be seen from the (static) equation of exchange:

$$MV = PT$$

Even if money M is constant, changes in velocity V can cause changes in national income PT. Moreover, a downward movement in velocity would lead to widespread unemployment if the price level is downward inflexible. (Recall that Keynesians generally argue that prices, especially wages, are very sticky in a downward direction.) Thus, a constant growth rate in the money supply, say Friedman's critics,

[8]Milton Friedman, *A Program for Monetary Stability,* Fordham University Press, New York, 1960, p. 98.

would not even eliminate the possibility of major economic disturbances arising in the monetary sector.

In summary, Friedman's monetary rule proposal is criticized on the basis that it would not necessarily lead to greater economic stability as he claims. Major destabilizing events could still occur in the real sector because of shifts in investment and in the monetary sector because of shifts in velocity. The main consequence of the rule, it is held, would be simply to tie the hands of the monetary authorities so that they could not do anything constructive about the ups and downs of the economy.

Beyond the somewhat technical criticisms of Friedman's proposal just discussed, his critics also charge that it is impractical for two reasons: The first of these is political. It seems extremely unlikely that the Federal Reserve will accept such a rule in the foreseeable future. And even if it did so, it is unlikely that it would be able to adhere to it for very long. Even a relatively mild inflation or recession would put the Fed under political pressure to "do something"—pressure it could not withstand for long.

The second charge of impracticality denies that the Federal Reserve has the technical ability to adhere to a rule. According to this criticism, the Federal Reserve does not have sufficient control over the money supply to ensure that it grows smoothly and steadily because the money supply is determined through the interactions of the banking system, the public, and the Federal Reserve. And while the Fed can dominate the money-creating process over a period of months, in the short run (a few weeks), its control over the money supply is a good deal less than perfect. The Federal Reserve could not, therefore, adhere to a rule of money supply growth even if it wanted to.

Friedman acknowledges that there is merit in this latter criticism. To answer it, he proposes some fundamental changes in the organization of the Fed—for example, the abolition of member bank discounting. But far more basic than these proposed changes is Friedman's acceptance of a proposal put forth in the 1930s for sweeping changes in the nature of commercial banking. This proposal is that commercial banks be required to maintain 100 percent cash reserves against their deposit liabilities. Such a change, if adopted, would eliminate commercial banking as we know it. Because it is so basic (one would be tempted to say *radical* if that word were not so often misused), an entire section will be devoted to this plan.

27-4 100 PERCENT RESERVE BANKING

In 1935 the economist Irving Fisher proposed a drastic change in the nature of American commercial banking.[9] The heart of Fisher's plan was to do away with fractional reserve banking and instead require banks to back their demand deposits with 100 percent cash reserves. In the spirit of the times, Fisher made this proposal

[9]Irving Fisher, *100% Money,* The Adelphi Company, New York, 1935. Laughlin Curry and Henry Simons made similar proposals at about the same time.

with the end view of stabilizing the banking system—to prevent future recurrences of the type that happened in 1933, when some 4,000 banks failed. The advent and subsequent success of the FDIC made Fisher's 100 percent banking plan (as it came to be called) generally moot for the purpose for which it was intended. But subsequent economists, most notably Milton Friedman,[10] have resurrected the plan for the purpose of giving the Federal Reserve absolute control over the money supply.

100 Percent Banking

How would such a plan work? The general idea is this: For all practical purposes, commercial banks as they now exist would be subdivided into two distinct institutions (although the two institutions might continue to occupy the same building). One institution would deal with demand deposits only and would be, in essence, a warehouse for money. People would bring money to it and receive (as now) a deposit against which they could write checks. Upon receipt of this money, the institution would either store the money in its own vault or in the district Federal Reserve Bank. The commercial bank would *not* be permitted to lend out any part of the money deposited with it. Instead, it would be required to maintain 100 percent cash reserves against all its demand deposits. The demand deposit aspect of banking would thus be reduced to storehouse and recordkeeping functions. It would accept deposits and clear and collect checks, nothing more.

The second institution into which banks would be subdivided would be lending institutions. These institutions would not obtain any funds from demand deposits. Instead, their source of funds for lending would be time deposits and sale of debt and equity to the general public. They would function very much like S&Ls and MSBs, except that their loan customers would contain a substantial proportion of businesses seeking short-term accommodation (i.e., traditional bank customers).

Advantages of 100 Percent Banking

The primary advantage of 100 percent banking is the one already indicated: It would give the Federal Reserve absolute control over the money supply. Recall that under the present system of fractional reserve banking, the money supply is determined in the short run by such nonpolicy variables as the currency/deposit ratio of the public and the excess reserve ratio of the banking system. Under 100 percent banking, neither these nor any other ratios would affect the size of the money supply. If the public decided to decrease its currency/deposit ratio, for example, deposits would increase and currency would decrease by equal amounts, leaving the money supply unchanged. Banks would not be able to create money. Similarly, banks would not be able to create money by decreasing their excess reserve ratio. Under 100 percent banking they would *have* no excess reserves.

Note that the 100 percent banking proposal virtually eliminates two of the Federal Reserve's three methods of monetary control. Variations in reserve requirements would be eliminated because reserve requirements (against demand deposits)

[10]Friedman, op. cit., pp. 65–71.

would be fixed at 100 percent. Borrowing from the Fed likewise would be eliminated because the deposit institution would never need liquidity and would not be permitted to lend. The sole remaining instrument of the Federal Reserve, open market operations, would be used by the Fed to control the money supply, and this control would be absolute. For each dollar of open market purchases made by the Fed, the country's money supply would rise by $1, neither more nor less.

Disadvantages of 100 Percent Banking

If 100 percent banking should be adopted, the present basis for the profitability of deposit banking would be eliminated. Currently, banks are profitable because when they accept, say, a $100 demand deposit, their excess reserves rise by about $80 or $90 and these excess reserves can then be lent at interest. Since this would be impossible under 100 percent banking, the presumption is that banks would have to impose high service charges on checking accounts. So high would these service charges be, indeed, that many people feel they would cause the public to substantially reduce its use of demand deposits. This would be a retrogression rather than progress, since demand deposits constitute a much more efficient payments system than currency. Friedman counters this criticism by suggesting that the Federal Reserve pay a subsidy to deposit banks in the form of interest on their reserves. But it is not clear that such a subsidy would be either understood or appreciated by the general public.

By far the main objection to 100 percent banking, however, lies in the sheer difficulty of getting from here to there. Banks do not now have 100 percent reserves or anything like it. To make an abrupt change would therefore require an outright gift of the needed reserves to the banking system. To move to 100 percent reserves gradually, e.g., by a secular rise in reserve requirements, would probably place a severe strain on the economy. Not only are commercial banks themselves a major United States industry, but their influence is felt in virtually all other parts of the economy. While it is doubtless true in principle that we should not forego permanent benefits because of transitional problems, many observers feel that the long-run benefits of 100 percent banking are not worth the short-run costs. Precise Federal Reserve control over the money supply, they argue, would not improve the stability of the economy sufficiently to be worth the trouble. Friedman, of course, disagrees.

Conclusion

The probability that 100 percent banking will be written into law is practically nil. Its immediate costs are too apparent and its ultimate benefits too hypothetical to give it widespread political support.

27-5 REVIEW QUESTIONS

1   Go back to the end of Chapter 19, and review the discussion of "rational expectations." If one accepts the concept of rational expectations, do you think he or she would also accept the concept of permanent easy money? Why or why not?

2   If a tight money policy depresses sectors of the economy that are considered socially desirable (such as new housing construction), how can one justify such a policy?
3   Give two advantages claimed for a monetary rule. Give two criticisms of such a rule.
4   If we had 100 percent banking, would the Federal Reserve have complete control over the (M_1) money supply? How?

28

The Lessons
of History

In Chapter 13 we discussed United States monetary history from the time of its beginning in our country to the time of the Great Depression. The purpose of that chapter was to show the necessity for the establishment of the Federal Reserve System and the FDIC. We now wish to pick up the thread of that discussion and unravel the skein of monetary policy down to the present. In doing so, however, the focus of attention necessarily shifts. As originally conceived, the purpose of both the Federal Reserve System and the FDIC was to defend the American economy against the severe financial disruptions that had plagued it—to put an end to the bank failures and financial panics of earlier years. The FDIC continues to perform this function. Indeed, it performs this function so well that it fades into the background of our monetary history, an unobtrusive servant of the community. The Federal Reserve System is different. Although the Fed continues to take its defensive role seriously, it has additionally been assigned the active duty of stabilizing the economy through monetary policy. And monetary policy is anything but unobtrusive. Decisions made by the Federal Reserve are the subject of continuous discussion, debate, and analysis. It is the historical record of these monetary policy decisions that is the focus of this chapter.

It seems to be a sort of rule for most people that the further back in history one goes, the less interesting are the details. Compensating for this, it also seems to be true that the lessons of history become sharper as the details fade. In most of what follows, we shall consequently try to avoid too many details and concentrate instead on the issues. Only in the last two sections, dealing with comparatively recent monetary policy, shall we refer to the mass of available data.

28-1 THE 1937–1938 RECESSION

In 1933, about 4,000 commercial banks in the United States suspended operations; in 1933, the Great Depression reached its bottom, unemployment being variously estimated at about 25 percent of the labor force; in 1933, the United States devalued the dollar from about $22 per ounce of gold to $35 per ounce; and in 1933, the Treasury embarked on an ambitious silver-purchase program designed ultimately to raise the price of silver. All these events had the effect of adding to the excess reserves of the commercial banking system. The large number of bank failures in 1933 meant that the weaker banks were being weeded out. Those that remained survived largely because of their strong position of liquidity, and the lesson was not lost on them. They wanted to preserve this liquidity, and one way to do so was to build their excess reserves. Additionally, the very low level of business activity meant that the demand for bank loans was practically nonexistent. This dearth of demand, coupled with the historically low levels of open market interest rates, made the opportunity cost of excess reserves virtually nil. The Treasury's silver-purchase program added to bank reserves. And, finally, the gold that flowed into the country following the devaluation of the dollar added huge amounts to bank reserves.

The excess reserves of the commercial banking system piled up. By 1935 they had (for member banks) reached the unprecedented figure of $3 billion. On the basis of the reserve requirements then in existence, this $3 billion was capable of adding $20 billion to the money supply, a huge amount by the standards of the time.

In 1935 the Federal Reserve system had no objection to this situation. The country lay in the throes of a massive depression, and the excess reserves simply had the effect of making money cheap. But in the following year, 1936, the Federal Reserve's index of industrial production rose by 12 points and wholesale prices began to advance. The economy appeared to be on the upswing, although unemployment remained high at about 14 percent. The possibility of economic recovery caused the Fed to view the banking system's excess reserves in a wholly different light. In a depression, excess reserves helped the recovery; but with the recovery actually under way, Federal Reserve officials began to see excess reserves as an inflationary threat. To remove this threat, the Federal Reserve hit upon the following scheme: It would use an increase in reserve requirements to soak up the excess reserves, thereby making its "credit policies more effective."

In July 1936, the Federal Reserve raised the reserve requirements for member banks. This rise still left approximately $1.5 billion in excess reserves, and a further increase in gold imports in the latter part of the year added another $0.5 billion to bank reserves, bringing excess reserves up to about $2 billion. This figure still seemed too high to the Fed, and so in January 1937, it announced that it was going to make two more increases in reserve requirements, the first to take effect in March and the second in May. The combined effect of these increases would be to place member bank reserve requirements at their legal ceiling. When the announcement was made, the Fed made it clear that the maneuver was not a move to a tight money policy, but was for the sole purpose of soaking up excess reserves. The announcement was made in January 1937. In February, the bond market broke, and interest rates rose sharply. In the second quarter of the year a recession set in—a recession within a depression. The turning point in the recession did not come until 1938, and it was not until 1940 that the economy recovered to its 1937 level.

The role of the Federal Reserve in *causing* the 1937–1938 recession remains a matter of some controversy among economic historians. Other things, especially a tighter fiscal policy, were occurring at the same time. Some historians blame these other events, while some blame the Federal Reserve. All are agreed, however, that the Fed's decision to raise reserve requirements precipitated the relatively high interest rates in early 1937. For in making this decision, the Federal Reserve had overlooked two very important elements in the situation: First, the excess reserves were distributed unevenly throughout the banking system. Although some banks might have been able to contemplate the higher requirements with complacency, other banks were forced to sell earning assets in order to meet the proposed new standards, and it was to some extent the sale of these securities that caused the bond market to break.

Beyond this (and probably more important) was the *attitude* with which most banks regarded their excess reserves. These reserves were excess only in the sense that they were not legally required; they were not excess in the sense that the banks thought of them as superfluous. On the contrary, in 1937 banks had just survived the worst banking crisis in history. Times continued to be unsettled, and the banks had a very strong demand for excess reserves, i.e., reserves that were available for use and not legally encumbered. When the Fed raised reserve requirements, therefore, banks sold securities to try to maintain their *excess* reserve position. As a result, the market broke and, at the least, the economic situation was worsened.

Lesson   Excess reserves and superfluous reserves are not the same thing.

28-2   THE "PEGGING" EPISODE: 1941–1951

By 1941 interest rates had fallen to extremely low levels. Difficult as it may be for us to imagine today, the yield on Treasury bills was less than ½ percent, and on long-term government bonds it was only slightly above 2 percent. When the United States entered World War II in December 1941, the Treasury decided it wanted to keep things this way. The Treasury knew that this war, like other wars before it, would be financed in large part by a huge increase in the public debt. And, like all borrowers, the Treasury wanted to be accommodated at low rates of interest. With the Federal Reserve's willing acquiescence (and, indeed, leadership[1]), a monetary policy was therefore adopted to maintain the low, prewar, depression interest rates throughout the wartime period. This monetary policy was accomplished by having the Federal Reserve "peg"[2] the government securities market.

The Federal Reserve's pegging policy was accomplished very simply: The Federal Reserve agreed to buy an unlimited amount of government securities at fixed prices in the open market. Since the Fed was willing to buy the securities in any amount offered, it was in effect establishing a support price, i.e., a price below which the securities could not fall. But, as we have seen, there is an inverse relationship between bond prices and yields. Consequently, if prices cannot go down, yields cannot go up: A floor under the prices meant a ceiling over the interest rates.

The Federal Reserve pursued its policy of pegging interest rates throughout World War II (1941–1945) with considerable success. Interest rates remained low, virtually frozen at their prewar levels. But while the policy of financing the wartime expansion of public debt cheaply was successful, another policy was sacrificed to accomplish it: monetary policy. Consider. When the Federal Reserve buys government securities, bank reserves rise. These are open market operations and, as we have seen, are the primary method used by the Fed to control the money supply. If, then, the Federal Reserve agrees to buy unlimited amounts of securities at fixed prices, it loses control over its open market operations. And in losing control over open market operations, it loses control over the money supply and hence over monetary policy. As one historian of the period stated: "The Federal Reserve became in effect a slot machine that would always pay off; anyone could insert into it an unwanted government obligation and receive in return an amount of money equal to the support price."[3]

The Federal Reserve's sacrifice of monetary policy at the altar of wartime finance was not immediately harmful. Throughout the war years, price controls and consumer rationing were in force so that the inflationary effects of the expansion of the money supply were largely suppressed. But shortly after the war, all government controls were removed. In 1946 prices began moving upward very rapidly and continued to do so until a recession intervened in 1948. The classic response of the central bank during a period of severe inflation is to pursue a tight money policy, but the Federal Reserve did not do this. Instead, it continued to hold to its wartime policy of pegging interest rates at low levels (although some minor adjustments in the rate structure were made). Indeed, it was not until a fresh outbreak of inflation occurred as a side effect of the Korean War that the Federal Reserve finally abandoned its pegging policy in March 1951.

[1]Elmus R. Wicker, "The World War II Policy of Fixing a Pattern of Interest Rates," *Journal of Finance,* June 1969, pp. 447–458.

[2]"Pegging" is something of a misnomer. A true peg would have prevented rates from falling as well as rising, whereas the Fed's policy was only to keep them from rising. By weight of custom, however, we shall use the word "peg."

[3]Lester V. Chandler, *Inflation in the United States, 1940–1948,* Harper & Brothers, New York, 1951, pp. 191–192.

The willingness of the Federal Reserve to peg the government securities market during the war years is understandable. During a war, all policies become subordinated to the single goal of winning, and monetary policy is no exception. But the willingness of the Federal Reserve to continue its pegging policy throughout the five years after the war is puzzling. It can be explained in part by the widespread fear, shared by the Federal Reserve, that the economy would collapse back into its prewar depression state after the war was over. Perhaps a more basic explanation, however, is that by the end of the war the Fed had become so accustomed to being dominated by the U.S. Treasury that it took five years for it to reassert its independence. Whatever the cause, the effect was that the Federal Reserve contributed materially to the postwar inflation.

Lesson   Controlling interest rates is a Keynesian policy. Controlling the money supply is a monetarist policy. Pegging the government bond market is no policy at all.

28-3   BILLS ONLY: 1953–1961

Shortly after the Federal Reserve removed its peg from the government securities market in 1951, it became concerned about the behavior of the government securities market. This market had led a very sheltered life during the ten years of the pegging episode, and it was not clear how well it would cope with its new-found freedom. As a consequence, the Federal Open Market Committee set up a special subcommittee to study the situation. This subcommittee came to the conclusion that the government securities market was indeed in poor health. Furthermore, the subcommittee said, the appropriate cure was for the Federal Reserve to confine its open market activities to trading only in short-term Treasury bills; stated negatively, the Fed was *not* to trade in long-term bonds (except to prevent market panics). This recommendation was accepted by the Federal Reserve in 1953, and subsequently became known as its *bills only policy.*

The analysis of the subcommittee ran as follows: The government bond market, it said, lacked "depth, breadth, and resiliency." A market with *depth* is one in which there is a substantial volume of buy and sell orders immediately below and above the existing market price. A slight movement in price will then cause these orders to be placed so that the price moves in a slow and orderly manner. (The opposite of a *deep* market is a *thin* market, a term that may be familiar to the reader.) By *breadth* the subcommittee meant a wide variety of market participants, and by *resiliency* it meant an ability for the market to recover from its ups and downs.

The reason for this lack of depth, breadth, and resiliency, the subcommittee charged, was that the Fed was conducting its open market operations in long-term bonds as well as short-term bills. Since the Fed was not a profit-maximizing institution, its buying and selling activities were viewed by the market as unpredictable and therefore erratic. In the short-term market this made little difference since prices of short-term securities move over a very narrow range in any case. But in the long-term market price movements are substantial (see Chapter 7 for an explanation). Government securities dealers, in particular, therefore faced the possibility of taking major losses on their inventories of long-term bonds because of Fed intervention in this market. The dealers were consequently backing away from the long-term market. They were behaving more like brokers than dealers; that is, they were matching buy and sell orders but were not taking a position in the market themselves.

If the subcommittee's analysis was correct, then a substantial improvement in the government bond market could be accomplished by keeping the Fed out of it. For if the Fed confined its open market operations to short-term bills, then its "erratic" influence on the bond market would be eliminated. The Federal Reserve accepted both the subcommittee's analysis and its recommendation. In 1953 it adopted the *bills only* policy for the conduct of open market operations.

The bills only policy had a number of critics (many of whom were inside the System itself). The critics complained, first, that the Federal Reserve was entirely too concerned with the welfare of the government securities dealers (a complaint that may still be heard today). But much more basic than this was the complaint that the Fed had voluntarily given up an important part of monetary policy. Recall that in the traditional Keynesian theory of the macroeconomy it is the *long-term* rate of interest that constitutes the transmission mechanism linking the monetary and real sectors. By dealing only in Treasury bills, critics charged, the Federal Reserve was giving up whatever direct influence it might have over long-term rates. True, they said, the Fed could still cause the short-term rate to change, and this, in turn, would cause long-term rates to change. But the responsiveness of long-term to short-term interest rates is not precise and consistent; a given change in the bill rate may be associated with various changes in the bond rate. Thus, in adopting the bills only policy, the Fed had agreed to try to stabilize the economy with one hand tied behind its back.

Finally, studies made after the bills only policy had been in effect for several years failed to uncover any evidence that it had improved the performance of the government securities market. Neither depth, nor breadth, nor resiliency, insofar as those concepts can be measured, had increased.[4] Nevertheless, the Federal Reserve did not abandon the bills only policy until 1961, seven years after it first went into effect. And when the policy *was* abandoned, it was not because of the arguments raised by its critics nor even because it had apparently failed to improve the government securities market. It was abandoned because the Fed decided to adopt another controversial policy that was wholly incompatible with bills only. The new policy was called *operation twist* and is described in the following section.

Lesson   Giving up a lot to get very little happens to sophisticated people, too.

28-4   OPERATION TWIST: 1961–1965

In 1959 and 1960 the performance of the economy left a great deal to be desired. Unemployment rose above 5 percent of the labor force and remained there until 1965. The growth rate of real GNP was sluggish. People began talking about

---

[4]Dudley G. Luckett, " 'Bills Only': A Critical Appraisal," *Review of Economics and Statistics,* August 1960, pp. 301–306.

"economic stagnation" as they had in the 1930s. In the presidential election of 1960 one of the slogans adopted by John F. Kennedy was "We must get this country moving again." These concerns about the growth rate of the economy, of course, had implications for the conduct of monetary policy. For, as we have seen, monetary policy can stimulate investment expenditures by making interest rates low, and a higher rate of investment means a higher rate of economic growth. If monetary policy was to do its part in getting "the country moving again," therefore, the indicated policy was one of cheap money.

But by 1960 another economic problem had also surfaced: the balance of payments deficit.[5] Although the United States had been running a deficit in its international sector for several years, this deficit was not taken seriously at first. Indeed, in the mid-1950s it was considered by many to be a good thing. The world economy, many held, was starved for additional liquidity, and a United States payments deficit would provide the needed dollar and gold reserves for other nations. Besides, many people at first refused to accept our deficit as persistent, arguing instead that it was transient and would be reversed in short order. By 1960, however, people expressing both these viewpoints had lost much of their credibility. It was becoming increasingly apparent that the United States payments deficit was not reversing itself, and that gold reserves were dwindling at an alarming rate. Officials of the Federal Reserve became more and more concerned over the balance of payments deficit.

The appropriate monetary policy for a deficit country to follow is tight money. As indicated in Chapter 25, short-term capital tends to move to those financial centers having the highest interest rates. Therefore, if the Federal Reserve could have raised interest rates in the United States, enough short-term capital might have been attracted to ease the payments deficit markedly. But this threw the Fed into a dilemma: The goal of balance of payments equilibrium required tight money and high interest rates, but the goal of economic growth required easy money and low interest rates. It was a policy conflict. For interest rates clearly could not be both high and low at the same time.

Or could they? Someone in the Federal Reserve had a bright idea. The reasoning went like this: Insofar as economic growth is concerned, it is *long-term* interest rates that are important. That is, it is the long-term rate of interest that is the critical policy variable in the investment decisions of business people. But insofar as the balance of payments deficit is concerned, it is *short-term* interest rates that attract short-term capital from one country to another. Might it not be possible, therefore, for the Fed to have its cake and eat it too by raising short-term interest rates while keeping long-term interest rates low? The Fed decided to try it. Because such a policy involved reshaping, or *twisting,* the term structure of interest rates, it became known as *operation twist.*

Operation twist involved both the Federal Reserve and the Treasury. For its part, the Federal Reserve was to conduct "swaps" in its open market operations. To

---

[5]Recall that at this time the United States (and also the rest of the world) was on a fixed exchange rate system. Thus the problem was a true payments deficit, not a decline in the foreign exchange value of the dollar.

explain, suppose the Fed were to simultaneously buy long-term government securities and sell short-term Treasury bills. The effect of these two actions on bank reserves would cancel out; that is, the Fed would be selling exactly as much as it was buying. But the sale of short-term securities would presumably raise short-term interest rates while the purchase of long-term bonds would keep their rates from rising. The role of the Treasury was approximately the same. In its debt management operations the Treasury was to concentrate its efforts in marketing short-term securities, thereby increasing their supply, lowering their price, and raising their interest rates.

One point about operation twist should be immediately apparent: It was wholly incompatible with the Federal Reserve's bills only policy because the Fed could not engage in open market swaps while at the same time staying out of the long-term bond market. Accordingly, in 1960 the Federal Reserve began buying securities with maturities of up to fifteen months. Then, in early 1961 the Fed announced that it was "purchasing in the open market U.S. government bonds and notes of varying maturities, some of which will exceed five years." This statement marked the death knell of the bills only policy and the birth of operation twist.

Operation twist continued as Federal Reserve policy until about 1965. By that year the growing escalation of the war in Vietnam had put the United States economy under sufficient inflationary pressure that the policy conflict of the Fed was resolved. The inflation called for tight money, and so did the balance of payments deficit. All systems were go, and the Fed began its tight money policy that led eventually to the famous credit "crunch" of 1966.

But what about operation twist? Was it successful? This question can be subdivided into two other questions: Did operation twist actually change the relationship between short-term and long-term interest rates? and, Did operation twist succeed in reconciling the conflicting goals of economic growth and balance of payments equilibrium? The studies that have been made of the first question suggest that operation twist probably did have some effect on the structure of interest rates, but that this effect was very slight.[6] However, this conclusion should not be confused with the notion that operation twist was doomed to failure, i.e., that the Fed *could* not twist the yield curve. For, after all, the Fed had successfully maintained a given pattern of interest rates for ten years during the 1941–1951 pegging episode. Instead, the very slight impact of operation twist probably reflects an underestimate by the Federal Reserve of the amount of open market intervention necessary to the successful achievement of its goal. Additionally, the Treasury's commitment to operation twist was a good deal less than total. The limited swaps of the Fed were offset, to some extent at least, by the Treasury's issuance of long-term bonds.

Since the Federal Reserve did not change the yield curve much, the answer to the second question remains in doubt. Certainly the two goals of economic growth and balance of payments equilibrium were not reconciled during the 1961–1965

[6]See Franco Modigliani and Richard Sutch, "Innovations in Interest Rate Policy," *American Economic Review*, May 1965, pp. 178–197.

period. Moreover, one research study,[7] based on previous empirical estimates, concludes that they could not have been reconciled even had operation twist been successful. The thrust of this study is that international capital flows are responsive to *long-term* as well as short-term interest rates and that domestic investment is responsive to *short-term* as well as long-term interest rates. Consequently, the *net* effect of raising short-term rates relative to long-term rates would have been negligible.

Lesson   To achieve two independent goals, it is necessary to have two independent policy variables. It is by no means clear whether long-term and short-term interest rates are two policy variables or one.

28-5   CREDIT CRUNCHES: 1966 AND 1969

In the early months of 1966 the American economy went into "boom" conditions. The expenditures associated with Vietnam caused an increase of $10 billion over 1965 in the defense budget. Other federal government expenditures and state and local spending also expanded. In the private sector, both business investment and consumer spending were major expansionary forces. As a result of these factors, the economy moved upward sharply. Unemployment fell below 4 percent for the first time in ten years; the Federal Reserve's index of industrial production rose by about 9 percent; and the GNP (measured in current dollars) increased by about 8½ percent to some $740 billion. In short, the economy was booming. But the boom carried with it its own set of problems. Along with the rise in everything else, prices began to move upward. Prices of consumer goods rose by 3.3 percent, as compared with an annual average rate of increase of 1½ percent in 1961–1964 and 2 percent in 1965. Thus, between 1964 and 1966 the economy moved from what many felt was a period of stagnation to a period of prosperity and beyond—inflation.

Responding to these inflationary pressures, in December 1965, the Federal Reserve raised its discount rate from 4 to 4½ percent. And in February 1966, the Fed really began to put the brakes on. Nonborrowed reserves of member banks—total reserves less member bank borrowings—rose very slowly between February and June. At the same time, the conditions of high prosperity in the economy at large put the banking system under extraordinary loan pressure. Banks responded by increasing their borrowings at the Fed, and interest rates moved up.

The tight money policy reached its peak during the summer months of 1966. Big banks in particular found themselves facing exceptionally large increases in the demand for business loans, but the Fed continued to restrain the flow of unborrowed reserves into the banking system. Caught thus between the loan demands of their customers and the tight money policy of the Fed, the banks scrambled for additional funds. Member bank borrowings from the Fed rose to more than $700 million. Active use was made of the federal funds market, and the rate on these funds rose

---

[7]Myron H. Ross, " 'Operation Twist': A Mistaken Policy?" *Journal of Political Economy*, April 1966, pp. 195–199.

to 6 percent, well above the discount rate. Many banks dumped their federal, state, and local government securities at substantial losses in order to accommodate loan customers. Some of the very large banks borrowed in the Eurodollar market at rates exceeding 7 percent. Money was very tight indeed.

However, the summer months of 1966 are noteworthy for more than just being a period of very restrictive monetary policy. Of particular interest are the interrelationships that developed among bank-issued negotiable certificates of deposit (CDs), Regulation Q, and nonbank financial intermediaries. Negotiable CDs, it will be recalled, are a money market instrument developed by commercial banks in the early 1960s. Because CDs are based on bank time deposits, they were at that time subject to Regulation Q, the regulation by which the Federal Reserve places a ceiling on the interest rate banks may pay on time deposits. In December 1965, the Federal Reserve raised this ceiling rate to 5½ percent. It was thought at the time that this ceiling would give banks adequate room to compete for funds in the face of rising rates on open market debt instruments. And so it did—temporarily. But by the middle of the summer in 1966, interest rates on short-term, open market paper had risen sufficiently that the 5½ percent ceiling became binding. Banks increasingly experienced difficulty in marketing new issues of CDs as former buyers began switching to higher-yielding Treasury bills, commercial paper, and the like. The commercial banks pleaded with the Fed to set a new, higher ceiling on time deposits, but in vain. In fact, the Fed did just the opposite. It *lowered* the ceiling rate on time deposits of less than $100,000 to 5 percent; additionally, it raised reserve requirements on time deposits exceeding $5 million from 4 to 6 percent.

Why did the Federal Reserve do this? Because it had a problem, and at the heart of the problem lay the nation's savings industry. As we discussed previously, a substantial part of the nation's savings are channeled into the three main types of financial intermediaries: S&Ls, mutual savings banks (MSBs), and life insurance companies. By the spring and summer months of 1966, these institutions were faced with a very serious problem of *disintermediation*. Hardest hit were the S&Ls. As open market interest rates rose above the ceiling rates these institutions were permitted to pay on their deposits, sophisticated depositors began switching from S&L deposits to other kinds of debt instruments, most notably bank-issued CDs. The net inflow of funds to S&Ls dropped sharply during 1966, and, during the four months of January, April, July, and October, they actually experienced net *outflows*. Disintermediation also occurred at MSBs, though less severely. And, as explained in Chapter 27, life insurance companies experienced a substantial rise in their policy loans, which reduced their *net* inflow of funds.

The process of disintermediation that occurred in the summer of 1966 caused widespread concern about the stability of the savings industry. But the concern went beyond even this. For S&Ls, MSBs, and life insurance companies are major investors in residential mortgages, and because the flow of funds into such mortgages was severely curtailed, the construction of new houses went into a slump. In the year preceding October 1966, new housing construction fell by some 40 percent. As can be imagined, this situation was vociferously protested by the construction industry, Congress, and prospective home buyers.

Regulatory officials were very much aware of these developments. But while the problem was clear, the solution was murky. One possibility was for the Federal Home Loan Bank Board to raise ceiling rates on S&L deposits, but it was felt that if this were done, the S&Ls would be caught in an impossible price-cost squeeze, or "crunch." When interest rates paid on deposits rise, they rise for *all* deposits; but when mortgage rates rise, they rise only on *new* mortgages. To raise S&L ceiling deposit rates, therefore, would have sent S&L costs soaring while their income moved upward at a much slower pace. Thus, it was judged that raising S&L ceilings would be as great a threat to the stability of the S&L industry as was disintermediation.

Given that the S&L deposit rate ceiling could not be raised, the Fed could not raise the ceiling rate applicable to commercial bank CDs. To do so would almost certainly have resulted in commercial banks bidding funds away from the savings industry, thereby making the process of disintermediation much worse. Additionally, the primary concern of the Fed continued to be the inflationary pressures in the economy, and the last thing it wanted was to give banks additional capacity for lending to businesses.

Caught on the horns of this dilemma, the Federal Reserve attempted a series of selective controls. As indicated, the ceiling rate on small time deposits (less than $100,000) was lowered from 5½ to 5 percent. The purpose of so doing was to make the banks weaker competitors for small savings accounts, thereby strengthening the competitive position of S&Ls and MSBs. The 5½ percent ceiling rate on large CDs, while not lowered, was not raised. What was raised was the reserve requirement against time deposits—from 4 to 6 percent. This had the effect of making funds acquired through the sale of CDs more expensive for banks. Whereas before banks could relend $96 for every $100 of CDs they sold, now they could lend only $94. Finally, the Federal Reserve attempted to use moral suasion to discourage banks from lending to businesses. On September 1, 1966, they sent a letter to all member banks admonishing them to slow down their expansion of business loans.

In the autumn of 1966 the situation abruptly reversed. Slack began to appear in the economy, largely owing to the decline in residential construction and a sharp drop in business spending for inventory accumulation. In October the Fed decided to move no further toward restraint, and in December monetary policy was shifted in the direction of ease.

The economic events of 1969 are in many ways similar to those of 1966 and therefore will not be described in detail. In June 1968, the Congress had finally taken measures designed to make fiscal policy more restrictive. Federal expenditures were cut by about $6 billion, and a 10 percent surtax was levied on personal and corporate income taxes. It was hoped that these measures would cause more of the burden of the fight against inflation to be borne by fiscal policy, thereby easing somewhat the share that monetary policy was required to carry. The general idea was that a restrictive fiscal policy would reduce demand while an easy money policy would stimulate production (supply). The combination of the two was supposed to check the upward thrust of prices without causing a recession. For a variety of reasons (which continue to be debated), it didn't work that way. By December 1968, it was clear that prices were continuing their rise at an unabated pace. Additionally, the balance of payments position of the United States was deteriorating rapidly. Faced with both these problems, the Federal Reserve adopted a tight money policy.

By virtually any indicator one cares to use, monetary policy throughout 1969 was extremely tight. The M_1 money supply rose only slightly, while the M_2 money supply actually declined by year end. Interest rates rose to such heights that it was necessary to go back more than a century to find precedents. Free reserves (excess reserves less member bank borrowings) fell, at one point, to less than –$1.1 billion. At the same time, banks were inundated with loan requests, and, as in 1966, banks scrambled for funds. They borrowed in the federal funds and Eurodollar markets; they borrowed from the Fed; and they dumped their holdings of open market securities.

Again, as in 1966, the process of disintermediation began. Net inflows of funds to savings intermediaries were sharply reduced. Banks found CDs difficult to sell at the prevailing ceiling rates, and the outstanding volume of CDs fell drastically. These events reduced the funds available in the mortgage market, and once more the residential construction industry found itself depressed while the rest of the economy was booming. Although the Federal Home Loan Bank Board attempted to intermediate by borrowing in the capital markets and expanding its advances to S&Ls, its efforts in this direction were insufficient.

In mid-February 1970, the Federal Reserve adopted a less restrictive policy. But it did so with mixed emotions. Industrial production was down, real GNP was not rising, and unemployment was up. But there was no sign of a halt in inflation, and the balance of payments situation was getting progressively worse.

Lesson   The 1966 and 1969 crunches illuminate a number of aspects of monetary policy. One of these is that Regulation Q can be used as a selective credit control weapon. But following close on the heels of this lesson is the further observation that regulation begets regulation: If it had not been for the existence of Regulation Q in the first place, then it is at least arguable that there would have been no need for a selective control. And a final thought: It seems clear that residential construction is highly sensitive to tight money. But if we then take measures to protect this industry from the adverse effects of tight money, are we not by the same token reducing the ability of monetary policy to stabilize the economy?

28-6   INTERNATIONAL CRISES: 1971 AND 1973

The first few years of the decade of the 1970s were years of extraordinary economic events. The United States economy seemed to lurch from one crisis to another. During the four years 1971–1974, we experienced a fundamental change in the international payments system from fixed to floating exchange rates; double-digit inflation; the worst recession since World War II; severe shortages of basic materials, especially petroleum; and a period of comprehensive wage and price controls. Even in "normal" times, the conduct of monetary policy is not easy; in times of such turbulence as these, it is exceptionally difficult. In this section we shall examine the international financial developments of those years, which eventually culminated in the most fundamental change in the international payments mechanism of the past 200 years—the system of floating exchange rates.

Events Prior to 1971

In the mid-1950s, the United States began running an almost continuous deficit in its balance of payments. This deficit, which was not at first alarming, became cause for considerable official concern by the mid-1960s. At that time the deficit was averaging about $2 to $3 billion annually and our gold stock and other international reserves were steadily dwindling. Analysis showed that the cause of the deficit was due primarily to capital movements; our merchandise balance was in surplus by about $5 billion during most of this time.

To stem the capital outflow, in 1964 the United States instituted the interest equalization tax, a type of exchange control designed to deal with capital account items. This control (since discontinued) had the effect of imposing a tax on the purchase of foreign securities by United States citizens. In 1967, the Federal Reserve System began the Voluntary Foreign Credit Restraint Program, which restrained the foreign lending engaged in by United States banks and other financial institutions —again, a form of exchange control. But these measures were not enough to correct our payments deficit. In April 1968, gold sales to support the price of gold in the private market became excessive and the United States, along with six other countries, moved to the two-tier gold-price system. This system meant that the central banks of these countries would thereafter neither buy nor sell gold in the private market but would trade in gold only with each other. Thus there would be two prices for gold: the *official* and the *private*.

The Crisis of 1971

The United States balance of trade moved from its traditional surplus to a deficit position in the late 1960s. Capital flowed out of the country, especially to West Germany, and by early 1971 a sense of impending crisis began to prevail. Interest rate differentials between the United States and other countries widened, capital outflows continued, and most European currencies were forced hard against the ceiling of the 2 percent band permitted by the IMF rules of the time. Speculative hot money moved especially into marks in anticipation of a revaluation (the opposite of a devaluation) by the German authorities. On May 5, 1971, the Bundesbank bought $1 billion in the first forty minutes of trading and then withdrew from the market. Their efforts to support the ceiling mark-dollar rate had been defeated by the speculators.

The inability of the German central bank to support the dollar in the face of heavy speculative trading touched off an entire series of events in the foreign exchange markets over the next several weeks. The German mark and the Dutch guilder were floated, and the Swiss franc and the Austrian shilling were revalued. The international monetary system was in general disarray. In the week ending August 14, 1971, speculative trading against the dollar became extremely heavy. On August 15, a Sunday, President Nixon announced Phase I of his new economic program, which was designed to check inflationary pressures in the United States and bring the foreign exchanges back under control. Domestically, wages and prices were frozen for a ninety-day period. Internationally, a 10 percent surcharge was put on dutiable imports into the United States (an exchange control), and it was announced that the United States would be no longer convert dollars to gold even for foreign central banks.

The measures taken by the President seemed to have little influence in stabilizing the international payments system, however. Indeed, between August and December 1971, things got progressively worse. Virtually all nations, while continuing to adhere officially to the pre-August 15 parities among currencies, said they would no longer accept the upper limits of the IMF's 2 percent band. France moved to a two-market system in which there was a *commercial* and a *financial* market for currencies. Japan, after a valiant effort, found it could no longer hold to the official exchange rate with the dollar. To make matters worse, there was an increasing tendency for nations to adopt exchange controls of one type or another. These generally chaotic conditions raised the spectre of a worldwide recession, and fragmentation of the world economy into restrictive currency blocs. Minor political irritants became abrasive.

It was in this general atmosphere that representatives of the so-called Group of Ten[8] industrial nations met in December 1971. What emerged from this meeting was the Smithsonian Agreement, which was hailed by President Nixon as the "most significant monetary agreement in the history of the world." The Smithsonian Agreement contained three major provisions: First, the United States agreed to drop the 10 percent surcharge on imports imposed the previous August. Second, the IMF band was widened from the original 2 to 4½ percent. But by far the most significant aspect of the Agreement was the complete realignment of official currency parities. The official value of the dollar in terms of gold was changed from $35 per ounce to $38 per ounce, a devaluation of almost 10 percent. The Swiss franc, Swedish krona, and Italian lira were also devalued, but not by so much. The British pound sterling and French franc were held at their old parities, which meant they were revalued with respect to the dollar. And, finally, the German mark, Dutch guilder, Japanese yen, and Belgian franc were revalued with respect to their previous parities.

In retrospect, considering what was to occur not much more than a year later, it is easy to be derisive about the "most significant monetary agreement in the history of the world." No doubt the President's speech writers did exaggerate. But it is nevertheless true that the currency realignments of the Smithsonian Agreement were historically unique, representing a degree of monetary cooperation among sovereign nations never before achieved.

The Crisis of 1973

The short-lived nature of the rate structure set by the Smithsonian Agreement illustrates very well the difficulties inherent in trying to establish equilibrium prices

---

[8]The United States, Switzerland, Sweden, Italy, West Germany, Japan, The Netherlands, Belgium, The United Kingdom, France.

by governmental decree. In May 1972, the European Community countries decided to hold their currencies to a 2¼ percent band relative to one another while maintaining the 4½ percent band relative to the rest of the world. It was a band within a band—a "snake in a tunnel," as it was called in the market. In June 1972 a speculative run on the pound forced the British to abandon their agreement at the Smithsonian and with the other European Community countries: The pound was floated. This, together with a very large Japanese payments surplus and United States deficit in the fall of 1972, kept the market uneasy for the rest of the year. Rumors were rampant that the Smithsonian parities could not be maintained.

In January 1973, something happened that seemed like a small thing. The Italian government decided to move the lira, not a particularly critical currency, to a two-market system. Because of the close financial connections between Italy and Switzerland, however, the Italian move put pressure on the Swiss franc and the Swiss authorities permitted the franc to rise above the Smithsonian ceiling rate. Speculators quickly came to the conclusion that the same thing would happen to other currencies, especially the German mark. By February 12 and 13 speculation against the dollar had grown so heavy that the European and Japanese exchange markets were closed; the Germans alone had bought about $6 billion in an effort to maintain the dollar-mark ceiling.

On February 12, 1973 (a Monday), President Nixon announced that the dollar was being unilaterally devalued from a central value of $38 to $42.22, that is, by about 11 percent. Simultaneously, the Japanese announced they were floating the yen, and the Italians that they were floating the lira. It was hoped that these measures would be sufficient to stem the speculative tide, but they weren't. By March 1 there was once more a massive speculative movement against the dollar, and the dollar fell to its (new) floor. On March 11, 1973, several European countries—Germany, France, The Netherlands, Belgium, Denmark, and (later) Norway and Sweden— went on a *joint float* system, which meant that they would maintain a 2¼ percent band among their own bloc of currencies but would float this bloc against the dollar. The Japanese yen, Swiss franc, Italian lira, Canadian dollar, and British pound continued to float independently. For all practical purposes, the world had moved to a floating exchange rate system.

Lesson Many economists—probably most—believe that a system of floating exchange rates is superior to a system of fixed exchange rates. Perhaps someday we shall learn to discard old systems and adopt new ones without going through the trauma of economic crises.

28-7 RECESSION WITH INFLATION: 1971–1974

As indicated in section 28-5, the credit crunch of 1969 was terminated by the slowdown in economic activity in 1970. Real GNP moved sideways in the fourth quarter of 1969 and then sagged by about 1 percent in the first quarter of 1970. Unemployment rose from about 4 percent at the beginning of the year to 6 percent by May. Notwithstanding the deteriorating industrial situation, however, prices continued their upward climb, and the balance of payments situation remained bad. The Federal Reserve was thus on the horns of a dilemma during the first few weeks of 1970. A liberal monetary policy would help unemployment and production but worsen the inflation and balance of payments deficit; a tight money policy would do the reverse. The Fed consequently vacillated until about mid-February, and then moved in the direction of greater ease. Throughout the remainder of the year, the Federal Reserve supplied substantial reserves to the banking system via its open market purchases.

1971

The first few months of 1971 continued very much like 1970: easy money, unemployment, and inflation. Added to these economic woes was the balance of payments crisis. The Federal Reserve's dilemma refused to go away: Whichever way it moved, the Fed would worsen some aspect of the economic situation. Given this paralysis of policy conflicts, the Nixon Administration decided on a new strategy: wage and price controls.

On August 15, 1971 (a Sunday), President Nixon announced Phase I of his new economic policy. The international aspects of this policy—the surcharge on imports and suspension of the convertibility of the dollar—have been described. Domestically, the President used his authority to put a ninety-day freeze on wages and prices and proposed a reduction in taxes. Conceptually, the plan was straightforward. Fiscal policy was to be used to bring the unemployment rate down while direct controls were to be used to keep prices from rising as this was happening. After ninety days, the President said, the Phase I freeze would be replaced by Phase II, an indefinite period of flexible price controls. In this manner, the apparently conflicting goals of full employment and price stability were to be reconciled.

What role monetary policy was expected to play in the new economic policy was not clear, but the role it *did* play was to reinforce fiscal policy. With prices held in check (temporarily) by Phase I, the Federal Reserve continued its expansionary policies throughout the remainder of the year.

1972

In retrospect (with the aid of 20-20 hindsight vision), 1972 was a crucial year for monetary policy. But this is in retrospect. At the time, things seemed to be going rather well. Measured by most indicators, 1972 was a good year for the American economy. Real output of goods and services (GNP) rose by 7.6 percent from the fourth quarter of 1971 to the fourth quarter of 1972. This growth rate was particularly impressive when contrasted with the 5 percent increase of the previous year and the decline in 1970. Furthermore, the unemployment rate fell from a 6 percent level at the beginning of the year to about 5 percent at year end. The rate of inflation, moreover, abated somewhat, although it certainly did not stop. The consumer price index moved up by only (!) 3.4 percent in 1972. To what extent the slowdown in inflation was due to Phases I and II remains a matter of controversy. It seems likely that some of the slowdown was due to these direct controls, but other factors were also at work. Most important among these other forces was a substantial increase in productivity (output per man-hour). The most negative aspect of the economy in 1972 seemed to be the balance of payments. Despite the currency realignments of the Smithsonian Agreement in December 1971, the United States balance of payments stayed in substantial deficit throughout 1972 and was a continuing source of official concern.

Monetary policy was expansive in 1972, although the brakes were gradually applied throughout the year. The M_1 money stock increased at an annual rate of 8.3 percent; the M_2 money stock (M_1 plus commercial bank time and savings deposits other than large CDs) increased at a 10.8 percent annual rate; and the M_3 stock (M_2 plus deposits at MSBs and S&Ls) increased by 12.9 percent. Bank reserves expanded, but the demand for reserves was even greater. Interest rates, especially short-term rates, consequently adjusted upward. Nevertheless, by the end of 1972, interest rates still had not regained the levels reached in the summer of 1971. Despite the upward movement of interest rates, the Board of Governors refused to approve any changes in the discount rate; it stayed at 4½ percent, the amount that had been set in December 1971. Finally, two adjustments in Federal Reserve regulations late in the year had a positive effect on bank reserves. These adjustments were of a technical nature and were not aimed at meeting any objective of monetary policy; one dealt with the structure of reserve requirements of member banks, and the other dealt with the check-clearing mechanism of the Fed. Nevertheless, their net effect was to supply about $1 billion to bank reserves.

The easy money policy of the Federal Reserve in 1972 was designed to spur the economy on to full recovery from the 1970 recession. Perhaps the chief ingredient in this decision was the unsatisfactory rate of unemployment. As noted previously, unemployment stood at about 6 percent of the labor force in 1971, and although it edged downward to 5 percent by the end of 1972, this still was not considered satisfactory. A 5 percent rate was substantially above the prevailing 4 percent definition of "full" employment and even further above the 3.5 percent rate that in previous years had been associated with capacity utilization of the nation's productive facilities. With prices to some extent, at least, being held in check by direct controls, it apparently seemed to Fed officials that the economy still had a good deal of slack in it.

This impression was mistaken. By the closing months of 1972 the economy was operating much closer to capacity than was generally understood. Perhaps the main reason for this lack of understanding was that a shift had occurred in the composition of the labor force. In particular, many young people and women had entered the labor force—two groups with an above-average unemployment rate—and the effect of this was to raise the average level of unemployment in the economy. Thus, in 1972 a 5 percent unemployment rate put our industrial capacity as close to full utilization as a 4 percent rate had in previous years. Judged in these terms, monetary policy was probably much less restrictive in 1972 than it should have been.

1973 and 1974

The year 1973 will be long remembered as the year in which inflation exploded. Early in the year, Phase II of President Nixon's new economic policy was terminated, to be replaced by Phase III. Phase III shifted the emphasis of the program from direct controls over prices to voluntary compliance with certain guidelines. But the depressant effect of direct price controls in an economy in which there was some slack could not be carried over to a voluntary program in an economy in which serious shortages were beginning to appear. Prices spurted upward at a rate not seen since the Korean War, twenty-two years earlier. In June 1973, prices were once again frozen ("Freeze Two," as the irreverent called it) for a period of two months, to be replaced by Phase IV. Over all, consumer prices rose by 8.8 percent during 1973.

There were a number of contributing causes to the inflation. For one thing, the Administration's economic policy may have had something to do with it. Holding down prices by direct controls also meant distorting resource allocation, and these distortions, in turn, meant the creation of "artificial" shortages in some industries. Additionally, the general weakening of the international value of the dollar caused import prices to rise. At the same time, crop failures throughout the world raised the price of agricultural commodities in the United States as well as abroad. Thus, while our balance of payments actually moved from deficit to surplus in 1973, the cost of this turnaround was a higher United States price level. Finally, a major factor contributing to the inflation was the energy shortage in general, and the petroleum shortage in particular. In the final quarter of 1973 mid-Eastern oil-producing countries put an embargo on crude oil. Although the embargo was lifted in early 1974, in the meantime oil prices had been quadrupled. Not only did this mean an extremely steep price rise in a fundamental raw material (energy) and hence a general rise in consumer prices, it also meant severe dislocations in our industrial capacity. For a number of our industrial processes had been predicated on cheap energy, and when oil prices rose so dramatically, plant and equipment that were economically viable under the old price structure became a dead-weight loss under the new. Economists at the Federal Reserve Bank of St. Louis, for example, have estimated that the fourfold increase in the price of imported petroleum wiped out about 4 or 5 percent of our industrial capacity.[9]

The economy got steadily worse in 1974. Real GNP began to decline in the first quarter and, while it recovered slightly in the second and third quarters, declined even further in the fourth quarter of 1974. The unemployment rate rose from about 5 percent at the end of 1973 to 7 percent at the end of 1974. This rise in the unemployment rate was one of the most rapid in the postwar era. And, as though this was not enough bad news, inflation became worse. By year-end 1974, the consumer price index was rising at an annualized rate of about 14 percent.

What was monetary policy during this time? Clearly, the Federal Reserve was on the horns of a dilemma—and the horns were very sharp indeed. For with

[9]Robert H. Rasche and John A. Tatom, "The Effects of the New Energy Regime on Economic Capacity, Production, and Prices," *Federal Reserve Bank of St. Louis Review,* May 1977, pp. 2–12.

unemployment and prices both rising, the Fed was damned if it did and damned if it didn't. In 1973, responding to the inflationary pressures in the economy, the Fed tightened up. The rate of increase in all three money supply measures (M_1, M_2, and M_3) slowed moderately, and interest rates advanced sharply. By mid-1973, the federal funds rate was about 10½ percent and Treasury bills were priced to yield more than 8½ percent; both rates established historical highs. Monetary policy eased somewhat later in the year, however, and continued that way into 1974 as the Federal Reserve attempted to accommodate the industrial dislocations and rising unemployment rate associated with the oil embargo. In February, however, the lifting of the oil embargo became assured, and the Fed once more began to put the monetary brakes on in an attempt to stop the raging inflation. The growth of the money supply was slowed, and by midsummer interest rates were once more setting historic highs. In June, the federal funds rate stood at 13½ percent, and about a month later the Treasury bill rate approached 9 percent. With the whole complex of short-term rates moving rapidly higher, the Federal Reserve raised its discount rate to 8 percent—an unprecedented figure.

In the late summer of 1974, the worsening employment situation and the slowdown in industrial production caused the Fed to reverse its tight money policy. Prices were still going upward at an annualized rate in excess of 12 percent, but the Fed apparently felt that the continuing high rate of inflation was due to the momentum built up over the previous several months, and that the number 1 problem had become the worsening recession. Monetary policy continued to ease throughout the remainder of 1974.

Lesson Monetary policy can create demand, but it cannot create supply.

28-8 RECENT MONETARY POLICY

The recession of 1974 came to an end, and recovery began, in the spring of 1975. Although the unemployment rate remained stubbornly high (at about 8 percent) in the early stages of the recovery, it eventually began to decline toward the full employment level of about 5 percent. But while the performance of the economy measured in terms of unemployment and production improved slowly but steadily as the decade came to a close, our performance with respect to prices was not good; the inflation rate declined from its peak of 14 percent in 1974 to about 8 or 9 percent during the rest of the decade, but did not go below that level. Month after month and year after year, the authorities continued to look for a cessation in the inflation, but they were continually disappointed. By 1979, as the decade closed, inflation had clearly become the nation's number 1 economic problem.

The high inflation rate of the late 1970s was, of course, a matter of grave concern to most Americans. All their pay raises, it seemed, were immediately canceled by higher prices. Worse, since the pay raises put them into higher income-tax brackets, many Americans found that their take-home pay at the higher prices forced them to reduce their living standards. Political agitation to "do something" about inflation became formidable. And beyond the consumer's woes with inflation, two other apparently inflation-related problems emerged: the declining value of the dollar in the international exchanges and the relatively slow pace of new capital formation in the American economy. The declining value of the dollar against such currencies as the Japanese yen and the German mark seemed to be due, in large part, to comparative inflation rates: Investors did not want to hold funds in a currency whose buying power was steadily depreciating. And American business people apparently felt that the rising cost of constructing new capital, coupled with the uncertainties surrounding an inflation-ridden economy, made capital formation too risky to undertake.

As a result of these developments, the Federal Reserve adopted a policy of *gradually* reducing the growth rate of the money supply. Their reasoning went that somehow the inflationary expectations that had been build up over a period of years had to be broken—that such things as pay raises *in anticipation of more inflation* had to be eliminated. The problem was that too sudden an application of the monetary brakes might break the back of the recovery and plunge us back into a recession of the magnitude of the one we had experienced in 1974. A gradual reduction of the growth rate in the supply thus seemed to give promise of reducing inflationary expectations without causing a major recession.

Lesson   It is a neat trick to chart a course between a rock and a hard place.

28-9   REVIEW QUESTIONS

1   In 1935, commercial banks in the United States held about $3 billion in excess reserves. In 1978, excess reserves were about $60 million. Why do you think excess reserves have declined while the economy has grown?
2   Explain what is meant by "pegging" interest rates. How does this result in a loss of control over open market operations?
3   In 1969, the Treasury raised the minimum denomination on Treasury bills from $1,000 to $10,000. Why would they do this?
4   Do you think recent monetary policy has been too tight, too easy, or about right?

Index

RUNAWAY

Books by Clarissa Watson

RUNAWAY

Clarissa Watson

New York   1985   *Atheneum*

For my husband

Library of Congress Cataloging in Publication Data

Watson, Clarissa.
    Runaway.

    I. Title.
PS3573.A848R8 1985   813'.54   84-45633
ISBN 0-689-11521-0

Published simultaneously in Canada by McClelland and Stewart Ltd.
Composition by Maryland Linotype Composition Company, Inc.,
Baltimore, Maryland
Manufactured by Fairfield Graphics, Fairfield, Pennsylvania
Designed by Harry Ford
First Edition

R U N A W A Y

1

The sun was as pale and wan as I was. It was not quite eight A.M., an hour in late March when neither human nor heavenly bodies in Gull Harbor are quite prepared to face another day.

My aunt, Lydia Wentworth, was an exception. But then, she was always an exception. And right now she was cantering along in front of me with the revolting *joie de vivre* of a drill sergeant leading his luckless charges off to a harrowing day in the field.

There she was, in her dove gray riding habit, her right leg hooked elegantly around the saddle pommel, sitting as easily as if she were serving afternoon tea. Well, she'd been brought up with her right leg hooked around a side-saddle pommel. As had I, thanks to her. Only today I was riding astride and in jeans—you don't ride side-saddle on an out-of-control locomotive.

She'd been turning up at my house like this for two weeks. Never any advance warning—she'd just suddenly appear, clattering around in my driveway, riding her favorite gray mare, towing some bad actor for me, and halooing and whistling until she roused me from my downy cot and sweet dreams. I do not approve of violent activity in the early morning, and to me eight A.M. is dawn. Sleep is the only civilized pastime at that hour.

She kept a fair sized stable at her estate, The Crossing. Mostly the horses were retirees from her rather extensive racing establishment and the majority had mouths of iron and manners to match, as I was finding out.

"What you need is some challenging exercise," Aunt Lydie

3

had announced to me in her most formidable voice when I came back from France after a disastrous affair. "You're drooping about. Why is it that you are always attracted to scoundrels? Why can't you fall in love with that nice Oliver Reynolds? Oh, well . . . so am I, I suppose. And I can tell you that there are only two cures for a broken heart . . . violent exercise or a new lover."

She had been subjecting me to the first ever since and it was getting exhausting. I was afraid the morning canters would go on with increasing vigor until either I found a new man or she ran out of spirited horses. It was all very well for her to go careening along ahead of me on her gray mare—the mare, after all, was a model of perfect gaits and manners. Whereas I was being subjected to nothing less than the rack.

There had been rain sometime during the night so that the occasional fugitive drop slipping from a branch made a surprisingly loud noise as it fell, even above the muffled sound of our passing. From the corner of my eye I was aware of spears of onion grass rising from the brown forest cover and the rust of mosses greening themselves for spring.

La Coquette, my aunt's mare, bobbed along like a goody-goody little girl on her way to dancing class. My snorting steed and I plunged along in her delicate wake like a bark in a killing sea, with me standing up in my stirrups and almost falling on my horse's neck in an effort to keep from running my aunt and her mount straight into the ground. My arms had turned to spaghetti: a hundred and eight pounds of thirty-six-and-a-half-year-old female are no match for a ten ton Goliath.

We rocketed along like this for another ten minutes or so. I was puffing and out of breath. Godzilla (as I had mentally christened him) was, on the other hand, just getting into the spirit of things, if his death grip on the bit was any indication. I prayed for succor. An earthquake. A cyclone. A hurricane. Any act of God that would end the torment. I am too old to be fighting with a horse.

What I got was a flock of geese.

They were a tightly disciplined flock of Canadas and they

4

came sweeping in very low, a winged fighter squadron hedge-hopping across the countryside. The noise was deafening, a mad cacophony of quacks and honks and automobile horn noises.

Godzilla decided instantly that he had been strafed. He took off as if he had a ticking bomb underneath his tail, almost knocking my aunt and her mare off their feet.

"Give him his head," Aunt Lydie screamed thinly after my fast disappearing form. "Give him his head and he'll go home!"

Give him his head? He already had it. And the bit. And anything else his heart desired.

We burst out of the woods like a rocket and took to the open fields, acres of which—carefully fenced—surround every noteworthy property in Gull Harbor . . . and there are plenty of them. I had absolutely not the foggiest idea of where we were . . . first of all I was too busy trying to cling to the mad monstrosity beneath me to chart a course and secondly I was accustomed to approaching people's houses by the front drive like a lady and not from the surrounding fields, like the Mau Mau. Ordinarily I can ride a horse with a piece of very thin thread in its mouth; but this was ridiculous—my arms were coming out at the sockets. If it was an athletic contest (and it was), I was already a loser.

I glanced over my shoulder just once and saw my aunt lift her mare's head, turn her neatly, and gallop off in the direction from which we'd come. Probably gone to get an ambulance and reserve a bed in the Gull Harbor hospital, I thought bitterly as she vanished.

After that I kept my full attention on the business of staying aboard, with visions of broken bones and full body casts to help keep me focused on the importance of staying exactly where I was, however uncomfortable it might seem at the moment.

As far as my boggled eye could see there were fields and post-and-rail fences and more fields and brush hedges and so on, apparently ad infinitum. Godzilla saw the same thing and liked what he saw—he was snorting with excitement, exactly like a dragon, only there weren't any flames. He was on course and galloping like an express train—head up, ears switching back and

5

forth, assessing the landscape. I had this weird feeling that I was in the hands of a professional.

We skimmed through the first jump, making the hedge rock. Before I even caught my breath we were approaching a second well-pruned hedge. Godzilla took it so deep into the branches that I felt them graze my hips. I could just imagine my aunt Lydie sitting on a hilltop, surveying the slightly disorganized scene, and saying with unabashed self-satisfaction, "You see, Persis, what a little exercise will do for you?"

The next few fences were post and rail and Godzilla treated them with respect, clearing them cleanly and neatly. He was beginning to get the feel of the course.

Now there were more hedges. Godzilla stood off and took them from a great distance, plunging deep into them to save time and energy. I wondered if my legs were bleeding beneath my jeans.

Godzilla was pacing himself now. He wasn't even puffing. I began to relax and enjoy the ride just the littlest bit. The crazy old beggar seemed to know exactly what he was doing, which was certainly more than I could say of myself.

Rather to my surprise, I recognized one of the houses that flashed by in the distance as we pursued our hurly-burly course across the meadows . . . I'd been on that particular terrace many times for cocktails. I was an accepted fixture at all the social events in Gull Harbor. Not because I was Persis Willum, starving artist . . . Gull Harborites are not impressed by starvation. On the contrary, I was welcome because I was the niece (albeit an impoverished one) of Lydia Wentworth, who just happened to be one of the wealthiest women in the world. Furthermore, I was youngish, not bad looking, and knew which fork to use at table. Put it all together and you have all the ingredients you need for social success in Gull Harbor. Not that it mattered to me.

This particular terrace belonged to Elmsworth, one of the great mansions of the North Shore. And that meant we were on our way to The Crossing—admittedly by a circuitous route but nonetheless on our way. My foxy old traveling companion of the

6

moment knew exactly where he was and what he was doing. Next would come Blairfield, carted over rock by rock and stone by stone from Italy in 1889 by old Ramsey Blair. Then we would be at Tribute, Courtney Lassiter's modest but elegant holding that was the last bastion before the nine hundred acres of Lydia Wentworth's The Crossing, the greatest property of them all. I decided by some quick calculation that we would have traveled approximately four miles . . . the exact distance of the Maryland Hunt Cup, which I had been told the equine monster beneath me had won twice when he was in his salad days.

Visions of our arrival at the stables now overwhelmed me, the scarcely concealed sniggers of the grooms already ringing in my ears. The horse would be lathered up and foam covered . . . an unpardonable sin. I would be wind-whipped, perspiring, and disheveled . . . equally unpardonable sins. They would whisper behind my back as they cooled Godzilla out. It wasn't fair, I told myself resentfully.

We charged across Blairfield's horizon. And, I thought, still dwelling on my impending arrival at The Crossing, I shall have to beg for a ride home. Too awful.

Blairfield disappeared astern and the high hedges of Tribute rose up in the distance. The moment I saw them, all concern for my arrival at Aunt Lydie's disappeared. If Godzilla attempted those hedges I might never arrive at Aunt Lydie's at all.

Tribute was an exception to the general North Shore landscape. A neat, four acre, hedge-enclosed square, it was plunked down between the two giant estates of Blairfield and The Crossing as if a monster pinking scissors had made a slight mistake in cutting out their mutual border. A long, narrow driveway, like a breathing tube, ran down to it from the tree-lined road that marked the southern edge of the estates, and Tribute itself was completely invisible from the road. It was a surprising little place—unexpected in that particular setting. The present English owner had made it more surprising by enclosing it in high hedges.

And I knew those hedges: they were killers. Five feet tall and a good three feet in width. Worst of all, they concealed a chain link fence topped with barbed wire. A member of the Gull Harbor police force had told me about it. "A regular fortress," he'd said, approvingly. The local police thought we should all arm ourselves to the teeth and take extraordinary precautions in these days of increasing robberies.

I saw those hedges looming up at me, ever bigger, and I began to pull desperately on the left rein, hoping to turn the horse so that he would make a slight detour and thus miss Tribute completely. Godzilla had seen the hedges—his ears were pointed straight at them—and it appeared he had no intention of avoiding their challenge. I pulled with all my strength. His neck did not bend. He took dead aim and we charged, devouring the intervening field in a ground-eating gallop. A great mushroom cloud of impending doom seemed to rise and hover over us.

The hedges came nearer and nearer. I wondered if it was too late in my ill-spent life to pray. Visions of smashed and broken equine and human backs and necks and legs flashed in front of my eyes.

Godzilla changed his tempo. He seemed to gather himself together, giving his tail an extra flip, like a rocket charge. I felt him shudder. I closed my eyes. And we were flying through the air, branches smashing around us. There was plenty of sudden, crackling noise with our passage.

Then we hit the ground, right lead foot first and the rest following smoothly—he didn't even stumble. I snatched at the reins, helping him lift his head up for balance, and we continued on our way, not pausing to consider the damage behind us. We had landed on deep green lawns behind the one-story miniature French château. My quick glance made note of imposing copper beeches surrounded by ivy, cement urns filled with more ivy, friendly sculptures in stone of squirrels and a fox, brick pathways winding here and there, and the kind of furniture one leaves outside year round.

This outdoor furniture had been set up, as if for a meeting, at the far side of the garden. And until the moment of our entry, it had been occupied by about a half dozen men who appeared to have been concentrating their attention on a collection of papers spread out on a glass-topped metal table. With our explosive appearance on the scene, they scattered as if they had been bombed, quite as astonished to see Godzilla and me as we were to be there.

I had no time to dwell on the intricacies of the situation: my horse was crossing the lawn in great spine-jolting leaps, sinking deep into the well-kept turf with every step, and the hedge at the far side of the property was coming at us all too fast. That he had cleared the first seemed miraculous. Could he do it again?

I was dimly aware of a cacophony of shouts and what sounded like curses from the garden behind me but there was no time for apologies. I leaned far forward in the saddle to take my weight off the horse's back and help make the impossible jump possible. Godzilla punched his way in and out of the spongy lawn—a kangaroo on a pogo stick. He gathered himself together and hurled his body at the greenery as if at an adversary. We were airborne, soaring. It was lovely. Something whizzed by on my left. I paid no attention. Probably throwing rocks at me, I thought. Never mind, I'll apologize tomorrow. Meanwhile, we're flying. We're over. I'm safe.

Godzilla alighted on the other side of Tribute's enclosure with a certain air of self-congratulation, well pleased to see that he had not lost his touch. We were on Wentworth land now, and he seemed to know it. He began to ease himself up—although he was by no means winded by his efforts—falling from a gallop to a slow canter to an easy, swinging trot. I was overjoyed to realize that we would not, after all, appear at The Crossing's stables lathered and foaming. Horse and rider would arrive together at the barn in more or less decorous partnership. I would make up something to explain Aunt Lydie's absence.

And tomorrow morning—or even better, this very afternoon —I would hie myself over to Sir Courtney Lassiter's house, bearing armloads of flowers, to apologize for wrecking his beautiful lawn, already green so early in the spring.

Within ten minutes we were clattering into the cobblestoned

Tudor stableyard, more or less cooled out and in reasonably good order, I thought.

The first groom to see us, who happened also to be the head groom, shattered my illusions.

"Mrs. Willum," he cried. "Whatever happened to you?"

I couldn't believe it. How could he possibly know what I had been through? How could he possibly have read the ignominy of my morning's adventure?

"What-do-you-mean-whatever-happened?" I mumbled, swinging myself down from the by now docile steeplechaser. That's when the pain hit me for the first time . . . when I braced myself with my left hand to vault out of the saddle. It wasn't exactly pain, really . . . the sensation was more that of a sharp and relentless stinging.

I looked at my arm, where the head groom was also staring, horrified. The sleeve of my Brooks Brothers cotton shirt was nicked and a torrent of bright red, healthy looking blood had issued from the neat little aperture.

I unbuttoned my cuff and pulled up the sleeve to expose my upper arm. No question about it, the blood was mine—my very own. The groom and I looked at each other.

"A branch?" I asked. "We were jumping. . . ."

He shook his head and gave rapid orders to an underling who was standing next to us, holding Godzilla's head. There was something about bandages . . . there are always plenty of bandages in a stable, even though they're generally used for wrapping horses' legs.

Then he turned back to me.

"A branch," I repeated. But I saw doubt and curiosity in his eyes.

I stared down at my arm.

Then I remembered. There had been *something* when we took the last hedge—something whizzing by.

But it was absurd. Courtney Lassiter mistake me for an intruder? He would have recognized me at once. Courtney Lassiter shoot at a woman? Never. He was a gentleman.

No—it was absolutely out of the question. People in Gull Harbor shoot at clay pigeons, live pigeons, assorted unfortunate wild game, occasional rabbits and crows (although these latter are rather frowned on), but never, absolutely *never* at dogs, foxes, horses, or people riding with or on them. And Courtney Lassiter of all people? Out of the question.

I looked the head groom firmly in the eye. "A branch," I repeated with finality. Then I marched up to the big house to wait for Aunt Lydie to make her appearance and arrange to have me driven home. I would ask if I could stop at Tribute to apologize to whoever was in residence and offer to repair the damage Godzilla and I had done to the lawn.

In due time she appeared, every silver-blond silken hair in place, exuding unruffled elegance. I don't think even being run away with would have disturbed her eternal savoir-faire.

I made my suggestion: could we stop at Tribute on the way home? Would the chauffeur (my aunt did not drive) mind? I'd made such a mess of the lawn. . . .

To my astonishment she refused.

"But Aunt Lydie, that mad horse of yours jumped right over Courtney's hedges. I ruined the lawn. I ought at least to. . . ."

"Absolutely not."

"But. . . ."

"Persis, I forbid it."

"But I. . . ."

"Persis, I have the keys to Tribute. Courtney left them with me. He always does."

Then it dawned on me. Courtney Lassiter had not been present among the men in his own backyard. Of course . . . there had been a note in the gossip column of the *Gull Harbor Trumpet* yesterday afternoon and I'd forgotten it until now. "About that devastating Courtney Lassiter," it said. "Rumor has it he will not return from the south of France for another two weeks or so, a bit of news that will leave the local belles desolate."

So Courtney Lassiter was away on another of what Aunt Lydie referred to as his "marvelously mysterious disappearances."

Well, there was nothing new about that—he came and went from the Gull Harbor scene with the independence of a reasonably affluent and active international bachelor of advanced middle age.

But if he was indeed still in France, who was at Tribute? Why a meeting outdoors, as far as possible from the house and its amenities? Why so early in the morning? *Was* it a meeting after all?

I began to understand.

"You mean that the people I told you I saw shouldn't have been. . . ?"

"It is a distinct possibility, Persis."

"Then don't you think we ought to call the police?" I reached for the telephone.

"No. Wait."

I still had my hand on the phone. It was on a Queen Anne table directly beneath a Velázquez. It was the first, and probably the only time in my life, I did not pause to admire the painting.

I stared instead at my aunt. She looked a little pale, I thought, even beneath her exquisite ivory everyday pallor.

"No," she repeated. "Bobby Blessing called early this morning to say that I must surrender the keys to no one unless he says it's all right. I assume that includes the police."

"But. . . ."

"No." She was very firm. When my aunt gives an order there is no question of disobedience. "We will *not* call the police, Persis. Bobby Blessing is the most intelligent man I know. He is the most important. Also, he is Courtney Lassiter's best friend. I trust him implicitly. The police would ask for the keys and I must honor Bobby's request. We will call Bobby Blessing."

"And he will decide. . . ?"

"Exactly. That is precisely what I mean."

And call Bobby Blessing is what we did. I'm still not sure I understood why, but it is what we did.

Instantly.

* * *

12

In the next few minutes my aunt subjected me to a performance that took me straight back to the nursery. She was the Nanny; I was the obedient child.

First I was commanded to give Bobby Blessing a brief telephone account of the episodes at Tribute. I did so, answering his one or two questions as briskly as possible.

Then I was ordered to leave the room while Aunt Lydie continued to chat with him. I did so, standing rather foolishly in the hallway contemplating a Picasso clown, a Turner seascape, and a Monet garden on the wall opposite me.

After a few minutes my aunt put her head out of the library door and commanded me to go downstairs where Roberts, her favorite chauffeur, would be waiting with a car to drive me home.

I protested a little. "But what's going on, anyway? Tell me, please."

The small rebellion was not a success. "Please have the goodness to do as I say, Persis. I'm still on the telephone."

I did as she said. Roberts was waiting, as advertised, and we drove to my house in silence—his polite, mine sulky. I was still sulking as I stripped off my horse-smelling clothes and stepped into the shower, holding my left arm outside the curtain like a fishing pole to keep it dry. This, I sniffed to myself, was *my* adventure, after all. It was Godzilla and I who had stumbled on . . . what had we stumbled on?

Anyway, I had earned by pain and humiliation and a possible bullet wound the right to an explanation of the morning's events. And if no one was willing to give me such an explanation I would be forced to take steps on my own.

Oliver Reynolds, the man I never get around to marrying, has often pointed out that Lydia Wentworth is not the only willful member of the family. And I suppose there is a certain amount of truth to the accusation. In addition to my willful determination not to marry again, he could point out a growing collection of painful scrapes and bruises from other ill-fated and willful adventures, like the disastrous affair with the wrong man in Touquiet, France, from which Lydie was helping me to recover, and my chasing missing paintings around the world, which had led to my getting involved with the FBI—and worse.

Except that I wouldn't call such behavior willful: I would say it had more to do with independence, and not liking to be pushed around.

Anyway, I would return to Tribute.

But this time I would not appear as a wild-eyed hoyden on horseback. I would make my second visit as a sedate country lady. With luck, I wouldn't even be recognized.

I pulled my most Gull Harbor, and therefore noncontroversial, sweater and skirt from the closet, placing my confidence in the conservative country Braemar look. A string of not too ostentatious matched pearls—always a symbol of probity. Too bad about the twenty-twenty vision: gold-rimmed eyeglasses would have added a nice touch.

And finally, a Red Cross pin prominently displayed on my bosom.

I surveyed the result in the pier glass mirror. Not too bad an imitation of the golf-bridge-tennis playing matrons of Gull Harbor, I thought. No one would suspect that I was really an artist. Or that I was the recent, unwilling passenger who had crossed the lawn aboard a runaway monster horse. Or, in fact, that I was I.

I noted with special pleasure that there was only the slightest of bulges beneath my yellow sweater to betray the bandage supplied by Lydia Wentworth's head groom and I was further pleased to note that the medication he'd applied with the bandages was doing its stuff . . . all I could feel was a very slight soreness. Aunt Lydie had been saying for years that horse doctors and horse medications were the only ones she would trust, and now I was inclined to agree.

I made one last pass at my unruly hair with the brush and climbed into my Mustang and was off.

The trip back to Tribute was definitely more comfortable than the previous one, although I confess that it didn't seem any faster. Of course, we were now taking the long way around—not half as exciting but infinitely easier on the nervous system. The countryside, in the first tremors of gathering itself to burst into bloom, was calm and peaceful.

Seen from the front as I wheeled down the long drive, Tribute looked bland and self-satisfied—the last place on earth where anything especially interesting would be going on. This was deceptive because Tribute had actually been built because of interesting goings-on.

It was an old scandal. Ramsey Blair—the original one—came back from Paris in the nineteen hundreds with a mistress, whom he set up in New York. A. K. Wentworth—Aunt Lydie's grandfather—saw her driving in Central Park and was sorely smitten. The lady liked both gentlemen and refused to choose. Both gentlemen refused to give her up. The result (the men were business tycoons and very pragmatic) was not to duel or to draw straws, but to compromise in the most civilized manner: they built Tribute between their two properties and shared. Eventually the lady acquired enough money and jewels to afford to run away with Blairfield's handsome English butler.

As I approached Tribute, smiling a little at the unconventional arrangement that had caused it to be built, I kept glancing in awe at the hedges that paced my progress, astonished that Godzilla and I had ever succeeded in clearing them safely. They looked bigger and more forbidding than ever from my little car.

The turn-around in front of the house was pure Gull Harbor—adorned by two stone statues (swans, this time), eight big stone urns that would blossom with flowers as the weather warmed, and well-raked bluestone edged neatly with red brick. On either side of the front door were white wrought-iron carriage lamps on standards. Tribute was not a big house—it was more like a graceful pavilion, small and compact. I parked my car, straightened my Red Cross pin, and trotted up to the front door. I pressed the doorbell. Somewhere inside the house musical chimes responded. The door opened with surprising suddenness and I found myself

15

facing a small oriental wearing a cream-colored coat and the subtle but unmistakable politeness of a gentleman's gentleman.

"Sssssss?" At least, that's what it sounded like—a word composed solely of S's, like escaping steam.

"Is Mr. Lassiter at home?" I knew he wasn't, but it was a beginning.

"No home, Missy." He began to close the door.

"Just one moment, please." I stuck my foot in the door, giving every indication of being about to enter. "May I speak to whoever is in charge in his absence? It is important."

The oriental gentleman (I had decided, based on nothing at all, that he was Japanese) burst into a long and indignant harangue, from which I extracted the words "all glone," and what sounded like "glood bly." Whatever he was *actually* saying, it was obvious that he was offering me no encouragement, and in an accent that was definitely comic opera.

But I was refusing, as brazenly as I dared, to get the message.

"It is a matter of the Red Cross. We are approaching every resident. It is the annual drive. Mr. Lassiter has always been one of our most enthusiastic supporters . . . he will want to see me."

I hoped that some of this speech was penetrating his Eastern composure. Did he understand a word? I couldn't be sure.

Meanwhile we were standing shoulder to shoulder and eye to eye, and looking past his slick black head I could see straight through the drawing room and out the large French doors in back. The outdoor furniture was back in place on the terrace. No one appeared to be around. Most curious of all, I could see no sign of the torn-up earth Godzilla's hoofs had left behind: every single piece of turf had been replaced.

"Missy glo now?" The manservant's glossy black eyes were fixed on mine.

I looked back at him, wondering.

All of us in Gull Harbor leave house keys with our neighbors when we go away . . . in case of broken pipes, burglaries, fire, or any of the hundred and one crises that occur when a house is left empty. Aunt Lydie was Lassiter's nearest neighbor, even though the distance between their houses was measured in acres rather than feet. Since Lassiter often traveled, she probably had her own set of keys.

A manservant would also have a set and he might very well have returned in advance of his master to get the house in order. But I didn't recognize him, although I'd often been a guest at Tribute. Of course it was perfectly possible that he was a new servant. Then who were the people I'd seen on the lawn? Why had they been admitted in Lassiter's absence? Where were they now? What had they been up to? I didn't like this black-eyed sibilant stranger.

And his coat didn't fit.

I tried once more, already feeling defeated. "I should like to speak to Mr. Lassiter if he's in residence. If he's not here, I should like to know where I can reach him and when he will return." I used my most imperious voice, copied faithfully—after years of study—from my aunt's. If this little hissing teakettle was legitimate, he would surely respond to the notes of command.

He responded, all right. But I couldn't understand any of the tirade that followed—most of it was in what I supposed to be Japanese, with a word or two of English tossed in at random. But something in his stance—a sort of over-all tensing of his body—convinced me not only that he had understood everything I'd said but that he was an interloper. An intruder.

He didn't belong here. I was suddenly sure of it. Tribute probably had an elaborate burglar alarm system—everybody in the area does these days. But given know-how and time, even the most elaborate and sophisticated protection system can be circumvented. If this was the typical Gull Harbor installation, it would send an alarm directly to the Gull Harbor police. To neutralize the system? Simple . . . cut the telephone wires.

I backed out of the doorway. He followed, still talking in a high staccato. I edged gingerly toward my car, intent on making a quick departure. I scanned the grounds as far as I could see on both sides of the house in a sort of desperate last look around before climbing into my car. He closed the door behind me, probably happy to see me go.

Then I saw the telephone pole, looking like only a telephone pole in beauty-conscious Gull Harbor could look, namely not like a telephone pole at all but like a part of the breathtaking landscape, or as much so as man could arrange. Only someone as determined as I would have noticed it hiding among the evergreens at an aesthetically pleasing distance from the house and dressed, greenly, in climbing vines.

I was out of the car instantly and across the lawn, poking about among the vines. And there it was—dangling like a participle at the end of an extremely long and embarrassing sentence. A cut wire.

The oriental gentleman's voice came from behind me. "Would you care," he said in faultless English, "to step inside?"

I would not care to. Most definitely. But I had no choice. He struck like a cobra. One of his arms locked around my neck. The other twisted my arm behind my back.

I tried to keep my head—remember what to do. Kick . . . kick backward at his knees. Kick hard and he'll loosen his grip.

But he didn't. So much for what they tell you about self-defense.

I tried to claw at the arm around my neck. It was no contest. I remember thinking—he's so little . . . how can he be so strong? The arm around my neck increased its pressure relentlessly. I couldn't breathe.

I thought, this time I've really done it. This time I'm going to die.

Aunt Lydie and Oliver will be furious.

18

2

My first thought—purely automatic—was, I don't suppose that I shall ever be able to speak again.

Then my unfocused eyes sorted themselves out and registered the form that was bending over me and I wondered, if I have died and gone to heaven, why did I wait so long?

I was instantly ashamed. There is something déclassé about getting carried away with the first presentable man that comes along. Part of it could have been relief and gratitude: he was holding me in his arms (and not as if he intended to murder me) and gently pouring brandy, drop by drop, down my throat. It was like swallowing a sword. But then the burning pain subsided, to be followed by a euphoric glow. The sensation was splendid.

"Her color's better now. I think she'll be all right. Why not put her in that chair? It looks comfortable."

Bobby Blessing's voice came from somewhere behind me. Then I was scooped up and rearranged gently in a big leather chair. I was in the library at Tribute, a room that was typically Gull Harbor down to the last piece of hand-rubbed wood paneling: the ubiquitous English hunting prints . . . the ever-present French toile curtains . . . the well-laid fire waiting for the match . . . the leather-topped desk . . . the easy chairs . . . the TV built into the bookcases which themselves were filled with leather-bound volumes in perfect order . . . the bar, cleverly concealed in a niche in the wall. Perfect—everything perfect.

There were, however, two atypical notes to rescue the room from utter banality—a leather-covered chair fashioned from the horns of Texas steers and a buffalo rug, smelling faintly of moth balls. Bobby Blessing was seated in the chair with the rug curling stiffly around his feet. He looked like a cross between a spider—for he was all arms and legs—and a cattle baron.

Actually there was one more thing to save the scene—the man who was now leaning against the bar, which was open, and smiling at me. A man that good looking would save any scene.

"I think you'll live," he said. "He never intended to kill you, or he would have, whoever he was."

"Must have heard us coming down the drive. Took off. Probably down the service road. Left you lying in the front hall. So stupid of you to be here." Bobby Blessing looked crossly at me and my sense of well-being evaporated. It was a little like having the pope displeased. Bobby Blessing had that kind of power.

I suppose he was the most distinguished man in Gull Harbor, where distinguished citizens are anything but a rarity. You could probably say that he was a diplomatic jack-of-all-trades: he'd held three cabinet posts, been advisor to five different presidents, and headed countless special diplomatic missions.

But his power was more subtle than all that. At seventy, he was still in daily touch with Washington, a kind of permanent minister without portfolio to the American government, and his influence seeped into countless secret and unsuspected quarters.

All of this I knew from my aunt, who adored him. I also knew that he was the last man in the world I wanted to be angry with me.

"Whatever made you do such a stupid thing? Why did you come here? Your aunt told you not to, didn't she?"

I tried to think of something intelligent to say and couldn't. Then I tried to say I was sorry. But all that came out was a series of unattractive croaks, like a raven.

Blessing's expression softened a little. "There, there . . . don't try to speak. I suppose it was the eternal female curiosity. My wife was like that—couldn't bear not to look into everything—like a cat, you know." He got up—in stages . . . a wooden ruler unfolding. "Well now, Alex, as the young lady's more or less all right, let's get on with what we came here for, shall we?"

The man at the bar nodded and stepped swiftly into the hall and out of sight. It was as if someone had turned out the light, which was strange because his hair was black and his skin was perfectly tanned. Maybe it was the eyes . . . they were very blue. Electric blue.

"Alexander Dana," Blessing told me, as if it explained everything. He began to poke about among the bookshelves.

I produced a croak of interrogation.

"Lawyer fellow with Lassiter's bank. Got a call from Washington last night. Asked me to let him in here today . . . looking for something." I heard the desk drawers being opened.

From my chair beside Lassiter's bar I could see across the hall into the dining room, where Dana now came into view. He was obviously looking for something but no lawyer with a bank ever looked for something the way Dana was doing now. He was unscrewing light bulbs and poking among the fixtures. He was examining the moldings. He was feeling the trompe l'oeil panels with his hands and then scanning them with some sort of instrument. Every movement was swift, light, sure. In the span of only a few minutes he was through and had moved out of sight again into another area.

I got up unsteadily and leaned into the bar, searching for the brandy. Another drop or two might complete the job of anesthetizing my throat . . . I had never yearned more for speech.

Bobby Blessing was rooting about among the fireplace logs, a performance I found absolutely extraordinary in a man of his age and dignity. I discovered the brandy and administered it to myself. The result was miraculous: bits and pieces of my voice were restored.

"Looking for what?" I cried, happy as a diva newly recovered from laryngitis. "They had lots of papers at the meeting this morning outside on the lawn."

"Where, exactly?"

21

"Off in the far corner."

"So they wouldn't be seen by someone coming to the front door." His voice was grim. "Wasn't a meeting at all. Going over what they found."

My voice was still scratchy and uneven, but it was back in service. "Looking for what?" I repeated, somewhat desperately this time.

"Anything unusual. Anything that doesn't fit the pattern . . . Lassiter's pattern." He was dusting his hands with an immaculate monogrammed handkerchief. His hands were long and bony like the rest of his frame, which itself was a frail monument to enduring ulcers.

Alexander Dana was back in the room, his return swift and silent. I couldn't believe I hadn't noticed him come back, but I hadn't.

"Anything?" he asked Blessing.

"Nothing," Blessing replied. "You?"

"Negative. Cleaned out. Not even a scrap of burned paper. Very professional."

Blessing grunted.

"Drink?" I asked them. They looked so disappointed I wanted to do something to comfort them. They agreed to whiskey and soda, which I fixed. We sat in silence after that, Dana on the corner of the desk, Blessing in the longhorn chair, and me beside the bar. I was longing to ask more questions, but their mood was so black I didn't dare.

Finally their glasses were empty.

"Might as well get going," Blessing said. "You well enough now to go home, Persis?"

I wished that I had the nerve to pretend I was too faint to drive. Then I could request the services of Alexander Dana, who was otherwise about to disappear from my life like the proverbial puff of smoke. A typical Gull Harbor lady would have done it: those women are tigers where men are concerned and they believe in the law of the jungle.

Instead I tried to temporize. "You said anything that doesn't fit the pattern, didn't you? Could it be anything that doesn't fit the pattern of the house?"

"Could be." They both looked at me with interest.

"Well, there are a couple of things. The buffalo rug, for instance."

"Nothing there."

"The chair . . . those horns."

"Obvious. But we checked anyway. Negative."

"The bar."

"The bar?"

I might never have noticed if it hadn't been for the words Marseille and Maures. I knew those places well and my attention was automatically arrested.

"Didn't you see?"

They both came over to the bar and frowned at it. Even when he frowned Dana looked marvelous—a little more dangerous and macho and marvelous.

"It's nothing but wallpaper made from the reproduction of a French newspaper. What's so unusual about that? Every bar and bathroom in Gull Harbor features French wallpaper with smart remarks on it. Who pays any attention? Who, in fact, reads French?"

True enough, the local landscape abounds in examples of French powder room wit—it is the last gasp in chic these days. It is also true that most Gull Harbor men don't know a word of French. They seem to harbor a suspicion that to know French is slightly decadent and best left to the ladies or to hirelings. One of my chief responsibilities at the art gallery where I earn my meager living is to translate all French correspondence for my employer, Gregor Olitsky.

"Well, I read French, and even though the type is so small as to be nearly indecipherable I can just make it out because I have good eyes. Let me translate."

And I did.

It was pages one and four of *Le Provençal*, Marseille, reproduced over and over again and set at different angles to make an endless pattern which was tiny but actually very handsome. The *Le Provençal* masthead was in a bright, orangy red and everything else was in black and white. Reading it wasn't easy, but it could be done.

The date was Friday, August 12, 1977.

Page one was ablaze with headlines, all of them celebrating catastrophes:

"Les enquêteurs sur les traces de l'assassin de Monique," screamed one. *"New York respire! Le 'Fils de Sam' enfin arrêté!"* cried another. *"Un réseau de 'traite des blanches' découvert entre la Belgique et le Midi. Quatre arrestations,"* proclaimed a third.

One headline was special because the story pertaining to it took up most of page four. LE DOUBLE CRIME DU MASSIF PRÈS DES MAURES . . . LES PISTES S'EFFONDRENT UNE À UNE.

The entire center of page four concerned itself with this story, so prominently headlined on the front page. Under the great black headline, LA FORÊT DES MAURES GARDE SON SECRET, there was a four column report of the deaths by gunfire (*"froidement tués à coups de revolver"*) of two British citizens, Mr. and Mrs. Broderick-Smith, found dead beside their Ford Cortina. The colonel in charge of the investigation was quoted as stating that robbery was not necessarily the motive for the crime. There were no clues—no record of the Broderick-Smith's activities before their deaths, although it was assumed that they were on a camping vacation. London was quoted as saying that neither of the deceased had any family. There was a rumor that Scotland Yard was sending an investigator. A witness was quoted as having seen two motorcyclists near the scene of the crime, which took place in an area where the terrain was much favored by the fans of *"la moto verte."* The witness confessed that the two motorcyclists would be impossible to identify since they were wearing helmets and the typical leather garb of their genre.

I had glanced at this lead story in a purely cursory way, thinking to myself that it was an odd sort of thing to reproduce in wallpaper and deciding that the left hand side of the page, which contained a detailed account of the arrest of the mad killer known

24

as Son of Sam, was probably the reason for the bizarre choice. A lot of people had followed the Son of Sam story—maybe Lassiter thought it made an amusing conversation piece for his bar. Gull Harbor is high on conversation pieces.

But when I happened to look at the headline beneath the story on the two murders in the hills of Maures, I was startled . . . and fascinated. While the two men searched the house around me, I read it through twice.

First the headline caught my attention. DES SIMILITUDES TROUBLANTES, it announced. And the similarities listed below could indeed be called troubling.

Between the years 1952 and 1977 no fewer than eight British citizens had been murdered within the roughly triangular area that joined Marseille, Menton, and Manosque. In 1952 Sir James Drumm and his wife were assassinated near Lurs and the case was still considered extremely controversial. In 1964 another representative of *"L'Establishment Britannique,"* Sir Duncan Oliver, was shot in Cannes, where he had lived during the Second World War. In 1973 the body of Jeremy Michael, a British officer in retirement, was discovered on the Promenade des Anglais in Nice. Two months later John Cartland Basil, another British subject, was found assassinated near Pelissanne. In 1975 Prentice Courtney, ex-RAF pilot, was found murdered in Menton. Finally, the deaths of the Broderick-Smiths.

The crimes, the news story reported, had many points in common:

1. All of the victims were British.
2. All the men belonged to the same generation, ranging from sixty-one to seventy-five years of age.
3. All had been involved in World War II.
4. All were very familiar with the southeast of France . . . one lived there (Michael) . . . one was born there (Oliver) . . . the others had been coming to the area over a great number of years (Drumm, Basil, Broderick-Smith, Courtney).

5. During the war, Sir Duncan Oliver had directed, from Cannes, an important branch of the affiliated Resistance. Jeremy Michael had worked directly with him. Basil had been attached to the S.O.E., the special British branch of the service operating in France in very close association with some of the principal branches of the Resistance. According to British authorities, Sir James Drumm had not played "any particular role" during the war—yet he was knighted by King George VI for "*services rendus au titre du ministère du Ravitaillement.*" As to Prentice Courtney, "ex-RAF pilot," killed at Menton, he would have been forty-two years old in 1942—an age when one no longer piloted Spitfires and Mosquitos. Why then, was he identified by Britain as an RAF pilot?

Was it not possible, the story demanded, that Drumm, Oliver, Michael, Basil, Courtney, and Broderick-Smith were all killed for the same reason . . . and by the same assassin?

"*Alors,*" the writer concluded cryptically, "*roman policier? Voire. . . .*"

Blessing and Dana listened to my reading of the material with fierce concentration, Blessing hum, humming to himself, Dana in silence. I re-read it several times. It seemed a very long time before they spoke . . . the power of their concentration was such that I would not have been astonished if the newsprint had leapt off the wall.

"That's it," Dana said, finally turning away. "If he had any detailed . . ." He seemed to have dismissed the wallpaper. ". . . but I seriously doubt that he committed anything to writing . . . he was too professional for that."

"Agreed." Blessing came over and put his arm around me in what I suppose was a gesture of affection, although it felt more as if someone had dropped a bundle of sharp sticks onto my shoulders. "Well, well. Very original—very amusing. But we've come away empty-handed. Very clever of Lassiter, actually. Very. Poor bastard."

26

I looked from one to the other. "Clever?"

"Well, certainly different. A sort of 'lest we forget old British heroes' every time he mixed a drink. There must have been others since that was written."

Dana didn't look pleased and I thought I heard him mutter "stupidity" beneath his breath but I wasn't sure.

"Of course," Blessing continued, "Lassiter always was a conceited ass. I hate to admit it, but it's true. Always thought the British were smarter—that *he* was smarter than anyone else—thumbing his nose. Really believed he was superior, like all those Brits."

It seemed to be a total non sequitur, much more worthy of my aunt than of Bobby Blessing. I decided to ignore it. "You said you're coming away empty-handed. What exactly are you. . . ."

"Just couldn't resist, could he?" Blessing was talking over me at Dana and this time I distinctly heard Dana say, "Stupid."

It was too much. My frustration made my voice rise half an octave.

"Well, there's one thing you must know . . . why are you calling Courtney Lassiter a poor bastard? Why?"

This time they answered.

"Because he's dead, Persis." There was a kind of rage in Blessing. "Dead. He was found on the Boulevard Canebière in Marseille."

"Yesterday morning," said Dana.

The triangle joining Marseille, Menton, and Manosque.

"Oh, no." Dead in Marseille.

One corner of the triangle.

"He was shot eight times at close range."

"Like an assassination!"

"Like an execution." Dana's voice had a January chill.

Blessing shrugged. "That's the way punks operate today. Kill you for a dime. In any case—dead. We're trying to find some necessary papers. A will. All that. And by the way, we'd appreciate it if you didn't say anything about his being dead. Not just yet, please. No one even knows he was in France and there are details to be worked out. Better not have everyone thrashing about —until we find the will and his other papers, that is. Agreed?"

"Agreed." A will, maybe. Important papers, definitely. And it was a safe bet that Blessing and Dana weren't the only ones looking: Godzilla and I must have jumped right into the middle of a search. "But as I seem to be an unwitting participant in this affair, couldn't you give me some idea of what it's all about?"

"Don't know ourselves." Bobby had the grace not to look me in the eye as he said it: he was obviously lying.

"Sorry. We can't." Dana was at least polite.

"Oh," I said.

There didn't seem to be anything else to say.

As it turned out, I did not drive myself home. Dana drove me, but it wasn't to my house, where there was some slight chance I could invent a delaying action that would hold him in place while I got to know him better. It was instead, after a brief conference with Blessing and a hushed telephone call by the latter to someone who could only have been my aunt, back to The Crossing.

"Your car will be picked up by one of the chauffeurs and returned to your house. You're in no condition to drive yourself. And you ought to be at your aunt's where you will be properly looked after until you recover." This was Blessing.

"But all I have is a sore throat. I can look after myself perfectly well."

"Absolutely not. In these incidents there is always danger of delayed shock."

"My housekeeper, Mrs. Howard. . . ."

"She's not there at night, is she? No—it's The Crossing. Your aunt won't hear of anything else. Anyway, she thinks you need to be fed."

And The Crossing it was.

28

3

My esteemed aunt, Lydia Wentworth, is a famous lady.

Not that she wants to be. In fact, her one proclaimed desire in life is to be anonymous.

"A lady's name appears in the press on only three occasions," she is fond of announcing, ". . . when she is born . . . when she is married . . . and when she dies."

By those standards, as she is now in her dazzlingly handsome mid-sixties, her name should have appeared twice: on the occasions of her birth and her marriage. But she has never married and I think she never will, although she views men with undisguised enthusiasm. She is afraid, I am persuaded, that men wish to marry her for her very impressive fortune.

In actual fact and to her horror her name is in the papers all the time. She complains that she can't understand it, but everyone else can. She's one of the wealthiest women in the world. She's beautiful. She has an opulent life style. Fabulous jewels. Houses around the world. The oldest limousine in captivity and a world-famous art collection.

But in her mind's eye, she is just a simple person living a simple life and doing charitable works when she can. I, Persis Willum, have come under the heading of charitable works ever since I was ten years old and my parents had the misfortune to vanish at sea while cruising the Bahamas.

"Most unfortunate," said my aunt and proceeded to do her duty, shepherding me into adulthood, albeit from a more-or-less safe distance. "I find children alarming," she confessed; and sentenced me to boarding schools round the clock—a sentence sweetened, when she felt particularly robust, by occasional trips to the races in England or Normandy and house parties with assorted nobility in the south of France. "It is important for a young girl to learn the amenities," she had said, and taught me to ride sidesaddle, to curtsy to grownups and, after I was sixteen, to drink a "brut" champagne from the proper flute and to distinguish between a Bordeaux and a Burgundy.

It was an interesting education and I adored her.

An interesting education. Except that she didn't educate me about men. "They're lovely," was all she ever said on the subject.

So at eighteen I married and educated myself.

And by the time he had drunk his way through my modest inheritance and into the grave I knew all I wanted to know: namely that it's all right to fall in love but marriage is dangerous. At thirty-six I have occasional attacks of falling in love, but not many. My luck has not been good, my record has not been shining, and my choices have not been enviable.

"You really ought to marry again," my aunt is always saying, which isn't fair considering her own antipathy to the marital state.

Lydia Wentworth is quixotic. I long ago resigned myself to the fact that she has one set of rules for herself and a completely different set for the rest of the world. "You're not bad looking, my dear, particularly now and then." And she would shake her silver cap of platinum hair, flash her jewels, and gaze at me with momentary interest before going off on an entirely different subject.

It was like Beauty telling the Beast to have hope. Although actually I'm not that bad. I'm medium tall and medium blond and there's nothing wrong with my legs, I'm told. In fact, there are days when construction workers and men in manholes carry on wildly.

I scratch out a sort of living by running Gregor Olitsky's chain of art galleries and selling an occasional painting of my own. I have a car and a house and Mrs. Howard to clean it and that's about all. In fact, I *like* my little house and I *like* my little life and my reaction to the prospect of a sojourn at The Crossing was comparable to that of the peasant being dragged into the palace and ordered to enjoy it.

But I was here and there was nothing to do but surrender joyously to my fate.

As fates go, it was strictly first class. The minute I set foot in the great hall I found myself coddled and pampered and fed quantities of throat-soothing honey from The Crossing's own hives and plied, between times, with quantities of fine food and drink.

My arrogant cat, Isadore Duncan (so named by my housekeeper, Mrs. Howard, a notorious nonspeller, because "she's always jumpin' around,") had come along with me and she took to her new life like a duck to water. In short order she had the servants enslaved and Aunt Lydie's myriad small dogs subjugated.

I, too, was seduced by my surroundings. Was I under house arrest? Had Blessing ordered Aunt Lydie to keep me out of his hair? It didn't matter—the hot-and-cold-running service and free-flowing luxury were wildly appealing. Being poor may be good for the creative juices, as starving artists have bravely maintained, but a short wallow in luxury is good for everything else.

There were also great quantities of vintage champagne to seal my fate.

"So good for the health," my aunt said.

"Which?"

"All of it."

And she was right. I prospered.

Roberts reported with horror that my car was in desperate need of a complete overhaul. Happily, I gave him permission to take it apart. Why would I need a car when I was perfectly content to stay where I was?

Blessing and Dana hadn't totally abandoned me. Occasionally they appeared like twin visions bearing photographs for me to examine. Aunt Lydie always absented herself on these occasions. She detested unpleasantness of any kind: when faced with anything disagreeable she simply ignored it.

The attack on me had been disagreeable.

The photographs Dana and Blessing produced at regular intervals were always of oriental types. They looked more or less alike to me. I could identify none of them.

"I'm sorry. I'm not good at oriental types. And anyway, I was mostly interested in the telephone pole and the garden and his nonfitting coat."

"Don't be absurd, Persis. Lydia keeps talking about your 'artist's eye.' Let's see it." Blessing was accepting no excuses. As usual.

Dana was nicer.

In fact he was very nice.

Nicer with every passing day. He even turned up now and then without Blessing. There was always a good reason . . . more photographs, a question to be answered.

He rarely spoke. He didn't have to. I found myself, rasping less and less, talking my head off. I chattered away about everything imaginable. And he listened with grave courtesy as if he had a serious concern for every word I spoke. It was very flattering.

Courtesy—he was old-fashioned about that. And when he smiled it was like a gift.

At the same time there was something about him that was unreachable. There was a reserve that attracted me; I kept wanting to find the person beneath the person I saw every day. I sensed fire. But I never saw it. He was always unruffled and composed and yes, a little cold.

But I didn't believe that he was really cold. He was complex —that was it. Unfathomable. Little hints of another person kept flickering through the dispassionate surface.

I'm Aries; and Aries is always seduced by the unanswered question. Heedless, headstrong Aries.

If I ever wondered why an estate lawyer had the time to linger at Gull Harbor and The Crossing, I didn't wonder much. I was too happy to have him around.

You're not falling in love, I told myself sternly.

As if I wasn't.

4

Within a few days Blessing and Dana arrived with a photograph I *could* identify.

I looked at it once and nearly toppled over. There was no mistaking this oriental gentleman: I felt my throat begin to swell, my voice begin to disappear. I was back at Lassiter's front door with unrelenting hands gripping me.

"He's the one."

Dana and Blessing, those two specimens of super-cool, suddenly lit up. Blessing almost allowed himself to smile; Dana's India sapphire eyes shot out beams of light.

"Persis, are you sure?"

"I'm absolutely certain. Who is he?"

"Nobody you'd invite to tea."

"I could guess that much. But exactly who is he? I think I'm entitled to know: I've been shot at and nearly strangled during this affair."

"It will be better for you the less you know."

I felt my temper rising. "I am not a child. You insult me."

So they offered a soupçon. "All we know about him is that he was formerly a member of something called the Mitzu Brigade."

"I never heard of it."

"Not surprising. It's one of those obscure terrorist groups."

"Is that all you're going to tell me?" Apparently it was, but I couldn't accept a lone crumb—I wanted the whole cake. I had an idea. "Does this have anything to do with the article last month in the *Gull Harbor Trumpet*?"

"*Trumpet*? Good Lord, Persis—who reads the *Trumpet*?"

"Well, I do and maybe you should."

"Are you serious? What article are you talking about?"

"An article warning us that there had been a rash of international bank hold-ups and kidnappings for money which Interpol expects to spread to the USA. Somebody's trying to raise huge sums of money and the *Trumpet* was warning Gull Harbor's millionaires to guard their flanks. Terrorists, they said."

They were silent.

"What were you doing—really doing—at Lassiter's the day you rescued me? Why won't you say? What was a member of the Mitzu Brigade doing there? What *is* the Mitzu Brigade? Who is doing what to whom and why?"

Dana picked up the photograph. "Thank you for letting us annoy you with this."

Bobby began the slow rise from his chair, section by long, brittle section. Either he or the chair creaked slightly. "Damn lucky for us you have a good eye, Persis."

"But—"

Once again it was no use.

"We must rush off, my dear. Sorry."

And that's exactly what they did. I felt like a spanked child —one who might burst into tears of rage and disappointment at any moment.

5

The next day they were back. This time it was at my request.

Aunt Lydie and Isadore Duncan and I were just finishing luncheon. It was after the salmon soufflé and the fresh peaches. Actually, Isadore was still picking delicately at her soufflé, which had been served to her on one of the best china plates and placed on the floor next to the white wicker basket-bed Aunt Lydie had bought her and which she refused to set foot in—she was a table-top cat.

Gull Harbor mail is delivered to the front door by a lady who drives a red, white, and blue jeep and is extremely polite. Nobody keeps a mailbox anymore—there's too much vandalism by people who drive out to Long Island to vent their resentment of the rich by smashing mailboxes.

Today she was later than usual and it wasn't until after our coffee was served that Jennings appeared with the mail on a silver tray.

There was one letter for me. It was covered with colorful stamps and the return address was Sir Courtney Lassiter, Tribute, Gull Harbor, N.Y. USA 11771.

I reached instantly for the telephone. "Bobby—there's something here. I need you at once."

"Of course. What is it, Persis?"

"A letter."

"Yes?" A mere letter obviously did not alarm him.

"It's from Courtney Lassiter and it's addressed to me. Bobby —he's been dead for days."

"Hang on, Persis—I'll be right there."

"I can't open it—I just can't." Even I could hear the hysteria in my voice.

For once Blessing was sympathetic. "Of course you can't. Damn the mails, anyway. I'll get Dana and we'll be right there."

He was as good as his word.

"It's the mails," Blessing repeated reassuringly when they arrived, slightly breathless. "They've gone to hell all over the world. It's everywhere—especially France. He must have mailed it the day they . . . the day he died. You did the right thing in calling us. Now don't you worry. We'll take care of everything."

He took the letter from me. I hadn't even realized I was still holding it.

Dana made comforting rumbles. I wanted to bury my head in his shoulder and close my eyes but I didn't think he'd permit it. So I kept my eyes on Blessing. Still wearing driving gloves, he was holding the letter and slitting it carefully with a silver fruit knife he had taken from the luncheon table. How meticulous he is, I thought dully.

He read the letter several times. Then he passed it to Dana. Dana was equally meticulous: he held it by the corner with his white handkerchief. Did they really hope to pick up fingerprints after all the people who had handled it?

I began to feel well enough, now that they had opened the letter, to be curious. "What does it say?"

Dana shook his head. "We'll check for prints to be sure it's genuine. . . ."

Blessing followed up. "Strange sort of thing for Lassiter to do. First of all, why write you? Second, the message . . . it's scarcely his sort of thing. Wants to know about a certain . . . what exactly does he say?—'street photographer' of the nineteen thirties. A man named Praha. 'Very obscure,' he says. Long before your time, Persis—that's what's odd. Says he was obscure. Nothing in the books about him."

They stood there and looked at me, Bobby very tweedy and

36

country squire-ish and Dana very knock-you-dead in an open blue shirt and blue sweater exactly the color of his eyes.

"Well, you are something of an art scholar," Dana said finally. "I suppose you might know—or at least be able to find out."

Blessing continued to eye me speculatively. "I suppose it could be genuine, although God knows it's atypical as all hell. Ever heard of this what's-his-name—Praha fellow?"

"No." If God was ever going to strike me dead, now was the time.

They continued to stare at me—two men who had asked a question of what they considered a sort of two-legged art computer and trustfully, confidently, expected it to spit out an answer.

"Sure?"

"Certain. The letter must be a fake."

"*Sure* you don't know this fellow—Praha?"

"I'm sure. It would have been before I was born and, anyway, photography is not my field. Never heard anything about him."

It was only a little lie. I knew nothing about Praha, but I had heard his name.

It was the kind of name one remembered.

"Could I?" I reached for the letter.

They didn't give it to me. Instead, Blessing put it carefully in his coat pocket, handling it fastidiously with his gloved hand. "Sorry, Persis. You understand."

I understood, all right. I understood that it was the last straw. Once again Blessing and Mr. Alexander-Mysterious-Dana were insisting on telling me nothing, even though I was the one who had been shot at and strangled. They wouldn't tell me about the terrorists and now they wouldn't even let me see my own letter—the letter that was sent to *me*. Did they think I was incapable of handling the information?

Yes, I understood. I understood that they were shutting me out again. Once too often.

37

I'm not the type to make a passive victim: I take a very dim view of being shot at and strangled.

"I understand." I understood that I now had two scraps of information which they did not have. They believed we were the only ones who had known Lassiter was in the south of France. They did not read the *Trumpet*. An oversight. *Someone* knew. And they did not know about Praha.

I had two small scraps—very small. But I was going to run with them. I owed it to myself.

Then I remembered that my car was out of commission. I'd have to talk someone into giving me a ride to the gallery. I'd talk Gregor's alcoholic secretary, Withers, into letting me borrow the gallery van.

And run.

Maybe I'd tell Bobby and Dana later.

Maybe I wouldn't.

6

The first thing I did after I picked up the van (Withers, rattling her beads in the closet where she kept her favorite brand of Scotch, hadn't even noticed me take the keys), was to call Ed Simms at his dingy institutional green office at the FBI. Or maybe it was puce: the paint was so old one couldn't really tell.

Simms was an old friend. I'd once helped him uncover a treasure trove of missing masterpieces and he owed me, as they say.

He wasn't there. Naturally. No one in New York is ever there the first time you call.

So I headed for the *Gull Harbor Trumpet*. The *Trumpet* was a pretty quiet place except on Mondays, when they typed up the newspaper and put it to bed. Two harried and vastly underpaid local housewives batted out almost the entire six-page weekly single-handed. The truth is, they were more like martyrs than housewives: they even solicited and pasted up the ads. The only things they didn't do were the so-called society column and the editorials. These were produced by the Editor-and-Publisher.

Today happened to be Wednesday. A citizen burning to present the *Trumpet* with news of an ax murder would either have to push a note under the door (no one answered the bell) or find a phone booth and telephone. In the latter case he would be forced to leave a message on an answering machine. "This is your local newspaper, the *Gull Harbor Trumpet*, Long Island's best. If you have a message for us, begin speaking when you hear the tone and we will get back to you at our earliest convenience."

I, however, was not misled by any of this. Light years ago, in an idle moment, I had written an art column for the *Trumpet* and I was therefore familiar with the Inner Workings, unanswered door bells and answering machines notwithstanding.

What I knew that nobody else knew was that the Editor-and-Publisher was in there tending her clippings, and tending them with all the loving care great gardeners lavish on their gardens.

The clippings were her personal religion. With fearsome dedication she combed, day after day, *The New York Times*, the *Daily News*, the *New York Post*, the *International Herald Tribune*, the *Wall Street Journal*, the *Cleveland Plain Dealer*—everything she could lay her hands on in the way of a major publication, many of them foreign, searching for things that might have a Gull Harbor point of view. It made the *Trumpet* seem terribly *au courant*. As a result *The New York Times*, the *News*, the *Post*, the *International Herald Tribune*, and the *Wall Street Journal* also combed the *Trumpet*'s pages for items they could rewrite from *their* point of view. After all, some of the most newsworthy persons in the world lived in Gull Harbor or its environs. The only difference was that it didn't take them as long to browse through the six-page *Trumpet*.

Her name was Kate Cochran, but she answered only to Cochran; and she was right where I knew she'd be—in her office, clipping items.

Cochran was not your average Gull Harborite. For one thing, although she was still handsome, she was the only person in a community of immaculate dressers who always looked as if she had never quite managed to get to bed all week, let alone to change her clothes. For another, while guarding the honor of Gull Harbor and its citizens with a loyalty bordering on the fanatic, she was gleefully irreverent toward those same citizens, chastising them in print and to their faces with a lack of respect that only a peer would dare employ.

"You must understand Cochran," people said, forgiving her. "She was briefly at school in Paris in the thirties—the Sorbonne—

and she fell in with Gertrude Stein and that crowd and turned into a sort of precursor of today's Hippies."

"Sure I met Stein," she would answer. "I was invited to her salons a couple of times—met Hemingway, Braque. She thought I was cute. But I was just a kid, for God's sake. I can hardly remember her . . . or them." She had never married although she had a lovely long body and a marvelously sculptured head and nose and an El Greco kind of special good looks.

She was sitting today at a desk that was approximately the size of a map table in a war room, every inch of the surface smothered in half empty Coke bottles and papers of one kind or another. When she saw me in the doorway she shoved her glasses up into the unkempt turmoil of her hair and smiled with undisguised pleasure.

"Persis!" Gesturing with a huge pair of library scissors. "Come sit down. Where have you been hiding?" For some reason Cochran had always liked me. I suspect that she considered me a fellow Bohemian.

She pushed back from her desk and emptied an overflowing ashtray into the metal scrap basket beside her desk. "What's up?"

A wisp of smoke rose immediately from the scrap basket and without even taking her eyes from me she reached for an open Coke bottle and emptied it on the would-be conflagration. The smoke subsided instantly.

"I need to know who told you Sir Courtney Lassiter was in the south of France." With Cochran it was best to be direct. She did not like to waste time.

"Lassiter?" She ran her fingers through her exuberant gray-blond curls until she found one lock of hair that was too long. Without hesitation she clipped it off and dropped it in the scrap basket. "You, too, Persis? I didn't know you were attracted to older men. All the widows and divorcées in Gull Harbor have been calling me for weeks asking where he is."

"I'm not attracted to older men."

"Then there must be a story in it. Promise to let me have it

41

first." She studied me with deepening interest. "What could it be about, I wonder? Well, never mind—you'll tell me when you're ready, I trust."

I laughed. "At this moment, it's just personal curiosity." Trying to sound a bit mysterious.

"All right—I won't press. Let's see—I log every call I use in the column. Self protection. It was Nadia Milonsky—here it is. She didn't say it was confidential. I'd called to ask if she'd give me an interview and if it was true she was doing a portrait of the president—remember, he'd just turned down somebody else's?"

He said it belonged in a home for the blind. "Yes."

"The bit about Lassiter just slipped out. She asked me not to mention the presidential business, but said nothing about Lassiter. Inferred I might have an interview if I didn't use it during her lifetime."

"Typical."

"I remember now. She wouldn't discuss the president but she said she was working on four new portraits."

"I didn't see their names in your column."

"No. Same thing. Feels that they might not want their names in print. Everyone's scared of being kidnapped."

It was true: none but the super-rich could afford a Milonsky portrait. A Milonsky likeness on the wall was proof of having arrived, socially and financially.

"Who? Telling me isn't the same as having it in print. I'd love to know."

"Why not? No harm in it. All she mentioned was not having it in print. The whole community probably knows by now."

"I'm always the last to know."

"Me, too." She offered me a newly opened Coke and when I declined, drank it herself. I waited patiently.

"It's always like that," she continued finally. "People swear me to secrecy and then I find out the whole world's been publishing it. Well, here it is."

She scribbled down four names and handed them to me.

I read the list. "They have one thing in common—they're pretty international."

"*Everybody* in Gull Harbor is international."

"They're all more or less newcomers."

She sighed. "Everybody else has already been painted by Milonsky. She runs through millionaires the way Montezuma's Revenge runs through Mexican tourists. It's like the great society photographers in the forties and fifties. If you're not 'done,' you haven't arrived."

"Speaking of photographers . . . do you remember when we were planning an exhibition of twentieth-century photographers at the gallery? We never got our act together, but while we were considering it I called you for advice?" Cochran was a gifted and highly skilled press photographer. It was how she had started out with the New York dailies before her family bought her the foundering *Gull Harbor Trumpet* to play with. She seldom bothered with photography today—she had slaves to do that, freelance.

"At the North Shore Galleries? I remember."

"And you said we must not overlook a French photographer of the thirties named Praha?"

"The 'lost photographer.' I remember."

"You said I must try to find his book, *Parisian Nights*."

"They talked about him at Gertrude Stein's. They were all crazy for anything new. And they couldn't stand it because nobody knew who he was. They had to know everything and everyone, otherwise what use is it to be the avant-garde?"

"What did they say?"

"He was a genius. Prowled the streets of Paris by night, taking pictures of prostitutes, pimps, and criminals at work."

"You remember all this?"

"Of course—even then I had a nose for a story." She clipped off another curl—frowning, distracted, remembering. "He published a book, *Parisian Nights*, and before anything but a few critics' copies reached the public the publisher's warehouse burned

43

down. Then Praha's studio caught fire and the original glass plates were destroyed. You can imagine that Stein's circle would have sold their souls to see a copy: everyone was buzzing."

"You saw the book?"

"No one saw it that I know of."

"Do you think it was destroyed on purpose?"

"Parisians love to talk. Their version was—and they also love *l'amour*—that a society lady visited the Paris *boites* for amusement . . . it was la mode in those days. She met a pretty young man in one of the bistros and there was an affair. She did not know that he was a petty criminal—he said he was a sculptor's assistant and maybe he was that, too. One day he tried to blackmail her—either she pay him what he asked or he would tell the husband. When she threatened to go to the police, he killed her and her two children. Then he decamped with her jewels and someone began the campaign to destroy *Parisian Nights*."

I was watching her: she had lit two cigarettes and stubbed them both out after a couple of puffs. Now she coughed, the racking, phlegmy cough of the smoking addict.

When the seizure had passed she continued, gasping a little. "There could only be one reason, we decided at Stein's . . . there must be a photograph in that book of Praha's by which the petty criminal could be identified as a murderer of women and children."

"What happened?"

"Nothing. Except the war. It came. Praha disappeared. Nothing was ever the same."

Cochran felt around for her glasses and put them back down on her nose. She picked up a copy of this morning's *Times*. "Anything else?"

"No. Thanks."

"My pleasure." She began to clip, the long silver blades slashing swiftly through the newsprint. "Just remember, I get first crack at any story."

"I'll remember."

It seemed a safe enough promise to make.

7

I tried Ed Simms again after I left the *Trumpet*. I called from the telephone booth at the service station on Bay Boulevard and this time he was in.

"I need something, Ed."

He sighed. Everyone was sighing at me today. It made me feel unpopular. "Any use asking you why?"

"Not really. Just take it on faith."

"I suppose it's something you needed to know yesterday?"

"Approximately. But don't worry, it's nothing confidential."

"Oh? That would be a change, at least." He sounded weary. But then he always sounded weary. "What now?"

I had a mental imagine of him slouched over his desk, running his fingers through the short blondish stubble of his crew cut. He was the only man I knew who still wore his hair short. He would be in a gray suit. He was always in a gray suit. And his brown shoes would have thick crepe soles. They always did.

"Nothing much—nothing that will get you fired, anyway. I just want to know if any of the following citizens is Public Enemy Number One." I didn't know very much about Milonsky's new clients. Maybe one of them was bad news. Maybe one of them had known Lassiter and ordered his assassination. After all, they were people who might well be familiar with the Marseille-Menton-Manosque triangle. I rattled off my list and added Nadia Milonsky for good measure: it was she who had actually told Cochran that Lassiter was in the south of France.

There was a pause. Then Simms sighed again. "All right, if

45

that's all you want I'll run it through the computer. It will take a minute. I'll call you back. Where are you calling from?"

I gave him the number. "There's one more thing, Ed."

"There always is," he said resignedly.

"Something called the Mitzu Brigade . . . is it some kind of Japanese chowder and marching club?"

He came to life. The line betwen us crackled with sudden energy. "Hardly, Persis. Don't mess with those boys: their business is kidnapping and murder. Why are you asking?"

"People keep mentioning them. And are you serious—murder?"

"Never more so. They started out as a few Japanese experts in the oriental arts of killing. Now we believe they're a highly trained coalition of murderers from all over—a super death squad —serving a world network of terrorist groups. They're trained in Bulgaria . . . we think by the KGB, but we have no proof. Have you read the *Times* today?"

The question surprised me. "Not yet." My mind had been on other things.

"Then let me read you an item." I heard the rustle of papers. "Here it is. Page four. Headline: 'DUTCH MILLIONAIRE KIDNAPPED ON AMSTERDAM STREET.' The story says, 'Three people kidnapped the chairman of the giant Heikel oil refineries as he walked to his limousine tonight, the police reported. The officers said the abductors pushed him into an orange van and sped away. The kidnappers fell on Ryhs Heikel, fifty-nine years old, about seven P.M. as he left his office.' There are more details, Persis. I'll skip those. But the last paragraph is significant. 'Two other major kidnappings have occurred in the Netherlands within the last three months. One tycoon was freed upon payment of a $4.3 million ransom, the other upon the payment of $8 million. There have been similar kidnappings in other western European countries in recent months. A special terrorist team is believed to be behind them, although no one has claimed the responsibility.' End of quote, Persis."

46

I didn't like the sudden pain I felt in my stomach. "Fund raising?"

"Exactly."

"By the Mitzu Brigade?"

"Or a section of it, working for a terrorist alliance called the Coalition."

"How do you know?"

"We have our informants. We know how it works."

"How?"

"It's sad. I mean, the way they're recruited. Often they're idealists, believe it or not. 'Entre dans la lutte armée,' they're told, 'and you will know adventures and women and violence and class war and the grands hotels.' Often it is the 'class war' that attracts them, especially if they are students, or poor."

The man who tried to strangle me—a student? Anything was possible. "What happens to them?"

"It is a long apprenticeship. They must give up everyone they know and love . . . everything. Their values are tested and changed. And it is a boring, painful process. They are always tested, watched, assessed. And finally, if he is judged good enough to serve, the recruit is placed in contact with a 'regular.' The executive committee will then decide in what capacity he will serve."

"It all sounds very exact."

"All very military. And for the elite . . . the truly gifted and dedicated . . . the Mitzu squad. There will be months of special training. Languages. Professions—cover professions. Weapons. Sten guns . . . Beretta 95Ss . . . 375s . . . Tokarevs . . . bombs. There are specialists in aircraft, missiles, ships, security. By the time they're through training, they wouldn't hesitate to kill their own mothers. The Coalition has one declared objective: to upset the balance of power in the world. That requires funds—mainly to buy arms. 'Chercher l'argent' is their main occupation and the Brigade is their main tool—through murder for pay, kidnappings."

"Could any members of the Mitzu Brigade be in the United States?" I knew they could: I'd met one. But I asked anyway.

47

"You bet they could." All of Simms's weary indifference was gone. "We're one hundred percent sure. We believe they have agents here staking out likely kidnap possibilities. We're taking all possible preventive measures. But if they succeed, we'll be forced to advise for the first time in history that the ransom be paid: Italy lost three prominent men by not getting up the ransom on time, England lost a member of the House of Lords. They're killers. Ruthless."

"And what about assassinations? There's been a rash of them. Minor figures to begin with—NATO and Common Market officials, generals, government officials. Car bombings. Shootings. I've been reading the papers. Will it start here now?"

There was a pause. Good old Ed Simms. Careful. Honest. Stodgy. Incorruptible. Then: "We live in bad times, Persis. Sometimes I think morality is dead."

I knew what he meant because I knew Ed Simms. I also knew he was saying that he did expect it to start here.

"The computer, Ed?" There was no use asking him any more questions.

"I'll get back to you in a few minutes."

"I'll be waiting."

We were both too depressed by our conversation to say anything more.

While I waited for the pay phone to ring I thought about the first time I had heard Praha's name.

Last year.

It was at the time of the annual art auction on our one and only Gull Harbor educational television channel, channel 21.

Every year all of us in Gull Harbor work for it as volunteers, cajoling and threatening everyone we know into giving up their old china and moose heads and bric-a-brac and treasured bibelots for the benefit of 21. Afterward we help sell the same things on camera.

I hate to think of the number of artists and collectors I have browbeaten into donating to the cause. And, while there are fantastic bargains to be had, I am perfectly sure that some day the Almighty will punish me for the glowing things I have said on the air about certain objects thrust upon me willy-nilly to sell to the highest bidder.

That year I was squeezed onto a folding chair in an ante-room awaiting my turn on camera. All around was a scene of semi-controlled madness. Cameramen were suspended from the ceiling . . . crew members and aides crawled about on hands and knees to avoid being caught on camera . . . principals struggled not to become entangled in cables and equipment. Paintings appeared on the monitors upside down. Occasional passing legs received star billing. Names and copy were now and then transposed, with hilarious results.

The anteroom was even more chaotic than the studio itself. All about me, like flotsam clinging to the sides of a dock, were deer heads, floor lamps, roll-top desks, jardiniers, spitoons, umbrella stands, pottery dogs, batik wall hangings, mysterious sculptures, Chinese bowls, outsize paintings, nineteenth-century bronzes, and hundreds of other fascinating items.

I sat with my feet jammed in among boxes of donations and prayed that I would be asked to auction something I wouldn't have to lie about.

And that's when I heard Praha's name.

"The sons of bitches sold the Praha book," someone said.

I turned my head. Two disheveled men in shirt sleeves—volunteers—were leaning among the odds and ends behind me drinking Sprite from cans.

"I thought you were going to bid on it?" Vaguely interested.

"I was. Did you see it? No? Praha was some photographer. Artistic, you know. But the insides of brothels and all that. I tell you—great. Paris. Those women. . . ." Eyes brightening. "Came in with a bunch of stuff from some rich old recluse . . . you know, the one that died last year. There aren't supposed to be any copies left."

49

"So what happened?"

"They got a telephone bid before it came up . . . for so much money they couldn't refuse and they let it go. The one condition was that the guy remain anonymous."

"So you can't buy it back."

"That's right. Couldn't afford it anyway, from what I hear."

"Tough luck."

"You said it! It was some book."

And that was the first time I heard Praha's name.

Cochran had been the second.

The telephone in the street-side booth jangled right on schedule. I leapt out of the van where I had been waiting and answered by the fourth ring.

"Persis?" He sounded a little more cheerful. "No Public Enemy Number One on your list—sorry. But I can't say they're solid citizens because, except for Milonsky, none is a citizen yet."

I guess I was relieved. "Could you run them down for me? Remember, you owe me."

"No harm. You probably know it all anyway. Let's see . . . Marcel Martin is French. Made his fortune in pornographic films —you didn't know that, I suspect. Officially, he advertises himself as a producer of art films. You don't care where they were born and all that . . . just bare facts, right? Unmarried. Takes his yacht to France every summer. Wants to become an American citizen."

Martin. I'd seen him around. Typical small Frenchman. Attractive enough. "Art films? Well, well. Next?"

"Hans von Berger. Buys and sells aircraft around the world. Makes tons of money. Supplies Third World countries. Probably makes crooked deals but no overt dishonesty apparent."

Von Berger. One of those blond German gods. The hit of Gull Harbor society. He and Martin both had the hostesses in a flaming flap. Von Berger stood out in any crowd. But Martin was no slouch either—both were marvelous at kissing the hand without actually touching it.

50

"Hallsey Bryce," Simms went on. "He's supposed to be an inventor but no one has ever seen visible proof of anything he invented. English. Rolling in money. Must be at least seventy years old. His wife's about fifty years younger. French."

Bryce. A brutal looking, glowering sort of man with a pretty child-wife trotting from party to party at his heels. I'd met the whole list here and there at this or that party.

"And Milonsky?" I asked.

"Countess Milonsky, if you please. Claims to be Russian aristocracy—the woods are full of them. Father was an aide to the tsar. Claims to be in her sixties. Came here from France where the family fled after the Revolution. Immensely successful. Seen everywhere but won't allow press interviews or photos. Guards her privacy. Guards the privacy of her clients, too. She's painted three presidents and two queens and everyone else who counts."

"And they've all bought houses here?"

"You're where they run on the fast track, kid. And Persis . . ."

"Yes?"

"Don't go mucking about for once. Be careful, will you? Just because nobody's Public Enemy Number One doesn't mean they all play nice."

"Don't be silly, Ed. When have I ever mucked about, as you put it?"

"When haven't you? I get this weird feeling every time you call. You're a nice kid, Persis. But sometimes you don't have a whole lot of sense."

"Yes, yes—I understand." I was anxious to end the conversation. I didn't need a lecture from Ed Simms: I got enough of them from Aunt Lydie and Oliver Reynolds, both of whom seemed to think I couldn't walk across the street without deliberately falling under a car. Not that they hadn't—at times—had reason on their side.

"Please, Persis, listen to me." Every word was laden with pained sincerity. "This time call me before you get in trouble?"

I touched my throat. I touched the spot on my arm where

the bullet had grazed me. I wanted to assure him, to say that of course I would call him before I got in trouble. But I couldn't. I was already in trouble.

"Thanks ten zillion, Ed," I said.

"Oh—and there's one other thing."

"Yes?"

"In case you think I'm kidding . . . that terrorist consortium . . . the Coalition . . . remember this . . . it has one reason for being, one single purpose: the overthrow of the western governments as we know them, the destabilization of the world as it now exists, the death of the western democracies. Do you understand, Persis?"

"Oh, God," I said. And I hung up.

8

After I hung up I thought briefly of going back to The Crossing and just sitting down and quietly thinking things over. But then I remembered that Aunt Lydie was giving a luncheon for an ambassador the next day, and thought better of it. The Crossing would be buzzing with activity. There would be a million workers swarming all over the place. It was definitely neither the time nor the place for sweet contemplation.

I ought to return the van. After all, I had more or less pirated it, swearing poor old Roberts to secrecy as he drove me to the gallery where I stole the keys from Withers's desk and the sacred van more or less from under her nose.

But it was glorious to be on my own for a few hours. I had, I realized, been a virtual prisoner all this time, albeit a pampered one. It was fun to be free.

And the van was full of gas.

I ought to make the most of it.

And I ought to begin with Nadia Milonsky, the indomitable countess. She seemed to be the star of this affair.

I straightened my shoulders and strengthened my resolve, feeling like a knight girding himself for battle, except that my noble steed was an art gallery van. Well, people had gone into battle less well mounted than that.

Nadia Milonsky.

It takes a collection of very special gifts to be the foremost portrait painter in the world, which was currently the position occupied by Nadia Milonsky. There had been many great ones in the past: Velázquez, Goya, Van Dyck, Ingres, Rembrandt, Monet, Renoir, Sargent, Degas, Eakins. To survive, the artists had to be as temperamental, eccentric, tough, and overbearing as their clients. The will of the subject more often than not had to submit to the ego of the painter for there to be a successful outcome. In most cases the artist won. But there had been many occasions in which the sitter and the artist engaged in a monumental clash. These contests often ended in the death of the portrait, as for example, in the case of the famous "lost" portrait of Churchill painted by Graham Sutherland—Churchill could not tolerate the artist's version of him and so the portrait disappeared.

Painters of kings and princes, history has showed, could not be milque-toasts. Madame Milonsky was not a milque-toast.

Still, she always managed her affairs with consummate grace. And no one had ever destroyed one of her portraits.

To begin with, she was, as she frankly admitted, a "society artist," catering to the wealthy and the powerful. The deep psychological aspects of the sitter did not interest her. What she looked for in a subject was the best possible view, presented in the most illustrious and luxurious setting. "I want to do portraits," she once said, "that will make all my sitters . . . even a hundred years from now . . . look like kings and queens." If the client was short, she made him look tall by raising the sitter's chair and painting him from below. If the client was fat, she veiled the body in shadow. If the client was ugly, she found a single attractive feature and dramatized it. No came away dissatisfied.

Furthermore, there was snob appeal. She was very chic. As a child of the Russian court, she explained casually, she spoke five languages impeccably. Her jewels were the equal of anyone's. She had painted everyone of importance and traveled everywhere in doing it. She was elegant, imperious, and amusing.

She was, in short, a personage. And she was about to paint four people, one of whom might have known Lassiter was in the south of France.

54

I had to talk with her. I like to do everything right now. Aunt Lydie says it's my fatal weakness. She has a new fatal weakness for me every week. So does Oliver Reynolds.

I had to talk to Nadia Milonsky because in everything you must begin at the beginning, and the beginning had been Lassiter's trip to France. At least, it had been the beginning for me. His being in France had precipitated his assassination, and that had drawn men into his garden. Their presence had, in turn, dragged me into the affair. Now the question was, who knew Lassiter was in France before he was killed?

Someone had told Nadia Milonsky . . . someone who knew. So I had to see her.

But it wasn't, of course, easy. When I called her house an ancient male retainer who could scarcely speak English informed me that she was at Kennedy Airport, about to fly to France. Kennedy Airport is a place to which only a madman would drive himself in mid-day. The traffic is abominable; so is the parking. And there was a time limit.

I strapped myself in, clenched my teeth, said a prayer, and took off like Fred Fearless fired from the cannon. And when I opened my eyes I was there. So was Nadia Milonsky, dominating everything as far as the eye could see.

She was standing near the Air France ticket counter. Her steel gray wig, so lofty and curled and eye-catching that you never noticed her face, was firmly in place. So were her corsets. She dominated the scene with the serene nobility of the Winged Victory of Samothrace dominating the hordes that toil upstairs at the Louvre.

She saw me and her voice soared easily above the mob. "Persis . . . what a magnificent coincidence! You are going to Paris, too?"

Her newest young secretary was at the first-class counter, almost invisible behind a mountain of matched luggage. There had been several young secretaries over the years, all of them handsome and bulging with muscle.

Madame had divorced herself from the boring preflight details and was standing aloofly to one side.

"They're trying to make me pay overweight: they always do," she whispered in a tone designed to shake the rafters. "It's always the same battle. And me, an old lady like me—why do they harass me? And a starving artist at that!" The diamond encrusted gold pin on her shoulder flickered dimly in agreement.

"Your paints and canvases?" I pointed to the luggage.

"No. My clothes, I'm afraid. It's always the same battle— they *will* not understand that I must make a good appearance."

"Your houseman told me you were off to Paris for two weeks . . . I thought perhaps it was a commission."

"My dear Persis—this is not entirely a working expedition. . . . Oh, no. But it's partly work. That child who's married to Hallsey Bryce . . . too young to have any character so the gown must be superb. We'll pick one in Paris. Not that there's any urgency—he won't allow her to be done until I'm through with him—the male ego is astonishing. But it's a good excuse. I'll do the great couture houses by day and a few small dinners by night. It will be such fun. I will arrange to have you invited, too, Persis . . . you're a charming addition to any party. I can't think, as a matter of fact, why I haven't done your portrait."

I could think why: Madame's fees varied between $200,000 and the unthinkable, depending on the client. I couldn't afford either end of the spectrum.

"I'm not going to Paris, Madame."

She wasn't listening. "You really have stunning cheekbones. And I've noticed your eyes—sometimes they're green, sometimes they're gray. Very fascinating." She was studying my face with fierce, professional concentration. It was as if a giant spotlight had been turned on me. I squirmed.

"I'm truly flattered. But. . . ."

"I do think, however, that your hair could be improved, if you'll forgive my saying so. It needs civilizing. It needs direction. There's a great new man at Arden's. . . ."

"It might have been the wind in the parking lot. Also, I was running to catch you."

The spotlight snapped off. "To catch me?"

"Yes. I had to drive like a madman to get here in time."

The murky dark eyes flickered. "How strange. Why did you do that?"

Her secretary had left the ticket counter and chose this minute to interrupt. "Madame—the money. . . ."

"Gracious, Armand—can't you do anything by yourself?" Then, turning back to me and speaking in the same ear-shattering whisper, she confided, "It has to do always with money. He's no good at it, I'm afraid. None of them are. But he's very useful in other ways. As an escort, for instance. He barely understands the language, and that's good. Also he's safe, being a *cycliste.*"

"Cyclist? You mean he's a bicyclist?"

"Heavens no, Persis . . . I mean what I say—a *cycliste* . . . something to do with pedals. Isn't that the proper French word? Gay, my dear. Light as a feather and no threat at all sexually. It's perfectly lovely. Now stay right here—you look divine—and I'll settle this and be right back."

She turned from me and moved with great dignity toward the counter, steaming past the five or six other first-class passengers waiting in line with the insouciance of a mighty steel-topped ocean liner passing a string of dinghies.

There was a brief exchange. It ended with Madame digging in her purse and emerging with a gigantic role of money from which she counted out a collection of bills to lay before the awe-struck Air France clerk. In a credit-card world, it was given to few to see such wads of the real thing. The luggage was then piled on the conveyor by the gasping young secretary, who watched with relief as it slowly disappeared.

Madame swam with stately nobility back to me.

"That's that," she said without rancor. She snapped her bag shut with a loud click. "Now why did you come rushing out here to see me? What's it all about?"

57

I took a big breath. "It's about Sir Courtney Lassiter."

"Lassiter? I don't believe it." Her voice soared. "I *don't* believe it. You, too? Is every woman in Gull Harbor on his trail?"

"No, Madame. I didn't come here to chase Lassiter. I just want to know who told you he was in France?"

"Why come all the way here for that?"

"Something about the house," I mumbled. "Need to be in touch. Thought that person would know. . . ."

"That antiquated Beau Brummell . . . that obsolete roué? Who would care where he is? The equipment, I'm sure, needs an overhaul." She released a peal of laughter that could be heard throughout the terminal. People set down their luggage and stared.

I tried not to look as astonished as I was feeling. Madame and Lassiter? Could they have been partners in some final geriatric fling?

Again the great laugh ricocheted around the waiting room. "Dear girl, I haven't the faintest idea who told me. Can't remember. Unimportant to me. Sorry. I can't concern myself with old fossils turned out to grass by their services. British Intelligence— shipped over here to finish out his days passing back useless scraps of noninformation through the Old Boy network. Silly old goat. Passé. Finished. Who cares where he is?"

"Intelligence? You know that?"

"I don't know, silly girl—just guessing. But why else would Bobby Blessing be sponsoring him? Surely you know that Bobby was a charter member of the OSS when it was all society and the best schools? First they played polo and rowed for their schools, then they all went to war and joined the OSS. My dear, we Russians come from a civilization schooled in such things . . . I can smell it a million miles away."

A slight exaggeration, surely; yet it made a mad kind of sense. Two old men, still playing cops and robbers.

One of them now dead.

I tried once more. "I was hoping you would remember who told you he was in France. It would be so helpful, Madame."

She pretended to mop her eyes, as if tears of amusement were spilling out of them. They weren't. "Courtney Lassiter . . . imagine you thinking his whereabouts were so important I'd remember who told me. Child, he's an old has-been. And dull, dull, dull." Having disposed of the unfortunate Lassiter, she turned to more interesting things. "I'll see you in a week or so, Persis. I'm coming back for the Artists' and Models' Ball—I must support my own. So must you, being in the trade, as it were. What are you coming as? I'm thinking of Catherine of Russia, the empress, you know. It's a good thing occasionally to remind everyone that there was such a thing as a Russian aristocracy."

In the recent confusion I'd completely forgotten about the Ball. "I hadn't thought."

"And there's the cocktail party on Martin's yacht before. Ah, *les nouveaux riches! Quand même, je suis très contente qu'ils soient mes clients. Mon Dieu*—I suppose I shall spend a fortune on myself in the couture houses this week, but I must, after all, be decently turned out for all the summer fêtes, don't you agree?" A slight film glazed her eyes as she contemplated the festivities to come: it was at such social events that she harvested new clients.

The couture houses were not my territory, so I plunged off on another tack. "Madame, do you ever work from photographs?" It was just something to say. But I might as well have asked her if she tore the wings from butterflies.

The great curl-crowned head swung on me fiercely. "Photographs? That's heresy, young woman."

"I didn't mean to insult you. Forgive me."

There was a thunderously silent pause. Then she relented. "Of *course* I work from photographs. How else would I get anything accomplished? Can you imagine the queen of England, for instance, posing for all the hours required to do a decent portrait? Some artists make a plaster cast of their sitters' bodies to save their having to sit. I take photographs."

"Are you good?"

"Acceptable. I learned in Paris before the war. I know all I need to know for my work."

I wanted to pursue it. "I'm a terrible photographer. Who taught you?"

But the secretary was back. "Time to move upstairs, Madame."

She did not rebel. "All right, Armand—I'm coming. My dear Persis, I'm so sorry you're not joining us. Imagine your coming all the way out here to ask about a broken down old rake."

Armand took her by the elbow and began to shepherd her through the crowds toward the escalator. He was like a small child towing a magnificent remnant of Imperial Russia—a remnant resplendent in a purple velvet suit and a diamond and pearl pin with matching earrings that would have given a jewel thief a heart attack.

Just before they disappeared I thought I heard a trumpet blast. But it was only Madame.

"The Ball," she cried: and vanished in the general direction of heaven.

So that was that. Nadia Milonsky, whom I had hoped would provide the answer to one of the two puzzles I had kept from Blessing and Dana, had evaporated before my very eyes, together with any hope I might have of learning who had been aware of Lassiter's trip to the south of France, a trip that Blessing had said no one knew about.

She didn't remember. She was on her way to Paris. And even when she returned, I couldn't go on asking her. She'd said she didn't remember, and from the way she said it, I knew it was final.

What next?

That, at least, was a question I could answer.

Next was the Lydia Wentworth luncheon for the ambassador to Bonn.

9

I tend to forget that my aunt, Lydia Wentworth, lives life at a very high and speedy level. I forget because, despite her limousines and her racing stable and her art collection and her houses scattered carelessly here and there around the world, she is quite without airs. It makes one forget.

Her reception for the ambassador to Bonn reminded me.

The Russian–East German–West German–American situation was touch and go. Things were so ticklish, in fact, that the ambassador had been called back to Washington for a Cabinet-level conference. Now he had his instructions and was about to rush back to his post.

But not before he saw Aunt Lydie.

"He's an old beau," she told me, "and he insists on lunching with me before his plane leaves for Bonn. You'll love him—he's handsome." She and I share a *tendresse* for handsome men.

Aunt Lydie's idea of lunching with the ambassador was to invite a zillion Republican millionaires to join them for a "snack" at The Crossing and to organize everything on literally a day's notice. Orders flew this way and that. The broad acres of The Crossing disappeared beneath a carpet of caterers, decorators, florists, tent raisers, car parkers, security people, and waiters. A year's work was accomplished in hours.

"It must be done right," my aunt kept saying. "Philip is the most important man in the world at this minute. One word from him and countries will fall." My aunt is great at exaggeration.

"Is he married?" I asked, feeling a twinge of sympathy for any wife who had to contend with Lydia Wentworth.

She looked pleased. "Oh, no—there was never anyone but me. I didn't want to marry. I still don't. He was sweet about it— he said he'd wait for me forever." The word "forever" appeared to give her pause: she took a deep breath and fixed me with an anxious eye. "Do you think he'll find me still attractive?" She held her breath and waited.

I gave her the right answer because it was true. "He'll find you smashing."

The glamorous, glittery lady relaxed. "I do hope you're right."

She'd put on her new Galanos dress for the occasion, and as if that weren't spectacular enough, she was wearing the famous Wentworth pearls.

"Oh, yes," I assured her, "he'll fall at your feet."

And he did. But not exactly the way I'd meant it.

The luncheon looked like an Impressionist painting come to life.

Aunt Lydie decided that it should be held outdoors. She had consulted the *Farmer's Almanac* and it gave her the go-ahead.

"Sunny and mild, it says. The *Almanac* has never betrayed me." And she gave orders for the gardens to be resodded, the hedges clipped, the intricate brick walks weeded, the five fountains turned on and acres of blooming flowers brought from the greenhouse at the eleventh hour and set in the dirt of the borders in their pots so that they could be whisked back again when the last guest departed.

Her faith in the *Almanac* was almost but not quite boundless—she hedged her bets by contracting for four pink tents to be placed at strategic intervals in case the unthinkable occurred.

"But it won't," she said confidently.

And it didn't. It wouldn't dare.

The day had dawned exactly as planned—the air was soft with spring and the sun shown. A pink canopy, edged by potted rose trees, led from the cobblestone front courtyard to the three acres of gardens. The spring garden was already in bloom, ablaze with daffodils and tulips .The greenhouse gardeners, thirty strong, had created the rest.

Dark green hedges formed intricate patterns in counterpoint to the equally intricate maze of brick walks. White wrought-iron chairs and tables had been artfully scattered throughout, the tablecloths echoing the color of the tents. Every table was graced with moss baskets of white and pink and red flowers. Fresh flowers and tendrils of live ivy climbed up the tent poles.

At the end of the series of gardens—the centerpiece of the whole exquisite picture—was a Chinese folly. It was designed in three soaring arches built of teak in a half circle and embellished with complicated oriental latticework through which the trees in the background formed a green setting. On either side, bas-relief extensions in airy oak patterns concealed wings of brick. The tops of these, screened by potted greenery, formed a terrace reached by winding iron stairs. Seated here was an orchestra. Their orders were not to stray from Cole Porter and they didn't. Below the two wings were a kitchen and a pantry in which the caterers operated like an unseen hive of bees.

In the middle of the large arch, star attraction for the entire view, was a bigger than life-size bronze sculpture of a troop of gypsy acrobats created by one of Aunt Lydie's favorite sculptresses, Rhoda Sherbell. It was a surrealist work, elongated and exaggerated, in which a male acrobat, a masterpiece of ropelike musculature, balanced a girl on his upraised hands. She could have been flying. Two other dancers looked on, poised on their platform like aerialists. They were all almost but not entirely naked, their costumes scanty and rococo, their expressions detached and other-worldly. Lydia Wentworth liked show-stoppers.

She had invited over two hundred guests and they were drifting around the gardens like figures in a dream ballet. The ladies wore large and elaborate hats—hats were the rage this year. From a distance they gave the impression of enormous peonies floating across the green.

Perrier and white wine flowed. An endless series of dishes

63

appeared . . . cold salmons and veals in aspic and vegetables that looked like flower gardens in bloom and soufflés that rose airily and never fell and quiches of every type and dessert crêpes made before one's eyes and champagnes so great that just holding them in a glass was an honor.

Naturally Aunt Lydie and the ambassador were the catalysts . . . the action flowed around, but never far from them. He was answering questions, chatting, bowing, smiling graciously, but never taking his eyes from my aunt for an instant. She was right —he was handsome.

The scent of money was everywhere, cloying, clinging. There was an ex-king. Afghanistan, I think. There were high-level diplomats. There were senators and governors. There were golf, tennis, and racing greats. Broadway was there. Hollywood, too, with two producers and a clutch of movie stars. There were a couple of oil sheiks. ("I hope they're not planning to buy Gull Harbor," my aunt whispered behind their backs.) Oliver Reynolds was there, of course, following me around like a faithful dog. And Nadia Milonsky's four new portrait commissions were there, mingling proudly with her old ones and trying hard to look blasé, as if they were invited to Lydia Wentworth's every day. Martin was rushing around kissing hands and talking too much in his thick French accent; Bryce's uninteresting little wife was doing the same. It was a mistake: in these circles Overspeak spelled Underbred. Never mind, I told myself—they'll learn. The Milonsky portrait is the first step. And Martin has already managed to corner everyone with the party on his yacht. Would Gull Harbor ever discover that his money came from porno films? Probably not. They'd rather be drawn and quartered than admit they'd even heard of one.

Hans von Berger's head was a golden tower surrounded by fluttering lady moths attracted to the golden light. His problem was not Overspeak—he was barely opening his mouth. He inclined his elegant body this way and that, smiling, his beautiful head nodding politely. There was something familiar about him—but what? I decided I was imagining things.

Hallsey Bryce stood against a boxwood hedge, glowering . . . a sinister spider waiting for a bug to fly into his web. But who, I wondered? Was he already bored with his child bride? I watched the arrogance with which he shook off the one or two polite guests who tried to be nice to him. And I wondered.

Looking at them all there together, I couldn't imagine which one might have known about Lassiter. He was a lady's man, according to Nadia Milonsky. Could it have been Bryce's wife? Had she a mysterious past? Had Lassiter known her before she married Bryce? Possible, I supposed. Martin . . . he was French . . . he had a yacht . . . yachts went to the south of France. Was he the one? Von Berger. Very, very possible—an aircraft dealer went everywhere and knew everyone. Yes, very possible. And Bryce, the inventor with no visible inventions. What about him? He looked mean enough to order anyone's assassination. Suppose he'd learned that Lassiter and his wife. . . .

But it was all idle speculation. What did I actually know? Nothing.

The party swirled around me and especially around Aunt Lydie and the ambassador. You couldn't see my aunt's silver head because of the crowds surrounding her and her guest. I wasn't doing badly, either. I was wearing a very modest dress but the skirt was slit to alarming heights.

The music was great. A few guests were dancing. I blessed my aunt for having the party outdoors: indoors the noise would have been deafening.

I tried to keep an eye on the four new Milonsky commissions but it was difficult. They had split up after their first greeting and were now lost in the crowd.

I looked around to see who else was present.

Bobby Blessing was there, naturally, looking quite out of sorts, and Dana—Dana was one of the men not following me: in fact, he scarcely looked my way. Cochran was there, but as a guest because she was Gull Harbor, not as the Press: Aunt Lydie never allowed the Press. And at the very last possible instant— Madame Milonsky. She appeared on the terrace with the unexpectedness of a booming thunderclap on a flawless summer day and cried out in a voice guaranteed to reach the last row in any balcony: "My darlings—I hadn't the least idea when Lydia invited me that I'd be able to get back from Paris for this occasion; but *there* was Laurence at dinner last night and when he heard my problem he lent me his private jet so I could be here to greet my beloved Philip, whom I haven't seen since the portrait in Bonn five years ago. And that heavenly man—the plane is waiting to take me back!"

It was so well done that there was a burst of applause and a rush forward to greet her as if she, and not the ambassador, were the true star of the occasion.

"Sporting old girl," said the ambassador.

"Scene stealer," said my aunt, who was an expert one herself.

"Champagne, champagne," said Nadia Milonsky and everyone had champagne and toasted her.

It was in the middle of this that Aunt Lydie gave me the signal that the ambassador was about to depart. "He'll just creep away, Persis . . . he doesn't want to break up the party. Keep an eye on things for me while I slip out to the car to say good-bye. I'll be right back."

They moved away casually. They paused behind an enormous Chinese vase filled with spring flowers. Then they disappeared.

I did as I'd been told, drifting from group to group, chatting with everyone and trying to be Aunt Lydie. Chatting wasn't easy: even outdoors the noise level was astonishing.

Still I heard it. Or maybe I sensed it—it could have been that. Nor was I alone: it was the waiters—they stopped whatever they were doing and, for the briefest of seconds, were still and listening. Then they were moving—fast. They were running. I ran too. Because I knew about the waiters. They were Security.

The tableau vivant was arranged in the courtyard, at the very steps of Lydia Wentworth's house.

Except that it was really a tableau mort.

She was there, standing on the next-to-the-bottom step like a waxwork image. The ambassador lay at her feet, his gray hair very

66

red, the unreal red of a Halloween wig that had been dyed, even so, a more bizarre than usual color.

There were men crouched in firing position. There were bodies. There was a strange, burned smell to the air.

It was a frozen second during which no one moved, as if afraid to spoil a perfect composition.

Then there was an explosion of action. Shouts. Men running. Walkie-talkies crackling. Sirens in the distance. Men bending over the ambassador at Aunt Lydie's feet.

She alone had not moved. I could tell from her waxen look that she was in shock.

"The kind of attack you can't stop," someone said.

"They infiltrated the drivers," said another voice. "The chauffeurs."

"Aunt Lydie—please. . . ." I put my arm around her.

She was in a trance. "I never saw it happen."

"Please—let's go in. They're doing everything they can for him."

"He's dead." I could barely hear her.

"Oh, Aunt Lydie. . . ."

"He promised to wait forever. And forever came."

She turned and walked into the house. Her back was very straight. But I knew she was crying. Blessing was at her side. So was I.

"Take care of her," he ordered, as she stepped inside. He stared at the devastation behind us.

"It has begun," he said.

10

There was no thought now of my going home. Aunt Lydie needed me. She wouldn't need me long: she would stop grieving in a week or so and after that it would be as if the ambassador had never existed. It was her way of dealing with catastrophes. But for the moment she needed me.

So I stayed—through police and detectives and reporters and press photographers and, almost as bad, through endless friends who called night and day to inquire after Aunt Lydie's health and to learn what inside facts they could about the shooting.

Mercifully the ambassador's funeral was held quietly at Arlington and my aunt was too "ill" to go, so we were spared that.

"It can't help now . . . it's all over for him. So why put ourselves through it?" And she didn't budge from her bed.

Not once did she ask who was responsible for the assassination: it had happened, and the "why" of it didn't interest her. But it interested me. The trouble was I couldn't find out anything about it. No one took credit for the attack. Ed Simms was not answering my phone calls and Blessing and Dana were elusively nonpresent. I tried to reach them several times. I had decided to tell them the little I knew that they did not know. The ambassador's assassination had convinced me that it was time. But they seemed to have disappeared and nobody was about to say where. There wasn't anyone else I dared talk to. I would have to wait for their reappearance.

The press remained occupied with the Ambassador to Bonn Affair, as they called it, for several days. Having no hard information, they trotted out all their favorite terms and flung them about at random like an overage baseball pitcher hurling balls toward home plate in the fond hope that one would turn out to be a strike. "Terrorists," "trained assassins," "international plot," and "upsetting the balance of power" were terms that surfaced often.

But after a period during which no real information made itself available, they lost interest and abandoned the hunt.

The minute they did Lydia Wentworth revived.

"I think I'll go to Paris in a week or so." She was leafing through the *Times* and drinking her morning coffee, both with more energy than she'd displayed in days.

"Really?" I was surprised. It was a sudden recovery, even for her.

"I must look after my health. Nobody loves a sick woman."

I noted with some amazement that she was looking quite splendid again. "That's true."

Did I sound sardonic? I may have, because she plunged her nose deep into her newspaper and didn't look at me.

"This Dutch kidnapping," she continued after a long pause, ". . . they'll never bother with me. I have let it be known to my men of affairs that not one cent is to be paid if I'm kidnapped."

Her color had come back and her eyes were sparkling. She was definitely on the mend. I'd had no time for anything but her since the ambassador's death: now, maybe, I could get my act back together. Lassiter . . . Praha . . . there was so much to think about. And I had to find Blessing and Dana: I had to tell them.

She was still talking. "Not one single solitary cent of tribute is to be paid on my behalf if I am ever 'snatched'—I believe that's the word?" She loves to be up to date. "And I've let it be known everywhere. So that's that. If anyone's sniffing around with an eye to putting the snatch on me, they'll soon give it up."

No one who really knew Lydia Wentworth could imagine that she'd pay one penny of ransom: even bankers were not as hard to separate from their money as she.

She rattled the newspaper for emphasis, then continued. "It's so interesting—the president is going to France in two months. It's

69

for a Super Summit of all the Western heads of state to see if they can't douse the flames of the Bonn-Kremlin situation. If conflict breaks out—and Russian tanks are already poised on the West German frontier—all of western Europe will be involved. That's what it says here. Of course, it's nonsense. Jiggs says he will straighten it all out and the flap will die without a whimper."

I knew what Jiggs she was talking about—she meant the president of the United States. They were long-time friends: Lydia Wentworth's support had a lot to do with his being in office.

I wasn't as optimistic as she. "Perhaps . . . but there's always the Near East business."

"Tempest in a hookah." She laughed, very pleased with herself. I refrained from mentioning that a hookah and a teapot do not serve the same purpose: a hookah is for smoking, of which Aunt Lydie does not approve.

She poured some hot water into her coffee from the silver Guernsey jug on her tray. "I talked to Marianne and Jiggs this morning. They'll dine with me in Paris so I must go over in advance—the house needs looking after." A wild exaggeration if ever I heard one. Her Paris staff was so excellent that even the Rothschilds had tried to seduce them away from her.

But I didn't demur. "Of course you must, Aunt Lydie."

"Marianne says she's going mad trying to choose her wardrobe for the trip. She doesn't know if they'll travel by plane or barrage balloon. The Secret Service is so hysterical after the attack on Philip that nobody knows the plans."

"One can't blame them."

"I'll go shortly after the Artists' and Models' Ball. It's a cause we must all support—those starving artists. What are you wearing? It's in the bowels of New York City, you know."

People in Gull Harbor will go to the ends of the earth to dance around in fancy dress. I don't understand it; but that's the way it is.

I had forgotten again. "I haven't thought of anything."

"You must. My dear, you've been wool-gathering for days. You promised."

70

A small flicker of excitement stirred within me. Dana was certain to be a wonderful dancer—I could tell by the way he moved. I would think of something wildly seductive and clinging —I do have a good figure. We would dance the night away.

But Bobby Blessing resurfaced to break the news, by phone, that Dana would not be back. "He's gone. Called back to Washington."

"Did he leave a message for me?"

"None. He's a busy man, Persis."

I combed the newspapers for a clue. I don't know why. Perhaps it was some dim idea that his disappearance would have a link to current events. But nothing seemed pertinent: the press was single-mindedly preoccupied with the fact that the French had developed a successor to Exocet which could search and destroy both surface and sub-surface craft. From all the uproar it was obviously a happening of some import, but not to me. All I was interested in was Alexander Dana. Wherever he was, it would have something to do with Lassiter. That was the only thing I considered a certainty.

My good spirits departed as suddenly as a houseguest when the weather turns bad.

The single note of cheer was a call from Kate Cochran.

"Persis? Try Marcel Martin."

I wasn't tracking. "For what?"

"For what you want to know."

"About . . . ?"

"About the photographer, Praha. I've just been at Martin's house doing an interview about international cruising and I've learned from the host himself that he's the proud owner of one of the world's most complete libraries of pornographic literature. He considers it a collection of great art."

"Did you see . . . ?"

"He showed me everything. A big paneled room *full*. Wow! Even I did some blushing. But no Praha."

My heart sank. "Oh."

"So I asked him . . . how come you don't have this famous

book by Praha? It's one of the most famous unseen books in the world. Every great collection should have it. And you know what he said?"

Now my heart began beating again, very fast. "What?"

"He said, I do. Probably the only copy left. But I don't keep it here. Sorry I can't show it to you. The implication was that it was in a bank vault somewhere, right?"

"Right."

"But you know collectors, Persis—you know them better than I do. They like to look at their treasures, not lock them away. So . . . want to bet it's somewhere where he can lay his hands on it whenever he wants? After all, it has to be the star of his collection."

"Somewhere near. Like. . . ."

"That's it . . . like his yacht. The last place anyone would think he'd keep something that valuable. And I'll never be invited there. I'm not chic enough, but you are. I know that you're all going there before the Ball."

"You're right, Cochran. If I find it, I promise I'll tell you about it the minute I do."

"You'll find it, Persis. Call me instantly. I'm betting on you."

I was glad she was so confident.

11

A string of gleaming limousines and bright taxis wound like a sinuous black and gold serpent through the grubby streets of Hell's Kitchen on New York's west side. Ordinarily, Hell's Kitchen is not a neighborhood knowledgeable New Yorkers frequent after dark: but tonight it was transformed, at least on the route to the KIKI Klub, which was hosting the Artists' and Models' Ball. The streets had been stripped of their garbage —the sidewalks swept of their drunks. No one was being mugged.

All this had happened by order of the mayor himself because a collection of famous art patrons was venturing out of its platinum-lined lairs to mingle with the Bohemian inhabitants of New York's famous lofts.

I was driving in style in my aunt's aged limousine with its Lalique bud vases, its ample running boards, and its venerable chauffeur, Roberts, at the wheel. Sharing the ermine lap robe with me was Lydia Wentworth and perched uncomfortably on the jump seat was Bobby Blessing.

We were creeping along patiently behind an enormous hired limo which in turn was following a long line of assorted expensive vehicles from which an occasional masked head emerged to demand why we were progressing so slowly. The costumes dimly visible inside the cars gave the whole procession a vaguely Alice-in-Wonderland look.

The trip in on Martin's yacht had been in itself a Wonderlandlike experience. We had boarded the *Greater Gatsby* at Seawanhaka Corinthian Yacht Club, helped aboard by uniformed stewards. Drinks had begun to flow immediately, as barmen struggled to keep their balance once we were under way, and maids teetered about the deck with hors d'oeuvres and stumbled up and down the steps to the galley below.

I was definitely not the smash hit of the evening, costume-wise, as they say in New York. By the time I finally realized that there was no way—absolutely none—that I was going to escape this soirée, the Gull Harbor locusts had denuded the costumers and there was nothing left but a third act curtain *Chorus Line* dress. Well, not exactly a dress—but tailcoat, top hat, mesh stockings, and cane, all in gold.

The plot was to have our cars meet us at the South Street Sea-port to transport us to the Ball. I was cadging a ride with Aunt Lydie: at a party like this it's nice to go first class all the way.

There were probably a hundred and fifty guests on the yacht. Floating down Long Island Sound with a hundred and fifty char-acters in fancy dress is not an everyday experience. Even Aunt Lydie was startled. I'm not sure who Aunt Lydie herself was supposed to be and I didn't dare ask; but she was done up in yards and yards of pink tulle and pink feathers and pink-dyed pearls. The moment we boarded the *Gatsby* she looked around and peered wonderingly through her pink silk and pearl-encrusted mask. "Persis," she demanded, "who *are* these people? I'm sure that I don't know any of them!" As she spoke a cloud of pink feathers separated themselves from her headdress and floated down around her, creating a rather celestial effect.

"Well, you certainly recognize me," said a Kodiak bear.

"Oh, *you*, Bobby. Of course. But you kept warning me."

I looked around with a sort of bedazzled interest. The scene was already quite bizarre. What would it be like, I asked myself, after a drink or two?

"That big Cossack has to be Nadia Milonsky," the Kodiak bear announced.

"I thought she was going to be Catherine the Great of Russia?" She'd practically promised.

"She found just in time that Sonny Thrasher's wife was com-

74

ing as Catherine, though heaven knows she's not Russian . . .
actually, she's from Mobile, I believe." My aunt snorted a little—
she was not mad about Mobile. Too hot.

"The mayor of New York is here as a Mets' ballplayer."

"And the governor's a Yankee . . . he always was a money
man." Aunt Lydie wasn't being critical, just pragmatic. "But the
mayor's always been for the underdog."

I looked around for Hallsey Bryce and his wife and for Von
Berger and our host. I never did find Bryce but he must have been
there because his wife, sweet and demure as Little Bo Peep, was
sipping champagne from the same glass as a big, handsome
Musketeer I recognized as Ronald Chunk, the real estate tycoon.
So much, Bryce, for marrying a child.

I spotted Hans von Berger in the milling crowd. He was not
hard to find because he was dressed as the compleat World War I
German flyer, complete with goggles and white scarf. He cut quite
a dashing figure and I heard him telling people he was wearing
the actual flying costume of the famous ace, Von Richthofen. "I
collect flight memorabilia," he said to the crowd of admiring
women clustered around him. It is absolutely necessary in Gull
Harbor to collect something.

"Ah," they all cried, wigs and masks and hoop skirts bobbing,
"How romantic!" They would probably have said the same thing
no matter what he was collecting. Once again I found him
familiar; once again I was baffled as to why.

The yacht gave a sudden lurch just then and a Marie An-
toinette fell down the stairs into the main saloon, where she
remained in a stately heap until champagne was brought and she
was assured that nothing had been broken. Whereupon she rose
and rejoined the revelry.

"That woman is from Connecticut. Greenwich, to be exact."
The way Bobby Blessing said it you would have thought Greenwich was Outer Siberia. "What would you expect?"

Just then I spotted Martin. He cut a rather startling figure
as Nijinsky in L'Après-Midi d'un Faun. He was, in fact, wearing

75

next to nothing. I wondered if he wouldn't freeze before the night was over. Then I saw that he was dragging a goatskin robe behind him.

"She's just under one hundred feet long," I heard him explaining to the little group of oddities that surrounded him. "Ninety feet, three inches, to be exact. That's so she can go through the Panama Canal without paying the fee on ships of one hundred feet and up."

It seemed a good enough reason to me.

"Where was she built?" someone demanded.

But I never heard the answer because Young Abe Lincoln (Oliver Reynolds, actually) had appeared on my port side. "Persis . . . don't forget, you're saving the first three dances for me. You gave your word."

"Did I?"

He looked disapprovingly at my gold sequined mask and mesh clad legs. "Maybe it should be four."

"Don't forget me." It was Gregor Olitsky, my employer. He had come as the Eiffel Tower, a rig so impractical that I was sure he would never get off the yacht, let alone onto the dance floor. One of his sculptors had made it for him—I'd been hearing rumors off and on for months. It was an exact ten-foot replica of the *Tour Eiffel* with Gregor hidden inside the aluminum central cone. Oliver took one look at this ungainly apparition and drifted discreetly off to starboard.

"Damn it, Persis, how am I going to dance in this thing?" Gregor is a marvelous dancer and ladies will stop at nothing to get into his arms on the dance floor.

"I think you'll have to take it off."

He did not want practical advice. "But damn it, Persis, I had it specially built! You're clever—what can I do?"

I knew my employer: he would make a dramatic entrance at the Ball if it killed him. "If I were you, I'd hire two or three of the *Gatsby*'s crew to go with you and prop you up," I advised. "I can't understand how you ever got up the gangplank in that thing in the first place."

76

"I didn't. I dressed here."

"In Martin's stateroom? Which way is it?"

Gregor gave directions. I started off.

Pathetic little bleats of anguish followed me. "Persis—don't desert me . . . I can't move and I need champagne."

"I'll send some." I kept going. If I didn't find the book soon it would be too late. We'd be at the dock before I knew it.

The stateroom was more like a presidential suite than an ocean-going bedroom. The paneling was walnut, the furniture was William and Mary, the paintings were original Gainsboroughs, and the carpeting was oriental. Next to the enormous bed was a bookcase with a dozen or so volumes. I wasted no time but sat carefully on the satin bedspread and began to check them out. *Parisian Nights* was number six, right in plain sight, just like *The Purloined Letter*.

I went through it once, swiftly. I went through it again, slowly.

Then I heard footsteps. They were brisk, authoritative. And they were headed my way. I dove into the adjacent dressing room. It had a long counter with a long mirror above it. By standing behind the door and leaving it ajar I commanded a perfect view of bookcase and bed.

A massive Cossack marched into the room. Without an instant's hesitation, the figure moved to the bookcase and began to examine the books. When the correct one turned up, the Cossack undid his tunic and stuffed the volume inside. Then the Cossack turned and quick-marched out of the stateroom and through the saloon.

I left the stateroom and dashed up the companionway. We would soon be docking in Manhattan. I must not let Nadia Milonsky out of my sight. More specifically, I must not let *Parisian Nights* out of my sight.

12

The entrance of the KIKI Klub was bedlam. TV camera crews jostled the arriving guests. Microphones were thrust into masked faces. Guests struggling to press inside were further frustrated by ticket takers demanding credentials.

The large number of exotic masks didn't help matters .Some stood out a foot or more from the wearer's head and contributed to the disorder.

Aunt Lydie and Bobby disappeared. I don't know how we got separated but they must have been recognized as VIPs and whisked inside while I was still trapped behind someone wearing a giant lampshade.

The logjam broke unexpectedly; and everyone was swept inside with the swiftness of rushing flood waters.

I don't know what I had expected . . . a long winding staircase, perhaps, down which sultry models would glide like goddesses. Gentlemen adoring them. Flowers. Violins.

This was something else—more, I suppose, like the original Balls of the twenties and thirties. There were some painted naked bodies. There was the heavy smell of pot. There were affluent types pausing to sniff cocaine.

The lighting was early Stygian. Body pressed to body in uninvited intimacy. Somewhere in the infernal gloom rock music howled and pounded. The human stream flowed slowly and relentlessly in that direction: I was carried along.

On a balcony to our left there was more TV. I saw the "7" on a camera. I saw Roger Grimsby, the anchorman, bathed in brilliant artificial light and looking every inch as celebrated as

78

the celebrities he was there to interview. A murmur of "Grimsby, Grimsby," swept through the crowd as we oozed past and he smiled down at us, like a pope.

"And there's Ginevra, this year's top model," someone shouted ecstatically, as if he had just been permitted a vision.

"Oh . . . ahhhhh," we all moaned.

"And there's Luciana Marino in red, the TV personality." I loved the way the populace identified everyone we ought to be impressed by.

"Ahhhhh . . . oh."

There she was indeed, standing right next to Grimsby and looking spectacular with her black hair pulled back into a heavy pigtail and her body swathed in a bullfighter's brocade cape. I looked for Oliver, but I didn't see him. Nor did I see Aunt Lydie or Nadia Milonsky.

We squeezed into a new room, leaving the balcony behind. It must have had a bar because people began passing plastic glasses back like a bucket brigade at a number one disaster. A spirit of almost unbridled friendliness now took possession of everyone.

"Ever been to a gig like this before?" a Miss Piggy mask demanded of me.

I shook my head and pulled my sequined mask across my face. I thought it would make me seem unfriendly. I thought it would discourage Miss Piggy.

A flash went off—we were too jammed together even to jump. Someone was photographing a model who was backed into a niche in the wall. She was wrapped in transparent gauze. I was glad Oliver wasn't with me—he would have been scandalized. Oliver is a Puritan.

My mask was beginning to make me feel claustrophobic. A woman up ahead was apparently in the same predicament. She was done up as a perfume flask with NORELL printed in large letters across her back.

"This place is a firetrap," she cried. "I'm leaving!" But she didn't.

She was correct, of course—it was a firetrap. But how to get out?

"Drink?" A glass of wine arrived, passed by unseen hands. It tasted rather foul. I wondered why, for the price everyone had paid to attend this affair, a passable wine couldn't be served to relieve the agony.

I still couldn't see Oliver. Would he ever be able to find me? It was insufferably hot. Retreat was out of the question. And where on earth were Lydia, Nadia, and Blessing?

I tried to save my sanity by transporting the scene to Paris and imagining myself being carried into a ballroom by the Japanese artist Foujita, as I'd read about it in the past. I would be sitting in a large golden birdcage—and probably naked.

It didn't work: I couldn't imagine it. I was at the wrong ball in the wrong city and I wasn't with Foujita . . . I seemed to be with Miss Piggy. The best I could hope for was simply to drift along and assume Oliver would find me wherever I finally came to rest.

Where I finally came to rest was the Disco Room, a particularly black Hades rent by blinding flashes of light that increased the disorientation already made unbearable by the deafening noise.

"Isn't it great?" someone screamed. "That's the Special Effects Committee."

"Baby, baby . . . show me some stuff," moaned Miss Piggy, still with me through our agonizing journey. "Dance?"

There didn't seem to be any choice. I downed the last gulp from my plastic glass and tossed it into the air, striving to get into the spirit of things.

"Baby, baby, light my fire." Miss Piggy was getting ecstatic.

I wasn't keen on lighting Miss Piggy's fire, but I tried to be polite and I let my hips move to the music.

A new body appeared next to mine, this one wearing a white plaster mask surrounded by a halo of aluminum discs from which dangled other plaster masks in miniature. For an instant I thought it might be Oliver because the new body was so tall. Then I remembered that he was Young Abe Lincoln tonight. I decided that I was having a delusion—my head felt queer. That *terrific* wine, I thought.

Bam . . . bam . . . bam went the music.

I reached toward White Mask to steady myself. "Excuse me. My knees feel funny." It wasn't just my knees . . . everything felt funny.

White Mask wasn't sure he'd heard correctly. "Did you say you feel *sick?*" he shouted.

"No—funny." All I wanted was air. I had to get out . . . breathe . . . walk around. I must not make a fool of myself in this crowd.

White Mask was helping me. So was Miss Piggy. Between them they were clearing a path. "Sick . . . sick," they were saying and people were moving aside.

I tried to hold my head up, but it kept drooping to my chest. My eyes closed. I was losing touch. I could hear remarks as we passed, but they sounded very far away.

"Drunk, poor thing."

"No wonder."

"No. On something, probably."

"Don't be sick on me, if you don't mind."

It was humiliating.

I caught a glimpse of a Guardian Angel beret. Helping, of course. "Make way, make way."

"Back door, please," one of my rescuers said. I was grateful: imagine if the TV cameras at the front door had caught me leaving the Ball in that condition—whatever that condition was.

We changed direction, sliding through a side door and into an adjacent building, stumbling through the dark toward a gleam of light in the back. I could barely see. I could not walk at all.

We were outdoors and they were helping me into a car. I no longer felt sick—just tired. I remember thinking how wonderful it was that there happened to be a car waiting.

Doors slammed. The engine started; and we eased softly into motion.

"Don't be scared." I felt my sleeve being pulled up. I wasn't frightened; and I didn't resist. I couldn't have resisted—I was drowning in inertia.

"This will make you feel better." I felt a prick.

Then nothing.

Nothing at all.

13

I love dreaming. Maybe it's because my dreams are invariably pleasant. I am inclined to dream about beautiful landscapes or wonderful food or dancing with somebody fascinating in front of the Acropolis on a moon-drenched night.

Aunt Lydie, on the few occasions when we have discussed the phenomena, has always maintained that pleasant dreams are the result of a pure conscience.

"I, myself," she proclaims, "have never had a nightmare. Neither have I ever done anything of which I am thoroughly ashamed."

Few mortals, including yours truly, can match this claim. But then, Lydia Wentworth is not an ordinary mortal.

Nonetheless, for whatever reason, my dreams are usually delightful and I've often wished I could have more of them. Like the one in which Craig Claiborne and Pierre Franey teach me to cook. Or the one in which my simple little watercolor is bought by the Metropolitan Museum of Art. I'm also fond of the one in which I kiss a frog and turn immediately into a beautiful princess, although I realize that the real story doesn't end quite like that.

This dream started out pleasantly enough. Mostly it was about Marcel Martin. He was wrapped in his goatskin and we were whirling around the deck of *The Greater Gatsby* in one another's arms. I was cold, and he offered gallantly to include me in his fur wrap but I declined: it might interfere with our dancing and I didn't want that.

The orchestra was sitting in the rigging wearing fantastic

animal masks and they were playing something with an insistent Africanlike beat. Martin and I were dancing to it perfectly at first and everybody was applauding, some of them even daring to tap me on the cheeks and shoulders as I whirled by to be certain that I noticed their applause. Everyone was there. I recognized them all on the sidelines. I couldn't make out what they were wearing and they were a little blurred, like scenery seen from le Train à Grande Vitesse, which is the fastest train in the world. But they were there, all right. All of them.

As I said, in the beginning Martin and I were dancing perfectly and everyone approved. Our feet never missed the beat and I floated in his arms as perfectly as if we had been born to dance together. He was smiling at me, his eyes level with mine because he wasn't very tall. "You're wonderful, Persis . . . a wonderful partner. I will dance with you forever."

How nice he is, I thought, floating lightly in his arms. We will go on like this forever while they all applaud.

But gradually the beat changed. We began to stumble. Was it the music? Were we, perhaps, growing tired?

The beat was heavier now—more demanding. It was harder to follow, although louder. What were we supposed to be doing? The tango? The rumba? The merengue? What?

The audience was no longer applauding: they were shouting at us now. "No . . . no. Wrong . . . wrong. You must do better . . . better."

I was freezing. Martin wrapped me inside his goatskin robe and although my body was next to his it didn't help the cold.

"Better! Better! You must do better!"

We stumbled and fell. And when I was finally back on my feet Martin was gone. Bryce was there. But was he? I couldn't tell because of his mask. Von Berger? But no. Where was the golden hair? Nathalie Bryce? What did she really look like, anyway? I had forgotten. She was forgettable. Who were these people and why had they come to the ball if they didn't want to dance? Couldn't they ask the orchestra to play something civilized— something without that mind-altering beat?

84

But the orchestra wouldn't listen, wouldn't change. So I ran away. I pushed my way through them all, remembering to be polite because I didn't want to offend anyone. "Excuse me, please . . . excuse me. I'm so very sorry but I can't talk to you just now. I must leave, you see."

And somehow I did leave. I don't remember how I got off the yacht—that part is blurred like the faces. But I was on the dock, running. I was running toward a building. And as I approached, it exploded. Flames were everywhere . . . flames in oranges and tomato reds like one of Aunt Lydie's favorite dresses. How beautiful, I thought. Which didn't make sense, because how could a burning building be beautiful?

I should have been afraid. I knew it. I mean, suppose someone was still inside?

But there didn't seem to be any question of that. Whatever was inside was already destroyed. I knew that, too. There was nothing, nothing to be done. Except to admire the beauty of the fiery glow against the black night.

So I just stood and watched. I think I must have been crying at the same time because I heard myself saying "No . . . no . . . no . . . no." But I didn't know why.

Then I saw the figure. He was hunched over and he was running, running, running for his life. He ran in the shadows along the walls of the buildings that lined the street—old buildings and the street scarcely wide enough for a car to pass. I knew he was running for his life and I wanted to run with him, to help.

"Wait—wait . . . I'll come with you."

But I couldn't keep up. He was too far ahead. And anyway, I was freezing—and damp, now, too.

And someone was calling my name.

Someone was wrapping me in warmth.

And calling gently, softly.

"Persis. Persis." Pleading. "Persis. Please."

14

It was like seeing the same movie twice. The cast was the same: the dialogue familiar. Once again the form that was bending over me made me suspect that I had died and gone to heaven.

"Her eyes are open. Persis?" It was Dana.

Bobby Blessing's voice came from somewhere. It had the usual faintly scolding tone, the subtle but unmistakable inference that whatever I'd done should *not* have been done, or done better. "Surely, Persis, you must remember something. All this nonsense about Miss Piggy. How about some practical information? Be a little helpful, please."

"Her color's better. She'll be all right." Dana was plumping up the pillows behind my head and smoothing back my hair. His hand felt cool. "Poor Persis . . . you've been having a hard time, haven't you?"

I wasn't sure, for an instant, that we weren't back at Lassiter's. Then I recognized the French bergères, the escritoire. I was in my room at Aunt Lydie's.

"Alex?"

"Try to make sense, Persis. All you talk about is Miss Piggy and somebody called White Mask." Blessing again.

"Alex—what happened?" I was half sitting up now.

"You're at The Crossing. We had you brought straight here. You're all right. Don't worry." His eyes were so close to me that I had an impulse to step into them and drown in their endless blue.

Bobby sounded furious with me. "You gave us the slip before

we got in the front door at the ball and the next thing we knew some fellow walking his dog at three A.M. on the beach found you lying in the wash, overdosed on drugs. Luckily it was just before the tide came in or it would have been bye-bye Persis Willum. We've had them drying you out ever since. It's cost your aunt a fortune, turning this room into a hospital complete with medics and nurses, but she didn't want any publicity."

"I'm sorry." The ball—had I given them the slip? I tried to remember. It seemed far away and unreal.

Dana still had his hand on my forehead. "She didn't give us the slip; she was deliberately separated from us. They wanted us to think she'd met someone and gone off for a weekend . . . that ambiguous phone message to the house . . . she'd be found later overdosed and drowned. Everyone would assume it was all about drugs."

"So we had to set up what amounted to a private clinic here because we couldn't take a chance on the hospital reporting . . ."

I felt tears in my eyes.

Dana saw them. "Don't listen to him, Persis. He's upset because we were scared: we thought we'd lost you. And now you must tell us everything you remember because it will help us find whoever did it."

I tried, for his sake. "I was at the ball. It was crowded. Hot. We got separated—there was someone in a lampshade. You were all gone. The wine was terrible. I began to feel queasy—ill. They helped me out, Miss Piggy and . . ."

"White Mask. Yes, we know. What else?"

"A car waiting. I fell asleep. I think I slept a long time. Then questions—always questions I couldn't answer. They were cross."

"Who, Persis? Who was cross?"

"I don't know."

"Try to remember."

But it was absurd. They'd never believe me. "Cocteau. Beauty and the Beast. A lion. A frog. A bird."

"Masks," said Dana.

"What did they ask? Remember, Persis—think."

I tried. I really tried. "Well—like a song."

It was the last thing they expected. "A song?"

"Over and over. A refrain. Over and over."

Blessing spoke to Dana as if I weren't present. "The drugs made it seem like that. They were hammering away at one theme."

"Theme—yes, that's it. It was a theme. Like iambs. Like the Morse Code. *Las*-it-ter . . . *Las*-it-ter . . . *Las*-it-ter." It didn't seem like a name to me any more, just a series of notes fiercely accented.

"That's it." They were speaking to each other again and they seemed relieved. "Wanted to know whom she saw in the garden . . . if she could identify . . . wanted to know if she was there on purpose . . . what she knew about Lassiter . . . how big a threat she posed . . . not kidnapping—knew Lydia wouldn't pay . . ."

"All I wanted to do was sleep," I told them.

They didn't listen. "Luckily she didn't know much; but they still tried to kill her . . . and they're on Lassiter's trail . . . moving fast . . . we'll have to move faster."

"Sleep," I said insistently. "I just wanted to sleep."

This time they heard.

"Of course you wanted to sleep . . . that was part of the drug psychology—answer our questions and you can sleep. But now—you're not sleepy now?"

"A little. Not much."

"To be expected. She's still not detoxified." The way he said it, Blessing managed to make it sound faintly immoral. I didn't know what he meant, but it certainly hadn't the cachet of being debriefed, for example. It was more like being defleaed. It was undignified. Unworthy.

I made a great effort, turning to Dana. "If you will please help me sit up a little straighter?" I made my eyes as big as possible to show that I was completely and splendidly de-everything-ed and I stared at Blessing. "If you would be kind enough to order some tea?"

Dana did and Blessing did. And when the tea arrived (it was English Breakfast so I assumed it must be morning), I called up

Aunt Lydie's most queenly tone. "And now, gentlemen, you will explain what this is all about."

"You're not well enough. Later, when you're stronger, Persis."

"Now," I said. *"Right now."*

And they knew I meant it.

15

"If you're sure . . ." Dana began. "This isn't easy stuff, you know."

"I'm sure."

"Let me." Blessing took over—habit of command, I suppose. He pulled out a gold-tipped black cigarette and made a ceremony of lighting it. "Care for one, Persis?"

I couldn't imagine anything I would care for less at the moment. "No, thank you."

"Damned good. Sobranie . . . made from a blend once reserved for a grand duke at the court of St. Petersburg, so they say."

"Oh."

"You don't mind? Good. Well, then, let's begin."

"I would like that, please. I have been through a lot. I should like to know why."

"Of course. You've earned the right." Blessing blew a long, lean cloud of smoke. "It has to do with money—more than half a billion dollars, to be specific."

"Depending on the rate of exchange, over 500 million dollars today." Dana put in.

"And there are two groups after it—two groups who have been after it for more than forty years: the British and the Russians."

"Three now," Dana added. "We've joined the hunt."

"Russians?" My hands had turned unaccountably cold. I slipped them under the down comforter to warm them.

"No proof, of course. But it began with Czechoslovakia, now part of the Eastern Bloc. It began with Czechoslovakian gold."

Blessing paused to pour a second cup of tea. He had called for a carafe of rum and he poured a judicious two fingers of it into his teacup.

"It was the beginning of World War II—the Czech government was falling: it had already been dismembered by the Munich Pact. Before he resigned, the president of Czechoslovakia, Eduard Benes, made plans to rescue his country's gold—fifty million dollars worth of gold bars—one thousand tons of gold then worth thirty-five dollars an ounce, today worth $373 an ounce. The English agreed to help and to hold the gold in trust until the restoration of Czech independence—a day that never arrived.

"The gold was removed in small quantities and melted down. It was possible to do this because the central Czech bank normally shifted gold from branch to branch over a period of thirty days and thus no suspicion was aroused.

"The melted gold was then poured into dozens of different molds which were painted with opaque paints and packed in rust inhibitors for shipping. The Czechs were great merchants; these molds for replacement parts—for polished steel gears, connecting rods—were typical of their shipping activities. False papers were supplied: the material crossed the border one shipment at a time and rendezvoused in France. It was then up to the British to get it out."

"They did?"

Blessing ignored the interruption. He was not to be rushed. "The British named the operation Boomerang, for the obvious reason that the material was to return eventually to its source. A team of British Intelligence officers was in charge. The French Resistance and a few Czech patriots supplied the manpower. The plan was divided into separate phases, with a different British officer in charge of each—for security reasons. Unfortunately the planned points of exit were shut one by one by the Germans, the swiftness of whose victories surprised everybody. The gold moved from point to point, like a chess game."

"Three years," Dana said under his breath. "Three years of failure."

"And forty years of failure since," Blessing muttered angrily.

It had all happened so long ago; it scarcely seemed germane. "It's a fascinating story. But what does it have to do. . . ."

"Patience. It has everything to do with you—with us." Dana put his finger to his lips to suggest my silence.

Blessing continued, oblivious. "The final desperate plan was to transfer the material to a British cruiser that would rendezvous near Marseille. The convoy snaked its way across Europe to the south of France."

I tried to imagine what it must have been like—this fortune in gold trapped inside an occupied country with no way to get it out. Germans everywhere. The bombing raids. The war.

But I couldn't. It had no reality. It was only pictures in a book—images on a screen. I am an artist. My life is visual. And I couldn't add the final reality that comes to an artist from being present and seeing with his own eyes. It was so far merely an adventure story and that was all.

"The cruiser—it came?"

"The cruiser never made the rendezvous. It was lost en route. And after that the whole affair went to hell." Failure—any kind of failure—did not please Bobby Blessing. He filled his teacup with rum and drank it down without pausing.

"The gold," said Dana, "disappeared into thin air. There was a massacre at the transfer point. The gold vanished. Someone in the operation knew those molds were solid gold. But how? Either by wit or because he had been told. Perhaps some of the cosmoline rubbed off; perhaps he could distinguish by weight . . . there are a number of possibilities, all presupposing either a traitor or a technician or both."

Blessing was calmer now. "The Brits sent survivors of their team down there year after year—matter of honor with them. As each appeared to get close to the answer he was murdered. Lassiter was the last. We were friends from the old days. He must have been getting close this time for them to set the dogs on him, poor bastard."

"I'm so sorry. And the Russians?"

"Naturally they know about the lost gold and they'd like to get their hands on it to finance their campaign to upset the western powers by backing the Coalition. Terrorism is expensive. The Russians don't want to show their hand publicly by passing out funds, so they encourage the Coalition to do its own fund raising, and they even help out now and then. We know they've lost agents in the Marseille region. And it's obvious they've inspired the Mitzu Brigade to go on the hunt for the gold."

"Because they were at Lassiter's?"

"Exactly. We believe somebody overpaid Mitzu to eliminate Lassiter . . . murder for hire is one of their fund raisers, of course. Mitzu got suspicious—the area was right . . . the victim was right . . . the history of the other dead Englishmen was right. They scented the lost gold. Hence the sacking of Lassiter's house. Hence your kidnapping and interrogation. . . ."

"Hence everything. Hence you wouldn't let me leave Aunt Lydie's—trying to protect me. And the murder of the ambassador . . . that means the destabilization plan is beginning here?"

"The activities of the Coalition change what might have been purely a British affair into everyone's affair. If the Coalition's agents get their hands on that half billion dollars," Dana said, "they can buy weapons like. . . ."

"If they get their hands on that more than half billion dollars before we do we can all begin to imagine the unimaginable." Blessing stamped out his cigarette furiously. It crumbled into black dust from the frenzy of his attack.

Dana had a faraway look. "I think she can imagine."

And the president was traveling to France.

"Is a submarine safe?"

They didn't think it was a foolish question. "There's a new weapon. . . ."

"For sale?"

93

"Everything is for sale if you have the price."

I didn't want to hear any more. I slipped down in the bed until the comforter touched my chin. I closed my eyes.

"It's been too much for one day," Dana whispered. "Let's go. Let her rest."

He was right. It had been.

I heard them tiptoe out. I heard the door close. I think, surprisingly, that I slept.

16

I slept off and on all that day and into the next. When Hannah, Aunt Lydie's personal maid, appeared with my breakfast tray I found that I felt like a new woman. I was definitely clear-headed, definitely strong, definitely cured.

And I realized that I had definitely forgotten to tell Blessing and Dana about Praha and what I'd learned.

Now Dana had disappeared again and Blessing wouldn't be back until evening.

Aunt Lydie was around, though. She popped her head in just as I'd finished my bath and was pulling on a pair of white cotton jeans.

"Oh, excuse me, Persis. I'm glad to see you're up and about."

"So am I, Aunt Lydie." I pulled on a white knit shirt and went to the dressing table to examine myself in the mirror. I looked a little thinner, but otherwise none the worse for wear.

My aunt stood behind me and examined me with a quizzical eye. She was done up in a beige and white Chanel suit. Ropes of pearls and gold chains cascaded down the front of her white silk blouse. Her handmade Italian shoes, I noted, were also beige and white.

"Persis," she said, "don't you ever wear skirts? You have such attractive legs."

"Not practical," I told her. "I'm a working girl."

"You young people—always practical. She's wearing trousers, too."

"Who's wearing trousers?" Aunt Lydie is a mistress of the non sequitur.

"The young person waiting to see you downstairs. She's called every day since the ball . . . since you've been out of commission. I didn't realize that you were such good friends."

"What young person, Aunt Lydie?" Sometimes she could be maddeningly vague and this was one of the times.

"The child who's married to that cross-looking man, Hallsey Bryce."

"*She's* waiting to see me?" I couldn't imagine it. I don't think I'd spoken to her more than five or six times.

"Indeed she is. What a dear little thing—so concerned about you. And parked right here on the doorstep this morning. I think the least you can do is to see her, even though she does wear trousers. I've put her in the morning room." And she went dashing off, heels beating a bright staccato on the hallway floor, calling back something about having to do some shopping and then back for an appointment and then to the races because she had a horse running. A few seconds later I heard the Austin Princess start up in the cobblestone courtyard and knew she was on her way.

I put on my lipstick and went downstairs to see—what was her name?—Nathalie Bryce.

"Good morning. Aren't you nice to come see me."

She jumped up when I came in the room. I'd always thought her an uninteresting looking little thing: her eyebrows almost met over the bridge of her nose, her features were not refind, her body tended to be stocky. When the bloom of youth was gone she would be in trouble. All these things were obvious to the artist's eye though probably not yet visible to anyone else. And today she was not at her best—she looked harassed and worried.

"Oh, Mrs. Willum . . . thank God!"

Her slacks were too red. Too baggy. Too long. Her hair was too short. Her shoes had those funny V-shaped heels the French were featuring this year. And her stockings were colored—the wrong color—too bright, almost purple.

But the odd thing was that there was something appealing about the disastrous nonorganization of her appearance . . . the kind of appeal one finds in a puppy that trips over its own feet and knocks things over with its wagging tail.

There was also something appealing about her perpetually worried look. Seeing her now, I realized that I had almost never seen her when she didn't look worried. There was in her appearance something of a lost child who is not entirely certain of his welcome at the first door he knocks upon.

Funny. A girl with a husband like Hallsey Bryce, who drove the most expensive cars and had bought one of the most expensive mansions in Gull Harbor. What did she have to be worried about?

It didn't make sense.

"Oh thank God," she said again. "Thank God! He's out of town—I don't know where. Thank God you're here."

It seemed an unlikely thing to say. "Please call me Persis, Nathalie. What is it? Are you in trouble?"

Her hands were clasped together so tightly that her knuckles were white.

"I saw them take you away at the ball."

I was instantly alert. "You did? How did you happen to notice?"

"We were on the balcony. I saw you come in. I wondered how you would ever join the rest of us, it was so crowded. Then they took you away."

"I see. Why, exactly, did it worry you? I was just feeling a little claustrophobic."

"It worried me because. . . ." With absolutely no warning she burst into tears. They cascaded down her cheeks as if a dam had burst. Perhaps it had. She made no effort to mop up the flood.

I pulled a handkerchief from my pocket and went to the rescue.

"I have to leave him." Her face looked like a watercolor portrait someone had left outdoors in a downpour—all the features appeared to have run together.

"Here, blow your nose, child. And for goodness sakes, stop crying. You're not making any sense. Leave whom?"

"First it happened in Belgium. They were nice people. So

kind to us. And a kidnapping. Hallsey was there on business for several months. He moved us to Norway. He was doing business with the government. Patents, he said. And again people were kind to us. Another kidnapping. Then Amsterdam. The same thing, only it was after we had come to America. I couldn't have stood to see again the fear and suffering."

It wasn't easy to understand her between the wrenching sobs, but I got the general idea. "Are you saying, Nathalie, that you thought I'd been kidnapped?"

"I can't tell you what I thought: I had to see you with my two eyes to be certain it was true that you were home and all right. I had to. Forgive me."

I have never seen a girl on the bare edge of a breakdown, but I was seeing one now. Her eyes were unfocused, her body totally uncoordinated. I put my hands on her shoulders, gently led her to the love seat beneath the window, and pressed her down among the pillows Aunt Lydie had needlepointed. They had little slogans. "Be reasonable—do it my way," said the one behind her head. "I'm perfect," said the one behind her shoulders. Aunt Lydie has spells of being domestic, but not very.

I sat down beside her and put my arm around her shaking shoulders. She buried her head in my white shirt and almost immediately I could feel wetness seeping through.

"I'm all right," I said. "You needn't have worried. They'd never kidnap me—nobody would pay the ransom."

"They didn't pay the ransom in Belgium and he was killed and dumped in the Wester Schelde. You don't know. . . ."

"Hallsey—your husband—surely you don't think. . . ."

"Think? I haven't been able to think coherently for months. I haven't been able to sleep. I wanted a father—I'd never really had a father. I thought he'd be everything . . . cherish and protect and love me forever. I would never have to worry about growing old—that was when father deserted my mother . . . she wasn't young any more. Hallsey was so much older . . . I would never have that fear. Fear? I never knew what fear was until now."

"But what do you fear?"

There was a long silence. Finally she spoke. "I fear *him*. I fear him because things happen where he is—nasty things. Seeing you being dragged out of the KIKI Klub decided me. They can't all be coincidences. Whenever we make an effort . . . 'be nice to them, Nathalie, they're important to me.' 'Smile, Nathalie—it's a man who likes young girls.' 'Go sit with the gentleman, Nathalie —he has a fondness for nymphets . . .' " Her shoulders heaved, and I thought for a moment she would be ill all over me and my now soggy whites. But I held her tight and gradually the rise and fall of her shoulders subsided.

I looked down at this child in my arms and thought how wonderful it was that she cared enough to be certain I was alive and well.

"When I saw them taking you . . . you were the only one in this whole place, aside from Madame Milonsky, who has bothered to be nice to me and *she* doesn't like my clothes . . . I had to know that you were all right. You understand?"

"I do. And as you see, I'm all right. What about you?" I hadn't thought about this girl for two consecutive minutes before. But now it was suddenly important that she should be safe.

"I'm leaving tonight. Marcel will take care of me. We're leaving for the south of France. He's making a film—Marseille is headquarters for his studio. It's cheaper, he says. And more agreeable. He has an apartment on the Boulevard Longchamp and later his yacht will come over and we'll live aboard her in the Old Port. At least he's young. And maybe, just maybe I'll get to star in a film."

Did she *know* what kind of films he made? Some people never make the right moves. But who was I to criticize? My life was a tapestry of wrong moves . . . a disaster of wrong choices.

"I hope you'll be happy." I was certainly the last to judge. But Martin?

"Please, don't tell anyone. . . ."

That she suspected Bryce of having people kidnapped? That she was running off with a porno king? They would think I was mad.

"Don't worry, Nathalie. I won't. But please let me know. . . ."

"You can reach me any time. Number eighteen, Boulevard Longchamp . . . I've already memorized it. It's going to be fun. I haven't had any fun for so long. . . ."

"I'm sure you will."

I walked to the door with her and watched her cross the courtyard to her gray Mercedes. She climbed in and then turned and waved to me.

"Good-bye!"

"*Au revoir.*"

But I couldn't help wondering if what I should have been saying was "*Adieu.*" It has an entirely different meaning.

It means, literally, "to God."

As I waved good-bye to her a yellow cab whirled into the courtyard, missing the Mercedes by inches.

17

It isn't every day that a great painter has need of advice, but apparently Nadia Milonsky did. And she must have needed it desperately, because she was inviting me to her studio, which had been off limits for as long as anyone could remember.

The message, delivered by hand by the Gull Harbor taxicab Madame employed for all her minor errands, arrived as Nathalie's car departed. It was scribbled in gigantic felt-tip pen letters on the inside of a flowery get-well card. Madame, obviously, was not fussy about her stationery.

I'm just back from a flying trip abroad to discover that I'm in the throes of painter's block. I've looked at the current portrait and I HATE it. Worse, I can't CURE it. Never happened before. Help! Cab will transport you to and from.
                                                              Nadia M.

Naturally I hurled myself into the cab: it never even occurred to me to say "no." I was so flattered I would have run there barefoot. Not even Madame's sitters had been inside that studio and when she entertained it was always at one of the Gull Harbor clubs. "Darlings, I hope you don't mind . . . my house is such a hovel." Work that required the actual presence of her sitters was executed in their own houses. Madame did the finishing touches privately in her studio, working from photos and without the presence of her clients.

As a sometime portrait painter myself, I could understand how it might happen—even to someone as skilled as the countess.

It happens to every painter sooner or later . . . there you are, painting happily away after a lifetime of successful portraits, and suddenly one of them goes bad and everything you do only makes it worse. You don't dare show it to the unfortunate subject—you're sure your career will be ruined. You work and rework it: it only gets worse. There's only one solution, finally, and that is the one Madame had chosen—bring in an experienced, outside professional. Nine times out of ten he will put his finger on the problem. Even more important, he won't talk.

So here I was on the way to Nadia's. And I owed it to my experienced eye and my reputation for discretion. I was thrilled. In my field Milonsky was a giant: to be invited to help her was like receiving a summons from Jupiter.

The cab turned on to one of the modest streets in mid-village. We were in the little area that constitutes Gull Harbor's "downtown"—home of the Gull Harbor Chemist, the Country Boulangerie, the Village Store, the Book Nook, the Full Glass (the most important merchant in town), and one or two other chic little enterprises necessary for the daily existence of the citizens. The taxicab dodged into a space between Never on Sunday (a lingerie shop) and the Big Cheese and there we were—in another world. Sitting behind neatly pruned privet hedges were a dozen or so unostentatious houses guarded by the square of shops around them like the interior of the Alamo by its walls and blockhouses. It was an area most of Gull Harbor didn't even know existed.

The cab deposited me in front of number twelve. "This is it," said the driver. "My orders are to be back for you in half an hour." The taxi drove off in a flash of yellow.

Milonsky's house was also yellow, but the genteel shade of watered-down lemon juice. It was encased in aluminum siding and surrounded by altogether unenthusiastic plantings of the most anonymous kind.

A manservant of indeterminate age greeted me at the door and led me without comment through a decently appointed living room and down a small hall to what must originally have been a downstairs bedroom. It was now Madame's atelier.

102

Madame was addressing her easel when I stepped in. She was addressing it with the gritty ferocity of a racing helmsman addressing the tiller of a recalcitrant sailing yacht.

"*Damn*—this portrait is going to finish by driving me mad. A disaster! I need your help, Persis. Where have I gone wrong?"

She stepped back, almost bumping into me, and threw out her arms in a gesture of martyrdom and despair. Specks of paint flew off her brush and splattered the canvas. She didn't seem to notice.

The atelier still had the air of a bedroom. There was no skylight, no sink, no linoleum floor. Instead there were two very ordinary windows without curtains and a clothes closet on one wall and tired looking green wall-to-wall carpeting. It was obvious from the carpeting that Madame was a neat painter despite her splashing brush. Obviously she was in the grip of fierce frustration at the moment.

Only the big studio easel in front of her and a high, upholstered sitter's chair—currently occupied by a spread-out and draped man's three-piece gray suit—proclaimed the room's true identity.

Propped on the easel was a portrait of Hallsey Bryce. It was more than half completed. Pinned to the back stanchion of the easel directly above the painting were several photographs of the subject which the artist was using for reference. In the photos Bryce was wearing the three-piece gray suit that was draped across the chair. The clothes were present: the sitter was not.

I studied the painting. If she wanted my help, she would get it, and honestly. I took my time. And as I looked, little worms of unease began to wriggle beneath my skin.

"What have I done?" she was asking. "I'm suicidal. This has never happened before. I've lost it and I can't get it back. Please tell me—where have I gone wrong? You know the man."

The ten-by-eighteen canvas had a hand-carved Hydenrich frame already placed around it, a trick employed by some portrait painters because they believe it easier to imagine the final result with the frame in place. On the wall opposite was a large mirror, another painter's trick: when things go wrong it is sometimes helpful to look at the canvas in reverse, as reflected in the mirror. Often unsuspected flaws show up in the mirror image.

I saw the problem almost at once. Without realizing it, she had caught the evil and corruption and viciousness of the man who was Hallsey Bryce, qualities he didn't show in public but that Nadia Milonsky's brilliant intuitive talent had reproduced without her even being aware of what she was doing. The result was a portrait that was alarming—actually frightening. But how could I explain? What could I tell her?

I found the portrait so loathesome that my eye strayed from it as I tried to form the words of a critique that would be helpful. Seeking respite, I gazed at the photographs thumbtacked on the easel. Bryce in profile. Bryce full face. Bryce three quarters. Different poses; different lights. Strange, disturbing, masterful photographs. Something tugged at the back of my mind. What was it?

"It's a wonderful painting, Madame." Might as well take the plunge. "No question of who it is. But . . ." I paused, still searching for the right words, "I think the smile is wrong. I think that man has a sinister smile . . . and you've caught it. Perhaps if you toned it down—although it looks just like him—it's certainly his smile . . . but I hate it . . . in person, I mean. . . ."

She was already working with the brush. In a dozen strokes the smile was gone. It changed the whole portrait. Bryce no longer looked like a decadent monster reveling in the spectacle of an enemy being burned at the stake.

"Magnificent, Persis. You've saved my life. By all that's holy, I'm grateful. You put your finger exactly on the problem. I never would have found it. Look—now he's the real Bryce . . . a bit cold, perhaps, but not so . . . weird." She was wearing a blue satin smock and I noted that there wasn't a speck of paint on it. Poor thing—she had really been in a state over the Bryce likeness.

"It's brilliant. Perfect."

The impressive nose twitched at the compliment and she sat down heavily on her painter's stool and gestured again with the sable brush. "That canvas over there against the wall . . . turn it around. I'd like to know what you think of it, as long as you're here and you've been so kind."

It was a finished portrait on a stretcher and not yet framed. The subject was Courtney Lassiter and the likeness was so good it was like coming face to face with the man himself.

"Madame—it's the best thing you've ever done."

She allowed herself to preen a little. "You think so? It does catch him, don't you think? I admit it. And by the way, he's never seen it completed. Have you heard when he'll be back? I've asked around but nobody seems to know. I don't understand. He promised. . . ."

She went no further: she didn't have to. I understood it all: her insulting remarks about him . . . her conversation with Cochran. She and Lassiter *had* been lovers and she thought he'd gone off and deserted her. Her call to Cochran had been a fishing expedition to see if Cochran knew his whereabouts. She was in love, and she feared she was a woman scorned.

I felt sorry for her, but what could I tell her? I had given my word.

And there was still something more. Something about those photographs. The artist's eye. . . .

"I don't know. Perhaps you could ask Bobby Blessing? He knows everything that goes on in Gull Harbor."

"I have, naturally. Nothing."

Lassiter and Milonsky—lovers. My head was spinning. Could it be possible . . . at their age?

But I knew it could.

And I knew I had to change the subject. I couldn't go on lying to her, pretending I knew nothing. I took a deep breath and looked frantically around the room. My eye lighted again on the suit Nadia had placed on the sitter's chair. And suddenly it clicked. No, it couldn't be . . . absurd. But, unbidden, the image of a Cossack formed in my mind.

I spoke without thinking. "What happened to the book?"

"Book? What book?" She wasn't alarmed, merely distracted. I don't think she really heard me.

"*Parisian Nights.*"

This time she heard. I had the impression that her whole body chemistry had stopped dead—no pulse beating, no blood coursing. I think that reaction was what confirmed it.

"I saw you take it." Unable to stop now. "I was in the dressing room." The book. The photographs.

There wasn't even a tremor in her voice. "What exactly did you see?"

"I saw you put it inside your tunic and leave."

"You think I am a thief?"

"No." Of course she was not a thief. She was something else —and the explanation was in front of me, tacked to the easel that held Bryce's portrait. "I think that before you were a portrait painter, Madame, you were a photographer." The answer was there before me.

The great face began to crumble.

I pointed to the photographs of Bryce. "No fancy lighting or lenses, no special equipment, no tricks. Yet they are obviously the work of a genius—obvious, at least, to the eye of another artist, though maybe not to anyone else."

"No."

"In those days young women did not wander the streets by night—not if they were nice young women. So you turned yourself into a man to be able to go where you wished and photograph the city as you loved it—by night. As a man you could venture safely into the darkest alleys of Paris." She was tall. Turning herself into a boy would be easy. Hair pushed up under a cap . . . baggy clothes . . . her camera. . . .

"What you say is ludicrous."

I went on, like a runaway horse. "Then came the attacks on you and your book. You disappeared. Eventually you came to America, as a painter—we all know that for the truly gifted, one form of talent melts easily into another. You were comparatively

106

safe here—who would believe the starving boy-photographer of Paris in the thirties was the great Madame Milonsky? But you are Praha, Madame. I know it now."

She pulled herself together, standing very tall and looking me straight in the eye. "No one will ever believe you."

"I do not intend to tell anyone."

"I would deny it. When I was Praha I was young . . . thin . . . timid . . . gentle . . . self-effacing. Today I am the opposite. Who would ever guess, except you? How *did* you guess? Was it the book? It had to be the book. You guessed when you saw me take it."

"That was the beginning, I suppose. Who told you Martin had it?"

"Cochran, in one of our chats." Her features were regrouping. And I'd thought Cochran's words were for me alone. "Where is the book now?"

"I destroyed it. I hope it is the last copy in the world and that I can now count on dying in my bed of natural causes. I intend to be buried in my best St. Angelo clutching my Renaissance silver hand mirror and a magnum of Perrier Jouet." She glanced at her wrist watch. "And now the cab will be waiting—it is time for you to go. I have another appointment."

I gave her my hand. I was really giving her my pledge. "I promise that I will say nothing. You have my word."

"Of course." She smiled. "No one would believe you, anyway. No one would care. I would deny everything and they would laugh at you."

She was right, and I knew it. And anyway, it was an old story. Who would care?

Then I remembered.

Lassiter had cared.

He had probably said something to her like, "Darling, I'm off to the south of France for a bit of business. I'll be back before you know it." Lassiter, never knowing she was Praha.

And Milonsky, waiting for a return that never happened,

had mentioned it to Cochran, hoping for a scrap of information. Milonsky, who never dreamed that Lassiter would be on the trail of Praha once he was in Marseille.

The irony of it haunted me all the way home in Nadia Milonsky's yellow taxicab.

18

Nadia Milonsky. Praha.

I crouched in my corner in the back of the cab and tried to get my wits together.

Should I have guessed the moment I saw the countess in her Cossack costume? Should I have guessed when she bridled so at my suggestion, made at the airport, that she might use photographs in her work?

Should I have guessed when Cochran told me she was the source of the information that Lassiter was in the south of France?

But how could I have guessed? I would have had to be some sort of genius to put it all together.

No—it was the theft of the book that told me finally. And the beauty of the photographs she had taken of her subjects. But only someone like me would guess from the photographs—only an artist. She was safe.

Because I would never tell. It was her secret and mine. She was a great artist twice over . . . a magnificent photographer and a superb painter. She was special. She was worth lying about to protect because the magnitude of her talent placed her above and beyond the rest of us.

I had given my word and it was sacred: I would never tell.

The yellow cab passed the entrance to Von Berger's estate and just on a whim I asked the driver to stop for a minute. The place was called "Fechtende Trappen," as if to advertise the glorious news that Von Berger was of German extraction. Fechtende Trappen boasted the usual long Gull Harbor drive to the main house, but with few leaves yet on the trees I could see through to the front turn around. Three Mercedes were parked there—two black and one light blue. With so many cars in evidence I deduced that I had a good chance of finding the airplane dealer in residence.

I was right.

A very military-looking aide opened the door and ushered me into a small paneled library to await Von Berger. He appeared in a minute or two, splendid in a pale blue V-neck sweater, gray flannels, and a yellow silk foulard embroidered with his initials.

"Mrs. Willum—what a pleasure." He was bending over my hand and I had a fleeting moment of panic over whether my nail polish was equal to the honor.

"I was just passing and thought I'd call on you. It's still one of the old-fashioned customs here."

"Very European—a custom I'm happy has not died."

"What a lovely house you have. It used to belong to friends of my parents. I spent many happy hours here as a child." I looked around me, remembering those times. I would certainly never have recognized the house today—it was as different as if it had never existed before. Everything was dark, ornate. The furniture was heavy oak; the single painting over the mantel portrayed Germanic ladies sporting about in what I assumed to be the Black Forest. The bookcases on either side of the fireplace contained not books but lead soldiers. From the unfamiliarity of some of the uniforms I assumed they dated from early Germanic wars. I definitely recognized several by the spiked helmets of the Kaiser's troops in World War I and the distinctive field uniforms of the German troops and officers in World War II.

Von Berger let me look while he lounged gracefully against the fireplace. He was, I confessed to myself, definitely a good looking devil. Not only was he tall and courtly and blond, but he had a neatly defined head and the arrogant bone structure of . . . of what? What was it that nagged at me?

"I see that you are a war buff," I said, looking at the shelves full of models.

"*German* war buff," he admonished politely. "My family were always military people, traditionally fighting officers in command of combat troops in the Imperial German Army. They fought under Frederick the Great. They served Bismarck. They died in World War I at Verdun. And my father did his duty in the last great war."

In other words, I thought, his father served under Hitler. But if he was a professional military man, what else would he do?

"I see. And you?"

He laughed. "My family is now dead . . . I was devoted to them. But they are gone. So I . . . I am a citizen of the world."

"You prefer not to live in Germany?"

"I prefer not to live next to the Russians, if you please. I do not mind working in Europe—I am there constantly on business. But I prefer to live here, in the United States, because America is the hope of us all." There was nothing melodramatic in the way he said it: he might have been discussing the breakfast menu, he was so matter-of-fact.

"And how did you happen to choose Gull Harbor?"

He shrugged. Even when he shrugged the motion was graceful. He threw out his finely-made hands in a gesture of amusement. "Who does not know of Gull Harbor? It is true that I knew no one in Gull Harbor when I first arrived, but I find that it is very easy to make friends—particularly in America. Americans are so generous with their invitations that in the few weeks I have been here I am sure I have met everybody I ought to know."

I'll bet you have, I thought.

"Does your business take you often to Marseille?" I asked.

His eyebrows rose over the pale, pale blue eyes. "Marseille? But of course—I go there occasionally on business. Why do you ask? Can I do anything for you when I am there the next time?"

I stood up. "Yes. Bring me back the true Marseille recipe for Tapinade, if you please. I had it once when I was there with my aunt and I loved it."

"I am not very interested in food," he told me coolly, "but I will try to remember." If my mention of Marseille had startled him for a moment, the intentionally frivolous request had re-

111

assured him, though not before I received a message: whatever he did with this aircraft, it was not totally honest—at least when he was dealing out of Marseille. Was it there that he conducted illicit business with Third World powers, supplying them with bombers and pursuit planes? Was I letting my imagination run away with me?

I didn't think so. There was something about the way he carried his head. He looked like a very beautiful bird of prey.

"Well, thank you for receiving me. And welcome to our simple little community."

He got the joke. "Thank you," he said, laughing.

"And I love your house. What does the name mean, by the way?" We were at the front door now and I pointed to the wrought-iron foot scraper with Fechtende Trappen lettered on it in small gold letters. I had noticed that even the rugs and draperies were made of a design created from the initials F.T.

"Fechtende Trappen means combat troops," he told me proudly.

"I see. Well, good-bye."

And all the way to The Crossing, on the final leg of my yellow cab journey, I kept thinking about that, too.

19

The Crossing was in an uproar when I returned. A gold and white van was parked at the door. "Van Clef et Fils, since 1867" was lettered on its side. It was brand new.

Aunt Lydie's favorite jeweler had arrived.

Inside there was turmoil. The staff was running about as if the world were expected to come to an end in the next fifteen minutes. Small dogs were yapping. My aunt was seated in the library issuing commands. No one seemed to be listening.

I tried to creep past without being observed, but a man I'd never seen before motioned me in. Aunt Lydie was excited.

"Persis—at last. Where have you been? I was halfway through my errands when I remembered that Mr. Ruinsky was coming today so I could select some new jewels for the Paris festivities. Mr. Ruinsky couldn't come himself, but he has very considerately sent his son and a whole new group of people to take care of me."

Mr. Ruinsky was the actual Van Clef of Van Clef et Fils and always had been. For thirty years he had been coming in person with a king's ransom in jewels for Lydia Wentworth to examine. It was always the same scenario: he arrived in an unmarked, bullet-proof car with a beautiful lady assistant and an armed bodyguard who remained present throughout. These encounters were marked by a certain pallor on both sides: Aunt Lydie blanched at the thought of the vast amounts of money she was about to spend—jewels were her fatal weakness—and Mr. Ruinsky paled at the prospect of the vast amounts of money he was about to make. Both, in short, were always in a state of anticipatory bliss.

Today my aunt was exhibiting her customary pallor. Ruinsky *fils* wasn't pale but he seemed jumpy. His father would never have approved . . . it was one thing to be pale with anticipation but never, by so much as a tremor, should the jeweler betray a sign of nerves. It is of paramount importance that a merchant peddling priceless jewels give the impression that the current transaction means nothing because there are many more eager buyers in the wings. It's part of the game, part of the mystique. It's how you get people like Lydia Wentworth in an acquisitive mood. Sweet indifference had always been Ruinsky's strong card, the card that unfailingly persuaded Aunt Lydie to open her checkbook.

But this young man was jumpy. It was apparent in the brusque way he motioned me into the room, eyes scanning the hall behind me. He didn't look or act the least bit like his father.

Nor did his two armed assistants follow the Ruinsky tradition: both wore dark glasses. *Père* would never have approved of that because it gave them an ever so slightly sinister look. With the father in charge, the guard had been so unnoticeable as to be almost invisible. Invisibility inspired confidence when such transactions were taking place.

There was also the obligatory lady assistant on hand. I had never seen her before, either, and she was a far cry from the elegant black-clad lady who was usually in attendance.

"Young Mr. Ruinsky insisted on waiting for you," my aunt said. "His father has been ill and so he has sent the whole second team today. I suppose it's a sort of try-out for you?"

Ruinsky *fils* nodded curtly. He motioned to one of the guards, who left the room swiftly. I heard the front door open. I heard his footsteps as he checked the courtyard.

My aunt was still talking. "His father told him you have a perfect eye, Persis, when it comes to selecting jewels that look well on me. In fact I think I do remember saying once that I would never spend more than fifty thousand dollars without asking your opinion."

I could see that the customary jewelry madness had so taken possession of her that a bomb in the courtyard wouldn't have caught her attention.

"I don't remember anything like that, Aunt Lydie."

"Neither do I, to tell you the truth."

"I thought not."

"In any case, I love having you here to give your opinion. This red dress—ordinarily I think red is rather vulgar but this one is an exception. I absolutely will *not* wear anything vulgar in Paris —I owe it to Jiggs and Marianne to make a good impression. The French think we have no chic—we must disabuse them. And the jewels must also be exceptional. What do you think, Persis . . . rubies? Rubies and diamonds? Diamonds alone?"

She signaled one of the parlormaids who had been pressed into service. "Please hold the dress up to Mrs. Willum. Someone put the rubies around her neck."

The *vendeuse* approached with a three-tiered ruby necklace. For several instants it dangled splendidly right before my eyes. Then it was clasped around my neck.

"Aunt Lydie. . . ."

"No—it won't do. So difficult to decide." She held up the other two necklaces and studied them fiercely, frowning with concentration. Ruinsky *fils* was fidgeting. Aunt Lydie didn't notice —she was too involved with her jewels.

"Aunt Lydie. . . ."

"I can't seem to decide. . . ."

Then I realized: she wasn't wearing her contact lenses. They were a recent addition to our lives, one she deeply resented and chose to rise above as if her vision were perfect.

The front door closed and the guard came back into the room. He exchanged glances with Ruinsky *fils*.

"We always serve tea when Mr. Ruinsky comes—why not have some now? I'm dying for a cup." It was the first thing I could think of.

Lydia Wentworth adores life's little ceremonies. "Perfect!

115

Your father always had a spot of sherry, too. And some little sandwiches, Jennings. Take the maids with you and see what you can do, quickly."

Jennings gathered up the maids. The younger Ruinsky seemed pleased. "I'll send my men to help."

Jennings started to protest, but I broke in. "Yes, do." Then in a low voice, as the disapproving butler passed me, "And be sure that the new chef includes the finger sandwiches."

Ordinarily Jennings is the most inscrutable of butlers, which is to say that no flicker of expression is ever allowed to cross his face. The present chef had been with my aunt for fifteen years, so there was a twitch—just a small one—of surprise. Then he marched out of the room followed by his little entourage of maids and men.

Ruinsky had produced his gun. It didn't surprise my aunt: his father, too, had always been armed. After all, he was carrying a king's ransom in jewels. She just rattled on.

"Now that that's settled, would you step into the powder room and actually put on the dress, Persis? I must see it *worn*. You don't mind, do you Mr. Ruinsky? Your father always let me do it this way. I like to match the gown and the jewels, you know."

"Miss Sherman will go with her." He seemed to be listening, but not to us.

"You think my niece will steal the rubies? Your father never minded: he knew my niece—jewels mean nothing to her."

He didn't answer. I realized he was listening to the group as they trooped downstairs.

My aunt shrugged and for the first time cast him a curious glance. "As you wish."

Miss Sherman and I stepped into the powder room.

It was by no means an ordinary powder room. In fact, it was by no means an ordinary room. The walls were covered with Vertes murals. The furniture was glass and steel Art Deco. The rug was hand-hooked by George Wells to match the deep blue and silver of the upholstery and curtains. These touches were all Aunt Lydie's, dating from her Art Deco period. But the most

116

astonishing touch was the contribution of her grandfather, the old tycoon A. K. Wentworth. On his European travels he had seen and fallen in love with Botticelli's *The Birth of Venus*. Being unsuccessful in his efforts to purchase the original, he had settled for commissioning copies of every size to be hung in each room of his Gull Harbor mansion. The job had kept several painters busy for several years. His granddaughter had long since thrown out the paintings, but his mania had not stopped there. At the same time he had commissioned Italian sculptors to do ten-inch-high bronze reproductions of the Venus to serve as water taps for every bathroom in his house. The basins were in the form of shells and Venus was flanked by two angels for faucets, also in bronze. Some of these fixtures were still in working order. The one in this room was in poor condition, the Venus in place but only loosely: she was waiting to be repaired.

"Do you mind if I wash my hands before I touch the dress? I'm a bit grubby—it's been a busy morning." I didn't wait for permission. Miss Sherman didn't look as if she'd give it. She looked to me like a lady who wouldn't be too fastidious. Maybe I had that impression because her fingernails were too curved and too red. Ruinsky *père* would never have approved.

I went to the basin and turned each cherub. Water came out from beneath the miniature shell on which the Venus stood and ran softly into the larger shell of the basin. I put my hand on the Venus.

"Miss Sherman . . . would you please check the hem of that dress before I step into it? I thought I noticed it coming undone. . . ."

Miss Sherman bent over. I lifted up the Venus and hit her on the head with all the force I could command. She crumpled without a sound. I took the dress from her, holding it over my arm to hide the heavy bronze Venus.

"Mr. Ruinsky . . . something's happened to your assistant— come quickly. She just toppled over—like that. Come!"

He was wary, motioning with his gun for my aunt and me to precede him. Aunt Lydie looked puzzled and started to protest, but thought better of it and obeyed. When she saw Miss Sherman on the floor she cried out in distress. "Oh, I hope she hasn't been ill on my rug . . . the flu . . . everybody's been ill . . . I hope. . . ." She rushed forward and tried to turn Miss Sherman on to her back.

Ruinsky motioned her away. "Don't touch her. Just get back." He leaned over, gun still in hand.

I lifted the Venus. A round cry of protest formed on my aunt's lips, but she never uttered it: the look I gave her would have silenced an entire Greek chorus.

The Venus struck again—harder than ever. It was the strength of desperation.

And Ruinsky dropped. It was a miracle. I thought we'd both be dead and instead there he was, draped across his assistant's body, their arms and legs mingling in an intimate but disorganized tangle.

"Persis," my aunt was crying, "have you gone mad? Attacking my favorite jeweler's son just as I'm about to make my selections?"

"He's not your favorite jeweler's son. You just weren't paying attention. No class. And too nerved up. And his men are busy right now tying up your staff downstairs. We need the curtain cords from the library . . . will you please get them?" I had Ruinsky's gun and Aunt Lydie went obediently to fetch the cords, rather—I imagine—to her own surprise.

"I don't understand," she complained as we rolled the false Ruinsky off the false Miss Sherman and proceeded to tie both of them up in knots. "Why isn't he my favorite jeweler? Isn't he the 'Fils' of Van Clef et Fils?"

"He is not," I told her, pulling tight a final loop. Neither victim of the bathroom Venus had budged; but they would soon. "We have to hope now that Jennings will set off his mad contraption and that help will arrive before those hoodlums come back upstairs. I know that Bobby Blessing assigned men to patrol the grounds after the ambassador's death."

"What mad contraption?"

"The New Chef."

118

"Oh my goodness!" She was remembering. Jennings had never trusted our conventional alarm so he rigged up his own anti-burglar system. The main ingredients were a button and a tape recording magnified to sound as if the house were under attack by the whole of Patton's Fifth Army. For months whenever we couldn't track him down he had always said he was busy with "the New Chef."

And just then the New Chef went into action. The cacophony was ear-shattering. Even I, who knew it was only the New Chef in action, was almost persuaded that our number was up.

"Come on, Aunt Lydie, let's go up to your room and bolt ourselves in until help arrives."

"But the jewels," my aunt cried. "I wanted the rubies and someone might steal them."

"Don't worry," I said. "They were copies. Good—but paste copies. You should have worn your glasses. I spotted it at once. Ordinarily you'd have noticed."

"Oh." Very embarrassed. "How could I have missed it? Is that what put you on to them—your artist's eye?"

"That—and their lack of class—Ruinsky would never have sent them out to represent the firm. Never."

"But. . . ."

In the midst of the New Chef's bombardment I now heard sounds of real gunfire. Then there was the roar of the van starting up and hurtling down the driveway. And shortly after that Blessing's voice. "Lydia . . . Lydia . . . where are you? Are you all right?"

"He's come," my aunt said. "I'm glad." A masterful understatement.

"But what did they want, if the jewels weren't real? I don't understand."

"I do. I understood the minute I realized they were waiting for me. They didn't want any surprises. You were about to be kidnapped in their fancy new van. We were. I was getting a free ride."

"You're not serious. Kidnapped? How idiotic."

"I know," I told her. "Why do you suppose I was desperate

enough to hit those people with your grandfather's beloved Botti-celli Venus?"

"I don't know. Why? I simply thought you had gone mad."

"Because," I told her, "I knew you'd *never* pay the ransom and I'm not ready to die."

She had the grace to look shamefaced; but she didn't con-tradict me.

20

The scene between Bobby Blessing and Lydia Wentworth that followed our deliverance was a classic battle of wills. Blessing was determined that Aunt Lydie should go into hiding where she could be properly protected from further kidnap attempts. Aunt Lydie was determined not to.

"I have all my preparations for Paris with Jiggs and Marianne: I don't have time to go into hiding, as you call it. Furthermore, it's an absurd idea. I've made it patently clear on many occasions that I will *never, never* agree to the payment of ransom."

"All very well, Lydia . . . but suppose they began to chop Persis up, bit by bit? An ear here—an eye there. Would you not send permission to your bankers under such pressure? Why do you think they waited for her?"

She thought about it. "They wouldn't dare. If they were caught. . . ."

"You'd better believe they'd dare. And suppose that didn't work: suppose we received one of your fingers—say that one, complete with ring. Do you think we'd hesitate to beg or borrow the money to get you back? Why are you so obstinately refusing to see the danger? What use will your money be to you if you are dead, and Persis, too?"

"I'm leaving it to orphans, and retired and homeless horses. It will do good for many years."

"Homeless horses! Really, Lydia—you can't be serious."

"I've never been more serious. I will not . . . I repeat *not* . . . pay ransom to anyone." She was utterly unshaken by the kidnap attempt: perhaps the reality of it had not yet dawned on her.

121

But Blessing did not surrender. "All the more reason, then, to see that you are not kidnapped. I've been working on a plan for weeks. I believe we could leave tomorrow morning. We will fly to Gatwick on one of those tourist flights—no one would ever suspect it was you and the flight is not uncomfortable."

"What did you say?" My aunt had never traveled less than first class in her life: she obviously couldn't believe her ears.

"It won't be bad, I promise," Blessing continued. "Then we'll take a small plane to La Baule where we'll be met and driven to Batz-sur-Mer. I've rented a large, quite wild-looking seaside house there—big enough to give you and Persis each a private floor and still leave plenty of room for my men, who'll double as servants."

"A tourist flight? I've never taken one." She had a faraway look in her eyes, like a child contemplating a whole counter full of forbidden candies. "I think it might be fun. And could we stay in a motel? I've never been in one. I'd like *that*, too."

Blessing didn't yet realize that he had her hooked and continued to unroll the details of his plan. "You'll be an English lady for this occasion: they're used to the English in that region and your accent isn't the least American. I think you'll find Batz amusing: they harvest salt, and there's the sea. We chose it because the house is well protected and because they're accustomed to the English renting big places for the season, which is almost upon us."

"June is the beginning," I said. "It's not yet June."

"I know. But we've put it out that one of you is an artist who likes to paint the sea in all seasons."

He'd been very thorough.

"I've never seen salt harvested," Lydia Wentworth said.

"You'll be on the Côte Sauvage—the Atlantic side: it's pretty spectacular. And if you can't live without the sophisticated shops and resturants, there's La Baule nearby. You'll love it, Lydia. I've spent a good deal of thought on finding you the perfect place. And there are the fishing fleets of Le Croisic. . . ."

"I've always wanted to go out on one of those bright-painted fishing boats," she said.

"It could be arranged." Blessing understood now that she was seduced. Like all the small international company of super-millionaires, she always went to the same chic places. But unlike them, she was endlessly curious about the rest of the world and hampered by the fact that people in her exalted tax bracket could not move about like the rest of us.

"How long will I have to stay?"

"No longer than it would have taken for you to get your Paris house in order. You'll be on hand in plenty of time to greet Jiggs and Marianne. By then the kidnappers will have turned their attention elsewhere: they need money *now*: we know that."

She looked delighted. "You mean you want me offstage just long enough for them to forget about me and concentrate on somebody else? All right—I agree. I'm not at all anxious to be dragged off in a van by types in moustaches and dark glasses. As long as you guarantee I'll get to Paris in time. . . ."

"You will."

They both looked relieved that the contest was over. My acquiescence was taken for granted by both sides.

21

Batz-sur-Mer, in Loire-Atlantique, Brittany, is a curious small town popularly believed to have been founded in 945, a town in which no one in his right mind would expect to find Lydia Wentworth, one of the wealthiest women in the modern world.

To begin with, it is a smallish, unpretentious place into which the sea has tentatively intruded shallow fingers to probe the surrounding fields. There are no great houses, no fine restaurants, no chic boutiques. The streets are narrow, the houses simple. On the Atlantic side, the ocean lashes mercilessly at the high cliffs and barren rocks that guard Batz from its fury. On the protected bays, the land has been cultivated for salt beds, and at the outskirts of the village housewives set up tables and place displays of their bagged salt on them, along with great sacks of potatoes and onions fabled for the special taste attributed to the saltiness of the surrounding fields. On weekends the roads leading from Batz are clogged with motorists stopping to buy the villagers' wares.

Aside from its salt, potatoes, and onions the village has just two other claims to fame: a large bronze statue of a beautiful Breton girl striding in from the salt marshes with a basket of salt balanced on her head and—just across from the church—a sabot maker whose flamboyant gifts as a promoter bring customers from miles around to buy his wildly diverse variety of wood-soled shoes.

My aunt fell in love with Batz-sur-Mer on sight. So far we were batting one hundred percent—she had also fallen in love with the economy flight to Gatwick and with the erratic small plane that flew us from Gatwick to the rain-swept airfield at La Baule, near Batz. I prayed that her good humor would last. We still had one hurdle to negotiate: her personal maid, Hannah, refused to fly and would not be with us for at least a week. In Paris Aunt Lydie always had a spare maid in attendance until Hannah's stately arrival by boat and train. In Batz, for the sake of security, there would be no personal maid but me. I did not anticipate that I would be a success.

Actually, there was one other hurdle, one that I also dreaded. Would she like the house—she who was used to every luxury and comfort?

I needn't have worried. The eccentric pile of timber and cement . . . a concoction that resembled a French chef's wedding cake gone made . . . delighted her. She loved the cliff. She loved the crashing waves at our feet. She loved the corridors and fireplaces and beams and parquet floors. Even the heavy furniture delighted her. "It's a true *maison de maître*," she exclaimed. "I've always wanted to live in one and now I shall—at least for a while."

"Do you really think you'll be happy here?" I was thinking of Hannah and how Aunt Lydie had not even packed her own pocketbook since she was a little girl.

"I'll be in seventh heaven. How do you pronounce this place? Batz as in baaaah as in sheep?"

"Yes."

"Extraordinary. I shall never master French pronunciation."

I was unpacking. Aunt Lydie was sitting on the edge of the bed, swinging her foot like a child.

"Why not put the gloves in that drawer . . . I'll never need them here. And the lingerie there. And by the way, what was in the package that taxi delivered just before we took the plane?"

That's the way she does things—delivers her blows when you're not looking.

"Oh." I thought frantically. I didn't realize she'd noticed. "Nothing."

"Nothing?"

"Well, just something from the gallery. Work. Gregor must be losing patience with my never being there."

She giggled. "I wouldn't worry if I were you."

I knew what she meant. If it pleased Aunt Lydie to have me trot around with her for the rest of her life, Gregor would be the last to object. He was mad about her.

Finally the unpacking was done. Not well, but done.

"Now that we've finished, I think I'll take a little beauty rest." She yawned.

"Exactly."

The package was lying where I had left it, on the bed in my room next to my pocketbook. It was about eight by ten inches in size, wrapped in plain brown paper, and tied with bright yellow kitchen string. Altogether an unimposing affair.

But I had a feeling . . .

As I touched it my heart began to beat a rousing tattoo.

It had arrived at literally the eleventh hour, delivered by Madame Milonsky's cab. I had carried it carefully in my hand from America to England, from England to France without once daring to look inside. I knew she would expect me to open it in privacy.

And finally I was alone.

My fingers trembled as I untied the string.

The wrappings fell away. There was tissue paper—layers of it. And finally . . . photographs.

They were black and white. They were not of Paris, I saw that at once. It was a different city. A different time and a different mood. There were girls. Soldiers . . . German soldiers. Boats. Bars. Wartime.

I saw the name of a bar, barely distinguishable in the light of a street lamp. "Café de la Canebière, Marseille."

Marseille. Praha had been in Marseille. It was not possible to mistake Praha's work . . . not possible to mistake the quality.

There was a note, penned in the usual flamboyant hand on the usual commercial greeting card. This one said "Happy Father's

126

Day." And she had scribbled "These are safer with you. Use as you see fit. I trust you. You will know what to do. And when to do it."

And that was all.

I went back through the photographs, studying them, searching for a face that might be familiar, the face of a murderer. No face stood out. There was nothing.

I looked at the note again. "You will know what to do."

But what was that?

22

The eight days before Hannah's arrival were a sort of idyll in which my aunt and I dwelt together in bucolic simplicity and pastoral charm. We took long walks along the littoral (followed at a discreet distance by Blessing's guard dogs). We lunched at a charming little resturant looking out on the breakwater. We counted the fishing boats at Piriac-sur-Mer and La Turballe. We strolled the beach at La Baule, bundled up against the spring winds and marveling at the young men already pitting their *planches à voiles* against the still-cold seas. We ventured to Pen Bé for *moules* and *huîtres*, plucked fresh from the ocean. We tasted *le salicorne*, the strange grass grown in the salt marsh beds. We dined at the three-star restaurant Bellevue Plage in La Baule and strolled the medieval streets and ramparts of Guérande. And one day, in an excess of ecstasy, we almost climbed aboard the three-story rococo merry-go-round in front of the Hôtel Royal in La Baule.

My aunt was like a child in a fairy-tale dream. Never once did she complain about my clumsiness as a drawer-of-baths, mixer-of-martinis, layer-out-of-clothes-for-the-day.

Never once did she chafe at the bit Blessing had imposed upon her—from her sunny disposition and total contentment one might have thought the sojourn in Batz had been her idea, carefully orchestrated for at least a year. She was amiability unparalleled to the guardians assigned to watch over her—even when her plans conflicted with theirs. It was, I finally decided, a reaction to the stresses of having the ambassador murdered before her eyes and almost being kidnapped, two events shocking enough to unsettle even so emotionally adjusted a person as my aunt. I kept telling myself that it was too good to be true and every day I woke up wondering if *this* was the day that would shatter the idyll. But nothing happened. She was charm itself.

Even the *International Herald Tribune* and its unsettling world news failed to upset her, although there was a slight tremor on the tranquil surface of our lives when an article appeared headlined: "WHITE HOUSE ALERT EXPLAINED. Security was tightened at the White House last night in response to intelligence reports that terrorists were planning a major attack on the American president, either here or abroad. . . ."

When she read it, Aunt Lydie (who had herself insisted that the security men drive to La Baule every morning to buy a copy of the *Trib*) threw the offending newspaper across the room. "Take it away," she cried. "It's a plot to keep Jiggs from the conference. They're trying to intimidate him! But he'll never submit to threats. I know Jiggs. He'll be in Paris, no matter how they try to scare him off. He's a great president and he'll be there to protect the western world. You can count on it."

That was the only flurry of excitement—otherwise the days passed without upset. If it rained, she loved the rain. If the sun ventured out she was enchanted. Every meal was bliss. She drank Gros Plant, the local wine, and pronounced it marvelous. She ate her first galette in her first Crêperie and adored it. She bought eight pairs of shoes from the sabot maker and ordered five more. I wouldn't have been surprised to wake up some morning and find her clad from head to foot in the local Breton costume.

And I could do no wrong in my role as Hannah. Although I was clumsy, inept, disorganized, forgetful, and totally inefficient, Aunt Lydie was all-forgiving. One would have thought she had stumbled into Paradise. Even Bobby Blessing's ever-present troops failed to annoy her with their presence.

But she knew the day would come when she would go to Paris: perhaps her pleasure was heightened by the knowledge that she would soon be wallowing in luxury in the company of some of the most powerful people in the world. Soon Hannah would arrive, soon Paris would call. And off she would troop, carefree and gay and quite forgetful of the unpretentious pleasures of Batz-sur-Mer which had given us refuge from the trials of our recent life on Long Island. My aunt could never resist the luster of the City of Light for very long. But then, who could?

In the meantime, here we were. It was restful and it was safe. But it was like being in prison. Everywhere we went, every waking hour I thought about Lassiter and Praha and the whole mad affair. What was it that Praha expected me to do? What?

I puzzled over it day and night, spilling my food, stepping into holes, almost being run down by cars in my foggy, distracted state. If my aunt noticed, she didn't say anything. Probably she attributed my worse than usual absent-mindedness to my efforts to serve as a competent ladies' maid.

"You will know what to do."

I studied and restudied the photographs.

Why couldn't I work it out?

23

I suppose I would have gone with Aunt Lydie to Paris; we all took it quite for granted that I would. But the telephone call from Bobby Blessing changed that. It must have been after lunch in New York because we were about to dine in Batz. My aunt likes to dine late.

"I have bad news," Blessing said. He was never one to feint if a straight blow to the jaw would suffice. He sounded as if he were in the next room, which made matters somehow worse.

My aunt motioned to me to get on the *écouteur*, that fantastic French invention which enables two people to listen, but not speak to, the caller simultaneously.

"What bad news, Bobby? Are my investments in trouble?" Naturally she associated bad news with finances: it was ever thus with people of superior means.

"No. No . . . never better, as a matter of fact. No—it's Nadia Milonsky."

I think my heart, for all intents and purposes, stopped beating. I didn't want to listen to what was to follow, but I listened anyway: I didn't know how to stop.

"Nadia? What has happened to her? Jiggs doesn't like the portrait she did of him?"

"Nothing like that, Lydia. I only wish it were. Far worse, I'm afraid."

"What could be worse for a professional portrait artist?" My aunt was being pragmatic but not imaginative.

"She's dead." He dropped it like that—without hesitation, without mercy.

"Oh, no." I could clearly hear in my aunt's tone the words "not this, too."

"I'm afraid it's true, Lydia."

"How?" She could scarcely ask the question.

"A senseless business. The police speculate that hoodlums broke into her house and, when there was no money to be found, killed her and that old man who worked for her and her secretary."

"Hoodlums looking for money? In Gull Harbor? You can't mean it." There had never been hoodlums in Gull Harbor. It was unthinkable. "There must be another explanation, Bobby."

"There isn't, I'm afraid. We think the secretary tried to oppose them and everyone was shot. The place was torn to bits— the police say they've never seen anything like it. Don't worry— she died instantly . . . a shot in the back of the head. The secretary and the old man were trying to defend her. Nasty business. I wouldn't have called, but I didn't want you to read it in the paper tomorrow."

"Do you think I should fly back?"

"For the funeral? Definitely not. I absolutely forbid it. It's the last thing Nadia would want—to put you in danger. No, Lydia . . . that's one of the reasons I called. I was afraid you'd read about it in the European press and insist on taking the next flight back. You must not do that—not under any circumstances. I absolutely forbid it."

"But I ought to. . . ."

"No. You're always so kind and generous. But this is one time when you must think of yourself first. Under no circumstances are you to return. It is too dangerous. I will not permit it. You will remain where you are. I will attend to the flowers and whatever else is necessary. Nadia would be the first one to understand—she was a European, after all, and Europeans know the value of life and the folly of risking it needlessly. No—you will not return. Hannah will be there in twenty-four hours and then in a few days you can go on to Paris to prepare for the president's visit. That is important."

He had said all the right things.

"I suppose you're right, Bobby—you always are. I've traveled all this distance because you wanted me to. I might as well stay because you want me to. You'll take care of everything?" She looked quite shaken.

"Of course."

"Good. Then, if you wish, I'll stay until Hannah comes and until you say it's safe to go on to Paris." I think Nadia Milonsky's death actually had frightened her—I'd never seen her so docile. I know it frightened me.

"Very good, Lydia. It won't be long—I promise you—maybe a week or so. I'll call and let you know when it's safe. My men will go with you—they'll take over at your Paris house."

"Very well, Bobby. Thank you." All three of us hung up.

"I'll wait until he tells me I may go," my aunt said meekly.

"Yes." I was glad she had promised him.

But I couldn't believe it. Hoodlums behind the Big Cheese? Robbers behind Never on Sunday?

Never. Never in a million years.

Nadia Milonsky was dead. How could it be? I had been with her only days before and she had been so strong, so vital, so alive —promising to die in her bed of natural causes and be buried with her mirror and her Perrier Jouet.

How was it possible? Could it be. . . .

Beauty and the Beast. The masks that hung over me, asking —always asking. Had I told them I'd seen her take the book? Had I?

Had I assisted at her death without knowing it? And she'd trusted me. "You will know what to do."

My aunt was looking at me in alarm. "Persis—are you all right? You look terrible . . . as if you were about to be sick. What's wrong?"

"I wish," I told her, "that I could die. Right now." And I began to cry. It was a shocking display: we don't blubber and moan in Gull Harbor. But I couldn't help it.

24

I had been in Marseille before, of course. But the circumstances had been different.

On those previous occasions I had arrived like a princess, stepping off a yacht in the Old Port with my aunt. Together we had dipped our elegantly painted toes in the vitality and excitement and implied danger of one of the most electrifying cities in the world . . . dipped our toes without ever getting them soiled. We had strolled the vast Canebière in our wide-brimmed summer hats, goggling at the crowds and drinking the refreshing juice made from grapes pressed before our eyes. As the streets darkened and the humming markets folded their wares we had returned to the sanctuary of our floating palace to drink champagne and admire the glittering lights of the city of sin and crime. This time I was arriving like everyone else, by a fast French train. It was all very fast: the sudden decision, a note for Aunt Lydie, a train from La Baule, and I was gone. I had telephoned ahead from Lyon to make certain that Nathalie Bryce was in town and, just as I had hoped, she had immediately insisted I stay with her. "You can walk from the station."

I studied the thickly carved doors of the Napoleon III town houses for the correct number. From the brass plates on many of the doors I had the impression that the area, while certainly far from run-down, had definitely seen better days. Many of the buildings now housed doctors and lawyers and individual apartments. Number eighteen, when I found it, was no exception: a brass plate informed me that the bureau of Martin Films, Executive Offices, could be found on the first floor. Martin *privé* was listed for the rest of the town house.

Nathalie met me at the door, looking radiant. Life with Martin evidently agreed with her. The pudgy face had been done over by someone with cosmetic know-how to dramatize cheekbones and eyes. She was a different girl.

"You'll stay here—we keep rooms for visiting VIPs and potential investors and they're all yours for now. From your bedroom you have a beautiful view of the golden Virgin that guards the city from the top of Notre Dame de la Garde."

"You're too kind."

"Not at all—I'm lonesome . . . Marcel is away all day and so far I haven't been offered any parts or even allowed on the set. Marcel doesn't want me exposed to pornography. He'd rather I stayed home and stared at the Virgin whereas I—for my part— would like some *real* excitement."

"The Virgin's pretty exciting—at least to an artist. She's more than forty feet tall and magnificently gilded and made of four hollow sections, an alloy of zinc and copper. Aunt Lydie and I climbed the circular staircase inside to get a view of the city through her eyes—literally. I'll take you . . . I think you'll find it exciting."

"Will you? And you'll have absolute privacy here to do as you want. But please join us for dinner. Marcel is looking forward to it. Every night, if you can."

"Gladly. And I have a favor to ask of him."

"He's very good about favors," she assured me solemnly. "In fact, he's very good about everything."

I sincerely hoped she was right. I was counting on it.

Could I count on Nathalie, too? I studied her, wondering. I needed an ally, but was she the one? My kidnapping, the attempt on Aunt Lydie, and finally the murder of Nadia Milonsky had forced me here. There had been no choice and I think I had known it the moment I opened the package with Praha's photographs. Nadia Milonsky had counted on me—believed in me. The arrival of the photographs had sealed the unspoken pact.

But whom could I count on? Martin? I needed him, surely. But could he be trusted? Nathalie? No, not possible—she was a child, an immature girl begging for something exciting to happen. I could give her that. But it wouldn't be fair.

"Show me the house, Nathalie. It looks beautiful."

She shrugged. She was used to wonderful houses. "I'm having my favorite decorator flown over. I don't like the way the place is done. I suspect all of Marcel's mistresses had a hand in it. They were mostly actresses, you know . . . and actresses have no taste."

Her lower lip jutted out in disapproval. Recalling how badly she had dressed in Gull Harbor, I quailed at the fate of the house. Still, as she gave me a tour of the place, I could see what she meant. Everything in every room was expensive—that much was obvious. But the melange of objects and tastes was staggering. I felt I was drowning in a sea of gilt and mirrors and armoires and tapestries and upholstery of conflicting patterns doing battle with oriental rugs of furiously disagreeing colors. Purples and dark greens and bright yellows and deep reds swirled before my eyes. There were puffs of brocade everywhere. Tassels. Fringes. Pillows and geegaws. It was enough to give you vertigo.

"A decorator. What a good idea." Any decorator would be preferable to the present state.

"It will give me something to do. I'm so bored. Marcel says I'm to have a free hand. He doesn't notice things very much."

Obviously. Or he couldn't have lived here.

"That's very nice of him." I sat down on a Louis seize chair with gold painted legs. Nathalie sat opposite me on a dark red Empire sofa under an oriental six-panel screen mounted on the wall. The screen was mostly orange and brown and dark green. Crystal lamps with silver shades flanked the sofa. There were two side chairs opposite done up in bright purple with cabbage roses in the design. I began to feel quite ill: it had been a long day.

A Vietnamese houseman served Pastis.

"He was a colonel at Dien Bien Phu," Nathalie offered. "Marcel rescued him from the Foreign Legion. You know that their headquarters are in Marseille."

"I know." It was one reason I was here.

"Marcel," she offered proudly, "is like that. He knows everybody."

"I suspected that." It was another reason I was here. "And are you happy, Nathalie? Is it working out? You're not sorry you left Hallsey Bryce?"

She looked better, certainly. And she seemed better. But one could never be sure. All this talk about excitement. . . .

She didn't answer directly. "You'll find Marcel is different once you get to know him. Not like Hallsey. Different. But still, you know, all men are the same in the end." She smiled at me and it was the crooked smile of a little girl, which didn't at all match the worldliness of what she had just said.

Her mood changed abruptly. "Finish your drink and we'll go down and take a coffee in one of the sidewalk cafés and watch the world go by. Because that's where the world is—in Marseille. Did you know that Von Berger is here? And I wouldn't doubt that Hallsey was here, too, searching for me and spying. Maybe we'll see them. And then, when we're thoroughly bored, we'll come back and dine with Marcel. No one dines before nine—so we have plenty of time. And whatever favor you have to ask of Marcel you can ask over cognac. He'll not refuse you, Persis . . . he's never been known to refuse a lady."

Von Berger and Bryce? Impossible. Too much of a coincidence. Still, if I was here, why not everyone else?

I put down my Pastis and jumped up. "I'm ready. Let's go."

As it turned out, we saw about a thousand people in the course of drinking three or four coffees.

But none was Von Berger. And none was Bryce.

25

Martin looked natty in a pink silk shirt, white foulard, white flannel slacks, and white buck shoes. Blinding, in fact.

"Did you know," I asked as we lingered over cognac after dinner, "that Nadia Milonsky was murdered in a robbery?"

"Appalling—we read it. The news was in all the papers. After all, she's an international figure. Odd, though—no photographs of her."

"She never allowed them to be taken. She was very private."

"Robbery—imagine. In Gull Harbor!" Nathalie was scandalized by the idea.

So was Martin. "I never thought, when I bought a house in Gull Harbor, that such a thing could happen there."

"It never has before."

"She didn't even get to start my portrait," Nathalie complained sulkily.

"She more or less finished the rest of us but Nathalie's wasn't even begun. I don't suppose you'd consider. . . ?"

"Not really. I'm not a portrait painter, Marcel. It's a now-and-then thing. I'm a *painter*. That's different. But I could suggest. . . ."

"I only want the best for her. As a favor, perhaps?"

The girl interrupted. I knew what she was thinking: I wanted a favor—he wanted a favor. "Excuse me, I must discuss tomorrow's marketing with the cook. She shops at dawn to get the best of everything." She left us, her silk caftan rustling mysteriously.

When her footsteps had died away, Martin lit a cigar and turned to me. "Why are you in Marseille? I, after all, have business here. But you . . . people like you don't come to Marseille."

"I came to see you, for one thing."

A short laugh exploded. He didn't believe me. "You're joking."

"No. In your profession you deal with a variety of people, do you not?"

His black eyes widened slightly. "I don't deny it. So?"

"Some of those people might help me."

"Oh? How?"

"A friend was killed here this spring." No one in Gull Harbor was supposed to have known where Lassiter was and Martin certainly wouldn't have met him—he was a late arrival in our community and Lassiter was long gone by then.

"I'd like," I continued, "to know why."

"All right. But why me?"

"Because you might have access to people who have heard something. Marseille is headquarters for the greatest of all mercenary armies, the Foreign Legion. It is made up of all types—criminals, murderers, escaped convicts, political *personae non gratae*—people of all kinds. Someone in that milieu must have heard *something*."

"I see. Anything is possible. His name?"

"Courtney Lassiter."

"Ah, yes, Lassiter. What happened to him?"

He was shot eight times at close range."

Martin allowed a long, slow whistle to escape. "Like that."

"Yes, like that."

"Information is hard to. . . ." he stopped. Nathalie had returned and was standing in the doorway.

"Who has been shot eight times?" She was just a little breathless, her kohl-rimmed eyes round with interest.

"No one, *Chérie*. We are discussing a possible plot for a film. Persis has presented me with quite a good idea."

"Oh." She sounded disappointed. "I thought maybe it was something real. Nothing exciting ever happens." She turned and went back to the kitchen. He waited until she was gone to speak.

"Any idea why he was in Marseille?"

I realized that I didn't really know. Something to do with the Marseille-Menton-Manosque triangle . . . something to do with Praha, with the gold. But what, exactly? I realized that I also knew next to nothing about Lassiter himself. "No."

"Well," Martin said, "the trail's cold, I'd say. But I'll make you a bargain. If I find out something useful for you, you will paint Nathalie. Agreed?"

"Done."

We shook hands. His handshake was strong and firm.

"I'll ask around," he told me. "But don't expect much, and not instantly—it will take a few days. Anyway, I'm relieved: there had to be a reason . . . people like you don't come to Marseille." He laughed the same short laugh, like a firecracker.

I studied him with interest. "You're an enigma to me, too. It's strange—you're not at all what I would expect."

He blew a mushroom cloud of cigar smoke and watched it ascend laboriously to the ceiling. "Why is that?"

"Well, for one thing, you don't look or act like a man whose occupation—or is it vocation—is pornography. You're too nice. You've been kind to Nathalie."

He laughed again. "Pornography is a business like any other. I inherited it from my father, you might say—he was an agent for the kind of seedy and kinky acts that played the *boîtes*—the night clubs—in the twenties and thirties. The natural evolution was pornographic films. We film them here because in Marseille it's easy to pick up people who will do anything for a buck. We market the films in Europe. America is just now becoming ripe for these things."

"Is that why you bought a house in America?"

"No—not at all. Every European is trying to buy property in America . . . we all want our money there. Nothing in Europe is safe: we're on the brink of war. America is the only place to be."

140

"All of you—you . . . Von Berger . . . Bryce?"

"Von Berger—there's a fellow who might help you. I saw him on the street the other day. Good looking fellow. Bones of a movie star. As for Bryce . . . there's a bad type. Mixed up with a gang of international criminals, I've heard. Finger man for terrorists. Just the fellow you need." He was smiling and his tone was heavy with sarcasm.

"Hallsey Bryce . . . he disappeared when he knew—" I stopped. There was no point in telling anyone that my aunt had nearly been kidnapped.

"That I was stealing his wife? Yes. But he did not make her happy. I shall."

"I'm glad. She's a nice child."

"I've been looking for just such a nice child all my life. A journalist who writes about crimes does not have to be a criminal. A man who makes pornographic films does not have to be a pervert. Does that answer your question?"

"It does. Now if you will help me. . . ?"

"I'll do my best. I'll try to find Von Berger—I've heard his father was a German officer who escaped into the Foreign Legion. I'll ask around among the people I know—as you say, I know a variety. I'll poke around in all the dark corners. And, if I succeed, you'll keep your part of the bargain."

"I will."

"Well," he said, "at least I'm relieved—my question is answered. As I said, people like you don't just come to Marseille."

"You may be right."

But then, neither did people like Courtney Lassiter. Nor, in the general run of events, did people like Nathalie Bryce or Von Berger or Marcel Martin, for that matter.

Everybody had to have a reaon. And that was the question, wasn't it . . . the reason?

26

The next few days were not exactly calm. I rose early and returned late, between times scouring the photography shops and galleries from Aix to Arles and St. Rémy to Les Baux. No one had heard of Praha. But I thought some of the looks I received were peculiar. Or was it my imagination . . . was I becoming paranoid?

Nathalie came with me once or twice. But she soon abandoned the chase, mostly because she was under the impression that I was doing art research, and it bored her. But she was kind enough to lend me her speedy dark blue Peugeot in which to make my rounds.

I visited the bureau of the newspapers *La Marseillaise, Le Meridional, Le Provençal* and *Le Soir* in my quest for information. Nothing.

It was in a bookstore on the Canebière that I finally had an inspiration. They had a display of photographs promoting a new book and it gave me just the idea I needed. An exhibit of photographs by Praha . . . if it were well-advertised, wouldn't it draw the murderer into the net . . . wouldn't he want to be sure . . . absolutely certain . . . wasn't it human nature?

I knew then—this was what I had to do.

I didn't waste a moment. I went immediately to the Musée des Beaux Arts. It was a logical beginning.

You have to climb to the top of the Boulevard Longchamp to get there. It is situated next to the Palais Longchamp, the climax to a stunningly Baroque series of cascading waterfalls and fountains topped by sculptured bulls and mythical marine figures.

I climbed the multitude of steps leading to the museum. I was starved: I had skipped lunch in my hurry to visit the Musée. The sight of a woman feeding twenty-two of the nearby zoological garden's wild cats, most of them kittens, honed my hunger and depressed my spirits. Suppose this didn't work? Suppose they weren't interested? What then?

I told myself not to expect too much. I knew that this museum was a treasury of early works, mostly from schools that have gone out of fashion and by artists now unmourned and unsung.

Still, it was a start.

Somewhat to my surprise the young director and her two equally young curators received me politely . . . maybe they didn't have many American visitors.

I had expected someone ancient, to correspond to the museum's collection—Petrus Paulus, Marius Engalière, Monnoyer, Francois-Marius Granet, Barrigue de Fontainieu. I had not expected children. Perhaps all the old curators had died off and been succeeded by their great-grandchildren. Nevertheless, the mention of Praha's name brought a quick reaction.

"Praha—we would give anything to see his work!"

"You've never seen it?"

"Never." That, of course, was scarcely surprising.

"Then. . . ?" How could they, buried in these archives, know of Praha?

They stood looking at me like three little boys. Their black hair was cut like boys' hair, their skinny little bodies were boys' bodies. They could have been three street urchins who had wandered into a museum by mistake. And they were as solemn as street urchins examining a stranger. After they had looked at me and then at one another they came—like children—to a wordless decision. "If you will tell us why you are asking about Praha, we will tell you what we know." I had the impression that we could be trading marbles. It was absurd—they weren't little boys—they were art people. But they were still people and they were curious.

"I have a small collection of his photographs. They were made

143

in Marseille. I was hoping you could help me find a place to exhibit them."

There was one of those pauses that is described in books as a stunned silence. The three little boys exchanged glances again. "Not here," the director said. "We are permanently fixed in *le temps passé*. But . . ." She paused, considering. "It would be the perfect thing. Photographs by a great photographer . . . photographs of Marseille to celebrate the new work of the great choreographer Roland Petit, also a great artist, for the Ballet National de Marseille opening at the opera house almost at once."

"It could be done: we can arrange it," the two curators added eagerly. "They asked us what we could give them by way of an exhibition for the lobby on opening night."

"How soon?" It was right . . . made to order . . . perfect.

"Ten days," they chorused. "We were desperate for an idea."

"And now," I told them, "it is your turn. How do you know Praha?"

"No one ever knew him. But there is a reward for any information about him or about anyone asking for him." They nodded in unison. "One thousand dollars, we're told. Eight thousand francs—a lot of money. One hears these things in Marseille."

Was I surprised? Perhaps. "A reward offered by whom?"

"We understand it's a matter of a post box. And now we must ask—these photographs . . . their provenance?"

"They were given to me by the photographer himself, to do with as I saw fit. Look—here is his note. Every photograph is signed on the back. And you can call the Waldheim Museum in New York to check that I am who I say I am . . . here are my credentials." I passed them my passport and wallet.

They fluttered over Praha's note, which was what interested them. There isn't a curator in the world who doesn't thrill to the notion of a coup such as this. "When will we see the photographs?"

"Tomorrow. I will bring them here. But there is one thing you must promise."

144

Three cropped heads turned to me simultaneously. The French don't like making promises any more than anyone else. "Yes?"

"My name must not be mentioned."

They thought it over and could find nothing wrong.

"You received the photographs in the mail with that note from the photographer himself," I continued. "You must say that."

They crossed the viewing gallery and conferred beneath an undistinguished French battle scene from the early 1800s. Their whispered consultation sounded, in that great chamber, like the humming of bees in a distant field. Finally they were finished.

"All right," they said when they returned. "Agreed. *C'est tout?*"

"No—that is not all."

And I told them the rest. They were all smiles and full of charm—I was not to worry . . . everything would be done as I wished. I knew that they would be on the transatlantic phone checking on me the moment I left the building; but there would be no trouble; the prospect of getting credit for having unearthed lost works by a lost artist would keep them cooperative. "Praha," I said to myself, "we have taken the first step."

27

I left the museum and walked slowly to Le Longchamp, the park that joins it behind the marvelous eighteenth-century fountains and charging bulls. It was a hot day, but in the shade of the park's flowering trees there was respite.

There was one unoccupied bench and I sank down on it. Youngsters bicycled happily on the paths around me. Grownups strolled by towing an endless variety of dogs. A miniature covered wagon full of children and drawn by four very small black ponies passed in front of me. I scarcely noticed any of it. I needed this time to think. My head was in a muddle. Things had to be sorted out. And here in the park, surrounded by laughing children and strangers, I might have the privacy in which to do it.

There were, it seemed to me, two different things happening.

First: the gold and everything that had to do with it. The gold had been stolen by someone unknown, and Lassiter, friend of Bobby Blessing, had been killed—together with six other colleagues—maybe more—in an effort to recover it. It might be safe to assume that, as they had all died near Marseille, the thief (or thieves) was still in this area. And I might reasonably assume that the $500 million dollars were also on hand.

Second: the Mitzu Brigade and the Coalition. This was essentially a different affair, having to do with a conspiracy to disrupt and destabilize the existing western world, a plan that required unimaginable amounts of money. The two situations overlapped by the merest chance, the tiniest whim of fate, because the man who stole the gold wished to have Lassiter dispatched and, in doing what he had probably done in the previous murders, had engaged paid assassins—in this case members of the Mitzu Brigade.

But in his zeal he overpaid, and the assassins—thirsty for money—found themselves in the same hunt for gold as the British. And the Americans, who had been in it unofficially before Lassiter was killed, had joined the hunt officially the moment Jiggs was threatened and the ambassador was assassinated. It was no longer just a matter of recovering lost gold: it was also a matter of keeping more than half a billion dollars out of terrorist hands.

All of that I understood. It gave me a headache, but I understood it. Barely.

But what about Praha? How did Praha and *Parisian Nights* fit into all of this? It was easy enough to understand the destruction of the book and the photographer's subsequent flight into anonymity. But why had Lassiter written to ask me about Praha just before he was killed? Why the interest in him in Marseille? And what had Praha been doing in Marseille, anyway?

There had to be some answers soon.

And the exhibition at the opera house had to be the catalyst.

28

The next few days were divided between Nathalie and the museum, where I helped the director and her assistants draft press releases for the Praha exhibition.

Nathalie and I industriously climbed the Virgin to peer out through her empty eyes at the port and the city spread languidly below, basking in the heat wave that had struck the south of France. Afterward we sipped *un jus de raisin* (1.50 fr.) on the Canebière and took a vedette from the Quai des Belges with ten Germans, an enormous Boxer on a chain, and two little girls with gold bracelets on each arm, to visit the Château d'If, the fortress in the harbor constructed by François premier and converted into a state prison in the seventeenth century.

I had never stopped at the fortress, although Aunt Lydie's yacht had passed it many times. "Too touristic," she always said, watching the crowds that clambered over the island and gazing with horror on those who had brought their swimming suits and were frolicking in the water. But my sensibilities were not so refined: I was eager to see the prison made famous by Dumas's Count of Monte Cristo who was imprisoned there—a childhood idol second only in my esteem to Athos of the Three Musketeers.

With Nathalie I was idle and almost carefree while I waited —hoping that Martin would come up with something. We shopped for shoes—Marseille was a multi-colored sea of shoes. We took Pastis in the sidewalk cafés. One night we even went to the races.

But I was also working. The press releases had been drafted and were beginning to appear. "Famous Lost Photographer's Work

Recovered." . . . "Mystery Genius Rediscovered" . . . "Lost Photographs of Marseille Go on Exhibit for Opening of Petit Ballet." Suddenly the press was full of Praha. Reporters leapt on the story —it had glamour, mystery, art. Petit announced in TV interviews that he had once seen a copy of *Parisian Nights* and considered it a work of genuis. Bookstores, newspapers, and even the museum were flooded with requests for information and a plethora of false leads about the location of copies of the book. Museums all over France combed their archives and regretfully announced that they could find nothing. Survivors from the world of arts and letters of the thirties were interviewed. Those who were not senile confessed that they had heard of but never met Praha. They recalled the affair of the destruction of the book. But that was all . . . and not very fruitful.

Then, too, there was the matter of framing the photographs for displaying. They had arrived in my hands in the simplest possible form—matted, backed by ragboard, and covered in polyethylene to protect the surface. The polyethylene was too cloudy for proper appreciation of the pictures and would have to be replaced by glass. The glass, in turn, required a frame. The museum, always—in true museum tradition—hard up for cash, spent a lot of time clanking around in its storerooms searching for frames that might be suitable. So far they had come up with nothing appropriate but the search was still on. And growing a bit feverish.

I left the details of labeling and documentation and installation to the museum staff, but even so there was a lot to do. The minute details of an exhibition are endless.

"But it's exciting," the director said, her short hair standing out from her head as if it, too, shared the general enthusiasm. "Usually it's so *dull* around here. All we work with is dead artists."

I didn't mention that Praha was also dead. I was the only one in the world who knew that. Or was I?

"It's exciting for me, too," I told her. "It must be the first time ever that these photographs have been on view. I feel like Christopher Colombus."

"Or Samuel de Champlain," the director said, ever the Gaul.

"Yes. Or Champlain." No point in inflaming the National Pride.

And suddenly Martin came up with something.

We had just finished dinner. Dessert had been a superb Algerian melon with Porto and I was euphoric—all food in Marseille seemed blessed with a special sun-drenched superiority that left me lazy and relaxed and scarcely capable of coping with high drama.

But that was what Martin was offering.

Nathalie had gone off to bed the minute coffee was served. "Forgive me," she yawned. "I'm so very sleepy. It must be the heat." We all felt the heat. But it wasn't that.

"I put something in her drink," he said.

"What!"

"We're going out. We have a rendezvous. And it's better if she doesn't know. She'll be all right in the morning." He might have been discussing the day's laundry, it was that cut and dried.

"You've found out something for me?"

"I think you'll find it interesting. Drink up. We're leaving."

There was an unseen vibration in the air around Martin that told me to beware, to pay attention, to guard my flank. Martin was still an unknown quantity. I had gambled on him.

We were in the foyer now. He rang for the lift. "All right, then. We're off."

The elevator arrived, hesitant as a debutante at her first party. He pushed me inside and pressed the down button.

"May I ask whom are we seeing?"

We were wedged in shoulder to shoulder in the tiny space. I did not find the proximity comforting. It was like rubbing shoulders with an iceberg.

"No names. And no questions." That was all.

The elevator, wavering slightly, continued its downward course.

"Can you at least tell me where we are going?"

150

"You asked," he said without bothering to look at me, "for my help, did you not?"

"I did," I admitted.

"Well, now you're going to get it."

The elevator stopped with a jolt and the door opened precipitously. But he blocked the exit. "There's just one thing."

I should have known there would be. There always is: it's just a question of what. "Yes?"

"I smell money in this—big money. You wouldn't be here otherwise. People like you don't come to Marseille. So it must be. And I intend to find out."

Money? I had thought I was here for Praha and even for Lassiter and six dead Englishmen—never for money. But hadn't it all begun with Czechoslovakian gold?

"Money? I don't know. . . ."

I never had a chance to finish.

"Well, *I* do. There's money. And plenty of it. And I'm going to get to the bottom of it."

He moved aside and allowed me to step out of the elevator. I stumbled and nearly fell, scarcely aware of where I was placing my feet, too alarmed to care.

He made no move to help me.

29

The street was dark and so was the café. I thought I made out the paint-chipped name CAFE DU PORT, but it was so dark that I couldn't be sure. I wondered if someone habitually shot out the street lamps here and decided, rather to my surprise, that they probably did.

Where were we? I hadn't a clue. Martin had driven like a madman around and around the tangled streets of the city (most of them made one-way in a hopeless effort to unsnarl the traffic) until I was thoroughly bewildered and disoriented. For one second —fleetingly—I thought I caught a scent of fish in the air, so perhaps we were somewhere near the waterfront.

One or two dim lights shown half-heartedly inside the café. It can't be the Old Port, I decided . . . nothing is this seedy there. We must be in the commercial area—that frightening maze of warehouses where the tankers anchor.

I could see a clutch of men clinging to the bar inside, as if they expected it to submerge momentarily. They never relinquished their grip nor turned to look at us. Perhaps they were professional nonwitnesses. It was a frightening thought.

Martin led me swiftly past the entrance and around to the side of the building where there was another door. It opened into a long dark hallway that culminated, finally, in a blacked-out room. He guided me by touch to a chair against the wall, navigating by the faint light that filtered in from the single bulb that marked the outside door. The hall smelled. The room smelled. Everything had the rank odor of clothes that had mingled too long with very dead fish. My stomach began to turn. I was going to be ill.

Then I heard it, and all my queasiness vanished. It was the faint stirring that meant we were not alone.

"Marcel?" I asked.

"Just be quiet and listen. There are two of them. They will speak in French. Do not interrupt, if you please. And do not under any circumstances light a match to look at them."

Light a match? I hadn't smoked a cigarette in ages. But I wished now that I hadn't been so virtuous. I would have given anything to see who was in the room.

One of them had begun to speak . . .hurriedly, nervously, and in heavily accented French. At first I couldn't catch the rhythm of it and then my ear adjusted: the accent was German.

"I was stationed here with the Wehrmacht. That was a long time ago. Afterward, I was in the Foreign Legion but this was before. One night we were ordered out . . . it was early in January 1943 . . . and piled into trucks and driven fast as hell down the coast. Maquis, they said. But it was over when we arrived. I was sorry about that . . . in those days fighting was *Glückseligkeit*—happiness. But it was finished. There must have been trucks . . . tracks were everywhere. Freight cars were burning. Bodies all around—some in our uniforms, and that was a curious thing. It looked like there had been an ambush, and a bloody one at that. I ought to know—I've seen a few in my time. North Africa . . . Belgium. . . ."

Martin broke in. "Go on."

"Afterward there was the usual sweep of the Old Port for information. Every petty criminal was rounded up and interrogated. The rumor was that a British cruiser had been discovered lying off shore to pick up some kind of special shipment and that she'd been sunk and the shipment ambushed. But by whom? If it was us, why the round-up? Well, ours was not to question.

"Anyway, a special railroad siding had been thrown up there so the cars could roll in with their cargo, whatever it was. The rails went all the way down to the beach—I saw them. Marseille harbor was bombed that night . . . the word was that it was a diversion. And in a few days there was the round-up in the warren of apartments and holes in the wall of the Old Port. There always was when something went wrong for our side. Thirty men were shot. Their names were on a list.

"We always wondered what it was about that night. We never heard. But a British cruiser—it must have been something big. So I've never forgotten."

A new voice broke in—this time it was in the unmistakable accent of Provence, thick and rolling.

"We never knew. And we were there too, some of us. In 1942 the Krauts occupied Marseille. They interrupted our business, those of us who brought things into the port. You know—not strictly legal, you might say. The French authorities had always been tactful . . . they understood the principal of live and let live. But the Krauts . . . they had to regulate everything. Ruin our livelihood. So naturally, every once in a while when the Maquis needed a hand we helped out. It gave us a chance to even the score a little.

"We got a call: extra men were needed for a night operation loading a ship. But we were late for our rendezvous—we had run afoul of a German patrol on the way . . . the Germans were very nervous that night. The rendezvous was for a small beach below the hills some miles outside the city. When we arrived there were bodies everywhere. Germans were loading up the last of a convoy of trucks and dispersing. It had been a massacre. Our people were lying all over the place. One of the Krauts, the one who seemed to be giving the orders, grabbed a flamethrower and began to torch the boxcars, yelling orders. It was like hell itself—you couldn't believe it was real. We hadn't been spotted yet—our orders were not to break cover until ordered. But at that moment some idiot jumped up and began to photograph the scene. We dragged the fool back down, but we'd been spotted and there was a lot of shooting before the Germans finally took off in their trucks."

154

I had been told not to speak, but it didn't matter. "The photographer—you knew him?"

"No. We were a motley bunch—a little of everything."

I hadn't expected better. I tried to imagine it. A country gobbled up by the enemy. A strange convoy snaking across Europe, trying to escape to England. A British cruiser sailing for a secret rendezvous. Bombs falling on the city for a diversion. And a collection of Maquis and criminals and patriots marching through the night to the rendezvous point, only to be met by disaster. A reckless photographer. . . .

It was long ago and it had no reality for me. "You—Wehrmacht—you said something I didn't understand. Bodies all around, you said . . . some in our uniforms and that was curious! What did you mean?" Martin had taken my arm roughly to try to silence me. But I had to know.

There was a long silence and I was afraid that perhaps I would not be answered. But finally the German spoke again. "Yes—it was a curious thing—I've always wondered. As I said, there were bodies all around. Most wore the kind of dark clothes the Maquis used at night. But others were in our uniform. Well, not exactly. Bits and pieces of ours. Maybe most wouldn't notice, but I did. I'm good at details—and I'd been in ordnance where you learn to notice military details. Things didn't match. Wrong jackets for trousers. Wrong caps for insignia. Mixtures of wrong decorations for wrong campaigns. It was exactly as if all the uniforms had been pulled out of a barrel and put on at random. And that's it."

"It's all we know."

"You're sure?" Martin demanded. "What about the cargo?"

There was no response from either of them.

"What was it? Where did it go?" Martin wanted an answer.

But he didn't get it. They were through. "We never heard. We don't know. Nobody knows. Whatever it was, it disappeared into thin air. There wasn't even a whisper—a rumor. Just gone."

Martin threw out an explosion of profanities. It was greeted by silence. Finally he stood up. "Oh, what the hell. And I called in a lot of favors! Let's go."

I got to my feet and followed him. Once again nobody at the bar gave us a glance as we passed outside.

We did not speak on the trip back: I was concentrating on trying to commit every word I'd heard to memory and I suppose Martin was doing the same. We wheeled and cornered across the city, doubling back on ourselves and executing complex patterns that could have inspired Roland Petit to create a traffic ballet. When we finally pulled up in front of eighteen, Boulevard Longchamp, we still had not exchanged a word.

Martin went through the ritual of locking the car that was part of the privilege of living in Marseille. I watched as he put the hand-written sign *"en panne"* (out of order) on the dashboard and tested each door. "O.K. Let's go in."

We started toward the building. Suddenly he stopped and took me by the shoulder and spun me around. There was nothing polite about it . . . it hurt. "Don't tell me there isn't money in this . . . I can smell it."

I tried to pull away. His grip tightened. "I won't stop until I find out. You've got a partner, Mrs. Willum."

We went into the apartment, the imprint of his fingers still deep in my flesh.

30

I did not sleep that night. Each time I drifted toward slumber I found myself sinking into a vortex of blood and flame and had to force myself awake.

Finally I picked up a book. When all else fails, a half hour or so of reading will relax the mind and permit sleep to take over.

It was a paperback I had discovered at the Canebière bookstore where I saw the photographs—something about Czechoslovakia—something I thought might serve as background. I read a few pages. It was very pedantic stuff, and almost at once the formula began to work . . . my eyes became heavy and the book kept falling on my chest.

I persevered. Read. Drift off. Read again. I was determined that when I did finally fall asleep it would be for the whole night. I didn't want to wake up a hollow-eyed, sleep-starved wreck of my usual self, which isn't movie star quality at best.

Read. Sleep. Read.

And suddenly I was sitting upright, eyes like cake plates.

Because there it was, right beneath my nose. "Praha is the Czechoslovakian word for Prague, its capital."

Praha—Prague. Nadia Milonsky was a Czech, not a Russian. She had created her Russian persona when she came to America. Just as she had created a large, noisy, bewigged, jewel-encrusted woman to hide forever the slim, shy, boy-photographer she had impersonated long ago. Masterful. Who would ever make the connection?

I sat there in bed repeating the name over and over again. Prague. Prague. Prague. I had to convince myself that it was real.

Because now I understood. She had fled to Marseille to lose herself in the teeming city . . . surrendering now and again to the irresistible impulse to photograph.

Now and then, as a Czech patriot and a French citizen, she probably helped the Maquis. Surely she had done so the night of the aborted attempt to save the Czech gold. It was partly a Czech operation: she was Czech. There could have been another photographer present, but I didn't believe it: it was Praha whose speciality was photographing at night.

Another part of the puzzle had dropped into place. I turned out the light, rolled over, and fell instantly asleep.

31

The first order of business when I awoke was to call the museum. I was full of energy. I had never felt better. I wanted to dance, or jump over a wall, or run a fifty-yard dash. I felt much too good. I warned myself: be careful, Persis—now is not the time to break a leg.

The museum director was pleased to hear from me. She was full of news. Suitable frames had finally been unearthed and if I would come immediately the young curators, who doubled as secretaries, restorers (or conservators, as they preferred to be called), framers, and general slavies would frame everything and have it ready to hang in ample time.

"I was certain we had something that would be appropriate . . . things have been accumulating in this museum for about two hundred years," the director told me calmly. "It's just a matter of patience and searching. Never give up, is my motto."

I was glad she was so cool. With the ballet opening just five nights away she had been shaving the details altogether too close for comfort.

"I was getting nervous." Maybe old age was creeping up.

"You needn't: we always manage in the end. But there is one thing we didn't anticipate."

My heart did its usual upward leap to resettle in the middle of my throat, a sure sign something was about to happen. "What?"

"We have already started taking the photographs out of their protective backing and polyethylene wrappings and we find now that we're one frame short. There's an extra photograph: it was doubled behind another. We'll have to make a decision: one photograph will have to be eliminated. Can you come right over?"

"I'll be right there." I was already tearing myself out of my jeans and flinging my body into something more suitable for the streets of Marseille where, whatever they do and however they do it, the ladies always wear dresses. After last night's interviews, I knew it was important not to stand out in any way: Lassiter and his colleagues had made themselves conspicuous by their inquiries about the lost gold. And they were dead. I didn't want to stand out from the crowd . . . being dead did not appeal to me.

32

The director and her assistants were skittering around in the museum storeroom like three hens in a granary. Each wore a blue-and-white striped apron that covered both upper and lower body and barely missed sweeping up the floor. They were brandishing hammers, finishing nails, and jars of gold-leaf paint in differing shades. Three three-star chefs preparing a banquet couldn't have been busier.

"At last!" cried the director, as if she had been waiting for hours instead of minutes. "We thought you'd never arrive. We must make a choice now."

"Where is the extra photograph?" My heart hadn't stopped pounding since the director mentioned it on the telephone. Praha had been present the night of the failed rendezvous with the British cruiser. Praha had stood up and attempted to take photographs in the midst of the melee. Praha had sent a packet of Marseille photographs to me, just before dying. Was it possible. . . ?

"Voilà!" they cried triumphantly in unison. Their voices were high and soft and delicate, even in their excitement. It is only after years of marriage that French women develop the voices of fishwives.

The photograph Praha had hidden was produced and thrust beneath my nose.

It was a night picture, of course.

But it was also a battle picture.

There wasn't any question—it had been taken the night of the battle on the beach. The back lighting, which generated dazzling contrasts of light and shadow, was produced by a blazing railroad car whose skeleton was clearly visible behind the flames. Bodies were scattered about at random and in shadow. Figures raced through the dark, guns ready, rifles leading bodies. Part of a truck was vaguely visible. They were there, those details, but they were essentially shadows to the scene.

All the photographer's energies had been centered on one man. He was center stage . . . a Shakespearian actor about to present a monologue. The flames behind him wrapped him in an eerie glow, like a heavenly body appearing to a saint in a vision. He was pointing his weapon directly at the camera, bringing the photographer into his sights before firing. It was a moment of frozen recognition between subject and cameraman.

But there was no recognition for me.

The main actor was back-lit. His face was in shadow. How frustrated Praha must have been, developing his film . . . how defeated by the lost opportunity. No doubt this was the best of what he had managed to snap that night on the beach—and it wasn't enough. The face Praha had tried to capture was a nonface.

And yet. . . .

I kept the photograph in my hand, lost in study.

There was something.

But what? It was impossible to make out the man's features. Impossible to establish an identity of any kind. So why did I have this feeling?

Something titillating. Something elusive.

I handed the photo to the director who was standing by, waiting for a decision. "We will not use this. And may I use your phone to call New York? I want to tell someone to come to the ballet. It is important."

I was already dialing Blessing's number. I heard the phone ringing in New York. He had to be there—especially with Dana gone.

But he wasn't, although it was barely six A.M. in New York.

"Mr. Blessing is out of town," his sleepy houseman told me, not impressed that this was a transatlantic call. He sounded outraged at being roused from his sleep.

162

"Have you a number where he can be reached?"

"I do not, but he may be checking in today—or maybe tomorrow. I'm not sure."

"When he does, will you tell him to call one of these numbers at once? And tell him I need him here in Marseille immediately." I gave him telephone numbers for and the address of the opera house and everything else I could think of.

"Very good. I will do my best."

I hoped he would: I had the feeling I would be needing Blessing, and soon.

There was still one thing . . . the most important one of all. The director finally mentioned it just as I was about to leave.

"I almost forgot. You made us promise to tell you if there were any requests to see the exhibition before opening night. There has been one request."

I had almost lost hope. "Who?"

"We don't know. The ballet received an anonymous donation of fifty thousand dollars in return for the privilege of viewing the photographs before dress rehearsal. The donor has expressed interest in buying the entire collection and the ballet wants me to welcome the benefactor in person. Another fifty thousand dollars has been promised this museum if I will; and we can use the money."

"Most interesting. Most generous." The bait had been set out and advertised: now it was about to be taken.

"So naturally I will be there."

"Naturally," I agreed. "And so will I."

"Ordinarily, as I promised you, you'd be welcome. After all, this donation would not be coming our way if it were not for you. But there is a serious problem: it was specified that I was to be the only outsider present."

"You are showing the collection before dress rehearsal?"

"Yes. One hour before. Privately. No one else is to be there."

"I will be there."

The director put the tip of the sable brush with which she had been retouching frames between her teeth and chewed on it distractedly. I understood her dilemma: was it wiser to safeguard the fifty thousand dollar donation to the museum, or did honor dictate that she allow me to come because it was the main condition I had exacted when I offered her the photographs?

Honor won. "All right," she said." Six P.M. sharp on Friday. Promise you won't let anyone know I said it was okay."

I would have promised anything. "Just don't give me away when you see me. I have a crazy idea." I laughed. It was a laugh of sheer nerves and tension.

She looked grim. "Fifty thousand dollars is no laughing matter. I hope we don't lose it because of you."

"I hope not."

But fifty thousand dollars didn't sound like much to me. Not when the stakes were over half a billion.

33

It must have been all the publicity about the Praha show at the Opéra Municipal that finally flushed Von Berger.

At least that was my theory.

He surfaced quite suddenly at the end of the day.

I had devoted the afternoon to Nathalie, driving her the ninety-two kilometers to Arles on swift autoroutes for a few hours' diversion. We parked in the Place de la République, lunched at the ancient Hôtel de la Cloître, and then visited the Musée Reattu on the banks of the Rhone to admire a collection of Picasso drawings. At least I admired them—Nathalie was not enthusiastic. "I don't understand them," she complained. "Anyway, Hallsey always said they were the attic-warmers of the future."

"Look at them with your own eyes," I advised. "Think for yourself."

She wasn't convinced. "I'll try." But it was obviously a failure. So we climbed to the Roman amphitheater and that was more to her taste, although what she really would have preferred was to have seen a bullfight taking place in it.

"I've never seen one."

"I hope never to see one," I replied.

"Well, an empty bull ring isn't very exciting."

Then she discovered the shops that ring the outside of the amphitheater, and that was exactly to her taste. She rushed into them one after the other, eyes alight and purse open. By the time we were ready to return to Marseille we were both laden down like two-legged beasts of burden. It seemed to me that she had bought everything her glance fell upon and I wondered if Martin wouldn't be furious when he saw the wild assortment of glassware and china and fabrics and pottery and other odds and ends she had acquired. But she didn't seem concerned so I wasn't either. All those mistresses must have accustomed him to orgies like this.

We got back to Marseille in record time and it was a good thing, because there it was—an invitation from Hans von Berger delivered by hand and written with an extravagance of flourishes on paper that bore an indecipherable crest. Would we come by for a drink this evening at six P.M.? He would look forward to receiving us, he wrote, and gave an address on the Boulevard Prado. He had already been in touch with Martin, he added, and Martin would meet us there.

"We will go, of course," Nathalie said. "It's really the first interesting thing that's happened."

"Do you know his house?"

"No. But it's a very chic address, I think. Mansions and the Turkish embassy and goodness knows what else. *Très, très chic.* We must also be very chic. There will be wonderful people there. He has probably taken Marseille by storm since he has been here, no matter how short the time."

It was my guess that he had taken Marseille by storm many moons ago, for this was not his first visit. I knew that much from our conversation in Gull Harbor. And a man like Hans von Berger would never keep a low profile—not with his good looks and golden hair. Women were, after all, the same the world over. The ones with the killer instinct would ferret him out no matter where he tried to hide. And a man with a house near Embassy Row couldn't be trying *too* hard to hide.

"Yes, yes," Nathalie repeated. "We must be very chic."

I made a mental trip through my wardrobe and groaned. "I don't think. . . ."

But Nathalie wasn't listening. She was dragging me down the hallway to her bedroom, which I hadn't been invited to see before. It was almost completely mirrored and anything that

166

wasn't a mirror was covered in red velvet. It was only two skips short of being a bordello. Those mistresses again, I wondered?

She flung open mirrored doors and began to root around in an enormous closet, pulling out dresses and flinging them around the room and across the bed and over the small upholstered chairs.

"What will it be? Oh, I'm so excited. The Ungaro that's way down on the hips? With a million strings of pearls and this big white hat? You like it?"

"Don't you think it's. . . ."

"What about this Yves Saint Laurent? It's the last thing Hallsey bought for me . . . you should have heard him moan. Millions for himself, but not one cent for me. You like it? I adore the melon with these crystal beads, don't you?" There were two round spots of color in her cheeks—two spots of color I had seen only once before . . . the night she drank champagne from the same glass as Ronald Chunk, the real estate baron.

"I. . . ."

"Or what about this Dior. Don't you love the shoulders? Or this Givenchy . . . one shoulder. I do have nice shoulders, don't you think? Or what about this black and white Guy Laroche?"

I was stunned. Was this the girl I had thought so badly dressed?

"All these clothes . . . I never saw you . . . I mean, I didn't imagine. . . ." I ran out of words.

She laughed and her laughter was gay and unaffected. The little lines of petulance habitually around her mouth had disappeared for the moment.

"You don't understand. I am a closet clothes horse. My men —they will never let me dress up. Always I must be the little girl. Hallsey fixed me permanently in time at approximately seventeen. *Toujours la jeune fille . . . zut!* With Martin it is a little better . . . he allows me to advance to approximately nineteen. With neither of them am I allowed to dress up and have a little fun and be a woman of the world. So I buy these beautiful clothes. And I try them on when I am alone. I dress up and prance around and smoke cigarettes from a long holder and practice walking with a slouch and a slink and dream of the time when I can do it all in public."

She began to pick up the dresses and hang them back in the closet.

"But surely, Nathalie, you could wear one of these. There must be something in that closet that would be appropriate."

She shook her head. "No. Not one. They won't do. Martin would be furious." The little lines of discontent were back around her mouth. "It will be the same all-enveloping caftan . . . it's the best I can do."

"Don't be absurd. Wear what you like. I'm sure Martin would approve." It didn't make sense. Why would two men buy her couturier clothes and then forbid her to wear them? Why would she have to fly to Paris for something suitable for her portrait?

She pulled open the doors to a second closet. It stood opposite a great full-length mirror and it was as crowded with gowns and hats and shoes as the first.

"These are from Rome. We made a flying trip there just for the fashions. I wanted to have my pick before they were shown in Paris. Valentino—you like it? This one I love with the dropped waistline. It's by Laug. Do you suppose a hat will be all right for six o'clock? No, no . . . Marcel would never allow it, even though he bought it for me."

We? Rome? That must have been Hallsey. A hat Martin had bought? And she was afraid to wear it?

"Try the Valentino, Nathalie. Let me decide."

She climbed into it, stripping to the buff in front of me without the least concern for modesty. The dress was white silk, low cut in front with cap sleeves and large black, yellow, red, and blue blossoms scattered artfully here and there.

A magnificent bit of dressmaking, one I would have given anything to own. But as she patted it into place over ample hips and pranced around the room I began to understand about the husbands. A strange transformation had taken place . . . the parlormaid had stepped into the queen's robes for a day and the

168

parlormaid had never looked more like a parlormaid. Nathalie was too young, too plump, and too ordinary for these extraordinary creations. She couldn't pull it off.

And something else . . . something that made no sense.

"Then why do they buy you all these expensive clothes if they won't allow you to wear them?" I could see now why they preferred not to let her prance around in these gowns—the strut and hip wriggling were absurd. But why buy them in the first place?

"Because, that's why." She stuck out an ample hip and pretended to puff on a long cigarette, chin in air, posing like a child trying to imitate a film star. "They know very well that I'll buy them myself if they don't, that's why."

Surely an empty threat. Each of these dresses cost thousands of dollars. "How?"

"Earn them."

"You're serious?"

"Oh, yes. Dewy youth and a French accent pay big money. And I always demanded a bonus—a trip to the couturier, you see. I always wore the very best. I worked only the highest priced hotels . . . the Ritz . . . the Plaza Athénée . . . the George V. Sometimes I went to London. I love the Connaught. All those lovely old men. I sit in the lounge with a Perrier. And presently one of them sidles up. 'Do you mind if I sit down?' Lustful old men, full of forbidden appetites, dreaming that this perfectly dressed young girl who has stirred their libidinous desires will somehow restore lost powers. And when they can't . . . oh, they are so pathetic then . . . it is a simple matter to ask for whatever one wants. Of course Marcel is different . . . he is young. But even he . . . from time to time. . . ."

She didn't finish She didn't have to. I understood.

No wonder her men refused to allow her to wear clothes that brought back her former profession. No wonder, further, that she didn't really fit them. Although, as I thought about it, a high-priced call girl didn't necessarily betray her career by looking out of place in fine clothes. There had been a girl at the Heart Ball in the Bahamas, I remembered, who far outshown anyone present in both chic and beauty—and she had turned out to be an octoroon whose profession was marrying and divorcing wealthy men.

But Nathalie—Nathalie was something else, a simple, lazy girl who probably didn't even understand the implications of living as she had lived and preferred marriage simply because it was easier, though boring.

"Ah well," I sighed. "Perhaps the caftan, after all."

"Perhaps." She stripped off the Valentino and put it back on its hanger with loving care. "Perhaps not even that. A simple skirt and blouse, I think."

"I think, too. Actually, you are most charming like that." It was true.

"But so boring." She hung the dress back on the rod with a dissatisfied snap.

"Tonight will be different."

She brightened. "I hope so."

"There will be interesting people to meet. You said so yourself." I wanted to cheer her up. I felt sorry for her. She was a child whose candy had been snatched away.

"It will be fun, won't it? Do you think it will be fun, Persis? We never go anywhere. And Marcel won't even let me have a part in his movies, although I know I can act and I'm not afraid of nude scenes."

I'll bet, I thought. But he wouldn't put her in a pornographic film. She was posing as his wife, after all. Suppose somebody recognized her?

"Never mind about Marcel's movies. Tonight will be exciting. You will meet new friends and you will be invited everywhere and you'll never be bored in Marseille again."

"Exciting. Yes, that's what I'd like. An exciting evening. Hurry and dress, Persis, and let's go. I've been longing for something exciting to happen."

As I dressed, I hoped she wouldn't be disappointed.

170

34

Nathalie was right—the street Von Berger lived on was elegant. Great plane trees cast luxurious shadows. Fine white Mediterranean houses peered out at us from behind wrought-iron gates. Even the exuberant Marseille traffic was subdued in passing, out of respect for wealth and power.

Nathalie was driving and she pulled up at the address Von Berger had indicated with a flourish and a squealing of brakes. "Driving is one of my sports," she had said earlier, and I believed her. On the way over she had given as good as she got from the other French drivers and had come out, I thought, just a shade the better of even the most daring. The chariot races in Nero's Rome couldn't have stirred the blood more than her careening progress across the teeming city had stirred mine. Our breathless arrival in one piece at Von Berger's gate convinced me that there was still a God in His heaven and I sighed with relief at the prospect of descending from Nathalie's infernal machine and relaxing in Von Berger's fine house.

But it was not to be.

A servant greeted us at the gate with new instructions. We were not, it appeared, to be allowed to alight. Von Berger had encountered difficulties with his schedule and would not be back in Marseille in time to entertain us here. Would we mind terribly meeting him at a rendezvous outside the city? He would be sure to get that far and the distance for us would not be an imposition. Naturally, since we were being so disagreeably inconvenienced, he would expect us to dine with him as well. Martin had been informed and would be present. The restaurant, La Bonne Auberge, was one of the finest on the Côte d'Azur. He promised it.

"La Bonne Auberge. I thought it was just beyond Antibes. That's not close." I remembered vaguely that I had dined there once long ago.

"I've heard of it, too. But it must be where he says it is. We can be there in thirty minutes. Twenty, if I put my mind to it."

"No please. Let's take our time." I was still disturbed and I tried to root around in my memory to fix La Bonne Auberge firmly in a geographic space. But it had been long ago. And furthermore, France was covered with places called La Bonne Auberge, just as it is covered with places called Villefranche and Le Mas and Le Moulin and L'Oasis and a million other things that come out in quadruplicate or worse throughout the country. The French have a theory that if you find a good thing you stick with it. So, now that I think of it, does everyone else.

Still, the unease persisted. "Nathalie, do you think we should? It's a long drive. And it will be dark."

She laughed. "Don't be silly, Persis. I'm a fabulous driver and it will be fun. And anyway, we have to go—Marcel is undoubtedly already on his way."

So the die was cast.

She wheeled the Peugeot around and we were off, Nathalie doing battle with the traffic while I deciphered the directions the servant had supplied in writing.

"I can't make too much of this map," I apologized, squinting.

"Naturally. That man was an Algerian."

"An Algerian? How did you know?"

"You can't miss the type. There are millions of them in Marseille. They'll do anything to make a franc. I must say that I'm surprised: you'd think Von Berger could find someone a little better than that to work for him."

But then we both forgot about it. After all, he was only a gatekeeper so what could one expect?

Nathalie hurtled across the city, the Peugeot screaming in and out among the columns of traffic like a demented greyhound.

We streaked past apartment buildings and soccer fields and commercial areas and camping grounds standing barren and lonely as they waited for the onslaught of summer. The kilometers flew by and Nathalie laughed aloud whenever she overtook a car and roared past it, clinging to the outer lane until the last possible moment before an approaching vehicle forced her back in line.

Now she began to sing in a high but piercing voice that carried clearly over the noise of the traffic around us.

"Milord," she crooned—that great lament-invitation of Edith Piaf. And I translated mentally as she sang. "Come on, mister, sit at my table and make yourself comfortable. Tell me your troubles and put your feet up on a chair. I know you, though you've never seen me. I'm only a tramp, a phantom of the street. . . ."

The notes were high and clear, but they were not the notes of Piaf. Nathalie may have lived a little of the chanteuse's early life, but that was the only similarity. The heart was missing.

She switched without a pause to Jo Dassin's "Allez Roulez," a song more suited to her style and she whipped through it with energy and verve.

Then it was back to Piaf. This time I joined her and the two of us sang at the tops of our lungs, vying with one another for the highest note and the longest held.

"Non, je ne regrette rien . . . nothing that's been done to me, good or ill. Everything's paid for, swept up, forgotten. I don't give a damn for the past . . . I'm starting at zero again. My life, my happiness, begins with you."

It sounded better in French, of course, and that's how we sang it . . . our voices trembling, Piaf style, and each of us thinking of someone. At least I suppose we were . . . I know I was thinking of Dana and feeling bereft and cheated and sad, just as Piaf intended. I don't know whether Nathalie was thinking of Martin or Bryce or if, indeed, she was thinking of anyone at all. Probably not. It is possible that she was just singing.

In any case, the caterwauling—and I'm afraid that's exactly what it was—made the kilometers fly. And by the time we had gone through "Le Chanteur des Rues," "Pauvre Pierrot," "Bye, Bye Louis," "Je Suis à Toi," "Les Mots d'Amour," and several others (repeating each one several times to perfect our performance) we had arrived at the *carrefour* where La Bonne Auberge was supposed to be found.

But there was nothing there. There was a crossroads, but there was nothing on it except a few rusty road signs to Nice, to Cannes, and—as always—to Paris.

We re-studied the map, both of us poring over it at the side of the road. There was no question—we were at the right crossroads. But where was the Auberge?

"We haven't made a mistake." Nathalie was puzzled but firm about that. "So it must be Von Berger who has erred."

"We'll have to ask. It's getting late."

"Such stupidity! And he's so good looking. Who would ever suspect?" She threw the car into gear and we were off, searching for a farmhouse.

They weren't hard to find. In fact we found three before anyone could do more than stare at us when we asked for the vanished restaurant.

The fourth farmer was articulate, but not very helpful. "No such thing around here, and I was born on this place. No Bonne Auberge, I assure you. Maybe in Antibes or Cap Ferrat or St. Tropez—that's where you find the good eating places . . . that's where the money is. Film stars, millionaires. If you're looking for good cuisine, that's where you'll find it."

Antibes. I knew I'd been there. But Antibes was too long a drive. Von Berger would never have expected us to meet him there.

I didn't like it. I hadn't liked it since the Algerian turned us away from his gate, refusing to let us turn into the drive.

The farmer went back inside and Nathalie and I sat in the car and stared at one another.

"What now?" She looked on the brink of tears with frustration and disappointment. Furthermore, we were beginning to be hungry. It had been a long time since lunch at Arles.

"I don't know. Let's think." But there was something else on my mind. "Did you notice the house?" It hadn't registered at the time but now a picture of it was materializing clearly in my mind.

"What house?" Houses bored her: she was solely concerned with restaurants.

"Von Berger's."

"I didn't see it. We never went in, remember?" Crossly, regretting it. Thinking I was crazy to be thinking about Von Berger's house when we couldn't even find Von Berger.

"I looked at it. Just a quick glimpse. And it didn't register at first."

"Well, what about it?"

"I'm not positive—but I had this strange impression."

She was impatient. That was the past: what she wanted to know was what to do with the present. "So?"

"I think it was empty." I'd said it and as I spoke I realized I didn't just think it—I was sure. It was one of those quick images that don't mature until later.

We were both silent, each of us considering the implications. Finally she spoke.

"What does it mean?"

"I don't know. Why would he ask us there if it was empty?"

"Maybe it was scheduled to be a housewarming. Maybe the furniture will come later."

"Maybe."

"Maybe everybody was supposed to bring something for the house and he forgot to tell us."

"It could be."

"And maybe everybody he invited will be waiting for us at the restaurant when we get there."

"Nathalie, there isn't any restaurant."

"I don't believe you." Her voice trembled and she spoke very loud to convince herself.

"I'm afraid it's true. There isn't any restaurant."

"But there *must* be. We have only to go on looking. One farmer doesn't know everything."

175

"We have looked. And it's getting dark."

"Well, I don't believe you. He wouldn't give us a map and everything if there wasn't a restaurant. I'm going to go on looking. It's a known fact that Algerians can't read and write and they certainly can't be expected to draw maps people can follow."

"That Algerian could write. La Bonne Auberge was lettered as clearly as anyone could have lettered."

"Never mind. It was an Algerian. So the restaurant could be right around the corner. And you only imagined that the house was empty—I didn't notice it. And I'm not going to miss a good time just because we can't read a map correctly."

She had made a decision. The car roared forward, spitting dirt behind it. In the hen house chickens woke up and cried out in alarm and a dog inside the barn began a deep-throated protest.

I shrugged and settled down in my seat. There was nothing else to do.

She was a tenacious searcher. We explored every road, poked into every cart track. We crossed and criss-crossed every intersection no matter how insignificant. We stopped and queried a half-dozen people. It grew dark. And still no Bonne Auberge.

Finally she surrendered. "We might as well go home and have something to eat. I'm exhausted and starved."

I was relieved. I didn't like what was going on and I didn't like Von Berger. The only reason I had consented to come was to learn what I could about why he was in Marseille and to try to find out if he was aware of the Praha show. As for me, my excuse for being in Marseille would be that I had read about Praha's exhibition and come especially on behalf of the gallery. No one could quarrel with that. And now here we were, in the country miles from Boulevard Longchamp—hungry, out of sorts, and wondering what had become of our much-anticipated evening.

We were too disappointed and dispirited to note the dim headlights at first. It wasn't until we had driven several miles that I became aware of them. Nathalie was too busy clinging to the winding road. I thought it odd that, despite the dark, they didn't use their brights. I turned in my seat to watch. They never came closer. They didn't drop back.

Suddenly the brights came on, and the vehicle speeded up until it was only a couple of car lengths behind us.

"My God!" Nathalie flung one arm up in front of her face, blinded. I reached in front of her and steadied the wheel. With the other hand I switched the rear-view mirror from light to eye-protecting dark. Nathalie's grip on the wheel tightened. "It's all right. I've got it."

"They must want to pass. Can you pull over a little?"

"Bastards. Why should I?" She was a combatant, not a driver.

"Because he'll blind you, that's why."

"Never! Pray to the Virgin." And she stayed where she was. So did the other car.

I protested again. No use: she had the bit in her teeth. So I settled down in my seat. It was the only thing I could do.

We went on like that. Nathalie stuck to her speed and so did the car behind, never varying its distance. In the brilliant light that bathed our front seat I could see the girl's lower lip jutting out in anger and determination.

Mile after mile. If we increased our speed, so did they. If we decelerated, they did too.

They didn't drop back. They didn't try to pass.

I was beginning to twist my fingers together to keep from speaking.

It was Nathalie who spoke first. "Bastards. Fresh kids. Playing chicken. Trying to scare us. Well, they won't scare me."

And she stayed her course. Once in a while she tried to lose them, but the Peugeot wasn't equal to the task. Once in a while she slowed suddenly. But they were expert drivers or else they could read her mind, because when she slowed suddenly so did they.

Finally we came to a straight stretch of road and we could see the lights of Marseille in the distance.

"Almost home." I had never seen a more welcome sight. I

didn't believe they were pranksters—not after this evening's itinerary. But I didn't want to frighten the girl. What good would it do? And now—so near the city—surely we were safe.

"Finally," Nathalie answered through tightly clenched teeth. "And you can bet I'll complain to the first 'flic' I see. Note the license number if you can, Persis."

She put her foot down on the gas and the Peugeot responded like a game pony, giving us all it had. But it wasn't enough. At that same moment, our pursuer shot forward, engulfing us in light. The girl was screaming at her Peugeot, calling on it for more speed, shrieking orders, exhorting and commanding.

"Nathalie—let them pass. Are you mad?"

But she wouldn't. And her Peugeot struggled with all its heart to obey.

But the pursuer was upon us. We drowned in the bright lights. Then it was abreast of us and careening along beside us. We were a team, charging at breakneck speed. Bright orange bursts came from the left. And then they were past, rocketing away from us into the night.

The Peugeot slowed. The Peugeot stopped.

There was absolute quiet.

We stared ahead, neither of us willing to say the unsayable. But somebody had to.

"Persis?" I could scarcely hear her. It was only a whisper in the night.

"I know."

"Is it true?"

"I think so. Yes."

"But it couldn't be."

We were quiet again, thinking about that.

Finally. "You saw?"

"I did."

"You're sure?"

"I'm afraid so."

"Did you see faces?"

"No. Did you?"

"No."

I could feel her shaking beside me. "You mustn't. We're all right. We have to get home, Nathalie. Don't go to pieces."

"I know. I can't help it."

"I'll drive."

"Please."

We changed places. She slipped over and I was the one who walked around the car and got into the driver's seat because I was, as it turned out, the stronger.

The Peugeot started up obediently.

The small voice beside me had only two questions as we crept quietly into Marseille.

"You saw it, Persis?"

"I did."

"They were shooting at us?"

"Yes, Nathalie." There wasn't any question.

Then why hadn't they killed us? Everyone else was being killed. Why wait so long to shoot at us? Why wait until we were almost back in Marseille? It didn't make sense. Was I going mad?

Martin was not there when we finally reached number eighteen, Boulevard Longchamp; but Nathalie wasn't alarmed. He had not, it seemed, ever attempted to rendezvous with Von Berger. The day's shooting had not gone well and everyone was working overtime in order to stay on schedule. There was a note from the maid saying that he would not be home until well after midnight.

Nathalie and I rummaged in the refrigerator for leftovers and thanked heaven he wasn't wandering around, like us, somewhere in the hinterlands searching for the nonexistent Bonne Auberge and being shot at by strangers in the night.

We toasted our safe return with a nightcap of Porto and fell into our respective beds, exhausted.

I didn't even stay awake long enough to admire the floodlit Virgin from my bedroom window. Which wasn't very grateful: maybe, after all, it was her gracious beneficence that had delivered Nathalie and me. Nothing would have surprised me that night.

179

35

I slept late the next morning and even so woke up exhausted. Nothing drains one's energy like a dark night, a fast chase, and a few bullets. My whole body hurt as much as if I had been in an automobile accident.

Well, I almost had.

Nathalie and Martin were not in evidence when I pulled myself together and staggered off to the museum around noon. And after that I was too busy to worry about anything except Praha and frames and installation and whether or not the Press would continue to cover the story as expertly as it had to date.

The young curators were as disorganized as ever while being at the same time as insoucient as ever. It was a perfect example of organized chaos.

Somehow I found the time to check on Von Berger's house by calling *La Marseillaise*. The foreign desk helped me out. I didn't even have to invent a story. All I said was I'd been invited to a party at a house near the Turkish embassy and no one was there. He asked for the address. I told him. In two minutes he was back to inform me that I must have had the wrong number—the owners of the house I'd gone to were diplomats currently posted to Djibouti. The house was empty, unfurnished, and for let.

I didn't ask about Von Berger. I thought I knew all I needed to know about him.

When I returned around six, Nathalie greeted me.

"Don't say anything to Marcel about last night." The two bright spots were back in her cheeks.

"But why not?"

"Because *I* haven't. After I got home I realized that last night was the most excitement I'd had since I got here. And if we tell Marcel he'll never let me go anywhere again. Imagine—the first time I'm out in Marseille without him and we get shot at. It's pretty wonderful when you think about it."

"It's wonderful that we weren't hurt."

"Even the car wasn't hurt. There isn't a mark on it. They were just trying to scare us. Well, I wasn't scared."

"I was."

"Oh, Persis, don't be an old woman. Nobody was hurt. I don't believe they intended to hurt us or they would have."

I wasn't so sure. "Maybe."

"In any case, be that as it may, don't tell Marcel. I am asking you—begging you."

How could I refuse. "All right."

"Promise?"

Reluctantly, because I believed it was wrong and that he should be told, I promised.

She clapped her hands. "You're a good sport. And you've made me very happy."

"It isn't fair to him, you know."

"Don't be silly. He's like Hallsey—always thinking about money. Only Hallsey has tons more—never mind about how he gets it—and Marcel has to scramble for his. I thought he was so rich. But he has to keep scratching. He likes to live like a king—big houses, yachts. But believe me, he earns every cent of it himself."

She sighed. Evidently she was disillusioned about the amount of his income.

"I like a man who works for his money," I said.

"Depends. Depends on how hard he has to scratch to get it."

And with that final word she went off to dress for dinner.

36

Dinner that night was from a menu selected by Martin; and it was so grand luxe I wondered if it was supposed to be a Last Supper. We began with champagne and proceeded to a series of glorious wines accompanying an hors d'oeuvres of *truffe en croûte*, a fish course of *filet de bar à la julienne des légumes*, an entrée of *noix de ris de veau aux champignons sauvages* (the mushrooms, so Martin informed me, flown in from the forests of Fontainbleau) a *plateau de fromages* and *les délices de Marjorie*. Marjorie was the cook and the '*délices*' were her sinful miniature fruit tarts.

Nathalie ate with unbridled enthusiasm; Martin with restrained dignity. I scarcely touched anything that passed before me: it was a matter of nerves.

"You 'guard the line'?" Martin asked after watching me push the food around plate after plate while scarcely sampling anything.

"*Oui—je garde la ligne. Je m'excuse, Marcel.*"

Nathalie, happy as a cat in cream, couldn't understand. "But it's so good, Persis. Why come to France, if not to eat?"

"Why, indeed?" The look Martin gave me was full of cynicism and inquiry.

"And anyway, you're thinner than I am by far. But remember, men don't like to go to bed with a skeleton . . . just bear that in mind."

Martin laughed and without comment lit his usual after-dinner cigar. The room was engulfed in smoke.

Also as usual, Nathalie coughed. "Marcel—you know I can't stand your cigars. I can't breathe."

He laughed again. "What I know is that you're longing to leave us and watch television. Always looking for adventure. What is it tonight?"

She was already on her feet: it was the evening ritual. "It's 'Dallas,' Marcel. Do come and watch. J.R. is just about to. . . ."

Martin waved her out of the room. "Run along. Persis and I will finish our coffee here and then join you."

She rushed out of the dining room and clattered down the hall. In a second we heard the sound of the music that heralded the beginning of her program.

He poured me a brandy and offered me a cheroot, which I politely declined, and we sat in companionable silence. He was very small and very compact and very neatly put together and I looked at him and thought about how much I needed someone I could trust. Everything was piling up on me.

He sat there like a perfect little miniature of a man, wearing a black velvet smoking jacket, rather warm, I thought, for this evening. His small feet were snugly encased in velvet slippers with his initials embroidered in gold. There was a gold bracelet on his right wrist and an impossibly thin Piaget gold watch on his left. The gold and black made a sharp contrast with his fawn-colored shirt and flannel trousers.

A perfect little dandy, I thought. Too perfect, maybe.

And then I thought, things have arrived at a critical point.

I must have someone to trust. Dana has vanished and Blessing hasn't appeared.

But was that someone Martin? Was he a man to be trusted?

I studied him, trying to disguise the intensity of my regard by watching through lowered lashes.

Somebody was trying to kill me. Hadn't there been a car pursuing us? Hadn't I been shot at—for the second time?

But was Martin to be trusted?

Well, I had to trust somebody, didn't I? I couldn't go on alone forever. And Martin had already helped me, after all.

"Could we close the door? I would like to speak to you."

And I told him. Not a word about last night. But everything else.

Everything.

37

Martin went out later that evening, saying he had a camera crew filming night scenes down at the Old Port. Nathalie begged to go with him. She said she never had any excitement. It seemed to me that between Nathalie and the young museum director someone was always complaining about the lack of excitement in Marseille; whereas I, for my part, found it quite exciting enough.

He explained to her patiently that he couldn't take her because it was a dangerous area. He'd be too busy to keep an eye on her, and he'd be worrying about her when he should be concentrating on his work. Further, it would be very late when he returned.

In fact, he never returned.

Nathalie had wanted excitement, and she got it. The police found Martin's body late the next afternoon. He was slumped over a picnic table at a parking stop on the autoroute outside the city. All day long people passing had thought he was a traveler taking a nap, until finally someone noticed the small black hole in the back of his head.

The police were not unduly upset. Death was as ordinary an event in Marseille as the ritual coffee or whiskey taken at the corner tabac before going off to work in the morning. People were murdered every day. For example, they pointed out, yesterday they had found the bodies of two men executed in the same fashion.

They had both been mercenary soldiers.

38

Somehow—I don't know how—we got through it.
Nathalie had him buried immediately.

"I want it over," she said.

She was convinced that it was her fault. Bryce, she was
certain, had ordered his execution. But Bryce was nowhere evident. Neither was anyone else we knew from home.

I was equally certain that it was my fault. After all, hadn't
I involved him in the Lassiter affair and wasn't such involvement
turning out to be a death sentence for everyone?

Like Lassiter and the six other dead Englishmen, he'd made
inquiries in the wrong places. Now, like them, and like the two
mercenaries we'd interviewed, he was very much dead.

It was the dreariest of funerals. Naturally, it rained. There
weren't many of us. His film crew and a few unimpressive-looking
actors. The museum staff, who had come as a courtesy to me.
We huddled under our black umbrellas like a collection of
mournful crows, noses dripping with a combination of tears and
raindrops, and shoes squishing wretchedly in the wet grass.

Then, as suddenly as it had happened, it was over.

Martin was gone. The film people were gone. The museum
staff was pursuing their business.

Nathalie shut herself in her bedroom for about half an hour
and then settled down to await the arrival of Hallsey Bryce: I was
sure she had been in touch with him and was expecting him
momentarily. Nathalie was a girl who had no intention of living
without a man—as long as he bought her clothes.

Marcel Martin had suffered an unfortunate accident. He was

gone. She would move back to her first protector. Life was like that. A girl had to look after herself. And maybe her sojourn with Martin had taught the tight-fisted Hallsey a lesson. Who could tell?

What would become of her? I didn't know, and I didn't have to worry about it, because she was a survivor. I would not abandon her. I would be at her side until help arrived. But there was another very pressing concern.

Because suddenly it was Friday, the day of the dress rehearsal.

39

The opera house was wreathed in quiet, its six Ionic columns the epitomy of unruffled dignity. Its frieze of classic figures gazed down at passers-by with monumental calm.

Anyone who knew anything about theater would know that the great house was holding its breath, waiting for the hour of dress to arrive.

The stage was silent. The fly floor was abandoned. The orchestra stalls were empty. The instruments were covered.

In an hour the scene would turn into chaos. But now the house slept.

I had come well in advance and stationed the car at the side of the small *Place* where I would have a clear view of anyone coming or going.

I saw the director cross the *Place* and approach the doors. She was very dignified today in a dark silk dress and white plastic earrings. A doorman let her in, ogling her slim, silk-sheathed body.

I had chosen a spot where my car would not stand out: others were moving about, arriving and departing. I ignored them and concentrated on the opera house.

Fifteen minutes passed. Another fifteen. Then two black Mercedes slid up and parked as close as possible to the entrance. Three men leapt from the first car and scanned the area. They were young, athletic, wearing dark glasses and three piece suits, neatly fitted.

They bounded up the steps to the main door and wrapped a smart tattoo. I saw the director let them in.

A minute or two passed during which I assumed they had

checked out the lobby, giving cursory attention to the scattered pieces of sculpture and checking the curved marble staircases on either side.

After a short time they emerged and nodded to the occupants of the second Mercedes. They opened the doors to the first car. Simultaneously a group of men leapt from the second automobile, surrounding someone who emerged from car number one, completely hiding the occupant from view.

Woman? Man? I couldn't tell.

All I could make out was a block of bodies in dark clothes. There was just no way anyone could have penetrated that tight-knit unit. Together, in a block, they swept into the building.

I counted to ninety. I thought it would give them the right amount of time. Then I was across the street and up the steps and knocking at the door. The director opened it. She gasped when she saw me.

I didn't blame her. I had seen enough of Marseille to know that there was just one kind of female who did not wear skirts— the delivery girls who carried messages and packages around the city. No one ever really looked at them: they affected a sexless image deliberately designed to put off the most amorous of males and to assure their getting in and out of offices in one piece.

Today I was one of those. I had taken my jeans and shirt to the park and rolled them in the dust. I had rented a pair of motorcycle boots and a white helmet from the boy who served juice at the *buvette* in the park. I carried a blue musette bag on which I had lettered UNISEX COIFFEUSE, HAIRDRESSERS TO THE STARS. It was very professional. The bag was filled with hairdressing equipment. It was my one chance to get inside the opera house.

"Delivery. Unisex Coiffeuse," I said.

The director was stunned.

"M. . . ."

I rushed to interrupt her, to stop her from saying my name, "I was told to deliver this hairdressing equipment before seven. I was told someone would be here to receive it."

"Ah, yes," she said, gathering her wits.

"So here it is—if you'll sign?" My eyes were moving around the room. Six men were watching. They had quick eyes and bunched muscles and they hadn't made up their minds yet what to do about me. I would have another moment or two to try to decide which of them was the important one before I had to leave.

And there was someone else. A woman. She was crossing the room, coming directly toward me. Disaster marching my way.

"Persis Willum," she was saying. "What a surprise. What are you doing in that ridiculous get-up?"

It was Kate Cochran. And she wasn't smiling.

40

She did it so smoothly that I doubt the director had any inkling of what was happening. First she linked her arm in mine; then one of the men swung in on my other side, and with astonishing speed we were out the door and in the back seat of the Mercedes with Cochran flinging a "thank you" and "the money will be deposited to the museum account" over her shoulder as we went. The rest of the party followed with equal speed and the two cars took off. I had not said a word. And with good reason—there was a gun pressed firmly to my back. I doubt if the director saw that, either.

When we were under way Cochran finally spoke to me.

"I'm sorry it's you, Persis. I've always liked you."

I chose not to examine the implications of that remark. "How," I asked instead, "did you find out about the exhibition?"

She laughed. "I clip newspapers—remember? *The New York Times* ran a story, among others."

The two cars were racing out of Marseille, weaving effortlessly in and out of traffic. The men did not speak. Looking at them and noting their bunched muscles and shifting eyes I understood them for what they were—thugs, Marseille brand. I could see bulges in their tight-fitting suits that meant every one of them was armed.

We were on the outskirts of Marseille before Cochran spoke again. "It's a shame about your being there, Persis."

I tried, although I didn't expect much. "I was there just by chance."

"In that costume?" She laughed again. It was not the kind of laugh that made you want to smile back. "No. And I'm sorry, truly sorry. But you pose a problem and it will have to be dealt with. But not by me." She did not speak again.

We had left the city behind and were winding our way swiftly along the edge of the sea. The terrain was getting rougher, more wooded. Houses were thinning out. So was the traffic: we flew past only an occasional "Deux Chevaux." The countryside became increasingly wild and unkempt.

We began to climb. There were no other cars now.

The surroundings became frankly hostile. We left the main road and turned onto a smaller one and after a few kilometers we left that one, too, and bumped onto an even more primitive trail, the Mercedes's springs suffering in martyred silence. To occupy my mind I tried to memorize our route, but it was hopeless . . . there seemed to be endless small trails overlapping one another in the piny woods and I had the impression that we were taking them all.

Suddenly we were plunging downward. I was sure that we had reached and passed the crest of the Corniche. Abruptly we began to climb again, still hurtling along at surprising speed. Up and down—a roller-coaster ride to . . . what?

When the wall appeared in front of us it was a total surprise.

There was no approach. We simply burst out of the woods like a bullet and there it was in a rough clearing, a high wall with an iron gate and roofs just visible inside the compound. There was a frantic barking of dogs—large dogs. The quiet sound of our motors had nevertheless put them into full cry. Yet the place had a tranquil appearance, like a typical south-of-France *mas*— walled properties are not unusual among well-to-do landowners in France. There was really nothing to suggest that this was an armed fortress.

So when two armed men suddenly appeared and looked into both cars, even examining the uninteresting contents of my hair-dressing bag, I was surprised. I shouldn't have been, but I was.

The examination was swift but thorough. Then we were motioned through the gate.

"Don't make trouble, Persis," Cochran said. "Just cooperate."

"With whom?" I hoped that I didn't sound as frightened as I felt; but the gun was digging into my side and it didn't inspire confidence.

I knew that we were on our way to meet the man who had been the cause of everything that had happened. In seconds now I would meet him face to face. It was for this that I had arranged the Praha exhibition. For this I had exposed myself in the opera house lobby. Everything had been for this . . .

Cochran was the unexpected particular, the detail that didn't compute.

But the man himself? I had a mental image, carefully assembled since the assassination of Lassiter and, scared though I was, I couldn't resist a small surge of excitement at the prospect of finally meeting him.

What would he be like? He would be a man of between sixty and seventy years of age—maybe even as young as fifty-five. He would be a recluse, not wanting to draw attention. He might be a man of many names, with a taste for the good things in life, even if he could only enjoy them in private. He would like expensive wines, food, art, women . . . why else would he rob and kill? He would be arrogant, cruel, ruthless, and amoral. He might even still be attractive to women—as certainly he had once been.

A sculptor's assistant, Cochran had said, so he would know a good deal about art.

A murderer. A killer. A man I was about to meet.

"Cooperate with whom?" I repeated.

"You will see in a moment. I suppose you read the same article I did and came rushing over here to see what it was all about?"

"Not exactly. I don't have your kind of income."

We were out of the car now and being escorted across a small courtyard and through the French doors of the foyer. Inside, the floors were parquet, the walls hung with what looked to me like medieval tapestries. At the head of the stairway that wound upward to the left was a large Rubens nude. We turned right and proceeded down a corridor lined with African masks. Whoever my host was, his tastes were eclectic.

We paused before a heavy chased bronze door. It must have come from some Italian Renaissance church—spoils of war in a long-forgotten French adventure abroad. One of our escorts knocked.

"Open up," Cochran called impatiently. "We have a problem."

The door opened with surprising suddenness, operated by some device at the fingertips of the man who sat behind the vast mahogany Chippendale desk at the far end of the room.

"The photographs?" His voice was harsh, his face in shadow.

"The photographs were all right. There was nothing. *She* is the problem . . . Persis Willum. She's smart. She's here. But why? She's in the middle of everything. What does she have to do with it? We must know."

Even in the poor light, even with the light behind him I recognized him as the man I'd seen twice in Praha's photos—Praha didn't need artificial lighting to get an accurate impression, even at night.

"You know my name; but I don't know yours." Daylight was fading fast. Cochran switched on a light. "You are. . . ?"

"Zed—just call me Zed. It won't matter."

I looked quickly around the room. Computers. Several TV screens. An assortment of paintings of the French school. A framed certificate from the city of Marseille—something about "invaluable service in wartime." A small statuette of the Virgin that guards the Old Port standing on the corner of his desk . . .I'd seen a million like it in the tourist traps that line the waterfront, but this one was different—it was gold.

"The statue is a memento?"

Cochran couldn't resist. "He is a hero of the city of Marseille. He saved the Virgin during the war."

That was it. Things began to fall in place with the precision of mail dropping through the slot in the front door of Gregor's gallery in Gull Harbor. A murderer who had been a sculptor's

194

assistant and understood casts and molds and metals, who understood handling statues on any scale. A massacre on a beach during
which a shipment of gold had vanished and after which dead
bodies in bits and pieces of German uniform were found. The
subsequent betrayal of the petty criminals of the Old Port, their
round-up and execution. Zed—savior of the Virgin. The gold reproduction on his desk.

Of course.

My throat closed with excitement. Nonetheless, I could speak
and the words came in a rush.

"And I know how he saved the city. I can tell you. Stop me
if I'm wrong."

I didn't give them a chance to stop me. "He knew all about
casting on a heroic scale. He had been a sculptor's assistant, probably a sculptor who did heroic figures for monuments and mem-
orials. That was in the beginning. The Allies were bombing the
harbor during the war; the city fathers were terrified for the safety
of the city's greatest treasure—the gilded Virgin. This man—Zed,
as he calls himself, went to them and said 'I can save your Virgin.
I will erect a substitute until the danger is over.' "

I was too excited now to worry about Zed or anything else
because the puzzle was unraveling itself perfectly.

"As I said, he had been a sculptor's assistant. He knew his
stuff. He made molds of the original Virgin and he and his men
substituted a Virgin made of solid gold—Czechoslovakian gold.
There was no danger—he knew from the Englishmen he worked
with that the Allies had agreed among themselves to spare the
monument."

The man in the window hadn't moved. Cochran seemed
stunned. "Gold? What gold?"

"Gold the British were trying to save for the Czechs. Zed was
part of a team trying to get it out of France. There was a rendezvous set up with a British cruiser. The cruiser never arrived,
probably its disappearance can be attributed to Zed. Anyway, he
hired mercenaries, put them in German uniforms as a cover,
massacred his own people, took off with the gold, and then be-

trayed his mercenaries to the Germans, who dispatched them. After the war he simply restored the original Virgin, melted down the false Virgin, and shipped the gold off to Swiss banks."

All these days I'd been staring at the Virgin in the harbor—climbing up inside her, studying her construction, admiring her golden glitter—but not until I saw the miniature of her in solid gold did it all fall into place.

"That, too?" Cochran said. She had been standing behind me. Now she stepped up beside me. We three were the only people in the room—our escort had left. "And Martin," she demanded, "what about Martin? The news came over the press wire that he was dead. Your handiwork?" She was addressing Zed, her voice tight with anger. He did not bother to respond, and she went on, with mounting fury. "Yes, I suppose it was. He got in your way somehow. Too many questions? And Nadia Milonsky—did you have to have her murdered? All I asked you to do was to get the book back and destroy it. But murder—you didn't have to do that. Lassiter, too. You're a monster. You kill for pleasure." She was actually shaking with fury from head to foot.

"Never for pleasure," he said virtuously, the way you might say "I never touch cigarettes." "You are too emotional. You have always known what I am—I make no apologies. And it was your idea to come here to make certain about the photographs." The only emotion he betrayed was in taking two steps toward her. In doing so he stepped into the light from the lamp Cochran had turned on. I could see his face now and the sudden recognition hit me a hammer blow exactly between the eyes.

"I had to. You know I had to. If there had been anything. . . ." She didn't finish, but she threw me an anguished glance I couldn't interpret. And yet . . . and yet. . . .

"It's all I've done for thirty years. Combing newspapers for anything that would threaten. Covering up. Guarding. Trying to make sure." She had herself tightly in hand now. Her tone was controlled, dangerous.

"I would thank you, except that I know you don't do it out of love for me."

196

"Especially not out of love for you. You are garbage."

This time he reacted swiftly. He took another two steps toward her, and with the two of them standing face to face, I finally saw it. I saw three faces together in a collage of features.

"Von Berger." I didn't even realize I had spoken aloud.

They turned to me simultaneously, two animals surprised in battle and now at bay.

"Of course. How could I have been so stupid—and I'm supposed to be an artist. Your son. It must have happened while you were a student in Paris, Cochran. What did you do, farm the infant out? Of course you did. To impoverished German gentry, I suppose. And he doesn't know. You must have been frantic when he turned up in Gull Harbor after all those years of protecting him. If he found out his father was a murderer. . . ."

"It would kill him." She said it as a fact, almost with relief.

"You warned Zed that Lassiter was coming—might stumble onto something. And you also went to interview Milonsky and saw the book. . . ." I began to understand about Cochran.

The telephone rang. Zed picked it up. Cochran paid no attention. Neither did I. We were absorbed in each other.

"Quite by accident. I was nosing around during the interview. I spotted it hidden among her art books. But I wasn't able to take it—she never left me alone for a minute."

Nadia hadn't destroyed the book after all. She had kept it as a reminder of an earlier form of her genius and it had killed her.

"I always kept in touch with him." She gestured toward Zed, who was listening on the phone. "I'm not proud. But it was in both our interests that no one should know he was a murderer. All I can say to defend myself is that I was trying to protect my son." She sighed. "I wish you hadn't come, Persis. You know too much—knew too much from the beginning. I thought at the start that I could use you, but when you turned up in Marseille . . . If you gave your word, perhaps. . . ?"

"That won't be necessary." Zed had put down the phone. "It seems you were followed from the opera house—the Mitzu Brigade. Our information is that they're on their way—we expect an attack at any moment. They are confident they can persuade me to tell them where to find the gold." He smiled. The smile surprised me. It had charm. "We've been expecting something like this for a long time. We're ready—more than ready. They will have a surprise." He opened the desk drawer. "A terrorist attack is a useful conceit: people are killed during such events."

"No," Cochran cried. "No more killing."

He smiled again and this time I saw front teeth that pushed into one another like the front teeth of a stable rat. "You needn't worry—she won't die alone."

"No. I won't allow it!"

"You've become a nuisance. Especially now that you know about the gold. And a danger. So very sorry." He did not look sorry; his eyes glittered and he was still smiling.

He brought the gun level.

Deliberate.

Unhurried.

Arm straight. Hand clenched.

Taking his time.

The gun steadied. With stunning speed Cochran threw the lamp at him. The room plunged into semidarkness.

Then came the sounds. The world reverberated and recoiled. There were five, six, seven great explosions. The sky lit up—the earth trembled. Bombs, I thought. They've crashed a truck through the main gate.

There was a pounding of gunfire in the compound.

Zed had recovered his balance. The gun swung in a small arc. I moved at the same instant and the bullet and I hit Cochran together. The weight of my body spun her sideways and she dropped. I heard him swear, saw the gleam of his shirtfront, registered the flicker of the ruby in his tie clasp. A fugitive bit of light hit the barrel of his gun: it was still pointed at Cochran. I felt in the bag slung over my shoulder for something—anything— to use as a weapon.

My fingers closed on a smoothness. I stepped up to Zed and struck at him. I heard the gun go off. I struck again. And this time he turned on me. I pressed the nozzle of the can in my hand and shot flood upon flood of hair spray into his unprotected eyes. He flailed with the gun. I felt a rush of blood down my forehead. He swung blindly again and again. I felt my right arm shatter and I dropped the can. My left hand searched desperately in the bag. I was going to fall. And when I fell. . . .

My good hand found something sharp and deadly but I couldn't hang on. Reality began to recede and I was drifting . . . drifting.

I think I saw Cochran. I think I saw the scissors plunge.

I think I saw him fall, silently, silently.

"Zed," I think I heard Cochran say. "Zed means zero."

I think; but I wasn't sure.

It could have been another bad dream.

41

"You might have told me that reports of your death would be vastly exaggerated. I would have worried less."

My aunt was drinking a Margarita. In preparation for a long hot summer to come, she said. We were all drinking Margaritas and lounging on the terrace at The Crossing—Aunt Lydie, Bobby Blessing, Oliver Reynolds, Alexander Dana, and I. I wasn't really lounging: I had too many stitches and too much plaster for that. But I was alive, at least, and present. The fruit trees in the distance were finishing their riotous bloom. The air was seductive. We were having a preview of summer.

"She certainly looked dead when we came to get her out of the hospital in Marseille," Oliver Reynolds said crossly. "She looked as if she'd burned all her bridges and decamped." Naturally, he was furious with me. He so often was.

Aunt Lydie tried to make light of it. She had forgiven me. "Dorothy Parker once read me one of her poems before she published it. She said, 'The clouds are low along the ridges, and sweet's the air with curly smoke from all my burning bridges.' I adored her, you know. Difficult, but witty."

Blessing was perched on a delicate wicker chair that was almost as fragile and bony as he. He overwhelmed it with his sheer, improbable length. "Funny, complicated affair, this Marseille thing. But then, they usually are."

"Tell us," Lydia Wentworth said, "all the secret things about the funny, complicated affair. You know I love secrets." She's like a child about secrets—she adores them.

"If there are secrets, you can't expect him to tell us, Lydia." Oliver was always correct about everything: he believed in playing the game, whatever it was.

But Blessing was willing, to a point. "Lassiter was British Intelligence trying to find out what had happened to a shipment of gold. The terrorist Coalition found out the gold existed and they wanted it, too. We called in Dana—terrorism is his speciality, you might say. And suddenly there we all were, wallowing in the same muddy waters. It was Persis who uncorked the bottle."

A slightly mixed metaphor, I thought, but apt. "You mean Godzilla and me?" It was hard to talk—my broken jaw was still wired. But I could hiss enough words to be understood.

"Absolutely. You two leapt, so to speak, right into the middle of the Coalition's death squad and that really got things rolling."

Aunt Lydie was charmed beyond measure. "Death squad? How fabulous."

"You should know, Lydia. They almost kidnapped you."

"Perfectly absurd of them," she said. "I never would have paid a penny."

Blessing chose to ignore that. "You, Persis, told everything you knew to Martin. He orchestrated the whole Von Berger thing to scare you into it. That was a good thing, as it turned out, but no thanks to you. He was a greedy little bastard and the minute you spilled it all to him he went right out to peddle it to the highest bidder. That turned out to be the Coalition, who promptly did him in. If they hadn't, Zed would have eventually. He knew from his sources that somebody was asking questions: he'd already done away with the two mercenaries."

"He was so nice to that girl, Nathalie," I said regretfully.

"He was a little rat." Bobby Blessing was always the realist. He brooked no sentiment. "To be specific, he sold the information you gave him to the Coalition and they followed you from the opera house. Zed was brilliant, actually."

"Brilliant?" This was Dana for the first time. Dana obviously had no kind words for the man who had tried to kill me.

"Brilliant," Blessing mused. "He knew they were looking for him and he was more than ready. They stepped into a trap. He had it all worked out. Except for two things."

"What two things?" Oliver demanded.

"First Dana. He and his team were on the Coalition's trail. They got there minutes after the Mitzu Brigade attacked. And—" he paused for dramatic effect. We were all hanging on every word. "And except for Cochran. He never dreamed she'd kill him."

I hadn't dreamed it either. It was true . . . literally true.

"Is she all right?" Aunt Lydie asked.

"She will be. It was a bad wound—just missed a whole roster of vital organs. But she'll recover."

She'd saved my life. And because of that no one would ever know what I knew. For public consumption, she had come to the opera house just as I had, to preview the exhibition. She had been taken off just as I had by Zed's men. That was the official story and that is how it would remain. Once again, we owed each other.

"And what about Hallsey Bryce?" my aunt asked.

Blessing laughed. "His portrait will hang him eventually. To be specific, his vanity will hang him."

The thought of Bryce being hanged did not unduly distress Lydia Wentworth. "Serve him right," she said with conviction.

"How," Oliver wanted to know, "did you work it out about the statue, Persis?"

"I'm only guessing, but I figure that Zed probably had each of its four hollow sections cut in half again and then, with winches and sandbags and a couple of trucks, they took it down and carted it away. All they would need was about ten men working three nights. Afterward it was easy enough for Zed to get rid of the men, and that was that."

"You really gave us a scare," Dana said, "when we arrived and found you and Cochran lying there in your respective pools of blood. I'm sorry not to have arrived in time."

"You arrived in time to save us. At least we're alive."

Aunt Lydie detested the Press. "Reporters are always turning up where they're not wanted." There was a certain amount of justice in her remark. On the other hand, I too had been turning up where I was not wanted ever since this affair began, though largely by chance.

"I'm just as guilty as she."

To my surprise, Blessing disagreed. "Without you, Persis," he said grudgingly, "we might still be trying to finish it. If you hadn't told Martin, and Martin hadn't told the Coalition and Dana hadn't followed the Mitzu Brigade. . . ."

I looked at Dana. He hadn't really been listening. He was looking over our heads and beyond us at some invisible point on the horizon. He looked like a thoroughbred just before it takes the bit in its teeth.

I reached out and took his hand in my good one and squeezed it gently. There was no answering pressure.

I heard my aunt's silvery laugh. "Don't be embarrassed, Alex. She's always like this in the spring."

I looked into Dana's crystal eyes and I knew he was already gone. This affair was over and he was moving on. He was not for me. Perhaps he was not for anyone.

"You are wrong, Aunt Lydie," I told her. "It has nothing to do with spring. I am just burning a bridge—a bridge I have never crossed."

For the first time I sensed summer in the air. I was free.

*Clarissa Watson is co-owner and director of
The Country Art Gallery in Locust Valley,
New York, which she helped to found, and
author of two other Persis Willum mysteries,*
The Fourth Stage of Gainsborough Brown
(1977) and The Bishop in the Back Seat *(1980).
Her interest in gourmet cooking has also
prompted her to edit* The Sensuous Carrot, *a
collection of artists' recipes from around the
world. She lives on the North Shore of Long
Island with her husband, a television executive.*